Children's
Literature
Review

Guide to Gale Literary Criticism Series

For criticism on	Consult these Gale series
Authors now living or who died after December 31, 1959	*CONTEMPORARY LITERARY CRITICISM (CLC)*
Authors who died between 1900 and 1959	*TWENTIETH-CENTURY LITERARY CRITICISM (TCLC)*
Authors who died between 1800 and 1899	*NINETEENTH-CENTURY LITERATURE CRITICISM (NCLC)*
Authors who died between 1400 and 1799	*LITERATURE CRITICISM FROM 1400 TO 1800 (LC)* *SHAKESPEAREAN CRITICISM (SC)*
Authors who died before 1400	*CLASSICAL AND MEDIEVAL LITERATURE CRITICISM (CMLC)*
Black writers of the past two hundred years	*BLACK LITERATURE CRITICISM (BLC)*
Authors of books for children and young adults	*CHILDREN'S LITERATURE REVIEW (CLR)*
Dramatists	*DRAMA CRITICISM (DC)*
Hispanic writers of the late nineteenth and twentieth centuries	*HISPANIC LITERATURE CRITICISM (HLC)*
Native North American writers and orators of the eighteenth, nineteenth, and twentieth centuries	*NATIVE NORTH AMERICAN LITERATURE (NNAL)*
Poets	*POETRY CRITICISM (PC)*
Short story writers	*SHORT STORY CRITICISM (SSC)*
Major authors from the Renaissance to the present	*WORLD LITERATURE CRITICISM, 1500 TO THE PRESENT (WLC)*

4

Children's Literature Review

Excerpts from Reviews,
m, and Commentary
on Books for Children
and Young People

Linda R. Andres
Editor

GALE

DETROIT · NEW YORK · TORONTO · LONDON

STAFF

Linda R. Andres, *Editor*

Sheryl Ciccarelli, Charity Ann Dorgan, Alan Hedblad, Motoko Huthwaite, Paul Loeber,
Sean McCready, Gerard J. Senick, Diane Telgen, Kathleen L. Witman, *Contributing Editors*

Marilyn Allen, *Assistant Editor*

Joyce Nakamura, *Managing Editor*

Susan M. Trosky, *Permissions Manager*
Maria L. Franklin, *Permissions Specialist*
Edna M. Hedblad, Michele M. Lonoconus, *Permissions Associates*
Andrea D. Grady, *Permissions Assistant*

Victoria B. Cariappa, *Research Manager*
Cheryl L. Warnock, *Project Coordinator*
Laura C. Bissey, Tracie Richardson, Norma Sawaya, *Research Associates*
Alfred A. Gardner, *Research Assistants*

Mary Beth Trimper, *Production Director*
Deborah Milliken, *Production Assistant*

Mikal Ansari, *Macintosh Artist*
Randy Bassett, *Image Database Supervisor*
Robert Duncan, Mikal Ansari, *Imaging Specialists*
Pamela A. Reed, *Photography Coordinator*

∞™ This book is printed on acid-free paper that meets the minimum requirements of American National Standard for Information Sciences—Permanence Paper for Printed Library Materials, ANSI Z39.48-1984.

Library of Congress Catalog Card Number 76-643301
ISBN 0-7876-1138-7
ISSN 0362-4145
Printed in the United States of America

10 9 8 7 6 5 4 3 2 1

Contents

Preface

Literature for children and young adults has evolved into both a respected branch of creative writing and a successful industry. Currently, books for young readers are considered among the most popular segments of publishing. Criticism of juvenile literature is instrumental in recording the literary or artistic development of the creators of children's books as well as the trends and controversies that result from changing values or attitudes about young people and their literature. Designed to provide a permanent, accessible record of this ongoing scholarship, *Children's Literature Review (CLR)* presents parents, teachers, and librarians—those responsible for bringing children and books together—with the opportunity to make informed choices when selecting reading materials for the young. In addition, *CLR* provides researchers of children's literature with easy access to a wide variety of critical information from English-language sources in the field. Users will find balanced overviews of the careers of the authors and illustrators of the books that children and young adults are reading; these entries, which contain excerpts from published criticism in books and periodicals, assist users by sparking ideas for papers and assignments and suggesting supplementary and classroom reading. Ann L. Kalkhoff, president and editor of *Children's Book Review Service Inc.,* writes that "*CLR* has filled a gap in the field of children's books, and it is one series that will never lose its validity or importance."

Scope of the Series

Each volume of *CLR* profiles the careers of a selection of authors and illustrators of books for children and young adults from preschool through high school. Author lists in each volume reflect:

- an international scope.

- representation of authors of all eras.

- the variety of genres covered by children's and/or YA literature: picture books, fiction, nonfiction, poetry, folklore, and drama.

Although the focus of the series is on authors new to *CLR*, entries will be updated as the need arises.

Organization of This Book

An entry consists of the following elements: author heading, author portrait, author introduction, excerpts of criticism (each preceded by a bibliographical citation), and illustrations, when available.

- The **Author Heading** consists of the author's name followed by birth and death dates. The portion of the name outside the parentheses denotes the form under which the author is most frequently published. If the majority of the author's works for children were written under a pseudonym, the pseudonym will be listed in the author heading and the real name given on the first line of the author introduction. Also located at the beginning of the introduction are any other pseudonyms used by the author in writing for children and any name variations, including transliterated forms for authors whose languages use nonroman alphabets. Uncertainty as to a birth or death date is indicated by question marks.

- An **Author Portrait** is included when available.

- The **Author Introduction** contains information designed to introduce an author to *CLR* users by presenting an overview of the author's themes and styles, biographical facts that relate to the author's literary career or critical responses to the author's works, and information about major awards and prizes the author has received. The introduction begins by identifying the nationality of the author and by listing the genres in which s/he has written for children and young adults. Introductions also list a group of representative titles for which the author or illustrator being profiled is best known; this section, which begins with the words "major works include," follows the genre line of the introduction. For seminal figures, a listing of major works about the author follows when appropriate, highlighting important biographies about the author or illustrator that are not excerpted in the entry. The centered heading "Introduction" announces the body of the text.

- **Criticism** is located in three sections: **Author's Commentary** (when available), **General Commentary** (when available), and **Title Commentary** (commentary on specific titles).

  - The **Author's Commentary** presents background material written by the author or by an interviewer. This commentary may cover a specific work or several works. Author's commentary on more than one work appears after the author introduction, while commentary on an individual book follows the title entry heading.

  - The **General Commentary** consists of critical excerpts that consider more than one work by the author or illustrator being profiled. General commentary is preceded by the critic's name in boldface type or, in the case of unsigned criticism, by the title of the journal. *CLR* also features entries that emphasize general criticism on the oeuvre of an author or illustrator. When appropriate, a selection of reviews is included to supplement the general commentary.

  - The **Title Commentary** begins with the title entry headings, which precede the criticism on a title and cite publication information on the work being reviewed. Title headings list the title of the work as it appeared in its first English-language edition. The first English-language publication date of each work (unless otherwise noted) is listed in parentheses following the title. Differing U.S. and British titles follow the publication date within the parentheses. When a work is written by an individual other than the one being profiled, as is the case when illustrators are featured, the parenthetical material following the title cites the author of the work before listing its publication date.

    Entries in each title commentary section consist of critical excerpts on the author's individual works, arranged chronologically by publication date. The entries generally contain two to seven reviews per title, depending on the stature of the book and the amount of criticism it has generated. The editors select titles that reflect the entire scope of the author's literary contribution, covering each genre and subject. An effort is made to reprint criticism that represents the full range of each title's reception, from the year of its initial publication to current assessments. Thus, the reader is provided with a record of the author's critical history. Publication information (such as publisher names and book prices) and parenthetical numerical references (such as footnotes or page and line references to specific editions of works) have been deleted at the discretion of the editors to provide smoother reading of the text.

- Centered headings introduce each section, in which criticism is arranged chronologically; beginning with Volume 35, each excerpt is preceded by a boldface source heading for easier access by readers. Within the text, titles by authors being profiled are also highlighted in boldface type.

- Selected excerpts are preceded by **Explanatory Annotations,** which provide information on the critic or work of criticism to enhance the reader's understanding of the excerpt.

- A complete **Bibliographical Citation** designed to facilitate the location of the original book or article precedes each piece of criticism.

- Numerous **Illustrations** are featured in *CLR*. For entries on illustrators, an effort has been made to include illustrations that reflect the characteristics discussed in the criticism. Entries on authors who do not illustrate their own works may also include photographs and other illustrative material pertinent to their careers.

Special Features: Entries on Illustrators

Entries on authors who are also illustrators will occasionally feature commentary on selected works illustrated but not written by the author being profiled. These works are strongly associated with the illustrator and have received critical acclaim for their art. By including critical comment on works of this type, the editors wish to provide a more complete representation of the artist's career. Criticism on these works has been chosen to stress artistic, rather than literary, contributions. Title entry headings for works illustrated by the author being profiled are arranged chronologically within the entry by date of publication and include notes identifying the author of the illustrated work. In order to provide easier access for users, all titles illustrated by the subject of the entry are boldfaced.

CLR also includes entries on prominent illustrators who have contributed to the field of children's literature. These entries are designed to represent the development of the illustrator as an artist rather than as a literary stylist. The illustrator's section is organized like that of an author, with two exceptions: the introduction presents an overview of the illustrator's styles and techniques rather than outlining his or her literary background, and the commentary written by the illustrator on his or her works is called "illustrator's commentary" rather than "author's commentary." All titles of books containing illustrations by the artist being profiled are highlighted in boldface type.

Other Features: Acknowledgments, Indexes

- The **Acknowledgments** section, which immediately follows the preface, lists the sources from which material has been reprinted in the volume. It does not, however, list every book or periodical consulted for the volume.

- The **Cumulative Index to Authors** lists all of the authors who have appeared in *CLR* with cross-references to the biographical, autobiographical, and literary criticism series published by Gale Research. A full listing of the series titles appears before the first page of the indexes of this volume.

- The **Cumulative Index to Nationalities** lists authors alphabetically under their respective nationalities. Author names are followed by the volume number(s) in which they appear.

- The **Cumulative Index to Titles** lists titles covered in *CLR* followed by the volume and page number where criticism begins.

A Note to the Reader

CLR is one of several critical references sources in the Literature Criticism Series published by Gale Research. When writing papers, students who quote directly from any volume in the Literature Criticism

Series may use the following general forms to footnote reprinted criticism. The first example pertains to material drawn from periodicals, the second to material reprinted from books.

¹T. S. Eliot, "John Donne," *The Nation and the Athenaeum,* 33 (9 June 1923), 321-32; excerpted and reprinted in *Literature Criticism from 1400 to 1800,* Vol. 10, ed. James E. Person, Jr. (Detroit: Gale Research, 1989), pp. 28-9.

¹Henry Brooke, *Leslie Brooke and Johnny Crow* (Frederick Warne, 1982); excerpted and reprinted in *Children's Literature Review,* Vol. 20, ed. Gerard J. Senick (Detroit: Gale Research, 1990), p. 47.

Suggestions Are Welcome

In response to various suggestions, several features have been added to *CLR* since the beginning of the series, including author entries on retellers of traditional literature as well as those who have been the first to record oral tales and other folklore; entries on prominent illustrators featuring commentary on their styles and techniques; entries on authors whose works are considered controversial; occasional entries devoted to criticism on a single work or a series of works; sections in author introductions that list major works by and about the author or illustrator being profiled; explanatory notes that provide information on the critic or work of criticism to enhance the usefulness of the excerpt; more extensive illustrative material, such as holographs of manuscript pages and photographs of people and places pertinent to the careers of the authors and artists; a cumulative nationality index for easy access to authors by nationality; and occasional guest essays written specifically for *CLR* by prominent critics on subjects of their choice.

Readers who wish to suggest authors to appear in future volumes, or who have other suggestions, are cordially invited to contact the editor. By mail: Editor, *Children's Literature Review,* Gale Research, 835 Penobscot Bldg., 645 Griswold St., Detroit, MI 48226-4094; by telephone: (800) 347-GALE; by fax: (313) 961-6599; by E-mail: CYA@Gale.com@GALESMTP.

Acknowledgments

The editors wish to thank the copyright holders of the excerpted criticism included in this volume and the permissions managers of many book and magazine publishing companies for assisting us in securing reproduction rights. We are also grateful to the staffs of the Detroit Public Library, the Library of Congress, the University of Detroit Mercy Library, Wayne State University Purdy/Kresge Library Complex, and the University of Michigan Libraries for making their resources available to us. Following is a list of the copyright holders who have granted us permission to reproduce material in this volume of *CLR*. Every effort has been made to trace copyright, but if omissions have been made, please let us know.

COPYRIGHTED EXCERPTS IN *CLR*, VOLUME 44, WERE REPRINTED FROM THE FOLLOWING PERIODICALS:

Appraisal: Science Books for Young People, v. 26, Winter, 1993. Copyright © 1993 by the Children's Science Book Review Committee. Reproduced by permission.—*Australian Book Review,* n. 121, June, 1990; n. 135, October, 1991; n. 167, December, 1994 & January, 1995. All reproduced by permission.—*Best Sellers,* v. 39, August, 1979. Copyright © 1979 Helen Dwight Reid Educational Foundation. Reproduced by permission.—*The Book Report,* v. 7, September-October, 1988. © copyright 1988 by Linworth Publishing, Inc., Worthington, Ohio. Reproduced by permission.—*Bookbird,* v. XVI, December 15, 1978; v. 34, June 15, 1996. Both reproduced by permission.—*Booklist,* v. 73, May 1, 1977; v. 73, July 1, 1977; v. 74, May 1, 1978; v. 75, October 1, 1978; v. 75, March 15, 1979; v. 77, November 15, 1980; v. 78, May 15, 1982; v. 79, January 15, 1983; v. 80, March 15, 1984; v. 80, April 15, 1984; v. 80, August, 1984; v. 81, September 15, 1984; v. 81, July, 1985; v. 82, April 15, 1986; v. 83, March 15, 1987; v. 84, October 1, 1987; v. 84, November 1, 1987; v. 84, November 15, 1987; v. 84, December 15, 1987; v. 85, November 1, 1988; v. 85, November 15, 1988; v. 85, April 1, 1989; v. 85, August, 1989; v. 86, September 15, 1989; v. 86, November 15, 1989; v. 87, September 1, 1990; v. 87, October 1, 1990; v. 87, October 15, 1990; v. 87, November 1, 1990; v. 87, March 15, 1991; v. 87, May 1, 1991; v. 88, September 1, 1991; v. 88, October 1, 1991; v. 88, November 15, 1991; v. 88, March 1, 1992; v. 88, June 15, 1992; v. 89, December 15, 1992; v. 89, March 15, 1993; v. 89, April 1, 1993; v. 89, August, 1993; v. 90, November 1, 1993; v. 90, December 1, 1993; v. 90, April 15, 1994; v. 91, October 1, 1994; v. 91, October 15, 1994; v. 91, November 1, 1994; v. 91, November 15, 1994; v. 91, February 1, 1995; v. 91, February 15, 1995; v. 91, March 15, 1995; v. 91, April 15, 1995; v. 91, July, 1995; v. 92, October 15, 1995; v. 92, November 1, 1995; v. 92, November 15, 1995; v. 92, January 1 & 15, 1996; v. 92, February 1, 1996; v. 92, May 1, 1996; v. 92, May 15, 1996. Copyright © 1977, 1978, 1979, 1980, 1982, 1983, 1984, 1985, 1986, 1987, 1988, 1989, 1990, 1991, 1992, 1993, 1994, 1995, 1996 by the American Library Association. All reproduced by permission.—*The Booklist,* v. 66, March 1, 1970; v. 66, May 1, 1970; v. 67, November 1, 1970; v. 70, December 1, 1973; v. 72, October 15, 1975; v. 72, November 15, 1975. Copyright © 1970, 1973, 1975 by the American Library Association. All reproduced by permission.—*Books for Keeps,* n. 36, January, 1986; n. 40, September, 1986; n. 47, November, 1987; n. 50, May, 1988; n. 55, March, 1989; n. 56, May, 1989; n. 60, January, 1990; n. 63, July, 1990; n. 77, November, 1992; n. 80, May, 1993; n. 85, March, 1994; n. 86, May, 1994; n. 89, November, 1994; n. 91, March, 1995; n. 94, September, 1995; n. 98, May, 1996. © School Bookshop Association 1986, 1987, 1988, 1989, 1990, 1992, 1993, 1994, 1995, 1996. All reproduced by permission.—*Books for Your Children,* v. 21, Summer, 1986; v. 22, Autumn-Winter, 1987; v. 26, Summer, 1991; v. 27, Spring, 1992; v. 29, Summer, 1994; v. 30, Spring, 1995. © Books for Your Children 1986, 1987, 1991, 1992, 1994 1995. All reproduced by permission.—*Books in Canada,* v. 12, December, 1983 for "Great Escapes" by Mary Ainslie Smith; v. 15, December, 1986 for a review of "The Curses of Third Uncle" by Mary Ainslie Smith. Both reproduced by permission of the author./v. 18, May, 1989 for a review of "Saltwater City" by Bruce Serafin.—*British Book News Children's Books,* September, 1986; March, 1987; March, 1988; June, 1988. © The British Book Council, 1986, 1987, 1988. All reproduced by permission.—*Bulletin of the Center for Children's Books,* v. 24, September, 1970; v. 26, March, 1973; v. 27, February, 1974; v. 28, February, 1975; v. 29, November, 1975; v. 29, May, 1976; v. 30, July-August, 1977; v. 31, January, 1978; v. 31, July-August, 1978; v. 32, November, 1978; v. 33, June, 1980; v. 34, November, 1980; v. 34, January, 1981; v. 35, December, 1981; v. 35, July-August, 1982; v. 36, March, 1983; v. 37, December, 1983; v. 37, April, 1984; v. 37, June, 1984; v. 38, October, 1984; v.

African actors preparing for a play, illustration by Leo Dillon and Diane Dillon. From *Who's in Rabbit's House?* by Verna Aardema. Dial Books for Young Readers, 1977. Pictures copyright © 1977 by Leo and Diane Dillon. Reproduced by permission of Leo Dillon and Diane Dillon. In North America by Penguin Books USA Inc.

Various woodland animals, illustration by Leo Dillon and Diane Dillon. From *Why Mosquitoes Buzz in People's Ears,* by Verna Aardema. Dial Books for Young Readers, 1975. Pictures copyright © 1975 by Leo and Diane Dillon. Reproduced by permission of Dial Books for Young Readers, a division of Penguin Books USA Inc.

PHOTOGRAPHS APPEARING IN *CLR,* VOLUME 44, WERE REPRODUCED FROM THE FOLLOWING SOURCES:

Allen, Pamela (outdoors), photograph by Ron Allen. Reproduced by permission of Curtis Brown (Aust) Pty. Ltd., for Pamela Allen.

Dillon, Diane and Leo Dillon, photograph by Lee Dillon. Reproduced by permission of Leo Dillon.

Fox, Paula, photograph by Jerry Bauer. © Jerry Bauer. Reproduced by permission.

Hopkins, Lee Bennett, photograph by Rocco Nunno. Reproduced by permission of Lee Bennett Hopkins and Curtis Brown, Ltd.

Hopkins, Lee Bennett with William C. Morris, photograph. Reproduced by permission of Lee Bennett Hopkins and Curtis Brown, Ltd.

Krull, Kathleen (outdoors), photograph by Paul Brewer. Reproduced by permission of Kathleen Krull.

McBratney, Sam, photograph. Reproduced by permission.

Yee, Paul, photograph by James Ho Lim. Reproduced by permission of Paul Yee.

Yolen, Jane, photograph by Shulamith Oppenheim. Reproduced by permission of Jane Yolen and Curtis Brown, Ltd.

Yolen, Jane (with children), photograph by Bruce Davis. Reproduced by permission of Jane Yolen and Curtis Brown, Ltd.

Children's
Literature
Review

Pamela Allen

1934-

Australian author and illustrator of picture books for children.

Major works include *Mr. Archimedes' Bath* (1980), *Who Sank the Boat?* (1982), *Bertie and the Bear* (1984), *A Lion in the Night* (1986), *My Cat Maisie* (1991).

INTRODUCTION

Pamela Allen is an author and illustrator best known for her picture books for small children. Since Allen's main audience is predominantly comprised of children who cannot yet read, her pictures and words work together on a page to convey the messages of her books. She carefully selects sounds that will convey moods, syntax that will determine the tone and speed with which a sentence is read, and words that will impart the most meaning to a child with an as yet limited vocabulary. "A very young child gets a lot of information from noises, more in a sense than they do from the actual interpretation of the meaning of a word," Allen explained in an *Australian Book Review* interview with Meg Sorensen. Because Allen gives so much attention to sounds and rhythms, her writing has been recognized for its poetry. Her language is simple, her text almost a cacophony, and her words beg to be shared. "I see my books as being read aloud," Allen revealed to Sorensen. "So I see a caring adult with a child and the opportunity for a book to be the catalyst to go on a journey."

Biographical Information

Pamela Allen was born in Devonport, Auckland, New Zealand in 1934. Throughout her childhood, she knew she "wanted to draw," and so she convinced her parents to let her attend art school. She graduated from the Elan School of Art at the age of twenty with a diploma in fine art but did not immediately pursue illustrating her own books. Instead she went on to attend Auckland Teachers Training College in the 1950s before working as an art teacher at Pio Pio District High School and Rangitoto College in New Zealand. Allen married Robert William Allen in December 1964, and it wasn't until she had her two children and moved to Sydney, Australia that she wrote and illustrated her first book. *Mr. Archimedes' Bath* was published to critical and popular acclaim.

Major Works

Mr. Archimedes' Bath shows Archimedes' discovery of water displacement. When a kangaroo, a goat, and a wombat join Archimedes in his tub and cause the water to overflow, he eventually realizes that each animal displaces water by his or her own weight. *Who Sank the Boat?* likewise explores a principle of science: balance. Five animals learn a wet lesson as they board a rowboat. A cow, a donkey, a sheep with her knitting, and a pig cause the boat to rock but not tip as they clumsily get in and then a wee mouse joins them and the boat capsizes. *Mr. Archimedes' Bath* and *Who Sank the Boat?* each have been recognized for fine, humorous drawings that complement the text. Zena Sutherland called the drawings in *Mr. Archimedes' Bath* "spaciously composed, humorous, and repetitive." Margery Fisher noted that the pictures in *Who Sank the Boat?* are perfectly allied with the "text that lends itself to chanting."

In *Bertie and the Bear,* a small child flees from a large bear who is then chased by an assortment of banging, tooting, and booming royalty and their entourage. The queen cries, "Shoo, shooo you monster YOU!" while a little dog yips, a captain blows his horn, and an admiral bangs a gong. The bear, surprised by the fuss on his account, begins to dance for the crowd. Bertie joins in, as do the others, replacing the hot pursuit with a happy parade. *Bertie and the Bear,* perhaps more than any of

Allen's titles, invites audience participation. According to a critic in *Publishers Weekly,* "Allen's expressive characters and the cacophonic effects add up to a different, very funny read." *A Lion in the Night* is the tale of an infant princess wishing her stuffed lion was real. It comes to life and kidnaps the princess for a nighttime run through fields and mountains. Like *Bertie and the Bear* they are pursued by a royal family. The lion returns to the castle ahead of everyone else, prepares breakfast, and then just disappears. Allen also wrote *Fancy That!* (1988), a story about a little white hen hatching six brown eggs in a very noisy henhouse, and *Belinda* (1993), the story of a farmer who dresses up in his wife's pink dress to appease a cow that has run off "mooing and trotting" all day instead of cooperating at milking time. Reviewers suggest that *Fancy That!* and *A Lion in the Night* be read aloud, with sound effects from the reader and audience. Similarly, Hazel Rochman thought that *Belinda*'s text and pictures recounting the chase of farmer and farm animals make "for slapstick read-aloud comedy."

Hidden Treasure (1987) and *My Cat Maisie* look at two hard lessons in life. In *Hidden Treasure* two brothers discover a pirate's chest while fishing. One brother pushes the other overboard and rows away with the treasure. He spends the rest of his life miserable, consumed with worry about protecting his treasure. The other brother swims home and lives out his days happily with his family. *My Cat Maisie* tells the story of a lonely little boy named Andrew. Andrew is enthusiastic when a stray cat wanders his way, but he is overzealous and too rough with his new playmate, who runs away in the interest of self-preservation. Andrew then gets a dose of his own medicine when the dog next door proves too aggressive a playmate for him. When the cat returns, Andrew has learned to be a gentler friend. Critics considered *Hidden Treasure* a vehicle for generating a discussion on what is important in life, and a critic in *Publishers Weekly* thought that *My Cat Maisie* helps to explain "some of the finer points of a potentially complex subject."

Awards

In 1980, the Children's Book Council of Australia commended *Mr. Archimedes' Bath* as Australia's picture book of the year. The book also received the New South Wales Premier's Award for best picture book and was commended by the Australian Book Publishers Association Book Design Awards. *Who Sank the Boat?* received the Children's Book of the Year Award from the Children's Book Council of Australia and the New South Wales Premier's Literary Award in the children's book category in 1983. In 1984 it received an honor diploma for illustration from the International Board on Books for Young People. In 1984, Allen again won the Children's Book of the Year Award from the Children's Book Council of Australia, this time for *Bertie and the Bear.* She won the New Zealand Library Association's Russell Clark Award for *A Lion in the Night* in 1986, and the Helen Paul Encouragement Award for *Fancy That!* in 1989; in 1990 *I Wish I*

Had a Pirate Suit was commended with the Australian Picture Book of the Year Award. *My Cat Maisie* received the 1991 AIM Children's Book Award in the picture book category, while *Belinda* was a 1993 honor book for Picture Book of the Year by the Children's Book Council of Australia, and *Mr. McGee Goes to Sea* received the Russell Clark Award for Illustration that same year.

GENERAL COMMENTARY

Meg Sorensen

SOURCE: "When Pom Pom Is Perfect: The Art of Pamela Allen," in *Australian Book Review,* No. 121, June 1990, pp. 44-5.

Every once in a while, in some dark corner of the gum nebula, something appears which the scientists call a molecular cloud. If you can happen to be lying awake, eyes despondently cast upon a godless sky, you would perhaps witness a shower of light. Hey presto—a million or so years later—a new star has formed.

And every once in a while, someone writes a children's book that matters, a Winnie the Pooh to thump, thump, thump down centuries of staircases, a rabbit hole to tunnel through time. And then there's Pamela Allen. First published in 1980, Pamela Allen has created a handful of picture-book masterpieces that, at best, are as pure as Pooh and rank up there with the Hey Diddle Diddles of Caldecott.

The praises of **Mr Archimede's Bath, Who Sank the Boat?, Bertie and the Bear, Mr McGee** and even the very simple **Fancy That!** should be sung loud and long, for these are the real thing. Like all great picture books for the very young, they are perfectly simple, yet I defy anyone, young or old, to read and re-read them and not be enchanted afresh every time.

The characters in these books exude life, caught at the highest point of action, and animated forever on the page. Every curve, stretch and twist communicates exactly the way they feel, the sentiment or momentum each embodies. Little fat figures skip across the page, legs astride in impossibly joyful angles. A bear bows with clumsy charm. This is the work of a thoroughly imaginative creative artist of no little skill, who has taken much time and care in order to get it right.

The best of her books don't bother with making sense, which is not to say that children can't understand them. On the contrary, one is reminded of the Groucho Marx quip that runs along the lines, 'Why, this is so simple even a child of five could understand it . . . somebody send for a child of five.' **Bertie and the Bear** ends with 'Pom Pom'. Lovely logic. Pom Pom—it makes perfect sense.

Pamela Allen knows how to talk to the natives. She'll beat drums, turn cartwheels, inflate a little man then send a bird to peck holes in his belly to bring him back down to size. She'll pile a cow, a sheep, a donkey, a pig and a mouse into a small boat with the kind of wicked humour that children adore.

I get a tingle of pleasure every time I look at the sheep in *Who Sank the Boat?*: she's placed her knitting neatly on the jetty in order to lower her ample woolly self into the boat. The whites of her eyes show wide as her two skinny little sheep's legs reach for the side of the boat, her belly angled precariously on the most extreme point of the jetty. A delightful moment.

With a Pamela Allen picture book, we are mesmerised from the first illustration—it is a deceptively simple yet completely enchanted world. Here, we can believe, anything is possible, thoroughly commonplace events being transformed into an imaginatively possible world. And when the curtain falls (a little troop of animals wending their weary way home, dripping wet from their adventure in the boat, Mr. McGee landing head first back into the bed from which he sprang) it's hard not to smile. Each fantastic journey takes us through a range of feelings towards a climax, from where those feelings are subsequently released. For a small child, this is a satisfying journey indeed.

Anyone can put three men in a tub, but it's the added rub-a-dub that matters. The poetry, for indeed this is what it is, of Pamela Allen's best texts, gets the pitch exactly right:

> Was it a sheep
> Who knew where to sit
> to level the boat
> so that she could knit

Although never lacking in spontaneous humour, the words are obviously very carefully worked to communicate meaning very clearly. And while much of the language is very simple, it is rarely obvious and never stoops to the cloying sweetness of many picture books. Words, especially in the early books, are not used to explain what the pictures haven't. They are there, working hand in hand with the drawings, like the beat of a drum behind a ritual dance.

Similarly, the action is far from clichéd and usually highly inventive. And, although it is often surprising, there is something familiar about it. No one in a Pamela Allen book is afraid to get their clothes dirty, wet, pecked or scrunched by bears and *Mr McGee* has flashes of slapstick that are pure Chaplin.

Herbert and Harry and *I Wish I Had a Pirate Suit,* her most recent books, are perhaps not as immediately accessible and ultimately less successful than the early titles. There is a little more logic and a lot more complexity so that they are a departure from the wonderful whimsical nonsense of *Mr McGee. Herbert and Harry* is very much a moral tale. It lacks the punch and flair of *Bertie and the*

Bear and the end is smug. If the intention was to instruct children on the virtues of giving rather than taking, the early title achieves this more convincingly, purely with its triumphant tone of generosity. However *Herbert and Harry* is far from devoid of value and similarly *I Wish I Had a Pirate Suit* has examples of the idiosyncrasies which can be enjoyed in Pamela Allen's earlier books. The characters claim the page in the same way, and there is at times the same courageous spirit embodied in the children's movement, but there is a point where the words try too hard and the result is laboured and confusing:

> That was a long time ago
> When I was only three
> Now I've grown bigger
> and the pirate suit fits me.
> Now I've got a pirate suit
> Although it's not quite new.
> I could be a captain
> With a sword and pistol too.

By this time, with only the discarded pirate suit to adorn the words, the story has missed a beat, lost its pace, and, when the younger brother appears with new courage, it's a little rushed. Perhaps the message here took precedence over the natural momentum of the picture book itself. . . .

[T]he picture books of Pamela Allen are very likely to be treasured by those who own them. They certainly have what it takes to join the ranks of enduring children's classics.

Meg Sorensen with Pamela Allen

SOURCE: "Interview" *Australian Book Review*, No. 121, June 1990, pp. 46-7.

[*Meg Sorensen interviewed Pamela Allen for* Australian Book Review.]

Sorensen: What do you believe makes a picture book work? Is it merely technique?

Allen: Adults buy books for children and many adults don't have an intimate experience of very young children. And so they bring to it what is their own perception of what a good picture book is. Those perceptions are not necessarily what works with a very young child. Brilliant artwork, impressive artwork, where you are bowled over by the enormous time and cleverness of it all, is not what a very young child is about.

If you look at something like *Little Black Sambo,* which is a very simple little drawing, it's the communication that's all important and for something to communicate to a very young child you need to *know* a very young child, because they have a different *journey* into perceiving meaning. They get their information from pictures. They get it from sounds, like 'rrrrr' meaning angry, the tone, quality, speed of the voice, *and* words—so you've got a much wider means of communicating with a very young child.

When I'm doing my books, I communicate from every angle I can touch.

Sorensen: Many of your books, especially the early ones, concern themselves with the 'real' world in the most cursory fashion. Is it that you think children want, perhaps even need, fantasy?

Allen: I don't come down heavily in that area—it's just that my books are conceptual, so I come to them not through an incident in real life, but through an idea in my head and then I shape them because I feel that a good picture book has a form. It's like poetry, it has a shape. And the more direct, the more economical I am with hitting the nail on the head *exactly,* the stronger my communication will be and, you know, that's why I don't actually like doing backgrounds. I like to cement the material I present so there isn't anything in the way of the message.

Sorensen: *Herbert and Harry,* first published in 1986 and just re-issued by Puffin doesn't have the whimsy of *Bertie and the Bear* which I love so much. It has a very definite moral message. Was this what you wanted to achieve?

Allen: *Herbert and Harry* was a bit of an odd-bod book, as you've picked up on. It's not meant for the very young and it's the one book that's not applicable to the very young—they're not on about values at that age. It was an idea I had . . . I wanted very much to evoke discussion on values, and it was a very simple idea that I thought would be readily available for any age group who wanted to open a discussion on values. That's how I see it being used. In fact, all my books have to be shared experiences and it's what you bring to them that makes them come to life. They open something.

Sorensen: Is *I Wish I Had a Pirate Suit* a conscious change of direction? In your other books you are in the fantasy right from the start, anything goes, while here there is a transition mechanism.

Allen: Yes that's true, but I haven't really thought of it the way you are presenting it. I started off in the real world and the play they had was the fantasy. Of course the book is about relationships and the fact that in childhood, if you've got someone older around, you are always the younger child and the older child is always bigger physically. The insurmountable relationship is that someone is dominating your life. Really the only way out of it is through the way you *feel.*

Sorensen: So you give the boy in the story the courage to deal with this?

Allen: The power.

Sorensen: Your texts always appear wonderfully simple, yet you work language like poetry. As a visual artist, did the poet in you come naturally or did you have to labour to achieve it?

Allen: I certainly approached my very first book with the knowledge that I was skilled in drawing. I had no consciousness that I could write anything, but I had a strong confidence that I knew about pre-school children, so I had two skills I felt sure about. I didn't think I could write, but in *Mr Archimedes' Bath,* which was my first attempt, I sorted it out in my head and I said to myself, 'this is the area you are not secure in, set yourself rules, write words, use words that communicate exactly what you mean. Don't allow yourself any extravagance, any irrelevancies and make sure that every word you use is exactly what you mean.' That was my head thinking about how to go about writing that book. Since that time, I've got more confidence and I've grown to realise more about language and I've delighted in the idea that the voice has speed. I can use rhythms, noises. A very young child gets a lot of information from noises, more in a sense than they do from the actual interpretation of the meaning of a word.

Sorensen: *Bertie and the Bear* is obviously a very carefully worked book, yet it appears so simple and spontaneous. How did you achieve that?

Allen: I personally feel that *Bertie and the Bear* is my best book. I don't regret anything about it. It was very much a conceptual idea. I didn't start off with what you see in the book. I had an idea that there was a fold or margin, and that in one half of the book I had embodied anger and where the centrefold was, there's a change of heart. Everything at the back was the same as what was in the front—the only thing that was different was how you *felt.* When the bear believes that all this noise is a gift he doesn't feel angry anymore, he feels different. I've still got all the same elements, the noise and the people, but the world has changed.

Sorensen: Since *Bertie and the Bear,* have you become more intellectual with your books?

Allen: No. Some books obviously I like more than others. I don't think of them all with the same affection and I keep trying to make another book. I like *Fancy That!* very much too. It's not pretending to be more than it is. It's very available. I always keep a special place for the text in my books because I'm writing for children who can't yet read. They are in the process of picking up clues to texts, unravelling things and therefore I have the few words that are necessary so that they are available to the child to decipher. Part of that is giving the text a special place *on* the page so that the meaning is not obscured in any way.

I think of a picture book as having a shape, a form—it has an introduction, it has a middle, it has a climax, an end. It's got a very definite shape for me. For me, also, it's about pace. You have to turn the page to get the next bit of information.

Sorensen: Childhood may well be a time of wonder and innocence, yet it can also be frightening. Do books help children to face fears or should they be a means of escape into a world where those fears don't exist?

Allen: Oh no! I think books are a means to understanding the world and, in my case, I see my books as being read aloud. So I see a caring adult with a child and the opportunity for a book to be the catalyst to go on a journey. So in the case of *I Wish I Had a Pirate Suit* you can't read it without talking about it. I don't think you'd have what it offers, which is the means to resolve the lack of power in the younger child. Through fantasy, courage, your own spirit, you can overcome the real physical disadvantage that is built into the situation.

Sorensen: What do you think, in general, of the picture books published in Australia?

Allen: What happens with publishers is that they're always looking to publish another picture book because they've got a market out there that hasn't seen that picture book at all, and so they're not interested in publishing old, well-loved picture books. I feel they could better serve the public if, through the selective process, those that were really valued were kept alive.

TITLE COMMENTARY

📖 *MR. ARCHIMEDES' BATH* (1980)

Kirkus Reviews

SOURCE: A review of *Mr. Archimedes' Bath,* in *Kirkus Reviews,* Vol. XLVIII, No. 5, March 1, 1980, p. 281.

"Mr. Archimedes' bath always overflowed. And Mr. Archimedes always had to clean up the mess"—despite the fact that he always shares his bath with a kangaroo, a goat, and a wombat. And so Mr. Archimedes decides to find out "where all this water is coming from." As one by one, then all together, the animals are removed from the tub, Mr. Archimedes notes that the water still goes up and down but doesn't overflow. "Eureka! I've found it!" he shouts when he discovers that the level after he gets out is just the same as before he got in. "We make the water go up," he continues as they all get in and the tub overflows again. "There are just too many of us in the bath, that's all." But this obvious observation is really not much to scream about. Allen's Archimedes stops where the real Archimedes began in the official story; and Allen doesn't even draw any conclusions or generalizations from the phenomenon she does have him catch on to. The menage as pictured seems to be having a lot of fun jumping in and out of the round footed tub with flabby, pink, Mr. A.; but where's the fun of making a dummy out of Archimedes for children who never heard of him in the first place? At first, Allen seems

to be onto a good thing here, but she lets it go down the drain.

Zena Sutherland

SOURCE: A review of *Mr. Archimedes' Bath,* in *Bulletin of the Center for Children's Books,* Vol. 33, No. 10, June, 1980, p. 185.

An Australian author's version of Archimedes' discovery is illustrated by line drawings (tinted on alternate pages) that are spaciously composed, humorous, and repetitive. Sharing his large, round tub with a kangaroo, a goat, and a wombat, Archimedes is bothered by the fact that the tub always overflows; he tries various combinations of animals and finally concludes that each creature displaces water by its own weight. Allen doesn't go into physical principles, but pares the idea down to a level comprehensible to the read-aloud audience, and she does it with good humor and flair.

D. A. Young

SOURCE: A review of *Mr. Archimedes' Bath,* in *The Junior Bookshelf,* Vol. 44, No. 5, October, 1980, p. 231.

Mr. Archimedes wrestles with the problem of his overflowing bath with his friends the Kangaroo, the Goat and the Wombat. Each gets the blame for mess on the bathroom floor until Mr. A by simple scientific deduction realises that it is their awkward bulk which displaces the water from the bath on to the floor. Eureka!

The text is short and the pictures splendidly full-page. It is not the legend as I remember it but it makes an amusing tale which is pleasant to look at.

Judith Sharman

SOURCE: A review of *Mr. Archimedes' Bath,* in *Books for Keeps,* No. 86, May, 1994, p. 10.

Mr Archimedes is wonderful—as he wobbles in and out of the bath, as he orders his friends about in experimenting with every permutation he can come up with, we see science truly in action! The inevitable climax of Eureka just leaves one and all with wide grins of satisfaction and glints of future experiments at bath time twinkling in our eyes. This is not a new book but a timely reissue of an old favourite.

P. Thompson

SOURCE: A review of *Mr. Archimedes' Bath,* in *Books for Your Children,* Vol. 29, No. 2, Summer, 1994, p. 7.

This is science through story and explores the simple

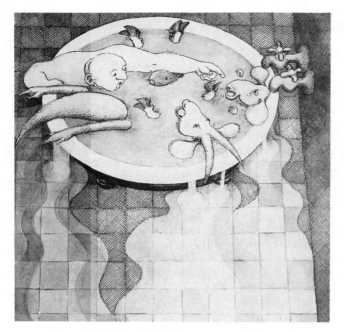

From Mr Archimedes' Bath, *written and illustrated by Pamela Allen.*

problem of changing water levels, Archimedes' principle in fact, in a charming, simple and funny way.

Mr. Archimedes and all his animals—wombat, goat and kangaroo—get into the bath together and it overflows. Whose fault is it? Most children realize what the problem is long before Mr. Archimedes, but nonetheless, they become fully involved with the excitement of predicting. The text is very repetitive, inviting children to join in. The illustrations are simple and uncluttered, but very funny; the goat with his eyes tightly shut, the kangaroo with his long fat tail, not to mention Mr. Archimedes himself with his bare bottom! This is a lovely book which, along with **Who Sank The Boat?** also by Pamela Allen, introduces young children to science in a wonderful and memorable way.

📖 *WHO SANK THE BOAT?* (1982)

Lucy Micklethwait

SOURCE: "One to Ten and Beyond," in *The Times Literary Supplement,* No. 4146, September 17, 1982, p. 1003.

Who Sank the Boat? [is] by New Zealander Pamela Allen, author and illustrator of the award-winning *Mr Archimedes' Bath*. She continues on the theme of water and the bulk of things therein. A cow, a donkey, a pig and a sheep and a tiny little mouse decide to go for a row in the bay. Do you know who sank the boat? "Was it the cow / who almost fell in, / when she tilted the boat / and made such a din? / No . . .". As in *Mr Archimedes' Bath* the text could have been fuller, but no matter. This is only

Pamela Allen's second picture book. Her ideas are good and her illustrations are very fine.

Margery Fisher

SOURCE: A review of *Who Sank the Boat?,* in *Growing Point,* Vol. 21, No. 4, November, 1982, p. 3990.

Simple jokes work best. Here, five animals plan an excursion in a dinghy, dubious about weight as cow, donkey, sheep and pig each step clumsily in: but it is the last passenger, the mouse, who decides the matter. A neat, positive use of wash and line and of grotesque shapes, in a style reminiscent of Burningham, allies perfectly with a repetitive doggerel text that lends itself to chanting.

E. Colwell

SOURCE: A review of *Who Sank the Boat?,* in *The Junior Bookshelf,* Vol. 46, No. 6, December, 1982, p. 218.

A brief rhyming text in large type tells the story—a simple one—of five friends who hope to go for a sail one sunny morning. The friends are a cow, a donkey, a pig, a sheep (with her knitting) and a tiny mouse. Four of them scramble aboard with some difficulty but with the fifth there is disaster. At last the reader knows who *did* sink the boat. Subdued, the animals plod home wet through, the mouse, quite unrepentant, skipping gaily behind.

The colours are pleasant, the animals unsentimentalised and amusing and there is a repetitive phrase. 'Do you know who sank the boat?' which helps to hold the child's interest.

Kristi Thomas Beavin

SOURCE: A review of *Who Sank the Boat?,* in *School Library Journal,* Vol. 29, No. 8, April, 1983, p. 97.

As a cow, a donkey, a sheep and a pig hop aboard a row boat, each escalates the boat's imbalance and dramatically lowers its level in the water until the final would-be occupant, a little mouse, lands them all in the drink. The text, which begins as prose, launches into rhyme on the sixth page, and every other page of verse contains a sepia-toned drawing that looks suspiciously like a rejected study for the full-color illustration that appears—more carefully drawn—on the recto. This might work in a silly but satisfactory way for a very young story hour, but whether it "teaches . . . the principles of balance," as the jacket claims, is anybody's guess.

📖 *BERTIE AND THE BEAR* (1984)

Zena Sutherland

SOURCE: A review of *Bertie and the Bear,* in *Bulletin of*

the Center for Children's Books, Vol. 37, No. 8, April, 1984, p. 141.

There is some rhyme and quite a bit of rhythm in the text of a boisterous cumulative story that begins with a bear chasing little Bertie, predatory gleam in eye. The queen (plump woman, red crown) chases after the bear, the king after the queen, the admiral (his gong rivalling the king's trumpet blare) after the king, et cetera. "All this for me?" The bear is so flattered he bows, turns cartwheels, and dances; in a lame ending, the procession continues with Bertie dancing after the bear. This doesn't have the substance or humor of the author's *Who Sank the Boat?* but it's fun to read and certainly it's fun to look at the ebullient figures in Allen's running frieze.

Ilene Cooper

SOURCE: A review of *Bertie and the Bear,* in *Booklist,* Vol. 80, No. 16, April 15, 1984, p. 1186.

A zesty cumulative tale that has some similarities to the old favorite, *Drummer Hoff.* Readers first see Bertie on the title page, looking over his shoulder, on the run. Turn the page and you'll know why. A big brown bear is after him. But Bertie is not without friends, and a fat queen shoos away the bear. The King follows the Queen, the Admiral is behind him, and the Captain, General, and Sergeant bring up the rear. Each has a musical instrument and plays LOUDLY on the move; but instead of being scared off, the bear turns around, stands up, bows very low, and says, "All this for me? Thank you." He then does a few cartwheels and a very bearlike dance. Suddenly, instead of being chased, he is leading a parade. The comical pictures are done in brisk colors, and the amusing mélange of characters veritably skips across the pages. Put this one on your story-hour list, and prepare for the sound effects.

Publishers Weekly

SOURCE: A review of *Bertie and the Bear,* in *Publishers Weekly,* Vol. 225, No. 16, April 20, 1984, p. 88.

Aimed accurately at little boys and girls who love to giggle and who take to nonsense in the round, Allen's picture book won't miss. Energetic cartoons in strong colors illustrate the doings set afoot by the bear that chases a small child, Bertie. The queen shouts, "Shoo, shooo you monster YOU!" and runs after the bear. With blasts on his trumpet, the king joins the pursuit, followed by the admiral (banging his gong), the captain (blowing his horn) and other members of the royal household. The banging and tooting and booming and shooing stop the bear. "All this for me?" he asks, bowing low and then favoring the crowd with an exhibition of cartwheels and fancy dancing. And Bertie dances after the bear so peace and good feeling are restored. Allen's expressive characters and the cacophonic effects add up to a different, very funny read.

Mary M. Burns

SOURCE: A review of *Bertie and the Bear,* in *The Horn Book Magazine,* Vol. LX, No. 3, June, 1984, pp. 317-18.

In attempting to outrun his pursuer—a large, toothy bear—little Bertie attracts an assemblage of rescuers, each with a different method of solving the problem. The Queen, a formidable figure in a print dress and opaque blue stockings, shouts "'Shoo, Shoo'"; the king, equally natty, blows a trumpet; the Admiral, Captain, General, and Sergeant, armed respectively with gong, horn, flute, and drum, follow in order. Bringing up the rear, a nondescript gray dog contributes penetrating yips to the clamor. The result is an "IN-CRED-IBLE noise"—an apt and straightforward statement accompanied by a double-page panoramic view of the discordant procession. But the denouement, in which the bear is revealed as less fearsome than at first supposed, is surprising, reassuring, and perfectly logical, given the joyous tone of the book. Yet knowing the outcome should not prevent one from reading it again and again, for the onomatopoeic text invites audience participation. Although the brightly colored, slightly cartooned figures are somewhat reminiscent of Pat Hutchins's creations, the overall effect is different, for the illustrator has wisely eschewed background detail to emphasize action and story. An engaging picture storybook in the classic tradition, imaginatively conceived and thoughtfully designed.

Kathy Piehl

SOURCE: A review of *Bertie and the Bear,* in *School Library Journal,* Vol. 30, No. 10, August, 1984, pp. 55-6.

To save small Bertie from the large brown bear chasing him, the Queen, King, Admiral, Captain, General, Sergeant and little dog each contribute plenty of noise to frighten the monster. "Bong-ng-ng." "a-rooty toot-toot-TOOOT" and "yip, yip, yip . . ." wash across the pages in colorful cacophony. Instead of being frightened by the din, the bear dances in appreciation of the jangling melody. Bertie ends by following him—"pom pom." Like all books in which plot is enhanced by sound, this one must be read aloud for full appreciation. However, the multicolored words that flow above the scenes are almost visual sounds, and the bear's impromptu ballet is delightful. Large, uncluttered illustrations and sparse text make this a natural for story hours.

A LION IN THE NIGHT (1985)

Paula Neuss

SOURCE: "Roaring Around," in *The Times Literary Supplement,* No. 4302, September 13, 1985, p. 1014.

"There once was a baby . . .", the book begins; but this is no ordinary baby, for it lives in a castle "with the King, the Queen, the Admiral, the Captain, the General, the Sergeant and the little dog". Furthermore, the baby is "she"—we are presented, in fact, with a captive princess, waiting to be rescued. The handsome prince appears here in the shape of a large, friendly lion.

Pamela Allen's pictures bring the romantic story down to earth—the baby is shown, strip-cartoon style, through the confines of her cot, alternately bawling and struggling to get out, and then realizing that her toy lion is small enough to slip through the bars. "She made a wish", and the rest of the book illustrates what this was. The queen wakes to see a lion stealing her baby. In a parody of A. A. Milne, "the Queen woke the King" who woke the Admiral, and so on down the line in a comic-strip series of characters with remarkable hats, from Babar crowns for the royals to the Sergeant's feathered and peaked creation. In these and their pyjamas, they chase the baby and the lion across and around the pages, waving mops and brooms. Now the lion and the baby take to a boat, looking for all the world as if they were going to visit Maurice Sendak's Wild Things. "Into the boat / and across the sea / Across the sea / and over the mountains / Over the mountains / and into the fields / And there the lion stopped." With a roar spreading over four pages he blows the pursuers back the way they have come, in a manner reminiscent of Scarface Claw's attack on the dogs in Lynley Dodd's *Hairy Maclary from Donaldson's Dairy,* whose rhythms are echoed here too.

The lion turns back to the castle, but the others have to run all the way round another page until they come full circle. King of the castle, the lion now reverses the game by letting everyone in. In a picture strip like a row of stickers we see them eating breakfast, with the lion feeding the baby a great number of tasty things, including a big bowl of strawberries and red jelly. He disappears in the morning but so does the baby—the last picture shows the empty cot with the soft toy on its side.

The influence of Sendak is marked, in both the illustrations and the tale. Mickey's toy plane, a dough vehicle in *In the Night Kitchen,* undergoes a metamorphosis similar to that of the lion. But it is a frequent feature of dreams that familiar waking things are transposed in them. This baby's dream is archetypal (the little girl waiting to be seen and saved). What makes the book so good is its balance of the fearful and the friendly. The baby's anger and loneliness are allayed by the warm, thick hair of the lion (which resembles the Queen's) and the bright clothes of the followers.

M. Crouch

SOURCE: A review of *A Lion in the Night,* in *The Junior Bookshelf,* Vol. 49, No. 5, October, 1985, p. 209.

If Pamela Allen shows a little of the influence of Sendak, especially in her lion, her work is by no means derivative. *A Lion in the Night* is a useful addition to the library of true nursery tales, with a text full of familiar and simple words but with a few new ones to enrich the young child's vocabulary. Marching with them, and cleverly matched to them, is page after page of excitement as the lion, with the kidnapped but willing baby, crosses field and forest, mountain and sea, pursued by the royal household from King to Sergeant and little dog. The story is a satisfying dream fantasy, the drawing full of well-observed and amusing touches. I missed Ms Allen's previous two books published in this country. On the evidence of *A Lion in the Night* here is another Antipodean to show the Old World how it should be done.

Denise M. Wilms

SOURCE: A review of *A Lion in the Night,* in *Booklist,* Vol. 82, No. 16, April 15, 1986, p. 1216.

A royal baby has a royal fit when she's put to bed one night while it's still light. She cries and makes a wish; just what that wish is becomes clear when, in the middle of the night, a lion speeds off with the baby on its back. The king, queen, admiral, captain, general, and assorted others follow in hot pursuit as the lion races far afield— all the way over the mountains and back to the castle again. When the king and queen and their cohorts return, the lion roars, "Ha! Ha! I'm King of the castle and you're the dirty rascals." Afterward, everyone has breakfast and the lion disappears—though not really. As the final picture shows, he's become the stuffed toy that appears so unobtrusively in the story's opening spread. The power-reversal theme will appeal to young psyches, and the full-color pen-and-ink drawings bring a sense of fun that matches the tale's exuberance.

Kirkus Reviews

SOURCE: A review of *A Lion in the Night,* in *Kirkus Reviews,* Vol. LIV, No. 8, April 15, 1986, p. 633.

A nighttime romp, first published in Australia, from the author/illustrator of *Who Sank the Boat?* and *Bertie and the Bear.*

The infant daughter of the King and Queen makes a wish and is whisked away by her toy-turned-real lion; her family pursues them over mountains, through fields, and across the sea. As morning nears, they grow tired, so the lion invites them all back to the castle for breakfast. Afterwards, "because it was morning, the lion just disappeared."

Allen's funny drawings, full of lovable characters and amusing details—the pursuers, in striped pajamas, are deployed across the double spreads in a series of rhythmical dances to echo the wonderfully cadenced text. The dream-adventure makes the night exciting, but leaves baby safe and sound when the sun rises, in this fantasy that begs to be shared aloud.

Joan McGrath

SOURCE: A review of *A Lion in the Night,* in *School*

Library Journal, Vol. 33, No. 1, September, 1986, p. 114.

This very slight story has a baby's wish come true. Tired of lying powerless in her crib, the frustrated baby chooses one of those magic nights when the moon is out and the tide is full to make her escape. Her toy lion becomes enormous and fierce, to carry her out of her parents' castle, over the fields, into the forest, past the church, into the boat, and so on in a circular chase, with the frantic castle-dwellers in pursuit. When they approach too closely, the lion disperses them with a roar. He and the baby are in control—until the morning, when the great lion disappears, and the stuffed toy is back in baby's crib. Allen's cartoon-like watercolors with pen and ink are amusing but inconsequential. Overall, this book is unmemorable: not to be compared with stronger wish-fulfillment drama such as *Where the Wild Things Are.*

HIDDEN TREASURE (1987)

Publishers Weekly

SOURCE: A review of *Hidden Treasure,* in *Publishers Weekly,* Vol. 232, No. 14, September 25, 1987, p. 109.

Allen's newest book presents a disarming look into the meaning of "treasure." Herbert and Harry are brothers who enjoy being together until they discover a treasure chest while fishing. The ensuing rift over ownership leaves Harry swimming for shore and Herbert escaping with the treasure. Herbert's concern over the treasure—that Harry or someone else will find it—turns the find into a lifelong burden as he searches for an impenetrable hideout so he can sleep without worry. His is a life of constant vigilence, while Harry, who "had no treasure," is surrounded by plump grandchildren and is "always able to sleep soundly." Allen's vibrant line-and-brush color illustrations show page after page of Herbert's burgeoning problems and then, with one revelatory picture of Harry, shows how the brothers' paths have drastically diverged. A bit of a moral and a lot of fun.

Ilene Cooper

SOURCE: A review of *Hidden Treasure,* in *Booklist,* Vol. 84, No. 6, November 15, 1987, p. 557.

Two brothers, Herbert and Harry, live together, work together, and enjoy each other's company. Then one day while in their fishing boat, they haul up what looks to be a pirate's chest, and the trouble begins. A fight ensues over the treasure's rightful owner, and Harry, pushed overboard, swims safely home. Herbert, however, rows away with the trophy; over the years he lugs it through a forest, carries it up a mountain, chips through a rock to make a hiding place for it, buys lots of guns to protect it, and grows to be a very old man who lives in a fortress with nothing but the wooden chest for company. Harry, on the other hand, with no treasure to worry about, sits

surrounded by his grandchildren, a happy man indeed. This is a message with a story, rather than vice-versa, and it's clever if not subtle. Vivid illustrations accented with cross-hatching have appeal, but the book will be of most interest to adults wishing to start a dialogue with children on the nature of happiness and what is important in life.

Mary M. Bush

SOURCE: A review of *Hidden Treasure,* in *The Horn Book Magazine,* Vol. LXIV, No. 1, January-February, 1988, p. 49.

Through the combination of a simple, straightforward text and finely detailed, striking illustrations, Australian picture-book artist Pamela Allen has created a powerful, contemporary interpretation of the old adage: "Money is the root of all evil." But she teaches without preaching, for she lets events speak for themselves, wisely resisting the temptation to intrude with an authorial commentary. Consequently, her story line remains a model of economy as she traces the contrasting fates of two brothers, Herbert and Harry, who are best friends and partners until one day, while fishing, they discover a great treasure. Immediately they become enemies, each claiming the reward until Herbert ends the argument by pushing Harry overboard. Harry, a strong swimmer, returns to the safety of his home and does not reappear until the story's end. Fearful that Harry might attempt to reassert his claim, Herbert rows to a deserted stretch of land, travels through a forest and then to the high hills, where he eventually creates a fortress to protect the treasure. For years, constantly on guard, "He cannot sleep. While Harry, who had no treasure, has always been able to sleep soundly." Although the narrative adequately differentiates between them, it is the accompanying illustrations that underscore the dramatic differences. Solitary Herbert stands armed atop his mountain peak; Henry, wearing comfortable slippers, sits on a sofa reading to his four loving grandchildren. Because of the close alliance between text and art, the illustrations play an important role in this picture book. The artist's use of crosshatching to create a stylized, three-dimensional setting gives a sense of space and time. Against this background her carefully exaggerated figures, distinguished by a cartoonist's sense of line, capture the irony of the situation with the timing of a true storyteller.

Jeanne Marie Clancy

SOURCE: A review of *Hidden Treasure,* in *School Library Journal,* Vol. 34, No. 7, March, 1988, pp. 156, 158.

When Harry and Herbert, two brothers, pull a treasure chest into their fishing boat, it signals the end of their companionable life together. In their struggle Herbert wins the treasure. Determined to keep it from Harry, Herbert searches for ever-safer places to hide the chest. His miserly quest finally ends atop a lonely mountain—isolated and fortified. Yet Herbert, always unable to sleep for

One night, when she had been
put to bed while it was still light,
she made a wish.

From A Lion in the Night, *written and illustrated by Pamela Allen.*

worry, still cannot rest. Meanwhile, Harry, who has never had trouble sleeping, lives a peaceful life surrounded by his loving family. Allen's colorful, cartoonlike watercolors reinforce the message of her short original tale. Herbert grays and balds before readers' eyes, emphasizing the depth of his lifetime obsession, and his stark and rocky surroundings point up the emotional barrenness of his life. In contrast, Harry glows within the warmth of his family circle. Allen's simple style and vocabulary makes for an effective readaloud or an excellent choice for young independent readers, yet this implicity belies the theme and content of her tale. What at first glance might appear to be a story for preschoolers might actually find its best audience with elementary school children—particularly in conjunction with a discussion of fables.

MR. MCGEE (1987)

E. Colwell

SOURCE: A review of *Mr. McGee,* in *The Junior Bookshelf,* Vol. 51, No. 6, December, 1987, p. 267.

Mr. McGee and his cat live under a tree quite contentedly

until one morning Mr. McGee makes the mistake of eating the 'wiggly skin' of his apple. This has an astonishing effect for he grows in size so rapidly and becomes so fat that he rises in the air like a balloon. It is an enjoyable experience, as can be seen from the pictures, until a bird mistakes him for a tasty morsel and punctures him in three places. Mr. McGee falls but, fortunately, on to his bed. He resumes his life as usual, a happy man pleased with little things.

The slight story is told in rhyming couplets and complemented by the large pictures, dominated by the tree. Children can watch Mr. McGee dressing, garment by garment, and inspect his domestic arrangements.

Some know-all child will notice that, although he has been punctured (in three places), he is still fat.

Brian McCabe

SOURCE: "Simply Entertaining," in *The Times Literary Supplement,* No. 4420, December 18, 1987, p. 1413.

Mr McGee by Pamela Allen is a refreshing and inspirational tale . . . It is the story of an eccentric character who lives under a tree and is transformed into a human balloon. He is just beginning to enjoy his floating existence when he is brought down to earth by a bird with a sharp beak. Though it is a simple tale simply told, it has a vital spark of magic. Pamela Allen shows that simple language need not be banal.

FANCY THAT! (1988)

M. Crouch

SOURCE: A review of *Fancy That!*, in *The Junior Bookshelf*, Vol. 52, No. 3, June, 1988, p. 129.

Fancy That! appeared first in Australia, but its message is universal. It is about communication. To all the enquiries of her farmyard neighbours the little red hen replies only 'Took.' The 'tooks' become more vociferous, the concern of the white leghorns more anxious, until the little red hen, having made sure that she is presentable, gets off her nest and reveals six fluffy chicks. 'Took!' indeed. Even the rooster joins in the celebrations. Pamela Allen draws with simplicity and directness, just as the matter demands. Her text is less than 200 words long, and one would not want a word more or less. It has that kind of perfection that passes unnoticed. Surely a winner with the smallest readers.

Margaret A. Bush

SOURCE: A review of *Fancy That!*, in *The Horn Book Magazine*, Vol. LXIV, No. 5, September-October, 1988, pp. 610-11.

Barnyard domesticity is happily conveyed in this simple, satisfying tale of a little red hen and her six brown eggs. Effectively structured, the story begins with a bright clear watercolor scene establishing location. "At the bottom of our garden is a red tin shed." A rooster and three white hens surround the shed. The next few pages build a cumulative scene inside the shed. There is a blue box containing straw, six eggs, and the red hen sitting on them. An ensuing dialogue between the chickens is the crux of the story and is likely to invite participation by young children. "'Took,' said the red hen. 'Really?' said the first white leghorn." When the preening red hen steps off the nest, the reason for her excitement is revealed to be six newly hatched chicks. The shed becomes noisy with a loud chorus of "took-took-tooking" followed by the cheeping of the chicks. When the rooster joins in, the chicks hop off the nest and follow their mother out into the yard. "'Fancy that!' said the little red hen." Brief narrative in large print faces many of the pictures; in all cases the noises of the chickens spill across the pages in hand-drawn red letters. The amazed and raucous chickens are depicted with clarity and good humor, and the understated plot helps make the book very engaging for story hours.

Jeanne Marie Clancy

SOURCE: A review of *Fancy That!*, in *School Library Journal*, Vol. 35, No. 4, December, 1988, p. 78.

In a box inside a shed is a nest on which there sits a little red hen. Proudly and patiently, she sits on her six brown eggs while the fancy white leghorns fuss around her. "Took, took," she replies. Finally, after carefully primping and preening, she stands to reveal her six yellow chicks. "Cheep, cheep!" The three white leghorns proclaim, "Took, took, took . . . !" and the rooster crows, "Cock-a-doodle-do!" And the little red hen is the star of the barnyard. Fancy that! Although *Fancy That!* initially sounds like one of Allen's cumulative tales, it lacks the chain-of-events momentum and rollicking rhythms of *Bertie and the Bear* and *A Lion in the Night.* The sole source of drama here is the little hen's secret. However, the book's graphic clarity and the simplest of plots make it a natural choice for toddlers, especially when one considers their fascination with animal young and animal sounds. Executed in Allen's signature style, the colorful line and wash illustrations are just the right size for group presentations. Simple lavender borders surround both the illustrations and the text but cannot contain the tooking, cheeping, and cock-a-doodle-doing of the farmyard fowl as they celebrate the new arrivals.

Moira Small

SOURCE: A review of *Fancy That!*, in *Books for Keeps*, No. 63, July, 1990, p. 8.

Immediate curiosity is aroused by the first page when it says 'At the bottom of our garden is a red tin shed', and page by page a discovery is made about what's inside. A simple story about a red hen sitting on her eggs with some white hens for company, and the most satisfactory ending produces a boxful of chicks. This shiny book has all the ingredients to make it perfect for a small child; it's clear and simple yet invites anticipation. The illustrations have humour and their meaning is plain. Definitely to be recommended for 3–5 year-olds.

I WISH I HAD A PIRATE SUIT (1990)

M. Hobbs

SOURCE: A review of *I Wish I Had a Pirate Suit*, in *The Junior Bookshelf*, Vol. 53, No. 6, December, 1989, p. 260.

In *I Wish I Had a Pirate Suit,* Pamela Allen has captured vividly the protracted frustrations of a small child who is always made to play his older brother's games. Peter moves on from pirate games to circuses, but by now his brother is old enough to stand up for himself and the "lion" unexpectedly turns. The visual narrative complements the text and develops it. Peter in his pirate suit exudes noise and insufferability as, vigorously drawn, he proceeds across an empty page with his sword and pistol.

The eyes of the reluctant little brother who has no pirate suit and has to be crew to Peter and endure his mean and bossy tormenting also interpret the text: expressive, uncertain, wistful, then contentedly self-assured. The story moves from and back to the living-room armchair, through a series of bright simple tropical scenes, the most heart-rending of which shows Peter at ease, galleon at anchor in the bay, under a sunshade beside a palm tree, having speared a (roast) jelly baby on his sword, while little brother proffers another on a plate: "He's eating all the jelly babies and there's nothing I can do."

S. J. Evans

SOURCE: A review of *I Wish I Had a Pirate Suit,* in *Books for Your Children,* Vol. 27, No. 1 Spring, 1992, p. 6.

My 5-year-old has never spoken these words to me out loud, but she immediately empathised with the book's title. In fact, I suspect we are both secretly more in love with the title of the book than the story. However, it has worn well over many readings, and will appeal especially to younger siblings who have put up with older children bossing them about. The little boy in this story is endlessly downtrodden in his older brother's games, but at least in his fantasies he can imagine turning the tables. Pamela Allen's pictures are colourful, cheerful redrawings of Pugwash themes.

MY CAT MAISIE (1991)

Betsy Hearne

SOURCE: A review of *My Cat Maisie,* in *Bulletin of the Center for Children's Books,* Vol. 44, No. 9, May, 1991, p. 209.

The best way to learn respect for animals is by animals' response to mistreatment, and Andrew is a prime candidate for a lesson. He's lonely, but the cat that strays into his arms runs quickly away after being squeezed, twirled ("Let's be helicopters and whizz round and round"), and submitted to games of fire engine and acrobat. As Andrew chases the fleeing cat, a neighboring dog plays rough with *him,* leading Andrew to gentler behavior when the cat reappears through the window to sleep on his bed. Allen's full-color compositions are simple but spiced with expressive action; this Australian award-winner has a warm and knowing way of projecting the world of small children—for their own enjoyment.

Margot Tyrrell

SOURCE: A review of *My Cat Maisie,* in *Magpies,* Vol. 6, No. 2, May, 1991, p. 20.

This is a book with a strongly child-centred opening: "Once upon a time there was a little boy called Andrew who didn't have anyone to play with." Andrew's efforts to play with a stray cat which comes to visit are so over-enthusiastic that the cat refuses to stay. Gradually, with the help of the dog next door who "gallumphs" all over Andrew, he learns the need to be caring and gentle. The illustrations are vibrant and full of movement—and so true-to-life, as anyone who has ever had a cat and an overly loving child, will testify! This is a book with a positive message conveyed in a beautifully designed and appealing way.

Publishers Weekly

SOURCE: A review of *My Cat Maisie,* in *Publishers Weekly,* Vol. 238, No. 23, May 24, 1991, p. 57.

Learning how to be a friend is one of life's most important lessons—and one that often has to be learned the hard way. So it proves in Allen's (*A Lion in the Night*) winsome tale. Friendless Andrew is thrilled when a scruffy stray cat turns up on his doorstep, but in his eagerness to play he's a bit too rough, and the kitty vamooses. Lobo, the frisky dog next door, turns the tables on the boy, who soon learns what roughhousing really means. A kinder, gentler Andrew emerges, ready to be a better friend when Maisie reappears—this time for keeps. Without being stodgy or didactic, Allen's ingenuous story and puckish illustrations (the feckless feline's array of expressions are priceless) help to convey some of the finer points of a potentially complex subject.

Kirkus Reviews

SOURCE: A review of *My Cat Maisie,* in *Kirkus Reviews,* Vol. LIX, No. 11, June 1, 1991, p. 727.

The big boy next door has a big dog named Lobo, but Andrew has no one to play with. He welcomes a stray cat with altogether too much glee ("Let's play wild Indians and you can be the horse"); the cat bolts. A daunting attempt to play with the obstreperous Lobo gives Andrew a salutary taste of the cat's feelings; when she creeps back that night, he welcomes her gently and the two make friends.

The message here is presented nicely in the events, which this prize-winning Australian conveys in a nicely compact text sparked with graphic words like "gallumphed" and in wonderfully expressive illustrations. Sturdy little Andrew is the image of his plump, comfortable mother, who has the same irrepressible gleam in her eye; his relentless activity is reiterated in each deftly observed posture. A perfect blend of text and pictures to make an entertaining story.

Lauralyn Persson

SOURCE: A review of *My Cat Maisie,* in *School Library Journal,* Vol. 37, No. 9, September, 1991, p. 226.

When a stray cat shows up at Andrew's house, the boy is

so delighted that he becomes overly excited. The cat, alarmed by the child's exuberance, takes off. Andrew follows and runs into the neighbor's playful dog, Lobo, who overpowers him just as the boy overpowered the cat. Andrew gets a second chance when the cat scratches at his window and he strokes her "gently, very very gently." Allen's simple picture book features a single line of action, no extraneous characters, concise but not bare-bones language, emotions with which children can identify, and a satisfying conclusion that also carries a nicely understated message. The illustrations are also successful. The characters are all expressively and sometimes humorously depicted; Allen's pen-and-ink and watercolor paintings convey a strong feeling of movement and action, and her use of white space for visual emphasis is especially effective.

📖 *BLACK DOG* (1992)

Kevin Steinberger

SOURCE: A review of *Black Dog,* in *Magpies,* Vol. 6, No. 4, September, 1991, p. 30.

With *Black Dog* Pamela Allen is moving into a new direction, away from her usual infant readership. The richly coloured ink drawings in her characteristic style remain and enhance the haunting, lyrical quality of the deceptively simple metaphorical story.

Christina lives with Black Dog on the edge of a forest. In spring, summer and autumn they rollick together in rumbustious play. Winter arrives creating a bleak landscape, the trees shed their leaves. Pitying the hungry birds, Christina spreads crumbs on the ground and waits for a response. One day she thinks she sees a flash of blue, "a strange and wonderful blue bird." From that moment she dreams of the bird and spends all her waking hours hoping for a glimpse of it. At the same time the dog's demeanour sadly changes as he is shunned in her quest for the blue bird. But just before spring arrives, she hears a sound, rushes outside, and from the top of the newly-greening trees flies Black Dog. He crashes to the ground to be cuddled by the chastened girl.

It is an abstract tale; the reader must ruminate over the link between the imagined blue bird and the dog's attempt to fly. There is much symbolism that opens the story up to different interpretations. Young readers might recognise the essential theme of love and rejection, however, it will be best appreciated by an older audience. Perhaps Allen's best work to date in both story and illustration.

Meg Sorensen

SOURCE: A review of *Black Dog*, in *Australian Book Review*, No. 135, October, 1991, pp. 53-4.

From Pamela Allen's first publication in 1980 it was clear that here was a creator of picture books with all the glow, gesture, din and dance to capture the attention, engage the imagination, teach, show, tickle and excite small children. Some of the early picture books (***Bertie and the Bear, Who Sank the Boat?*** and ***Mr Archimedes Bath***) are classics—picture books for the very young that are as bold, bright and beautiful as has been published, anywhere, anytime. ***Herbert and Harry***, published in 1987, was less successful, but foretold a more serious, weighty tone (message) which the delightful ***My Cat Maisie*** pursued. Maisie's success lay in the combination of strong message with all the visual lightness, joy and clarity of the earlier books.

Black Dog succeeds in going deeper again, into territory where few modern storytellers dare to travel—delving confidently and with profound accomplishment into the psychological realm of fairy tale. Beneath the manifest simplicity of a picture book for young children lies a substance and complexity to match the brothers Grimm.

Championing the virtues of fairy tales, Bettelheim says that 'the fairy tale's concern is not useful information about the external world, but the inner processes taking place in an individual'. And while ***Black Dog*** may appear to be a picture book about a little girl and a dog, beneath the surface a journey is taking place which leads inexorably to the illumination of a simple truth—the blue bird of happiness may well abide in the black dog of reality.

The knowing of this kind of truth can only be truly achieved through what Bettelheim called an 'internal process', for even though as an adult I may intellectually know the formula, my heart (which has its own say in the way I act) so quickly forgets. Fairy tales teach the heart to remember. This cannot be achieved through what Bettelheim calls 'abstract ethical concepts' (although a legion of right-minded instruction manuals thinly disguised as picture books may suggest otherwise), 'but through that which seems tangibly right and therefore meaningful to him (her)'. In other words, through the medium of a simple, brief, clear story a child is taken through an experience which teaches her or him something significant about life. The story, of course, must work equally hard both at engaging the child's consciousness in the journey and at the impression made on the psyche at the point of resolution. Profound stuff for a picture book, but Pamela Allen has pulled it off.

'Black Dog and Christina lived together in a little house near a forest.' The stage for the fairy story is set: small house, small child, big forest—no clutter of adults or any other meddling references to the 'real' world. Christina and Black Dog are happy, until the little girl thinks she glimpses 'a flash of blue . . . a strange and wonderful bird'. She forgets the dog, pines and dreams of the blue bird. 'In this way the winter passed.' (It is interesting to note here the significant change in the style of Allen's text; the language has none of the explosive exuberance of her earlier books, but is pared down, understated—a melancholic whisper befitting the passing on of a timeless wisdom. This is the language of fairy tales and Allen is not for a moment out of her depth.)

The story continues throughout the winter as, cast aside by the pining child, Black Dog becomes more and more dejected. (Here Allen's skill as a creator of picture books really comes to the fore as she visibly separates the dog in the black and white of its misery from the coloured longing of the little girl.) Finally to try to win back his friend, the dog takes to the tree tops and tries to fly. No heart can be left untouched by the sight of Black Dog falling helplessly to earth trying pathetically clumsily beautifully to imitate the flight of a bird.

We at ABR [Australian Book Review] had some terrible moments wondering whether the dog had actually died. Although the text tells us that 'his heart was beating fast', he looks frighteningly lifeless, lying limp in the arms of the repentant child. This raises yet again the complex question of whether the small child should be confronted by the reality of cause and effect. In life sometimes the lesson does come too late and too hard—the real chance to grasp the moment of happiness lying at our feet is lost, as our eyes remain fixed on the chimera we thought we saw in the treetops. The question is, of course, should small children be subjected to the harsh sad truth that humans are not always saved by the flash of insight and bravery just in the nick of time? In fairy tales there is almost always resolution in hope; good deeds and lessons learnt lead to fine rewards. I think it's safe to assume that Black Dog lives happily ever after too. It is certainly safe to assume that Christina's journey led to understanding—a journey offered to every child blessed with an adult to read them this wonderful book.

M. Hobbs

SOURCE: A review of *Black Dog*, in *The Junior Bookshelf*, Vol. 56, No. 2, April, 1992, p. 52.

This is a moving, rather frightening fable, wonderfully illustrated by Pamela Allen's expressive round-eyed Christina and her adoring Black Dog. The gay abandon (one *must* still be able to use that term!) of movement in the early happy scenes before winter comes, outside the little house near the forest where they live, contrasts sharply with the bare, grey tree trunks in serried ranks and the tangible cold, as Christina and Black Dog scatter crumbs from her loaf for the birds. The two watch them come from the window—until she glimpses a strange and wonderful blue bird. The illustrations chart her obsession with this chimaera and the gradual exclusion of Black Dog, until at last she thinks she sees it fly again: Black Dog has risked his life in an attempt to provide for her what she wants and regain her love. Christina apparently comes to her senses in time. This is a haunting little story, both in words and pictures.

Moira Small

SOURCE: A review of *Black Dog*, in *Books for Keeps*, No. 80, May, 1993, p. 7.

The story of a black dog and a girl called Christina who are best friends. They have great fun together until one day Christina starts dreaming about a beautiful blue bird and forgets to play with Black Dog. Eventually he manages to get her attention by pretending to be the blue bird flying up in the trees; only when he falls and hurts himself does Christina realise how much she loves him. What a good way of understanding how painful it can be to love and to feel jealous—something small children often need explained. I'm sure this book will help enormously.

BELINDA (1993)

Kevin Steinberger

SOURCE: A review of *Belinda*, in *Magpies*, Vol. 8, No. 2, May, 1993, p. 26.

Routine is the keystone of life on the farm of old Tom and Bessie. Each day Tom works in the garden and Bessie milks Belinda the cow. And the dog, cat and pig wait patiently for their certain drink of milk. They are, all of them, creatures of habit. But when Bessie's trip to the city interrupts that routine, chaos reigns on the farm; Belinda refuses to let Tom milk her. A comical battle of wits ensues until Tom triumphs with a highly amusing, ingenious ploy—a masterstroke of lateral thinking.

Belinda represents a superb harmony of words and pictures. Pamela Allen's charming illustration style has varied little over the years but each new book is invested with a freshness that appeals to new and familiar young readers. Here again is an energetic romp across broad white space, over and around large-print text, of the two adversaries brightly coloured and fetching in loose, exaggerated line. The text is longer than usual but not a word is wasted. It reads aloud superbly, sustaining the story and teasing out Tom's predicament with much amusing repetition.

The book's clear, uncluttered design deserves commendation and is sure to stand out for infant readers with its striking simplicity. No one could resist the pink bordered cover portrait of the rather winsome Belinda.

Janet Taylor

SOURCE: A review of *Belinda*, in *The School Librarian*, Vol. 41, No. 2, May, 1993, p. 53.

Bessie has gone away for the day leaving Old Tom to milk Belinda the cow. Belinda is reluctant to cooperate, to say the least! Should he speak nicely to her? Should he tempt her with a juicy carrot? Eventually, he has to disguise himself to win Belinda's confidence.

The book's text is large and clear, and used in such a way as to give extra emphasis at certain points. Every page is set out in an individual way. Pamela Allen's illustrations are bold, boisterous and extremely funny. Portions of the story are repeated or echoed, reminiscent of a nursery rhyme, which makes *Belinda* an excellent book to be read aloud or read with a young reader. Overall, it is easy to recommend this book highly to all readers, young and young-at-heart.

Kirkus Reviews

SOURCE: A review of *Belinda,* in *Kirkus Reviews,* Vol. LXI, No. 11, June 1, 1993, p. 715.

Bessie milks Belinda every day, while Old Tom grows vegetables; but when Bessie goes to visit her daughter, Old Tom is to do the milking. "There's a good girl," he croons, whereupon Belinda declares her intentions with "one almighty kick." She's faster than he is, and also smart enough to snatch the carrot he offers before escaping. But Old Tom is clever: Disguising himself as Bessie, he gets milk for himself as well as the family dog, cat, and pig; and the only evidence, when Bessie comes home, is mud on the hem of her dress. Allen's lively story is as succinct and neatly honed as a folktale, while her deftly designed illustrations—pen-and-watercolor figures silhouetted on clean, white pages—are splendidly witty. Plump, cheery Bessie is a fine foil for bearded, bald-topped Tom, whose slight, agile figure is amusingly repeated across the spreads, counterpointed by his rope or his flying bucket. A delightful offering from this much-honored New Zealander/Australian; perfect to share with a group.

Elizabeth S. Watson

SOURCE: A review of *Belinda,* in *The Horn Book Magazine,* Vol. LXIX, No. 4, July-August, 1993, p. 439.

Humor abounds in this tale of Belinda the cow and her hapless master, Old Tom. When Old Tom's wife, Bessie, goes off to visit her daughter and leaves him to tend to Belinda, trouble begins. Not only will the cow not give Old Tom any milk, she leads him a merry chase—"mooing and trotting, mooing and trotting . . . What WAS Old Tom to do?" The farmyard appears to have a milkless future until Old Tom finds a comical, if not strictly plausible, answer. The text flows beautifully, with a strong rhythmic refrain and expertly employed repetition that enforces the fun. The simple, whimsical pictures are the perfect accompaniment to the lighthearted text. An outstanding readaloud.

Debra S. Gold

SOURCE: A review of *Belinda,* in *School Library Journal,* Vol. 40, No. 1, January, 1994, p. 80.

Bessie and Old Tom enjoy their serene life in the country and vigorously attack their personal chores to keep things on an even keel; every day, she milks Belinda and he works in the garden. However, events take a drastic turn for Old Tom when Bessie visits her daughter in the city

overnight. The highly responsible job of milking the cow is then delegated to him—and Belinda has a mind of her own. But this man refuses to be bested by the animal and comes up with the perfect solution: he puts on his wife's pink dress, rubber boots, and straw hat, and lo and behold, the cow thinks he's her beloved mistress. The final result is milk in abundance. Allen delivers a zany story of stubbornness and determination through a simple text that bounces along with a light and breezy tone. Its clever use of repetition and crisp sentences beg to be read aloud. The watercolor illustrations with India-ink crosshatchings are manipulated with great flair to create small, comical figures that are often shown in a series to create an animated effect. Children will revel in the sheer silliness and appreciate the creative solution.

Mr. MCGEE AND THE BLACKBERRY JAM (1993)

Mandy Chootham

SOURCE: A review of *Mr. McGhee and the Blackberry Jam,* in *Magpies,* Vol. 8, No. 5, November, 1993, p. 25.

The resourceful Mr McGee, as fresh as ever after the eventful *Mr McGee Goes to Sea,* is back to sort himself out of another pickle. In a fit of pique, the gentleman declares that he must have blackberry jam instead of marmalade on his bread. Accordingly, he sets out with resolution to find a source of blackberries. But an unfortunate encounter with a group of curious heifers puts a stop to his plans to pick blackberries and make jam.

This is an excellent choice for preschool storytime programmes. For reading aloud, the combination of a brisk rhyming text, strong, but concise storyline and neatly rounded conclusion allows plenty of scope for expression and audience participation.

The pictures balance precisely with the text and add the right touches of humour and incidental action which enrich the story. Once again, the book has achieved the high standard of technical and creative expertise in terms of design, typography, layout and clarity of illustration which is now a hallmark of Allen's work.

Very suitable for reading aloud to children aged between 3 and 5 years. Highly recommended.

Carol Woolley

SOURCE: A review of *Mr. McGhee and the Blackberry Jam,* in *The School Librarian,* Vol. 42, No. 1, February, 1994, p. 15.

In this latest offering from Australian author Pamela Allen, Mr. McGee decides he wants blackberry jam on his bread rather than marmalade, and sets off in search of the desired fruit.

With simple illustrations and a clear rhyming text, this humorous picture book will appeal to preschoolers as well as to those learning to read independently. It is obvious that the book was written for the Australian market since it includes several words that may have to be explained to young readers, for example, 'billy can' and 'kookaburra'; but hopefully this will not detract from their enjoyment of the story.

CLIPPITY CLOP (1994)

Nola Allen

SOURCE: A review of *Clippity-Clop,* in *Magpies,* Vol. 9, No. 5, November, 1994, p. 23.

Clippity-clop employs the features of many of Pamela Allen's entertaining picture books from effective design and typography to humorous illustrations and rollicking text. A little old woman and a little old man share a common problem and the same resources with which to solve it—a heavy load to be delivered by obstinate donkeys.

As the title suggests, this story, bursting with sounds, requires an energetic rendition. The typography varies in size, font and placement indicating changes in volume, speed and rhythm. Speech balloons from two other characters provide another perspective of the story and opportunity for further reader participation. The clever use of white space and the main action of the story draws the eye from left to right across the double page spreads. Even the book's glowing cover festooned with carrots hints at the colloquialism that is about to be explored. One quibble with the depiction of the man is that he does not look old whereas the little old lady at least sports long, greying locks!

Once again, this Australian author/illustrator discovers a way to teach and entertain preschool children within the pages of a picture book.

Linnet Hunter

SOURCE: A review of *Clippity-Clop,* in *Australian Book Review,* No. 167, December, 1994 & January, 1995, pp. 60-1.

Pamela Allen's approach exerts a much tighter control over the page. A little old woman, a little old man and two stubborn donkeys are the bare elements of *Clippity-Clop* and its simplicity is utterly deceptive.

The written text occurs only in the bottom quarter of the landscape format, while the visual text is placed above it, across the full double page spread. The horizontal line is used to full effect to increase the sense of travelling distance as the donkeys gallop, rear up, refuse and plod along it, variously enticed by carrots and sticks.

Allen's use of white space is as interesting as her strengths with posture, gesture and the broken line penwork which imbues each captured moment with the movement of moments both previous and yet to be.

She is very playful with the form of her texts. This one is, as pointed out on the end paper, a soundtrack which tells us onomatopoeiacally the sounds which accompany each action, and the type is variously italicised, enlarged over a word, reduced or placed end to end like bricks. This gives read aloud clues (whisper, shout or sing) and also ensures that it becomes part of the picture and the graphic appeal of the page. Pre-readers seem to appreciate the shapes of letters, so black and clear.

Even the most monotonous reader will find themselves unable to resist performing it exuberantly; a book to play with and in.

Additional coverage of Allen's life and career is contained in the following sources published by Gale Research: *Contemporary Authors,* Vol. 126; *Contemporary Authors New Revision Series,* Vol. 53; and *Something about the Author,* Vols. 50, 81.

Leo Dillon

1933–

Diane Dillon

1933–

American illustrators.

Major works include *Why Mosquitoes Buzz in People's Ears: A West African Tale* (by Verna Aardema, 1975), *Ashanti to Zulu: African Traditions* (by Margaret Musgrove, 1976), *The People Could Fly: American Black Folk Tales* (by Virginia Hamilton, 1985), *The Tale of the Mandarin Ducks* (by Katherine Paterson, 1990).

INTRODUCTION

Collaborating since the late 1950s, Leo and Diane Dillon

are highly regarded husband-and-wife illustrators of children's books. Each an individually gifted artist, the Dillons have combined their talents on a variety of projects, including book jackets, album covers, and other commercial art, but they have largely focused their efforts on children's literature, claiming that the field offers the greatest opportunities for artistic freedom and experimentation. Often praised for their versatility, the Dillons have demonstrated their ability to convey a variety of styles, creating effects similar to those of African batik, medieval woodcuts, art nouveau, and Japanese *ukiyo-e* images. This flexibility of style is likewise apparent in the range of their projects, which include illustrations for African folk tales, Scandinavian and Greek epics, literary classics, science fiction, fantasy, and concept books. Their works have been called bold and imaginative, and the Dillons are frequently noted for their innovative artistic techniques, including their use of a specialized frisket—a kind of stencil—combined with pastels. Beginning each work on a conceptual level, the artists hash out ideas together and then begin sketching in pencil. Later, the images are refined as the piece is passed back and forth between the two, errors are corrected, and finally color is added. In producing each work of art as a team, the Dillons have often referred to the creation of a third artist, whose talents synthesize their individual skills and allow for the creation of new styles and forms. In addition to praise for their experimental techniques, the Dillons have been lauded for the accuracy and the depth of their artistic research, particularly for their realistic and Caldecott award-winning paintings in *Ashanti to Zulu: African Traditions.* Leo and Diane Dillon believe that their art should not merely reflect a story, but enlarge upon it and render it with added depth and vitality. This is apparent in all their work, but perhaps more so in those instances when their illustrations are described as outshining the accompanying text.

Biographical Information

Diane (Sorber) Dillon was born in Glendale, California, on March 13, 1933. Her father was a teacher and her mother a pianist and homemaker. Although she demonstrated a precocious artistic talent as a child, she received very little formal training until she enrolled in Los Angeles City College in 1951—prior to this both of her parents had expected that she would marry and raise a family instead of pursuing a public career. In 1952, Diane contracted tuberculosis and spent nearly a year in convalescence. After recovering, she moved in with her aunt and uncle in order to attend Skidmore College. Unhappy there, she transferred to Parsons School of Design, where she met Leo Dillon, in 1954. Leo Dillon was born eleven days prior to Diane in Brooklyn, New York. His parents had emigrated from Trinidad and owned a small trucking business in New York City. They encouraged Leo's youthful interest in art, and enrolled him in art classes as a child. He attended Manhattan's High School of Industrial Arts (now Art and Design) and later served in the United States Navy between 1950–53. This period of military service allowed him to earn money for college through the GI Bill, and to enroll in Parsons School of Design in 1953. Although highly competitive at Parsons, the two artists each developed an immense respect for the other's talents and work. Following graduation in 1956, the two separated briefly and Leo began working as the art director for West Park Publications, but the couple were eventually reunited and married in March of 1957. Shortly thereafter, Leo and Diane Dillon decided to embark on a joint freelance career. In the late 1950s and early 1960s the Dillons operated under the name Studio 2, allowing them to produce work in an assortment of styles. By the 1960s they had earned considerable regard for their album covers and book jackets and had begun

illustrating children's books; among their first projects were Erik C. Haugaard's Scandinavian epics *Hakon of Rogen's Saga* (1963) and *A Slave's Tale* (1965). They experienced even greater fame in the following decade with the publication of the highly successful *Why Mosquitoes Buzz in People's Ears* and *Ashanti to Zulu.* Concurrently, Leo Dillon worked as an instructor in artistic method at New York's School of Visual Arts between 1969–77. In the ensuing years, the Dillons have continued to illustrate books for children and adults and to experiment with and develop new artistic techniques. Likewise, the artistic team has been honored with a variety of awards for their outstanding work spanning four decades.

Major Works

Over the course of their career the Dillons have been commended for their vast array of artistic creations designed to accompany the texts of children's books. Praised for elegant, stylized figures, rich imagery, realistic detail, bold lines, and sumptuous colors, the Dillons' illustrations have proved to be some of the most compelling in children's literature. Often their art evokes a powerful mood or setting, as in the memories of Aunt Dew rendered in soft brown and white for Sharon Bell Mathis's *The Hundred Penny Box* (1975). The stylized, full-color figures of *Why Mosquitoes Buzz in People's Ears* were thought by Ethel L. Heins to possess "a lush, forceful splendor which almost overshadows the humorous, naïve folk tale." In *Ashanti to Zulu,* the Dillons demonstrate their capacity for realism and detail. Their color paintings record the ordinary lives of a man, a woman, and a child from twenty-six different African tribes. For each illustration in acrylic, pastel, and watercolor, the artists endeavored to recreate an authentic setting and to include examples of regional clothing, wildlife, and dwellings. *Who's in Rabbit's House? A Masai Tale* represents another of the Dillons' books based upon African sources. For the work, the artists painted multiple, overlapping images of their human figures clad in animal masks in order to convey a sense of action and motion. The ornate illustrations of *Two Pairs of Shoes* (1980), a collection of two Middle Eastern folk tales retold by P. L. Travers, demonstrate the Dillons' ability to render complex detail and a sense of heightened activity, as well as capture the Persian atmosphere of Travers's stories. For Virginia Hamilton's retellings of African American folk tales entitled *The People Could Fly,* the Dillons adopted a more restrained and elegant approach in their art, creating their subtle, yet expressive figures in black and white. Patricia Dooley admired the "attenuated art nouveau curves; flat planes of muted color; and stylized, elongated forms" in Michael Patrick Hearn's *The Porcelain Cat* (1987). In order to create the images for *The Tale of the Mandarin Ducks,* an eastern fable about kindness and wickedness adapted by Katherine Paterson, the Dillons studied the Japanese woodcut style known as *ukiyo-e,* which dates from the seventeenth-century. Their graceful watercolor and pastel drawings in the work blend *ukiyo-e* with a more modern art deco style and are said to be as emotive as the story itself, leading Ann Banks to observe that "even the cruel lord's robe looks mean." The Dillons' talent for adapting various styles is likewise shown in *Pish, Posh, Hieronymus Bosch* (written by Nancy Willard, 1991), in which the fantastic and grotesque manner of the medieval painter is captured in their alternating sepia and full-color paintings.

Awards

The Dillons were awarded the prestigious Caldecott Medal by the American Library Association in 1976 for their illustrations in *Why Mosquitoes Buzz in People's Ears*, making Leo Dillon the first African American to receive the honor. The following year, the Caldecott committee again selected the Dillons for the same recognition, this time for *Ashanti to Zulu*—the only time the award has been granted two years consecutively to the same individual or individuals. *Ashanti to Zulu* also earned the Hamilton King Award for excellence in illustration from the Society of Illustrators, 1977, and was chosen one of *New York Times* Best Illustrated Children's Books in 1976. Among many other honors the Dillons have received are the Lewis Carroll Shelf Award for *Who's in Rabbit's House? A Masai Tale* in 1978 and the *Boston Globe-Horn Book* Award for picture book in 1991 for *The Tale of the Mandarin Ducks.*

AUTHOR'S COMMENTARY

Leo Dillon

SOURCE: "Diane Dillon," in *The Horn Book Magazine,* Vol. LIII, No. 4, August, 1977, pp. 422-3.

Diane Dillon is one of the finest artists I've ever known, and I realized it even before I met her. I was at Parsons School of Design in New York City when one day I noticed a painting hanging on the wall at a student exhibition. It was a painting of a chair—an Eames chair—and I knew it had to be by a new student because nobody in our class at the time could paint like that. I looked at the painting, and I thought, "I'm in trouble now!" This artist could draw. That was all right—I could draw too. This artist knew perspective, which is one of the most difficult things a beginner has to learn. And most important—this artist had the patience to *render*! This artist was a whole lot better than I. I figured I'd better find out who he was. *He* was Diane.

I hadn't spoken to her yet—in fact, I wasn't sure I was going to—when she came over to me and said, "You are very good." "Hah!" I thought. "Talented Miss Wasp is now going to condescend to tell one of the menials he's good. *I* know better." I said, "I see that one of your pieces is very nice too." And that pretty much set the tone of our relationship for the next several years.

One of the things about Di's work that's so incredible is her use of color. She can do things with color I can hardly believe—make reds look cool and blues look warm, things like that—because she really understands color. Once, after we were married, we were working on a piece and she mentioned very casually that we should do the color in pink and orange. "If we do it in pink and orange," I said, "that will be the end! I can't live with someone who'd do anything in pink and orange. We'll have to get a divorce!" We did it in pink and orange, of course, and a couple of years later everywhere I turned I was seeing things in pink and orange. It's a common combination now.

People wonder a lot about how we work together. But I don't think people ever realize how hard it was for us to learn how to blend our styles. It was years and years before we could pass a piece of work back and forth between us and not get into a fight. One time we were working on an illustration, and we just couldn't agree about the approach. It was a book jacket, I think, something about medieval knights. I thought the style should be rough and strong; Di thought it should be fine and delicate. We fought about it, but neither of us could convince the other, and neither was willing to compromise. We ended up using both styles—the bottom half showing the horses was done in woodcuts, or anyway, something that was rough and crude, and the top half, which showed the knights, was done finely and delicately. As I recall, it worked out all right, but I know how!

Things are good now, though. It used to be that one of us would do the actual drawing and the other would make comments or draw a change on a tissue overlay. But now one of us can just pass the piece of art to the other, and he or she can erase what's wrong and redraw right on the original. Our egos aren't at stake anymore.

As a matter of fact, everything's going well now. It's really one of the nicest times in my life. The art is good, and our son Lee, now twelve, is old enough to work with. I love working on things with him—like on the house. Once I was putting in a floor and Lee was helping me. I'd measured everything and shown him what to do, and we were both working away. In about ten minutes he came over to me and said, "I think your measurements are wrong." Very quietly. Very modestly. Very correctly. I let him measure the whole floor, and it's a beautiful job. He's wonderful. Having three artists in the house—or maybe it's four, since Di and I do so much work together—is better than anything I ever dreamed of.

Diane Dillon

SOURCE: "Leo Dillon," in *The Horn Book Magazine,* Vol. LIII, No. 4, August, 1977, pp. 423-5.

When I think about Leo, the first thing that comes to mind is his strength. Obviously he's strong physically, but that's not what I mean, although one strength is symbolic of the other. It's more a matter of endurance and remarkable patience—although he's terribly impatient waiting for rubber cement to dry! Leo is really a study in opposites. He's patient with the big things, impatient with the small. He has incredible conviction, and yet he is able to admit mistakes, to change his mind and his direction if he feels he has been wrong.

The most wonderful thing about Leo's strength, though, is his ability to transmit it to other people, to energize them, to act as motivator. He does this to many people, and he certainly does it to me. When we were first married, Leo had a job as an art director at a magazine. I was determined to be the model 1950s housewife, and that didn't include drawing or painting. Leo took this for a while, then he casually began bringing work home, encouraging me to work with him on design problems, easing me back into art. That was really the beginning of our working together as one artist, I think. Finally there was a blow-up and I got back to work!

Leo has incredible energy. I don't think he's ever quite understood that I need sleep occasionally; he feels sleep is a form of death—time spent not doing anything. In fact, until a few years ago he slept with his clothes on, so he'd be ready to go at a moment's notice.

Leo is, I think, the kindest man I've ever known—and really that's part of his strength and his ability to motivate people. He doesn't like crowds, big parties—things like that—but he truly loves people, and love radiates from him. He's concerned about how people feel, about what they think—of themselves more than of him—and he'll go out of his way not to hurt someone.

He can be tricky, though: "You're so much better at such-and-such," he'll tell me, implying, "Why don't you do it?" He had me balancing the checkbook for years before he sat down and explained to me a faster way to add! Obviously I wasn't better at it at all—but I'm still balancing the checkbook.

Someone asked us recently who was the perfectionist, and I'd say it was Leo, but sometimes it's hard to tell when you work so closely together. I do know, though, that our real feeling about aiming for perfection began with *Why Mosquitoes Buzz in People's Ears*. Suddenly it seemed that neither of us could tolerate even a tiny flaw, a minute speck on the black night sky, and we strove for artistic perfection on that book more than on any other except *Ashanti to Zulu*. In a way, when *Mosquitoes* won the Caldecott Medal, it was as much a reward for us as an award. We had worked harder to achieve perfection—although, of course, we didn't achieve it—than we ever had before, and people somehow knew it.

I don't want to end a biography of Leo without saying something about Lee, for he is so much our pride. Lee has always been a sweet spirit and very much a part of us, never against us in any way. Other babies may have been fussy and colicky, but not Lee—he even seemed to know when we had a deadline to meet. And now that he's growing up, he probably understands us better than anyone,

puts up with our quirks, and stands now on his own in a beautiful way.

GENERAL COMMENTARY

Phyllis J. Fogelman

SOURCE: "Leo and Diane Dillon," in *The Horn Book Magazine,* Vol. LII, No. 4, August, 1976, pp. 378-83.

Diane and Leo Dillon were born just eleven days apart in the month of March and both recall loving to draw for as long as they can remember. Although there are other similarities in their backgrounds, there are also great differences.

Leo was born and brought up in Brooklyn, New York. His parents came from Trinidad to this country as adults, and it was here that they met, married, and had two children. But because their formative years had been spent in the West Indies, they could not perceive the true state of race relations in the United States—a fact that was to be partly an advantage for their son but also an enormous burden. Not knowing they were supposed to stay in the ghetto, Leo's parents made sure that they lived in the best neighborhood they could afford. Mr. Dillon owned his own truck, and Mrs. Dillon was a dressmaker. They rented at first and later bought a house on the same block in the East New York section of Brooklyn where they lived throughout Leo's childhood. This meant that Leo went to better schools than most Black children, for then even more than in the 1970's, ghetto schools got the fewest supplies and the least experienced teachers. His mother and father couldn't understand discrimination, so when the inevitable racial problems arose or when Leo was excluded from things everyone else took part in, they blamed their son, refusing to entertain the possibility of discrimination.

Leo had to cover up his true feelings at school in order to cope. At the same time he was not allowed to discuss his feelings and anxieties at home. So out of necessity the young boy became secretive and something of a loner. Since he could always draw well, he turned wholeheartedly to art which became both a source of pleasure and the main outlet for his feelings. His talent made Leo the center of attention at school and saw him through many painful times. "I could always draw my way out of bad situations," Leo recalls.

His parents encouraged him. They were proud that he was so talented, and they always bought him paints and art supplies. But the thought never occurred to them that their son would pursue art as a career. They, after all, had come to the United States during the Depression, and the few artists they saw were on the dole.

His mother and father had always planned that Leo would

study medicine or law, and they knew, of course, that he had to go to high school before college. What they didn't understand and Leo didn't tell them was that the high school Leo had chosen would not prepare him for these professions. Leo went to the School of Industrial Arts in Manhattan which now, in its modern building on East Fifty-seventh Street, is called The High School of Art and Design. It was marvelous for Leo. He loved it, and the four years he spent there were years of bliss. For the first time he belonged. Race was irrelevant in this school; art was important. None of the students felt threatened—they were coming together to do creative work, which was all that mattered.

It was here that Leo met and was taught by Benjamin Clements. "Clements was a great teacher, an excellent draftsman, and a gentle person. He shaped my life." After four happy years Leo made up his mind to join the Navy, a determination which was to serve two purposes: First, it allowed him to put off the decision of what to do with his life, and second, it would make him eligible for the GI bill, providing him with money for college. Leo found the experience boring but bearable. The combination of his physical strength and drawing talent again pulled him through some difficult moments, particularly with white sailors from the Deep South. After leaving the Navy he worked for a while with his father, building up the business. Then, on the advice of Benjamin Clements, he enrolled in Parsons School of Design.

Diane was born in Glendale, California. She always knew she wanted to be an artist, and therefore she drew all the time. Her father was a high school teacher, and her mother was a pianist and an organist. Although her family always lived in Southern California, they moved thirteen times, so Diane and her older brother attended two elementary schools, three junior high schools, four high schools, and three colleges. The one constant in her life, other than her family, was art.

As a child Diane had no formal art training except during her eleventh year when she took oil painting lessons one hour a week from an octogenarian. Although her parents encouraged her artistic talent, their general attitude was that, while it was nice for her to have this ability, it really wasn't important since she was expected to get married and be taken care of. "I went through a classic period as a proper young girl when I wanted to be a nurse," says Diane. She also fleetingly considered being a stewardess and very briefly went to modeling school, but she really was determined to have some kind of career in art. During her high school years there were a number of discussions about money for college. Diane's parents decided that if there was enough money for only one, her brother would go to college, since it was his work that would matter in later life.

The summer she completed high school, Diane worked at Lake Tahoe and earned enough money to pay for her tuition at Los Angeles City College, which she attended for two years as an art major while her family lived in Hollywood. She started in fashion design but switched to advertising after a year. Then she contracted tuberculosis and spent a year in a sanatorium, reading most of the time. Then Diane went to live in Schenectady, New York, with an aunt and an uncle who sent her to Skidmore College, where she again majored in art. She commuted for a semester, but traveling was a great waste of time, and in her second semester she moved onto the campus. Diane recalls that she didn't fit in at Skidmore and never felt she belonged. After a year her art instructor told her there was nothing more she could learn there in art unless she was interested in weaving or jewelry. She wasn't, so after her third semester she transferred to Parsons.

For the first time she felt at home. She began attending classes in the summer, and one of the first things she noticed was a painting of Leo's. When she saw it, her immediate thought was, "If that's the kind of work that's done here, I'll never be able to compete. I don't belong here." She was intrigued by the enormous talent of the student who could do such work, and she asked about Leo. She was told he was a loner, that he took his lunch and ate it down by the river. Diane, who by all accounts was rather shy and unaggressive, introduced herself. Leo gave her the distinct impression that he wasn't interested. Shortly after this their class had to move to another room, and Diane sat next to Leo. Later she found out he was furious, since he'd hoped to have the drawing board to himself. Leo had always been the best artist in their class at Parsons and had had no serious competition until Diane arrived. He felt Diane was better than he was, and he became very competitive. In the beginning he didn't even want to talk to her. Diane, too, was very competitive, but Leo recalls that she never showed it.

While at Parsons these two highly talented students experienced similar unpleasant incidents that each remembers vividly. One instructor took Leo aside and told him that although he was an excellent artist he wouldn't be able to get work in the art field because of his race. Another instructor told Diane he hated talented females because they always got married and had babies, and all the talent and training were wasted. Despite these discouraging comments, both of them continued to learn as much as they could and planned careers in art.

Diane and Leo both speak of their three years in school together at Parsons as a time of intense competition, anger, and constant fighting. Although after a while they fell in love, their rivalry didn't end, and their different backgrounds caused them a great deal of suffering. Eventually they became so miserable they decided to separate. After college Diane moved to Albany, and they cut off all communication. But they discovered that they were even more miserable apart than they had been together, so Diane returned to New York, and they decided to get married. Both families were against their marriage because of the racial difference, but Leo and Diane were determined; and once they were married their fighting stopped.

At that time Leo was an art director for a magazine, and Diane was the only woman artist in the advertising agency she worked for. Diane soon left her job to be a proper housewife in the accepted 1950's fashion. She concentrated on cooking, specializing in intricate hors d'oeuvres to go with the cocktails she served Leo when he arrived home from work. Every day Leo would ask her what she had done, and she would point to the gourmet food. This nightly exchange continued until one evening Leo became furious with Diane and told her she was wasting her talent. The next night there were no drinks and no hors d'oeuvres. When Leo asked Diane what she had done, Diane pointed instead to a painting.

Now Diane and Leo decided to do freelance work together. They had spent three years in rivalry and competition and were too happily married to risk that again, so they decided to collaborate on everything. They had no money in the bank and no freelance work yet, but Leo, who found his nine-to-five job unbearable, quit. Thus began the Leo-and-Diane-Dillon collaboration which has continued throughout the twenty years they've been married.

The next two years were a time of intense poverty. Often they didn't even have enough money to go on the subway to pick up a job someone had asked them to do. During this time Leo's father fortuitously had a number of deliveries to make in their neighborhood. Once or twice a week he would appear with a bag of groceries, explaining that he had a job on the next block and thought he'd drop in. Diane says it was only after that period had passed, and Mr. Dillon never seemed to have any more trucking jobs in their neighborhood, that they realized what he'd been doing.

On February 28, 1965, their son Lee was born. Soon afterward, they bought their own brownstone house in Brooklyn, fondly called Dillons' Folly, which they have been renovating ever since. Their partnership continued in everything: art work, child care, and running the house.

During their first years the Dillons had worked together on album covers, advertising, magazine illustrations, movie posters, and paperback covers. While continuing their other art work, they now did book illustration, too, and in 1968 my relationship with them began when I called to ask them to illustrate their first picture book, *The Ring in the Prairie: A Shawnee Legend,* [edited by John Bierhost and Henry R. Schoolcraft,] which The Dial Press published in 1970. Illustrating children's trade books offered them a kind of freedom they had never before experienced; no one told them what to draw or asked them to repeat a style. And I believe it is this creative freedom which allows these enormously talented artists to capture the essence of a story and to select the style and technique that perfectly complements it.

In 1969 the Dillons began teaching at the School of Visual Arts while continuing their art work. The course is "Materials and Techniques," and at first Leo and Diane taught it together. Later they each had a separate class. Diane left teaching in 1972, but Leo continues.

Although Diane, Leo, and I have worked on only four books together—the fourth, *Ashanti To Zulu: African Traditions* by Margaret Musgrove, is not yet published—not a week goes by without some artist walking over to one of their paintings on my office wall, gazing in admiration, and saying in wonder, "I don't know how they do it."

"Frisket with pastel and watercolor," I say, if it's the jacket painting for *Beind the Back of the Mountain.*

"No," is the inevitable reply, "I mean I don't know how they work together on the same painting."

"Neither do I," I used to say, "but when I find out I'll let you know."

And now we all know, to some extent, at least. But the more I know, the more I marvel—at their talent as artists who collaborate so completely; at their amazing ability to capture so sensitively such warmth, humor, and feeling in art as stylized as that for *Why Mosquitoes Buzz in People's Ears;* but mainly I marvel at these remarkable human beings who make seemingly impossible things work because of their particular wonderful qualities.

Phyllis Borea and Jo Yanow

SOURCE: "Leo & Diane Dillon" in *Communication Arts Magazine,* Vol. 25, No. 2, May-June, 1983, pp. 42, 44.

Prompted by the women's consciousness movement several years ago, some people wanted to know why Diane's name came second in their signature. Why not switch it around—make it Diane and Leo?

They wouldn't consider it. The signature is the "company name" for their art. Married for twenty-five years, the Dillons have evolved a technique of working that is so intimate that they pass the art between them as each, in turn, takes it a step further. They speak of their work as being yet another person, a third being that emerges from their two minds. "It's as if the work is itself," they explain philosophically.

To understand this unique attitude you only have to spend a few hours with them in their tall, narrow house in one of Brooklyn's neighborhoods. In this house, they say, they have created their own world where they have been able "to become free from thinking in stereotypes." From here it takes a messenger only 20 minutes to deliver assignments to clients in Manhattan. It's the best of both worlds.

The house figures dominantly in their conversation because so much of their toil is in it. They have been remodeling it, brick by brick, floor board by floor board, since its acquisition, 23 years ago. Each time they thought a floor was finished, they'd move the studio there. Currently, they work in the sun-filled top floor, up four flights of unfinished stairs (no railings). Leo says they have a plan for the house but that plan keeps changing. "What's time?" he asks. "Doesn't matter, does it?"

Though Diane admits there are things she'd rather be doing than sawing wood, she adds, "On the other hand, what would we be doing if we weren't working on the house?"

Tools they use in the house, hammers and saws, plus chisels, electric erasers and myriad artisan's instruments are employed extensively by them in their illustrations for book jackets, children's books, record album covers, soap packages and other assignments. In their view, the word artisan—in the old and true sense—carries with it the noblest of ideas about one's endeavor. Illustrations have been made with paint mediums of every variety and also with wood, copper, silver, ivory, thread, paste. After conceiving an idea about using marbleized papers as the borders for a painting for the cover of the book *Child of the Morning* they decided it was time to get a vat and learn to make handmade paper. (This soon led to teaching themselves bookbinding.) For a map for *Great Ages of Man* they created a clay relief. They have hundreds of such examples.

The Dillons met at Parsons, but nobody should get the idea that the collaboration was immediately smooth and easy from the start. They explain that it grew through trial-and-error and, while they were drawn inexorably to the work of the other right off, they were tremendously competitive as youngsters.

Diane grew up in California, studied for a year and a half at Skidmore College, then transferred to Parsons in New York. She recalls entering with feelings of apprehension about the fast-paced scene there and immediately spotted the wonderfully realistic work of an intense, hard-driving fellow named Leo Dillon. She wanted to flee.

Born in Brooklyn, Leo attended the High School of Industrial Arts (now Art and Design). He served in the United States Navy during the Korean War where he was put in charge of the paint locker aboard ship. For extra money he did portraits of shipmates' girlfriends, using house paint (this worked out to be excellent training, he claims). When he first saw the "individual graphic style" of the newcomer Diane at Parsons he recalls being apprehensive "because she had so much talent."

Their initial collaborations involved design. Their illustrations were done independently. Illustrating together grew out of a recognition that it was the only answer to a true partnership for them. A first practical step in this direction was an early woodcut style they developed; the hard edge art made it easy for one to pick up a line where the other left off.

The Art of Leo & Diane Dillon, a 1981 book by Byron Preiss (Ballantine Books), explores their proficiencies as a team. Preiss waxes poetic about the "magic" in much of their work. There are elements in the pictures hard to pin down. They like to add elements that you may not notice the first time you look, a rustic scene in a small corner, people who are also animals, a mood made by a strange color.

"Even when it's not called for, we create a story—to keep us interested along with the viewer," says Leo.

"The typical boy-girl romance would never go to us. The pretty pink-cheeked white kid . . . we have wanted books that showed beautiful pink-cheeked black children, Indians, or whomever," says Diane.

One might wonder if they get a first crack on ethnic assignments. The Dillons say they do on children's books, but not on other things.

Their technique is the "vocabulary," they explain, and it starts with the drawing, as precise as it can be. Detailed, immaculate drawings go to the client.

As for techniques and applications, they have many of their own. One is multiple frisket. For example: over the face of a woman done as a frisket rendering with pastel dust (rubbed into the surface of the paper), they lay yet another frisket. This can be repeated for different double images. Or: They might make an intarsia, a mosaic of small pieces of wood, to create a picture.

Courses on materials are given more frequently today, but they were uncommon 10 years ago when the couple conducted a class on materials and techniques at the School of Visual Arts. To the surprise of the administration, and of the Dillons, it was over-subscribed. Teaching gave them the chance to master other approaches. They would assign students a technique they didn't know, then "cram" to figure out how to do it for the next session. SVA provided them with a studio room for experiments.

Students also were taught about research. How far the Dillons carry this point is shown in their art for *Ashanti to Zulu,* a book on the peoples of Africa which won a Caldecott Award, given annually by the American Library Association for best children's book art. The author's text lacked pictorial details and there was just no way they could compose pictures from the manuscript. They undertook their own version of "Roots" for each of the tribes. And what a colossal job they gave themselves! Determined to include in each illustration a man and woman, animals, dwelling and local terrain, the research took them three months. (The art only needed a month to complete.)

As a footnote to the thoroughness of their research a publisher once sent them, as part of the background he provided, a piece of art they had done years earlier.

These days their son Lee, 17, an art student (painter and sculptor), sometimes helps out his parents, drawing in background figures. Apart from the emergence of Lee as an artist, other things have been changing for the pair, as well. Diane is president of the Graphic Artists Guild, becoming an advocate for better communication between client and artist and among artists. "Artists shouldn't feel isolated or confused when it comes to procedures, pricing and other aspects of business anymore," she says. This is a giant step out for an individual who had felt she was too shy to teach the SVA class. The necessary speechmaking and appearances after winning two Caldecotts literally "forced them to leave the cocoon." And, in spite of other awards as well, the Hamilton King (Society of Illustrators) and Hugo for Science Fiction and Fantasy, they say they never realized that anyone else was noticing their work.

All roads still lead to Brooklyn and the Dillons prefer not to be far from this work. They want to create "beautiful pictures." Art continues to go to clients "ready for hanging in a gallery," often contained in boxes they have made because they want it to stand for something of value.

"It's a question of quality—in a glass, a package, over the TV. Anything can be art. We consider ourselves to be *fine illustrators.*"

"Now this might raise some eyebrows, but we consider Michelangelo to have been an illustrator," concludes Leo.

Bookbird

SOURCE: "Leo and Diane Dillon," in *Bookbird,* Vol. 34, No. 2, June 15, 1996, p. 40.

Leo and Diane Dillon have earned a reputation for their commitment to excellence and outstanding range of styles. Through their versatility, research, and integrity as artists they constantly raise the standard for distinction in illustration. Their illustrations are highly suggestive of other cultures, although they take particular pride in depicting African American history and culture.

The Dillons were born 11 days apart in 1933—Leo in Brooklyn and Diane near Los Angeles. They met at and graduated from Parsons School of Design in New York City. A year later they married and gave up potentially lucrative jobs to pursue careers as freelance artists. During their early years, they learned to work together as a team on every piece of artwork, passing it back and forth between them. By the time they had begun to illustrate children's books, what they refer to as "the third artist" had emerged, displaying a unique style with sharp, crisp outlines.

The Dillons have won numerous awards, including the 1971 Hugo Award, the 1982 Balrog Award for Lifetime Contribution to Science Fiction/Fantasy Art, and the Coretta Scott King Award for illustrating *Aïda.* In 1976, the Caldecott Medal was awarded to them, making Leo the first and only African American to win the medal. The following year they were awarded the Caldecott Medal again, the only illustrators to win the medal in two consecutive years. Leo and Diane Dillon have devoted their lives to art and the challenges of the craft of illustration. Their hope is that their work conveys to young viewers the richness of the world around them and the beauty of the different peoples who share the world.

TITLE COMMENTARY

BEHIND THE BACK OF THE MOUNTAIN: BLACK FOLKTALES FROM SOUTHERN AFRICA (1973)

Betsy Hearne

SOURCE: A review of *Behind the Back of the Mountain: Black Folktales from Southern Africa,* in *Booklist,* Vol. 70, No. 7, December 1, 1973, p. 384.

A tricky crocodile, some heavenly maidens, an extremely stupid jackal, and a gluttonous farmer are among the many characters in this diverse collection of tales from various tribes. Some of the stories are fables, with a definite moral, while others are based on such familiar themes as winning the hand of a beautiful princess or outwitting a monster. The author of *Tales for the Third Ear, from Equatorial Africa* has maintained the atmosphere of the stories' origins in her spirited, entertaining retelling, and the strikingly patterned black and gray illustrations are outstanding.

Zena Sutherland

SOURCE: A review of *Behind the Back of the Mountain: Black Folktales from Southern Africa,* in *Bulletin of the Center for Children's Books,* Vol. 27, No. 6, February, 1974, p. 89.

Dramatic pictures in black, white, and grey are bold and stylized, with a high sense of design. The tales they illustrate are folk legends from half a dozen language groups of South Africa; trickster tales, witches outwitted, talking animals and magical skymaidens, stories of love and charity and hunger that reflect the concerns of people who live close to the land and are governed by the mores of their cultures. The writing style is smooth, and some of the tales are particularly suited for storytelling although all come from the oral tradition. A glossary and a list of sources is appended.

THE HUNDRED PENNY BOX (written by Sharon Bell Mathis, 1975)

Betty Lanier Jenkins

SOURCE: A review of *The Hundred Penny Box,* in *School Library Journal,* Vol. 21, No. 8, April, 1975, p. 55.

The Hundred Penny Box contains a penny for each year of Aunt Dew's life, and each penny symbolizes a memory which she shares ritually with her great-great-nephew Michael ("'1930,' Aunt Dew said 'Depression. Henry Thomas, that was my late husband, died. Died after he put the fifty-six penny in my box.'"). The young boy acts as buffer in the tug of war between Aunt Dew, who is stubborn and set in her ways, and Michael's mother, who wants to toss out the dilapidated old coin box. Mathis has etched wonderful characters in Michael as he champions the cause of his aunt, and Dewbet who is still feisty despite frequent changes in mood and periods of senile forgetfulness. With the Dillons' dark brown illustrations that look as if they were drawn from old, dim memories, this is an effective bridging of the generation gap.

Zena Sutherland

SOURCE: A review of *The Hundred Penny Box*, in *Bulletin of the Center for Children's Books*, Vol. 29, No. 3, November, 1975, p. 51.

Soft, misty pictures [by Leo and Diane Dillon] in brown and white reflect the tenderness that is the prevailing note of a touching story about a child and a very old woman. . . . Most of the story consists of dialogue, much of it between Aunt Dew and Michael, and while the author gives a strong picture of family relationships and family continuity, it is the love and trust between the two protagonists that is the dominant theme. Beautifully written, the restraint of the style makes the book's message of the love the more effective.

📖 *WHY MOSQUITOES BUZZ IN PEOPLE'S EARS: A WEST AFRICAN TALE* (retold by Verna Aardema, 1975)

Leo Dillon and Diane Dillon

SOURCE: "Caldecott Award Acceptance," in *The Horn Book Magazine*, Vol. LII, No. 4, August, 1976, pp. 373-7.

[The following is Leo and Diane Dillon's acceptance speech for the Caldecott Award, which they delivered at the American Library Associaton meeting in Chicago, Illinois, on July 20, 1976.]

Usually when a book is completed, we are on to the next, and behind-the-scenes details are forgotten. But this time is different. It's the first time in our lives we've talked more about a book after its completion than while we were working on it. It all started when Phyllis Fogelman, editor-in-chief of The Dial Press, called us and asked if we would like to illustrate a tale about animals based on a style we had used on the jacket for **Behind the Back of the Mountain** [written by Verna Aardema]. We were excited by the possibility of working on a kind of book we'd never done before, and Phyllis began looking for a good manuscript for us. A few months later she sent us Verna Aardema's retelling of the West African folk tale, "Why Mosquitoes Buzz in People's Ears." When we first read the manuscript, we were both amazed that in just a few pages there was such a wealth of material. Each paragraph was packed with action, each scene flowed into the next. The cast of characters was varied, and there was a wide range of emotion. There was humor, tragedy, seriousness, and silliness. Needless to say, we were delighted with the visual possibilities.

For the first time, we were about to illustrate a book that was truly for young children, a story that was perfect for reading aloud and one that young children would become intensely involved in. **Mosquitoes** wasn't our usual problem book. Over the years editors have called us when they've had a manuscript that would be difficult to illustrate. And in working on those books, we have, of course,

From Why Mosquitoes Buzz in People's Ears, *written by Verna Aardema. Illustrated by Leo and Diane Dillon.*

had to spend a great deal of time in the conceptual stages, thinking and rethinking the solution. For *Mosquitoes* the conceptual stage was very easy; this book, we knew from the start, would be fun to illustrate. We have had a few heated discussions in our twenty years of working together about whether or not art is fun, but on this book we agreed.

To us every book we accept is different, and each provides us with a chance to do things we haven't done before, a chance to grow and expand as artists. Every manuscript presents a new challenge. We have looked for new solutions to different challenges, tried out new styles, experimented with different approaches—not without failures, but also never without excitement and growth. One of the things we have avoided over the years is specialization. We have fought against limiting our styles ever since we began working together. When we first started free-lancing and took our portfolio around, we were frequently told by art directors that we had too many styles— they'd never remember us, and so, of course, they'd never have any work for us. Because of that we called ourselves *Studio 2* for a while instead of Leo and Diane Dillon. Somehow, art directors were able to deal with a variety of styles when they thought we were a whole studio full of artists.

We never hesitate to try a new technique on a job. In fact, we feel it is the only way to learn its possibilities and limitations. If you make a mistake on a trial piece, you can toss it out; but on a real assignment, you have to find a solution. For *Mosquitoes* the new technique we tried was airbrush, and we had to find solutions to the inevitable problems.

We believe that the role of the illustrator is *not* simply to duplicate the text, but to enlarge on it, to restate the words in our own graphic terms. That's why we enjoy working on children's books so much. In some fields, such as advertising and textbooks, illustrators are not expected to think and are sometimes given specific instructions on what to draw. But in children's trade books the artists have a great deal of creative freedom. We illustrate the text, of course, but we are also free to go beyond it or to pick out certain aspects and play them up.

Take, for example, a couple of the characters in *Mosquitoes:* the antelope and the little red bird. The antelope has a very minor part in the story—he is simply sent to bring Mother Owl and later the iguana before the council. We decided he really wanted a more important part—he wanted to be a star. So he began trying to get attention, peering out and grinning, hamming it up, until finally on one spread he is seen up front in the center, with a great toothy smile. You may have noticed he reaches the peak of his career on the cover of the Newbery-Caldecott program. The little red bird never appears in the text at all. We put her in one spread and became rather fond of her. We began to think of her as the observer or reader and added her to the other spreads. Thus on each page you will find her watching, witnessing the events as they unfold. On the last page, when the story is over, she flies away. For us she is like the storyteller, gathering information, then passing it on to the next generation. We were asked recently if the attention we gave the antelope reflected any feelings we might have of being unnoticed. We'd like to answer that tonight that certainly is not the case.

We were also fascinated by the filmlike quality of the story. So much happens within the space of two or three paragraphs, we felt that to leave any of the scenes out of the pictures would create a jumpy effect. We wanted the pictures to flow the way the story flowed. To accomplish this, we showed the same animal doing more than one thing on a page. We imagined that if we placed each page of the book side by side, the total effect would be that of a long scroll. The story would unfold with total continuity in picture form, and there would be no gaps. In drawing the animals, one of our first concerns was to show the expressions on their faces. We wanted to indicate human emotions that children could identify with yet retain each animal's distinct features. This was challenge enough, but the most difficult part was trying to put expressions onto a mosquito's face.

One important element of the text from our point of view is the repetition. In the beginning the series of events is laid before the reader as each one happens. Later, at the council, each character retells one of those events from his or her own point of view. We didn't want to show the same scenes twice—though we might have met our deadline if we had!—so we decided to focus on each character's perspective. In the pictures we tried to exaggerate each one's story, just as the animal might have done in retelling it. This approach seemed particularly appropriate to us, since at the time of the retelling, the animals are all trying to exonerate themselves. They're trying to put the blame on someone else: It wasn't *my* fault—it was the crow's; it wasn't *my* fault—it was the rabbit's! Hence, when Mother Owl stands before King Lion recalling the events as she thinks they occurred, the pictures show the monkey viciously attacking the helpless baby owlet. The reader, of course, knows that this is *not* the way it happened, and we have enjoyed hearing that children, with their keen sense of justice, protest, "NO! NO! It didn't happen that way!"

Since January we have had the opportunity to speak to a number of audiences about *Why Mosquitoes Buzz in People's Ears*. Invariably the reaction has been, "That's all fascinating, but how do you work *together*?"

We worked on *Mosquitoes* in the same way we work on all our books. After we read a manuscript we discuss it, tossing back and forth ideas about possible styles and techniques until we agree on what will work best. At this critical stage of concept, it is a great advantage having two minds working together—the ideas come twice as fast. Then we proceed to the next step. The drawings are done in pencil, then refined, and finally the finishes are done in color. On *Mosquitoes,* the color was done in airbrush with frisket, which is a form of stencil. One area is done and then masked out, or covered, and the next area is done. The black areas are painted in last, then glazed with blue or purple. But as for who does what—sometimes even *we* aren't sure. Each illustration is passed back and forth between us several times before it is completed, and since we both work on every piece of art, the finished painting looks as if one artist has done it. Actually, with this method of working, we create a third artist. Together we are able to create art we would not be able to do individually. By joining our talents in various combinations, we have several different styles available to us. As individuals we have our own styles and approaches, and we continue to work separately for gallery showings. Most people who are familiar with our individual work and our work together see a resemblance but agree that the third artist is, indeed, a separate person.

There is one more thing we would like to talk about, but we haven't been able to find a logical place for it in this speech—even though we've written several drafts since January. Now that we have a captive audience, and such a large one at that, we're going to talk about it anyway. We feel very strongly about craftsmanship: the tool that gives us the freedom to say what we want to say in our art. It is our vocabulary. An artist *must* know how to use and have control over media in order to express his or her ideas. When we first started teaching in the 1960's we were distressed to see the emphasis shifting from technique and craft to theatrics. Students were being given projects like drawing on a long sheet of brown paper and then wrapping themselves in it or going to the park and experiencing each other. Conceptual experience was emphasized, and although concept *is* important, it is useless without technique. Art is not accidental. Accidents happen; we do not want to rely on them, but rather take advantage of them when they occur. We are happy to see a shift back to an emphasis on craft.

In conclusion, we would like to say that receiving this award has reinforced our faith in what we believe. It has encouraged us to experiment further, to refine and perfect our work. I would like to add here that I was informed that I am the first Black artist to win this award. I felt proud when Tom Feelings previously won honors but never dreamed I would be standing here tonight.

We would like to thank Verna Aardema, whose story was an inspiration; Phyllis Fogelman, whose vision brought the words and pictures together; Atha Tehon and Warren Wallerstein, whose knowledge and perfectionism we relied upon; Ellen Teguis, Regina Hayes, Susan Pearson, Toby Sherry, and everyone else at Dial who worked with us. And to the Newbery-Caldecott Committee, which had the difficult task of making the decision, our very special thanks. We are extremely proud to be here tonight. Thank you.

Kirkus Reviews

SOURCE: A review of *Why Mosquitoes Buzz in People's Ears,* in *Kirkus Reviews,* Vol. XLIII, No. 19, October 1, 1975, p. 1117.

This tale from Africa is another of those cumulative goose

chases except that instead of pursuing an object, the game here is fixing the blame for an overlong night. As King Lion summarizes the chain of events after it's all straightened out, "it was the mosquito who annoyed the iguana, who frightened the python, who scared the rabbit, who startled the crow, who alarmed the monkey, who killed the owlet—and now Mother Owl won't wake the sun so that the day can come." Not one of your indispensable kernels of folk wisdom, but it is the kind of brisk go-round that can pick up a lagging story hour group. And though the stunning illustrations are not our favorite Dillons—they don't generate much life or involvement—their crisp cut paper look commands attention.

Zena Sutherland

SOURCE: A review of *Why Mosquitoes Buzz in People's Ears: A West African Folk Tale,* in *Bulletin of the Center for Children's Books,* Vol. 29, No. 3, November, 1975, p. 37.

A "why" story from Africa is retold with verve in a picture book that should delight young listeners and adult readers—especially those who may use it for storytelling—equally. A mosquito tells a whopping lie to an iguana who, muttering, fails to respond to the greeting of a friendly snake. The snake goes into a rabbit hole and frightens a rabbit . . . and this chain of events leads to an owlet accidentally killed and its mother failing to hoot and wake the sun. No sun? The lion calls a meeting of all animals, the chain is unraveled, and the mosquito is condemned. The cumulation will appeal to listeners, and the youngest children especially will enjoy the descriptions of sound (the snake moves "wasawusu, wasawusu . . .") and the surprise ending. The illustrations are magnificent, stylized and patterned pictures of animals, strongly-composed double-page spreads with plenty of white to set off the distinct forms and separate their parts, bold colors used with restraint and nuance. A handsome example of good bookmaking.

Carol Stevens Kner

SOURCE: A review of *Why Mosquitoes Buzz in People's Ears,* in *The New York Times Book Review,* November 9, 1975, p. 48.

Leo and Diane Dillon's colorful illustrations provide just the right sort of kaleidoscopic, jungle safari experience. Made of bright, puzzle-piece shapes, highly decorative like the African motifs they are based on, the animals are realistic enough to appeal to young children and draw them into the action. The repetitive patterns of feathers, leaves and scales complement the lilting rhythms of the text—the snake slithers "wasawusu, wasawusu, wasa-wusu," the monkey leaps "kili wili" and the iguana's head nods "badamin, badamin." I would never have imagined that a lion laughed "nge, nge, nge," but mosquitoes, it is certain, speak the same language all over the world.

Denise M. Wilms

SOURCE: A review of *Why Mosquitoes Buzz in People's Ears: A West African Tale,* in *Booklist,* Vol. 72, No. 6, November 15, 1975, p. 447.

Elegance has become the Dillons' hallmark; here, cut shapes of varying hues are assembled into stylized scenes to create a polished, dramatic visual panorama. Matching the art is Aardema's uniquely onomatopoeic text relating how a mosquito's silly lie to an iguana sets in motion a cumulative series of events that finally causes Mother Owl not to call up the sun. The resulting hardship ends only after King Lion traces the problem back to its source. An impressive showpiece.

Helen Gregory

SOURCE: A review of *Why Mosquitoes Buzz in People's Ears: A West African Tale,* in *School Library Journal,* Vol. 22, No. 4, December, 1975, p. 40.

A familiar folk tale, well told, of a series of misunderstandings beginning with the lowly mosquito and leading to the death of an owlet and Mother Owl's refusal to wake the sun. After the animals in council trace the catastrophe to the mosquito, her own guilty conscience sets her punishment through the ages. Stunning full-color illustrations—watercolor sprayed with air gun, overlayed with pastel, cut out and repasted—give an eye-catching abstract effect and tell the story with humor and power. This ought to be a strong contender for the Caldecott Medal.

Ethel L. Heins

SOURCE: A review of *Why Mosquitoes Buzz in People's Ears: A West African Tale,* in *The Horn Book Magazine,* Vol. LII, No. 2, April, 1976, pp. 146-7.

In a cumulative tale, a boastful mosquito triggers a concatenation of mischief-making events. Iguana, python, rabbit, crow, monkey, and owl all become innocent links in a chain of exasperating accidents. The tale of trouble finally ends when King Lion steps in and orders the offender punished. Some years ago, another version of the story was published—Benjamin Elkin's *Why the Sun Was Late*—in which satisfactory but undistinguished pictures accompany the straightforward storytelling. The new book, illustrated by two superbly gifted artists, presents an interesting, though disturbing, contrast; and it brings up some fundamental questions about the role of illustrations in picture books and about the delicate but crucial balance between graphics and text. Sophisticated in design and impressive in technique, the full-color spreads have a lush, forceful splendor which almost overshadows the humorous, naïve folk tale. The characters, looking like sculpturesque prototypes, seem inappropriate for a story which is not—after all—a legend of epic proportions but only a simple animal fable.

SONG OF THE BOAT (written by Lorenz Graham, 1975)

Denise M. Wilms

SOURCE: A review of *Song of the Boat,* in *Booklist,* Vol. 72, No. 4, October 15, 1975, p. 302.

"Flumbo walk about in Bonga Town. / He say How-Do to everybody, / But him heart no lay down, cause he no got boat. / Alligator did break him canoe." Once again Graham draws on the idiomatic English of West Africa to tell of Flumbo, who goes with his son Momolu to search for a tree he can fashion into a new canoe. The quest is realized through a dream of Momolu's in which the spirit people reveal to him "one fine tree, fine past all he ever see before." Out of it Flumbo makes a magnificent canoe, and after crediting Momolu, takes his family for a ride down the river. The Dillons' elegant woodcuts, overlaid with swaths of orange and plum, stretch rhythmically across the pages, furthering the fantastical mood of the story and setting a prize example of book design.

Gertrude B. Herman

SOURCE: A review of *Song of the Boat,* in *School Library Journal,* Vol. 22, No. 3, November, 1975, p. 62.

Woodcuts by the Dillons based upon African motifs, in black, brick, and tones of purple are as rhythmic and strong as Lorenz' story about a small boy who helps his father find the right tree for making a new canoe. As in earlier books in which the author retold Bible stories in the English "folk speech" of the Liberian people, the same poetic patterns appear here. "Flumbo make a fine canoe . . ." The author and artists make a fine book.

Anita Silvey

SOURCE: A review of *Song of the Boat,* in *The Horn Book Magazine,* Vol. LI, No. 6, December, 1975, pp. 584-5.

Told in the folk speech of West Africa, the story of Flumbo who goes in search of a new canoe resonates with language so strong and rhythmic that it elevates the simple adventure into a hero quest. Setting out with his son Momolu, "Flumbo look him small boy. / He say, 'The road I walk be long. Oh, / It be long past the legs of my small boy.' / Momolu look up and he say, / 'Elephant cross big hill; / Goat cross big hill same way.'" Eventually Momolu dreams of finding the gum tree from which they will carve the canoe, and on his awakening, the two seek and find it. And after the priests call the spirit of the tree, "Flumbo did make fine canoe, fine past all canoes!" The author has already produced a series of beautiful, well-crafted picture-book texts—this one is even more subtle than the others; but he has never had an illustrator who so captures the spirit of his work as do the Dillons. The woodcuts—some black and white and some colored with magenta and orange—present solid, often massive, figures against settings articulated with bold line. Like the text, the woodcuts feel indigenous to Africa, but, at the same time, both text and pictures retain a universal element.

Zena Sutherland

SOURCE: A review of *Song of the Boat*, in *Bulletin of the Center for Children's Books*, Vol. 29, No. 9, May, 1976, pp. 144-5.

Remember Graham's touching *Every Man Heart Lay Down*? In this story there is the same cadence and structure of language, the poetic English of African tribesmen: "Flumbo look him small boy. He say, 'The road I walk be long. It be long past the legs of my small boy.'" But his small son, Momolu, not only keeps the pace, but helps his father find just the right tree for making a boat that will replace the canoe broken by an alligator. Both the story and the style are beguiling, and the finely detailed illustrations, based on the style of African woodcuts, are strong and dramatic, bold in composition but intricate within the masses of figures.

ASHANTI TO ZULU: AFRICAN TRADITIONS (written by Margaret Musgrove, 1976)

Leo Dillon and Diane Dillon

SOURCE: "Caldecott Award Acceptance," in *The Horn Book Magazine*, Vol. LIII, No. 4, August, 1977, pp. 415-21.

[The following is Leo and Diane Dillon's acceptance speech for the Caldecott Award, which they delivered at the American Library Association meeting in Detroit, Michigan, on June 18, 1977.]

Last year, after the Caldecott Award was announced in January, we returned home from Chicago to work on *Ashanti to Zulu: African Traditions* [by Margaret W. Musgrove]. Our primary concern was to do a book that would show our gratitude for such an honor. We wanted our next book to be the best we had ever done. It would not only be a way of saying thank you, but also a way of proving to *ourselves* that we deserved the award.

For a long time we had been working in isolation. When art left our house, it was out of our hands. We had nothing more to do with the book it became, nor did we hear much about it. We received compliments from time to time, which were appreciated, but we were unprepared for the impact of knowing that people were watching. After the Caldecott we realized something was expected of us; now we had a challenge and a goal—motivation that had dulled over the years. The summer before we had been very depressed at how little we seemed to be moving ahead. Then the award came and with it a feeling of tremendous elation. The sky was the limit! Along with

that feeling of elation was a fear that somehow we had reached a peak in our career—would it now be downhill?

Ashanti to Zulu had been in the house and we had been thinking about it on and off for some time. Our first thought had been in terms of a very ornate decorative style, possibly incorporating each letter in the illustration. When we studied the manuscript more carefully, our concepts began to change. Margaret Musgrove's idea of showing the variety of peoples and customs in Africa appealed to us. There was an interesting fact about each of the twenty-six different groups; some we had never heard of before. How different this book about Africa was from the ones we grew up on. We imagined ourselves reading *Ashanti* as children and felt the excitement of wanting to know more. Any single group could merit a book of its own, and it seemed important to expand on the text, to show as much as possible about each people. As we were formulating our thoughts, we asked questions, such as, What do the people look like? What did they wear? What did the country look like? So we decided to show for each group, whenever possible, a man, a woman, and a child in costume, with an example of a dwelling, an artifact or a type of work, plus an animal from the area.

As we began the first drawing of the Ashanti, we quickly found that the decorative style we had in mind would not be adequate. Because of all the things we wanted to show, the drawings began to take on a more realistic style. To avoid a dry factual statement we wanted to combine realism with the elegance of a fairy tale, that would also be more interesting visually. In dealing with visual images we tend to look at the fairy tale as a vehicle that offers us the most freedom to do whatever comes to our minds. There is no limit to what we can imagine or create, because in fairy tales there are madly ornate costumes, baroque castles, fantasy landscapes, and wonderfully strange creatures to work with. We grew up believing that our ordinary lives were pallid in comparison.

But in *Ashanti to Zulu* the common people were the stars. The text for the most part deals with people in everyday pursuits. We began to appreciate the grandeur in ordinary living, in what actually exists. It is the intelligence in a person's eyes or the nuances of body language—things shared by all people—that make for real beauty. We strove to be accurate with the factual details but especially wanted to stress the things we all have in common—a smile, a touch, our humanity. We took artistic license with particular situations so that they reflected the tenderness that exists among all peoples. It didn't matter if the Ga man would ever be around when his wife was making foufou; the tenderness of his touch, the warmth passing between them is a universal truth. Or with the Quimbande it was irrelevant whether husband, wife, and children would sit down to play a game in the middle of the compound; the love and family closeness were true.

So far things were running smoothly, but not for long. We had no trouble finding information on the Ashanti, but when we got to the Baule we ran into a snag. In all our research material—and we have built up quite a personal research library over the years—we couldn't find an example of the crocodile symbol so prevalent in that area. And when we took stock of the rest of the book, we realized that some one thing was missing for almost every letter. Either we had no costume for the woman, or the type of dwelling was elusive, or the animal was hard to find. We began to doubt the practicality of showing all elements, but we still felt it was right—we didn't want to compromise.

Our usual procedure is to start at the beginning and do each page in sequence. This time we had to skip around according to the research materials we had at hand. So the next two pieces were the Masai and Tuareg, since they were the only ones we had complete information on.

It was about then that we realized this was *not* a simple alphabet book! All our previous books were folktales of a non-technical nature. They did not require extensive research. We would find photographs of the people of the area, look at their art and patterns as inspiration, something to base our style on. Once we had the basis, we could exaggerate and add our own ideas to that. An example is *Why Mosquitoes Buzz in People's Ears: A West African Tale*. That art was based on an African batik style with white line but ended up as a flat graphic style. We had occasionally been involved with work that required extensive research—we once illustrated an article about the fourth-century Greek theory of planetary orbits by Eudoxus—but we were provided with the information needed. For *Ashanti to Zulu* we were on our own, and it was a completely new experience in research for us.

After compiling a long list of the specific items we needed, our first attack was on local bookstores for back issues of *National Geographic*. Illustrators' needs are visual rather than verbal. Descriptions help, but words conjure up different pictures for each listener. We could not afford to imagine what something might look like. We had to *see* it. After several days of going through dusty old magazines, we moved on to the picture gallery of The New York Public Library, a valuable collection to many professions but especially to artists. But even they lacked information on a number of things. So while one of us kept working at the drawing board, the other went to the Mid-Manhattan Library, then to the Schomburg Collection, and after that to the library at the Museum of Natural History.

Pages and pages of notes and more possible leads piled up, but we still lacked photographs. The more we read and learned about each group, the more we realized that each was unique. The customs were as varied as the types of peoples. The dwellings were far more varied than we had been aware of. Some were made of mud and wattle, some of stone or mud bricks, some of woven mats. Some were square, others were round. Some roofs were flat, others were conical. The clothing and patterns were specific, from the special blankets of the Sotho with their hats that repeat the shape of the mountains in that area to the ornate embroidered clothing of the Hausa. Even the style of hair had meaning, as did the jewelry. The peoples

themselves ranged from warm red tones through yellow ochres to ebony. There was no way of faking it. Like Europe, Africa is comprised of many peoples and customs, even more varied than our own continent.

By now we knew we were in trouble. We had several pieces done, but on most we were being stopped by some missing element. We called on Dial to help. They arranged for us to use the library at the United Nations, and as time got tighter and tighter, they searched for many of the remaining items on our list so that we could stay with the drawings.

Although we had completed the paintings for the jacket and poster and three of the inside pieces, much of the book was still at the sketch stage when we took a week off last July to go to Chicago for a very memorable time, blissfully free of research. But that research was still going on in New York while we were away. The people at Dial had our list of the still-missing items and were in touch with Margaret Musgrove and through her with experts on African culture at Yale. They were calling United Nations embassies, contacting publishers of obscure books, tracking down African experts, and doing further library research.

The last item that continued to elude us was the Lozi barge. We had found one photograph showing the front half from inside the barge, but we couldn't see the black-and-white stripes or the king's shelter that was so clearly described in the text. One of the Dial editors had the misfortune to move into our neighborhood and found herself researching by day and making house calls by night. After much searching she finally located a picture of the barge, for which we are eternally grateful.

Many of the details of all that research have become jumbled and hazy, but one thing we remember clearly is the pleasant and helpful attitude of the librarians who answered hundreds of questions about how to find things and spent hours helping us look them up.

We returned from ALA in Chicago on a Thursday afternoon. Thursday night our house-calling editor delivered the latest batch of research material. And on Friday morning we were sitting at our drawing boards again, finally ready to start the finished illustrations. By now we were months past our deadline. Our usual procedure is to complete all the artwork and deliver it in one package, as it's important for the flow of the book to be able to look back while we are working to see the color, the direction of the action, and the effect one page has next to another. Fortunately, however, this wasn't as crucial in *Ashanti to Zulu* because each page was really a complete story in itself and because each illustration was held together by the border. Everyone was now involved in our hectic schedule, so this time we sent in the finished paintings as we completed them, four or five at a time. First they were checked once again for accuracy at Dial and sent to the separator, who proceeded with the camera work on those pieces while we continued painting the next group of illustrations.

Finally the last piece of art was delivered, the camera work and several provings were completed, and we were ready to go on press. This was the first book on which we were able to experience the printing stage. We had always thought of the actual printing process as mostly a mechanical procedure, but we learned that a great number of creative decisions are made on press. We are more aware now than ever before of the importance of the dedication and cooperation of everyone involved at each step that a book goes through—from editorial to production to promotion.

We would like to thank Phyllis Fogelman for her guidance and understanding, and for the times when she had the vision to encourage our ideas, no matter how abstract they seemed. It is a pleasure working with her. Again we thank Atha Tehon, Warren Wallerstein, Susan Pearson, Regina Hayes, Ellen Teguis, Toby Sherry, and all the others at Dial for their care and talents in producing a beautiful book. We'd also like to express our appreciation to Holyoke Lithograph for their dedication to craftsmanship and accurate reproduction of the artwork. Since so few people ever see the original art, the printed work becomes the original, and to an artist this step is crucial. An African proverb seems appropriate here: Cross the river in a crowd and the crocodile will not eat you.

A thank you seems inadequate to express our appreciation to the Children's Services Division of ALA and to the Newbery-Caldecott Committee. Before we received the Caldecott Medal last year, we felt very discouraged. The award made a substantial change in our attitude and morale. We felt someone was looking at our work. The experience of people waiting twenty minutes in line to show their appreciation was humbling. We found that people knew of work we had done fifteen years ago. Your encouragement and recognition have given us the confidence we needed to go on for the next twenty years. (We hope!)

It has also made us examine who we are and who or what the third artist is. We each have our own distinct styles, but when we work together, as we do on all our children's books, we essentially create a third artist. We've never really allowed ourselves to examine that phenomenon too closely on the chance we might jinx it, but over the years we have blended our thoughts and styles together to produce art we couldn't have produced separately. In the beginning we worked pretty much by trial and error, but later, working together became automatic, the work passing from one drawing board to the other at different stages. When we first sit down to discuss a manuscript, we throw a lot of ideas at each other. Most of them are rejected immediately, as if we're just waiting for a particular idea. And the moment it hits, we both catch the excitement, and the visual images begin to flow. Even though one of us might not have thought at all in a particular direction, as soon as that idea is voiced by the other, it's as though it had always been there—it was just necessary to have it spoken. We've occasionally been able to tap this third awareness at other times in our lives, and there may be a relation between it and the similarity of

our tastes. Often we find one or the other of us saying, "That's what I would have done or chosen."

We've always known that in some ways the third artist was quite separate from our personal lives, because in times of anger, when husband and wife aren't speaking, the artist continues to communicate and produce. The fact that we are forced to talk and discuss a job dissipates the anger, and we make up sooner. It's easier to stay angry with your mate than it is with the person you work with, especially when the deadline is the next day!

We've never been able to predict totally what the final product of this third artist will be, since neither of us can actually see what the other is seeing, even though we agree on the words. The surprises have kept us interested. We rely on the advantages that a partnership and collaboration can provide, and we trust each other's judgment and taste. In the early days we worried about the loss of our individual identities, but we have found the third identity is as valid and real and as much *us* as the separate ones.

For illustrators the Caldecott Medal is the most substantial and respected award an artist can receive. The committee this year had difficult decisions to make. Their independence and freedom from extraneous considerations enforces the integrity and meaning of this honor. We are both *very* proud and will try to keep *your* standard of excellence. And a special thanks from the third artist who, after all, really produced the art.

Kirkus Reviews

SOURCE: A review of *Ashanti to Zulu: African Traditions,* in *Kirkus Reviews,* Vol. XLIV, No. 24, December 15, 1976, p. 1307.

From Ashanti to Zulu, 26 African tribes appear in a sort of slide show alphabet, each one allotted a lavish painting over a paragraph of text, with words and pictures joined in a formal, vaguely deco-style frame. This prescribed format gives a superficial air of sameness to the pictures even though the Dillons are careful to depict differences in headdress, dwelling structure, etc., and it gives the pages a static, stilted look which the illustrators do nothing to allay. The text, higgledy-piggledy, simply supplies a cultural snippet on each tribe: a general characterization of the Jie, herders in Uganda whose "men . . . roam with their cattle while the women do the farming," but only a fashion report on the Masai and a crocodile legend from the Baule. Nor is any distinction made between a custom peculiar to the tribe and, for example, the Fanti one of "pouring libation" with palm wine. Of course, the intent of the presentation is no doubt less systematic description than appreciation, and the Dillons' paintings fairly glow with appreciation—and the expectation of a like response. (Their sheen in fact not only glows but often glares, though the tones remain subdued.) At the same time, in a reversal of the usual division of labor, the pictures are crammed with information; a man, woman, child, home, artifact, and animal is conscientiously worked into almost every tableau. With no selective focus there's an exhausting much to look at—too much to effect the distillation achieved in the Feelings' Swahili counting and alphabet books, though of course this is certain to attract much regard.

Jane Abramson

SOURCE: A review of *Ashanti to Zulu: African Traditions,* in *School Library Journal,* Vol. 23, No. 6, February, 1977, p. 67.

Twenty-six African tribes—from Ashanti to Zulu; from the Sahara down to the savannas—file by in the Dillons' dazzling processional. Each framed tableau in lush tropical tones (parrot green, mango, aqua, lemon) offers a composite picture of a particular people, showing their regional dress, wildlife, type of home, etc. Unfortunately, the text, limited to a boxed paragraph below each picture, neglects to point all this out and, instead, is restricted to describing a folkway or custom. At best there are snippets of interesting information (e.g., the Jie who name themselves after their cows; the Tuareg men who wear veils and defer to the women); at worst the narrative sounds as if it were excerpted from old *National Geographics.* Still the artwork makes it all worthwhile; as beautifully designed as the famous Ashanti *kente* cloth, its stylized elegance manages to capture both the variety and vitality of African tribal life.

Barbara Helfgott

SOURCE: A review of *Ashanti to Zulu: African Traditions,* in *The New York Times Book Review,* February 20, 1977, p. 30.

Ashanti to Zulu, which has been awarded the 1977 Caldecott Medal for excellence in illustration, is a large, colorfully illustrated book that strives "to introduce the reader to 26 African peoples by depicting a custom important to each." A single custom can hardly convey much that is meaningful about any culture, and in that sense the book is severely limited. Within those limitations, however, interesting facts abound. . . .

Margaret Musgrove's prose conveys some of the diversity of African mores. The illustrations give them life. Leo and Diane Dillon, who were also awarded the 1976 Caldecott Medal for *Why Mosquitoes Buzz in People's Ears,* here surpass their previous efforts. Their 26 paintings include, whenever possible, a family, a dwelling or some artifact or animal indigenous to the area so as to reflect the world of the peoples they depict.

These are sophisticated illustrations, the colors rich yet subdued, the drawing stylized and subtle. Facial characteristics vary from subject to subject, but all bear the same air of mystery. *Ashanti to Zulu* is an exotic book for those ready to look beyond the familiar.

Paul Heins

SOURCE: A review of *Ashanti to Zulu: African Traditions,* in *The Horn Book Magazine,* Vol. LIII, No. 2, April, 1977, p. 179.

In brief texts arranged in alphabetical order, each accompanied by a large framed illustration, the author introduces "the reader to twenty-six African peoples by depicting a custom important to each." Her purpose is to "give the reader not only a feeling for the vastness of the African continent and the variety of her peoples but for the place that tradition holds at the very heart of African life." In fulfilling her purpose, she has been aided immeasurably by the illustrators; and the pictures, which admirably embody the subject matter of the book, are worthy of independent discussion as works of art. In most of the paintings the artists "have included a man, a woman, a child, their living quarters, an artifact, and a local animal" and have, in this way, stressed the human and the natural ambience of the various peoples depicted. Without falling into banality or conventionality, the paintings, for which pastels, watercolors, and acrylics were employed, suggest the idealism and dignity of murals. The clearly limned figures often recall the contours of African wood sculpture but are subordinated to the carefully composed placement of diagonals and parallels. The jewellike effect of the blues, greens, and reds, often presented in patterned contrast, are likewise subordinated to the overall tawny tonality of the pictures. The controlled, rich art successfully glorifies the great variety of folkways found among the Black peoples of Africa.

WHO'S IN RABBIT'S HOUSE? A MASAI TALE (retold by Verna Aardema, 1977)

Kirkus Reviews

SOURCE: A review of *Who's in Rabbit's House?* in *Kirkus Reviews,* Vol. XLV, No. 19, October 1, 1977, p. 1041.

Much ado among the animals, with an unseen monster occupying Rabbit's house and threatening everyone who comes near; with Rabbit herself intervening when the strong-arm eviction methods of Jackal, Leopard, Elephant, and Rhinoceros would destroy house and housebreaker alike; and with insignificant, overlooked Frog finally out-bluffing the fearful creature . . . who turns out to be "only a caterpillar." Like *Why Mosquitoes Buzz in People's Ears,* this is neither the most pregnant nor the most involving of illustrated African folk tales (nor is Aardema a rhythmic storyteller), though again like *Mosquitoes* . . . , it's crisp and commanding. The Dillons turn the characters into identically clad human players in animal masks, they allow the masks to change expressions (no less veracious than the masks themselves), and they make of the whole another artificial, but admittedly dazzling performance—more theatrical than dramatic.

Ruth M. McConnell

SOURCE: A review of *Who's in Rabbit's House?* in *School Library Journal,* Vol. 24, No. 3, November, 1977, pp. 41-2.

Exuberant and inventive artwork runs away with this re-telling of a Masai folk tale, pictured as if put on in a village setting by masked actors who, in effect, become the animal characters. Rabbit asks a succession of neighbors to help rid her house of a fierce, hidden stranger, who calls himself Long One. Only Frog succeeds, by pretending to be a spitting cobra. Long One turns out to be a very scared caterpillar, who runs off as all the animals laugh. The players, huts, and tree-silhouettes stand out boldly in rich earth tones against a pale ground and white sky. The warm hues of the actors' robes, their dark brown limbs dramatically posed, and their mobile, fantasy-beast heads all join to form colorful and dynamic patterns on each page. Motion is shown by re-drawn, slightly overlapping animated figures (it may have to be pointed out to children that, for example, a double-spread showing six rabbits is one rabbit in six different stances). Aardema has inserted sounds ("FUUU! fumed the rhinoceros . . . Up and away went Rabbit—WEO over the lake! Then—NGISH!") to propel the action in her spirited text. But the illustrations have the last word, as two of an audience of curious lions on the horizon are shown exchanging glances of knowing incredulity as to the goings-on. A stunning performance.

Joyce Milton

SOURCE: A review of *Who's in Rabbit's House?* in *The New York Times Book Review,* November 27, 1977, p. 38.

Who's in Rabbit's House? reunites the Caldecott medal-winning team of Verna Aardema and artists Leo and Diane Dillon. The Dillons, who have built their reputations on elegant interpretations of African source material, present this story in the form of a play, acted out by Masai villagers wearing expressive animal masks (a piece of artistic license, by the way). Moreover, the Dillons employ a nonliteral, freeze-frame style of depicting motion. It's a technically ambitious undertaking, but Verna Aardema's earthy onomatopoetic voice is an energizing force. Here, once again, the little guy triumphs. After Leopard, Elephant and Rhino have bungled the job, it is none other than Frog who flushes the monster that has holed up in Rabbit's house. That the much feared "Long One" turns out to be merely a boastful caterpillar is double confirmation of the power of bluff, and caterpillar's surprise appearance gives the artists a chance to end their "play" with a visual splash. Overall, the African setting is used to infuse a simple plot with drama and individuality.

Zena Sutherland

SOURCE: A review of *Who's in Rabbit's House? A Masai Tale,* in *Bulletin of the Center for Children's Books,* Vol. 31, No. 5, January, 1978, p. 73.

A humorous Masai animal tale is told here as a performance by Masai villagers, and the characters are shown as people wearing animal masks. The story: Rabbit sits in her doorway every night to watch the other animals drinking at the lake. One night she comes home to hear a voice inside her house, behind a barred door, saying "I am The Long One. I eat trees and trample on elephants. Go away!" Jackal offers to burn the house to get The Long One out; Rabbit protests. Leopard attacks the roof; Rabbit sends him away. Frog, who's been amused by these and other abortive attempts, tries scaring the mysterious intruder, who proves to be a caterpillar. Rabbit goes back to sitting in her doorway, while Frog sits on a log, croaking with laughter. The illustrations, double-page spreads rich with color, are beautifully composed, although young children may be confused by the fact that there are three images of Jackal, for example, shown on the page that refers to a single jackal. The story is deftly told, with the action and humor that appeal to children, and the text is extended by the vitality of the illustrations.

Virginia Haviland

SOURCE: A review of *Who's in Rabbit's House: A Masai Tale,* in *The Horn Book Magazine,* Vol. LIV, No. 2, April, 1978, p. 156.

Although the artists have once again used an African tale for their text, they have not repeated themselves and, in fact, have produced their most successful picture book. The story, from *Tales from the Third Ear,* is told with colorful use of "authentic African ideophones": "She banged on the door, *ban, ban, ban!*" The folk tale tells how a chain of animals seek to help Rabbit, whose house is occupied by a creature roaring out, "I am The Long One. I eat trees and trample on elephants. Go away! Or I will trample on you!" The portrayal of the action as scenes in a drama is a brilliant conception for interpreting the sequence of attempts to remove the interloper. The play is performed by Masai villagers wearing animal masks. In the full-color illustrations the artists used a rich harmony of earth tones set off by the heavy use of black. Expressive eyes, ears, and arms indicate emotion, and the choreographic rhythm of the figures adds pulsing life. The page design permits ample space for text yet skillfully achieves a panoramic effect; a tree separating the two halves of each double-page spread acts as a unifying device.

D. A. Young

SOURCE: A review of *Who's in Rabbit's House?* in *The Junior Bookshelf,* Vol. 45, No. 1, February, 1981, p. 8.

The attempts at assistance by the rabbit's friends to rid his house of an unwelcome squatter all seem to involve damage to the little house. In the end it is the cunning of the frog which reveals the fearsome occupant to be merely a long green caterpillar. This charming African folk tale gives victory to the smaller creatures and puts the large boastful ones in their place. It is a thoughtful 'growing-up' story for young children. The illustrations are bold, colourful and striking. The story is acted out by Masai villagers wearing animal masks which make each double-spread a lively and attractive scene. The artists have cleverly used the technique of showing several phases of the action in the picture. A very successful example of British book production.

📖 *HONEY, I LOVE AND OTHER LOVE POEMS* (written by Eloise Greenfield, 1978)

Kirkus Reviews

SOURCE: A review of *Honey, I Love,* in *Kirkus Reviews,* Vol. XLVI, No. 6, March 15, 1978, pp. 308-9.

On every small (5¼ x 7¼), buff-colored page, a lovingly modulated little girl stands out in glowing black from a childlike, scratchy cartoon in tan. The Dillons' attractive illustrations are sure to lend an aura of class to the text, but with the same tone and format for every page, they don't bring out what little there is to feel about Greenfield's less textured poems. There are 17 short selections in all, varied in subject (love, fun, things, riding on a train), colloquial and undemanding, but never forceful. The funkiest, "Way Down in the Music," sounds more like Tin Pan Alley (" . . . I let it wake me / take me / spin me around and shake me . . .") than the cited Jackson Five, and overall the weak, unimaginative meter is a let-down: "Rope Rhyme," with the bounciest title, sounds more like a jog (" . . . Jump right up when it tells you to / Come back down, whatever you do . . ."); the inspirational intent of "Harriet Tubman" doesn't jibe with its light verse rhythms; and the title poem has some nice sounds and observations ("My cousin comes to visit and you know he's from the South / Cause every word he says just kind of slides out of his mouth") but goes on too long with the same monotonous beat. Nevertheless, easy to slide through—and the package will be admired.

The New York Times Book Review

SOURCE: A review of *Honey, I Love,* in *The New York Times Book Review,* April 30, 1978, p. 25.

From the cover on, **Honey, I Love** reaches out and pulls you in to a warm place. The poems by Eloise Greenfield show that you don't have to go on forever to say a lot. She writes this about a child's view of an elderly aunt: "What do peope think about / When they sit and dream / All wrapped up in quiet / and old sweaters."

The illustrations by Diane and Leo Dillon are a fine combination of sophisticated realistic drawings superimposed

From Ashanti to Zulu: African Traditions, *written by Margaret Musgrove. Illustrated by Leo and Diane Dillon.*

over happy little pictures that look child-drawn. Their superb reputation remains justified.

Sharon Elswit

SOURCE: A review of *Honey, I Love and Other Love Poems,* in *School Library Journal,* Vol. 24, No. 9, May, 1978, p. 55.

Greenfield herself can be heard through the voice of a young Black girl in this book of love poems. She speaks in an easy way, of everyday things, sometimes rhyming, sometimes not. Most of the poems don't attempt complex perceptions. Greenfield's child is younger and less intense than the women Nikki Giovanni's adolescents grow up to be; and she is older and less political than Lucille Clifton's Everett Anderson. About herself she says, "Honey, let me tell you I LOVE the laughing sound / I love to make the laughing sound." The strongest images come in portraits of other people, like her older brother Reggie who has forsaken his family for basketball and Aunt Roberta who sits "All wrapped up in quiet / and old sweaters." There are some awkward stanzas and prosaic lines, but the Dillons transform this quiet book into magic with soft, grey charcoal renderings of the young girl and her friends, overlaid with child-like brown scratchboard pictures embodying the images in the poems.

Zena Sutherland

SOURCE: A review of *Honey, I Love and Other Poems,* in *Bulletin of the Center for Children's Books,* Vol. 31, No. 1, July-August, 1978, p. 177.

Brown and white childlike stick figures are combined with soft, almost misty black and white pictures of beautiful black girls to illustrate sixteen poems about a child's love and enjoyment of people and places and doing things. The last poem concludes with, " . . . I love a lot of things / A whole lot of things/ And honey / I love ME, too." The poems have moments of vision, some felicitous phrases, and a consistency in showing a child's viewpoint, but they often have a less than poetic quality and seem merely fragmentary attitudes or reactions of rather prosaic calibre.

CHILDREN OF THE SUN (written by Jan Carew, 1980)

George Shannon

SOURCE: A review of *Children of the Sun,* in *School Library Journal,* Vol. 26, No. 9, May, 1980, p. 65.

Too long and poorly plotted, this literary legend tells of the sun's youthful actions including the euphemistic rape of an earth woman and the problems of the resulting twin sons. Carew's text is wordy and hampered by such self-conscious writing as "banished the lingering webs of sleep" and "yet not a drop of blood stained the innocent grass." The book's strongest element is the Dillons' illustrations steeped in warm sunlight but even these, though rich in color and texture, offer little life or movement. Multiple images replace energetic line and there is little flow between words and visuals. Author and artists are trying too hard. The result is overly dramatic poster pin-up material—a glamorous chest with little inside it.

Zena Sutherland

SOURCE: A review of *Children of the Sun,* in *Bulletin of the Center for Children's Books,* Vol. 33, No. 10, June, 1980, p. 187.

An original folktale incorporates some familiar mythic elements, and is beautifully illustrated by the Dillons, who here combine the fine sense of composition and color that is in *Why Mosquitoes Buzz in People's Ears* and the soft, melting technique they used in *The Hundred Penny Box.* Here all of the characters, mythic and human, are black, and the strong, beautiful faces are dominant notes amid translucent surrounding details. In the story, which falters intermittently, stylistically, a beautiful woman becomes impregnated by the arrogant Sun; one of the twin boys she bears covets greatness, the other goodness. One accidentally kills the other, but Father Sun melts the spear that had pierced his son's heart and brings him back to life; the sons stay with their father and there are three

suns in the sky until the power-hungry brother is killed by his Father Sun in a burning embrace as punishment for the havoc he has created on earth. The other son returns to earth to bring peace and harmony to humankind; while he is on this never-ending mission, his old mother weeps, and her tears flow down the mountain, "and the sea carries them to the shores of the whole world," the story ends. Not *much* too much in this weaving of episodes, but still—too much.

Joyce Milton

SOURCE: A review of *Children of the Sun,* in *The New York Times Book Review,* June 1, 1980, p. 20.

There's always cause for misgivings when a children's picture book is described by its publisher as "stunning." In the case of *Children of the Sun,* these misgivings are amply justified. Leo and Diane Dillon are talented artists who have won two Caldecott awards for illustration—for *Why Mosquitoes Buzz in People's Ears,* a retelling of an African folktale, and for *Ashanti to Zulu,* an album of African peoples. But here, the Dillons and their collaborator Jan Carew have embarked on a misguided quest for universal importance.

Mr. Carew's text is an inflated and sometimes incomprehensible pastiche of mythological themes. His tale concerns twin sons of Father Sun, one evil and one a Christ-like benefactor of mankind; however, there's no logic or consistency to the cosmos these twins inhabit. On one occasion, the irresponsible twin visits the earth and his solar emanations wreak havoc, turning "lakes into cauldrons" and "forests into torches"; at other times, the twins travel to earth without causing so much as a heat wave. As irritating as the story is, the Dillons' burnished, soft-focus illustrations do have their moments, and one picture of the White Crane who gives fire to mankind by striking his beak against a flintstone achieves a dreamy perfection. Overall, the effect of pages filled with swirling feathers, idealized profiles floating against the clouds and characters wearing sunburst halos, is not so much ennobling as excessive.

TWO PAIRS OF SHOES (retold by P. L. Travers, 1980)

Zena Sutherland

SOURCE: A review of *Two Pairs of Shoes,* in *Bulletin of the Center for Children's Books,* Vol. 34, No. 5, January, 1981, p. 101.

From Middle Eastern sources, Travers has chosen two stories for polished retelling; her prose has the cadence of the formal oral tradition of classical Middle Eastern folklore, with its ornate speech and courtly elegance. In *The Sandals of Azaz,* a courtier proves his devotion to his king and his humility in acknowledging his humble start in life; in *Abu Kassem's Slippers,* a humorous tale, a merchant keeps trying to get rid of an old pair of slippers and, with each attempt, gets into a situation where the slippers come back and he has to pay a fine. The stories would still be entertaining were they not illustrated, but the illustrations add immeasurably to the book: graceful, ornately detailed and handsome in composition, they have the rich formality of Persian miniatures. While the book can be used as a source for storytelling, it would be a pity to miss the beauty of the pictures, framed in elegant borders, that will be enjoyed by independent readers or those to whom the book may be read aloud, sharing the art.

Sally Holmes Holtze

SOURCE: A review of *Two Pairs of Shoes,* in *School Library Journal,* Vol. 27, No. 5, January, 1981, p. 55.

The rich, luminously colored paintings facing each page of text are detailed scenes of action and lively expression, telling much of the story and reflecting much of the culture. It is unfortunate that 70 percent of the page is comprised of borders—even the borders have borders. It is not that the paintings suffer from being small (4" x 6"), but that the book suffers from its pages being too large, resulting in unattractive, overfussy design.

The New York Times Book Review

SOURCE: A review of *Two Pairs of Shoes,* in *The New York Times Book Review,* January 4, 1981, p. 25.

Leo and Diane Dillon's artwork is admirably polished and resourceful in its illumination of the texts. But their intention of capturing the flavor of Persian miniatures is far more successful in the second, more stately tale than in the near-slapstick first. The illustrators' choice of a marbleized frame for the art in the opening tale detracts from the pictures' impact. The plain brown background in the second tale works better. Overall, however, the book's pictures have the effect of a too rich dessert; the surfeited eye soon longs for a simple white page to set off the complex illustrations.

Ann A. Flowers

SOURCE: A review of *Two Pairs of Shoes,* in *The Horn Book Magazine,* Vol. LVII, No. 2, April, 1981, p. 184.

As might be expected, the combination of a renowned writer with equally renowned illustrators has resulted in a literate and sumptuously beautiful book. The contrast between the two stories is echoed in the luminous illustrations. The first tale tells of a miserly, unsavory merchant, Abu Kassem, and of his comic and unsuccessful attempts to rid himself of his unlucky slippers; and the second is about the honorable Ayaz, the respected confidant and advisor of King Mahmoud, who never forgot his humble beginnings as a simple shepherd. The borders and

page decorations are works of art in themselves, and the surprisingly effective facial and bodily expressions of the characters are humorous or noble, as the occasion requires, even though the pictures remain within the formal genre of Persian miniatures. A tour de force, both visual and verbal, magnificent but not particularly childlike.

📖 *BROTHER TO THE WIND* (written by Mildred Pitts Walter, 1985)

Publishers Weekly

SOURCE: A review of *Brother to the Wind,* in *Publishers Weekly,* Vol. 227, No. 17, April 26, 1985, p. 83.

The Dillons will surely be candidates for a third Caldecott Medal for the magnificent paintings they contribute to Walter's magic tale. Influenced by African myths but an original, the plot is based on the yearning of a small boy, Emeke. Only his grandmother shares his trust in the power of the Good Snake to give Emeke the ability to fly. A long search in the company of skeptical animals ends when they arrive at the rock where Good Snake listens, then gives Emeke instructions to achieve his goal. Back at the village, everyone except the grandmother jeers at Emeke as he prepares for flight. But he's up and away, soaring, and changing the ridicule to applause. The color and imagination in the illustrations surpass everything the gifted collaborators have created in their honored career. This is a work of art destined for a permanent place in literature.

Gale P. Jackson

SOURCE: A review of *Brother to the Wind,* in *School Library Journal,* Vol. 31, No. 9, May, 1985, pp. 84-5.

The Dillons' illustrations reinforce the magical essence of the book with brilliant color, strong vibrant lines and the stuff of dreams illuminated. Rich in patterns and textures—the feathery clouds, the scaly snake, the jagged mountain—and color (the darkly ominous jungle contrasts with the light colors and airy feeling associated with the Good Snake), the illustrations display the Dillons' strong sense of design. This story of a boy's quest for, and eventual, flight, does in fact give readers room to soar.

Denise M. Wilms

SOURCE: A review of *Brother to the Wind,* in *Booklist,* Vol. 81, No. 21, July, 1985, pp. 1561-2.

Imaginative, detailed scenes play out the story, which the Dillons set in windowlike arched frames that are often brimming with drama. Literal story aspects are often interpreted in symbolic terms; for example, the laughing turtle's disbelief in Good Snake is echoed in a carapace whose angles show a mosaic of grinning faces, and the intelligence of Good Snake and the wind is depicted by an apparitionlike human appearing in the background. The colors are muted and the look is polished; this is an attractive, visually subdued presentation.

Charlotte W. Draper

SOURCE: A review of *Brother to the Wind,* in *The Horn Book Magazine,* Vol. LXI, No. 4, July-August, 1985, p. 446.

An ordinary story that evokes African folklore recounts how the young goat herder Emeke withstands the ridicule of his family and his village in order to learn how to fly. Encouraged by only his grandmother, Emeke consults with Good Snake, who "'can make any wish come true.'" Good Snake instructs Emeke to make a special kite and to wait for a special wind. Aided by wild animals, Emeke builds his kite and is borne on the wind from the mountain down to his village. Elements of folk legend—such as the wise woman, the oracular snake and its magic talismans, talking animals—contribute a timeless power to Emeke's lessons of faith and self-reliance. The illustrations emphasize the coalition of dream and necessity, which fuels Emeke's ingenuity. Vibrantly colored scenes of Emeke's daily life in the village are superimposed against personifications of the surreal forces which inspire his imagination.

📖 *THE PEOPLE COULD FLY: AMERICAN BLACK FOLK TALES* (retold by Virginia Hamilton, 1985)

Kirkus Reviews

SOURCE: A review of *The People Could Fly: American Black Folk Tales,* in *Kirkus Reviews,* Vol. LIII, No. 19, October 1, 1985, pp. 1088-9

The combination of Newberry winner Hamilton and the Dillons, two-time Caldecott Medalists, raises high expectations. It is especially noteworthy that they've combined their talents to present a collection of Black American tales—a folklore awesome in its richness, power and complexity. With all this in mind, we expect to find here nothing less than fire from the mountain. Though there is much to enjoy, and many parts are quite stirring (such as the title story), Hamilton has prepared a sampling of carefully and respectfully retold tales, not a living work of art.

A surprisingly facile introduction sets a restrained tone. And her forerunner, the complex figure of Joel Chandler Harris, is unfairly assessed. From reading Hamilton, one would not get the idea that Harris took enormous pains to reproduce the tales as he heard them, even when elements of the stories were incomprehensible to him.

The book is organized into four sections: animal tales, fantasy, supernatural and tales of freedom. The final one ("Carrying the Running-Aways: And Other Slave Tales of Freedom") is by far the most effective for the contemporary reader; the best of these stories convey great heroism, beauty and nobility. Less rewarding are the fantasy tales (with the exception of "Wiley, His Mama, and the Hairy Man"), and the supernatural tales (although they frequently entertain, and several would be excellent as read-alouds). The animal tales move the reader the least, and are rather lifeless.

Hamilton's approximation of dialect speech is laudable for its readability. The Dillons have lent handsome black-and-white paintings to the work, but they seem posed and static. Still and all, this is a useful collection and a valuable undertaking. Though flawed, it brings a good sampling of lore from the past to a new generation of readers.

Ruth M. McConnell

SOURCE: A review of *The People Could Fly: American Black Folk Tales,* in *School Library Journal,* Vol. 32, No. 3, November, 1985, p. 85.

The well-known author here retells 24 black American folk tales in sure storytelling voice. In four groupings she presents seven animal tales (including a tar-baby variant); six fanciful ones (including "Wiley, His Mama, and the Hairy Man" and a tale of which Harper's *Gunniwulf* is a variant); five supernatural tales (including variants of the Tailypo, John and the Devil—and a wild cautionary tale, "Little Eight John"); and finally, six slave tales of freedom, closing with the moving title story. . . . With the added attraction of 40 bordered full- and half-page illustrations by the Dillons—wonderfully expressive paintings reproduced in black and white—this collection should be snapped up.

Sean Wilentz

SOURCE: "Child's Play," in *Village Voice Literary Supplement,* No. 41, December, 1985, pp. 1, 16-9.

[Animals] . . . scamper through . . . Virginia Hamilton's collection of 24 Afro-American folk tales, **The People Could Fly.** Hamilton brings back to us, in fresh ways, one of the oldest storytelling traditions in our history. It is a handsome book, elegantly illustrated (in black and white!) by Leo and Diane Dillon. Its tales of tricksters and transcendence have a political bite, but no pat political lessons, a deadpan irony without cheap tricks, the surrealism of the oppressed, in which the craziest things do happen. More than that, Hamilton has the language. She has found a way to write in a black English that escapes sounding like Uncle Remus, and imparts a poetry you'll never get from the Brothers Grimm. Some years ago, working as a book clerk, I saw plenty of middle-aged black customers, and some whites, buying *Roots* as a treasured keepsake, a monument to Afro-American survival. **The People Could Fly** has at least as many claims to be a source of pride.

📖 *THE PORCELAIN CAT* (written by Michael Patrick Hearn, 1987)

Patricia Dooley

SOURCE: A review of *The Porcelain Cat*, in *School Library Journal*, Vol. 34, No. 3, November, 1987, p. 90.

"You scratch my back . . ." is the way the world, and this tale, works: an old formula but a reliable one, in an enchanted, elegant new guise. In this version the magician gets his basilisk blood when the witch gets her shellfish from the undine, who gets her mushrooms from the centaur, when the magician's apprentice climbs a tree to get him some ripe fruit (this is the weakest link). The point that "a bargain is a bargain" is clearly but amusingly made, and the conclusion is a clever surprise (somewhat muted by a puzzling final image). The Dillons create a magical nightworld for the tale, all attenuated art nouveau curves; flat planes of muted color; and stylized, elongated forms. Strange moonfaces haunt the starry sky, and cats hide behind trees and float in cloud-shapes above. (Don't miss the Escher-like endpapers.) This first Hearn-Dillon collaboration is a "smashing" success; a book to read, and to pore over.

Patricia MacLachlan

SOURCE: A review of *The Porcelain Cat*, in *The New York Times Book Review*, November 8, 1987, p. 50.

Leo and Diane Dillon's extraordinary pictures add great depth and meaning. "The moon was full and ripe," Mr. Hearn writes, and the Dillons' moon watches Nickon from page to page, beginning young and changing face and age as the night goes on. Cats and the presence of cats lurk everywhere; on the endpapers, in mist above the river, as cattails beside it. This beautifully designed book invites the reader to turn back to each picture so that the reader becomes part of the story. The surprising end pulls the reader farther, past the last page, when even the Sorcerer has given up on his untrustworthy magic, to the back of the book jacket. Then the reader realizes what we all may have once known, or known and forgotten: only the young truly know magic.

Ethel L. Heins

SOURCE: A review of *The Porcelain Cat*, in *The Horn Book Magazine*, Vol. LXIII, No. 6, November-December, 1987, p. 725.

In an elegantly designed and illustrated book a sorcerer sends his young apprentice to fetch an ingredient for a magic spell—a mission which in folk-tale fashion leads the boy into bargaining with three supernatural creatures. Plagued with rats, the sorcerer determines to prepare a concoction that will bring a porcelain cat to life; and finding that "a vial of basilisk blood" is required, he orders his boy Nickon to go and fetch it from the Witch Beneath the Hill. But the old hag will oblige only if Nickon can extract a favor for her from the Undine of the Brook—who, in turn, dispatches the boy on an errand to the Centaur of the Wood. The text is somewhat mannered: "The clear water rushed from the smooth stones and pink shells dotting the river's mouth; and soon a water maiden raised her lovely head. 'Yes, yes,' she spoke, in a whisper that would have silenced a storm at sea." But interpreted in highly decorative, often stately illustrations reminiscent of art nouveau with sinuous line and controlled energy, the story transcends itself. The artwork reflects both the fantasy and the sudden flip humor at the end of the book, and careful looking reveals a variety of cats, both realistic and imaginary, lurking in unexpected places and, surrounded by rats, leaping joyously all over the endpapers.

Betsy Hearne

SOURCE: A review of *The Porcelain Cat*, in *Bulletin of the Center for Children's Books*, Vol. 41, No. 4, December, 1987, p. 65.

In the tradition of sorcerer's apprentice tales, young Nickon is sent on an errand by his master. But Nickon does not bungle his task—to procure a vial of basilisk's blood for a spell that will bring a china cat to life to rid the Wizard's house of rats. The first magic creature he asks requires something that sends him to the next, and so on, until he succeeds, only to watch the animated cat shatter into a thousand pieces when it pounces on its first rat. The Dillons' art, parlaying the magic theme into objects with faces throughout the book, has the last say as a porcelain bird flies out of the china rubble at the apprentice's feet. So much for magicians and their charms. This ending will confuse some young listeners, who may also miss the irony of the magician going to so much trouble when there are cats depicted everywhere in the illustrations. The book is gracefully designed with art deco frames and still, rounded shapes that keep the humor mischievously low key, a tone set by the subtle text. A smooth, sophisticated blend, from wry wording to softly shaded endpapers sporting a tell-tale illusion, this is almost too sophisticated for its format.

📖 *THE COLOR WIZARD: LEVEL 1* (written by Barbara Brenner, 1989)

Denise M. Wilms

SOURCE: A review of *The Color Wizard*, in *Booklist*, Vol. 86, No. 2, September 15, 1989, p. 192.

Splashes of color bring the drab world of Wizard Gray to life. Red is his first pick, followed by blue and yellow; from these primary hues flows a rainbow of color. This lesson in how colors are formed spills forth in simple rhyme and intriguing pictures as the white-bearded man paints his house, his clothes, his animals, and even his dragons in the wide-ranging shades of his ample palette. A practical lesson in a whimsical package.

Gale W. Sherman

SOURCE: A review of *The Color Wizard*, in *School Library Journal*, Vol. 35, No. 15, November, 1989, p. 76.

The Dillons add their fine touch to *The Color Wizard*, a story in rhyme about a wizard who transforms his gray world into a colorful paradise. The Dillons' added note that explains color and light concepts makes it easy to expand this book's use beyond the language arts curriculum.

📖 ***MOSES' ARK: STORIES FROM THE BIBLE***
(retold by Alice Bach and J. Cheryl Exum, 1989)

Ilene Cooper

SOURCE: A review of *Moses' Ark: Stories from the Bible,* in *Booklist,* Vol. 86, No. 6, November 15, 1989, p. 656.

Bach, who has written numerous children's books, combines her talents with those of Exum, a biblical scholar, to present an entertaining yet thoughtful compilation of Old Testament stories. These 13 tales are based on new translations from the Hebrew, and the book's highly readable introduction explains how the authors chose and retold their material, often using modern archaeological finds to extend details of life in biblical times. Favorite stories are here—the creation of Adam and Eve, Noah's ark—but the authors have also included more obscure tales, for instance, the meetings between Saul and the medium at Endor and between Solomon and the Queen of Sheba. Each story is followed by notes, which add texture and nuance. The Dillons' dramatic gray- and black-toned artwork, bordered in vivid green, completes this evocative and useful work.

Patricia Dooley

SOURCE: A review of *Moses' Ark: Stories from the Bible,* in *School Library Journal,* Vol. 35, No. 16, December, 1989, p. 105.

The Dillons are such effective colorists that finding them confined to black and white here is initially dismaying—but only initially. The artists make the most of their *grisaille* by choosing night scenes or interior settings. These picture have detail, dignity, and drama, and their unusual design wizardry has a convincingly archaic flavor. The image of Moses dwarfed by towering walls of water is so powerful that scholars' objections (the crossing of the shallow sea was probably more a matter of weather than of wonder) might seem carping.

Paul Heins

SOURCE: A review of *Moses' Ark: Stories from the Bible,* in *The Horn Book Magazine,* Vol. LXVI, No. 1, January-February, 1990, pp. 84-5.

Working from the original Hebrew texts and ranging from Genesis through Kings, the authors have retold thirteen episodes from the Old Testament. Linguistically aware of the complex subtleties of the original, they have, in their title, taken advantage of the fact that Noah's floating houseboat and Moses's floating cradle—both vessels of salvation—were denoted in the Hebrew by the same word. They have chosen three narratives—those concerned with Adam and Eve, Noah, and the tower of Babel—as introductory to the other accounts, which reveal the origins of the Jewish nation: the exodus from Egypt, the incursion into the Promised Land, and subsequent events leading to the kingships of David and Solomon and beyond. The experiences and adventures of the patriarchs—Abraham, Isaac, and Jacob—as well as those of Joseph and his brothers have been omitted; and the authors have included "a number of stories that portray women as strong figures." Along with the idealized portraits of Moses's sister Miriam, Deborah the judge, and the queen of Sheba, such powerful if malevolent exemplars as Delilah and Jezebel have been presented—justifiably, since they are an integral part of the frank realism of the Old Testament. Strictly adhering to the original narrative frame of the stories, the authors have expanded the compressed style of the biblical accounts by using details from other portions of the Old Testament or from the findings of archaeologists; and they have skillfully combined authenticity with the fluent movement and dialogue of traditional storytelling. For each story Leo and Diane Dillon have made pastel and watercolor illustrations in black and tones of gray; using motifs from Egyptian and Assyrian art, they have combined their customary use of elaborate patterns with a strong feeling for implicit drama. Especially powerful are the depictions of the parting of the Red Sea and the witch of Endor's conjuration of the prophet Samuel's ghost. With an introduction, notes in the form of commentaries for each selection, and a bibliography.

📖 ***THE TALE OF THE MANDARIN DUCKS***
(retold by Katherine Paterson, 1990)

Leo Dillon and Diane Dillon

SOURCE: "The Tale of the Mandarin Ducks," in *The Horn Book Magazine,* Vol. LXVIII, No. 1, January-February, 1992, pp. 35-7.

[The following is Leo and Diane Dillon's acceptance speech for the Boston Globe-Horn Book *Award, which they delivered at the annual meeting of the New England Library Association in Hyannis, Massachusetts, on September 30, 1991.]*

When Virginia Buckley sent us the manuscript for ***The Tale of the Mandarin Ducks,*** by Katherine Paterson, we had no doubts about illustrating it. Not only was the story beautifully written, but it had a great message of compassion for other living creatures, and it was about honor,

Behind the curtain the actors prepare the set and the props, rehearse their lines, and don their masks.

From Who's in Rabbit's House?, *written by Verna Aardema. Illustrated by Leo and Diane Dillon.*

commitment, and the sharing of life's hurdles as well as good times.

Our first step after reading a manuscript is research. As a starting point, we get inspiration from the art forms of earlier periods in history. From there it is filtered through us. We are not concerned about deviating from that inspiration as long as we have the essence. For this story we went directly to the source—Japan. That sounds as though we're world travelers! Actually, we travel in books and libraries.

We have long admired a style of Japanese wood-block prints called *ukiyo-e* that was developed in Edo in the 1600s. *Ukiyo-e* means "pictures of the floating world," so named because the style and technique were developed to meet the needs of a newly prospering merchant class. The single-sheet format, combined with the wood-block process, made affordable editions of prints available on varying subjects portraying life of ordinary people. The nouveau riche were ripe for an art that spoke to their lives and needs, an art capable of changing with every shift in public taste.

In studying these prints, we realized that the line had the character of a brush line even though it had been cut from wood—very different from the sharp angular line of European woodcuts. The style is established in the line. The line varied from thick to thin as well as from black to gray.

Another discovery in studying this art was a frank acceptance of the gutter in bookmaking. Rather than trying to span it, the Japanese separated the picture, leaving margins on either side. This appealed to us since we're always trying to manipulate the art, keeping lines horizontal over the gutter so they will connect or placing a vertical device such as a tree in the center. We've been known to complain about the side-stitched book before, so here was our chance to avoid the problem altogether!

Since we did not have the time to actually cut the line in wood, we knew the line would be easy to transpose. We could work directly on paper with brush and ink. The large, flat areas of even, graduated color were not so direct. It took two-and-a-half weeks of trial and error working with different combinations of papers, brushes, and media. The simplest things are often the hardest to achieve.

We finally discovered that if we applied watercolor with a sponge rather than a brush, we could achieve the effect we wanted without streaks and brush strokes. Wood prints have a texture from the grain in the wood. Before we transferred the drawing onto the board, we used an ink eraser to texture the paper for a grainy effect.

The trial-and-error period at the beginning of each new book is painful. We wonder if this time it will beat us. It seems there's always a period early in the process when we're not sure of the technique or of ourselves. We have gained a certain amount of confidence over the years, but the creative process is always an unknown, and new techniques always have their mysteries. It may be the sense of danger that keeps us excited.

Since the underpainting with the sponge was a wet process, we had to work on a stiff surface that would not warp and buckle rather than the flexible surface required for the scanner, which is the preferred means of reproducing the art. Instead, the art had to be photographed first, which is one step removed; sometimes clarity and depth can be lost.

We would like to say that as artists we are concerned about the scanning process. Recently we were given instructions by a studio dictating the type of paper we must use and techniques we must avoid. They were working with a new scanner so sensitive that it picks up writing or irregularities on the *back* of the art. For us this is not progress. It is limiting our freedom to use what is most appropriate for a particular technique or effect.

We thank Riki Levinson for the beautiful reproduction and depth and subtlety of color and line. Often people are amazed that we work together, yet we are always working with a number of people who are part of the finished book. It is a group effort from author to printer. We feel we are accepting this award for all of us who had a hand in the making of *The Tale of the Mandarin Ducks*.

This award is very meaningful to us. It is a way of being reassured, after all these years, that we haven't "lost it" yet.

Betsy Hearne

SOURCE: A review of *The Tale of the Mandarin Ducks,* in *Bulletin of the Center for Children's Books,* Vol. 44, No. 1, September, 1990, pp. 14-5.

Great artists keep growing. The Dillons show more depth of line, color, and style than ever before in this original blending of Japanese art (ukiyo-e), art deco, and picture book illustration. Watercolor and pastel paintings envelop, without overwhelming, the text of a story about a pair of mandarin ducks, whose separation ultimately leads to a happy ending. A cruel lord captures the male for its plumage and then punishes the samurai whom he believes to be responsible for releasing the bird to return to its mate. The samurai refuses to betray the kitchen maid who really opened the cage and, reduced to the status of servant, falls in love with the kindhearted woman. The two are saved from a death sentence by the magical intercession of two imperial messengers, who lead the lovers to a snug hut in the woods before turning into a pair of mandarin ducks. Paterson's adaptation of a Japanese folktale (no sources given) is as graceful as the figures so skillfully drawn by the Dillons. The life-and-death drama is concluded with an unobtrusive moral: "Yasuko and Shozo . . . had many children who gave them much happiness—and a little trouble. But as they had learned years before, trouble can always be borne when it is shared." The Dillons' loving visual development of these two characters, curved together with flowing outlines, says even more than words can.

Carolyn Phelan

SOURCE: A review of *The Tale of the Mandarin Ducks,* in *Booklist,* Vol. 87, No. 1, September 1, 1990, p. 59.

A Japanese fairy tale, in picture-book format, about a Mandarin duck caught and caged at the whim of a wealthy Japanese lord. Separated from his mate, the bird languishes in captivity until a compassionate servant girl sets him free. The lord sentences the girl and her beloved to death, but they in turn are freed and rewarded with happiness. In the best fairytale tradition, their rescuers, ostensibly servants of the Emperor, turn out to be the grateful drake and his mate. The unity, simplicity, and grace of Paterson's writing find apt expression in the Dillons' watercolor and pastel illustrations. Resembling traditional Japanese prints in their strong, expressive lines, the horizontal pictures feature muted colors with warm undertones. The artwork, like the text, uses repeated patterns and motifs to good effect. The occasional positioning of a small, bordered picture within the larger double-page spread enables the viewer to see in two places at once, for example, the palace where the caged drake sits and the nest where his mate awaits him. A good choice to read aloud, this picture book offers children an appealing folktale expressed with quiet dignity.

Kay E. Vandergrift

SOURCE: A review of *The Tale of the Mandarin Ducks,* in *School Library Journal,* Vol. 36, No. 10, October, 1990, p. 111.

There is a quiet subtlety of tone in both text and illustration that perfectly captures the spirit of this Japanese folktale. . . .

The Dillons' watercolor and pastel paintings have the appearance of woodcuts with a luminous quality, conveying both the gentleness and the strength of the characters and of the bond of love between the two couples, human and duck. The illustrations are simultaneously powerful and ethereal with bold lines and fine details which, nonetheless, are more suggestive than definitive. This visual understatement is seen most clearly in the depiction of nature. Each tree, flower, or blade of grass hints of more behind. There is a grace in the flowing lines of the kimonos and beauty in the muted autumn/winter palette, giving a golden, blue-gray, or mauve glow to the various scenes. Although the obvious message of this tale is that of kindness rewarded, there is a more subtle message brought home in the final words, "trouble can always be borne when it is shared."

Ann Banks

SOURCE: "Love Is the Pot of Gold," in *The New York Times Book Review,* November 11, 1990, p. 42.

Long ago and far away, the storyteller begins—and we enter the dream zone of a folk tale, an improbable realm where animals talk, people fly and kindness is repaid. In *The Tale of the Mandarin Ducks,* a fable set in imperial Japan, good things happen to good people, and good ducks as well. So gentle is this story that wickedness is not even avenged. The worst that befalls the cruel and greedy lord who causes all the trouble is that his material desires are thwarted.

The story has been retold by the Newbery medalist Katherine Paterson in spare, stately language that flows as gracefully as the folds of a court kimono. The richness of Leo and Diane Dillon's illustrations provides a perfect accompaniment. Executed in watercolor and pastels, they are modeled on *ukiyo-e,* a style of early Japanese woodcuts. The colors are luscious, the line sensuous. Seldom has clothing been more expressively rendered, even the cruel lord's robe looks mean.

Ethel L. Heins

SOURCE: A review of *The Tale of the Mandarin Ducks,*

in *The Horn Book Magazine,* Vol. LXVI, No. 6, November-December, 1990, p. 754.

For their brilliantly conceived interpretation of the story, the Dillons acknowledge their debt to the beauty of *ukiyo-e,* a popular style of Japanese genre paintings and woodblock prints that developed in the seventeenth century and flourished into the nineteenth. To the flat, stylized elegance of *ukiyo-e,* the Dillons have added some of the realism, freshness, dynamism, and dramatic color contrasts of Western art; thus, while emphasizing atmosphere, they nevertheless rely on emotion and action to energize the visual storytelling. Beginning with the handsome endpapers and the exquisite title page, the book contains some of the artists' most splendid work.

John Mole

SOURCE: "Thereby Hangs a Picture," in *The Times Educational Supplement,* No. 3894, February 15, 1991, p. 31.

Stylisation of a . . . [linear] kind is to be found in Leo and Diane Dillon's imitation of 18th-century Japanese woodcuts to complement Katherine Paterson's **The Tale of the Mandarin Ducks**. Expressively conveying both the Samurai fierceness of court tyranny and the radiant love of the servant couple who survive their lord's wrath thanks to the pair of captive ducks whose release at their hands has occasioned it, these are memorable illustrations to a gentle text.

AÏDA (adapted by Leontyne Price, 1990)

Roger Sutton

SOURCE: A review of *Aïda,* in *Bulletin of the Center for Children's Books,* Vol. 44, No. 2, October, 1990, p. 42.

Like many **Aïda** productions, this one is lavishly appointed, with gold borders, opulently colored paintings, and delicate narrative friezes heading the text. While some of the paintings, such as the one of Aïda's moonlit confrontation with her father, are dramatically effective, others hide the drama in crowded patterns and colors. The friezes tell the story more clearly, conveying the passions of the story through formalized pose and gesture.

Barbara Elleman

SOURCE: A review of *Aïda,* in *Booklist,* Vol. 87, No. 3, October 1, 1990, p. 331.

Who better to retell the beloved, tragic story of the Ethiopian princess Aïda than the famed diva whose musical interpretation has transfixed thousands in opera houses around the world? Price has always had a special relationship with this opera and the heroine because, as she says in the afterword, "my skin is my costume." In a lengthy but smooth-flowing narrative, Price draws on her long association with the story to slim the libretto into a cohesive, credible tale. Captured by the Egyptians and made a slave to Princess Amneris, Aïda falls in love with the handsome military captain Radames, who returns her devotion, spurning the advances of Amneris. When her father is also seized by the Egyptians, Aïda tricks Radames into revealing an escape route. In a jealous rage, Amneris brands Radames a traitor and sends him to his death in a sealed tomb. Aïda secretly joins him there as the story closes. The Dillons magnificently capture the drama with powerful full-page illustrations that resemble stage sets. Huge marbled pillars, stark stone steps, and decorated walls are backdrops for the strongly realized characters, who are richly robed in intense, vivid colors. The page design is noteworthy: text and illustration are framed with stylized gold-flower motifs, while small visual vignettes that appear above the text on the left side of each two-page spread also carry forth the action. Ideal for reading aloud during an Egyptian unit, in music classes, to children attending the opera, or for the pure aesthetic experience.

Kirkus Reviews

SOURCE: A review of *Aïda,* in *Kirkus Reviews,* Vol. LVIII, No. 19, October 1, 1990, p. 1397.

Like last year's Fonteyn/Hyman *Swan Lake,* an elegant edition narrated by a star long associated with a major work. As Price explains in an eloquent note, she sees Aïda as "a portrait of my inner self . . . [whose] deep devotion and love for her country and for her people—her nobility, strength, and courage—are all qualities I aspire to . . ." Price's unpretentious yet dramatic retelling, like Fonteyn's, reflects her unique intimacy with the role. In their handsome art, the Dillons skillfully combine stylized, rhythmically arranged figures in decorative friezes; larger paintings in which expressive faces are set off by rich backgrounds in collage-like patterns; and unique borders delicately wrought of gold. A dignified tribute to a noble tale.

Ann Stell

SOURCE: A review of *Aïda,* in *School Library Journal,* Vol. 36, No. 11, November, 1990, p. 131.

A straightforward, sympathetic retelling of the story of the beautiful and noble Ethiopian Princess, Aïda, who, while enslaved in Egypt, is caught between her devotion to her father and her country and her love for Radames, young captain of the enemy army. The Dillons' dramatic, decorative style with their sumptuous use of color is perfectly suited to the opera's moving and tragic story. The book is elegant in its design. Full-page dramatic paintings opposite each page of text are supplemented by smaller pictures set in a strip above the text where profiled characters in the style of ancient Egyptian art repeat the story line. Gorgeous endpapers and border designs in gold car-

ry out the Egyptian theme and add to the richness and vibrancy of the book. All that is missing is Verdi's wonderful music. *Aïda* is particularly welcome as there have been few opera-story picture books of note.

John Rockwell

SOURCE: A review of *Aïda,* in *The New York Times Book Review,* December 2, 1990, p. 38.

The bulk of [*Aïda*] . . . is given over to a straightforward but flat retelling of the tale, unilluminating for those who know the opera and unevocative for those who do not. What redeems it are the glowing illustrations and overall design by Leo and Diane Dillon. The distinguished American artists, who have won two Caldecott Medals for books about Africa, offer a richly colored pictorial tapestry, inspired as much by Art Nouveau as by Egyptian and African motifs. It is their work that provides the compelling operatic analogue that Ms. Price's prose does not. Children might well be drawn to the opera by the pictures. Better yet, maybe the Dillons could be cajoled into designing a stage production of *Aïda.*

Mary M. Burns

SOURCE: A review of *Aïda,* in *The Horn Book Magazine,* Vol. LXVII, No. 2, March-April, 1991, p. 217.

Based on the opera by Giuseppe Verdi, this is book production in the grand style—from the elegant velvet black casing stamped with gold letters to the marbleized endpapers embellished with a stylized pattern of lotus blossoms and pods. Opera, it has been said, is the most baroque of art forms; certainly, the book's design underscores that concept. While not double-page spreads in the conventional sense, opposing pages are treated as complementary units: the text appears on the left surmounted by a friezelike series of figures that interpret the action; on the right, a full-page, full-color illustration focuses on a particular character or grouping, much as the spotlight would highlight the principal performer or performers. Price's appended "Storyteller's Note" provides the reader with insight into her personal affection for the opera as well as an understanding of the emotions that infused her unforgettable and unrivaled interpretation of "heavenly" Aïda, the Ethiopian princess whose love for the Egyptian commander Radames ultimately leads to tragedy.

THE RACE OF THE GOLDEN APPLES
(written by Claire Martin, 1991)

Hazel Rochman

SOURCE: A review of *The Race of the Golden Apples,* in *Booklist,* Vol. 88, No. 2, September 1, 1991, p. 56.

This romantic picture-book version of the Atalanta myth combines the styles of medieval tapestry with contemporary glitz. The language is a bit flat ("I'm sorry, Goddess") with little of the vitality of Evslin's colloquial retellings; it's as if the myth has been reduced to soap opera ("Suddenly he knew he had loved her since he first saw her"). The framed illustrations in glowing color are highly decorated, stylized in background but with extraordinary depth. They begin with spring and autumnal scenes in the forest where Atalanta is abandoned as a baby and raised by Diana to run like the wind. When Atalanta discovers she's really a princess and is summoned to her father's side, the setting moves to the court. Finally, there's the crucial race with her lover, which (as this version spells things out) she chooses to lose. The most dramatic pictures retain the mystery of myth (Venus flying down with the golden apples in purple light) and the glory of passion (Atalanta confronting her father in fury). Less interesting are the pictures that show her as a smiling blond coed running track.

Ann Welton

SOURCE: A review of *The Race of the Golden Apples,* in *School Library Journal,* Vol. 37, No. 10, October, 1991, p. 111.

The Dillons' illustrations are certainly impressive, but are somewhat below their usual standard, While the pastel borders are lovely, the pictures of Atalanta and the rest of the characters seem stiff and lifeless. This may have to do with the generally cool palette, relying largely on teal, or the fact that the acrylic paintings attempt to emulate tapestry. Whatever the reason, there is an occasional awkwardness, a sense of linearity where the line should flow, and in some pictures, proportions are off—arms or legs slightly too long, as if inspired by El Greco. Nonetheless, the book as a whole is arresting, and lacking other picture-book versions of this Greek legend of unstinting love, this is a solid purchase for mythology sections.

Betsy Hearne

SOURCE: A review of *The Race of the Golden Apples,* in *Bulletin of the Center for Children's Books,* Vol. 45, No. 3, November, 1991, p. 69.

The Dillons' deep-toned illustrations feature ornate patterning, an artistic context in which the heroine looks startlingly like Barbie. Both words and images, while striking in impact, suffer some tonal dissonance with the myth—because of overexplanation, in the case of the text, and glamorization, in the case of the art. Though the story cries out for simpler treatment, it still wields a certain power even within this format of brittle beauty.

PISH, POSH, SAID HIERONYMUS BOSCH
(written by Nancy Willard, 1991)

Carolyn Phelan

SOURCE: A review of *Pish, Posh, Said Hieronymus*

Bosch, in *Booklist,* Vol. 88, No. 17, November 15, 1991, p. 628.

For 500 years, Hieronymus Bosch's paintings have fascinated viewers with strange visions of grotesque creatures and odd twists on the routine. Imagining life with Bosch, Willard's fanciful poem introduces children to his young housekeeper, who's at the end of her tether: "I'm quitting your service, I've had quite enough / of your three-legged thistles asleep in my wash." Three-legged thistles are the mildest of the weird creatures who inhabit the unruly Bosch household, but the artist unsympathetically dismisses her complaints with a "'Pish, posh,' / said Hieronymus Bosch." The poem creates a believable nonsense world and lets the characters' good hearts bring a loving resolution to the problem. The Dillons' illustrations, lively sepia drawings alternating with larger, full-color paintings photographed in a decorative metal frame, reflect the inventive nonsense of the poetry, though without always capturing its tone. Made of gold-painted wood embellished with charming, fantastical figures cast in brass, bronze, and silver, the frame that encloses each painting is a fanciful delight; however, its use here lends an air of self-conscious artistry that removes the audience a step from the fantasy of the paintings themselves. From a practical standpoint, the volume's large size (12¼ inches by 11¼ inches, based on galley and jacket dimensions) makes it an unwieldy addition to many poetry collections in libraries, but it could be shelved with picture books instead. A showy original.

Betsy Hearne

SOURCE: A review of *Pish, Posh, Said Hieronymus Bosch,* in *Bulletin of the Center for Children's Books,* Vol. 45, No. 4, December, 1991, p. 109.

The Dillons have unleashed a riot of surrealistic creatures within each gilt-framed illustration. It's hard to resist poring over these topsy-turvy mutants claiming imaginative kinship with Bosch's own strange creatures. Although each composition is crawling with activity and is further complicated by gold figures decorating the frames, there's a largesse of creamy space that rests the eye, and the surfaces within the pictures are kept purposefully smooth and untextured to relieve the compression of shapes. Not every child will be able to figure out what's going on here, but then, not every child is literal enough to care—those who love Alice in Wonderland (and they're a select lot) will catch the drift enough to enjoy the wild energy of Dillon sights and Willard sounds.

Kenneth Marantz

SOURCE: A review of *Pish, Posh, Said Hieronymus Bosch,* in *School Library Journal,* Vol. 37, No. 12, December, 1991, p. 119.

One needn't know Bosch's paintings of nightmarish otherworlds to be intrigued by the fantastic cast of characters

Willard describes and the Dillons depict—although this visual parody is even more delightful to those familiar with the artist's work. The painter's housekeeper complains of the extreme frustration produced by the hordes of weird creatures that keep her from her proper duties, and she leaves. But she's followed by the lot who clamor for her loving attention, and she returns resigned to an active life with those who need her. Willard's verse has a Seusslike dash to it, most frequently rhymed couplets with unusual words and even odder references to things such as a "pickle-winged fish." All the words are hand-lettered in an unlikely mixture of upper-and lower-case letters in the same tones of warm brown used to create vignettes on the pages facing the full color scenes. And such illustrations they are! The Dillons' son has cast four winged beasties and intergrated them onto a gilt wood frame with a softly arched top. Inside the artists have painted scenes in the spirit of the 15th-century genius but in a more modern, post-Renaissance fashion. The setting and humans are realistically portrayed in period dress, the artist as a bit of a crackpot and his housekeeper as a young woman fed up with his madness. It's the "beehive in boots" and "three-legged thistles" that infest all parts of these scenes that are based on characters from Bosch's vision of hell. Only now the effect is comic rather than frightening. Once again the artists show their virtuosity, their ability to don the robes of another artistic period or place, and yet play the play in their own fashion.

Leonard S. Marcus

SOURCE: A review of *Pish, Posh, Said Hieronymus Bosch,* in *The New York Times Book Review,* December 22, 1991, p. 5.

The Dillons' illustrations are inventive, highly accomplished pastiches that freely borrow from (rather than imitate) the work of Bosch and other early Dutch painters. Like the text, the illustrations make a running joke of cataloguing the offspring of Bosch's fertile imagination, and much fun is to be had in trying to spot all the impossible creatures (some of them quite tiny) that riddle the bustling scenes.

But if cucumbers and candles all come alive, the story's two main characters both remain remote and largely unknowable in these pictures. In the absence of clear direction from the text, their reactions often look merely staged.

The frame in which the paintings are displayed isn't a painting of a frame but a photographic reproduction of a real one. Fashioned from silver, bronze and brass by the scultor-painter Lee Dillon, who is also the illustrators' son, the frame is both whimsical and grand. Glowing, three-dimensional images of the sun and of winged elf-musicians ornament its sides. A visual delight in itself, it's a work of art framing other works of art about an artist. Clearly, the "art part," in John Ashbery's phrase, has been amply attended to in this book for young readers; what's lacking is enough heart.

NORTHERN LULLABY (written by Nancy White Carlstrom, 1992)

Ilene Cooper

SOURCE: A review of *Northern Lullaby,* in *Booklist,* Vol. 88, No. 20, June 15, 1992, p. 1834.

Framed by the Dillons' magical evocation of the northern night sky, Carlstrom's soothing words—part poem, part lullaby—convey both grace and dignity. "Goodnight Papa Star / Goodnight Mama Moon / Bending your silver arms / down through the darkness." The young native American narrator, not seen until the last sleepy spread, calls to those in the natural world he finds so dear, bidding them all to rest in peace until the morning. Only the Northern Lights continue to stir as the child asks, "And when I turn over / Between sleep and dreams, / Northern Lights dance / your good night over me." With motifs and artifacts of Alaskan native peoples, though not of a single group, the panoramic spreads, in colors as deep and muted as the evening sky, are tender and moving. As one might expect of illustrations for a lullaby, these seem to spring from some illusive dream world beyond intellect and pretense: Grandfather Mountain, his face as craggy as his name, brushes back his hair made of new-fallen snow. Using subtle shading of airbrushed color, overlapped and shadowed for an unusual impression of depth, the Dillons' art here is as fine as any work they've done before. A felicitous collaboration.

Betsy Hearne

SOURCE: A review of *Northern Lullaby,* in *Bulletin of the Center for Children's Books,* Vol. 46, No. 2, October, 1992, p. 40.

"Goodnight Papa Star / Goodnight Mama Moon, / Bending your silver arms / down through the darkness." Natural elements and wild creatures are personified here in poetic and graphic forms, with a spare text and sweeping illustrations that both imply the vast, snow-covered spaces of the far North. Smooth dark portraits set into patterned masks and costumes give faces to Sister Owl, Brother Bear, Cousins Beaver and Fox, Auntie Willow and Auntie Birch, Great Moose Uncle, Wolf Uncle Gray, Snowshoe Hare, and landmarks of earth and water. A dark sky flecked with square snow flakes and rounded mounds of cloud and snow give a comforting organic feel to the lullaby, which will calm the most fearful toddler as it seems to have done the sleeping Native American child trundled on the last page. The format itself is spaciously designed, with double-spread pictures snuggled against a swathe of pebbled paper, at the bottom of which the verses are discreetly tucked. The end effect is both simple and sophisticated. . . .

Karen K. Radtke

SOURCE: A review of *Northern Lullaby,* in *School*

Library Journal, Vol. 38, No. 10, October, 1992, pp. 80, 85.

A sleepy baby says goodnight to the Alaskan countryside and its inhabitants in a free-verse poem. Each natural element or animal is represented by an anthropomorphized object—Grandpa Mountain, Great Moose Uncle, Auntie Birch. The verse is evocative, filled with subtle imageries of the cold, yet beautiful, country. However, the romantic text, with its inverted language patterns, makes for sophisticated reading. The Dillons' airbrush and watercolor illustrations do not portray any specific group; rather, ". . . they aimed at capturing the spirit of all native peoples from that land." Isn't it time that writers and illustrators stop characterizing Native Americans as one people? Each double-page spread effectively humanizes the symbolic text, utilizing the natural colors and patterns of the area. However, they, too, are sophisticated and a bit posed. A lovely book that is too abstract for young children and not specific enough for multicultural units.

📖 *MANY THOUSAND GONE: AFRICAN AMERICANS FROM SLAVERY TO FREEDOM* (written by Virginia Hamilton, 1993)

Betsy Hearne

SOURCE: A review of *Many Thousand Gone: African Americans from Slavery to Freedom,* in *Bulletin of the Center for Children's Books,* Vol. 46, No. 7, March, 1993, p. 212.

The real voice of history must be individual, and these thirty-some historical personalities give witness to slavery's toll on African-Americans. Each one speaks for thousands silenced. Hamilton shows her versatility here with an ambitious two-century story told in vignettes that never shortcut their subjects of complexity, however compressed the information. Part of her success derives from changing her rich, idiosyncratic fiction style into a straightforward prose that lets the facts speak louder than their presentation. This takes a lot of trust in the young audience and in the story itself, and Hamilton's faith is justified. From the "running away" of a slave named Somersett in 1671 to a South Carolina slave's celebration of the Emancipation Proclamation in 1863, these moving episodes run the gauntlet of tragedy, comedy, nobility, and trickery as each slave struggles to become free in whatever way is viable. One wins her case in court; another mails himself in a large crate from his plantation to an abolitionists' headquarters. One, in despair, cuts her daughter's throat (shades of Toni Morrison's *Beloved*) and jumps into the river with her baby when her family is recaptured. The baby drowns, and Margaret Garner is sold into the deep south, where she dies in the rice fields. A slave named Jackson poses as his light-skinned wife's maid, and they both fool a boatload of Southern ladies all the way from New Orleans to Cincinnati. These tales of high drama never run longer than a few pages, illustrated with some of the Dillons' most emotive, strongly shaped art in black and white. The frontispiece and closing illustration

alone speak volumes—a ship leaving a dungeon, with a broken doll on the floor; a family leaving a mammy-doll behind in a shack as they drive off in a mule-drawn wagon. The format is open, spacious, and inviting. This should be required reading for history curricula, but once introduced, it won't need to be. And don't cheat yourself of the opportunity to share it aloud. An index and bibliography are included.

Lyn Miller-Lachmann

SOURCE: A review of *Many Thousand Gone: African Americans from Slavery to Freedom,* in *School Library Journal,* Vol. 39, No. 5, May, 1993, p. 116.

The vignettes are lively, readable, and written with a poetic flair that distinguishes this book from most collective biographies for this age range. All of the stories shed a different light upon Hamilton's themes and the factual information she presents as an introduction to each theme. Her research is impeccable. The Dillons' black-and-white illustrations are refreshingly original, conveying the emotion and drama of the experiences described; text and visuals combine to create a powerful and moving whole. Reluctant readers and those with little prior knowledge will find this book unusually approachable with its short chapters, lively writing, and ample white space.

Mary Moore Easter

SOURCE: A review of *Many Thousand Gone: African Americans from Slavery to Freedom,* in *Hungry Mind Review,* No. 26, Summer, 1993, p. C3.

Halfway through **Many Thousand Gone,** I felt the need for an intermission of reflection just to absorb and recover from the cruelty embedded in the matter-of-fact history Virginia Hamilton compiles. The focus of the book, as suggested by the title quoted from a spiritual, is escape from bondage. The interior illustrations are extraordinary in stark black-and-white metaphor, economical statements that appear every few pages. Though there is only one full-color drawing, on the cover, it alone could provide many points of conversation for a child of early reading age.

📖 *THE SORCERER'S APPRENTICE* (retold by Nancy Willard, 1993)

Hazel Rochman

SOURCE: A review of *The Sorcerer's Apprentice,* in *Booklist,* Vol. 92, No. 5, November 1, 1993, p. 529.

The Dillons' full-page water-colors, exquisitely drawn in meticulous detail, show domestic uproar just about to burst out of the tight gold frames. In fact, there are a few tiny spot illustrations outside the frame on each page. The sorcerer's house has 57 doors and "knockers made of gnashing teeth"; there are eyes everywhere, and his creatures are neurotic, brooding, sinister, and clownish. Words and pictures work together perfectly to make us see that chaos is "very near"; everything is in a state of transformation. The more you look, the more shapes change and slither and leap out as something different. The best scene of all shows the sorcerer ordering the dishes to wash each other ("The spoons leapt up and scrubbed the plates"). He's in control. In contrast, when Sylvia's task is to make clothes for all the creatures, she can't control anything. She's overwhelmed; even the scissors try to bite her hand. In desperation, she pours the sorcerer's potion on the sewing machine—and creates the wildest nightmare. The machine reveals its monstrous teeth: it bursts from the house and hems the trees; it stitches the mountains, snips the moon, bites the sun, until the sorcerer returns and order is restored. In a lovely last line, Willard gives the old cautionary tale a moral for today: Sylvia has learned to turn "failures into fairy tales."

Betsy Hearne

SOURCE: A review of *The Sorcerer's Apprentice,* in *Bulletin of the Center for Children's Books,* Vol. 47, No. 5, January, 1994, pp. 170-1.

The team that produced *Pish, Posh Hieronymus Bosch* has set loose a mad menagerie of machinery, with Sylvia the sorcerer's apprentice overdoing her master's magic potion to help her with a sewing job ("Your first task is to make new clothes / for all the creatures in my care— / New caps, new capes, new vests and hose"). When the machinery starts multiplying, the magician awakes and breaks the spell; we leave ambitious, red-haired Sylvia on Mount Dragon's Eyes, learning magic at a more sedate pace. An assortment of strange but amiable creatures surrounds her, "while Sylvia teaches them to say / the spell she worked out yesterday / for turning pencils into pails, and failures into fairy tales." The carefully controlled verse is vintage Willard, and the carefully controlled art is vintage Dillons. Both are more smoothly crafted than spontaneous, but the story itself has a certain intrinsic chaos that overflows the book's gold-bordered formality, asserting a tension that will assure kids' response to the inventive details of rhyme and illustration. A note attests to the tale's long history.

Patricia Dooley

SOURCE: A review of *The Sorcerer's Apprentice,* in *School Library Journal,* Vol. 40, No. 1, January, 1994, pp. 116-7.

The Dillons have worked their usual magic on the illustrations. Clear, saturated colors and a touch of Art Nouveau style are vehicles for whimsy that is never cute or cloying. Detail-packed, the pictures beg for repeat viewing as the rhythmic verses roll on. A welcome return visit to a tale too long dominated by Disney.

Sam Swope

SOURCE: A review of *The Sorcerer's Apprentice,* in *The New York Times Book Review,* January 16, 1994, p. 20.

In Ms. Willard's updating, the sorcerer is Tottibo, a generic medieval wizard with glowering eyes and pointy ears who surrounds himself with various creatures and "beasts without a name." We never know what kind of magic Tottibo practices, but it feels dark even if it's not especially fearful. This vagueness is partly in the text and partly in the illustrations, which, while dazzling in their complexity and wonderfully detailed, have something a little tame about them, a little too bright, as if the talented Dillons were afraid to conjure something truly tenebrous. . . .

Nancy Vasilakis

SOURCE: A review of *The Sorcerer's Apprentice,* in *The Horn Book Magazine,* Vol. LXX, No. 2, March-April, 1994, p. 193.

Author and illustrators recharge this familiar cautionary tale, adding a sly feminist slant. A new apprentice to the magician Tottibo is given the task of sewing clothes for all the creatures, real and fantastical, that fill his teeming house. Sylvia's distressed assertion that she came to learn magic earns her a stern warning from her new master: "magic free of aggravation" requires practice. To demonstrate, he pours one drop of potion into a sink of dirty dishes, whereupon platters, plates, and saucers leap up and scrub themselves clean. Then he leaves Sylvia to the task at hand. The job seems overwhelming, however, as Willard and the Dillons in a delightful magic of their own breathe frenzied life into all inanimate objects. The thread, sprouting arms and legs, grows snappish, and buttons rollick and tumble, while the old treadle machine looks on. Exasperated, Sylvia picks up a bottle and pours on some magic powder, only to have the sewing machine run amok. "It stitched the dishes to the table, / it stitched the noodles to the ladle." It escapes out an open window and "like an unruly vine, / it sewed the muffins to the line / and appliquéd the lemon pie / and half a dozen dirty socks / across a famished stretch of sky." Tottibo returns to restore order, and in the last page he can be seen winging away on the back of a stork as a presumably wiser and well-practiced Sylvia turns "pencils into pails / and failures into fairy tales." The dancing, varied rhythms and the alliterative imagery of the poetry make this a read-aloud treasure. The book is a visual prize as well. Preposterous creatures swarm over cream-colored, gilt-bordered pages while small vignettes outside the frames open up each spread and advance the story line. The whole enterprise is a masterful and creative meeting of the minds between author and illustrators. The extensive source note at the end will give readers, whose interest will surely have been sparked, an opportunity to look for this story in one of its many other forms.

📖 *WHAT AM I? LOOKING THROUGH SHAPES AT APPLES AND GRAPES* (written by N. N. Charles, 1994)

Elizabeth Bush

SOURCE: A review of *What Am I?* in *Bulletin of the Center for Children's Books,* Vol. 48, No. 2, October, 1994, p. 40.

What am I, indeed. Four simultaneous concepts are three too many in this offering for the toddler set. First, it's a color-concept book, in which pages of concentric shapes each display four shades of a primary or secondary color. Second, it's a fruit-identification game, with two-line rhymes that hint at a fruit which is pictured on the following page ("I'm green, I'm nice / to eat by the slice." An avocado, of course). Third, it's a shape-identification book, in which geometric forms appear as die cut openings (a rectangle appears with the text "I'm blue, I'm small / I'm shaped like a ball," and a diamond shape peeks through to a banana). This is all going on at the same time, and then comes a let's-all-be-friends exhortation, with an arch of children's hands forming a "rainbow of the human race." The Dillons' double-page fruit paintings are quite luscious: large details of individual fruits facilitate the guessing game for the youngest viewers, while close-ups of foliage and symbiotic insects offer additional visual information for a slightly older audience. But this volume's hazily conceived mission and overload of contradictory visual and textual detail make it a weak choice for sharing with preschoolers.

Carolyn Phelan

SOURCE: A review of *What Am I? Looking through Shapes at Apples and Grapes,* in *Booklist,* Vol. 91, No. 6, November 15, 1994, pp. 605-6.

This rhyming picture book invites children to guess what is described in a riddling rhyme and shown through a geometrically shaped hole in the right-hand page. On the left side of the spread a series of concentric squares appears, for instance, a small dark red one in the center bordered by ever larger and lighter ones to the edge of the page. The facing page, white with a cut out square window showing only a bit of textured red hidden on the next page, has the words "I'm red, I'm round, I fall to the ground. What am I?" Turn the page to see a large, horizontal spread of apple boughs heavy with fruit and one big, beautiful red apple. The riddle's answer might be guessed from the verbal or visual clue, but it has nothing to do with the squares that figure so prominently in the design. This multiple-concept book would be stronger if it did not try to do so much, from the guessing game to the colors lesson to the fruits lesson to the shapes lesson to the final lesson "In places here, and foreign lands, / the rainbow can be seen in hands / that make the world a better place /—a rainbow of the human race." Still, the paintings of shapes and fruits are huge, handsome, and appealing in their simplicity. Nursery-school teachers looking for concept books will find a number of uses for this one.

Jan Shepherd Ross

SOURCE: A review of *What Am I? Looking through Shapes at Apples and Grapes,* in *School Library Journal,* Vol. 41, No. 1, January, 1995, p. 83.

This clever book is essentially a guessing game that encourages readers to name the colors, shapes, and types of fruit described in simple riddles and revealed by turning the die-cut pages. Vibrant graphics in photoreal detail show the tempting produce on its respective bush, tree, or vine. Charles ends the lyrical presentation with a reference to the "rainbow of the human race." A multifaceted, beautifully designed book that will serve a variety of needs, and will introduce several different concepts in a unique, entertaining way.

Mary M. Burns

SOURCE: A review of *What Am I? Looking through Shapes at Apples and Grapes,* in *The Horn Book Magazine,* Vol. LXXI, No. 1, January-February, 1995, p. 48.

A selection of fruit exquisitely rendered in full color is the focus of an imaginative concept book which introduces shapes and colors. A handsome still life in which different varieties of fruit are artfully arranged suggests the content of the succeeding pages. For each sequence, a simple rhyming question directs the reader's attention to the specific subject, which is hidden behind a two-inch labelled die cut of a geometric shape; the opposing page presents various shades of the color associated with that subject. The banana, for example, describes itself as follows: "I'm yellow, I'm thin, / you peel my skin. / What am I?" The following double-page spread supplies the answer in an interpretive botanical study. Audiences will also enjoy the lighthearted addition of one or more insect visitors in each composition to provide further stimulus for interaction. Unfortunately, the innate unity of the concept is marred by the forced introduction of the rainbow as a bridge to a multiracial assemblage of hands "that make the world a better place—/ a rainbow of the human race." The idea is worthy—but deserves better than placement as an afterthought. This jarring note aside, however, the book is unusual and aesthetically pleasing.

📖 *HER STORIES: AFRICAN AMERICAN FOLKTALES, FAIRY TALES, AND TRUE TALES* (retold by Virginia Hamilton, 1995)

Patricia (Dooley) Lothrop Green

SOURCE: A review of *Her Stories: African American Folktales, Fairy Tales, and True Tales,* in *School Li-*

brary Journal, Vol. 41, No. 11, November, 1995, pp. 111-2.

Outstanding interpreters of, and contributors to, black culture for children, Virginia Hamilton and the Dillons have produced yet another superb offering, of value to all ages and segments of our society. **Her Stories** contains 20 brief pieces, equally (if sometimes rather abitrarily) distributed in 5 sections: animal tales, fairy tales, supernatural stories, "folkways and legends," and true tales (including Hamilton's own account of this book's genesis). Vernacular rather than dialectal, the fluid writing recalls the oral sources of these tales (there is a source bibliography, and comments on provenance follow each tale). As the title implies, the stories all feature females, but there is nothing predictable about the roles they play. Funny, touching, scary, magical, and inspiring by turns, the characters are as varied as the narratives—and as the tastes of readers. The Dillons' electric-hued acrylic paintings (16 full-page, several vignettes, and an enticing jacket) catch the tales' multiple moods. The book is a gallery of beautiful women of color. Entrancing and important, this notable collaboration deserves a wide success.

Hazel Rochman

SOURCE: A review of *Her Stories: African American Folktales,* in *Booklist,* Vol. 92, No. 5, November 1, 1995, p. 470.

The storytelling is dramatic and direct in this collection of nineteen tales about African American females, beautifully retold by Hamilton in a wide variety of simple, colloquial voices and styles. ("There was this glory-looking young girl in the times when animals talked. She was Lena, beauty.") Animal tales, *pourquoi* tales, tales of the supernatural, legends, tall tales, and factual accounts are gathered in a large-size volume designed for group sharing, with big, clear type and wide margins. The stories also leave lots of space; the endings leave you wondering. The Dillons' glowingly detailed acrylic illustrations extend the horror, comedy, rhythm, and spirit of the tales, ranging from the glamour of the mermaid to the creepy terror of the Cat Woman to the legendary power of Annie Christmas, who was "coal black and tree tall."

Additional coverage of the Dillons' lives and careers are contained in the following sources published by Gale Research: *Major Authors and Illustrators for Children and Young Adults* and *Something about the Author,* Vols. 15, 51.

Paula Fox

1923-

American novelist and author of children's fiction.

Major works include *The Slave Dancer* (1973), *One-Eyed Cat* (1984), *The Village by the Sea* (1988, published as *In a Place of Danger,* 1989), *Monkey Island* (1991), *The Eagle Kite* (1995, published as *The Gathering of Darkness,* 1995).

For information on Fox's work before 1976, see *CLR,* Vol. 1.

INTRODUCTION

Fox's reputation as an outstanding writer for children is due to the many award-winning books she has written over the past thirty years. A versatile writer, Fox has written picture books for the very young and novels for young adults and adults. She is most noted, however, for her works that feature preteen and teenage protagonists. Often praised by critics for her willingness to explore sensitive and moral issues, including AIDS, homosexuality, and racism, reviewers also applaud Fox's spare writing style, visual language, and fully realized characters and settings. Moreover, Fox is valued for her keen understanding of young people, especially their relationships among peers and adults. Many of her books address themes such as death, abandonment, and mistrust, which reveal the human experience. Fox explained in her 1974 Newbery Award acceptance speech that her reasons for writing are "to discover, over and over again, my connections with myself, with others."

Biographical Information

Half Cuban and half Irish, Fox was born in New York City in 1923. Her father earned a living rewriting plays by other authors and writing his own. After doing this for a number of years in New York City, he, along with Fox's mother, traveled to Hollywood and England to work for film studios. Therefore, until age six, Fox lived with a minister and his elderly mother in a Victorian house overlooking the Hudson River. It was the minister who taught Fox to read and write, introduced her to many literary greats, and gave her the idea of becoming an author. At age six, Fox was sent to live in California and moved again at age eight to Cuba to live with her maternal grandmother for two years. During those years Fox attended a one-room school with eight other students of various ages.

When President Fulgencio Batista began his revolutionary rise to power, Fox was sent back to New York, but hardly saw her parents. By the time she turned twelve, the

young girl had attended nine schools. When she was old enough to work, Fox held a variety of jobs, including one as a machinist for Bethlehem Steel and one as a punctuator of fifteenth-century Italian madrigals for a music publisher. Fond of traveling, she continued to find jobs in cities abroad. For example, she became a stringer for a British news agency just after World War II, which allowed her to visit the war-torn country of Poland. She eventually returned to New York, married, and had two sons. After she and her first husband divorced in 1954, she attended Columbia University and then taught for a number of years. As her children became older and more independent, Fox had more time to write. In 1962 she remarried and by 1966 her first book, *Maurice's Room,* was published. She has written a number of works since then, for both children and adults, and has won many literary awards, including the prestigious Newbery Medal for *The Slave Dancer* in 1974.

Major Works

Set in the 1840s, *The Slave Dancer* features Jessie, a white thirteen-year-old street musician, who is kidnapped and forced to work on a slave ship. His primary job is to play his fife for the hungry, tired, and abused Africans, but he suffers other harsh experiences which tragically change his life. "So palpably was life aboard the *Moonlight* rendered that even those who claim that an examination of slavery should be the exclusive right of descendants of slaves and their friends were aroused," said Alice Bach. Set almost one hundred years later in 1939, *One-Eyed Cat* tells the story of eleven-year-old Ned Wallis, the son of a Congregational minister and a wheelchair-bound mother. Ned's parents forbid him to try out the new air rifle that his uncle gave him. Disobeying them, Ned finds the gun and fires it outside. He thinks he hits something and soon discovers a one-eyed cat. Possessed with guilt for injuring the cat, Ned goes through a rough period which ends when he sees the cat healthy and with family. Anne Tyler wrote that "the story can teach young readers about grown-ups' expectations of them."

The Village by the Sea relates the troubles of Emma, a ten-year-old girl who must live with her uncle and mean aunt at a beach town on Long Island for two weeks. To avoid her aunt, Emma accompanies one of the local girls to the beach, where they build a village from the unique treasures they find along the shore. It is not until after Emma returns home to her father that she understands her aunt's actions. Amy Kellman stated that "the cancerous effect of envy and the healing properties of love and self-esteem are driven home poignantly and with a gentle humor that runs throughout the book." In *Monkey Island,* eleven-year-old Clay Garrity becomes homeless after his father abandons the family and his mother disappears from their welfare hotel room. The young boy drifts to a local park nicknamed Monkey Island where many of the neighborhood's homeless congregate. Eventually, the young boy is reunited with his mother after a bout of pneumonia and placement in a foster home. Kay E. Vandergrift wrote that *Monkey Island* "both sustains a mood of apprehension and encourages readers to consider carefully the plight of the homeless." In *The Eagle Kite* Liam discovers his father is dying of AIDS. His mother tells him it was contractred from a blood transfusion; however, Liam suspects his father is homosexual. Embarrassed and confused, Liam tells his friends his father is dying of cancer. Eventually, Liam is forced to come to terms with his emotions. According to Hazel Rochman, "Fox avoids nothing about the dying and the anguish of survival."

Awards

The Slave Dancer won the Newbery Medal from the American Library Association in 1974, and Fox was awarded the Hans Christian Andersen Medal for Writing in 1978. *One-Eyed Cat* received the Christopher Award and became a Newbery Honor Book in 1985. In 1989 *The Village by the Sea* received the *Boston Globe-Horn Book* Award for fiction and also became a Newbery Honor Book.

AUTHOR'S COMMENTARY

Paula Fox

SOURCE: "Newbery Award Acceptance," in *The Horn Book Magazine,* Vol. L, No. 4, August, 1974, pp. 345-50.

Nearly all the work of writing is silent. A writer does it alone. And the original intention—that first sudden stirring of one's imagination—is made up of many small, almost always humble, things. Because a major effort of writing is reflection, which is silent and solitary, I place thought under the heading of the experiences I had while I was writing *The Slave Dancer*.

By thought, I do not mean the marshalling of one's intellectual forces to refute an argument or to bring about a temporary victory over what agitates and bewilders us. All such victories are, I believe, transient. By thought, I mean that preoccupation with what we feel and why we feel it, and the enormous effort we must make to educe from a tangle of impressions and fleeting images the nature of those feelings. In this sense, thought is the effort to recognize.

It is an effort carried out against formidable enemies: habit; inertia; the fear of change and what it will entail; the wish to preserve our idiot corners of safety, of being "right"; and self-righteousness—the most dangerous enemy of all, full of a terrible energy that would turn us away from pondering the mystery of existence towards its own barren pleasures.

This effort to recognize is an effort to connect ourselves with the reality of our own lives. It is painful; but if we are to become human, we cannot abandon it. Once set on that path of recognition, we cannot forswear our integral connections with other people. We must make our way towards them as best we can, try to find what is similar, try to understand what is dissimilar, try to particularize what is universal.

Once we accept the responsibility of our connection with others, we must accept that we are like them even in our differences; and if in one instance, we are not a victim, we can be in another. And if in one instance we do not persecute, in another we will. And if we have not experienced the ultimate shame and anguish of captivity, of utter helplessness, we have experienced—at some time in our lives—something approximate to it, something from which we can construe a sense of what it is like to be other than ourselves.

Thought and feeling and recognition are the fruits of effort, and some of them are bitter. Once, years ago, I had a fleeting notion while I was reading a news story about a man pursued by a mob which intended to hang him. I thought: I could have been the victim, and I could have been one of the mob. Victim and mob are composed of my kind. We need not forgive what is vile in ourselves, but we must try to understand what is vile. If we cannot concede that we are born into this world with a capacity for cruelty, we cannot act against it.

The cat may not die from curiosity; but without it, the cat will likely perish. This curiosity, this puzzlement about our own existence and the lives of other people, is not an idle thing. It awakens the imagination, and the imagination makes it possible for us to realize that our own experience of life is both special to ourselves and generic to our kind. When we understand the continuity, the indivisibility, of human experience, we can begin—timidly perhaps, and with many a backward glance to the illusory snugness of those idiot corners—to consider the fact of our union with all others. Against the habitual indolence of the imagination, curiosity pushes itself, asks its shocking questions, and shoves us up against the folly of our wish to remain singular—and unmoved.

Writing is immodest although the experience of it is full of chagrin, even of mortification. A writer dares to claim that he or she will tell you a story about people and circumstances you know the writer could not have known. Because writers have sovereignty over their own inventions, they appear to make an outrageous claim: They will tell you everything about the characters in their stories. This is a world, they say; and every stick of its furnishings—every gesture and grimace of the people who live among these furnishings—is true and revealed. But this is not what happens in life. In real life, we stammer, we dissimulate, we hide. In stories, we are privy to the secrets, the evasions, the visions of characters in a fashion which real life only permits us during periods of extraordinary sensibility, before habit has made us forget that the cries behind the locked doors are our own.

The effort of writing is to approximate being, but our books can only have a degree of success. As we all know, when we put away the book we have been reading and return to the consciousness of the moment, art is not life. Our own individual lives are not finished inventions, but questions we can only partly answer.

No writer can truly answer the question, "Why did you write that book about those people?" Because, though the story between the book's covers is finished, the impulse that generated the story has been a question all along. I write to find out. I write to discover, over and over again, my connections with myself, with others. Each book deepens the question. It does not answer it.

The ultimate experience of abandonment is to be abandoned; the ultimate experience of injustice is to feel its outrage in every part of one's life; of hunger, to be hungry; of violation, to be violated. And so the immodesty and claims of a novelist are appalling. Yet, lying just behind that immodesty is a nearly overpowering sense of how little one knows, of how one must labor with the stuff of one's own life and struggle against the narrowness of one's own experience of life. It *is* an appalling claim. Without that claim and without those stations along the way that fall far short of ultimate experiences but from which one can sense what it might be like to go the whole journey, no book can be written.

The story of human slavery is a terrible story. Yet how

one's heart clenches at the knowledge that there are those who wish it forgotten, even denied. The Spanish playwright Calderón said, "To seek to persuade a man that the misfortunes which he suffers are not misfortunes, does not console him for them, but is another misfortune in addition."

Last year, I saw on the television news an elderly woman standing in front of a half-completed housing unit in Newark, New Jersey. She was a picket among a group who were determined that such a housing unit for black people was not going to be built. Clutching her pocketbook close to herself, her face as shut as any vault door, she explained her action this way: "Why should *they* get special housing?" she cried. "Their people decided to come to this country on ships just like mine did."

They decided! Is it conceivable that this woman could actually have believed that the black people who were forcibly packed into slave ships, who perished by the millions, had decided upon such a fate? The belief of that woman is not "thought." It is the brute self, rising up to obliterate all other claims to a just life for fear its own claim is threatened. And it is that brute self which is the enemy of all justice. Surely that woman must have read, even in those textbooks of her own youth with their indecently hurried references to slavery, something of what really happened.

Yet even she, at the furthest outpost of denial, poses a question. Her stance in front of the television camera was one of alerted stupidity, which did not entirely conceal her fear and confusion. If I were to write a story about her, I would wonder what she had in that pocketbook, why she clutched it so fiercely, what she thought she was protecting, what she thought *special* meant, and why, during the middle years of her only life, she was walking in a picket line that sought to prevent other people from their rightful acquisition of shelter.

There are those who feel that slavery debased the enslaved. It is not so. Slavery engulfed whole peoples, swallowed up their lives, committed such offenses that in considering them, the heart falters, the mind recoils. Slavery debased the enslavers, and self-imposed ignorance of slavery keeps the mind closed and the heart beating too faintly to do other than insult and wound with such phrases as *special housing*.

There are others who feel that black people can be only humiliated by being reminded that once they were brought to this country as slaves. But it is not the victim who is shamed. It is the persecutor, who has refused the shame of what he has done and, as the last turn of the screw, would burden the victim with the ultimate responsibility of the crime itself.

When I read the records of the past, I sometimes wanted to turn away from what I was learning—to sleep. But as I read on and heard the words of the captive people themselves, as I began to feel the power of their endurance, I perceived that the people who had spoken so long ago of every conceivable human loss were not only survivors, but pioneers of the human condition in inhuman circumstances. They not only maintained life, they had nurtured it, and what they knew springs toward us, out of ashes, out of a holocaust.

To battle one's way into the past and to attempt to bring back what Lionel Trilling has called "the hum of the past" is to discover that history is a kind of fiction. We know that such a man was born and died, that such a battle was fought and lost, that such a charter was signed. Through personal records, drawings, artifacts of one sort or another, we can say to ourselves the past existed, *was;* that is how people dressed, this is what they ate, how they were buried. But that "hum" is another matter. We must invent.

And so what we write must, as E. M. Forster says, "go beyond the evidence." What we have for that task is our knowledge of ourselves in our own time. I lived for three months in New Orleans, near Rampart Street, where the line between black and white dwellings was then a stretch of pavement; and on the banks of the Mississippi, I used to eat my lunch—a "poor boy" sandwich, which, as a consequence of the inflationary tendencies of modern life, has come to be called a "hero." I spent years in Cuba when I was a child, living on a sugar plantation where no stick remained of the stocks in which slaves had once been punished only a few decades earlier. In ships' logs, I discovered weather, winds I would never feel, the names of currents I had not known existed, seas which I had not crossed. But once I was on a ship in a nearly disastrous storm at sea.

I wrote *The Slave Dancer* as a never-quite-to-be-freed captive of a white childhood in a dark condition. When I read a footnote in a book, the title of which I can't now recall, that said that slaver crews often kidnapped youthful street musicians and signed them on ships as slave dancers—for such were they called—something consonant with, or peculiar to, my own sense of myself set me on the course of writing my book.

Writing *The Slave Dancer* was the closest I could get to events of spirit and flesh which cannot help but elude in their reality all who did not experience them. Still, the effort to draw nearer is part of the effort of writing. It is not so different from the effort to understand our own infancies which become fictions because we cannot consciously recall them. Yet a few powerful images maintain their grip on our imaginations for all of our lives. If we are able to invoke even fragments of those images, we can, sometimes, despite formidable differences in circumstance, rouse them up in others. Little though we may feel we have in common, there is enough for us to take on the truest obligation we have—recognition of the existence of that which is other than ourselves.

Once I read a fairy tale of a poor fisherman who cast his net into the river and caught a genie in a bottle. Having released the genie, the fisherman and his wife wished for all the strange things we are supposed to wish for—worldly power and possessions, and a staggering number of cas-

tles. But this couple grew sated and wanted an end to wishing. Then they discovered the price of all that beneficence—the genie would not return to his bottle until they had guessed his true name.

In *The Slave Dancer,* I have made an effort to call the genie by his name. But the genie is not back in the bottle. Other efforts have been made and will be made. Each time, perhaps, we get a little closer to the fires of that holocaust which have burned for so many centuries, and so begin to put them out.

I am profoundly grateful to all of you for your recognition of my effort.

Paula Fox

SOURCE: "Paula Fox: Acceptance Speech—1978 H. C. Andersen Author's Medal" *Bookbird,* Vol. XVI, No. 4, December 15, 1978, pp. 2-3.

One morning, years ago when I was young, I was walking along the sea at a place called South Beach on an island off the coast of Massachusetts. At the edge of the waves, drying in the sunlight, was a small sealed bottle. Inside it, I could see a written card but the glass was too thick to make out what it said. I hurried home, and there with screwdriver and knife I extracted the cork and fished out the card. It was from the Department of the Interior of the United States Government. It told me that I had found a bottle that had been launched some months earlier in an effort to determine the meanderings of certain ocean currents, and that if I would fill in the appropriate places on the card with information as to exactly where I had found it, and on what date, the Department would be grateful, and, further, would be prompt in informing me where the bottle had been launched from originally. I filled in the information at once, went to the village post office to mail the card, and began to wait. Governments do not answer promptly, and it was a long wait, six weeks as I remember it. During that time, I spent hours in the library studying the coastlines of the world in atlases, and I daydreamed incessantly about the extraordinary places from one of which my bottle had undoubtedly come.

When the Government answered at last, I tore open the letter and, at once, gasped with laughter and chagrin. Laughter at the folly of my own imaginings, and chagrin at the truth. The bottle had been launched from South Beach on that very island where I was staying, and it had not left South Beach.

The astonishment which I so much wanted to feel those long years ago when I was waiting for news of that bottle, I now feel because of the news you have given me about my books, the news that currents unimagined by me have carried them so far.

With astonishment—and gratitude and delight, I thank the International Board on Books for Young People for awarding me the Hans Christian Andersen Medal.

We have all heard of the long argument about the difference between literature for children and literature for adults. And in the vast expansion in publishing for children that has taken place over the last century, we have all been affected, one way or another, by an elaboration of differences within the children's book world itself, controversies over age groups and age interests and age categories. What is often lost sight of in the din of contention is the universal power and endurance of a good story, a power expressed in a line I once read that speaks of "a tale which draweth children from their play and old men from their chimney corners."

The power of a good story is the power of imagination. And great imagining, Goethe wrote, is the imagining of truth, the effort to grasp truth through the imagination. It is the truth of life one finds in great stories.

It would be perverse and fatuous to claim that any 5-year-old child would find *Madame Bovary* or *Crime and Punishment* interesting. But that a child's interest is not likely to be aroused by Emma Bovary or Raskolnikov does not confirm a general division between child and adult, only a particular one. A particular division is not the heart of the matter. The heart of the matter, I believe, is that the art of storytelling is, ultimately, the art of truth. In the imaginative effort that lies behind a good story, there is no difference between writing for children and for adults. And if what children have read, or have had read to them, has not condescended to them, has not given them meretricious uplift and vainglory at the expense of truthfulness, and has awakened their imaginations, they may, later, want to know about Emma Bovary and Raskolnikov.

The Venerable Bede in his *Ecclesiastical History of the English People,* tells of the poet Caedmon, an illiterate cowherd who lived in the 7th century. Caedmon did not have the gift of song, and in the evenings when the harp was handed round in the monastic farmstead where he labored, Caedmon would steal away to the stables, ashamed that he could not sing.

One night in a dream, a stranger appeared to Caedmon and told him that he must sing. Caedmon asked, "But of what shall I sing?" And the stranger in his dream said, "Sing of the beginning of all created things."

That is the task for story-tellers. That is what literature for children and adults is about, all created things.

GENERAL COMMENTARY

Alice Bach

SOURCE: "Cracking Open the Geode: The Fiction of Paula Fox," in *The Horn Book Magazine,* Vol. LIII, No. 5, October, 1977, pp. 514-21.

The nomination of Paula Fox for the Hans Christian Andersen Medal is a splendid choice. Her novels touch the deepest human feelings; she enlarges our understanding of the human condition by establishing an authentic relationship between each of her protagonists and the reader. Each of her books is a meticulously crafted invention—not a reduplication of life. In an era when novels are served up with the speed of a cheeseburger, she has mercifully not been lured into the verbal fast-food industry. Paula Fox expresses her respect for children by never diminishing the events of their lives nor sentimentalizing their responses. Her novels written for children resound with the integrity and conviction of her novels for adults.

She understands that the work of a novelist is to tell a story and make the reader care what happens. She does not confuse this work with that of a social worker, who gets paid to tell teenagers what to do if they are addicted, abandoned, abused, or pregnant; nor does she confuse her function with that of a fortuneteller or an astrologer, who will predict during which month you may expect sorrow and how soon you may depend on happiness.

What sets her work so far above the gaudy blooms—the social workers and fortunetellers—who are knocking out books as fast as kids can swallow them, is her uncompromising integrity. Fox is nobody's mouthpiece. Her unique vision admits to the child what he already suspects: Life is part grit, part disappointment, part nonsense, and occasionally victory. She doesn't stain these victories with artificial coloring. One of her characters triumphs when he makes a choice which changes him and the way he sees himself or the people around him, even if no one else recognizes the change. And by offering children no more than the humanness we all share—child, adult, reader, writer—she acknowledges them as equals.

An integral part of all Paula Fox's books—from the elegant prose of the allegorical *The King's Falcon* to the unrelenting layer upon layer of brutality in *The Slave Dancer*—is language. Her books are *written,* not mumbled in the kiddie argot adapted by writers desperate to speak to the young reader. Nor has Fox ever resorted to verbal flash to authenticate her work; only writers who secretly believe children are different from us fill up the silence by shouting code words. They depend on a ten-speed bike, granola, or a "bionic" arm to forge a hasty bond, because they think their competition is comic books and situation comedies.

Paula Fox believes children have the right to know what to expect from life. She acknowledges confusion. Nowhere in her books does she imply there are solutions to grief, abandonment, loneliness. I suspect she remembers a child's frustration at being told, "Don't worry, everything will work out." What that statement really says is "Be silent. Keep your fears to yourself." By admitting to the universality of fear, puzzlement, and foolish behavior, she invites the reader to scream, to snicker, to laugh, to admit pain.

If a writer's intention is to engage the reader with dramatic action, he may choose to construct his novel around dire circumstances, such as murder, rape, addiction, or madness. The novelist's function in this case is analogous to that of a weatherman forecasting a hurricane or a tornado. Human disasters, like natural ones, generate their own excitement. The novelist uses his fictional storm to elicit responses of alarm, agitation, or anxiety.

Eschewing high winds for the flutter of daily happenings, Paula Fox creates a world in which the reader can locate himself. She draws us into the viscera of her novels by relating experiences we can share and recognizes that what we know to be true in life must also be true in the life of her characters. Her novels shimmer with gentle epiphanies, for she is incapable of creating the permanent bliss so often dished up in children's literature.

Paradoxically, it requires a great deal more thought for a writer to create a book that withholds conclusions than to build one that runs in a straight line linking every action to a waiting solution. If one writes of a boy stealing a loaf of bread and then describes him being caught and punished, the writer has a whole body of literature and a reinforced ethic on which to depend. But if the writer considers a boy who steals the bread and does not get caught, the fictive possibilities multiply. Writing about real lives that rarely run in straight lines takes prodigious thought. The author must never let his attention wander from the world of the book. Paula Fox describes this process in her Newbery Medal acceptance speech:

> By thought, I do not mean the marshalling of one's intellectual forces to refute an argument or to bring about a temporary victory over what agitates and bewilders us. All such victories are, I believe, transient. By thought, I mean that preoccupation with what we feel and why we feel it, and the enormous effort we must make to educe from a tangle of impressions and fleeting images the nature of those feelings. In this sense, thought is the effort to recognize.

Gus Oliver, called "stone-face" by his family and classmates, has a panoply of fears, among them night and the possibility of falling down an abandoned well concealed by the winter's snow. Gus is faced with a choice: to go into the dark night, cross the snow-covered meadow and search for his sister Serena's lost dog or to lie to Serena, the person he cares about most. The reader appreciates the enormity of Gus's struggle even though the author does not ornament his victory with loud ceremony. Gus returns with the dog in the early morning. He enters the kitchen, in which his family is preparing breakfast. We recognize that he has gained a measure of self-respect by his firm refusal to crack open his geode in spite of the urging of his brothers and sisters. This scene, which is also the conclusion of the novel, is quiet, like Gus himself. Fox knows there would be no hurdy-gurdy praise from Gus's acidulous family. Never stepping outside the story, she lets Gus reward himself.

> When he felt like it, he would take the hammer and tap the geode in such a way that it would break perfectly, in such a way that not one of the crystals inside would be broken.

But until then, until he wanted to, no one would touch it.

Journeys are undertaken by most of Paula Fox's protagonists, from the little boy's slapstick trip across the street in *Good Ethan* to Jesse's unforgettable months aboard the *Moonlight* in *The Slave Dancer*. After they return home, each character has learned something about himself. When Great-aunt Hattie acknowledges in *The Stone-Faced Boy* what Gus's trip must have cost him, she could have been talking to Ben Felix, who journeys to Boston to meet his father in *Blowfish Live in the Sea*; to Ivan, when he has returned from Jacksonville and seen his completed portrait in *Portrait of Ivan*; to James Douglas, who travels alone across Brooklyn to return a stolen dog to its owner in *How Many Miles to Babylon?* The reader joins with Great-aunt Hattie in saying to each of these boys, "'You must have been scared. How many times did you think of simply turning around . . . ?'" By living through his fear and completing his journey (or in the case of Jessie in *The Slave Dancer,* surviving his journey) each one triumphs for a while over circumstances he had expected would defeat him.

Blowfish Live in the Sea is a novel about Ben Felix, who has felt defeated for years. The reader sees Ben as he appears to his half sister Carrie, the narrator: Ben feels no affinity for his stepfather, and he wrote off his own father when he was six. Because we are kept outside Ben's thoughts, we know that the boy inscribes on every imaginable surface *"Blowfish live in the sea."* But we don't know why. Only at the conclusion of the novel does Ben explain this message, when he gives Carrie the dried-up blowfish his father claimed to have caught while exploring the Amazon.

After he has journeyed to Boston and confronted his father, Ben can let go of the terrible hurt he has suffered at learning the man is a phony braggart. Because accusation is so much easier than acceptance, we are compelled to respect Ben's decision to remain with his eccentric father and to help him in a dubious project—restoring and running a broken-down motel. Ben has succeeded in freeing himself from the anger that drove him to resist his father by the only available way—the secret meaning of his blowfish message. By Ben's acceptance of his father, Fox demonstrates her faith in the reader's ability to understand the vortex of the novel. She gives no cozy assurances that Ben will get his own act together, that the motel will be a financial success.

Most critics overlook Paula Fox's sense of humor, a vital element in her work. She is often described as a serious writer, whose books are concerned with the problems sensitive children confront. The label *serious* coupled with *problem* and the pejorative *sensitive child* combine to make one anticipate an experience of unremitting anguish, a book-length toothache. Conscious of what a light touch the writer must exercise in order not to turn worry into whine, Fox cuts through the fog of intense emotions with a beam of modest humor. She does not envelop us with Ben's feelings during the initial confrontation scene with his father. What we see is a fumbling drunk struggling to shave the other half of his mustache. What Carrie reports is the dialogue; what each reader supplies is Ben's emotions. Fox conveys pain without lingering over it.

Great-aunt Hattie appears in *The Stone-Faced Boy* driving a 1926 Stutz Bearcat, wearing crocodile shoes, and smoking a cigar. When Gus encounters her in the middle of the night, she does not dissuade him from his journey. She does not pry, she does not gush. She extracts from her amazing bag a pair of earmuffs and a geode, her kind of comfort. The reader grins at this autocratic eccentric who gives no thought to explanations. But we have not forgotten that Gus must now leave the house alone. Again it is the reader who supplies the emotion because Fox has presented a situation—the boy alone with the terrors of the night—familiar to all of us.

The author, like Great-aunt Hattie, does not provide explanations. She does not concern herself that a middle-class child reading *How Many Miles to Babylon?* may find James Douglas's whole life a problem. Living with three aging aunts in one room, sharing a bathroom with all the tenants on the floor, incapable of attention at school, and bullied by hoods, the boy led an existence which could have made the novel a pious tract about guilt and blame. But Fox is telling James's story, and the overcrowded tenement is where the boy and his family and friends live. "[H]e heard conversations, a few words on the fourth floor, a few more on the third and second floors, like pieces of string he could tie together."

James misses his mother terribly and has created a vivid fantasy of himself as a Black prince and of his mother, "her black hair tumbling down her back, dressed in a long white gown, stronger than anyone. . . ." One day his loneliness overcomes him, and he leaves school to go to an abandoned house, where he often plays. Because Fox never lets herself or her readers pity James, she awards him the respect and integrity all her characters share. The ways in which they are forced to live and the people they must live with are presented as part of the story, not as a plea for sympathy. Most important, she never exaggerates what they have accomplished. While inferior writers depend on superlatives to entice the reader, she tells a credible story because she has not aroused suspicions with overblown language. Within a few minutes James's emotions have ranged from the terror of his journey to return the dog and the proud anticipation of telling his aunts of his bravery to the unarticulated joy of seeing his mother waiting for him with his aunts. This telescoping of feelings, one immediately into the other, is a sensation children recognize and know to be true.

One of the finest examples of a writer's control over her material is found in *The Slave Dancer*. With an underplayed but implicit sense of rage, Paula Fox exposes the men who dealt in selling human beings. The horror, the ruthlessness, the moral abasement of these men's lives is often overlooked by writers eager to dwell solely on the humiliation of the slaves. The novel centers around Jessie, a young white street musician who plays the fife. He

is as much a captive aboard ship as the Blacks. Miraculously, the author never abandons her story for the heady self-indulgence of a polemic. The publication of *The Slave Dancer* did precipitate polemic from other quarters: A few individuals insisted that she had no business writing about a white teenager kidnapped by slave traders. Members of the Council on Interracial Books for Children would keep Paula Fox in chains, permit her to write novels stemming only from her own life experiences. So much for imagination. The members of this organization will have to relinquish their copyright on suffering if they are to preserve a vestige of credibility. Ironically, even this canard about *The Slave Dancer* trumpets the achievement of Fox as a novelist. So palpably was life aboard the *Moonlight* rendered that even those who claim that an examination of slavery should be the exclusive right of descendants of slaves and their friends were aroused.

The Slave Dancer is written with words that make one weep. Its conclusion is as cathartic, as devastating as that in any classic tragedy. The author risks her novel on the power of one stunning sentence: "I was unable to listen to music." How many writers gamble their work on the reader's ability to read? How much safer to supply molten conclusions.

For a writer to be judged great, for a novel to endure, the writer must resist safety, must not give in to the temptation to reach for simplistic conclusions. The best writers, like Paula Fox, reject the blanket of security that blinds them to wonder, to ongoing amazement without which they can offer us no fresh interpretations of the bits and pieces of our everyday lives. Fox provides an accurate metaphor for distinguishing creativity from representation in her novel *Portrait of Ivan,* a lyric celebration of various ways of perceiving reality. The most demonstrably accurate vision of reality is embodied in the figure of Ivan's father. A businessman who deals in facts, airline schedules, and stopwatches, he depends on photographs to recall the color of a car or the height of a tree outside his hotel room.

Before beginning to paint Ivan's portrait, Matt observes the boy, using the same techniques he later suggests to Geneva when looking at her drawing of a snake in *"The Book of Things. Volume One. Seen and Drawn by Geneva Colrain."* (Geneva's book is one of the details in fiction, like the Hatter's mad tea party or Toad's motor car, that becomes a gift from writer to reader.) "'You might try drawing it,'" Matt tells Geneva, "'in other ways besides being coiled up. Half-coiled, or hanging from a tree, or with its head resting on a twig. The more ways you draw it, the more you will understand what a snake is.'" When a writer bases his narration on what he has seen, he is creating a verbal portrait.

Contrapuntal to the portrait, Matt begins a crayon sketch, born of Ivan's dim recollections about his mother and a scattering of facts provided by Ivan's father. The sketch accretes as Matt learns more about Ivan's life as they travel south and as Ivan puts questions to his father. Gradually, Ivan moves from the black-and-white world his father guards to a world where what one imagines can be made to seem real. He tells Matt, "'I saw a picture of my mother. . . . I remembered her better before I knew what she looked like.'" While Ivan is satisfied with the finished portrait, it is the sketch that genuinely excites him. The real world has been fused with the imagined to form a separate entity. "The sledge had been filled up with people he knew. . . ."

A memorable novel is one in which we believe all the people and the sledge are real. Only a handful of writers can create such a world, one the reader perceives to be filled with people he knew. Paula Fox is among them.

Linda Silver

SOURCE: "From Baldwin to Singer: Authors for Kids and Adults," in *School Library Journal,* Vol. 25, No. 6, February, 1979, pp. 27-9.

So few authors write equally well for children and adults that Paula Fox and Isaac Bashevis Singer (who do) should be noted. Fox's polished prose is so restrained that at times it is cryptic. . . . Except for *The Slave Dancer,* Fox's novels have contemporary settings and are preoccupied with themes of isolation and non-communication. Almost all of her characters function within environments that are physically and psychologically hostile.

In *Poor George,* the title character is alienated from his wife and job and consumed with a sense of moral aimlessness. His new home, a suburban refuge, is broken into by a prowler; later, he is shot by a neighbor. The decaying city from which George fled (but to which he continually returns) is the home of James Douglas in *How Many Miles to Babylon,* where it becomes the symbolic representation of the real and spiritual slum within and against which James struggles. Economic security offers no comfort to any of the *Desperate Characters* of Fox's books: Ben Felix of *Blowfish Live In The Sea* has virtually dropped out of the human race; Gus Oliver, the *Stone-Faced Boy,* is beset by fears and loneliness; Ivan in *Portrait of Ivan* lacks a sense of self.

Squalor figures almost obsessively in Fox's writing for older children and adults. Skies are "the color of tallow," the air is viscous and grey, streets breathe "an air of decay and desolation," rain falls on "open refuse cans," and "animal excreta slowly liquified and refuse sidled sluggishly toward the drains." The opening chapter of *Desperate Characters* describes a woman emptying emptying garbage onto the ground; Annie Gianfala in *The Western Coast* has a tapeworm, an "obscene thing in her vitals." In *Blowfish* . . . Ben and Carrie come upon a Boston park where Carrie makes out "a few dark shapes of people moving slowly like fish in a dirty fishtank." These images parallel the emotional desolation felt by Fox's characters and nowhere do the two conditions merge more powerfully than in Jessie Bollier's nightmare voyage in the moonlight in *The Slave Dancer,* a story of profound human corruption. "All around me bodies shifted in ex-

hausted movement . . . I could barely draw breath, and what breath I drew was horrible, like a solid substance, like suet, that did not free my lungs but drowned them in the taste of rancid rot . . . With what I was sure was the last effort of my life, I heaved up the upper part of my body, but my legs had no leverage. I sank down. I began to choke." Awarded the Newbery Medal in 1974, this book shows Fox at her best, in part for what it is—morally serious art—and in part because it is free from the flaws found in some of her other writing. The worst of these is a tendency to create characters endowed with an excess of awareness: too perceptive, too able to articulate their own or other's problems. *The Stone-Faced Boy* suffers from this "novelistic" defect; as does *Portrait of Ivan.* Fox's unwillingness to explain or offer sympathy for her characters outside of what the story itself arouses shows a masterful command of the storyteller's art but can also have the effect of narrowing the range of empathy. With *The Slave Dancer* again perhaps the exception, Fox's books are easier to admire than they are to love.

John Rowe Townsend

SOURCE: "Paula Fox," in his *A Sounding of Storytellers: New and Revised Essays on Contemporary Writers for Children,* J. B. Lippincott, 1979, pp. 55-64.

Of the new writers for children who emerged in the United States in the later 1960s, Paula Fox was quickly seen to be one of the most able. Her books were unusually varied; each had a distinct individual character, but at the same time each was stamped with her own imprint. And they had an air of newness: not merely the literal contemporaneity which almost anyone can achieve but the newness that comes from looking at things with new eyes, feeling them in a new way.

In the 1950s and early 1960s, a traditional and generally reassuring view of children and their role had run through the work of the leading and well-established children's writers. Childhood was part of a continuing pattern—the orderly succession of the generations—and children were growing up to take their place in a known and understood world. As the 1960s went on, it was perceived increasingly that this pattern did not reflect reality. Families and societies were not stable; the older generation was not regarded, and did not even regard itself, as the repository of all wisdom, and it could not be assumed that young people were anxious to grow up and join it. The generation gap had opened up, and before long writers for young people were trooping into it, often in a worried, heavy-footed and anxious-to-be-with-it way.

Paula Fox was one of the small number of writers who brought quick sharp perceptions to the new and in many ways uneasy scene, and also an instinctive sympathy for the young who (just as much as their parents) had to deal with it. A recurrent theme in her work of the late 1960s, and again in *Blowfish Live in the Sea* (1970), is that of non-communication and lack of understanding between young and old. But she is not a writer who could be content to mine a single narrow seam. She has written both adult and young people's novels; she has produced picture books and younger children's stories; and her most substantial work on the children's lists up to the time of writing, the award-winning *The Slave Dancer* (1973), is a historical novel of weight and intensity which stands on its own, at a distance from her other books.

Her early books for children have central characters aged from about eight to ten, but one would hesitate to say that they are 'for' readers of such an age. The audience and the author's position in relation to it seem curiously fluid. One has no sense that the writer, as an adult, is *here,* in charge, handing it out, while the audience of children is *there,* duly taking it. If there is a message in the air, it is probably for someone quite different. The first two, *Maurice's Room* (1966) and *A Likely Place* (1967), are not telling children anything except a story, but seem rather obviously to be saying something to parents: don't fuss the child, let him grow in his own way. The two books are humorous, even witty, but in a way that one would expect to appeal to readers rather older than their heroes. And the third and best of the early books, *How Many Miles to Babylon?* (1967), whose hero is barely ten, was one of only two books specifically recommended for teenagers by Nat Hentoff in the *Atlantic* for December 1967. The conventional wisdom is that children and teenagers don't want to read about children younger than themselves, and this generally appears to be true. But it could be that discussion of the question betrays a more fixed attitude than Paula Fox would adopt. Who says who is to read what? Like many other writers, she raises the question 'For whom?', and as with many other writers I can find no answer except 'For whom it may concern.'

Maurice's Room is in fact a blessedly funny book; and as for readership, one can only try it on and see if the glove fits. Maurice at eight is dedicated to his collection of junk, which spills over everything. His parents feel he needs more constructive interests, and often discuss him with their friends.

> Some visitors said that collections like Maurice's showed that a child would become a great scientist. Many great scientists had collected junk when they were eight years old. Other visitors said Maurice would outgrow his collection and become interested in other things, such as money or armies. Some suggested to the Henrys that they ought to buy Maurice a dog, or send him to music school so that his time might be spent more usefully.

And his parents, with the best intentions, get everything wrong. The dog they borrow to be a companion to Maurice is in fact a dreadful nuisance to him, yet Mother is soon convinced that 'Maurice and Patsy are inseparable.' An attempt to get Maurice to learn an instrument is disastrous. The beautiful sailboat that Mr Henry buys Maurice for his birthday is forgotten while Maurice and friend grope for some old bedsprings lying on the bottom of the pond. 'If I had known you wanted bedsprings instead of a beautiful three-foot sailing ketch, I would have gotten you bedsprings,' says poor Mr Henry in despair. Finally,

Maurice's parents decide to move to the country, where they hope that everything will be different. And this time at least all is well, for although Maurice isn't terribly interested in the country as such, there is an old barn that already holds the nucleus of a promising new junk collection. It's a hilarious, subversive book, full of casual joys. One can see that Maurice will survive the well-meant but uncomprehending intrusions of adults, just as will Lewis in *A Likely Place.* Lewis, too, is fussed by the grown-ups, but is fortunately left by his parents in the charge of eccentric Miss Fitchlow, who goes in for yogurt and yoga, calls Lewis 'pal', and lets him off the lead. Which is just what he needed. It is a short, dry, subtle book; and if there is a lesson in it, then I suspect that, as in *Maurice's Room,* it is really a lesson for parents.

Paula Fox's third book, *How Many Miles to Babylon?,* is a longer novel of much greater depth and complexity. Its hero, James, is a small black boy living in Brooklyn, whose father has disappeared and whose mother has gone into hospital, leaving him in the care of three elderly aunts. One day he walks out of school and goes to play by himself in an empty house. In his mind is a story that his mother has really gone to her own country across the seas and that he is secretly a prince. Three small boys, not much older than James but tougher, capture him and make him help them work their dog-stealing racket. James travels frightening miles with them on the back of a bicycle, goes to a deserted funhouse on Coney Island, sees the Atlantic. At night he frees the stolen dogs, runs away, gets home to the old aunts, and finds his mother there. She is back from hospital; she is no princess and he no prince. 'Hello, Jimmy,' she says.

On the surface it is a straightforward story, with its strong plot about the fearful boy and the tough gang and the dogs and the juvenile racketeering. But there are strange undertones: the symbolic voyage, the 'other' story of James which is only hinted at. The action, although shadows are cast before and behind it in time, takes place within a day and a night. 'Can I get there by candlelight? Yes, and back again.' Both action and setting are almost dream-like; the landscape an intimately-known landscape yet glimpsed as if in shifting mists. Everything is experienced through James; and James himself is wandering in a mist of illusion, though eventually compelled by what happens to grasp at rough reality. It is felt in every page, but never said in crude terms, that James is a member of a sub-merged race and class, and isolated even within that. He is not a sharply-drawn character, nor meant to be, for the reader will suffer with him rather than observe him from the outside; but the minor characters—the three old aunts, the three young racketeers—are clear in outline, defined by the words they speak.

In one sense the outcome of *How Many Miles to Babylon?* is plain. James has proved himself, has faced the actual world, found and accepted his actual mother. He has come through. But to say that is not enough. Illusion and reality, the symbolic and the actual, are not to be so neatly separated. There is much in the book that the mind cannot simply deal with and eject. The inner mystery is something to be carried about and wondered at from time to time rather than be resolved.

The same might be said of *The Stone-Faced Boy* (1968), whose hero Gus—the middle child of five, about ten years old, timid, vulnerable, shut-off—goes out into the snow at night to free a stray dog from a trap. Gus, too, proves himself; finds the key that will help him to overcome his problems. But again this is not quite all. *The Stone-Faced Boy* is a winter's tale, with the quiet, real-yet-unreal feeling of a white landscape. There is a shiver in it, too: a ghostliness. The trap in which the dog is caught belongs to an old man, who takes Gus home to his cottage, full of the debris of the past, for a cup of tea with his equally old wife. And at one point the old man tells the old lady to show Gus how spry she is.

> She made a strange little jump and then, holding her skirt out with her two hands, she did a little dance in front of the stove, smiling, wobbling slightly, kicking one foot out, then the other. Then she fell back softly into the rocker, like a feather coming to rest.

On the previous page we have heard that the old lady 'had a light, free laugh, and to Gus's surprise the sound reminded him of Serena'. Serena is his younger sister, aged about eight: nice, dreamy, imaginative. Gus feels it is impossible for Serena to get so old. But of course she will; this delicate tying together of the two ends of life makes one of the book's many quiet yet admirable achievements.

Portrait of Ivan (1969) does not have the mysterious depths of *How Many Miles to Babylon?* or *The Stone-Faced Boy,* but has subtleties and satisfactions of its own. It is a brief novel about a boy of eleven who leads a dull, lonely life, walled in by well-to-do, conventional, adult-dominated surroundings. The walls about him begin to crack when he meets the painter Matt and the elderly reader-aloud Miss Manderby, and start collapsing rapidly as he potters about in a boat with a barefoot girl called Geneva. There is a key sentence to the understanding of one aspect of Paula Fox when Ivan realizes that in his life in the city

> he was nearly always being taken to or from some place by an adult, in nearly every moment of his day he was holding on to a rope held at the other end by a grown-up person—a teacher or a bus driver, a housekeeper or a relative. But since he had met Matt, space had been growing all around him. It was frightening to let go of that rope, but it made him feel light and quick instead of heavy and slow.

Ivan has needed space in which to open out, yet by a near-paradox, in order to open out he needs a framework, a context for his own life, a sense of who and what he is and how he got here. He has been living in what might be called a cramped void. It is something important when his friend draws for him the imagined sledge on which his mother, whom he never knew, left Russia as a child, a little girl who 'did not know she had begun a journey that led right to this room where her son now lay, half asleep'. That is a link that Ivan needed.

Ben, in *Blowfish Live in the Sea,* is eighteen and although the book is largely about him, the viewpoint is that of his half-sister Carrie, aged twelve. Though Ben is older than Ivan, his emotional position is somewhat similar, in that, just as Ivan needed the link with his mother in order to orientate himself, Ben needs to find his father. But Ben's father is not dead; he is a drifter, a pathetic, unsatisfactory person. Ben's mother has divorced and remarried, and Ben has a stable, prosperous home, but he is totally alienated. He has dropped out of school, got rid of all his possessions, and Carrie sees him as

> a tall thin person in a droopy coat with the collar up. The person's hands are shoved into the coat pockets; the threads that stick out from the places where buttons used to be are a different color from the cloth of the coat. When he walks, the person looks down at his feet as they move forward in cracked muddy boots.

'Blowfish live in the sea' is the message that Ben writes on brown paper bags, on unopened letters, in dust on windowpanes; and the explanation is that his father once sent him a blowfish—round as a soccer ball, stiff with varnish, orange and yellow and shiny—with a letter describing it as a souvenir from the upper reaches of the Amazon. Ben's graffito is a comment on this shabby deception. But when his father turns up, a perennial failure with nothing to his name but a seedy rundown motel, Ben decides to join him: 'He needs some help to get it into shape. He doesn't have hardly any money. . . . The place is a wreck.' We leave Ben starting on the carpentry, keeping his father off the drink; we don't know how long it will last, but we know it is something positive for Ben at last and will be the making of him.

This is the principal strand of the book, but there are others. Running through it all is Carrie's affection for Ben. As she looks at him, dusty and sad, with the rawhide thong round the hair that he won't get cut, Carrie remarks, 'Sometimes I thought I loved him better than anyone.' And in his desultory way Ben returns the affection; in fact there are traces everywhere of a loving, more open Ben. Although Ben belongs strictly to his time, and although people of his age already look different and behave differently, he is not in the least invalidated as a character by subsequent change. The underlying human nature can be seen quite clearly within the pattern formed by its interaction with outward circumstances.

Paula Fox is obviously much concerned with relationships between children and adults. She is conscious that in a complicated and rapidly changing society it is hard for the generations to live together satisfactorily. It will not do for grown-ups to think in terms of feeding a child into the production line and in due course drawing off an adult from the other end; but neither can young people really write off the older generation, ignoring it as irrelevant or hating it as the enemy.

Her books for younger children are a mixed collection, and in my view have not always been successful. They include a curious, way-out picture book *Hungry Fred* (1969), about a boy who eats his way through the contents of a house, the house itself and the backyard, and is still hungry. Then he makes friends with a wild rabbit as big as himself. 'The rabbit leaned against Fred. Fred smiled. He felt full.' It is difficult to see what young children will make of this. And although one accepts that a picture book, like a poem or story, does not have to be understood in literal terms in order to make its impact, there needs to be an imaginative power and unity which I do not find in *Hungry Fred,* and which the artist, understandably, could not supply. *Good Ethan* (1973), about a small boy who ingeniously solves the problem of retrieving his new ball from the wrong side of a street he has been told not to cross, is a simpler and more satisfactory conception, and benefits from pictures by Arnold Lobel which are exactly in key with it. Paula Fox is also the author of *The Little Swineherd and Other Tales* (1978); a group of short, folk-type stories set in the odd framework of an attempt by a duck—yes, a duck—to succeed in show business. The duck is promoting the actual storyteller—a goose who simply likes to tell stories—and there is dry satiric humour in the account of the duck's attempts at exploitation and his uncomprehending interventions in the creative process. But the book as a whole does not quite work. Russell Hoban would have done this kind of thing better. The title story, however, about the half-starved and neglected boy who takes over a smallholding when its owners disappear and has vastly improved it by the time they come back to reclaim their property, is a touching and memorable one; it would have been preferable, I believe, to present it on its own.

I have left until last the book which, so far, is Paula Fox's finest achievement. I do not think it could have been predicted from her earlier work that she would write such a book as *The Slave Dancer.* It is the story of Jessie Bollier, a boy who is pressed into the crew of the slave ship *Moonlight* in 1840 for a voyage to Africa, picking up a cargo of blacks to be sold in Cuba. This is a case where the discipline of writing for the children's list has been wholly to the benefit of the book as a work of art. The 'young eye at the centre' is no mere convention of the adventure story for children; it is the one perspective from which the witnessing of dreadful events can be fully and freshly experienced, and at the same time the moral burden be made clear. Jessie is horrified by the treatment of the slaves, but he is powerless to prevent it; moreover he is young, white, and one of the crew, and the oppressors are his fellow-countrymen.

Jessie plays the fife, and his job is to make music to which, for brief periods daily, the slaves can exercise. This is called dancing the slaves. The aim is to keep them (relatively) healthy and therefore marketable, in spite of the crowded and filthy conditions in which they live. A slave has no human value but has a financial one: a dead slave is a lost profit. As the voyage goes on, the slaves, crammed together in the reeking hold, become sick, half-starved and hopeless, most of them suffering from 'the bloody flux', an affliction that makes the latrine buckets inadequate. And Jessie finds that 'a dreadful thing' is happening in his mind:

I hated the slaves! I hated their shuffling, their howling, their very suffering! I hated the way they spat out their food upon the deck, the overflowing buckets, the emptying of which tried all my strength. I hated the foul stench that came from the holds no matter which way the wind blew, as though the ship itself were soaked with human excrement. I would have snatched the rope from Spark's [the mate's] hand and beaten them myself! Oh, God! I wished them all dead! Not to hear them! Not to smell them! Not to know of their existence!

The Slave Dancer is not a story solely of horror. It is also a novel of action, violence and suspense, culminating in shipwreck (which was indeed the fate of a slaver called *Moonlight* in the Gulf of Mexico in 1840; the actual names of her crew are used). Jessie and a black boy named Ras with whom he has made a precarious friendship are the only survivors; they reach land and there is a limited happy ending. Ras is set on the road to freedom; Jessie gets home to his mother and sister, is apprenticed, lives an ordinary, modestly-successful life, and fights in the Civil War on the Union side.

After the war my life went on much like my neighbors' lives. I no longer spoke of my journey on a slave ship back in 1840. I did not often think of it myself. Time softened my memory as though it was kneading wax. But there was one thing that did not yield to time.

I was unable to listen to music. I could not bear to hear a woman sing, and at the sound of any instrument, a fiddle, a flute, a drum, a comb with paper wrapped around it played by my own child, I would leave instantly and shut myself away. For at the first note of a tune or of a song, I would see once again, as though they'd never ceased their dancing in my mind, black men and women and children lifting their tormented limbs in time to a reedy martial air, the dust rising from their joyless thumping, the sound of the fife finally drowned beneath the clanging of their chains.

Those are the closing sentences of *The Slave Dancer.* Ultimately the book is not depressing; the human spirit is not defeated. But it is permeated through and through by the horror it describes. The casual brutality of the ordinary seamen towards the slaves is as fearful in its way as the more positive and corrupt cruelty of the captain and mate and the revolting, hypocritical crew member Ben Stout. For the seamen are 'not especially cruel save in their shared and unshakable conviction that the least of them was better than any black alive'. They are merely ignorant. Villainy is exceptional by definition, but dreadful things done by decent men, to people whom they manage to look on as not really human, are a reminder of our own self-deceit and lack of imagination, of the capacity we all have for evil. There, but for the grace of God, go all of us.

Is such knowledge fit for children? Yes, it is; they ought not to grow up without it. This book looks at a terrifying side of human nature, and one which—in the specific manifestation of the slave trade—has left deeply-planted obstacles in the way of human brotherhood. The implication was made plain by Paula Fox in her Newbery acceptance speech in 1974. We must face this history of evil, and our capacity for evil, if the barriers are ever to come down.

TITLE COMMENTARY

DEAR PROSPER (1968)

Kirkus Service

SOURCE: A review of *Dear Prosper,* in *Kirkus Service,* Vol. XXXVI, No. 7, April 1, 1968, p. 393.

Dear Prosper, begins this memoir of a self-educated dog, written to his abandoned next-to-last owner. He is an expert at running away, he explains to Prosper, recounting neglected infancy in a general store in New Mexico; indoctrination by canine companions on a cattle ranch; all work and no praise herding sheep; boredom as a pampered pet on Beacon Street, and the digs of a jealous chauffeur; the loose ends of life in a seedy circus; defection in Paris, his favorite place, and then Prosper, his favorite owner. But he is too old to keep up with an energetic boy, and certainly too old to face the prospect of going to school back in the States, so he slips away. Now he is settled in with an elderly blind man whose tempo matches his, and to whom he can be useful; they are both serene. . . . The clipped, economical telling is a departure from the author of *How Many Miles to Babylon?* and just right for the canine narrator. This is one smart pup who exploits but doesn't impersonate people, one dog tale that doesn't wag; kids will empathize with Frank-Juanito-Anthony-Boffo-Duke, maybe even moisten over *Chien* and his master, but they can't condescend—*Dear Prosper* puts dogs on guard, puts people in perspective. Different and should do nicely.

Margaret F. O'Connell

SOURCE: A review of *Dear Prosper,* in *The New York Times Book Review,* July 21, 1968, p. 22.

Dear Paula Fox: We're beginning to expect some of the freshest book ideas from you. Take this latest one, a real shaggy dog tale. No joke. At once piquant and poignant, it's as offbeat as *How Many Miles to Babylon?,* perhaps not as memorable, let's say it's closer in style to *Maurice's Room.* You took a chance setting it down as a dog's memoir, written by him in the form of a long letter to his next-to-last (and favorite) owner, but it works. We can't quite believe that a dog can learn to read and write by scanning the lost-and-found columns, but then who could growl at your making him such a witty, observant correspondent? His recollections of getting from Truth or Consequences, N. M., to Paris, France, and of the masters he's had, give us a new perspective on people and places in the world. Thanks to you, a dog's life seems downright adventurous.

HUNGRY FRED (1969)

Kirkus Reviews

SOURCE: A review of *Hungry Fred,* in *Kirkus Reviews,* Vol. XXXVII, No. 5, March 1, 1969, pp. 233-4.

The color is the key after Fred has eaten the apples in the bowl on the table, the bowl, the table, the rug in the dining room, the dining room . . . and in turn, the trees in the yard, the rest of the house and its furnishings, the grass in the meadow, he approaches a rabbit "Stay right there," says the rabbit, "I've heard about you" whereupon two shades of green brighten the monochromatic (but never monotonous) line drawings and color—literally and figuratively—what remains. It's the beginning of the end of gluttony for Fred: urged home by the rabbit, he finds his father making a new clay bowl, his sister knitting a rug, his mother planting trees. With the rabbit to lean on (and occupy a planting hole "from time to time"), Fred feels full—i.e. senses that there's more to life than a full stomach. Two off-beat talents (the author of *Stone-Faced Boy, et al.,* the depictor [Rosemary Wells] of *A Song to Sing, O*) are perfectly matched in this fable for all times: the laconic illustrations complement the easy, economical text, both epitomized by Fred's secretive smile. The obvious objection is just that obliqueness: kids will delight in all-devouring Fred but many will be puzzled by the outcome—Fred doesn't miss what he's consumed so there's little reason for him to appreciate its reappearance. Corollary (but not quite) is the obliviousness of his family contrasted with the attention of the rabbit. . . . An enigmatic imperative.

Nora L. Magid

SOURCE: A review of *Hungry Fred,* in *The New York Times Book Review,* May 4, 1969, p. 53.

A rousing success with adults and children alike, *Hungry Fred* is introduced by its cover, on which Fred is munching the leaves from a tree. On the title page, there is the staircase in Fred's house with a large chomp removed from it. Hungry Fred's ambitious gustatory career starts logically with apples, and proceeds with deadpan logic to the bowl, the table, the dining room rug and then the dining room. His family doesn't pay attention, but when Fred meets a large rabbit and says "I'm hungry," the rabbit says, "We've all noticed that." As Fred's relationship with the rabbit advances, his family copes with its predicament. The layout is particularly fine, because it staggers the astonishments; and Emily, who chose this one for its bunny, appreciated it far beyond the rabbit fact. The ending is subject to discussion and debate and may puzzle some children.

THE LITTLE SWINEHERD AND OTHER TALES (1978)

Paul Heins

SOURCE: A review of *The Little Swineherd and Other*

Tales, in *The Horn Book Magazine,* Vol. LV, No. 5, October, 1978, p. 516.

As in *The King's Falcon* the author employs a traditional storytelling mode—with a difference. The narratives are set in a framework: An entrepreneur of a duck decides he would like to become the manager of a goose who is telling stories to eight young frogs sitting on water lily pads. Attempting to persuade the goose to perform in public, he listens to five tales: "The Little Swineherd," "The Rooster Who Could Not See Enough of Himself," "Circles and Straight Lines," "The Alligator Who Told the Truth," and "The Raccoon's Song." Except for "The Little Swineherd," which is an apologue rather than a fable, the author—in the manner of Hans Christian Andersen—makes use of the anthropomorphic animal story. Ascribing human traits and foibles to members of the animal kingdom, she evaluates and satirizes mankind; however, instead of ending the tales in a conventional moralistic manner, she makes use of the open-ended conclusion of the short story form. Beautifully simple in language, cadenced in storytelling style, replete with dialogue, the narratives are full of concrete detail and humor; but it will take more than a superficial reader to understand why they end as they do. In each of the unconventional black-and-white illustrations [by Leonard Lubin] elaborately modeled figures or faces are set against a background of unshaded linear drawing.

Betsy Hearne

SOURCE: A review of *The Little Swineherd, and Other Tales,* in *Booklist,* Vol. 75, No. 3, October 1, 1978, p. 292.

These skillfully wrought stories are tied together by two characters who represent a common theme in the book, foolish appearance versus the wise heart. A goose comes to the pond every afternoon for the love of telling a good story to the frogs who listen. The duck is a flashy showman trying to convince the goose of a stage carrer under his management. In the first story a greedy couple abandon their farm and foundling swineherd for a more luxurious world, while the boy finds true wealth developing a home and friendship with a kind pedlar. The second tale features a vain rooster; the third, a cricket who tries to convince a millstone pony to walk "straight ahead" out into the world; the fourth, two researchers who are eaten by their crocodile subject; and the last, a young raccoon who learns to play her troubles on the flute, creating music instead of complaints. Each story is a small world unto itself and each animal a unique individual. There is no shortage of witty remark and observant proverb, either, but much of it may fly well over a child's head. Best shared aloud in class with a chance to discuss, but also entertaining for perceptive readers on their own.

William Jaspersohn

SOURCE: A review of *The Little Swineherd,* in *The Christian Science Monitor,* October 23, 1978, p. B2.

A goose tells tales to a duck who wants to put her in show business, and this eloquent raconteur limns a world of flute-playing raccoons and pompous roosters, of innocent swineherds and truth-telling alligators that recalls the worlds of Aesop and the Grimms. Paula Fox has some shrewd things to say through her goose about folly, animal and otherwise, and it's a tribute to both their talents that none of these six tales gets fouled in its own moralism. Nor is goose or human above a good joke—on the likes of behavioral science, for example, in the persons of two researchers, Fork and Clogg, bumblers harassing the aforementioned alligator. Too, Miss Fox and her goose know the fabulist's secret: that sometimes a story's best ending is no ending at all. Leonard Lubin's fluent illustrations are a perfect complement to this, Miss Fox's first book for children since her Newbery Award-winner *The Slave Dancer.* This is a magical book, perhaps best read aloud, and one sure to enchant even the sulkiest bedtime audience.

Zena Sutherland

SOURCE: A review of *The Little Swineherd and Other Tales,* in *Bulletin of the Center for Children's Books,* Vol. 32, No. 3, November, 1978, p. 43.

A new Scheherazade is created in a book of fanciful tales for the older or more sophisticated reader; many have sly digs at adult pursuits, such as the inane research project in "The Alligator Who Told the Truth," or in the behavior of the talent-scouting duck. It is the duck who hears a wise goose telling the first tale, "The Little Swineherd," and promptly decides that he can put the goose on stage. He listens to each of the tales she tells, five in all, and offers suggestions for improved performance, all of which are calmly ignored by the goose. The tales are amusing and wise, the style fluent and polished.

A PLACE APART (1980)

Kirkus Reviews

SOURCE: A review of *A Place Apart,* in *Kirkus Reviews,* Vol. XLVIII, No. 18, September 15, 1980, p. 1235.

Tory, 13, has just lost her father in an accident and moved to a new town with her mother when she meets Hugh—rich, arrogant, aloof, older (a high school junior), and, to her, totally fascinating. With her mother about to remarry and all of life a muddle, Hugh serves as a compelling, if unreliable, center. He wants to be an impresario and behaves now like a capricious puppeteer; when he drops her for Tom Kyle, a new boy at school, she waits to be picked up. Gradually and reluctantly, though, Tory has come to see the callousness in Hugh, and she summons courage to say no to him when she finds herself unable to complete the play he's been pestering her to write for a school performance. That's the end of her relationship with Hugh, but not of her involvement. When Tom Kyle is badly hurt in a car accident, essentially trying to prove himself, long-standing mass resentment surfaces and Hugh the "snob" is blamed. Tory alone argues for a fairer judgment, just as later only Tory is moved to visit Tom in the hospital. Tory's feelings for the Hugh she has glimpsed through the rare chink in his posture give some weight to her attachment and her later regret. We have seen similar hints of humanity in other such inaccessible figures, just as we have seen similar high school tragedies and mass reactions. However, Fox doesn't settle for a simple demonstration of consequences. Also, Tory's sometimes confused but always earnest attempts to sort things out give edge and undercurrent to the action; and her retrospective first-person telling, though it never gets ahead of the story, does show a seasoned perspective well beyond the outlook that Tory the subject starts out with. Everyday material, undistinguished plot, but sharpened by the Fox intelligence.

Zena Sutherland

SOURCE: A review of *A Place Apart,* in *Bulletin of the Center for Children's Books,* Vol. 34, No. 3, November, 1980, p. 52.

Victoria is thirteen when she begins her story; her father has recently died, she and her mother have moved to a small town, and she is quickly enthralled by Hugh, several years older than she. Oddly self-contained, Hugh dominates her thoughts if not her time, and Victoria admires him although her one other friend, Elizabeth, and her mother think he is a poseur. Hugh drops her for a new classmate, and then Victoria learns that Hugh is just as quick to drop Tom; finally, she sees that Hugh has no real affection for anyone, and what she misses is not Hugh himself but the way he had made her feel. When the breach comes (Hugh's family moves, and Victoria's mother is about to remarry and move also) Victoria is over her pain. This is almost an adult novel, subtle and percipient in its relationships, mature in its bittersweetness; the characters are firmly drawn and the style is grave and polished.

Anne Tyler

SOURCE: "Staking Out Her Territory," in *The New York Times Book Review,* November 9, 1980, p. 55.

I know a teen-age girl who seems to spend most of her library time opening books, reading their end flaps and slamming them shut "Fourteen-year-old Mary and her alcoholic mother. . . ." Slam. "When fifteen-year-old Laura learns she's pregnant. . . ." Slam. What she wants, she says, is a book about somebody ordinary. It could be somebody with a problem, if necessary, but does the problem have to be the most important part of the book?

The 13-year-old narrator of *A Place Apart* has several problems. Her father has died, she and her mother have moved to an unfamiliar town, and the boy who befriends her often confuses and troubles her. But the center of the novel is Victoria her self, not her problems; and Victoria makes a truly wonderful heroine—"ordinary" enough to win over any young reader, but also reflective, observant and articulate.

"I had a dream last night," she tells her uncle. "I dreamed I was a queen, and my crown was a circlet of those little brown pears you can buy in the market in the fall. And I was floating over land that was covered in mist."

"Your dream means that what you must do is find your own country," her uncle tells her.

In a sense, that's Victoria's biggest problem, and one that most adolescents will understand—locating her territory, naming it, making sense of what's happening around her. She used to believe, she tells us, that "if I could describe one entire day of my life to someone, that person would be able to tell me what on earth life was all about." But that was before her father died, and the year that's covered by "A Place Apart" is the period of time it takes her to regain, however shakily, some sense of order and security.

The issue of her confusing friend—a boy who enjoys manipulating people—is a major part of the plot, but it doesn't seem essential. Far more important is Victoria's grief for her father, which is palpable—fading, reviving unexpectedly and fading again. There's a moment, very shortly after his death, when Victoria's mother wakes her in the middle of the night and the two of them sit staring at each other. There's another, just before a vacation trip, when Victoria is stricken by the sight of two suitcases where once there were three.

Victoria's mother is beautifully drawn—a woman floundering but doing her best. When she thinks of remarrying, later in the story. Victoria doesn't approve; but the man is sympathetic and he tries hard, and Victoria realizes that. It's a relief—no black-and-white characters here, but the stuff of real life.

Her readers are complimented, you might say. Paula Fox trusts them to appreciate a story without gimmicks or exaggerations. She writes a honed prose, avoiding all traces of a gee-whillikers tone, and her language is simple and direct. *A Place Apart* is a book apart—quiet-voiced, believable and often very moving.

John Rowe Townsend

SOURCE: A review of *A Place Apart,* in *The Horn Book Magazine,* Vol. LVI, No. 6, December, 1980, pp. 648-9.

How does an author continue her career after publishing a book with the power, weight, and intensity of *The Slave Dancer?* Such achievements are not repeatable. Following her excursion into folk tale and fable with *The Little Swineherd,* Paula Fox has written a novel for young people in something like the manner of her *Blowfish Live in the Sea,* a first-person account of some eighteen months in the life of Victoria Finch, aged thirteen. After Victoria's father died, the girl and her mother move from Boston to a small New England town, where she makes school friendships, especially a self-deceiving and ultimately self-defeating one with a talented but selfish and exploitative boy called Hugh; at the end her mother is to remarry, and they are to move back to Boston. Although quite a lot happens, there is not much plot; the narrative proceeds from one significant incident to the next, producing ultimately what might be called a linear image of early adolescence. The book calls for thoughtful, attentive reading; it offers neither the old romantic view of boy-girl friendship nor the more recent insistence on menstruation and sexual fumblings. Victoria faces, across the great void of her bereavement, the true mysteries of adolescence: What is one to make of oneself, of other people, of relationships, of life and death and time? She does little more than survive the psychological perils that beset her. There is some joy but more anguish, and when her mother eventually tells her, "'It's as hard to be grown-up as to grow up,'" Tory replies "'It can't be harder.'" She has had a rough passage. Despite the insight and sensitivity one would expect from Paula Fox, the book is in many ways sad and slightly dispiriting. Remembering the emphasis the author placed in her Andersen acceptance speech on the power and importance of storytelling, one may find this novel a little thin and even a little disappointing.

📖 *ONE-EYED CAT* (1984)

Anne Tyler

SOURCE: "Trying to Be Perfect," in *The New York Times Book Review,* November 11, 1984, p. 48.

In Paula Fox's 20-odd years of writing for children, she has distinguished herself as a teller of mingled tales. Let other authors underestimate their young readers' intelligence however they will, creating entirely villainous villains and entirely heroic heroes—but Miss Fox trusts that even children know life is a complex, inconclusive, intriguingly gray-toned affair.

One-Eyed Cat is a story about an introspective 11-year-old boy, the only child of a minister and his wife, who is immobilized by arthritis. The year is 1935, the place is a small town in New York State, and Ned Wallis is the boy attempting to be the perfect person his parents believe him to be. Or perhaps we should say the person he *imagines* they believe him to be, for his mother confesses straight out that she's not your standard saintly invalid, and his father is a fine enough minister to be unsurprised by ordinary human error.

In Ned's case, the error is thoughtless cruelty. It so happens that a maternal uncle has brought him a loaded Daisy air rifle for his birthday. His father confiscates it, explaining that while the uncle's earlier presents—archeological treasures of various sorts—provided material for the imag-

ination, all that one can imagine with a rifle is "something dead." The rifle goes to the attic. But in the dark of night, Ned sneaks it outdoors for just one shot, and that's what sets the plot in motion. He shoots at a sort of shadow, although semiconsciously he knows it may be more than a shadow. His target is a cat, which loses an eye to Ned's bullet.

For Ned, the knowledge of his guilt marks the beginning of a new distance from his parents. "It was with the gun that his trouble had started. Yet the gun hardly seemed to matter now. It was as if he'd moved away, not to the parsonage next to the church, or to Waterville, but a thousand miles away from home. What did matter was that he had a strange new life his parents knew nothing about and one that he must continue to keep hidden from them. Each lie he told them made the secret bigger, and that meant even more lies. He didn't know how to stop."

Luckily, he has a chance to redeem himself. While he's helping an elderly neighbor with his chores, he sees the cat again and takes steps to feed and shelter it, all the while continuing to keep his guilt a secret. How he finally confesses—and to whom—makes for a genuinely affecting scene.

The story moves slowly at times, perhaps too slowly for younger readers, and it suffers on occasion from a sense of indirection. The uncle who brought the rifle, for instance, invites Ned to take a trip with him. With some reluctance, Ned accepts the invitation, but eventually he changes his mind and stays home. One feels that the author herself may have changed her mind; what was introduced as an important element of the plot peters out without having served much purpose.

Generally, though, *One-Eyed Cat* succeeds. It's full of well-drawn, complicated characters—Mrs. Scallop, the insensitive housekeeper who means well nonetheless; the lonely old man who waits for his grown daughter's postcards, even though she just sends him the same one over and over; and two very appealing parents. There's integrity in the plot, as you'll realize when the housekeeper tells Ned that his mother's disease was caused by Ned's birth. In a slicker story, Ned would have brooded over her words throughout the rest of the book and never let his mother know why. In *One-Eyed Cat,* he tells his mother at once, and she dismisses the notion conclusively—and anyhow, he never really believed it from the start.

Most important, though, is what the story can teach young readers about grown-ups' expectations of them. If I had a child right now in his middle years—old enough to land himself in some sort of mess, young enough not to know yet that his parents themselves are imperfect—I would offer him this book. It says clearly, but never too baldly, that parents are not so easily scandalized as all that, that what disturbs them more than their children's mistakes is the sense that their children are concealing serious worries. This is what makes *One-Eyed Cat* a book of real value.

Louise L. Sherman

SOURCE: A review of *One-Eyed Cat,* in *School Library Journal,* Vol. 31, No. 4, December, 1984, p. 89.

Ned Wallis, given an air rifle by his favorite uncle for his eleventh birthday, is stunned when his father, a Congregational minister, puts the gun in the attic, declaring that Ned is too young for one. That night Ned takes the gun outside, and fires it once. To his horror, he thinks he has hit something. Soon after, a wild one-eyed cat appears, and Ned is sure that the missing eye is the result of his shot. Ned struggles with his guilt over what he has done and the lies he tells to cover it for the rest of that year. It affects his relationships—with his mother, who is bound to a wheelchair by crippling arthritis; Mrs. Scallop, their malevolent housekeeper; Mr. Scully, an old man for whom Ned does chores; and Ned's school friends. Ned finds himself torn between hoping the cat will survive and wishing it dead so he will be relieved of his guilt. In an almost abrupt conclusion, he is finally able to share his guilt and fears with his mother after seeing the cat, alive and with family. Fox's writing is sure. Her characterization is outstanding, and she creates a strong sense of place and mood. the relationships among the characters are complex and ring true, while often filling readers with a sense of despair. *One-Eyed Cat* is a deep and demanding psychological novel. Its slow pace may limit its appeal, but those who persevere will be rewarded.

Ethel L. Heins

SOURCE: A review of *One-Eyed Cat,* in *The Horn Book Magazine,* Vol. LXI, No. 1, January-February, 1985, pp. 57-8.

In the mid-1930s Ned Wallis, the only child of a Congregational minister, lived in a "big, ailing old house" on a hill overlooking the Hudson River. Stricken some years before with rheumatoid arthritis, the boy's mother was an often helpless invalid; yet life was simple and serene, for the family was nourished by its mutual unspoken love. Only the housekeeper, the grumpy, overbearing Mrs. Scallop, was an irritating presence—"red and inflamed, like skin around a splinter"; they bore her self-righteousness with annoyance tempered by humor. Then, for Ned's eleventh birthday his uncle gave the boy an air rifle—which his father promptly forbade him to have. But in a strangely compulsive act Ned took the gun, stole out into the night, and shot—just once—at a dark moving shadow near the barn. Some weeks later, as he was doing chores for Mr. Scully, an elderly neighbor, the boy glimpsed a scruffy, sickly one-eyed cat, and he was haunted by the fearful certainty of what he had done. For months his guilt and shame engulfed him; inattentive in school, he spent more and more time with old Mr. Scully, both of them trying to keep the feeble animal alive. At home he was surrounded by his father's kindness and his mother's pain, and he felt imprisoned in the web of lies he had told in order to keep his terrible secret from his patient, bewildered parents. Then, one momentous sleepless night in the spring, with his mother's encouragement Ned came to terms with the truth and at last found reconciliation and release. In a rare, remarkable novel for children the pure clarity of the prose, its reticence, and its concrete sensual imagery recall the literary style of Willa Cather. The much-honored author writes with an artlessness that conceals her art, using the nuances of language to reveal the subtleties of human experience and to push back the frontiers of a young reader's understanding.

Patricia Craig

SOURCE: "A Shot in the Dark," in *The Times Literary Supplement,* No. 4294, July 19, 1985, p. 806.

Ned Wallis is an American eleven-year-old in the 1930s, son of a Congregational minister who embodies goodness, and a crippled mother whose outlook on things is more refreshingly wayward. When an uncle thoughtlessly presents Ned with an air-gun, the Revd James Wallis bears away the offensive object and stows it in the attic. From here it is retrieved by Ned, in a mood of defiance which comes on him in the night. Once the airgun is in his hands, he can't resist trying it out. "What is there to imagine with a gun?" his father has justly enquired. "Something dead." As it turns out Ned, after his single shot in the dark, doesn't have to take responsibility for a piece of wanton slaughter; but something nearly as beastly occurs. A cat turns up, and one of its eyes is missing.

This is a novel about guilt, tolerance, forgiveness, helpfulness to others, kindness to animals, the natural high spirits peculiar to the young, the need to curb these occasionally in the interests of thoughtfulness, and the inclusion in life of such distressing matters as illness and pain. With all this to communicate, Paula Fox has a job not to seem preachy and the didactic purpose never recedes sufficiently to allow incident or characterization a free run. Ned is engaging, and so are his imperfect uncle and mother; and Mr Wallis fulfils his function adequately. There is an unlikeable housekeeper who, you feel, has been inserted merely as a token non-charmer, and someone not at the centre of some piece of moral tuition for the hero. It is all—for all the clarity and amiability of the writing—just a little less than riveting to read about. Still, the handling of the cat is subtle and effective.

Margery Fisher

SOURCE: A review of *One-Eyed Cat,* in *Growing Point,* Vol. 24, No. 4, November, 1985, p. 4527.

Paula Fox is never obvious or heavy but every work she writes is measured and inevitable, contributing to a lucid and richly felt analysis of human relationships. *One-Eyed Cat* begins on the eve of Ned's thirteenth birthday. His uncle, a rare, much travelled visitor, has brought him a gun as a present; his parson father firmly puts this away, believing the boy is too young even for target practice and too vulnerable to the basic instincts which a gun could wake. Angry at his interference, Ned takes the gun from the attic at night and, wandering beyond their lonely house, fires at a moving shadow; later, helping their neighbour, old Mr. Scully, as he always does, he sees a cat with a wounded eye and blames himself for its condition. The storyline follows the months of autumn and winter in which Ned helps Mr. Scully to care for the cat, while the ebb and flow of his mother's serious illness somehow parallels this smaller concern, both keeping the boy's conscience alive and painful. Behind the story, and faithfully, skilfully integrated with it, Ned's moods from day to day and his relations with his parents, with the conceited overbearing housekeeper, with the old man, are gradually revealed to the reader. Paula Fox's prose is rich with images and dense with the interaction of feeling and action. The quality of her writing may perhaps be glimpsed in a random extract. . . .

But the book is so finely wrought that only a complete, deliberate reading of it can show how touching, how true and how stirring the latest of her remarkable stories is.

THE MOONLIGHT MAN (1986)

Hazel Rochman

SOURCE: A review of *The Moonlight Man,* in *The New York Times Book Review,* March 23, 1986, p. 48.

"Where was he? Where was her father?" For three weeks of the summer vacation Catherine Ames has been stranded at her Montreal boarding school, waiting for her father to come and get her. It's to be their first long time together since her parents divorced 12 years ago when she was 3. He finally calls, disarming, apologetic as always; and she crosses on the ferry to meet him in Nova Scotia, where they spend a month in a cottage near a seaside village.

He has always been an exciting romantic figure to her, a moonlight man. She hasn't known much about him from their snatched infrequent meetings. But when he arranged for the school in Montreal, insisting that she move beyond her mother's New York home, "Catherine wanted to do what her father wanted her to do." Now she hopes for a "splendid journey."

Two days after her arrival she discovers he's an alcoholic, a shambling monster in chaos that terrifies and disgusts her. She realizes why she had to wait all that time at school. After a night of drinking, he makes her drive his sodden friends home.

There's been little in young adult fiction with this kind of plain intensity since Robert Cormier's early novels. Paula Fox is an acclaimed adult writer and her children's book, **The Slave Dancer**, won the 1974 Newbery medal. In contrast to the formula young adult novels of frenetic action ("always on the edge of screaming," as one novel depicts the genre) and the therapeutic coming-of-age epiph-

anies (with teenagers talking about talking about feelings until they suddenly realize how to be instantly grown up), Miss Fox writes with wit and candor about painful change and growth. Her language is exquisitely controlled, reaching for meaning in the patterns and pauses of ordinary conversation, often in words of one syllable.

Bitterly ashamed, Mr. Ames promises to try to stop drinking and charms his daughter into forgiveness. In solitude, they begin to know each other. He cooks, reads aloud and talks about books he loves and places, especially Italy, where he promises to take her. For the first time they can "afford" silence. Sometimes he lectures her, challenging slick responses and "junk language" (What does she mean she "had" *The Ancient Mariner* in school?) Though he is warm to everyone, even fawning, Catherine sees that she surprises him and that he likes her. They laugh together, sometimes helplessly. In unguarded moments, she confronts his sadness. He is an aging writer, disappointed, drowning.

A few days before they leave, he gets drunk again. She finds him at an illegal still, on his hands and knees, barking for company like a dog. When he comes around, she rages at him, hurls cruel insults: he's nothing but a "moonshine man." Though she soon pities and forgives him, their relationship is changed. Facing her own cruelty ("she hadn't known she had it in her to be so mean") and the illusions that have kept her helpless, she begins to take responsibility for her actions.

Miss Fox's words do what her story says, showing, as in the novels of Anne Tyler, that the cadences of small talk and the concrete images of daily life hold the intense power of myth. Catherine's father is like the Ancient Mariner bum who staggers after her on a New York sidewalk. She and her father are at times as helpless as the crazy old crone they find shut up in the dark rural cottage down the hill. All that Catherine discovers in their summer retreat is also part of home and school and within herself: danger and affection; monstrosity and laughter; moonlight and glaring sun.

Romance is not denied by her painful new awareness and by her separation. She begins to miss her boyfriend, who skis and dances in the moonlight. Her father's way of seeing, his questioning of the familiar, will always be part of her, and so will her knowledge that they love each other. His stories about Italy will make her go there herself one day.

She has seen him dumb, helpless, insensible; she has also seen him struggle to see the truth. The novel's astonishing ending bares the painful ambiguity of that struggle: in reply to Catherine's tired cliche, "See you," as they part at the airport, he kisses her and whispers, "Not if I see you first."

Hanna B. Zeiger

SOURCE: A review of *The Moonlight Man,* in *The Horn*

Book Magazine, Vol. LXII, No. 3, May-June, 1986, pp. 330-1.

Paula Fox has crafted the story of a fifteen-year-old girl coming to terms with the emotions of a divorce that happened twelve years before and of a relationship with a father who has been an elusive but romantic figure in her life. Catherine has been anticipating this summer and her first long visit with her father since she was three years old. The day for her to be called for at her boarding school has come and gone with no message from her father. For twenty-one days she coaxes and argues the headmistress into allowing her to wait for him. Just as she has given up hope, a phone call from her father instructs her to come to a small town in Nova Scotia where he has rented a cottage for them by the sea. As soon as she is with him, her unhappiness with him slips away. He has an ability to use words and charm to win her over as if he is weaving a magic spell. For him, spending the intimate time with his daughter, whom he has kept at arm's length until now, is like shining the harshest daylight on the mirage with which he shrouds his failures. Catherine sees him as "a juggler keeping a lot of objects going at the same time . . . while remaining hidden behind them." In hiding from her, he also hides from himself. His beguiling ways and his excessive drinking are his way of "escaping from reason and obligation." He deprecates his former wife with her certainty and neat, orderly life as a daylight woman, and Catherine realizes how much he is a moonlight person: insubstantial and undependable, yet able to transform everything he touches. As their days together pass, Catherine alternates between seeing him as an aging, frightened, and weak man and someone who draws her irresistibly to him. "He was running all over her, drowning her in language. Still, she felt better. How did he do it?" Recovering from her anger after his final drunken binge, Catherine is able to look at his weakness with some pity and understanding. Although she can accept and love him as he is, for her, her parents' divorce is at last final.

Judith Sheriff

SOURCE: A review of *The Moonlight Man,* in *Voice of Youth Advocates,* Vol. 9, Nos. 3 and 4, August and October, 1986, p. 142.

Twelve years after her parents' divorce, 15-year-old Catherine Ames has the opportunity for a seven-week visit with her father, with whom she has had only brief visits since the divorce. Her 50-year-old father, however, is three weeks late picking her up at her Montreal boarding school. Finally, just as both Catherine and the headmistress agree that Catherine's mother must be contacted, her father calls, full of apologies, and arranges for Catherine to meet him in Nova Scotia. Catherine, so very eager to be close to her father, immediately forgives and travels to join him. Within two days Mr. Ames and friends are drunk and Catherine takes care of them. Soon she discovers that the vacation was instigated by her stepmother: "She said—if you never got a close look at me, you'd be wondering

about me all your life." And Catherine does wonder. Why does her father, a writer with two novels to his credit, earn his living by writing travel guides? Why does he live so much in a literary and alcoholic fog rather than in touch with the real world and his own daughter? Why his abrupt mood changes, his chauvinism, his lies and broken promises? But despite all the questions, the answers to which she only partly understands, it is a good visit in that Catherine really does come to know this stranger. Two days before their vacation is over, Mr. Ames again gets very drunk, precipitating a very honest and very painful quarrel.

As in Fox's Newbery Honor book, **One-Eyed Cat,** the story is not so much about *what* happens as it is about what the characters perceive about the events and their own actions. Fox's characters have great depth. and Catherine especially is notable for her realistic, yet ambiguous, feelings for her father. Her father's alcoholism is not treated in clinical detail but with great emotional sensitivity. When Catherine returns to her mother's home in New York, she realizes how glad she is to be there—and how glad she will also be to return to school; they all, indeed, do have lives elsewhere. In short, this is another artistic beauty, and surely another award winner from the talented Ms. Fox.

Sarah Hayes

SOURCE: "Breaking the Rules," in *The Times Literary Supplement,* No. 4365, November 28, 1986, p. 1344.

Catherine's father is late picking her up from boarding school—three weeks late. And instead of spending the summer in Rockport, as she had expected, he takes her to an odd little house in Nova Scotia at the back end of nowhere. Catherine knew her father would turn up eventually. She knew he would charm and entertain her in unexpected ways. She knew she would be disarmed. She did not know that her father was an alcoholic.

The word alcoholic is never used. Mr Ames is a drunk, a lush, a moonshine man; not a "problem". This is not a novel about learning to live with alcoholism, but a portrait of a wonderful, charming, doomed man who happens to drink. He drinks in a wild, blind, obsessional way. Catherine is only fifteen, but she is forced to turn out in the middle of the night and drive her father and his drinking cronies home. On one occasion, after a tour (for research purposes) round various local illicit stills, Catherine thinks he is dying. In his sober periods he goes on fawning and grovelling and charming and "drowning his daughter with language".

By the end of the summer Catherine can take no more. She is glad to return to her ordinary, tidy mother and her careful, caring stepfather. But she has changed. She sees the world differently: not as a place in which people are hopelessly flawed, and not even as a place in which weakness requires understanding and forgiveness. Paula Fox is not concerned with homilies. By the end of the summer Catherine has seen through her father's sickness to the person underneath, and he has opened her eyes and ears. Mr Ames bombards his daughter with books and words and ideas. He bullies her: "Don't be victim. It rots the brain." "Find a better word." "Be dignified." "Don't be a prig." "Don't condescend." Gradually Catherine learns to be true to herself, to trust her reactions and throw off the shackles of convention and fashion. She even learns to respect the humble sandwich.

The novel is painful; there is the suffering and self-hatred of the drunk, and the pain of living with him—with the broken promises, the lying and the charades of renunciation. But it is not an unhappy or depressing novel. Good times as well as bad lodge in Catherine's memory. Mr Ames is an exciting man to do very ordinary things with. And the landscape of Nova Scotia steals up imperceptibly to anaesthetise the hurt.

The Moonlight Man breaks all the rules for teenage novels. It has a cast of two, both of whom are bookish; there is no romance, no sex, no action; and the author dares to preach (though her sermon has a strange theme). Paula Fox challenges the reader to take another look at her or his assumptions, using the tragedy of the adult to break through the complacency of youth. Despite its sombre story and serious intent, her book remains quirky, humorous, intimate and readable—a triumph against the odds.

LILY AND THE LOST BOY (1987; British edition as *The Lost Boy*, 1988)

Betsy Hearne

SOURCE: A review of *Lily and the Lost Boy,* in *Bulletin of the Center for Children's Books,* Vol. 40, No. 11, July-August, 1987, p. 206.

Although there are three children central to Fox's new novel, the real heartbeat of the story is the Greek island where they are visiting for the summer. Each character—and especially the island—takes shape in the reader's mind through indelible scenes and sensory description. Lily is nearly twelve and the smartest of the lot, an observant, sharp-tongued girl wary of the reckless young stranger, Jack, who diverts her fourteen-year-old brother's attention and who ultimately plays out a role in a classic tragedy. Jack has been rejected by his mother and neglected by his father. It is inevitable, from foreboding hints in the text, that he will cause grief—as it turns out, the death of a Greek child with a close, loving family. The irony here is clear and striking, and the role of the protagonist, Lily, an interesting one in relationship to the boys' friendship. It is Lily who ultimately perceives and retrieves Jack from self-destructive isolation. As is her wont, Fox presents readers with a book that sustains thought with subtleties of tone and meaning. The dynamics of characterization also sustain attention, as does the close rendering of atmosphere: at one point, Lily tries to recapture a melody "like a little silver bird flashing in the woods; it vanished when you tried to fix it with your eyes." Along with the

American cast here, readers will be transported to another place, with another sense of time.

Ethel L. Heins

SOURCE: A review of *Lily and the Lost Boy,* in *The Horn Book Magazine,* Vol. LXIII, No. 5, September-October, 1987, pp. 615-6.

In an article in the January/February 1987 *Horn Book* Paula Fox spoke of her belief that the child has an instinctive sense of human affliction and is able to "feel intimations of hardships, of conditions, of experiences far beyond the range of his or her own experience." More subtly and sensitively than many writers for young people, she probes the emotional lives of her characters. From Williamstown, Massachusetts, two children and their parents come to live for a few months on Thasos, a Greek island in the northern Aegean Sea. Lily, nearly twelve, is haunted by the historic and mythic aspects of their village, "perched on the edge of the past," with its ancient amphitheater and ruined temples. There, she and her brother Paul, two years older, explore their extraordinary surroundings and quickly grow close to each other—until young Jack, another American, comes into their lives and alters the relationship. Silent, unsmiling, and restless, Jack is the son of an arrogant, eccentric expatriate who has achieved local admiration and fame for his superb skill at folk dancing. Constantly boasting of the boy's self-reliance, the father lays a heavy burden of unnatural loneliness on him. Lily dislikes and resents the boy but perceives his tragic situation and is moved to reluctant pity, while Paul is mesmerized by Jack's independent life and devil-may-care singularity; shutting out Lily, the two boys become friends. Disguising his bitterness with bravado and goaded by his father's dazzling performance, Jack flaunts his own acrobatic virtuosity on a bicycle until his recklessness propels him and others into catastrophe. Writing in a calm, conversational yet imagistic style, the author impressively conveys both the outer atmosphere of place and the inner, highly charged atmosphere of personal emotions. For Lily and Paul, distanced from their ordinary world, the exotic, isolated setting adds intensity to the shattering events; separately and together, they have been changed by the experience of suffering and loss.

Miranda Seymour

SOURCE: "From the Time of Gods," in *The Times Literary Supplement,* No. 4424, January 15-21, 1988, p. 70.

In the days when children still relished the Tanglewood Tales and Andrew Lang's storybooks, Greek mythology and history were absorbed at an early age. We need a Greek Astérix now to do for the warriors of Athens and Sparta what that comic-strip hero has so successfully done for the cohorts of Roman soldiers.

Both Paula Fox and Edward Fenton are concerned to stimulate interest in the forgotten tales of gods and heroes;

and both of these books tell a modern story in which the past is a strong and significant element. Fenton introduces a contemporary Odysseus, the old seadog Kapetan Sarandis, who is full of tales of gorgons and sirens. Fox cleverly uses a dramatic staging of *Iphegenia in Aulis* as the ominous prologue to her story's climax—the death of an innocent child. Wisely, both authors confine the educational aspect to discreet hints and allusions. The ancient past becomes a rich background for these lively stories of modern life in a Greek village as seen through the eyes of an American child.

Paula Fox has received several awards for her children's books. Her most recent novel, **The Moonlight Man,** examined the relationship between an adolescent girl and her father, a charmer, a liar and a drunk. The lost boy of her new book's title is Jack Hemming, who comes to the island of Thasos with his boasting, drinking, larger-than-life father, a man who can outdance and outdrink anyone on the island. Catherine Ames in Fox's earlier book was fifteen, old enough to examine her father with some detachment; Jack is younger and desperately anxious to emulate his father's cocksure arrogance.

Jack's arrival has a disturbing effect on Lily and Paul, the American brother and sister who were inseparable allies, joint explorers of their island paradise. Paul falls under Jack's spell; Lily, jealous and isolated, is more aware than her brother of Jack's private loneliness and of his need to capture attention and admiration. When Jack's desperate acts of bravura lead to a village child's death, Lily is the one who guesses where he has run to hide himself and who goes to help him. The summer on Thasos is her rite of passage, a first unacknowledged experience of love. Fox dramatizes the fragile nature of the children's relationships with great sensitivity and the life of the village is conveyed with colour and plenty of homely detail. Most impressive, however, is the way she evokes the brooding presence of ancient Thasos, contrasting a reassuring daylight island with the ghostly landscape of night, where Lily and Jack wander in moon-blanched ruins rules by the gods.

Penny Blubaugh

SOURCE: A review of *Lily and the Lost Boy,* in *Voice of Youth Advocates,* Vol. 10, No. 6, February, 1988, pp. 279-80.

Lily, 12, and her 14 year old brother Paul are living on the small Greek island of Thasos where their father has taken the family with him while he's on sabbatical from his teaching job in Massachusetts. He's picked Thasos as a temporary home because not many English-speaking tourists visit and he's determined to learn as much about Greece and the Greeks as he can first hand.

Both children seem to love the island, are progressing well in Greek and are happy with each other's company for the first time in several years. As the day to day frustrations begin to die down and the Coreys become more attuned to the pace of the island, it begins to be almost a paradise except, as Lily says, for the vipers.

Then one morning as the children are visiting the Acropolis, they see a strange boy about Paul's age. Excited and curious Paul goes over to meet him, but Lily feels herself drawing away. Once met, Jack Hemmings, an American living with his father further up the island begins to draw Paul in and Lily watches their new-found closeness drift away. At first she's angry with Jack, but as she watches and listens, as she sees Paul closing his family out and turning to Jack, she begins to wonder. Why is Jack never with his father? Why does his mother pay money to keep him away? Why do the islanders dislike Mr. Hemmings in spite of their admiration for his dancing?

Jack begins to spend more and more time with the Coreys and in spite of his ideas, things that drag Paul into delinquent situations, Lily starts to feel how much pain Jack carries. Finally Jack's recklessness takes the life of another child and after he runs away Lily feels that she must be the one to find him. Their return to Thasos makes her even more aware of his loneliness, but there's little she can do to help him. And finally, as the Coreys leave the island, Jack and Mr. Hemmings stand at the quay and watch, more separated together than they ever were apart.

This is a warm, poignant story that shows life in both its simplicity and its complexity. It paints a beautiful picture of village life in Greece, shows the goodness of life itself, but offers no easy solutions to the difficulties of living.

THE VILLAGE BY THE SEA **(1988; British edition as** *In a Place of Danger,* **1989)**

Paula Fox

SOURCE: "The Village by the Sea," in *The Horn Book Magazine,* Vol. LXVI, No. 1, January-February, 1990, pp. 22-3.

[*The following is Paula Fox's acceptance speech for the* Boston Globe-Horn Book *Award for fiction, which she delivered at the annual meeting of the New England Library Association in Springield, Massachusetts on September 25, 1989.*]

The Italian novelist, Cesare Pavese, wrote in his journal a few lines that speak eloquently about the struggle of writing and of the solace and significance of those moments and events which take account of that struggle. Pavese writes:

To have written something that leaves you emptied of your vital powers . . . to have poured out not only all you knew was in you, but all that you suspected and imagined, the turmoil, the shadowy visions, the subconscious; to have achieved that with long weariness and tension, learning caution through days of hesitation, sudden discoveries and lapses, concentrating all your life and energy on that one point; and then to realize that all this is as nothing unless it is welcomed by

some sign, some word of human appreciation. To lack
that warming response is to die of cold, to be speaking
in the wilderness, to be alone.

Human appreciation, warming response, are not in one's
mind while one is writing. If they are, a certain paralysis
takes place. Imagination plays possum; imagination is the
first casualty of self-consciousness. Apprehensions and
speculations about what that mysterious person, the reader, will think and feel and say about what one writes
brings work to a halt, and the daily self with its worries
and regrets, its fretfulness and vanities, exerts its tyranny.
But when a writer has luck, that self slips away and makes
room for something else, for the story told by a voice that
is, somehow, outside oneself, a voice which is often in-
distinct, a mumble, but which goes on and on until one
day, one hour, the teller knows the tale is done.

It is then, when the pages lie on the table, that a writer
wonders how on earth it came about, and where did it all
come from? And it is then that one appreciates a voice
saying, "Well! Look at this! Perhaps it is worth reading,
even reading the whole story!"

When I was very young, during the Second World War,
I got a job in a machine shop in New York City. I was the
only female there. I was a bit persecuted by the machin-
ists, who were both amused by and resentful of the presence of a girl among the lathes and grinders where industrial diamonds were produced. The shop was on the four-
teenth floor. There was a broad fire escape where, during
a break, we, the workers, were permitted to have a smoke
and a cup of coffee for a few moments. But the teasing
got me down. One early morning, as I walked from my
apartment to the shop on Irving Place, I began to tell
myself a story. When it came time for the morning break,
I began to tell the story to my fellow workers. I didn't
think about it. I just did it. To my astonishment, they
listened, and they wanted to know what happened next.

And so the next day, I told them. And the day after that,
I managed to come up with a new story just long enough,
ten minutes or so, for that morning break out on the fire
escape. They began to be nicer to me. After all, you don't
want to kill Mother Goose as long as she keeps talking.

I want to give you my heartfelt thanks for this lovely
award, this warming response.

Amy Kellman

SOURCE: A review of *The Village by the Sea,* in *School
Library Journal,* Vol. 34, No. 11, August, 1988, p. 93.

When her father is scheduled for surgery, Emma is sent
to stay with her Aunt Bea, a "terror," and her warm, mildly
eccentric Uncle Crispin. Although Emma wonders how
anyone related to her father could be a terror, she does
remember a visit when she was younger during which
"Aunt Bea filled the whole space of her memory just as
she had filled the chair." The novel is built on a series of

pushes and pulls, tensions and releases among the characters. Emma's anxiety about her father is allayed after the
successful operation, but the tension between her and her
aunt grows. That pull is relaxed when Emma and a new
friend build a miniature village of shells and other treasures from the sea. The final resolution of tension does
not occur until the very end of the novel when Emma
makes peace in her own mind with her aunt. The highly
visual language allows readers to see the characters emotionally as well as physically. For example, Emma is
thrown off balance by her aunt. "That was part of Aunt
Bea's being a terror. She forced Emma to think about
every single movement she made." The small cast of
characters are fully realized, as is the setting. Fox con-
jures up the house by the sea and the tiny village so that
readers will share the joy of its creation and the pain of
its destruction by Aunt Bea. The cancerous effect of envy
and the healing properties of love and self-esteem are
driven home poignantly and with a gentle humor that runs
throughout the book. Fox has given readers another treasure for reading alone or reading aloud.

Beverly B. Youree

SOURCE: A review of *The Village by the Sea,* in *Voice
of Youth Advocates,* Vol. 11, No. 4, October, 1988, p.
181.

While Emma's father is undergoing heart bypass surgery,
she must spend two weeks with Uncle Crispin and Aunt
Bea, "the terror," at their house on Peconic Bay. Their
house is totally unexpected—dirty cups and saucers are
on the porch, dirty clothes are scattered all over the house,
and dust balls are everywhere. Aunt Bea prefers to stare
at a Monet reproduction of the ocean rather than the ocean
itself, she speaks sarcastically, and she wears sloppy
clothes and plays solitaire. Emma's journal entry for her
first night is brief: "I'm here. Uncle Crispin is really nice.
The bay and the beach are great. Aunt Bea is ___." One
day Emma meets a girl about her own age on the beach,
and she and Bertie begin to construct a village from the
treasures they find as they explore the beach. Emma leaves
her aunt's house early in the mornings to escape and to
work on their project. Emma and Bertie are proud of their
project and finish it the day before Emma is to return
home. They invite Bertie's grandmother and Emma's aunt
and uncle to the viewing, but Aunt Bea refuses to go.
When Emma hears a noise during the night, she goes to
her village on the beach only to find it in shambles. On
the sand are beads from Aunt Bea's moccasins. Emma
doesn't understand why Aunt Bea would commit such an
act. Uncle Crispin says, "Envy's a coal comes hissing hot
from hell." When Emma gets her journal to share with
her father, she notices that her first and only entry is
finished; for Aunt Bea had sneaked into her room that
morning and written, "Aunt Bea is a sad bad old woman."

Fox tells a rich story of compassion and growth. Emma's
concern for her father and her trying to understand Aunt
Bea are aspects of her maturing. Emma is a bright young
girl whom readers will enjoy.

Rosellen Brown

SOURCE: A review of *The Village by the Sea,* in *The New York Times Book Review,* February 5, 1989, p. 37.

When our daughter had her first nightmare at the age of 2, my husband and I stared at her in consternation. Nothing terrible had ever happened to our protected darling; what imagined trauma could be so terrifying that it woke her screaming?

Foolish, loving parents realize soon enough how little control they have over their children's lives, let alone their imaginations or their discovery of all that lurks at the edge of the dark forests of possibility. The question eventually becomes, then, one of timing: how soon do we acknowledge—educate them in—danger, uncertainty, madness, death? From the Brothers Grimm to Katherine Paterson's *Bridge to Terabithia* to Maurice Sendak's return to Grimm in *Dear Mili,* writers for children have made themselves benevolent guides to sorrow and loss. Each measures out bitterness in a different-sized spoon and washes it down with a greater or lesser dose of sweetness. But the genuine writers don't flinch.

Paula Fox, whose fiction for young people has won Newbery and American Book Awards because it never stints on the complexity of her adult novels, has assembled a beautifully scaled small world in her 1989 Newbery Honor Book, **The Village by the Sea.** What feels, at first, as if it were going to be, uncharacteristically, a "problem" book, declares its premise in its first paragraph. Ten-year-old Emma's father is going into the hospital for what turns out to be open-heart surgery; she is being shipped off for safekeeping to an aunt and an uncle at a beach on Long Island. At so straightforward a declaration of situation the heart quails: not much separates that paragraph from the blunt description (to simplify the work of librarians and parents) that strips children's books down to the bones on the copyright page (and ends, like a slammed door, with the likes of "1. Aunts—Fiction. 2. Beaches—Fiction").

But by the end of **The Village by the Sea,** what's come clear instead is that Ms. Fox's structure turns out to be elegant, fine-boned, not abrupt, and the flesh on it is trim. This is not a book one crawls into to be hidden and protected. But it gives solace in its intelligence and honesty, and for many a child those qualities can be more reassuring.

In terror for her father's life, Emma goes off without complaint like the well-mannered child she is, to spend two bewildering weeks with a kind uncle and a brutally neurotic aunt, a recovered alcoholic who is unused to children. Worse, she is unable to summon up even rudimentary decency in the company of strangers. Aunt Bea is a wonderful, terrible character, frightening for anyone to confront, but especially for a child who is just learning what constitutes appropriate behavior. A loose cannon on a small deck, Bea is capable of saying the most unexpected things, sometimes fascinating, always hurtful. "She

doesn't care what the target is," Emma's father explains. "She wants to feel the stones leaving her hand." It is a hard thing to learn how sad such a woman is, since she is (supposedly) a grown-up.

Emma, confused, escapes to spend most of her time with a new friend constructing, out of found objects, an imaginary village on the beach, an ideal world—it has a library, a forest, an artist's studio, but no stores and no dentist's office. The perfect village, all pine bough, sea lavender and sand dollar, meets a fate unexpected but not implausible, given the characters. Emma's moment of recognition melds the disparate parts of the story into a hard solid with a cutting edge: like the individual (or the self) however beloved, like the family however strong, Emma's miniature haven is ultimately beyond her protection. She can only cherish the building of it, and then the memory.

Ms. Fox shows her respect for her audience by writing with her usual fine attentiveness. Emma sees "the white spark of an airplane's wing"; she hears "the steamy whisper of pouring tea." She and the adults talk a lot, unsentimentally, trying to capture difficult emotions, and only a certain kind of sober, patient child (and perhaps an accompanying parent) will want to listen. But those who do will discover, in the calm voice of a writer too realistic to simplify, what Keats said it took—"a World of Pains and troubles"—"to school an Intelligence and make it a Soul."

Sharon Scapple

SOURCE: A review of *The Village by the Sea,* in *The Five Owls,* Vol. III, No. 4, March-April, 1989, pp. 60-1.

In *Village by the Sea,* as in her other recent works, Paula Fox creates a situation in which the main character must deal with two conflicts simultaneously. Unhappily, ten-year-old Emma must visit her Uncle Crispin and Aunt Bea at Peconic Bay during the two weeks her father is hospitalized for open-heart surgery. Emma's parents are sympathetic; they regret having to send her away, for they know, as does Emma, that Bea is a difficult woman, a terror. What Emma is not told is that Bea is alcoholic. The story is tightly knit as Paula Fox deftly balances Emma's concern for her father's life and her fear of Aunt Bea's unpredictability.

Emma is a perceptive child, and she frequently comments on what Crispin and Bea say or do. She notices, for example, that Crispin's voice "often had a pattering effect like a light rain falling on a roof." Sometimes the patter made her restless. Aunt Bea's statements about people were "like being punched in the same spot over and over again. You got a kind of ache just listening to her, and the ache didn't go away." Although living with Bea was like "putting one foot behind her to ease the screen door so that it wouldn't bang," Emma is empathetic and she wonders what thoughts pass through Bea's mind as she tears the flesh on her fingers.

Paula Fox's knowledge and understanding of how children cope with dysfunctional family systems are accurate. She writes knowingly, from the inside. Emma is a survivor. She learns how to avoid conflict; she is forced to think about every move she makes.

Throughout her visit, Emma maintains her sense of humor and her musings are clearly child-spoken. Once, to avoid Aunt Bea, Emma seeks relief on the porch. As she sits down in one of the old rocking chairs, Emma imagines all six of them filled with identical Aunt Beas, rocking all day and "cackling" about how horrible life is until they tipped their chairs right off the edge. Later on, Emma speculates that Bea drank so much tea that "there must be rivers and brooks and still ponds of tea throughout Aunt Bea's body."

In the end, the reader will be glad Emma decides to reveal to her father only the happy hours she spent with her friend Bertie building the village by the sea. From items found on the beach—blue and green beach glass, wood, green sea lettuce, sea lavender, bubble shells—she and Bertie construct a village that looked "more real than if it had been life-sized." It was Emma's refuge, a place where "hours flowed like the waves of the bay."

Though *Village* is a truthful text, it bears a disturbing sadness. Emma's decision not to tell her father about two of Bea's more malicious acts toward her perpetuates the unwritten rule that what occurs inside a dysfunctional family must remain unspoken. Perhaps it is at this point that the text becomes more adult than childlike.

Barbara Sherrard-Smith

SOURCE: A review of *In a Place of Danger,* in *The School Librarian,* Vol. 37, No. 3, August, 1989, pp. 113-14.

It will be good news for school librarians and their clientele if subsequent titles in this new series of trade paperbacks from Orchard Books are as compellingly readable and agreeable to look at and handle as [*In*] *a Place of Danger*. Plot and characterisation live up to the promise of the first arresting sentence: 'All that afternoon, and through supper, a question Emma wanted to ask her father stuck in her throat like a piece of apple skin.' The question haunting twelve-year-old Emma is whether her father will recover from the serious heart operation he is to undergo. While he is in hospital, she is to stay with his half-sister, and she feels, with some justification, that her destination is as much a 'place of danger' as her father's. This aunt, whom Emma hardly knows, is always referred to in the family as a terror, and Emma's memory of her as intimidating and unsympathetic proves well-founded. The aunt's behaviour is at times alarming, even violent, always baffling. She seems to take a perverse pleasure in needling her husband and her niece. Her childish tantrums and inexplicable rages dominate their lives. Emma realises there is something lopsided about her, as though she had lost her balance a long time ago and couldn't get

it back. Emma survives with the help of her uncle, a young neighbour who befriends her, and the tranquil beauty of the North American shore where they live. Finally, she comes partially to understand this strange household, to sympathise with them; and she realises with a maturity beyond her years, that love can take many forms. Many readers will identify with this teenage heroine involved in a family crisis, who is forced to discover that adults can have serious and puzzling failings. Endearingly lacking in confidence at times, she emerges as a strong positive character whose experiences linger in the mind long after the novel has been read. There is a sense of urgency throughout the book which is sustained by the spare distinction of the writing. A welcome addition to middle and senior school libraries.

Margery Fisher

SOURCE: A review of *In a Place of Danger,* in *Growing Point,* Vol. 28, No. 3, September, 1989, p. 5217.

Paula Fox consistently plans her fiction with a balance of interest, slanting action and emotion toward a young hero or heroine but giving full measure to the adults whose partial control may be for good or ill. *In a Place of Danger* uses the familiar plot of a girl on a visit to virtual strangers with the most impressive, broad view of people and their interactions. Emma's father is to undergo major heart surgery and the weeks spent at the seashore home of Aunt Bea and Uncle Crispin are, first of all, shadowed by the girl's anxiety and then by the alarmingly brusque and wayward behaviour of Aunt Bea, a huge, hostile, tea-swilling woman whose moods are treated with respect and yet (as Emma slowly realises) with reservations by her quiet, perceptive Uncle. Emma does escape from the claustrophobic atmosphere of the bungalow in visits to the beach, where she and a girl staying nearby build a village out of shells and beachcomber finds which helps both of them through difficult days; but in the end Aunt Bea even destroys their pleasure in 'Deer Haven' as the 'hot coal of envy' which Uncle Crispin has tried to explain over-rules the tormented woman's efforts to behave sensibly. There is nothing sensational here but a calm, steady progress through sparse narrative and scrupulously selective dialogue, along a road towards the understanding of personality. Areas of perception allow for readers of varying degrees of sensibility, some of whom may feel the plight of self-tormented Aunt Bea to be the most interesting aspect of the book.

MONKEY ISLAND (1991)

Kay E. Vandergrift

SOURCE: A review of *Monkey Island,* in *School Library Journal,* Vol. 37, No. 8, August, 1991, pp. 164, 166.

Eleven-year-old Clay Garrity's family had been what most people would consider an average family—until the magazine his father worked for went out of business and he couldn't find another job over the next year. Clay then experienced the gradual decline from that normal existence to one of abandonment by his father, the move to a welfare hotel and, at the beginning of the story, the disappearance of his mother who, with the added burden of a difficult pregnancy, is unable to cope with the daily struggle for survival. Clay eventually comes to a small park scornfully called "Monkey Island" for the homeless who live there. Here he is taken in by two men who share the wooden crate that offers them some shelter from the cold November winds. These three become a sort of family, holding on to some sense of humanity in a brutal and brutalizing world. For all of its harshness, *Monkey Island* is also a romanticized view of the world. Although Clay is not spared the hunger, fear, illness, and squalor of the streets, there is still a distancing from the more immediate types of violence that exist there. He is always on the edge of such danger, but no incidents actually touch him. In the end, it is pneumonia that brings him back into the social services system. After ten days in the hospital, the boy is placed in a foster home and shortly thereafter is reunited with his mother and baby sister in a conclusion that readers desire but that may strain credibility. This is a carefully crafted, thoughtful book, and one in which the flow of language both sustains a mood of apprehension and encourages readers to consider carefully the plight of the homeless, recognizing unique human beings among the nameless, faceless masses most of us have learned not to see.

Ellen Fader

SOURCE: A review of *Monkey Island,* in *The Horn Book Magazine,* Vol. LXVII, No. 5, September-October, 1991, pp. 596-7.

Eleven-year-old Clay Garrity awakens in the welfare hotel where he and his pregnant mother have lived for the last month to find his mother gone. His search for her leads him to a nearby park, where he becomes part of an encampment of homeless people, but a bout with pneumonia brings Clay's situation to the attention of the social service agencies, which place him with a foster family while they continue the quest for his absent mother. Although he is well cared for in the foster home, Clay especially misses the two homeless men who had become his surrogate family and who had helped him survive. He repeatedly visits the park until he meets up with one of the men, who has taken significant steps to better his life. In a poignant and promising ending, Clay, his new baby sister, and his mother, who now has a job, move into their own apartment. They have hope that Clay's father, who had deserted them after becoming depressed and defeated about his inability to find a job, will eventually reappear. Fox's story is neither an indictment of society nor a vehicle to proffer solutions for a growing national problem. It is instead an emotionally powerful story of one family's travail, one child's anxiety and fear, and the people who help that child until he and his mother are reunited. These are characters readers will understand and care about; Clay's universal struggle with the issue of what

constitutes a home, his bewilderment over his abandonment by both his parents, and his ambivalence at his reunion with his mother are expertly and honestly played out. The novel individualizes the problems of homeless people and puts faces on those whom society has made faceless; readers' perceptions will be changed after reading the masterfully crafted *Monkey Island*.

Roger Sutton

SOURCE: A review of *Monkey Island,* in *Bulletin of the Center for Children's Books,* Vol. 45, No. 2, October, 1991, p. 36.

"He was eleven years old and he had never felt so alone in his life." Clay's mother has disappeared, pregnant and without her coat, from the squalid hotel where they lived; his father had left weeks before, when the family still had their own apartment. And Clay leaves too, finding makeshift refuge and friendship in a small city park. Although he finds kind protection from Buddy, a young black man, and Calvin, an old alcoholic, Clay's life in the park is cold and tiring, scary and uprooted. There's a man who gives out coffee and doughnuts, but the police send him away; Clay and Buddy scrounge from trash barrels or buy food with the proceeds of can returns. Too many recent novels about homelessness are romantic adventures filled with exciting dangers and homeless "free spirits"; this book is simple and honest, true to its story of one lost boy. The dangers here are cold and hunger and street gangs; the homeless are "people trying to find better ways to sleep on stone." Although there's some occasional speechmaking via Calvin and Buddy, Fox's writing is always direct and quiet, and all the more so when she's describing hard things, such as the "hot silence" of an unspoken family fight, or being abandoned by a sad mother: "it was terrible that she had done that." Clay finds his mother after being hospitalized for pneumonia; and, despite his deep emotional wounds, the miracle of baby Sophie and the sustaining spirit of Buddy allow him to trust again the possibilities of family.

Dinitia Smith

SOURCE: "No Place to Call Home," in *The New York Times Book Review,* November 10, 1991, p. 52.

One autumn morning 11-year-old Clay Garrity wakes up in a welfare hotel in Manhattan and discovers that his mother has left him. Clay's father. who has also disappeared, is an unemployed magazine art director. His mother, until recently, had a job working with computers. Clay is white, he has been to good schools (he can read "Robinson Crusoe")—an atypical homeless child. He is the hero of *Monkey Island,* Paula Fox's delicate and moving novel, one of the first describing middle-class homelessness for young readers.

The sight of homeless people pushing shopping carts down the street or sleeping on benches in local parks has become a fact of life, and for children they are the ultimate representation of a terrifying fantasy—of parents leaving, of loss and displacement. How does a writer make the unbearable bearable without violating the basic truth of the situation?

Ms. Fox, who has won an American Book Award for children's fiction for her novel *A Place Apart,* the Hans Christian Andersen Medal for her collected children's work and a Newbery Medal for the young adult novel *The Slave Dancer,* has written a relentless story that succeeds in conveying the bitter facts.

She depicts life in a welfare hotel precisely the way Clay's pregnant mother needs the sound of a portable radio all the time to drown out her increasing despair, the way the woman next door cares—alone and lovingly—for her retarded son who sits all day watching television, "his feet turned out like a duck's feet." The elevator is a "a poison box," the halls are littered with trails of coffee grounds from leaking garbage bags. A trip to the bathroom can be a dangerous journey.

Eventually, Clay makes his way to a city park—called "Monkey Island" by thugs who prey on homeless people there. Like most of the newly homeless, Clay has trouble sleeping. The recent arrivals "were in a panic for days," one character observes. "They were also the angriest if someone or something woke them up in the middle of the night." Life is a constant, primal search. A portable toilet at a construction site is a gift, a broken water fountain means no way to wash that day. For an old woman, counting her few possessions over and over again is "a kind of housekeeping."

Although the focus of Ms. Fox's story is a middle-class family, she never lets us forget the way race and class affect destiny. When Clay catches pneumonia, his black friend, Buddy, wants to take him to a hospital but knows a taxi probably will not stop for him. "*Nigger* is the longest word I know," says Buddy.

Eventually, Clay is placed in a foster home where people are kind. But, one wonders, how will Ms. Fox ever resolve Clay's abandonment? Will she stage a scene of false forgiveness? When Clay and his mother *are* finally reunited, his mother *doesn't* ask Clay to forgive her. "Sorry can't erase all that," his mother says. She can only hope that one day she and Clay will find a way "to go on caring for each other that's . . . beyond *sorry.*"

Cathryn M. Mercier

SOURCE: A review of *Monkey Island,* in *The Five Owls,* Vol. VI, No. 3, January-February, 1992, p. 64.

Paula Fox's troubled characters quietly dominate novels of introspection and reflection. *Monkey Island* both follows that tradition and breaks from it. Like Gus, *The Stone Faced Boy,* Clay wears a set mask to project his inner frailty—vulnerability proves an unaffordable luxury

threatening his physical and emotional survival. A contemporary Hansel, Clay is abandoned by his father, then his mother, and finally "the safety net" of Social Services. Forces of weather and harsh cold, the blank stares or accusatory faces that pass him by on the street, further drive Clay into himself.

Simultaneously, the novel tells an active story. Realizing his mother's desertion yet unwilling to give up hope for her return, Clay, like Hansel, learns the path from his new "home" to the last place he shared with his mother. He moves constantly to survive, to keep warm, and to keep from being noticed. Riddled with doubts, traveling alone, feeling fragmented and numb, Clay lives in shadow. In the park, an island of temporary refuge, he meets his "fate" in Buddy and Calvin. They make room for him, share with him, and create a place for the forgotten child. With only themselves to offer, the young black man, Buddy, and old white man, Calvin, begin to patch up Clay's emotional wounds with illuminating kindness.

Fox remains true to herself and her characters. Calvin and Buddy do not parent Clay. They assume responsibility not because Clay is a child but because he's an individual human being in need. A victim of adults, Clay loses the innocence of a child without becoming an adult. He remains a child in search of nurturers and seeking warm human embrace. His limited life experience defines him still: an eleven-year-old boy, abandoned.

In some books, characters look to each other as a way of holding onto themselves. *Monkey Island* cries for a more extensive human community for survival and sustenance. Clay learns that "families can let you down." At the end of the novel, Clay's reunion with his mother doesn't instill much hope; however, Clay's Hansel now has a baby sister, Sophie, a Gretel to whom he'll hold on as firmly as he does Buddy. Underpinning it all, Clay feels lucky and knows he has found angels in the world. Luck and angels may be amorphous, unreliable concepts to build a life on, but suffused with hope and possibilities, they can serve as anchors.

As she does with Jessie in *The Slave Dancer* and Ned in *One-Eyed Cat,* Paula Fox creates a character in bewildering, morally incomprehensible circumstances and trusts her readers to recognize and challenge these complexities. What rescues all three characters is the tenacity with which they grasp precarious human connections. At the heart of *Monkey Island* is the call to morality, to compassionate humanity. The book's most haunting image remains the single word of graffiti Clay writes with his red crayon: STOP.

Victor Watson

SOURCE: "Rite of Passage," in *The Times Educational Supplement,* No. 3985, November 13, 1992, p. 11.

The hero of *Monkey Island* is an 11-year-old boy called Clay, who is abandoned by his mother. Without her, Clay cannot stay in their filthy and dangerous apartment. After some aimless wandering, he joins New York's "cardboard city", where he is befriended by a dying alcoholic and a young black man. "Monkey Island" is the contemptuous name the local youths give to the small park where the down-and-outs live in their makeshift shelters. Clay, supported by the zany philosophical benevolence of his new companions, endures violence and extreme hardship.

There is a happy ending of sorts, because mother and son—both changed by their experiences—are reunited and provided with a better flat to live in.

This story might have been a recipe for sentimentality, but Paula Fox concentrates throughout not on Clay's feelings but on his thoughts—his obsession with *Robinson Crusoe,* his puzzlement at shouted and scrawled obscenities, his fragmentary memories of his father, his understanding of the fact that "being a child . . . made no difference at all". This concentration on understanding leads to its own understated climax when we are told that Clay is filled with a "spooky hilarity" to realise "that he had real thoughts of his own".

For readers in a hurry, Paula Fox's detached and economical narrative provides a swift and dramatic rite-of-passage experience; more attentive readers will appreciate that her sparse telling makes possible a disciplined realism entirely appropriate to her subject.

📖 *AMZAT AND HIS BROTHERS: THREE ITALIAN TALES* (retold by Paula Fox, 1993)

Betsy Hearne

SOURCE: A review of *Amzat and His Brothers: Three Italian Tales,* in *Bulletin of the Center for Children's Books,* Vol. 46, No. 7, March, 1993, pp. 210-11.

"No sooner had the tiny rooster led his friends into the house than he felt chicken feathers around his feet. 'I don't care for these feathers,' he said. 'They make me wonder where the chickens have gone.'" With sly humor and classic restraint, Fox styles a folktale reminiscent of "The Bremen Town Musicians"; here, five animal friends who've been savaged by a wolf find his house in the woods and get even. In another tale, a variant of Joseph Jacobs' English folktale "Mr. Vinegar," a widow and her son, Cucol, collect a bag of gold abandoned by frightened thieves (like Mr. Vinegar, Cucol drops a door on their heads from a treetop) and best the villagers who have taunted them. Without violating folkloric compression, the author manages to personalize archetypes, as in her consideration of the widow's son: "Cucol was not backward, only very slow in reaching a conclusion, and as is true for most people, it was often the wrong one." Fox also respects the laws of folklore justice; when, in the trickster tale of the title, Amzat's two villainous brothers try to take away his humble inheritance, their punishment is cheerfully merciless. These three stories, illustrated with

canny pen-and-ink hatch drawings [by Emily Arnold McCully], will make delicious fare for independent readers, but don't neglect to share the book aloud with younger listeners as well. After all, Fox heard them from Floriano Vecchi—whom she introduces in the preface as an Italian transplanted to New York City—and has passed them on in the belief that "stories do not disappear. They last longer than anything else."

Ilene Cooper

SOURCE: A review of *Amzat and His Brothers: Three Italian Tales,* in *Booklist,* Vol. 89, No. 14, March 15, 1993, p. 1316.

Fox heard these stories from a childhood friend, who heard them from his grandfather, who lived in a mountain village in Italy and in turn had heard them from his own grandfather. As Fox says in her introduction, she has also added her own touch to the tellings, continuing the "great rope that ties the generations together." In the first tale, the title story, Amzat and his wife outsmart Amzat's two mean spirited brothers, who want to take the couple's meager possessions. One caveat: Amzat, the good brother, kills an innocent shepherd to accomplish his own aims, and this might bother more sensitive children. "Mezgaleten," a variation of "The Bremen Town Musicians," features a group of animals that does in a nasty wolf. The last, "Olympia, Cucol, and the Door," introduces a mother and son as foolish as any to be found in folktales. Despite their Italian origins, the stories lack a strong sense of place; still, the tales are robust and vital, and the characterizations sharply cut. [Emily Arnold] McCully's pen-and-ink drawings appear frequently and add zest. An excellent choice for reading aloud.

Kirkus Reviews

SOURCE: A review of *Amzat and His Brothers: Three Italian Tales,* in *Kirkus Reviews,* Vol. LXI, No. 8, April 15, 1993, p. 528.

A fine novelist passes along three stories told by Floriano Vecchi, born near Bologna (who heard them from his grandfather, b. 1850, who got them from his), explaining that these tales survive—with changes and additions in each generation—though Florian's village was destroyed in WW II. The stories—rich with folkloric themes, uncompromisingly unsentimental, and imbued with the kind of humor that makes the ironies of the human condition more endurable—are much enriched by Fox's wry, graceful retelling. In the title story, two angry men try to defraud their cheerful younger brother of the stony hilltop that's his meager patrimony; twice, Amzat tricks them harmlessly, but the third time his retribution is startlingly severe: he hoodwinks them into killing their wives and then themselves; an innocent bystander also perishes. "Mezgalten" is an intriguing variant of "The Bremen Town Musicians," lively with dialogue and incident. In the third tale, two village outcasts (neither too bright: "to Cucol a thought was . . . a beautiful cloud of meaning that he liked to study for a long time before he tried to make sense of it") end up with their persecutors' wealth largely because of Cucol's amusing stupidity. [Emily Arnold] McCully's frequent sepia drawings seem to have lost some delicacy in enlargement, but her caricatures complement Fox's wonderfully incisive depictions of human foibles. Not to be missed.

Nancy Vasilakis

SOURCE: A review of *Amzat and His Brothers: Three Italian Tales,* in *The Horn Book Magazine,* Vol. LXIX, No. 4, July-August, 1993, pp. 468-9.

Explaining in her preface how these stories have come down to her "as a kind of unwritten library that is passed from generation to generation," Paula Fox has added her own distinctive voice before sending them on their evolutionary way. In the first tale, clever Amzat and his wife foil his greedy brothers' schemes to cheat him out of his property. The second story is a variation of "The Bremen Town Musicians," in which a rooster, ewe, donkey, cat, and dog band together to kill a wolf who has tormented them. And in the final story, this one in the noodlehead tradition, the author introduces Olimpia and her simpleton son Cucol, for whom a thought was a "beautiful cloud of meaning that he liked to study for a long time." Hounded out of their home by their neighbors, they go off into the woods, where through a series of slapstick misadventures they end up with an enormous bag of gold. Mother and son live out the rest of their days in wealth and luxury, while those villagers who had been the cause of their exile are reduced to living in the hovel that the two had abandoned. Paula Fox has retained the darker elements that are as much a part of folktales in their original forms as the humor. Justice is imposed with harsh and obliterating finality. Amzat's revenge on his brothers results not only in their deaths but in the death of an innocent shepherd as well. Emily McCully's drawings, with their heavy deep brown lines and animated characters, pick up both aspects of these intriguing tales.

WESTERN WIND (1993)

Betsy Hearne

SOURCE: A review of *Western Wind,* in *Bulletin of the Center for Children's Books,* Vol. 47, No. 1, September, 1993, pp. 9-10.

Eleven-year-old Elizabeth Benedict believes the reason she's being sent to spend August with her grandmother in a primitive Maine island cottage is the newly born brother on whom her parents lavish attention. Paula Fox uses an isolated situation, as she has done before, to delve into a child's deepening awareness—here, of her grandmother's value as a person, a painter, and an elder facing death with dignity. Through interactions stripped bare by a simplified life devoid of electronic distractions or electric

conveniences, the two characters replace their formal connection with an affectionate respect that contrasts ironically with the one other family on the island, who comprise an odd mix of overprotection and underestimation of each other. Elizabeth, her grandmother, and the vulnerable young island boy whom Elizabeth rescues in more ways than one, are fine portrayals of individualistic independence at different stages of a life spectrum. Always spare, Fox's style especially suits this taut narrative, into which she slips similes that are frequent but consciously plain to suit the setting: a bay is "like a tray holding bits of land on its metal-blue surface"; "the family is really like a small country"; "birds swooped and rose like torn strips of paper"; Elizabeth sees "a yellow bar of sunshine like the light at the bottom of a closed door" or stifles "a laugh that was rising in her throat like a bubble in a bottle" or watches interest fading from someone's face "like light dimming in a room." These are primarily visual images—almost cubist like some of Gran's paintings—but they become less decorative than inherent to plot and pace, as when Elizabeth realizes that the cottage room seems "beautiful, almost like a person she had begun to love" or when the supporting posts in the same room, which "had suggested trees or columns to Elizabeth, now looked like the stout wooden bars of a cage" around the island family fearful of having lost their little boy. It's seductive to start quoting a good writer, but perhaps Fox summarizes her own book best: "Make it up," orders the boy in soliciting Elizabeth to play his imaginative game. "You just need a little bit of a thing to start a story. Pretty soon, there's everything!"

Karen Hartman

SOURCE: A review of *Western Wind,* in *Voice of Youth Advocates,* Vol. 16, No. 5, December, 1993, p. 290.

Eleven-year-old Elizabeth Benedict is angry and hurt. She thinks her parents, caught up in the excitement of a new baby, are sending her to visit her grandmother in Maine to get her out of the way. Gran, an artist, summers on a small island inhabited only by herself and the dysfunctional Herkimer family. Elizabeth has no time for Mr. and Mrs. Herkimer or their sullen fourteen-year-old daughter, but she is drawn to their son Aaron, a small boy Gran describes as a strange child whose parents are "awfully nervous about him."

Elizabeth slowly learns to enjoy the isolation and beauty of the island, the primitive living conditions, her Gran's stories of the past, and the company of Aaron. Elizabeth often takes Aaron with her on her walks around the island, and she seems to understand and tolerate his behavior much better than his own family. It isn't until Aaron is lost and Gran and Elizabeth help the Herkimers hunt for him that Elizabeth finds out the truth about why she was sent to spend a month with her grandmother. The strain of hunting for Aaron is too much for Gran, she becomes very ill and sends Elizabeth for help. Mr. Herkimer calls the Coast Guard and then tells Elizabeth the truth—her grandmother has serious heart problems. Gran ends up in the hospital and Elizabeth realizes her parents sent her to Maine because Gran is dying. Elizabeth learns to accept and love her new brother, and she learns just how special her Gran was—a woman who shared her memories and who gave Elizabeth unconditional love. Fox has written a heartwarming story for middle school readers. Readers will relate to Elizabeth's confusion about her parents' intentions and her feelings for a rather eccentric grandmother.

Maeve Visser Knoth

SOURCE: A review of *Western Wind,* in *The Horn Book Magazine,* Vol. LXX, No. 2, March-April, 1994, pp. 198-9.

Elizabeth feels she has been exiled from her home in Massachusetts to spend the summer with her grandmother on a tiny island off the Maine coast. Since the birth of a baby brother, which Elizabeth declares is "disgusting" at her parents' advanced ages, Elizabeth has felt replaced and unwanted. Reluctantly, she finds herself at her grandmother's primitive cottage, where she must spend a summer with paintings, poetry, and a rather unfathomable old woman. Gradually Elizabeth comes to appreciate her grandmother, and as she observes the Herkimers, the only other family on the island, she learns about the different kinds of family love. She develops a friendship with Aaron, the young, overprotected boy in the Herkimer family, and when Aaron runs away in the middle of a terrible storm, Elizabeth and her grandmother join the frantic search. Though Elizabeth finds the terrified boy, her grandmother collapses from the strain, and Elizabeth belatedly learns that her grandmother is very ill. She then realizes that the summer was arranged not to send her away, but to give her important time with her grandmother before her death. *Western Wind* is a quiet story of relationships and character. Elizabeth and Aaron both grow through their friendship and their exposure to another, different family. By the end of her month on the island Elizabeth has learned a great deal more about both her grandmother and herself. The small summer island is another central character in the book—moody, stark, bewitching, and integral to the events as they unfold. Fox's beautiful prose gives a rich dimension to the story about the struggle to adjust to change within a family and within oneself.

Cyrisse Jaffee

SOURCE: A review of *Western Wind,* in *The New York Times Book Review,* April 10, 1994, p. 35.

To her dismay, 11-year-old Elizabeth Benedict has been sent to stay with Gran for a month by her parents, who have just brought home a new baby. Not surprisingly, Elizabeth is resentful and sullen, and the prospect of spending August with her "unpredictable and ungrandmotherly" Gran only adds to her unhappiness.

Gran—Cora Ruth Benedict—a painter whose attitudes and words are often as sharp and pointed as the rocky land-

scape she loves, has left the picturesque but tourist-ridden charm of Camden, Me., to settle off the coast on rustic Pring Island. Unsentimental, proud and opinionated, Gran is a stickler for proper English usage, honesty and clean living.

So Elizabeth must grapple not only with the lack of electricity and indoor plumbing and with Gran's silences, but also with loneliness and boredom, fueled by the anger she feels about being abandoned by her parents. Meeting the only other family on the island—John and Helen Herkimer and their children, Deirdre and Aaron—doesn't seem to offer any solace, either.

Deirdre is sarcastic and unfriendly, and Aaron is a precocious, hyperactive child whose antics earn him a lot of attention. (It's no coincidence that the dynamics of the Herkimer family echo those of Elizabeth's.)

It is Aaron who animates the story. Like Elizabeth, he knows that his behavior allenates other people. "Sometimes when someone hugs me," he tells her, "I feel like an eagle has got me in its claws." It is the boy's disappearance one foggy night that reveals and tests the intricate ties—and love—that have bound these people together.

Despite the weakness of its minor characters and its somewhat melodramatic plot, *Western Wind,* in the tradition of the best young-adult fiction, manages to capture the essence of Elizabeth's transformation from a self-absorbed adolescent to a more tolerant, loving person. The lessons she learns are about making connections, which, as the skillful Paula Fox eloquently demonstrates, is what life, and art too, are all about. "We cannot forswear our integral connections with other people," Ms. Fox said in 1974 when she accepted the Newbery Medal for her novel *The Slave Dancer.* "I write to discover, over and over again, my connections with myself, with others. Each book deepens the question. It does not answer it." Within its familiar framework, *Western Wind* will gently lead the reader along the unsteady path toward discovery.

THE EAGLE KITE (1995, British edition as *The Gathering Darkness*)

Hazel Rochman

SOURCE: A review of *The Eagle Kite,* in *Booklist,* Vol. 91, No. 11, February 1, 1995, p. 1003.

Liam's father is dying of AIDS. He got it from a blood transfusion, Liam's mother says. My father has cancer, Liam tells his girlfriend. But Liam remembers what he has made himself forget, that more than two years earlier he had seen his father embrace a young man on the beach. Now, through the long, dreary months of the illness, while his father lives alone in a rented cottage on the shore, Liam goes through a tangled mess of denial, anger, shame, grief, and empathy. As in Fox's *Village by the Sea,* there's an unkind relative, an aunt who knows she's mean and is helpless to be otherwise. And as in **One-Eyed Cat**, the sick parent is flawed, funny, gentle. Fox writes in ordinary words about universal things: love and death and lies and also time and memory—how they seem and what they are. The story confronts our deepest fears: what if the scarecrow beggar out there on the street, the statistic in sex-ed class, the demon of the howling mob came right into our comfortable home? Scenes burn in your memory: that embrace on the beach, the suppressed fury in the pauses of conversation. Fox avoids nothing about the dying and the anguish of survival. The plain note Philip leaves for his wife and son says it all: "My two dears. There's hardly anything left of me."

Claudia Morrow

SOURCE: A review of *The Eagle Kite,* in *School Library Journal,* Vol. 41, No. 4, April, 1995, pp. 150, 153.

Liam, a high school freshman, learns that his father is dying of AIDS. Suddenly, his comfortable family is in pieces, and his father has gone to live in a seashore cottage two hours from the family's city apartment. Distanced from both parents by secrets each of them seems compelled to keep, Liam remembers having seen his father embrace a young man years before—a friend, his father had said. In the remainder of the book, Liam and his parents wrestle with truths that encompass not just disappointment and betrayal, but intense love. This is far more than a problem novel. AIDS is integral to the plot, the issue is handled well, and the character who has AIDS is portayed sympathetically, but the book's scope is broader than that. It is a subtly textured exploration of the emotions of grief that will appeal to the same young people drawn to Mollie Hunter's *A Sound of Chariots* and Cynthia Rylant's *Missing May*. Dramatic tension is palpable, sustained in part by a dazed, timeless quality in Liam's slow reckoning with loss. The characters are neither idealized nor demonized, and Fox's take on Liam as a confused, seethingly angry, tight-lipped, surreptitiously tender teenager has the ring of authenticity. Some in the target audience may find the action too slow or the mood too dark, but those who persevere will be rewarded by the novel's truthfulness.

W. Keith McCoy

SOURCE: A review of *The Eagle Kite,* in *Voice of Youth Advocates,* Vol. 18, No. 2, June, 1995, pp. 93-4.

Liam Cormac's dad has AIDS. It's hard enough being thirteen and learning every day about the new you. Now he has to learn about the father he thought he knew, and understand what has become different. Liam has to understand his mother, too, and how this has changed her and other people and how AIDS changes their attitudes.

The time covered by **The Eagle Kite** is a brief, but intense, portion of one young boy's life. With Liam, we experience the betrayals, the estrangement, and the anger

that goes with the sudden knowledge that your father is not the man you thought you knew, that you know the truth behind the lies, and that you have lied to yourself, as much as any of the adults have. The illusions of childhood always have to be given up, but we want to give them up gently, not have them broken as savagely as Liam breaks his kite.

Fox's spare prose enhances the emotions that are buffeting the Cormacs. It is as bleak as only the disease and its wake can be, yet the story is not without a sense of completion and recovery at the end. Even though Philip (the father) dies, Liam and his mother have learned to love him again. They know that he will still live for them, not as the sick man of the past two years, but as the spirit that attracted them once and always.

Nancy Vasilakis

SOURCE: A review of *The Eagle Kite,* in *The Horn Book Magazine,* Vol. LXXI, No. 4, September-October, 1995, pp. 608-9.

Liam Cormac was ten years old when he saw his father on the beach embracing another man. He has never spoken of the incident and has repressed the memory of it—until now, in his first year of high school, when he learns that his father is dying of AIDS. The family, unable to confront the truth of Philip Cormac's homosexuality, enters a period of denial and individual withdrawal. Philip leaves their apartment and moves into a small cabin on the New Jersey shore. Liam and his mother speak little to each other and visit Philip once a month. The time spent with him is awkward, silent, and ultimately unfruitful. Liam makes frequent treks to the public library where he furtively hunts up information about the disease. He suppresses his questions and fears and knowledge from everyone, and his resentment grows until he feels compelled to hurl at his father the full force of his anger. He travels alone to his father's cabin on the day before Thanksgiving, and the two finally begin to talk. To his surprise, Liam learns that his father feels as powerless as he, and that he is in the midst of his own search for understanding. Philip's dying becomes a time of dignity and reaffirmation for all three members of the family. Paula Fox has taken on a difficult subject and suffused it with a beauty of form and style that is distinctively her own. The evolution of Liam's emotions from voiceless anger and an abiding sense of loss to acceptance and love, a journey paralleled by his mother's, is described with painstaking honesty. This will be a hard novel for teens to absorb, but well worth the effort.

Judith James

SOURCE: A review of *The Gathering Darkness,* in *Reading Time,* Vol. XL, No. III, 1996, p. 34.

This short five-chapter story covers a range of emotions and themes. The illustration on the cover captures the gloom and pathos in the lives of thirteen-year old Liam Cormac, and his parents Philip and Katherine. Philip has AIDS, and the story deals with the disintegration of the family as Philip is dying, and the resolution of the hurt and trauma suffered by his wife and son. Especially his son, when he discovers his father's illness is not caused by a contaminated blood transfusion, and he observes his father's meeting with his lover.

This is an honest, painful book about adults and homosexual relations, as seen from a young adolescent's view point. The story arouses many emotions but does not overindulge in sentimentality—although Liam and his mother have a level of maturity not always found in the real world when they accept Philip's sexuality at the end of the story. Paula Fox writes very well, allowing the emotional turmoil and tension of this family to come through.

Additional coverage of Fox's life and career is contained in the following sources published by Gale Research: *Authors and Artists for Young Adults,* Vol. 3; *Contemporary Authors New Revision Series,* Vol 36; *Contemporary Literary Criticism,* Vols. 2, 8; *Dictionary of Literary Biography,* Vol. 52; *Junior DISCovering Authors (CD-ROM); Major Authors and Illustrators for Children and Young Adults; Major Twentieth-Century Writers;* and *Something about the Author,* Vols. 50, 81.

Lee Bennett Hopkins

1938-

American poet and author of fiction, nonfiction, and picture books; editor.

Major works include *Mama* (1977), *Surprises: An I Can Read Book of Poems* (selected by Hopkins, 1984), *Voyages: Poems by Walt Whitman* (selected by Hopkins, 1988), *Good Rhymes, Good Times* (1995), *Been to Yesterdays: Poems of a Life* (1995).

INTRODUCTION

Hopkins is a prolific and respected poet and anthologist who has also contributed to the genres of fiction and nonfiction. As a poet, he characteristically addresses the thoughts, feelings, and activities of children in simple, direct poems that use the formats of metric rhyme and free and concrete verse. Although his original work receives positive critical attention, Hopkins is perhaps best known as the compiler of a variety of thematic collections that represent classic and contemporary American poetry. As with his own verse, Hopkins's anthologies are praised for their strong child appeal; addressing such subjects as animals, holidays, the circus, urban living, and farm life, the collections are often noted for introducing young people to poetry in an accessible and enjoyable manner. Hopkins includes rarely anthologized, but familiar, poems and verse in his collections. He also creates whole anthologies on particular poets, such as Langston Hughes, Carl Sandburg, Walt Whitman, and Harry Behn. In these works, Hopkins focuses on the poems that he feels will speak most directly to a young audience; the volumes also include his prose introductions to the poets. Most critics consider Hopkins's anthologies to be both unusual and inviting, and they consistently praise the selection of material in them as well as the respect for the poets that his books reflect. Throughout his career, Hopkins has worked with a number of well-known illustrators such as Ann Grifalconi, Lisl Weil, Tomie dePaola, Ben Shecter, Fritz Eichenberg, Hilary Knight, and Charles Mikolaycak, and his works are acknowledged for the complementary nature of their texts and pictures. Called "a true master collector" by Kathleen Whalin and "the indefatigable anthologizer" by Liz Rosenberg, Hopkins is regarded as an authentic champion of American poetry for children. A critic in *Juvenile Miscellany* notes that Hopkins's "immersion in poetry, past and present, text and illustration, places him at the heart of children's literature."

Biographical Information

Born in Scranton, Pennsylvania, Hopkins spent most of his early years in urban Newark, New Jersey. He once noted that his only exposure to reading was "movie mag-

azines, comic books, and an occasional adult novel that my mother passed on to me." Hopkins was the oldest child in the family, and he spent most of his days and nights working at odd jobs to help his family financially. Although Hopkins was often absent from school, he met a teacher, Mrs. Ethel Kite McLaughlin, who "introduced me to two things that had given me direction and hope—the love of reading and the theatre." It was Mrs. McLaughlin who inspired Hopkins to become a teacher. He attended Newark State Teachers College (now Kean College of New Jersey), majored in education, and after graduation became a sixth grade teacher in Fair Lawn, New Jersey, where he taught for six years.

Hopkins received his master's degree from the Bank Street College of Education in New York and became a resource teacher, setting up special programs and classes. In trying to help fourth through sixth graders with reading problems, Hopkins discovered that poetry was the solution. "I began a love affair with the genre, reading as much of it as I could find," he said. When his term as a resource teacher ended, he became a consultant for Bank Street's Learning Resource Center in Harlem, began submitting articles to professional journals, and published a successful book on language arts enrichment for disadvantaged elementary school children. Inspired by the death of Langston Hughes, whose works he had often shared with his students, Hopkins compiled *Don't You Turn Back: Poems by Langston Hughes* (1969), his first anthology for children. After leaving Bank Street, Hopkins worked as a curriculum, educational, and literature consultant for several publishing companies while serving in such professional organizations as the National Council of Teachers of English and the International Reading Association and speaking to children and educators around the country. He also hosted *Zebra Wings,* a fifteen-part television series that describes different styles of writing. However, his writing and editing is still of utmost importance to Hopkins—"Writing," he has noted, "is my life, my love"— as is his interest in poetry. "I strongly believe," he once wrote, "that poetry should flow freely in our children's lives; it should come as naturally as breathing, for nothing—*no thing*—can ring and rage through hearts and minds as does this body of literature."

Major Works

Although known primarily as a poet and anthologist, Hopkins received favorable responses for his first two works of autobiographical fiction, *I Loved Rose Ann* (1976) a two-part story in picture book form about a one-sided romance, and *Mama,* a novel for middle graders about a boy whose single mother is a kleptomaniac. Hopkins is especially lauded for his characterizations of the title character of *Mama,* a brassy but devoted and hard-working parent, and her concerned son, who like his mother is never named. A critic in *Publishers Weekly* referred to *Mama* as Hopkins's "not-to-be-missed first novel," and Zena Sutherland wrote, "You'll remember Mama." Hopkins is also the author of *Mama and Her Boys* (1981), a sequel in which he names his characters— Trudy Kipness and her sons, narrator Chris and preschooler Mark—and describes how the boys try to find their mother an appropriate suitor. Of his collections featuring the poems of individual poets, *Voyages: Poems by Walt Whitman* was particularly well-received. In this work, Hopkins chooses fifty-three poems and excerpts from the poet's oeuvre and organizes them in sections representing Whitman's youth, his travels, the people with whom he came in contact, and his feelings on aging and death. Considered an especially fine introduction to Whitman for teenage readers, *Voyages* is lauded by Nancy Vasilakis as a "well-conceived and elegantly produced anthology. . . . The volume brings joyfully to life the poetic vision of the archetypal American poet." Hopkins is also highly regarded as the compiler of two collections of poetry for the very young child, *Surprises: An I Can Read Book of Poems* and *More Surprises: An I Can Read Book* (1987). Part of a popular series for beginning readers, the volumes present short, easy-to-read poems about the everyday lives of children in both rhymed and unrhymed formats. A reviewer in *Publishers Weekly* commented that *Surprises* is such "a good idea that it's a wonder this is the first of its kind." In their assessment of *More Surprises,* a critic in *Kirkus Reviews* demanded,

"Let there be more anthologies of this sort for young readers!"

Recently, Hopkins has written three books—an informational book and two volumes of poetry—that reflect his own life. In the picture book autobiography *The Writing Bug* (1992), he describes his early life as well as what inspired him to become a writer, while in a second picture book, *Good Rhymes, Good Times,* he collects the original work he has published over the last twenty years. A critic in *Publishers Weekly* referred to *Good Rhymes* as a "joyous collection" and added that "Hopkins brings freshness and immediacy to his subjects." With *Been to Yesterdays: Poems of a Life,* Hopkins described the events of his thirteenth year, which culminated in his decision to become a writer, in twenty-eight poems of three or four words per line. Reviewers note both the emotionality and economy of the poems and find the collection an especially affecting work; Kathleen Whalin called *Been to Yesterdays* "a rare gift, a careful exploration of one life that illumines the lives of all who read it" while Susan Dove Lempke noted that Hopkins achieved "in very few words what many prose authors take chapters to tell." In addition to his poetry collections, picture books, and stories, Hopkins is the author of an informational book on African American history, a book of riddles about food, and several books for adults; in this area, Hopkins is well regarded for his books on teaching and language arts as well as for compiling two collections of interviews with popular authors and illustrators of children's literature.

Awards

Several of Hopkins's works have been chosen as notable books by the American Library Association and the National Council for Social Studies; he has also received several child-selected awards. In 1980, Hopkins was named an honorary doctor of law from Kean College and received the Phi Delta Kappa Educational Leadership Award. He was given the International Reading Association Manhattan Council Literary Award in 1983 and was named the National Children's Book Week Poet in 1985. In 1989, Hopkins received the Silver Medallion from the University of Southern Mississippi for his lifetime contribution to children's literature.

AUTHOR'S COMMENTARY

Lee Bennett Hopkins

SOURCE: "Report of a Poet-in-Residence," in *English Journal,* Vol. 62, No. 2, February, 1973, pp. 239-43.

The Coordinator of Creative Writing Programs for the New Jersey State Council on the Arts, Debra Stein, approached me to serve as Poet-in-Residence at the Wayne Valley High School in Wayne, New Jersey. This program is a part of a statewide project that brings poets and writers into the New Jersey schools to introduce literature and teach writing. Most of my work in the field of education has been with elementary-aged students in Grades Kindergarten through 6. Approaching students of high school age was indeed a challenge. Since many students, regardless of their age, approach poetry with distaste, I decided to start from the very beginning—going back to the poetry of childhood and within four weeks' time, one day a week, continue on "through life" to poetry written by adults for adult audiences. . . .

Over the four-week period spent with the students and their teachers, I was able to go beyond the prescribed curriculum, bringing to students a wide variety of poems and poets. During each session we discussed just about every type of form from couplets to free verse; from short verse forms (haiku, cinquain, sijo) to experimental forms (concrete poetry, found poetry). I could best describe the total experience as an opening-up process in that students were exposed to a multitude of types of poetry. In addition just the exposure to a living, grown poet in the classroom opened the avenue to the writing world for the students.

Louisa Dette, one of the teachers whose sophomore English classes I visited, commented that it was surprising to see the boys in her classes writing poetry, for poetry is a subject for which they rarely expressed much enthusiasm.

The experience was a rich one for me. I talked about poetry, read poems by the score, saturated the students with words, thoughts, and images such as they never heard before.

The total experience was not all positive. Several teachers and students did not agree with me on many counts. Several hold fast to the belief that the only way of poetry is to dissect it word-for-word to get full meaning, full impact. Several disagreed with me when I talked about getting master poets' works into the heads and hearts of the very youngest child. Why shouldn't a child of five or six be read some of the poems by William Carlos Williams, Langston Hughes, or Carl Sandburg? "Nonsense!" responded several participants. "You have to be able to analyze and dissect these poets' words and thoughts before a poem can have true meaning."

And I replied, "Nonsense!" back to them. "All you have to do to love a poem is to *feel* it. Then it's yours—forever."

In summary, the students searched their minds and hearts, they opened up without and within, they thought, they wrote, they shared, they expressed a spectrum of emotion—most were with me all the way. And I am positive that many will think of poetry as something more than memorizing a Shakespeare sonnet or worrying whether they'll pass the vocabulary test of the meanings of hidden words and phrases from lines written by Ben Jonson or Yeats. I gave them poetry—a fresh look—and many will

remember for a long, long time to come that poetry is pleasure!

Lee Bennett Hopkins

SOURCE: "Immersed in Verse," in *CBC Features,* Vol. 42, No. 1, January-June, 1989, p. 7.

I chuckled upon receiving a letter from the Children's Book Council, inviting me to write this piece for *Features.* At that very moment, I was immersed in verse, completing columns for "Poetry Place," the feature I have done monthly for *Instructor Magazine* since 1980. Rarely does a day go by when I am not in the midst of reading and selecting poetry for children and young adults.

I have taught elementary school for six years and have participated in various aspects of the world of education for nearly thirty years. Most of my anthologies stem from past teaching experiences and are the types of collections I wish I had access to for sharing with my students when I was in the classroom every day. Currently, my frequent and productive associations with today's classroom teachers have helped me to identify what I think is needed in the marketplace.

Since the late 1960s, I have done many collections based on specific themes. It was in the classroom that I realized that poetry can be used effectively to turn on above-average, average, and reluctant readers throughout the grades. And, oh, what it can do to bolster the self-concept of children everywhere.

Children's likes and dislikes depend on the type of poetry they are exposed to from the earliest age. In recent years the publication of books of light verse such as Shel Silverstein's volumes has opened doors to poetry for countless youngsters.

Few people understand the lengthy process one goes through in putting together an anthology. My books start with a theme. The first step is to research the topic to see if or how it has been done before. Then, the long, long process of selecting poems begins, reading every book of poems by past and contemporary authors from A (Arnold Adoff) to Z (Charlotte Zolotow)! To compile a collection I easily read thousands of verses before I begin to make selections.

Balance is important in an anthology. I want many voices to reach children's ears so I rarely use more than three works by the same poet. I also try to envision each volume as a stage play or film, having a definite beginning, middle and end. The right flow is a necessity for me. Sometimes a word at the end of a work will lead into the next selection. I want my collections to read like a short story or novel—not just a hodgepodge of works thrown together aimlessly.

My files for *Dinosaurs* date back over ten years. Here, my own concept got in my way. Doing endless research,

I found a host of light verse about the beasts of yore. But I knew this wasn't the approach for me. My concept for *Dinosaurs* was to present a nonfiction account, encompassing their earliest days on earth through to their extinction. Few works were available to meet this need.

Over the years I have nurtured a group of people who are scattered throughout the country and who I fondly call my "take-out poets." I write to each of them, telling them exactly what I am looking for. They usually come through. Thus, *Dinosaurs* contains eight specially commissioned works never before published.

There is a method to my madness in pursuing these writers: it brings fresh voices to readers and, it gives these writers the chance to become recognized and have their works reprinted. I am always in search of new talents because there are so few poets writing for children. I want to encourage as many as I can. I have a great sense of pride when the right poems come to me in the mail.

Once a collection comes together, it goes to an editor for suggestions. I listen to editors and appreciate any comments they might have to make a collection the best it can be.

Once approved, an artist is selected for the book, and I begin the long permissions hunt. Each poem used must be cleared with the original copyright holders and paid for. This process easily takes six months, and involves an enormous amount of time and the back-and-forth exchange of letters, contracts, etc. From when "the idea" strikes, it is well over two to three years before a book is published.

Some books happen in curious ways. One afternoon, during lunch with my editor, Charlotte Zolotow at Harper & Row, I said to her, "The 'I Can Read' series has been in existence since 1957. How come there has never been an 'I Can Read' book of poetry?"

Charlotte thought this was a viable idea—one no one had ever proposed before—and that I should do it.

Several weeks later when I received the guidelines for an "I Can Read" book, I knew *why* no one ever had done it. No poem could be more than thirteen lines, including the title, and no line could contain more than thirty-six characters, including spaces and punctuation marks! This was indeed a challenging project. A simple idea which took me over two-and-a-half years to complete.

With the success of *Surprises,* I was on my way to two more "I Can Read" volumes—*More Surprises,* and the forthcoming *Questions*.

Side by Side came about via the staff at Simon & Schuster. Grace Clarke had arranged for Hilary Knight and me to have lunch to discuss the possibility of doing a 96-page, full-color volume for young readers. Hilary and I became instant friends. The book was painless, a delight from start to finish.

Side by Side also gave me the opportunity to do a book that I had long wanted to do—a volume combining the work of past masters such as Robert Frost, Edward Lear and Lewis Carroll, with poems of such contemporary greats as Myra Cohn Livingston, Eve Merriam, and Aileen Fisher, as well as newer voices. Here was the chance to include such classics as Carroll's "The Walrus and the Carpenter," Lear's "An Alphabet," and Follen's "The Three Little Kittens," placed side by side with contemporary voices and thoughts.

For me, any day without a poem is just another day on the calendar. *Every* day is poetry time! So—happy poetry-ing to each and every one of you.

GENERAL COMMENTARY

Anthony L. Manna

SOURCE: "In Pursuit of the Crystal Image: Lee Bennett Hopkins's Poetry Anthologies," in *Children's Literature Association Quarterly,* Vol. 10, No. 2, Summer, 1985, pp. 80-2.

In his introduction to Paul Janeczko's anthology of modern poetry, Lee Bennett Hopkins pays tribute to the unique inward perception that poets bring to everyday experiences:

> The poet takes the ordinary and makes it extraordinary, revealing life, translating and distilling visions of experience to each individual. The poet causes us to think and wonder and feel more and more intensely until we begin to see life as a crystal image.

As one of America's most prolific anthologists of poetry for young people, Hopkins has spent his career trying to make the crystal image accessible to children. He has published over thirty anthologies since 1969, when *Don't You Turn Back,* his acclaimed selection of Langston Hughes' poems, appeared on the market. Hopkins has also hosted and been consultant for "Zebra Wings," a fifteen-part Educational Television program that involves children in creative writing; and for teachers of poetry he has written two vigorous and practical texts, *Pass the Poetry, Please* and *Let Them Be Themselves,* the latter a result of his experiences teaching writing to children in Harlem. In addition, Hopkins' column, "Poetry Place," is a monthly feature in *Instructor* magazine.

Although Hopkins offers children a generous selection of mostly short, mostly contemporary, and mostly American poetry, his anthologies include highly cadenced nursery and Mother Goose rhymes, zany nonsense, and light verse of varying quality. In fact, the poems Hopkins selects, particularly the ones he chooses for very young children, are a surprisingly mixed lot, including both technically sound, emotionally honest pieces and predictable and sentimental verses that are an insult to the child's sense of wonder. On the one hand, Hopkins has a fine ear for poetry that reveals what Helen M. Hill has described [in "How To Tell a Sheep from a Goat—and Why It Matters" in *The Horn Book Magazine*] as "a wholeness or soundness of thought, perfection of technique, and sincerity of tone," which characterize poetic integrity; on the other hand, he is often attracted to poems that contain such banal language, such forced rhythm and rhyme, and such deadening piety that they are a perfect fit for the category of poetry that Kornei Chukovskii, as cited in Haviland's *Children & Poetry,* reserved for poems that could "cripple [children's] aesthetic taste, disfigure their literary training . . . condition them to a slovenly attitude to the written word, and block off [their] appreciation of genuine poetic works."

Consider, for example, Hopkins' popular six-part holiday poetry series: *Hey How for Halloween!, Sing Hey for Christmas Day, Good Morning to You, Valentine, Beat the Drum, Independence Day has Come, Merrily Comes Our Harvest In,* and *Easter Buds are Springing,* all published by Harcourt. In *Halloween,* Hopkins devised a format that has remained consistent throughout the series: abundant illustrations in traditional colors, lavender in *Easter,* for example, and amber in *Harvest;* approximately twenty brief, frequently anthologized pieces mostly by modern and contemporary American poets; and a loose arrangement that generally moves from anticipation for what the holiday promises to a focus on the special feelings and incidents that distinguish it.

The problem begins with the design of the holiday anthologies. The entire series lays out such an overwhelming visual feast that there is little room to savor the few good poems which deserve special attention. In *Halloween,* for example, Janet McCaffery's dramatic black and white sketches crowd the small pages and envelop the poems, leaving far too little space for the reader's imagination to flourish under the influence of e. e. cummings' spirited word play in his untitled poem which begins "his whist/little ghostthings" or Myra Cohn Livingston's "The House at the Corner" in which the subject and form of the poem are inextricably connected:

> The house at the corner
> is cold gray stone,
> where the trees and windows
> crack and groan,
> so I run past
> fast
> when I'm all alone.

Furthermore, the tone and content of the illustrations often conflict with, rather than enhance, many of the selections. In *Harvest,* Schecter's uninspired pen-and-ink illustrations of a large cast of Pilgrim children and adults, many of them with silly facial expressions, trivialize the few serious selections, such as Myra Cohn Livingston's "First Thanksgiving," an eloquent reminiscence about a time of peace and camaraderie, and Aileen Fisher's "All in a Word," a celebration in rhymed couplets of the sights,

sounds, and smells associated with Thanksgiving. These pictures translate the poem's images into literal, rather than interpretive, visual impressions, and when a selection is awkward and contrived, this only draws attention to its lack of substance. Such is the case with Alice Crowell Hoffman's "November's Gift":

> November is a lady
>   In a plain gray coat
> That's very closely buttoned
>   Up around her throat.
> And after she's been roaming
>   All around the town,
> She reaches in her pocket,
>   Deep, deep down,
> Then pulls out a present,
>   And with laughter gay,
> Says to everybody,
>   "Here's Thanksgiving Day."

Here, the poem's inappropriate rhythm, facile rhymes, and condescending tone are punctuated by Shecter's facing, full-page illustration of a larger-than-life female figure who, as a personification of November, rises high above a boy and a miniature town. The result is an altogether monotonous experience that makes no demands on the reader's imagination.

Hopkins' most recent works constitute an eclectic potpourri of topical anthologies that further reveal his determination to provide children with poems they can immediately relate to, often sacrificing technical skill to relevance. Just as profusely illustrated as the holiday poetry series, these recent anthologies focus on a variety of topics, some threadbare from overuse, others somewhat appealing if not notably original in concept: children's bedtime rituals and nighttime concerns (*Go to Bed!*); the habits and habitats of fairy folk and wee creatures (*Elves, Fairies, and Gnomes*); the ordinary and whimsical happenings that occur throughout the course of a typical day (*Morning Noon and Nighttime, Too*); the textures of experiences that have been filtered through the child's perspective (*By Myself*); the infectious and exuberant energy of the circus (*Circus! Circus!*) and prayers, lullabies, and dreams that celebrate life and living (*and God Bless Me*).

Hopkins has also gathered a cycle of poems about nature (*To Look at Anything, Moments,* and *The Sky is Full of Song*) and a thin cluster of poems about a variety of animals (*My Mane Catches the Wind, I Am the Cat,* and *A Dog's Life*), all of these marketed for the eight to twelve set. Further, *A Song in Stone,* Hopkins' tribute to the uniqueness of city experiences, was named a Notable Children's Book of 1983 by the American Library Association, an honor he received for *Don't You Turn Back,* his anthology of Langston Hughes' poems, and, more recently, for *Rainbows are Made,* a thoughtfully arranged selection of Carl Sandburg's poems accompanied by Fritz Eichenberg's, though occasional, wood engravings.

In those rare instances when Hopkins is in charge of poems

that combine fresh ideas, rhymes and rhythms appropriate to the topic and mood, and images that jolt the senses, he orchestrates his material and orders it into a distinctive pattern that takes shape under the guidance of the tone and emotional characteristics of the poems rather than a superficial concern for their topical similarities. In *Rainbows are Made* he uses several of Sandburg's highly metaphoric "Tentative (First Model) Definitions of Poetry" as section headings, allowing them to serve as frames and structures for serious and witty poems about people, language, ordinary objects, nature, and, in the final section, about the sea and the night, topics which though never directly filtered through the child's point of view are charged with childlike perspective. The effect is a tight thematic focus, a center of attention from which Hopkins controls the pieces as though he were overseeing the theme and its variations in a satisfying musical score. In the section reserved for poems about ordinary objects, Sandburg's definition ("Poetry is a shuffling of boxes of illusions buckled with a strap of facts") sets the stage for selections that interestingly play with appearance and reality. "Paper II" is a case in point:

> I write what I know on one side of the paper and
> what I don't on the other.
> Fire likes dry paper and wet paper laughs at fire.
> Empty paper sacks say, "Put something in me,
> what are we waiting for?"
> Paper sacks packed to the limit say, "We hope we
> don't burst."
> Paper people like to meet other paper people.

Rainbows also works because of its design. Since one of Eichenberg's somewhat surreal wood engravings precedes each section, the illustrations help to establish mood and to define a section's topic without getting in the way of the poems themselves. The selections are therefore given the space to breathe on large, uncrowded pages.

Like *Rainbows, A Song in Stone* is notable for its effective design and the enticement of selections that demonstrate a variety of inventive rhythm and rhyme patterns consistent with the moods and feelings evoked and the memorable experiences treated in the poems. *The Sky is Full of Song,* which was chosen by *School Library Journal* as a Best Book of Spring, 1983, is substantial in what it has to offer despite its thinness. A cycle of thirty-eight brief poems that highlight, with increasing intensity, various incidents that distinguish each of the seasons, *Sky* is a combination of clear, open pages, bold print, sharp, full-color linocuts that cleverly enhance the selections, and an array of highly compressed, colorful poems like Judith Thurman's "Rags":

> The night wind
> rips a cloud sheet
> into rags,
>
> then rubs, rubs
> the October moon
> until it shines
> like a brass doorknob.

Equally effective is David Ignatow's "The City," a spare little piece with a delightfully defiant tone:

> If flowers want to grow
> right out of the concrete sidewalk cracks
> I'm going to bend down to smell them.

The fact that Hopkins is capable of putting together a lucid and substantial anthology that can both challenge and delight the child's curiosity and imagination makes it that much more difficult to accept the glaring inconsistencies and lack of control which permeate so much of his work, as though he were only occasionally aware of Kornei Chukovskii's belief that children's poetry "must have the skill, the virtuosity, the technical soundness of poetry for adults." Thus, in *Morning Noon and Nighttime, Too* versifiers such as Steven Kroll, Bobbi Katz, Margaret Hillert, the team of Stacy Jo Crossen and Natalie Anne Covell, and Hopkins himself, some of them Hopkins' favorites who appear in several of his anthologies, detract from the authentic sentiments of David McCord ("This is My Rock"), Felice Holman ("Things That Happen"), and Judith Thurman ("Zebra"), who write not so much as children but from an enduring awareness of childhood, an ingredient too often lacking in Hopkins' anthologies.

In "Poetry Unfettered," noted British poet and educator Leonard Clark reminded us that because poetry has the potential to heighten children's awareness and to enhance the development of their personality, discriminating selection is essential when it comes to choosing poems for them. Drawing attention to the anthologist's responsibility, Clark wrote, "The importance of choice cannot be overstressed. What we should aim at is to choose poems which, because of their evocative nature and economy of statement, reveal the world to children, as it was in the beginning, is now and ever shall be." What must matter as well is the technical soundness of the poems we offer children, for the power and endurance of a poem's revelations depend on the poet's skill with language. As Helen M. Hill pointed out in *The Horn Book Magazine,* "The better the poem, the better the experience . . .". Since Lee Bennett Hopkins reaches such a large audience of children with the poems he continues to select, he too needs to be reminded that children deserve much more than a flawed crystal image.

TITLE COMMENTARY

📖   ***DON'T YOU TURN BACK: POEMS BY LANGSTON HUGHES* (selected by Lee Bennett Hopkins, 1969)**

Kirkus Reviews

SOURCE: A review of *Don't You Turn Back,* in *Kirkus Reviews,* Vol. XXXVII, No. 23, December 1, 1969, p. 1270.

Perhaps the greatest tribute to Langston Hughes is not the publication of this book, although it is a fine collection, but the fact that so many of the poems will be familiar from other anthologies (at least three have given titles to books: *I Am the Darker Brother; Hold Fast to Dreams; Black Like Me*). Loosely grouped by theme (Negro-ness, hopes, the sea), the poems come from several periods of his life although there is nothing representing the querulous confusion of his last years: e.g. "The Negro Speaks of Rivers," "The Dream Keeper," "Daybreak in Alabama" and "Snail" are here but "Ballad of the Landlord" and "Black Panther" are not. However, this does include some lesser known hymnlike poems and a few in dialect, such as the conversational "Baby": "Albert! / Hey, Albert! / Don't you play in dat road. / You see dem trucks / A goin' by. / One run ovah you / An' you die. / Albert, don't you play in dat road." Ann Grifalconi's woodcuts, in handsome brick red and black, convey both sense and essence. ***Don't You Turn Back***—look ahead.

Booklist

SOURCE: A review of *Don't You Turn Back*, in *Booklist*, Vol. 66, No. 13, March 1, 1970, p. 847.

According to the editor, who read the works of Langston Hughes to students of all ages during his travels around the country as consultant to Bank Street College of Education's Harlem Center, the 45 poems contained in this volume are those which evoked special feelings from young listeners and readers. The short poems, enhanced by [Ann Grifalconi's] striking two-color woodcuts, are presented in an inviting format.

Zena Sutherland

SOURCE: A review of *Don't You Turn Back*, in *Saturday Review*, Vol. LIII, No. 19, May 9, 1970, p. 47.

Working with inner-city children in Harlem schools, Lee Hopkins discovered that they responded spontaneously to the poems of Langston Hughes. Collected here are some of those that were particularly enjoyed. Most of them are brief, childlike in their simplicity, and timeless in their interpretations of black dreams, sea-longing, or the triumphant affirmation of faith. Dramatic woodcuts [by Ann Grifalconi] and dignified format help make this a tribute to a fine poet.

Zena Sutherland

SOURCE: A review of *Don't You Turn Back*, in *Bulletin of the Center for Children's Books*, Vol. 24, No. 1, September, 1970, pp. 10-11.

Handsomely illustrated with woodcuts [by Ann Grifalconi] in black, red, and white, a good collection of poems by Hughes, many of them written early in his career. The poems are grouped in four sections: "My People," "Prayers and Dreams," "Out to Sea," and "I Am a Negro." Direct and succinct, the poems have a sensitive and elemental simplicity that have made them particularly popular with the black children with whom Lee Hopkins has worked.

IMPORTANT DATES IN AFRO-AMERICAN HISTORY (1969)

Janet G. Polacheck

SOURCE: A review of *Important Dates in Afro-American History*, in *Library Journal*, Vol. 95, No. 6, March 15, 1970, p. 1195.

A not at all inclusive book, chronologically arranged, that offers brief paragraphs concerning people and events important in Afro-American history. Among the many omissions are Denmark Vesey, Marcus Garvey, Richard Hatcher, Eldridge Cleaver, Dick Gregory, and Rap Brown; the author includes Wilt Chamberlain but excludes Bill Russell, who has not only been a great athlete but who has contributed thoughtful statements on race problems through his speeches, articles, books, etc. The material that is presented would be useful for planning calendars, programs, or displays, and for quick reference; the many black-and-white pictures scattered throughout the book are very familiar but useful for identification. Despite its omissions, this is a useful beginning reference tool for students not yet able to handle the far superior *A Pictorial History of the Negro in America*.

Julia Bartling

SOURCE: A review of *Important Dates in Afro-American History*, in *Booklist*, Vol. 66, No. 17, May 1, 1970, p. 1102.

Notes on important Afro-American events and personages past and present arranged by the days of the year and divided into monthly sections each of which is preceded by an African proverb. Illustrated with numerous photographs most of which are portraits of outstanding black Americans. An index makes this a useful quick reference on Afro-American culture as well as an interesting and timely book for browsing.

THIS STREET'S FOR ME! (1970)

Marjorie Lewis

SOURCE: A review of *This Street's for Me!* in *Library Journal*, Vol. 95, No. 16, September 15, 1970, p. 3039.

Seventeen short poems about child life in the city, specifically on a play street. Familiar to city children will be the subjects: subways, gum-machines, frankfurter sellers, fire hydrants, shoe-shine boys, and the play street itself. But the liveliness and bustle of urban life aren't evoked in the dull, trite versification which lacks the rhythm that might have made the poetry memorable—or at least vigorous. One or two of the poems (e.g., **"All For a Penny"**) are onomatopoetically pleasing: "Clinkle / Clinkle / Clinkle / Chug-a-chug-a-chug-a- / Plop! / Gum. / Yum!," and there is a nice concrete one about a fire escape (though it would have been more effective had it been done on a single page rather than split between two facing ones). Generally, however, [Ann] Grifalconi's crayon drawings in rust-brown and black, with their vitality and distinctive style, are far superior to the poem.

Julia Bartling

SOURCE: A review of *This Street's for Me!* in *Booklist,* Vol. 67, No. 5, November 1, 1970, p. 227.

Noteworthy for their graphic rather than their poetic quality, these 17 original modern poems, accompanied by full-page illustrations [by Ann Grifalconi] in soft shades of brown and black, depict familiar city sights and activities from a child's viewpoint. Of immediate appeal to urban children, the picture book of poems offers a pleasurable vicarious experience to suburban children and will be useful with classes studying city and country life.

CHARLIE'S WORLD: A BOOK OF POEMS (1972)

Zena Sutherland

SOURCE: A review of *Charlie's World,* in *Bulletin of the Center for Children's Books,* Vol. 26, No. 7, March, 1973, pp. 107-8.

Poems about the weather, toys, the zoo, city sights, Christmas, the delight of having one's own room . . . such are the subjects for a collection of poems that record images rather than reflect moods. Although there is little innovation in the poetry, the combined appeals of rhyme, rhythm, and familiar sights and objects may appeal to the independent reader, since the poems are simply written. The illustrations [by Charles Robinson] are mediocre.

Margaret A. Dorsey

SOURCE: A review of *Charlie's World: A Book of Poems,* in *Library Journal,* Vol. 98, No. 6, March 15, 1973, p. 995.

Twenty-one poems centering on the life of Charlie, a young city dweller: the contents of his pockets, a skyscraper under construction, the sun shining "through the sparkle / of / TV antennas," friends, the zoo, Christmas, etc. Almost every poem appears on a double-page spread. Unfortunately, the 9¼" x 6¼" book is printed predominantly in dull blue and green which deaden the otherwise well-done pen sketches [by Charles Robinson]. The mediocre effect of the illustrations will turn off young browsers; however, teachers and storytellers may find some of the selections useful.

KIM'S PLACE AND OTHER POEMS (1974)

Nancy Rosenberg

SOURCE: "A Tree Grows in Print," in *The New York Times Book Review,* May 5, 1974, p. 38.

Another easygoing picture poetry book is **Kim's Place**, by Lee Bennett Hopkins. It provides a quick glance at everyday experiences in short, pedestrian verses ("The city is the place to be. / The city is the place for me.") The subjects are homey and child-centered—losing a tooth, writing a name, eating some watermelon—and two of the fourteen poems champion girls' equality lightly but firmly. Lawrence Di Fiori's illustrations are quiet and capable, although on the last page the nighttime sky obscures the text.

Kirkus Reviews

SOURCE: A review of *Kim's Place,* in *Kirkus Reviews,* Vol. XLII, No. 10, May 15, 1974, p. 531.

Kim is a girl, which constitutes the chief asset of these thirteen short everyday rhymes about a small child's everyday world. Kim catalogs the unexceptional possessions in her room, writes her name on the sidewalk, and tells us how everything looks green through sunglasses, how the puppy sleeps on her bed instead of his own, and how a tooth fell out after she stopped jerking and pulling on it. Hopkins characteristically includes scenes of urban fun ("The city is the place to be, / The city is the place for me") and, without a twinge of irony, immediately follows some current conventional wisdom complaining that Kim's food comes prepared from the store and the kitchen oven isn't used with the equally current and conventional (but possibly incompatible) assertion that "Girls Can, Too" do whatever boys do; then there's a follow-up on Kim's ambition to be an astronaut. . . . But proper values do not a poem make and **Kim's Place** is no livelier than **Charlie's World**.

Daisy Kouzel

SOURCE: A review of *Kim's Place,* in *Library Journal,* Vol. 99, No. 10, May 15, 1974, p. 1466.

These 16 poems, accompanied by pedestrian wash drawings in muted yellow, putty and gray [by Lawrence Di Fiori], attempt to describe the thoughts and activities of a little girl. The title poem and **"Question"** are pleasant enough, and there's a plug for women's lib in **"Girls Can, Too!"** However, on the whole, the verse is devoid of the musicality, wistfulness, introspection, and humor which can be found in similar collections for this age group. . . .

Zena Sutherland

SOURCE: A review of *Kim's Place,* in *Bulletin of the*

Center for Children's Books, Vol. 28, No. 6, February, 1975, p. 95.

A collection of poems spoken by a small girl is illustrated [by Lawrence Di Fiori] adequately in quiet colors. Some of the writing is free, some is in metric rhyme that occasionally falters; some of the poems bear no relation to sex role, like "How do dreams know / just when to creep / Into my head / when I fall off to sleep?" and others are definitely a girl's poems, as in **"Girls Can, Too!"** The author seldom achieves sharp imagery but he does have a persistent awareness of a child's concerns and a child's viewpoint.

I LOVED ROSE ANN (1976)

James A. Norsworthy, Jr.

SOURCE: A review of *I Loved Rose Ann*, in *Catholic Library World*, Vol. 48, No. 2, September, 1976, p. 90.

Each story usually does have at least two sides as is cleverly shown by Hopkins in this story about Harry and Rose Ann. An excellent book for stimulating class discussion and to foster trying to see the views of others. Sepia and white illustrations [by Ingrid Fetz] perfectly convey the mood and everchanging tone of the text. Highly recommended for grades K-3.

Judith S. Kronick

SOURCE: A review of *I Loved Rose Ann*, in *School Library Journal*, Vol. 23, No. 1, September, 1976, p. 101.

A two part story about the thwarted romance between a pair of school-age youngsters. Harry, who is the initiator of the romance, tells his side first: Rose Ann, the object of his affections, has spurned all his advances—special Valentines, flowers, and so on. In the second half, Rose Ann says she likes Harry Hooper very much but is put off by the "dumb" ways he has been acting lately. She concludes by saying she is more interested in her friendship with her girl friend than "loving Harry or Larry" (his rival). Expressive realistic, pen-and-ink sketches [by Ingrid Fetz] complement the story. The young picture book format, however, may strike the potential audience (second and third grade independent readers) as too childish. Also, question: why can't Rose Ann and Harry just be friends? Must there be a romance?

MAMA (1977)

Publishers Weekly

SOURCE: A review of *Mama*, in *Publishers Weekly*, Vol. 211, No. 8, February 21, 1977, p. 79.

Here is the not-to-be-missed first novel by the popular anthologist, writer, teacher and host of the TV series,

"Zebra Wings." His story of a too-resourceful mother and her two inner-city sons rockets along, inducing tears and laughter with each scene. Mama changes jobs as the need to provide specials for her "Troops" arises. As Easter nears, she works in a department store and comes home with a complete spring wardrobe for each boy. When she feels they could use more meat, she cleans house for a butcher and his wife and depletes their freezer. With Christmas on the way, Mama takes her stand at the holiday counter of a five-and-dime; soon, the family's little flat is crammed with glittering ornaments. By now, the older boy is terrified of the consequences if Mama is caught stealing and makes up his mind to find a solution for the problem. He does, in a touching but unsentimental finale.

Kirkus Reviews

SOURCE: A review of *Mama*, in *Kirkus Reviews*, Vol. XLV, No. 7, April 1, 1977, p. 351.

Mama is a nonstop talker—whether proclaiming her preference for plastic plants or complaining about the bills from Con Edison, "whoever he is"—but what she says has little to do with what her son wants to know: namely, what's behind the little games she makes him play with her every time she changes jobs. At the department store it's the Easter outfits game with the boys carrying home shopping bags every Wednesday and ending up the best-dressed kids at church; when she keeps house for a butcher and plays the meat game, the family has wonderful dinners every night of the week; and at the five and dime where she goes to work just before Christmas, the ornaments game results in an extravagantly decorated tree, along with three baby Jesuses and eighteen Wise Men. Her worried son, the nameless narrator, feels a little better when a kindly neighbor suggests that this is Mama's misguided way of "telling her love" for her two fatherless boys, and that showing theirs might be the best way to stop her. But he feels even better when Mama takes a job at the laundromat where doing her own laundry is part of the deal and there's not much else she can take. It's little more than a sketch, and a softened projection at that, but Mama clearly deserves a break. Give her a hearing.

Betsy Hearne

SOURCE: A review of *Mama*, in *Booklist*, Vol. 73, No. 21, July 1, 1977, pp. 1652-3.

Unlike many adult characters in children's literature, Mama is very complex. She shoplifts, she talks endlessly and obnoxiously (except about whatever she wants to avoid), and she prizes all things plastic; you know she would be a royal pain to live with. And yet she is so loving, resourceful, transparent, and even—finally—flexible that you want to hug her and give her all you can, just as her son, who narrates the story, does. As he watches her go from job to job and gradually forces himself to the awareness that she is stealing, he himself becomes a more complex character; he can and does reject stealing without rejecting his mother. While the younger brother is left undeveloped, he is important to the feeling of family unity developed as a whole. There is a subtle ending in which Mama, realistically enough, does not change but rather shows potential for acceding to the influence of her son's real needs. Young readers can absorb this slice of humanity through the gently humorous dialogue and situations, as well as the empathetic narrator's exposed feelings.

Zena Sutherland

SOURCE: A review of *Mama,* in *Bulletin of the Center for Children's Books,* Vol. 30, No. 11, July-August, 1977, p. 175.

You'll remember Mama. Tough, cheerfully vulgar in her tastes (she scorns real flowers, preferring plastic; she scoffs at African violets because they're foreign flowers), passionately dedicated to seeing that her two sons whose father has decamped have everything they need. But Mama also wants the boys to have everything they want, so she steals. When she works for a butcher, she steals steaks; when she works in a department store, she steals clothes; when she works at the five-and-ten, she steals more Christmas tree ornaments than a single tree can hold. The story is told by the older boy (the children are never named) in a convincing narrative; he becomes aware of Mama's thievery and anguishes about it, but he knows it is done for love. The ambivalence he feels is perceptively portrayed, and the strength and tenderness of his mother's love is touching, but it is in the character of Mama, made vivid through her words and deeds as well as through her son's troubled love, that Hopkins excels.

Whitney Rogge

SOURCE: A review of *Mama,* in *School Library Journal,* Vol. 24, No. 2, October, 1977, p. 114.

An over-drawn unconvincing character with an aphorism for every occasion, Mama steals clothes for her children from her department store job, steaks and roasts from the butcher and, from the dime store, an abundance of Christmas decorations including 18 wise men, all in plastic (her favorite substance). The plot revolves around her eldest son's slow realization that the packages his mother asks him to sneak home from her various places of employment are hot goods and on his attempts to deal with the problem. After consulting a sympathetic neighbor, the child decides all his mother really needs is love and at the book's end, the dilemma is temporarily solved because Mama has a new job in a laundromat where all she can plunder is soap. Hopkins treats large-scale shoplifting, coupled with using a child as accessory, as a minor eccentricity of an otherwise sterling character and his glib assumption that kleptomania can be cured with affection and a change of scene is distressing. Although the author does convey the young boy's almost frantic concern about his mother's thieving, the book's sitcom style doesn't do justice to the seriousness of the theme.

A-HAUNTING WE WILL GO: GHOSTLY STORIES AND POEMS (1977)

School Library Journal

SOURCE: A review of *A-Haunting We Will Go: Ghostly Stories and Poems,* in *School Library Journal,* Vol. 23, No. 9, May, 1977, p. 78.

Younger readers who like friendly ghosts will enjoy *A-Haunting We Will Go: Ghostly Stories and Poems,* selected by Lee Bennett Hopkins. The 13 stories, by such authors as Walter R. Brooks, Elizabeth Yates, Sorche Nic Leodhas, and Moritz Jagendorf, are divided into three sections: modern short stories of the supernatural; stories in which the ghostly occurrences may have natural explanations; stories in the traditional folk tale mold. An open format and many black-and-white illustrations [by Albert Whitman] will tempt browsers to start reading.

Barbara Elleman

SOURCE: A review of *A-Haunting We Will Go,* in *Booklist,* Vol. 73, No. 17, May 1, 1977, p. 1343.

A collection of 13 short ghostly tales sure to appeal to young readers intrigued with "things that go bump in the night." Stories included by authors such as Aileen Fisher, Elizabeth Yates, Sorche Nic Leodhas, Ruth Manning-Sanders, and Lee Bennett Hopkins vary from puzzling mysteries ("The Ghost in the Orchard") and funny encounters ("The House That Lacked a Bogle") to troubling experiences ("Gray Man's Warning"). [Albert Whitman's] gray-shaded drawings, more amusing than scary, illustrate the text. Good for enjoying around the campfire as well as for reading alone.

TO LOOK AT ANY THING (selected by Lee Bennett Hopkins, 1978)

Betsy Hearne

SOURCE: A review of *To Look at Any Thing,* in *Booklist,* Vol. 74, No. 17, May 1, 1978, p. 1439.

Illustrating poetry, where images flourish in the imagination, is tricky business; but this interplay between thoughtful verse and expressive photography brings greater meaning to each and encourages careful scrutiny. [John] Earl's specialty is figures or "faces" in nature—flowers, wood, ice, a skyline. Each well-reproduced black-and-white photograph suggests a world of thoughts and associations, which Hopkins has shaped by the lyrics of Walt Whitman, Robert Frost, Patricia Hubbell, Carl Sandburg, Langston Hughes, and others. Children will want to stare a while, then choose their own accompanying poems, or perhaps write them. The art here is really worth slowing down for and living with a while. "Whatever you have to say, leave / the roots on, let them / dangle / And the dirt

/ just to make clear / where they came from" ("These Days" by Charles Olson).

Sharon Elswit

SOURCE: A review of *To Look at Anything*, in *School Library Journal*, Vol. 25, No. 3, November, 1978, p. 64.

The pictures came first in this poem in the picture, picture in the poem collaboration. [John] Earl tugs at viewers' powers of observation and humor to find the anthropomorphic spirits in his black-and-white photographs—faces in whorls of bark and driftwood, dinosaur bodies in ice capped stones. Hopkins meets the visual challenges with 23 poems, drawn mostly from moderns—Zolotow, Sandburg, Frost, Lilian Moore, Gary Snyder, Langston Hughes. It works—the poems haven't been anthologized too often; the poems and pictures are appropriately paired; the game of finding trolls and elephants in sylvan scenes isn't forced and doesn't limit the words. One major regret is the design, however; it makes self-conscious use of image repetitions that don't always have a purpose, monotonous gray tones, inappropriate sizing and coy placements on the page, in many cases sabotaging the material.

Curriculum Review

SOURCE: A review of *To Look at Any Thing*, in *Curriculum Review*, Vol. 18, No. 1, February, 1979, p. 44.

Look carefully and you can see faces in nature, faces like those in John Earl's photographs in this book. In addition to the work of this highly perceptive observer and talented photographer, this large book contains Lee Hopkins's clever choices of excellent poems by such poets as Robert Frost, Mark Van Doren, Langston Hughes, and Walt Whitman. The skillful layout does credit to the poems and pictures. For example, a photograph of ice on rock formations in a river looking like dinosaurs quenching their thirsts is accompanied by Patricia Hubbell's "When Dinosaurs Ruled the Earth." As the poem is printed on four pages, six prints of the photograph appear, getting smaller and finally fading into near invisibility or "extinction." Although the poems are always apt, students should be encouraged to discover their own poem or prose passage, or better yet, they should try to write their own poem for their own face found in nature.

WONDER WHEELS (1979)

Booklist

SOURCE: A review of *Wonder Wheels*, in *Booklist*, Vol. 75, No. 14, March 15, 1979, p. 1145.

Mick Thompson's first love is roller skating—a talent he is carefully cultivating in order to win a place in the line-up of an amusement park show; his second turns out to be Kitty Rhoades, whom he meets at his local roller rink.

While much of his energy goes toward practicing for his skating audition, Mick still has time to get to know Kitty, whose home life, he discovers, is the antithesis of his own happy one—especially in relation to her problems with a psychotic ex-boyfriend that even Mick doesn't learn about until it is too late. Though superficialities and awkward pacing make the story seem stilted and overdramatized, it has a likable teenage protagonist and simply constructed characters and situations. Not intended for teens with reading difficulties, but more suitable for that audience.

Joyce Milton

SOURCE: A review of *Wonder Wheels*, in *The New York Times Book Review*, April 8, 1979, p. 32.

Wonder Wheels at first promises to be a "Saturday Night Fever" on roller skates, geared to the younger set who do their dancing at the rink instead of at the disco. The characters are 17 but act younger, and when Mick Thompson rejects his sometime skating partner for Kitty Rhoades, a new girl at the rink, one assumes that his biggest problem will be persuading Kitty's mother to let her go out on dates. Not so. Kitty is soon murdered by a psychotic former boyfriend. Mick is then left alone to contemplate Kitty's demise while staring at his empty coffee cup: "A few minutes ago you were full—brewing and steaming with life. Now you're empty. Things can become empty so fast in life. So damned fast!" Fortunately, Mick recovers from this state of mind in time to correct the one flaw in his skating routine—droopy boxer shorts—and win his first national skating audition. The point seems to be: we all have to die; all the more reason for not wasting our good years by wearing tacky underwear. The sentiment is not a romantic one, however, and by the time we reach the scene of Mick's grand skating finale the author himself seems to be skating in five directions at once. Stay out of his way, and let this particular circuit of "life's merry-go-round" career past you.

Patricia Ann Reilly

SOURCE: A review of *Wonder Wheels*, in *Best Sellers*, Vol. 39, No. 5, August, 1979, p. 168.

Wonder Wheels, whirling out from two contrasting family circles, revolves around the love, life and death experiences of two young-adult roller skaters who frequent the rink which gives this novel its title.

Mick Thompson, the seventeen-year-old star of the roller skating rink, is the embodiment of traditional upper middle-class values in a stable family life style; Kitty Rhoades, the seventeen-year-old neophyte at the rink, is the composite of all the insecurities and turmoil of a shattered home life; Kenneth Delaney, the sadistic twenty-year-old "man-of-the-world," is a type that young readers will readily recognize. Mrs. Rhoades adds to the complexity of the bittersweet love triangle by constantly nagging Kitty to date Kenneth, the "ideal" potential husband.

Kitty knows otherwise, but she cannot confide in her ranting, raging mother, nor in her senile, doting Grandma Perkins who adds to the confusion in the home.

Although the story of young love is an oft repeated one, Hopkins' use of local color and stark reality lend credibility to the plot. With almost a Dickensian geographical exactitude, the author includes street names, bus stops, and places in the New Jersey environs. The conflict, rising action, and suspense concerning Kitty's "secret" are well drawn—not as tautly, of course, as in *Romeo and Juliet,* but as convincingly and harshly real as current news reports.

Hopkins' treatment throughout the novel, from simple details to the surprise ending, is in good taste and merits an "A" classification for the Young People's Book.

📖 *MAMA AND HER BOYS* (1981)

Kay Webb O'Connell

SOURCE: A review of *Mama and Her Boys,* in *School Library Journal,* Vol. 28, No. 2, October, 1981, p. 142.

Mama's single-parenting two boys, preschool Mark and fifth-grader Chris. They're a loving family who work hard to make their life together happy—Mama is a laundress who's highly respected by her boss, the boys are top students and dutiful sons. When the boss proposes to Mama, the family stability is threatened: the boys don't want Mr. Jacobs for a father. The appealing characters resolve their problems; the boys find Mama a good man, and the family circle is complete. But there is a bothersome aspect of this book. The dust jacket shows a white trio, but the book's characters seem Black, especially Mama and her boys. There's no concrete mention of color or ethnicity, but the implied ethnicity is confusing, especially within the contemporary urban setting and a human-interest focus. These misgivings about the book's realism undermine the story's warmhearted tone.

Zena Sutherland

SOURCE: A review of *Mama and Her Boys,* in *Bulletin of the Center for Children's Books,* Vol. 35, No. 4, December, 1981, p. 70.

The story is told by the elder of two young brothers, as it was in *Mama* but in this sequel the boys have names, Mark and Chris. They worry because Mama might marry her boss, Mr. Jacobs, but that comes to naught; they are more accepting of the possibility that she might marry Mr. Carlisle, the school custodian—and indeed, by the end of the book, that's clearly imminent. This has less vigor than the first book, a difference reflected in the cover art by Ted Lewin; in the first book Mama was brassy, tough, vulgar, fiercely loving and lovable, while in the sequel she's loving but protective rather than tough, boringly repetitious rather than brassy. Perhaps because

there is no deep problem here (like the anguish about knowing Mama was a thief) the book is less affective than its predecessor; it is also weakened somewhat by the precocity of the younger brother's conversation.

Publishers Weekly

SOURCE: A review of *Mama and Her Boys,* in *Publishers Weekly,* Vol. 220, No. 24, December 11, 1981, p. 62.

Hopkins's lighthearted and touching story concerns further events in the lives of the Kipness family and friends, featured in *Mama.* Divorced and dedicated to bringing up her sons Mark and Christopher with love that involves strict discipline, Mama is a strong woman. She surprises her sons by dithering, however, when she begins to share a piece of big news: Mr. Jacobs, who owns the laundry where she works, has proposed. Mark and Chris make it obvious that they don't welcome the idea at all, so Mama refuses Mr. Jacobs. But Mark unknowingly gets a second courtship going by introducing Mama to Mike Carlisle, the janitor at his school. Mike becomes a frequent visitor at the Kipness home, calling Mama "Trudy." The author packs the ensuing incidents with merriment and an understated lesson about different kinds of love and companionship.

📖 *RAINBOWS ARE MADE: POEMS BY CARL SANDBURG* (selected by Lee Bennett Hopkins, 1982)

Publishers Weekly

SOURCE: A review of *Rainbows Are Made,* in *Publishers Weekly,* Vol. 222, No. 24, December 17, 1982, p. 75.

[Fritz] Eichenberg's strong, handsome woodcuts strengthen as well as reflect the images in 70 poems, chosen carefully by Hopkins from nearly 1000 by the late Pulitzer Prize winner. The editor's sensitive introduction traces Sandburg's universal appeal to his genius at using language as an art to share thoughts about people and what matters to them. The rugged verses express almost countless feelings—about love, hate, nature and human-made things. "Lines Written for Gene Kelly to Dance To" is one of the merry lyrics in the book. There are many more that call for shouts of joy and laughter, among the poet's serious questions about the stupidity of war and the fever to acquire material things: "Money buys everything except love, / personality, freedom, immortality, / silence, peace." Hopkins, a well-known anthologist, presents his most impressive collection. . . .

Barbara Elleman

SOURCE: A review of *Rainbows Are Made,* in *Booklist,* Vol. 79, No. 10, January 15, 1983, p. 679.

"He makes us think, see, feel, take notice," Hopkins says

of Carl Sandburg in his brief but adroit introduction, succinctly proving his point with 70 carefully, chosen verses by one of American's greatest poets. The handsome volume is shaped into six groupings, each headed by one of Sandburg's own definitions of poetry from *Good Morning, America;* for example, "Poetry is a series of explanations of life, fading off into horizons too swift for explanations." In these sections Hopkins has gathered verses dealing with views of people, wordplay, observations of the world, nature notes, and thoughts of night themes. Topping off this extraordinary offering are six splendid wood engravings, plus a frontispiece of Sandburg. [Fritz] Eichenberg, one of the foremost engravers working today, expands on the strength and sensitivity of these much-admired poems and brings a new dimension to them.

Zena Sutherland

SOURCE: A review of *Rainbows Are Made,* in *Bulletin of the Center for Children's Books,* Vol. 36, No. 7, March, 1983, p. 133.

Carefully selected, this assemblage of Sandburg poems includes many that are not often included in collections of his work intended for young readers. The poems have been grouped in six sections: poems about people, about the night, about the sea, about nature, about everyday objects, and about words and language. The quality of the writing is matched by the strong, dramatic wood engravings [of Fritz Eichenberg], one for each section, and is set off by the spacious format. Title and first line indexes are provided.

Mary M. Burns

SOURCE: A review of *Rainbows Are Made,* in *The Horn Book Magazine,* Vol. LIX, No. 2, April, 1983, p. 180.

Compiled by Lee Bennett Hopkins. Illustrated by Fritz Eichenberg. In a handsome volume seventy of Carl Sandburg's poems are presented in an inviting and aesthetically pleasing format. The introduction indicates that the choices were intended to demonstrate the elements particularly characteristic of Sandburg's work: his interest in people; his vigorous imagery; his ability to see what is wondrous, challenging, or puzzling in the familiar; his gift for capturing a variety of emotions in everyday language arranged, as in "Cool Tombs," to create a haunting refrain. Quintessentially American, Sandburg's voice is that of the pioneer—gruff and plain-spoken yet endowed with a particular vision. His definitions of poetry reflect an effort to marry the transcendent and the mundane and to give concrete form to abstraction. Consequently, the decision to use several of these definitions for divisional headings is an inspired one, for it provides the opportunity to relate the poet's themes and theories to practice. Thus, the statement "Poetry is a search for syllables to shoot at the barriers of the unknown and the unknowable"

precedes such poems as "Is Wisdom a Lot of Language?" "Bird Talk," and "Different Kinds of Good-by." Included in this section is "Metamorphosis," which asks, "When ice turns back into water does it / remember it was ice?" For each of the six sections the artist has created full-page wood engravings in which representational images are combined into impressive interpretations of the introductory quotation. Some, like the frontispiece portrait of Sandburg, are relatively conventional; others suggest the surreal landscapes of the imagination. With indexes of first lines and titles.

Linda Wicher

SOURCE: A review of *Rainbows Are Made,* in *School Library Journal,* Vol. 29, No. 7, March, 1983, p. 196.

Rainbows Are Made offers some 70 short poems by Carl Sandburg and groups them by theme: the seasons, the sea, the imaginative mind, etc. Each theme explores different aspects of poetic creativity as envisioned by Sandburg and illustrated by Fritz Eichenberg's wood engravings. Eichenberg has truly captured the power and vigorousness of Sandburg's verse in images somewhat reminiscent of Blake's spiritual incarnations. The poems have been carefully chosen and placed so that each can be discovered and examined as a gem. No dates are appended to the poems; Hopkins' introduction, however, provides adequate biographical information and an overview of the poet's life work. While not as comprehensive as *The Sandburg Treasury,* **Rainbows Are Made** does not limit itself to poems for children and about childhood as the earlier collection does. Yes, there is an index of first lines and titles. This is, above all, a handsome collection and, secondly, a useful one for the elementary or secondary school library.

A SONG IN STONE: CITY POEMS (selected by Lee Bennett Hopkins, 1983)

Publishers Weekly

SOURCE: A review of *A Song in Stone: City Poems,* in *Publishers Weekly,* Vol. 223, No. 27, July 8, 1983, p. 65.

[Anna Held] Audette's splendid photos faithfully illustrate every scene in the poems selected by Hopkins for his latest anthology. The title comes from the collection of Langston Hughes, *City:* "In the morning the city / Spreads its wings / Making a song / In stone that sings." Lyrics about umbrellas like flowers in the rain, the city dump, pigeons, junkyards, unending construction and a myriad of metropolitan sights catch the imagination in the unusual book. Myra Cohn Livingston, Maxine Kumin, Eve Merriam, Felice Holman, Lillian Moore and Hopkins himself are among the many distinguished poets represented. Harry Behn has the last word in "From an Airplane": "Night settles on earth, / and the blue city becomes / a nest of fireflies."

Peter Neumeyer

SOURCE: A review of *A Song in Stone: City Poems,* in *School Library Journal,* Vol. 30, No. 5, January, 1984, p. 77.

Some of the poems in this collection are accomplished, a few, like Merriam's "Stray Cat," are outstanding and the black-and-white photographs [by Anna Held Audette] are set in artful juxtaposition. However, the metrical or poetical variety is distinctly limited. The majority of the poems have a melancholy urban tone, addressing pigeons who "seldom try the sky" and grownups who "rush . . . crush . . . scurry . . . flurry." Norma Farber's melodious lullaby addresses the "city children" sleeping in the "rumble, babble, beep"; Langston Hughes' poem sees a benevolent city spreading "its wings / Making a song / In stone that sings" and three lines aborted from a Harry Behn poem end the volume serenely. As may be appropriate for *A Song in Stone,* almost every verse is a verbal snapshot; there is little drama, little action, in perhaps half. Like the new, diminished Hershey bar, this mini-collection of 20 poemlets or snippets by 17 poets is not nearly the value you once could get—say in Nancy Larrick's rich collection, *On City Streets,* which it so resembles in format.

HOW DO YOU MAKE AN ELEPHANT FLOAT? AND OTHER DELICIOUS RIDDLES (1983)

Eva Elisabeth Von Ancken

SOURCE: A review of *How Do You Make an Elephant Float? and Other Delicious Riddles,* in *School Library Journal,* Vol. 30, No. 3, November, 1983, p. 78.

Poet Lee Bennett Hopkins has written a dreary little book of riddles vaguely based on the topic of food such as, "What turns without moving? *Milk. It can turn sour.*" Most of the riddles, though touted as original, have come by this way before (some often); few are funny. The confusing format—riddle questions at the top of the page, answers in small type at the bottom—makes it difficult for young riddle fans to find the answers. The illustrations [by Rosekrans Hoffman] in gray and lavender are amusing, but they cannot carry the load. With the many really funny riddle books available, let this elephant sink.

Zena Sutherland

SOURCE: A review of *How Do You Make an Elephant Float? and Other Delicious Riddles,* in *Bulletin of the Center for Children's Books,* Vol. 37, No. 4, December, 1983, p. 69.

Like many books of riddles for children, this runs a narrow spectrum, from some fairly clever puns to such bland riddles as "When is it proper to serve milk in a saucer?" "When you feed a cat," or such nonsense as "What is green and noisy and very dangerous?" "A herd of thundering pickles." Some jokes are tossed in that are not

riddles; the comic grotesque drawings, lavender-tinted, have humor. Everything has to do with food; adults may groan, but children will probably repeat the riddles ad infinitum. Possibly ad nauseam.

SURPRISES: AN I CAN READ BOOK OF POEMS (selected by Lee Bennett Hopkins, 1984)

Betsy Hearne

SOURCE: A review of *Surprises,* in *Booklist,* Vol. 81, No. 2, September 15, 1984, p. 137.

With section titles like "Who to Pet," "At the Top of My Voice," "Boats, Trains, and Planes," "Rain, Sun, and Snow," and "Goodnight," these 38 poems offer beginning readers a chance to try some verse, which especially lends itself to the exercise by virtue of rhymes, short lines, and lively images. These brief selections are particularly unintimidating, and Hopkins has managed to vary the light tone with poets like Nikki Giovanni, Gwendolyn Brooks, Norma Farber, Karla Kuskin, Dorothy Aldis, Langston Hughes, and other popular poets to whose work each of these might serve as a springboard. The vocabularly is consistently simple without seeming restricted, and the vividly colored pen drawings [by Megan Lloyd] pack a lot of action as well as balancing the large print for relief of struggling young readers. A friendly book with subjects that will connect with children's everyday lives and lend a little music along the way to counter the choppy prose of most early reading texts.

Ethel R. Twichell

SOURCE: A review of *Surprises,* in *The Horn Book Magazine,* Vol. LX, No. 6, November-December, 1984, p. 769.

Short poems in an I-Can-Read book comprise a collection that seems just right for beginning readers wanting to browse at their own pace. Ranging from the whimsical to the absurd, most of the poems touch on familiar experiences or unanswered questions of the very young. In one, a much-loved teddy bear offers reassurance to a child on awakening in a dark room while another captures the exhilaration of hollering at the top of one's voice. The easy-to-read poems are limiting as an introduction to the excitement or beauty of language, but the catchy rhymes, small jokes, and quirky turns of phrase are appealing. Colorful detailed pictures [by Megan Lloyd] accompany each verse, serving both to illustrate and to embellish with their own understated humor.

Publishers Weekly

SOURCE: A review of *Surprises,* in *Publishers Weekly,* Vol. 226, No. 17, October 26, 1984, pp. 104-5.

Poet-anthologist Hopkins has collected poems for the

*Lee Bennett Hopkins with William C. Morris
at an ALA conference, 1984.*

outstanding I Can Read list, such a good idea that it's a wonder this is the first of its kind. Beginners are sure to discover their thoughts and feelings in lyrics about subjects that are part of a child's world, as expressed by Norma Farber, Aileen Fisher, N. M. Bodecker, Elizabeth Coatsworth, Russell Hoban and others, including Hopkins himself. Extremely bright tones of yellow and red add verve to [Megan] Lloyd's illustrations. There is a regrettable slip in the index: "Covers," by the gifted Nikki Giovanni, is listed, but her name is omitted. This error will undoubtedly be corrected in future editions. Meantime, small boys and girls will have the pleasure of enriching their imaginations by reading or listening to the pithy, musical lines on pets, bugs, traveling, weather, nighttimes, daytimes.

Zena Sutherland

SOURCE: A review of *Surprises,* in *Bulletin of the Center for Children's Books,* Vol. 38, No. 3, November, 1984, pp. 47-8.

Neatly framed, small-scale drawings [by Megan Lloyd] that are vigorous, sometimes humorous, seldom graceful, illustrate a collection of poems for the beginning independent reader. A few of the selections have a note of bland contrivance, but most of them are either good or

very good in their brevity, simplicity, freshness, and vision. The book should also be useful for reading aloud to very young children.

Nancy Palmer

SOURCE: A review of *Surprises,* in *School Library Journal,* Vol. 31, No. 4, December, 1984, p. 96.

The surprise here is that no one ever thought of this before. Hopkins, that ubiquitous compiler, has put together a first-rate collection of poems from the proverbial star-studded cast: X. J. Kennedy, Myra Cohn Livingston, Nikki Giovanni, Russell Hoban, Eve Merriam, Langston Hughes, Christina Rossetti, Carl Sandburg and on and on. These 38 poems, most previously published elsewhere, employ short words and simple language to tell their tale or paint their picture and often make good read-alouds as well as smart choices for beginning readers. Kids will enjoy the range of topics—from bugs to boats to goodnight—and the inclusion of both new and familiar material. [Megan] Lloyd's illustrations are witty reflections of the poems, drawn in pinks, yellows, oranges, greens and browns and neatly framed on each page. An index of authors and titles makes the book useful as an anthology as well as a beginning-to-read.

MORE SURPRISES: AN I CAN READ BOOK (selected by Lee Bennett Hopkins, 1987)

Kay E. Vandergrift

SOURCE: A review of *More Surprises,* in *School Library Journal,* Vol. 34, No. 2, October, 1987, p. 121.

More Surprises is a collection of simple and enjoyable poems, but it lacks surprises. Most of the poems are readily available elsewhere, and the six subject groupings do not work effectively to give insight into individual poems or into relationships among them. The inclusion of "An Historic Moment" in the "Some People" grouping or "Whistling" with the "Body Parts" puts an inappropriate focus on these poems, forcing readers who pay attention to headings to notice, for instance, the shape of the lips more than the child's desire to whistle. Among the 35 poems one finds Zolotow's "People," which sets a mood; Hoberman's "Brother" and Bodecker's "Ruth Luce and Bruce Booth," which play with language; and many others that create vivid images, capture the cleverness of childhood, portray quieter happy times, or evoke an explosion of laughter. Hopkins' own poem **"This Tooth"** is one of the few with a sense of surprise, and his **"Good Books, Good Times!"** sums up for beginners what reading is all about. [Megan] Lloyd's illustrations are, with few exceptions, colorful and cheerful, working better with the humorous poems than with the more serious ones. Lloyd appears to have been limited by the page layout, which, in order to contain the longer poems on one spread, crowds the illustrations into a narrow strip at the top. Astute adults sharing these poems with children can use the acknowledgements to go back to original works by Aldis, de Regniers, Fisher, Kuskin, Livingston, and Zolotow for other poems appropriate for new readers.

Ilene Cooper

SOURCE: A review of *More Surprises*, in *Booklist*, Vol. 84, No. 3, October 1, 1987, p. 326.

This is the perfect compilation to teach the joys of poetry to very young children. Words and rhyme schemes are simple enough for beginning readers to handle themselves, and the offerings by poets such as Aileen Fisher, William Cole, Karla Kuskin, and Jack Prelutsky are filled with humor and verve. There's a selection about a man who loses his head and another about a nose with a cold that does nothing but blow. The full-color artwork [by Megan Lloyd] varies in size from small bordered scrolls to full-page pictures. This companion to *Surprises,* also edited by Hopkins, is a sheer delight.

Kirkus Reviews

SOURCE: A review of *More Surprises,* in *Kirkus Reviews,* Vol. LV, No. 19, October 1, 1987, pp. 1463-4.

Thirty-five poems for beginning readers—including work by N.M. Bodecker, Christina Rossetti, Mary Ann Hoberman, and William S. Harris—in this sequel to the first I Can Read poetry collection, *Surprises.*

In both rhymed and unrhymed verse, these poems talk about brothers who are brothers, poetry (Harris: "The man said, after inventing poetry, / 'wow'"), noses and ears, whistling, school concerts, lions, birds, witches, worms, open fire hydrants, weather, books, and loose teeth (Bodecker: "'Lithen,' said Ruth / 'I've a little looth tooth'"). Poems are arranged in six arbitrary categories: "Some People," "Body Parts," "Living Things," "How Funny," "Hot and Cold," and "In School and After." But some of the funnier poems are not in the funny compartment; the nature and seasonal poems are less exact than the others; and the illustrations [by Megan Lloyd] are perfunctory, though cheerful.

Still, while the quality of the poems is uneven, there is enough here to catch early recruits for poetry's cause. Let there be more anthologies of this sort for young readers!

Betsy Hearne

SOURCE: A review of *More Surprises,* in *Bulletin of the Center for Children's Books,* Vol. 41, No. 5, January, 1988, pp. 91-2.

Continuing one of his best ideas—anthologizing poetry into an easy-to-read format—Hopkins includes 35 selec-

tions by Karla Kuskin, Mary Ann Hoberman, Jack Prelutsky, N.M. Bodecker, and others who display a knack for simple, entertaining rhymes. The rhythmic repetition, humor, and narrative quality of pieces like "If You Ever Meet A Whale" (anonymous) or "My Nose" (Dorothy Aldis) make them natural practice material. Although these are not difficult to find elsewhere, their appearance here is convenient and reinforces teachers' using more creative approaches to reading by exercising skills with inventive language and imaginative literature.

SIDE BY SIDE: POEMS TO READ TOGETHER (selected by Lee Bennett Hopkins, 1988)

Publishers Weekly

SOURCE: A review of *Side by Side: Poems to Read Together,* in *Publishers Weekly,* Vol. 234, No. 11, September 9, 1988, p. 135.

Sprinkled throughout this cheery volume of familiar poems are pictures of people reading—a lady in a straw hat reading to a toddler on an old-fashioned porch, a kangaroo reading to babies in her pouch. True to the title, the poems collected are perfect for reading side by side. There are story poems; counting rhymes; verses about seasons, holidays and animals. Every page is filled with [Hilary] Knight's rollicking watercolors of exuberant, bright-eyed children. What will ensure this book's popularity, however, is the inclusion of poems many parents and grandparents will remember, including "A Visit from St. Nicholas," "The Three Little Kittens" and "The House that Jack Built." Fun for all members of the family, this is both a nostalgia-filled and a living collection.

Ellen Mandel

SOURCE: A review of *Side by Side: Poems to Read Together,* in *Booklist,* Vol. 85, No. 5, November 1, 1988, p. 487.

The subjects of [Hilary] Knight's sprightly illustrations in this collection of perennial and promising candidates for poetry favorites are agile, active children and frolicking animals that engage the reader with every glance. Among holiday inclusions are Lydia Maria Child's "Over the River and Through the Wood" and Clement Moore's "Visit from St. Nicholas." For everyday sharing there are "I Went to the Animal Fair," "Poor Old Lady" (who swallowed a fly)—both anonymous offerings—classic contributions from the likes of Robert Louis Stevenson, Lewis Carroll, and Robert Frost, and contemporary selections from Nikki Giovanni, Karla Kuskin, and Arnold Lobel, among others. With the rhythmic, sometimes narrative verses, and the joyful antics of the characters prancing across the pages, this collection offers visual as well as aural treats for children and adults to savor together.

Kathleen Whalin

SOURCE: A review of *Side by Side: Poems to Read Together,* in *School Library Journal,* Vol. 35, No. 4, December, 1988, pp. 98-9.

The title is appropriate not only because the selected poems are so perfect for reading aloud, but because of the perfect integration of the poems and [Hilary] Knight's illustrations. As in his *Twelve Days of Christmas,* Knight extends the meaning of the grouped poems with accompanying scenes that create their own subtext. The book is arranged by seasons. Hopkins shows the strength of a true master collector. His selections embrace Mother Goose, traditional songs, and modern poets such as Eve Merriam, Langston Hughes, and Robert Louis Stevenson. A book worthy to sit side by side with Prelutsky's *Read-Aloud Rhymes for the Very Young* and some of Hopkins' other collections.

📖 *VOYAGES: POEMS BY WALT WHITMAN*
(selected by Lee Bennett Hopkins, 1988)

Hazel Rochman

SOURCE: A review of *Voyages: Poems by Walt Whitman,* in *Booklist,* Vol. 85, No. 6, November 15, 1988, p. 565.

Hopkins has selected 53 poems and excerpts from poems to introduce this classic American poet. A brief overview describes Whitman's life and his radical and enduring influence. Then the poems are arranged in five sections covering more than 40 years, including Whitman's view of his youth, his journeys ("Song of the Open Road"), the people he met, the mourning of the Civil War ("When Lilacs Last in the Dooryard Bloomed"), and his sense of aging and death. Full-page black-and-white illustrations by [Charles] Mikolaycak introduce each section: a heroic youth rises from the emigrant cradle "endlessly rocking" on the ocean; a traveler reads on his back under a tree by a river; the face of Lincoln broods above the war dead. In addition, a few small circular illustrations are scattered throughout, including a lovely cat's face accompanying "I think I could turn and live with animals." A spacious, handsome edition that helps make accessible a poet of vigor and sensitivity.

Kirkus Reviews

SOURCE: A review of *Voyages,* in *Kirkus Reviews,* Vol. LVI, No. 22, November 15, 1988, p. 1680.

Another inviting, well-crafted introduction to an American poet's work, and a companion to *Rainbows Are Made: Poems by Carl Sandburg*.

"Shut not your doors to me proud libraries, for that which was lacking . . . yet needed most, I bring . . ." For all its other beauties, Whitman's poetry seldom strikes young readers as funny, making this opening sally all the more startling. Hopkins follows a brief biographical introduction with 53 selections from *Leaves of Grass,* mostly short—though "When lilacs last in the dooryard bloom'd" is here in its entirety, arranged in five broadly thematic groups. The poet's dense rush of words is counter-balanced by a spacious layout, and many of his images are reprised in gray but suitably dramatic full-page illustrations [by Charles Mikolaycak], as well as occasional head- or tail-pieces.

Readers who find Frasconi's *Overhead the Sun* too brief and picture-bookish will welcome this handsome new sampler.

Kathleen Whalin

SOURCE: A review of *Voyages,* in *School Library Journal,* Vol. 35, No. 4, December, 1988, p. 130.

Fifty-three selections from Walt Whitman's poems, roughly spanning the poet's journey from youth to old age. As in *Rainbows Are Made,* to which this book is a companion volume, Hopkins shows his deep respect for this American poet. The Whitman of *Voyages* is, indeed, a searcher for truth and a celebrator of the human spirit. The book's layout, with its clear typeface and [Charles] Mikolaycak's strong black-and-white drawings, reinforces the dignity of the text. Whitman's images deserve the focus that a book such as *Voyages* gives them. There is a brief biographical introduction and an index of titles and first lines.

Nancy Vasilakis

SOURCE: A review of *Voyages: Poems by Walt Whitman,* in *The Horn Book Magazine,* Vol. LXV, No. 1, January-February, 1989, pp. 86-7.

Illustrated by Charles Mikolaycak. A well-conceived and elegantly produced anthology consisting of fifty-three selections that represent the work of this important American poet from the beginning of his career to the end of his life. The volume is divided into five sections, comprised of Walt Whitman's musings on the places of his youth, his journeys through the United States, themes relating to the Civil War, those celebrating the self, and finally, his poems about old age and dying. Along with some of the poet's better-known titles, such as "Out of the Cradle Endlessly Rocking," "When Lilacs Last in the Dooryard Bloom'd," and several selections from "Song of Myself," Hopkins has included some revealing and frequently overlooked poems on the war and ruminations on his death. Walt Whitman is remembered primarily for his poems celebrating life; it is humbling to note with what reverence he still regarded the world during his final years, which were marked by infirmity and poverty. The choice of Charles Mikolaycak to illustrate this book, intended to serve as a companion volume to *Rainbows Are Made: Poems by Carl Sandburg,* is a happy one. The artist's handsome, massive drawings are a perfect complement to Whitman's vigorous and unorthodox lines. The volume brings joyfully to life the poetic vision of this archetypal American poet, ending with the especially apt choice, "Now Lift Me Close," which includes the lines: "What you are holding is in reality no book, nor part of a book; / It is a man, flush'd and full blooded—it is I." Index of titles and first lines.

Liz Rosenberg

SOURCE: A review of *Voyages,* in *The New York Times Book Review,* March 26, 1989, p. 19.

In April 1862, Emily Dickinson wrote to the editor Thomas Wentworth Higginson, "You speak of Mr. Whitman. I never read his book, but was told it was disgraceful." Dickinson was 31, her remark almost certainly tongue-in-cheek, yet there's no doubt Mr. Whitman's "disgraceful" book would have been considered unfit reading for the young. There's evidence in *Voyages: Poems by Walt Whitman*—a selected Whitman geared to teen-agers—that a certain uneasiness remains to this day.

No one, on the face of it, seems better suited to young readers than Whitman; with his "barbaric yawp," what Emerson called his "terrible eyes and buffalo strength." The central, heroic I of his poetry is brash, braggardly, overheated, sexy, vacillating ("Do I contradict myself? / Very well then, I contradict myself"), democratic, soulful—in short, he smacks of the eternal adolescent. *Voyages,* edited by the indefatigable anthologizer Lee Bennett Hopkins, is an ideal project in theory. It should be a wonderful book—as was *Rainbows Are Made,* Mr. Hopkins's selections from Carl Sandburg.

But there are at least two problems. One is that Mr. Hopkins doesn't have the same bright, intuitive feel for Whitman he had for Sandburg. He calls Whitman a "caring, daring, sharing" poet—words to make any teen-ager wince.

Another, more serious problem is that Whitman is not, in fact, an easy poet for the young. Even Galway Kinnell, editor of *The Essential Whitman,* remarks. "The poems of Walt Whitman meant little to me when I read them in high school and college." For all his seemingly adolescent energy and passion—perhaps because of it—he is really a poet of adult wisdom. His extremism, his philosophizing, his rantings and fumings will appeal to a very rare bird among teen-agers.

Moreover, *Voyages* is watery Whitman at best. It shows us the Good Gray Poet—the Boy Scout's Whitman, quaintly Americana, robust, squeaky-clean, a bit preachy: "Remember, fear not, be candid, promulge the body and the soul, / Dwell a while and pass on, be copious, temperate, chaste, magnetic." Charles Mikolaycak's static full-page drawings loom over the poems, but do little to enhance the book. Arranged as a poetic chronol-

ogy of sorts. *Voyages* takes us through a rough biography—a project magnificently achieved in Whitman's life-long work, *Leaves of Grass,* which constitutes the mythologizing of a man, Walter Whitman, into Walt Whitman, "one of the roughs," as he called himself, "a cosmos."

This is a literal-minded condensation with little hint of the rolling long-breathed rhythms and dashing exclamations that constitute Whitman's genius. Mr. Hopkins's selection of poems is quirky, consisting largely of short, little-known works, and unsatisfactory snippets of the long great poems, all from the 1891-92 "Deathbed" edition. The only long poems reprinted here in full are "Out of the Cradle Endlessly Rocking" and "When Lilacs Last in the Dooryard Bloom'd," proving again that we find it less frightening to expose our young people to death than to sex. Nearly all of Whitman's greatest works—"Reconciliation," "I Saw in Louisiana a Live-Oak Growing." "On the Beach at Night," "A Noiseless Patient Spider," "Passage to India," "Crossing Brooklyn Ferry"—are missing, although Mr. Hopkins has selected a few lesser-known beauties that are particularly apt for the young, including "A Clear Midnight" and "A Leaf for Hand in Hand."

Mr. Hopkins is a well-meaning editor, but it takes a keen appreciator to put together a volume of selected poems so as to provide, in the critic Lawrence Clark Powell's words, "meat for the young to grow on and medicine to heal the older who have been hurt by life." This was beautifully accomplished by Lee Bennett Hopkins himself in the Sandburg book, by Mr. Powell in *Poems of Walt Whitman,* in *Edna St. Vincent Millay's Poems Selected for Young People,* and by Robert Frost in his own collection, *You Come Too.* What counts in each individual instance is to serve best the poets themselves and the young readers in whom they live.

Susan Schuller

SOURCE: A review of *Voyages: Poems by Walt Whitman,* in *Voice of Youth Advocates,* Vol. 12, No. 2, June, 1989, p. 131.

In this anthology of 53 poems, Hopkins presents a selection of Walt Whitman works that should serve as a fine introduction for adolescent readers. Arranged in five groupings, the poems span Whitman's life and represent the themes of youth, journeys through America, slavery and the Civil War, self discovery, and old age and death. Some of his most famous poems, such as "Out of the Cradle Endlessly Rocking" and "When Lilacs Last in the Dooryard Bloom'd" are included along with selections and excerpts from other verse. This is a handsome edition, from the quality of paper and typeface to the black and white sketches by Charles Mikolaycak that subtly enhance the text. A brief biographical introduction and index of titles and first lines are included in this companion volume to Hopkins' *Rainbows Are Made: Poems by Carl Sandburg.*

📖 *ON THE FARM* (selected by Lee Bennett Hopkins, 1991)

Lee Bock

SOURCE: A review of *On the Farm,* in *School Library Journal,* Vol. 37, No. 10, October, 1991, p. 110.

With his usual instinct for selecting poetry by outstanding poets, Hopkins has gathered 16 short selections that will appeal to children. All of them share a voice that is consistently quiet, contemplative, and not silly, raucous, or nonsensical. In combination with [Laurel] Molk's sunny watercolor illustrations, this creates attractive pages that children will linger over. Many of the entries speak to what were once common experiences in our previously rural society—basic experiences such as greeting each farm animal joyously, clicking a stick down a "pickety" fence, or listening to the rooster's crow. Other poems are more universal: Myra Cohn Livingston's "Prayer," for example, and Patricia Hubbell's "October Morning"—"It's an apple-dumpling dandy day." All in all, this a fine collection.

Carolyn Phelan

SOURCE: A review of *On the Farm,* in *Booklist,* Vol. 88, No. 3, October 1, 1991, p. 333.

Prolific anthologizer Hopkins presents 16 short poems about farms and farm animals. While there is a common theme, each poem is illustrated individually, cast with different characters, different settings, and different seasons. [Laurel] Molk's appealing watercolor artwork will draw readers to the book, though, occasionally, its diffuse prettiness diminishes the more cogent imagery of the poetry. The verse itself is well chosen. A good source of read-alouds for the young, especially where books on farms are in demand.

📖 *THE WRITING BUG* (1992)

Nancy Vasilakis

SOURCE: A review of *The Writing Bug,* in *The Horn Book Magazine,* Vol. LXIX, No. 5, September-October, 1993, p. 616.

These three autobiographies [Verna Aardema's *A Bookworm Who Hatched,* Jean Fritz's *Surprising Myself,* and Lee Bennett Hopkins's *The Writing Bug*] continue the Meet the Author series, a timely and well-conceived project that earlier introduced Cynthia Rylant, Rafe Martin, and Jane Yolen to young readers. These are attractively formatted picture-book biographies, liberally sprinkled with full-color photographs and ideally suited to those younger students who are curious about their favorite authors. While these first-person narrative accounts provide some basic, factual biographical data, they concentrate for the most part on the creators' lives as writers. All three authors take a slightly different slant on the topic. Verna Aardema offers a few particulars about the book production process. Young readers might also be interested to learn that as a child she began thinking up stories in a secret backyard hideaway she escaped to in order to avoid helping with the dishes. Jean Fritz writes of her lifelong fascination with explorers, describing her own research and writing as an exploration through history. The autobiography by Lee Bennett Hopkins gives a slightly fuller picture, referring to his early career as a teacher and alluding in an indirect way to a less than idyllic childhood in a single-parent family. Still, the emphasis is on the positive aspects of his current life. All in all, these biographies give just enough factual information and personal commentary to satisfy readers and report writers in the second and third grades.

M. Jean Greenlaw

SOURCE: A review of *The Writing Bug,* in *The New Advocate,* Vol. 7, No. 3, Summer, 1994, p. 212.

This "Meet the Author" series provides clear and simple autobiographies for younger children, allowing them to peek into the life of some of their favorite authors. Lee Bennett Hopkins writes briefly of his childhood, then tells how he got hooked into writing. It will be interesting for children to read that "There isn't a day that goes by that I'm not reading poetry or working on a poem of my own." His work day is described, as well as the pleasures he enjoys in his home and in nearby New York City. Hopkins' dog Dude is featured, along with a poem inspired by Dude's overnight stay at the vet. Color photos [by Diane Rubinger in *The Writing Bug*] add to the feeling that one really does get to meet the author.

📖 *GOOD RHYMES, GOOD TIMES* (1995)

Kirkus Reviews

SOURCE: A review of *Good Rhymes, Good Times,* in *Kirkus Reviews,* Vol. LXIII, No. 11, June 1, 1995, p. 781.

A poet known for his theme-based anthologies collects nothing but his own work in a pretty picture book.

A few new poems—including **"Mother's Plea," "Split," "Winner"** and the succinct **"Winter"** (NEVER / quarrel / with / winter. / It / ALWAYS / wins.)—join with old favorites, including the title piece, exhorting the joy of reading, **"Valentine Feelings," "Sing a Song of Cities," "Behind the Museum Door," "Puppy," "Overnight at the Vet's," "Cat's Kit,"** and more. [Frané] Lessac's vivid multicultural urban landscape is as accessible as Hopkins's enthusiastic verse; adults will find this a pleasure to read aloud, with its celebration of events important to children: the loss of a tooth, a new puppy, or a Valentine from someone special.

Hazel Rochman

SOURCE: A review of *Good Rhymes, Good Times,* in *Booklist,* Vol. 91, No. 21, July, 1995, p. 1881.

Well-known anthologist Hopkins has collected 21 of his own children's poems published over the years. Rooted in the small events of a child's day, from jiggling a loose tooth to cuddling a pet, the poems are very simple, usually no more than one or two words to a line, with some affectionate wordplay and "good rhymes." [Frané] Lessac's brilliantly colored illustrations in folk-art style set the poems in a vital multicultural city neighborhood.

Publishers Weekly

SOURCE: A review of *Good Rhymes, Good Times,* in *Publishers Weekly,* Vol. 242, No. 27, July 3, 1995, pp. 60-1.

This joyous collection of 21 original poems, written between the early '70s and the present, deftly depicts a sense of delight and wonder in everyday experience. Hopkins brings freshness and immediacy to his subjects, whether a loose tooth, the city in the hush of snowfall, or summer fruits ("No matter / how / hot-burning / it / is / outside / when / you . . . cut deep / into / a / fresh, ripe watermelon / coolness / comes / into / your / hands"). [Frané] Lessac's energetic illustrations boldly enhance the text; painted in primary hues, their compelling, naïve quality seems both childlike and folkloric. Brush stroke dabs suggest, alternately, raindrops scattering from clouds, sparks from a fire, or blades of grass in a park. While the compositions as a whole are clean and simple, intricate patterns decorate quilts and drapes, plates and packaging. The bright spontaneity of the art pulls the reader into a cheerful city milieu captured throughout the seasons, a world that is matter-of-factly multicultural. An uncluttered layout offers plenty of white space, allowing the luxury of lingering over a page and truly savoring each poem.

Margo Wecksler

SOURCE: A review of *Good Rhymes, Good Times,* in *Children's Book Review Service,* Vol. XXIII, No. 14, August, 1995, p. 158.

These lovely, zippy poems were written especially for this age group; they're brief, but descriptive, explore things and emotions and are illustrated [by Frané Lessac] with delicious detail: bricks, blades of grass, butterfly wings. There is a nice gender, race and age mix of people in the pictures so many people will feel like the book is really for them.

Sally R. Dow

SOURCE: A review of *Good Rhymes, Good Times,* in *School Library Journal,* Vol. 41, No. 8, August, 1995, p. 135.

Here, prolific anthologist Hopkins has gathered 21 of his own light-hearted poems, many of which have been published elsewhere, into an engaging collection that captures the wonder and exuberance of childhood. The simple verses express childlike sentiments on a variety of subjects, from pets to favorite pastimes, from the awesomeness of thunderstorms to the quiet magic of the seasons. [Frané] Lessac's vibrant, primitive paintings, many of which depict urban life, are equally childlike and enormously appealing. Attractive design with spacious layout on large pages guarantees a wide audience. The title says it all—*Good Rhymes, Good Times.*

BEEN TO YESTERDAYS: POEMS OF A LIFE (1995)

Lenore Rosenthal

SOURCE: A review of *Been to Yesterdays: Poems of a Life,* in *Children's Book Review Service,* Vol. XXIV, No. 1, September, 1995, p. 10.

In his deceptively simple poetry, Hopkins relates from his childhood. In no more than three or four words per line, he sketches touching, joyous experiences that could be from anyone's life. A boyhood picture of the author is on the cover with snapshots of him and his family inside. The soft charcoal sketches [by Charlene Rendeiro] match the mood of the poems. Children will probably not pick up this slim volume, but parents and teachers reading the poems may spark some interest.

Kathleen Whalin

SOURCE: A review of *Been to Yesterdays,* in *School Library Journal,* Vol. 41, No. 9, September, 1995, p. 209.

This autobiographical cycle of poems is a rare gift, a careful exploration of one life that illumines the lives of all who read it. **Been to Yesterdays** chronicles Hopkins's 13th year, the year he moved from Pennsylvania to New Jersey, the year his parents divorced, the year his grandmother died, the year he knew he'd be a writer. Each poem is a model of emotional economy. The author writes of seeing packing boxes and knowing the family must leave a too-expensive apartment ("Stowed in cardboard / corners / memories rest / quietly / in paper chests"); he reflects on his grandmother's death and his growing up ("no more / sitting on / Grandma's knee / no more / smiles / or kisses / or joy / no more / darling / no more boy.") The spare elegance of the poems is matched by a spare, clean book design—the words are surrounded by white space and a few pen-and-ink sketches [by Charlene Rendeiro]. Like Cynthia Rylant's *Waiting to Waltz,* this book offers rich biography in a clear, poetic form. Readers will rejoice that Hopkins decided "To / make / this world / a whole lot / brighter / when / I grow up / I'll / be / a / writer."

Susan Dove Lempke

SOURCE: A review of *Been to Yesterdays,* in *Booklist,* Vol. 92, Nos. 9 & 10, January 1 & 15, 1996, p. 823.

Hopkins distills the experience of his middle-grade years into 28 poems of poignant clarity, achieving in very few words what many prose authors take chapters to tell. The first poem, with its too sprightly picture-perfect family, will make readers suspect that the future holds "another long drawn-out night / another bitter, brutal fight" ending in "the dreaded word—*divorce.*" The Woolworth store is a recurring motif in the poems, including the heartbreakingly honest **"Clutching,"** in which Hopkins learns from his mother that the lady with the kind smile and dark skin is a "nigger," not, according to his grandmother, a good word to choose, because "some words / can hurt / when you/blurt'em out. / Cause / undue sorrow. / Cause / undue pain." Hopkins transforms bleak events into crystalline moments, concluding with his resolve as a 13-year-old to "make the world a whole lot brighter" by becoming a writer. Good reading and an excellent, unconventional choice for teachers doing units on poetry and autobiography.

Journal of Adolescent and Adult Literacy

SOURCE: A review of *Been to Yesterdays: Poems of a Life,* in *Journal of Adolescent and Adult Literacy,* Vol. 39, No. 5, February, 1996, p. 423.

Lee Bennett Hopkins, a poet and a compiler of more than 50 poetry anthologies, opens his heart to readers to tell about his childhood. With quiet spirit the poet expresses his feelings about his parents' divorce, his mother's struggle to survive, his dreams of becoming a writer, his love for his grandmother, and his views of Christmas. Some poems are sad, like **"When,"** when his father leaves; most poems are tender, like **"Smile,"** a description of his "picture-perfect family." Through the eyes of a young boy these simple, emotion-filled poems capture the pain of divorce and its effect on a family. As a bonus, charming end papers show snapshots of Hopkins as a young boy, of his family, and of his house in Scranton, Pennsylvania.

Additional coverage of Hopkins's life and career is contained in the following sources published by Gale Research: *Authors and Artists for Young Adults,* Vol. 18; *Contemporary Authors New Revision Series,* Vol. 29; *Junior DISCovering Authors (CD-ROM); Major Authors and Illustrators for Children and Young Adults; Something about the Author,* Vols. 3, 68; and *Something about the Author Autobiography Series,* Vol. 4.

Kathleen Krull

1952-

(Also writes as Kathleen Cowles, Kathryn Kenny, and Kevin Kenny) American author of fiction and nonfiction.

Major works include *Gonna Sing My Head Off! American Folk Songs for Children* (1992), *Lives of the Musicians: Good Times, Bad Times (and What the Neighbors Thought)* (1993), *The Other Side: How Kids Live in a California Latino Neighborhood* (1994), *Wilma Unlimited: How Wilma Rudolph Became the World's Fastest Woman* (1996).

INTRODUCTION

A noted author of fiction and nonfiction for young people, Krull is admired for her ability to stimulate reader's interest in the lives of others. With works ranging from music anthologies, biographies, and picture books, Krull's well-paced, conversational writing style is easily accessible to children and has earned her praise from critics. In her books about the arts, the author is noted for encouraging interest in musicians, authors, and artists by providing humorous tidbits of information and showing readers the human side of these legendary figures. Critics also applaud Krull for her in-depth investigations into the lives of children from different cultural backgrounds. In her works, she seeks to show young readers how much they actually have in common with people whose lives are seemingly different. Of her own writings, Krull said, "I aim for making my books as fresh as I can—using words and combinations of words that only I would use."

Biographical Information

Born in Fort Leonard Wood, Missouri, Krull grew up in Wilmette, Illinois. Interested in becoming an author at a young age, she practiced by writing *A Garden Book* while in second grade and *Hairdos and People I Know* as a fifth grader. After graduating magna cum laude from Lawrence University in 1974, she accepted a job at Western Publishing to begin her career in children's literature and saw her first book in print while employed there. In 1979, the author took a position as managing editor at Raintree Publishers, followed by a two-year stint as a senior editor at Harcourt Brace Jovanovich where she helped begin a children's book department. Leaving the industry in 1984 to pursue freelance writing and reviewing, she has since remained involved with aspiring authors by conducting workshops, offering lectures, and teaching classes at universities. Krull stated that in addition to using her own hobbies for inspiration, she writes with an eye toward what children are interested in and tries to recall what books and subjects she enjoyed as a child. She once admitted, "My 'hidden agenda' is always to create books that will mean as much to readers as books have meant to me."

Major Works

Out of a "fear that traditional music was losing its place in the lives of children," Krull set out to produce *Gonna Sing My Head Off! American Folk Songs for Children*, a well-received compilation of sixty-two American songs selected and arranged by the author. She not only included traditional tunes such as "I've Been Working on the Railroad" and "Yankee Doodle," but also songs which are more recent in origin, like Pete Seeger's "If I Had a Hammer" and Leadbelly's "Good Night Irene." In addition, Krull, who studied music along with English in college, prefaced each title with a brief introduction detailing the historical background behind each song and offered lighthearted instructions for singing each song. In *Lives of the Musicians: Good Times, Bad Times (and What the Neighbors Thought)*, the author continued to keep children interested in music by exploring the lives of famous musicians. Krull fleshed out the offbeat lives of sixteen men and women with amusing and interesting anecdotes combined with standard biographical information. Critics praise Krull for providing intriguing personal details about the composers and thereby dispelling the intimidation surrounding the world of classical music.

Finding a receptive readership, she continued in this same down-to-earth style with other books about the habits, quirks, and idiosyncracies of famous authors and artists.

Krull's books reveal her interest in the everyday events of children's lives as well as adults. In her book *The Other Side: How Kids Live in a California Latino Neighborhood,* part of the "World of My Own" series, the author followed the varied lives of three Latino children living in California's Chula Vista near the Mexican border. She recorded how these children maintain and balance two different cultures and languages, one at home and one away from home. At the same time, though, Krull determinedly emphasized that these children share the same experiences as other American children. Krull wrote three other books in this series, focusing on Native American, Chinese American, and African American youths. Krull has also created an inspiring picture book biography. *Wilma Unlimited: How Wilma Rudolph Became the World's Fastest Woman* details how a sickly, polio-stricken child was able to persevere through paralysis, racism, and poverty to become the first woman to win three gold medals in a single Olympic competition. Critics admired Krull's ability to bring the near mythic life of Rudolph down to earth and to interest children in such a sensational female athlete.

Awards

Gonna Sing My Head Off! American Folk Songs for Children was named a Children's Choice Book of 1993 by the International Reading Association and the Children's Book Council and an American Library Association Notable Book of 1993. *Lives of the Musicians: Good Times, Bad Times (and What the Neighbors Thought)* was listed as a Golden Kite honor book for nonfiction by the Society of Children's Book Writers and Illustrators and as a *Boston Globe/Horn Book* honor book for nonfiction, both in 1993. *Wilma Unlimited: How Wilma Rudolph Became the World's Fastest Woman* was named an American Library Association Notable Book of 1997.

TITLE COMMENTARY

SOMETIMES MY MOM DRINKS TOO MUCH (with mother, Helen Krull, 1980)

Zena Sutherland

SOURCE: A review of *Sometimes My Mom Drinks Too Much,* in *Bulletin of the Center for Children's Books,* Vol. 34, No. 5, January, 1981, pp. 96-7.

This is less a story than an amplification of a situation; told by Maureen, an only child who appears in the illustrations [by Helen Cogancherry] to be about nine years old, it states Maureen's sadness and worry about her mother's drinking, and the way she has at times been embarrassed by Mom's behavior when Maureen's friends were present. Dad explains that it's sickness, that Mom still loves Maureen even when she acts angry; at times, he, too, acts angry at Maureen when she thinks he is really angry at her mother. The only action in the story is that Mom, with her employer's agreement, goes to a hospital and has arranged for supportive therapy on dismissal. Dad says candidly that they hope she will get over the illness of alcoholism, but that they can't count on it. As a story, this is tepid; as an explanation of the pattern of alcoholics, it's a bit simplified, so that it's easy to absorb but certainly not fully explanatory, especially in eliding any mention of the possible causes of alcoholism.

Lynn H. Aspey

SOURCE: A review of *Sometimes My Mom Drinks Too Much,* in *Science Books & Films,* Vol. 16, No. 5, May-June, 1981, p. 273.

This is an excellent book for young readers! The definitions and problems associated with alcoholic mothers (or parents, regardless of sex) are clearly stated and should be easily comprehended by young children. Topics covered include how the child feels about a parent's drinking problem; how family members feel embarrassment and helplessness; how other children perceive the child's alcoholic parent; how important the teacher's role can be; and how treatment is available but not always effective. Alcoholism and family relationships and problems are dealt with sensitively and compassionately. I would recommend this book highly to all young children since it will help them to gain insights and knowledge about an intensifying social problem that affects growing numbers of young people and adults alike. Any parent or teacher facing and dealing with this problem, either with their own children or children in a classroom, should find this book a valuable teaching tool—perhaps a good "ice breaker."

GONNA SING MY HEAD OFF! AMERICAN FOLK SONGS FOR CHILDREN (1992)

Roger Sutton

SOURCE: A review of *Gonna Sing My Head Off!,* in *Bulletin of the Center for Children's Books,* Vol. 46, No. 2, October, 1992, p. 47.

Krull's informative notes and Garns' versatile pastel illustrations enhance this collection of sixty-two American songs ranging from the tried-and-true traditional, such as "I've Been Working on the Railroad," to modern composed songs that have entered the folk canon, such as Malvina Reynolds' "What Have They Done to the Rain." The arrangements, which include guitar chords, are clean and simple ("without being boring," as the compiler/arranger correctly notes), easy enough for adults remembering long-ago piano lessons as well as for kids just beginning. Krull's tempo and tone directions ("Spunky," for "Oh, Susanna," "Like an opera singer," for "I Gave My Love a Cherry") are clever without cuteness, and the wide variety of the anthology—work songs, cowboy sagas, spirituals, protest songs, etc.,—encourages an equal variety of possibilities for use, including classroom sing-alongs, bedtime story hours, and family recreation. [Allen] Garns does an admirable job of wedding image to music: "Down in the Valley" faces a full-bleed picture of a pastoral setting framed by prison walls; his sketch for "Stewball" streaks a racing horse and rider against a vibrant aqua sky. The notes that preface each song give interesting bits of both musical and American history; first-line and song-type indexes are appended. Handsome, useful, unstuffy and lots of fun, this is the perfect contemporary companion to Margaret Boni and the Provensens' classic *Fireside Book of Folk Songs,* an antecedent Krull acknowledges in her preface.

Ann Stell

SOURCE: A review of *Gonna Sing My Head Off!* in *School Library Journal,* Vol. 38, No. 10, October, 1992, p. 105.

"From California to the New York Island," this book was made for you and me! Hard as it is to believe, *Gonna Sing My Head Off!* is the first serious collection for young readers since Ruth Crawford Seeger's memorable *American Folk Songs for Children.* Margaret Boni's *The Fireside Book of Folksongs* and Tom Glazer's *Treasury of Folk Songs* are also library staples. Hang on to them; there's surprisingly little overlap here. Of the 62 folk songs Krull has selected, only 21 are in Glazer's larger compendium. Some classics from Seeger's title are not in this one, but Krull has amassed so many outstanding selections that no one will be disappointed. She pays tribute to many of our folk singers by including "Joe Hill" for Joan Baez, "Good Night Irene" and "Rock Island Line" for Leadbelly, "If I Had a Hammer" for Pete Seeger, and "So Long, It's Been Good to Know You" for Woody Guthrie. The oversized book itself is handsome, uncluttered, and accessible. Short, readable paragraphs accompany each entry and tell a little of its history. The musical arrangements are easy to follow. There is a helpful index of song types as well as of first lines. [Allen] Garns's warm pastel drawings evoke the many moods of the music with great success. His rich palette, use of perspective, and energetic lines add verve and variety to this sparkling sampler. Librarians, teachers, parents, and children who get a hold of this book are sure to sing their heads off.

Kirkus Reviews

SOURCE: A review of *Gonna Sing My Head Off! American Folk Songs for Children,* in *Kirkus Reviews,* Vol. LX, No. 19, October 1, 1992, p. 1257.

Citing the splendid *Fireside Book of Folk Songs* as inspiration, Krull gathers 60 lively favorites, old and new, with contemporary appeal—protest and work songs, games and dances, spirituals, nonsense, love songs, etc. Her arrangement is creative: alphabetical order leads to some nice serendipities, e.g., ending with some searching w's—"What Have They Done to the Rain?"; "Will the Circle Be Unbroken?"—and "Yankee Doodle," while an index of song types brings out many other connections. Krull provides simple musical arrangements and fascinating brief introductions to the songs' histories, including recordings by well-known singers from Pete Seeger to the Beach Boys. These are not all pure folk, but they've all been widely sung as if they were, and Krull is scrupulous in accounting for their diverse origins. Even her instructions for singing are fun: "Unladylike"; "As if you're seasick." Only [Allen] Garns's illustrations, on almost every spread, are a bit uneven: some seem perfunctory in their choice of subject and in execution; but, elsewhere, he uses the lush tones of his pastels to better advantage in energetic designs, deftly sketched vignettes ("Joe Hill") or glowing, evocative scenes. An inviting book. Index of first lines.

Oscar Brand

SOURCE: "These Songs Were Made for You and Me," in *The New York Times Book Review,* November 8, 1992, p. 44.

Gonna Sing My Head Off presents 68 familiar songs, including a few of Woody Guthrie's best, organized alphabetically by title in a handsome format. Ms. Krull previously edited *Songs of Praise,* a collection of hymns. Her choices here are as wide-ranging as a stampede, and often just as unpredictable.

The songs include Steve Goodman's "City of New Orleans," a popular hit for Arlo Guthrie in 1972; the ancient "Riddle Song"; the 1908 rouser "Take Me Out to the Ball Game," and the 1930's labor anthem "Joe Hill." The variety of the selections will probably fascinate as many adults as children.

Ms. Krull has carefully researched the origins of the songs, although she may not be aware that "The Erie Canal" is a 20th-century creation, or that the melody she uses for "Stewball" is a recent copyrighted version.

But it's important to note that in these arrangements the keys are eminently singable, the chords easily playable. The drawings by Allen Garns are eloquent, and *Gonna Sing My Head Off* is totally enjoyable.

📖 IT'S MY EARTH, TOO: HOW I CAN HELP THE EARTH STAY ALIVE (1992)

Virginia G. Schuyler

SOURCE: A review of *It's My Earth, Too,* in *Appraisal: Science Books for Young People,* Vol. 26, No. 1, Winter, 1993, pp. 31-2.

This colorful book discusses how children can help the "earth stay alive." The illustrations [by Melanie Hope

Greenberg] are bright and effective. The children pictured are multicultural and varied. The twelve ways to help the earth to stay alive are simple and yet understandable for the intended audience. Wouldn't it be great if this book were translated and distributed worldwide! Children are anxious to help "save the earth." Primary teachers will enjoy reading this book to their students. It provides information to build upon.

JoAnn M. Valenti

SOURCE: A review of *It's My Earth, Too*, in *Appraisal: Science Books for Young People*, Vol. 26, No. 1, Winter, 1993, pp. 31-2.

The last three pages of this 30-some page hard cover, pricey book, aimed at very young readers, offers a list of twelve ways children can help protect the environment. The list, which will have to be read to most of the targeted audience of what I feel should be pre-schoolers, suggests basic acts of socially responsible as well as environmentally responsible behavior. Children are told to save trees by using a lunchbox rather than paper bags, to ride their bikes or walk before asking to go somewhere in the family car, not to litter the beach, and to brush their teeth without leaving the water running. All of this is well and good, especially an admonishment that bugs are not all bad and should be escorted outside rather than automatically squashed; however, I wonder how parents will take to item number one, which tells children not to take more food than they can eat in order to avoid waste. Unless much has changed, getting children to eat healthy things, such as peas and carrots, or to eat enough in general is a problem in many families.

There are less expensive and longer lists of ways children can positively affect the environment available. . . . This very simplistic approach may be a useful starter book for the totally unenlightened child and/or parent. I hope there are none. On the other hand, the author's general message about greed might be necessary to reach some audiences.

📖 LIVES OF THE MUSICIANS: GOOD TIMES, BAD TIMES (AND WHAT THE NEIGHBORS THOUGHT) (1993)

Publishers Weekly

SOURCE: A review of *Lives of the Musicians: Good Times, Bad Times (and What the Neighbors Thought)*, in *Publishers Weekly*, Vol. 240, No. 8, February 22, 1993, pp. 96-7.

Red was Mozart's favorite color. Beethoven was a slob. Clara Schumann's concerts were so popular that police had to be called in for crowd control. In this enthralling work, Krull dishes 16 of the movers and shakers in musical history—from Vivaldi and the "three B's" (Bach, Beethoven and Brahms) to Gilbert and Sullivan, Woody Guthrie and Scott Joplin (early critics of his ragtime accused it of causing permanent brain damage and ruining

people's morals). Readers who thrive on offbeat information will be delighted by the splendid array of fun facts lurking in these informative and accurate snapshot biographies. Krull masterfully distills the essentials of each musician's life into snappy prose, an attitude echoed in the book's lively, playful design (the introductory page for each musician, for example, contains not only pertinent information but tantalizing, often cryptic "kickers" as well—the one above Brahms's name alludes to his checked underwear, which audiences occasionally glimpsed when the absent-minded conductor forgot to fasten his suspenders). [Kathryn] Hewitt's caricatures feature full-sized heads on tiny bodies—a slant that plays up the quirky presentation. She, too, has an eye for detail, pulling out appropriate visual tidbits from the text—Bach's prized silver coffeepots, for example, grace a page corner. Even those only remotely interested in music will be hooked by these living, breathing anecdotes—the stuff of which the best biography is made.

Carolyn Phelan

SOURCE: A review of *Lives of the Musicians: Good Times, Bad Times (and What the Neighbors Thought)*, in *Booklist*, Vol. 89, No. 16, April 1, 1993, p. 432.

In a radical departure from most collective biographies written for children, this book is never dull. From its opening quotation ("The more of us musicians there are, the crazier we all become."—Erik Satie), to its colorful illustrations, to its fascinating details ("Not until he was almost thirty did [Franz Lizst] stop playing with toy soldiers"), the book makes its statement with style. Beginning with Vivaldi and ending with Woody Guthrie, the selections provide a few surprises, but the 19 composers profiled include many whose music children might hear, perform, or write reports about, such as Bach, Beethoven, Chopin, Gershwin, Joplin, Prokofiev, Verdi, and Gilbert and Sullivan. Others, such as Boulanger, Shumann, and Satie, will be less familiar, but no less interesting. Krull strives to show how these famous and creative people lived in their lives, noting in her introduction that in their music "they had a perseverance and single-mindedness that led not only to success, but also to eccentricities, sometimes amusing, sometimes sad." A marvelous full-page caricature of the biographee opens each section of the book, followed by a few pages of biography and another, smaller illustration. While there's no subject index or source notes here, the back pages include a glossary of musical terms, an index of composers, and a bibliography for further reading. [Kathryn] Hewitt's stylized paintings interpret the surroundings and personalities of the musicians with panache. Although the writing is occasionally choppy, this unique volume represents a welcome departure from the cold, idealized, "marble bust" approach to children's biographies of musicians.

Kirkus Reviews

SOURCE: A review of *Lives of the Musicians: Good*

Times, Bad Times (and What the Neighbors Thought), in Kirkus Reviews, Vol. LXI, No. 8, April 15, 1993, p. 532.

A collection of anecdotes about 19 musicians from Vivaldi to Woody Guthrie that's offered "as a way of getting closer to the musicians—and the music"—but that may only distance readers from traditional music by portraying it as an incomprehensible milieu populated by odd characters. Apparently chosen with more regard for the picturesque (Chopin's cherished silver goblet of earth from his native Poland, Clara Schumann's penchant for wearing a different white dress every night) or the bizarre (the full chamber pot under Beethoven's piano, Chopin's deathbed request that his body be cut open before burial) than for authenticity, a number of the incidents related are apocryphal; several have long since been called into serious question or specifically refuted by responsible scholarship. Although the attention given to 20th-century figures (six entries) is laudable, the selection is eccentric: Stephen Foster but not Schubert, Gilbert and Sullivan but not Wagner, Satie but not Debussy. An attractive volume with eye-catching full-page watercolor caricatures, but the information is too inconsequential and too unreliable to be of much use.

Beth Tegart

SOURCE: A review of Lives of the Musicians: Good Times, Bad Times (and What the Neighbors Thought), in School Library Journal, Vol. 39, No. 5, May, 1993, p. 117.

Bravo! A collective biography that is informative and fun to read. Krull has compiled an enjoyable assortment of sketches on 16 famous musical giants that will have readers rushing to the stereo. In three or four pages each, such masters as Vivaldi, Mozart, Beethoven, and Tchaikovsky; popular composers such as Gilbert & Sullivan, Joplin, and Gershwin; and even folk hero Woody Guthrie are profiled. Gossipy, nitty-gritty personal habits and quirks are presented, along with a sense of appreciation for the musicians' lives and times. [Kathryn] Hewitt's full-page caricatures are surrounded by important details. In subdued but striking colors, she captures the personality and temperament of these composers. This is a humorous, delightful, appreciative treat. While it doesn't have enough information for reports, it's a fine, personalized way to introduce children to the creators of great works that are a part of every music curriculum. The book has a helpful list of musical terms, an index, and an excellent bibliography. It belongs in every library and on every music teacher's desk.

Jim Gladstone

SOURCE: A review of Lives of the Musicians: Good Times, Bad Times (and What the Neighbors Thought), in The New York Times Book Review, October 3, 1993, p. 31.

Joe loved to snack and favored both herring and eggnog!

Nadia relaxed by soaking in exotic bath oils!

Wolf wrote letters to his terrier, Bimperl!

If Joe, Nadia and Wolf's mail went to a ZIP code like, oh, 90210, or if Joe, Nadia and Wolf had hair to die for in their new rap video, kids would eat up the preceding factoids. Wolf would seem all the more lovable and approachable because he missed his pup. Nadia's sex appeal would crank up a notch. And Joe—that wacky Joe!—well, there's no accounting for taste, but his oddness is part of his charm, no?

Joe, Nadia and Wolf, however, are neither prime-time Icons nor Top 40 faves. They're Johannes Brahms, Nadia Boulanger and Wolfgang Amadeus Mozart as sketched in Kathleen Krull's quirky volume of music lore, *Lives of the Musicians: Good Times, Bad Times (And What the Neighbors Thought)*. And while dead composers of unfashionable music are not the types whose innocuous domestic "secrets" generally raise hairs on the backs of prepubescent necks, Ms. Krull may be on to something.

To most preteen-agers (heck, to most American adults), classical music isn't attached to individual names and faces. Rather, it is a singular, incomprehensible creature, a massive beast of orchestral *Sturm und Drang* that is too foreign to be approached, let alone enjoyed. Ms. Krull tackles this problem with an interesting technique: rather than try to explain why the classics may be richer than current pop, she borrows pop's sales techniques and applies them to great composers. Quoting the cellist Yo-Yo Ma, she writes: "Beethoven thought that through his music he could change the world. Today, rock musicians are virtually the only ones who think that."

Turning these tables, Ms. Krull culls inconsequential tidbits, the sort of stuff that fills Tiger Beat magazine and MTV News, and uses them to create portraits of the masters that give children individuals to whom they can relate. We learn that one of Beethoven's favorite foods was macaroni and cheese, that Frédéric Chopin was embarrassed by his "huge" nose, that Giuseppe Verdi collected peacocks and cacti. Slight stuff, yes. But undeniably intriguing.

Elementary school music teachers will probably adore this book. Having failed to get pupils' attention with pronouncements like "We will next listen to a piece written in 18th-century Vienna," they can now use real grabbers like "The guy who wrote this piece was wild for macaroni and cheese."

Lives of the Musicians successfully humanizes 20 important figures through Ms. Krull's bright thumbnail sketches and the illustrator Kathryn Hewitt's droll accompanying caricatures. While most of the subjects can reasonably be pegged as "classical" composers, a few show her to be rather idiosyncratic herself. What's Stephen Foster doing in this crowd? And Woody Guthrie? Still, when there's so little children's literature available about *any* music, let us rejoice when we're treated to a passage as jauntily peculiar as Ms. Krull's description of Erik Satie's apartment—"The room reminded people of an immense spider web. One of the two pianos was buried under newspapers. There was gymnastic equipment, but no bed, just a hammock."

Ms. Krull edited *Gonna Sing My Head Off: A Treasury of American Folk Songs for Children,* which provides concise historical backgrounds for a variety of time-honored tunes. While some composition-specific information is offered in "Musical Notes" at the end of each chapter in *Lives of the Musicians,* one does wish the biographical essays stirred up a bit more of an urge to listen to the composers' music. Nonetheless, there's lots of appealing stuff here and the composers will surely endure another wee bit of neglect. After all, we're not exactly dealing with the New Kids on the Block.

📖 **CITY WITHIN A CITY: HOW KIDS LIVE IN NEW YORK'S CHINATOWN (1994); THE OTHER SIDE: HOW KIDS LIVE IN A CALIFORNIA LATINO NEIGHBORHOOD (1994)**

Hazel Rochman

SOURCE: A review of *City within a City: How Kids Live in New York's Chinatown* and *The Other Side: How Kids Live in a California Latino Neighborhood,* in *Booklist,* Vol. 90, No. 16, April 15, 1994, pp. 1530-31.

Part of the World of My Own series, these two lively photo-essays illustrated in full color capture what it's like to be an immigrant child in a strongly ethnic neighborhood. Each book focuses on at least two children from two different families, so that there's a sense of individual differences within a common culture rather than a vague stereotype. The account of New York City's Chinatown moves from the tourist's view of an exotic place to a candid account of what it's like to grow up in those crowded, noisy, sometimes scary streets. The book on the California Latino neighborhood is generally more upbeat, especially about the young people's continuing contact with the other side of the border, a place they often return to even as they grow up in the U.S. In both books, bilingualism is a crucial issue—what languages the young people speak at home, how they learn English, how they act as guides and translators for their parents. Krull is the author of several fine books, including *Gonna Sing My Head Off* and *Lives of the Musicians.* She writes here with an informal, chatty style, weaving together information about family, friends, school, religion, holiday celebrations, and career plans as well as facts about clothes, musical and TV tastes, and food (pizza's the universal favorite). The book design is occasionally confusing, with different photographs [by David Hautzig] sometimes crowded together, but the warm, intimate photos show what's special about the kids and their neighborhoods and what is universal.

Roger Sutton

SOURCE: A review of *City within a City: How Kids Live in New York's Chinatown* and *The Other Side: How Kids Live in a California Latino Neighborhood,* in *Bulletin of the Center for Children's Books,* Vol. 47, No. 9, May, 1994, p. 291.

In a welcome pair of "at-home" versions of the colorful cultural profiles we've been seeing about kids in other countries, Latino children in Southern California's Chula Vista and Chinese-American children in New York City's Chinatown here talk about how they've learned to mediate two cultures, the one they were born into and the one to which their parents have brought them. In many ways, these books are a model for the genre. They're strongly focused on the young subjects, there's a greater emphasis on daily life than on exotic foods or "festivals," and the color photos are plentiful, sharp, and unposed. *The Other Side* shows Mexican-American kids in school; out with their friends; traveling to Tijuana, seven miles away, to see relatives (and doctors—medical care is much cheaper there). *City within a City* similarly follows its subjects through daily routines of school and family life. General facts and controversies (illegal immigration, bilingual education) are successfully drawn from the anecdotal portraits, although *City* demonstrates some ambiguity over the number of Chinese living in New York. Each book has a map, a reading list, and an index; further volumes in the series are planned.

Kirkus Reviews

SOURCE: A review of *The Other Side: How Kids Live in a California Latino Neighborhood,* in *Kirkus Reviews,* Vol. LXII, No. 10, May 15, 1994, p. 701.

A perceptive documentary portraying three Mexican-born children, Pedro and Francisco Tapia and Cinthya Guzman, and their community in Chula Vista, between San Diego and the border. All fluently bilingual (Cinthya is considering medical school), they describe learning English in an American school and how they use two languages in their daily lives, the advantages of living in the US (cleaner, better education), and reasons for frequent visits back to Tijuana (to see family and get cheaper medical treatment; it's also safer). Though Krull mentions problems faced by Latino immigrants (one of several sidebars discusses stereotypes) and describes their customs and culture, she emphasizes the stable, disciplined family life these three young people enjoy and what they have in common with other American kids. The lively, thoroughly detailed account is well served by the candid color photos [by David Hautzig] on every spread. A fine resource.

Publishers Weekly

SOURCE: A review of *City within a City: How Kids Live in New York's Chinatown* and *The Other Side: How Kids*

Live in a California Latino Neighborhood, in *Publishers Weekly,* Vol. 241, No. 22, May 30, 1994, p. 58.

These attractive debut titles in the A World of My Own series combine lively photography and simple text to introduce two very different communities. Each book focuses on specific children who live in the area, describing their routines at home, in school and with friends. Emphasis is placed on the joys and problems of participating in two cultures. *City,* for example, examines how many Chinese young people act as interpreters for immigrant parents, how Americanization affects tradition and how individuals learn to incorporate old attitudes with new opportunities. In *The Other Side,* three Latino children cope with transitions between their California neighborhood and the Mexican town of Tijuana, where many members of their families still live. Krull (*Lives of the Musicians*) makes skillful use of quotes from the various subjects, allowing their voices and experiences to command center stage. [David] Hautzig's (*DJ's, Ratings, and Hook Tapes*) candid photos tend to emphasize daytime street scenes in *City,* while *The Other Side* displays a more dramatic range. Sidebars address additional topics of interest, such as stereotypes, art, food and the history of the communities; helpful maps provide reference.

Anne Connor

SOURCE: A review of *The Other Side: How Kids Live in a California Latino Neighborhood,* in *School Library Journal,* Vol. 40, No. 6, June, 1994, p. 139.

In this engaging look at three Latino children who live in the border town of Chula Vista, Krull presents a positive view of the immigrant experience. In a straightforward and readable style, she shows three children who have successfully adapted to a new culture and language, while maintaining close ties to their extended families in Tijuana. Basing her portraits of Cinthya, Francisco, and Pedro on interviews, she adds insight into their social situation with brief essays on Mexican culture, stereotypes, and influences of immigration on California. While her subjects clearly have a good life, she does briefly mention the more difficult existence of many Latino immigrants—especially those who have entered the country illegally. With many glowing full-color photographs [by David Hautzig] and simply stated social commentary, this is a useful and valuable addition to library collections.

Susan Pine

SOURCE: A review of *City within a City: How Kids Live in New York's Chinatown,* in *School Library Journal,* Vol. 40, No. 7, July, 1994, p. 111.

Through conversations with two 12-year-old residents, Chao Liu and Sze Ki Chau, Krull presents an overview of life in New York City's Chinatown, making brief observations about crowded streets, vegetable stands, tourists, immigrants, crime, gangs, holidays, food, stereotypes, and traditions. Unfortunately, there is not enough solid information here for report writers, and Chinese youngsters may find the text's many generalizations hurtful. A photograph of four teenagers playing handball on a graffiti-filled court does not necessarily mean "signs of gang activity . . . "; and it is unlikely that Chao's first language is English if his parents do not speak it. To describe the local cuisine as looking to an outsider like it comes "from another planet" is insulting; it is also not accurate to describe the New Year Festival as "more frightening than festive" to children. The author notes that many non-Catholic Chinese attend Catholic school, but neglects to point out that in New York many non-Catholics attend parochial schools. Some of the descriptions of Chinatown are also applicable to other ethnic communities in New York, and so the presentation of the Chinese experience as totally unique is misleading.

Rhonda Cooper

SOURCE: A review of *City within a City: How Kids Live in New York's Chinatown,* in *Kliatt,* Vol. 30, No. 6, November, 1996, p. 26.

This book uses text and photos to tell the story of two Chinese-American twelve-year-olds living in New York City's Chinatown. The narrative discusses the children's relationship with their parents, their likes and dislikes, and their aspirations. Along the way it also serves as a travelogue to the neighborhood that houses at least 250,000 Chinese Americans, and is often a first stop for both legal and illegal immigrants to the States. Although the Chinatowns in major American cities remain popular tourist attractions, and most Americans have at least a slight familiarity with Chinese cuisine, information on the lives and beliefs in those Chinese-American communities is less readily available. This book provides insights into how these two children feel about growing up in Chinatown, how the assimilation process affects their families, and how much like other American kids of their generation they really are. Sidebars about the history of Chinatown, Chinese food and medicine, and cultural stereotypes are valuable additions to the main narrative. The nearly 40 color photos [by David Hautzig] in this volume visually complement the text by showing the reader the everyday life of these children and the other inhabitants of their neighborhood.

LIVES OF THE WRITERS: COMEDIES, TRAGEDIES (AND WHAT THE NEIGHBORS THOUGHT) (1994)

Publishers Weekly

SOURCE: A review of *Lives of the Writers: Comedies, Tragedies (and What the Neighbors Thought),* in *Publishers Weekly,* Vol. 241, No. 31, August 1, 1994, p. 79.

As seductive as Krull and [Kathryn] Hewitt's *Lives of the Musicians,* this compendium of brief biographies of literary luminaries is as much fun as a tête-à-tête with a gossipy friend. Krull knows exactly how to captivate her audience; she goes right for the juicy stuff, adding to historical fact the kind of chatty incidentals and amusing anecdotes that put flesh and blood on dry literary bones. Hans Christian Andersen, for example, "was known to hug trees," and Edgar Allan Poe, at 27, married his 13-year-old cousin. Emily Dickinson and Mark Twain shared an eccentricity—they both dressed solely in white. Jane Austen ate chocolate for breakfast, and Jack London liked to pose outrageous challenges to his houseguests—swallowing live goldfish, perhaps, or pushing peanuts up their noses. These exuberant thumbnail sketches are ably matched by Hewitt's sophisticated caricatures, which will delight sharp-eyed readers with their many visual references to particulars and oddities about each of the subjects. A must-have for the reference shelf.

Kirkus Reviews

SOURCE: A review of *Lives of the Writers: Comedies, Tragedies (and What the Neighbors Thought)*, in *Kirkus Reviews*, Vol. LXII, No. 18, September 15, 1994, p. 1275.

Another colorful, enthralling excursion into our cultural heritage from the author and illustrator of *Lives of the Musicians*. Krull has selected 20 (dead) literary figures that are—or should be—familiar to young people. All, with the exception of Lady Murasaki, are European or American, and most are from the last two centuries. Arranged in order of birth, each gets one of [Kathryn] Hewitt's polished, huge-headed portraits, a three-to-six-page biography, and a handful of "Bookmarks," miscellaneous notes in smaller type. It's hard to stop reading; if the chapter titles aren't enticement enough ("Ugly Duckling or Little Mermaid? Hans Christian Andersen"), the first sentences ("Robert Louis Stevenson spent his whole life either ill in bed or out having thrilling adventures") will be. Krull expertly sets the hook with well-turned phrases and arrays of tasty facts: Frances Hodgson Burnett owned a dollhouse with a working shower; Jane Austen "was a world-class aunt"; Zora Neale Hurston studied voodoo practices. Sources are not specifically cited, but the author inserts sufficient notes of caution (regarding Langston Hughes's homosexuality, for instance) to establish credibility, and an excellent, nonscholarly bibliography is appended.

This may not be the *only* book you'll need on these writers—for one thing, their quirks get more attention than their works—but you'll have to look far to find a better *first* one.

Deborah Stevenson

SOURCE: A review of *Lives of the Writers: Comedies, Tragedies (and What the Neighbors Thought)*, in *Bulletin of the Center for Children's Books*, Vol. 48, No. 2, October, 1994, p. 53.

In a companion volume to their *Lives of the Musicians*, the duo of Krull and [Kathryn] Hewitt offer a collection of literary lives. The nineteen writers featured are a varied lot: some are American (Mark Twain, Edgar Allan Poe), some not (William Shakespeare, Jane Austen); most wrote in English (Zora Neale Hurston, E. B. White) but some did not (Murasaki Shikibu, Miguel de Cervantes); most are writers of children's books or of literature now frequently read by children (Hans Christian Andersen, Robert Louis Stevenson, Isaac Bashevis Singer). The biographies are thumbnail sketches, gossipy and confiding about the experiences and whims of their subjects in a way that personalizes Famous Authors without diminishing them in kids' eyes; the book won't expand kids' understanding of the literature much, but it will help them put real people to the bylines. The colored-pencil and watercolor art offers droll, big-headed caricatures reminiscent of the *New York Review of Books* as well as small vignettes of aspects of that author's life or interests (some of the vignettes represent awfully peripheral aspects, such as roach powder for E. B. White's brief stint, mentioned in the text by all of three words, of selling the stuff). Young bookworms especially will enjoy the pageant of personalities, but many kids will relish the appropriate bio when used in conjunction with that author's literature—try it as a come-on for a readaloud.

Lauren Adams

SOURCE: A review of *Lives of the Writers: Comedies, Tragedies (and What the Neighbors Thought)*, in *The Horn Book Magazine*, Vol. LXX, No. 6, November-December, 1994, pp. 745-6.

The author and illustrator of *Lives of the Musicians* have created another eclectic collection of biographical sketches, this time featuring twenty of the world's most famous literary figures. Presented in chronological order by date of birth, the selection of writers begins with Murasaki Shikibu, the first-century Japanese author of *The Tale of Genji*—considered by some to be the world's oldest novel—and concludes with Isaac Bashevis Singer, the Jewish-American storyteller who died in 1991. As in *Musicians,* Krull provides basic biographical details and carefully points out those aspects of her subjects' lives that remain unknown. But once again she excels at weaving in the more gossipy pieces of information: headstrong Emily Brontë once cauterized her own arm with a hot poker after being bitten by a rabid dog, telling no one until after the wound had healed; Langston Hughes was so fascinated by death that, as a child, he once ran away to spend the night in a morgue. These juicy tidbits, combined with other details of personality—impeccable Charles Dickens never had a hair out of place; flamboyant Zora Neale Hurston was buried in a bright pink gown—create striking, albeit brief, portraits. Krull's witty text is perfectly complemented by [Kathryn] Hewitt's quirky illustrations, which also highlight unique details: E. B. White, for example, is shown with a spider web strung beneath his arm, spelling out the word *terrific*. Brief notes called "bookmarks" at the end of each bio provide only scant information about the subjects' literary accomplishments, but this fascinating introduction may well entice young readers to further exploration of those works accessible to their age level and will surely generate memorable impressions to last until future encounters with these great writers. A highly entertaining production for all ages.

📖 *MARIA MOLINA AND THE DAYS OF THE DEAD* (1994)

Stephanie Zvirin

SOURCE: A review of *Maria Molina and the Days of the Dead,* in *Booklist,* Vol. 91, No. 4, October 15, 1994, p. 436.

Although intended for a younger audience than [Kathryn] Lasky's book [*Days of the Dead*] above, this also focuses on the celebrations of one Mexican family. Instead of choosing a real family, however, Krull follows a fictional one as it prepares for and experiences the Days of the Dead. The fictional framework is somewhat thin, with the family eventually moving to the U.S., where Maria, with childlike naïveté, looks forward to being "richer than we were in Mexico" and celebrating Halloween. Krull makes clear that revelry is part of the holiday celebrations, but her narrative is rather solemn. Fortunately, [Enrique O.] Sánchez's paintings lighten the mood, their broad palette and pastel colors adding a pleasant, yet still suitable lift. Particularly noteworthy is the story's ending, in which Maria discovers that the spirits of her ancestors can still be honored in her new home—but in a slightly different way. Krull's appended notes add much to the telling, and a recipe for the traditional holiday bread will make the holiday experience more concrete.

Francine Prose

SOURCE: A review of *Maria Molina and the Days of the Dead,* in *The New York Times Book Review,* October 23, 1994, p. 30.

Maria Molina and the Days of the Dead, by Kathleen Krull, illustrated by Enrique O. Sánchez [has] a familiar style that might be termed picture-book ethnic. (The faces are sweetly pretty, impassive, with uniformly dark cocker spaniel eyes.) The plot follows Maria's family to the graveyard on *los Dias de los Muertos* to honor the spirits of her grandmother and brother, who died when he was a baby. Meanwhile Maria's mind is on emigration: "If I lived in the United States, I, Maria Molina, would not be in a graveyard tonight. I would be out trick-or-treating on Halloween, with enough money to buy lots of candy and a fancy costume." By the book's conclusion, Maria's dream has come true. Her family has moved to the United States, where she celebrates Halloween but preserves her ethnic heritage *and* her brother's and grandmother's memories with a household altar and homemade *pan de los muertos,* the traditional bread of the dead.

Jessie Meudell

SOURCE: A review of *Maria Molina and the Days of the Dead,* in *School Library Journal,* Vol. 40, No. 12, December, 1994, pp. 77-8.

Maria's infant brother and her grandmother have died in the last year, and the girl and her family honor them during the Days of the Dead celebration. As her mother explains the various Mexican customs involved, readers, too, learn about them. Comparison to Halloween is smoothly woven into the narrative. After it is over, Maria's parents move north to the U. S., later sending for their children. Krull does an excellent job of showing how a family can leave its homeland and carry their culture with them while accepting their new land. She describes the traditional foods and concludes with additional facts about *los Días de Muertos* and a recipe for "Bread of the Dead." [Enrique O.] Sánchez's illustrations, done in earth tones, capture the flavor of the celebration. While skeletons appear in many of the pictures, children will not be frightened, as others show the fun people have during this period. A wonderful choice to introduce children to a custom with which they are not familiar, and a reassuring story for those who are trying to keep old traditions in a new country.

📖 *BRIDGES TO CHANGE: HOW KIDS LIVE ON A SOUTH CAROLINA SEA ISLAND* (1995); *ONE NATION, MANY TRIBES: HOW KIDS LIVE IN MILWAUKEE'S INDIAN COMMUNITY* (1995)

Roger Sutton

SOURCE: A review of *Bridges to Change: How Kids Live on a South Carolina Sea Island* and *One Nation, Many Tribes: How Kids Live in Milwaukee's Indian Community,* in *Bulletin of the Center for Children's Books,* Vol. 48, No. 6, February, 1995, p. 204.

Following up her journalistic portraits of kids in New York's Chinatown and in a Latino neighborhood in Southern California, Krull here looks at life in Milwaukee's Indian community and in the African-American towns on the Georgia Sea Islands. Both books are crisply designed and written, focusing minority experience through the daily life of a few ten- to twelve-year-old children, always acknowledging the fluid borders between cultural specifics and the larger American society. Thirza and Shawnee are both students at the Milwaukee Indian Community School, which, along with providing instruction in the usual run of subjects, gives Indian kids from many tribes a cultural context for their studies: Shawnee, for example, constructs a science-fair experiment to see whether a hogan or a tepee better retains heat. Travis and Martha receive daily lessons in black history from their families, their school, and most pervasively the rich historic legacy of the freed slaves on their island of St. Helena who built their own communities after the Civil War. Sharp color photographs [by David Hautzig] show the kids in a variety of ordinary diversions (going to the mall, riding bikes) as well as participating in ethnic traditions; each book is a blend of the culturally specific and the everyday that will draw in the reader who wants to read about "kids like me." An up-to-date reading list and an index concludes each title.

Julie Corsaro

SOURCE: A review of *Bridges to Change: How Kids Live on a South Carolina Sea Island,* in *Booklist,* Vol. 91, No. 12, February 15, 1995, pp. 1080-1.

The latest entry in the A World of My Own series profiles two 10-year-old African Americans, Travis and Martha, living on St. Helena, a beautiful coastal Sea Island of South Carolina. Krull strikes a noteworthy balance between the details of the children's everyday lives—family, school, hobbies, favorite food (pizza, in both cases), aspirations—and a broader set of issues. The latter range from the history of slavery in the region and the related development of the Gullah language, to changes brought about on the once-isolated island by bridge building and real-estate development. There is one flaw: Krull flounders with disputable statements such as, "The Uncle Remus stories originated here." The simple, conversational quality of the text is matched by the informal full-color photographs [by David Hautzig]. Appealing in its own right, this briskly written book can also provide a context for listening to the scary folktales found in [Mary E.] Lyon's *Raw Head, Bloody Bones* (1992).

Kirkus Reviews

SOURCE: A review of *One Nation, Many Tribes: How Kids Live in Milwaukee's Indian Community,* in *Kirkus Reviews,* Vol. LXIII, No. 4, February 15, 1995, p. 227.

Krull tells the story of Thirza Defoe and Shawnee Ford, two Indians (a term she says is "increasingly preferred over" Native American) who attend the Milwaukee Indian Community School. Funded by a high-stakes bingo hall run by Potawatomi Indians, the school has students from many different tribes. In addition to other subjects, they learn about Indian culture and gain a sense of pride in their heritage. The school stresses the importance of preserving Indian culture and downplays differences among tribes.

This is a competent portrait of an unusual community, engagingly depicted through the experiences of two of its children. [David] Hautzig's full-color photos are technically superb in further chronicling the life of contemporary Indians.

Anna DeWind

SOURCE: A review of *Bridges to Change: How Kids Live on a South Carolina Sea Island* and *One Nation, Many Tribes: How Kids Live in Milwaukee's Indian Com-*

munity, in *School Library Journal,* Vol. 41, No. 3, March, 1995, pp. 214-5.

Bridges tells about two African-American children who live on South Carolina's St. Helena Island, where isolation and tranquilty give the impression that this is a place where time has stood still. Long-time residents speak a distinctive blend of English and West African languages known as Gullah. Yet, in spite of the island's exotic aspects, these youngsters resemble typical American kids in many ways. *One Nation* introduces an Oneida/Ojibwa girl who is a talented solo hoop dancer and an Ojibwa/ Comanche/Mexican boy. They are both students at the Milwaukee Indian Community School, which incorporates Native American cultures into every aspect of its curriculum. In both books, descriptions of the young peoples' domestic lives, written in an informal, child-oriented style, are interspersed rather jarringly with boxed factual information on the Gullah influence and African ties, or on Indian history and contributions to the world. Large, full-color photographs [by David Hautzig], one or more on almost every page, and the use of the subjects' own words bring these children to life.

Richard B. Woodbury

SOURCE: A review of *One Nation, Many Tribes: How Kids Live in Milwaukee's Indian Community,* in *Science Books & Films,* Vol. 31, No. 4, May, 1995, p. 114.

The unique Milwaukee Indian Community School is described through the lives of two Indian students, a girl and a boy, ages 11 and 12. The school preserves and transmits traditional Indian skills and knowledge (including languages) and also has a regular curriculum, from history to science to computers. Focusing on two students makes it possible to emphasize their daily lives, habits, activities, interests, and future hopes. The problems and pleasures of living in two cultures are discussed, ranging from the traditional sweat bath at the time of the new moon to video games in the mall. Indirectly, the book urges tolerance and understanding of those who are different from ourselves, describing insults and misunderstandings that Indians suffer. (They are said to prefer the term "Indians" to "Native Americans.") A brief sketch of Ojibwa Indian history is included. The many attractive color photos [by David Hautzig] add a great deal of information and vividness to the text, but the oversimplified map of Wisconsin shows only 3 of the 10 reservations in the state.

V IS FOR VICTORY: AMERICA REMEMBERS WORLD WAR II (1995)

Mary Harris Veeder

SOURCE: A review of *V Is for Victory: America Remembers World War II,* in *Booklist,* Vol. 91, No. 21, July, 1995, pp. 1875-6.

An entertaining, informative book that works even better

for browsing than for start-to-finish reading. Breadth and selection of material, not depth, are the strong points. Postcards, posters, headlines, and personal letters, as well as the expected selection of photographs, help give young people a taste of the World War II experience—the home front, the battlefield, and the political front. A section on the Holocaust is followed by a chapter on Japanese American internment camps, and there's brief discussion of prejudice in the armed forces. The brightly colored pages and clever design will lure readers, who will find the book a rich source of topics for grandparent-child conversation. A chronology and a bibliography are appended.

Susan Dove Lempke

SOURCE: A review of *V Is for Victory: America Remembers World War II,* in *Bulletin of the Center for Children's Books,* Vol. 48, No. 11, July-August, 1995, p. 387.

A note on the cover calls this "a book for families commemorating the 50th anniversary of the Allied victory," and, as a browsing book for adults to use with children to discuss World War II, it works well. Children without the background knowledge to put references such as the Cold War into context will be hopelessly confused, especially because much of the information is scattered in captions. The captioned material—pictured memorabilia such as postcards, ration books, posters, and newspaper headlines, and profuse photographs of both the famous (movie stars, politicians and generals) and ordinary people (the soldiers and the civilians waiting at home)—is the book's strong point; the book's design, with such items framed in period shades of chartreuse, pink, and maize, contributes greatly to its impact. In her introduction, Krull discusses the effect the war continues to have on life today and suggests that children talk to older relatives about the war. She outlines a few of the events leading to the war, and for the most part presents the American perspective, though the subject most fully covered is the Holocaust. Other chapters cover civilian life, soldiers, weapons, and the Japanese-American internment camps, and Krull gives a good overview of important people from both the Allied and Axis sides. Because there has been little summation of the events of the war, the chapter on its conclusion loses impact: Paris' liberation is not so thrilling when its occupation has been barely touched upon. The final chapter, titled "Lasting Effects," contains a loosely related hodgepodge of information from post-war devastation to the U.N. to Doctor Spock to General Colin Powell. Also included are a sketchy chronology, a bibliography (with children's books highlighted), a period map, and an index.

Russell Freedman

SOURCE: A review of *V Is for Victory: America Remembers World War II,* in *The New York Times Book Review,* September 10, 1995, p. 35.

Historic photographs . . . figure prominently in Kathleen Krull's *V Is for Victory: America Remembers World War II,* but the approach here is very different. Ms. Krull surveys all of World War II, touching on topics ranging from the origins of the war to its lasting effects. Sections on the Holocaust and Japanese-American internment camps are particularly graphic and compelling, and brief profiles of wartime personalities offer a lively run-down on who was who.

But the emphasis is on the pictures—some 150 wartime photographs, many as familiar as the flag-raising at Iwo Jima, supplemented by full-color illustrations of weapons, medals, war bonds, ration books and other World War II artifacts. Illustrations on virtually every page are accompanied by briskly informative captions that make up the greater part of the book's text. Many of the black-and-white photos are reproduced as blue-tinted halftones and are laid out against color backgrounds. The result suggests a bright scrapbook of the war, a procession that's the graphic equivalent of sound bites and that invites browsing rather than sustained reading.

An elaborately designed book like this deserves more meticulous editing. A caption gives the date of Franklin D. Roosevelt's death as April 4, 1945, while the accompanying newspaper headline announcing his death is clearly dated April 13 (he died on April 12). A photo of "a recent Army draftee, with newly shorn hair," actually shows a young soldier with a full head of neatly parted hair; he is displaying his military equipment for inspection on the bunk directly in front of him, not in the background as the caption states.

Claudia Moore

SOURCE: A review of *V Is for Victory: America Remembers World War II,* in *School Library Journal,* Vol. 41, No. 10, October, 1995, p. 164.

Colorful pages replete with archival photos, postcards, posters, letters, and realia present a visual and textual scrapbook of the war years. Krull covers the preliminary events, Pearl Harbor, life at home, military service, the Holocaust, weapons, and lasting changes and effects brought about by the war. Chapters are introduced and end with appropriate overviews, but the bulk of the text is comprised of explanatory comments associated with the illustrative material. Some are in boxed inserts of contrasting colors. Individual battles are not discussed. The index is detailed and sufficient to help researchers. Some pages are a bit difficult to read as print is sometimes superimposed onto an enlarged monochromatic photograph. Billed as "a book for families," this title begs to be shared; students are encouraged to ask relatives about their memories of this time. But even if appropriate grandparents are not available, all readers will benefit from this visual feast of an era that continues to influence our lives today.

Norma A. Sisson

SOURCE: A review of *V Is for Victory*, in *Voice of Youth Advocates*, Vol. 18, No. 4, October, 1995, p. 252.

The author clearly has done her homework in writing this book. It is full of facts which describe the attitudes and situation surrounding World War II. This is a pictorial book which has graphics over graphics and print over graphics which makes the reader think that the information is secondary to the pictures. The photos are placed at angles which at times is distracting. There is little that is consistent in the format except for the chapter titles which are even different colors. However, the information in the book is exceptional. The author tells of the war effort in which Americans rushed to enlist and were enthusiastically patriotic. The book gives an excellent picture of how it was to live and work in the United States during that time. There is an abundance of information which is long enough on the various subjects, but not so long as to overwhelm the reader. The writer does not shy away from telling the reader about the ethnic prejudice toward the Japanese Americans. There is a biographical section on the major players of World War II. The additional parenthetical information is of great assistance to define terminology and explain other helpful information. I highly recommend this book for all school libraries.

📖 *LIVES OF THE ARTISTS: MASTERPIECES, MESSES (AND WHAT THE NEIGHBORS THOUGHT)* (1995)

Kirkus Reviews

SOURCE: A review of *Lives of the Artists: Masterpieces, Messes (and What the Neighbors Thought)*, in *Kirkus Reviews*, Vol. LXIII, No. 19, October 1, 1995, p. 1432.

Krull vigorously beats more dust from the rug of High Culture with this followup to *Lives of the Musicians* and *Lives of the Writers*. Although all but one of her 20 choices worked in the Western tradition—and more than half in the 20th century—they make a diverse crew. Among the familiar names for young readers are da Vinci, Michelangelo, Warhol, Rembrandt, Chagall, Duchamp, Rivera, Kahlo, Cassatt, O'Keeffe, Matisse, van Gogh; among the lesser-knowns, William H. Johnson, Katsuchika Hokusai, Sofonisba Anguissola, Käthe Kollwitz. All of them had unique talents and vision, and it's that uniqueness that Krull zeroes in on, salting her accounts with the entertaining, often outrageous anecdotes that readers have come to expect. She also mentions the love interests, sexual preferences, spouses, and other aspects of the artists' lives that were important to their work. [Kathryn] Hewitt decorates each biography with one of her funny, stylish caricatures plus a smaller picture that features redrawn versions of characteristic figures or motifs; some readers, however, may feel perturbed that none of the artists' works are directly reproduced. Fresh, spirited, and unconventional.

Carolyn Phelan

SOURCE: A review of *Lives of the Artists: Masterpieces, Messes (and What the Neighbors Thought)*, in *Booklist*, Vol. 92, No. 5, November 1, 1995, p. 468.

From the eclectic series that began with *Lives of the Musicians: Good Times, Bad Times (and What the Neighbors Thought)* comes a volume devoted to visual artists. The subject seems well suited to Krull's format: informative short biographies that focus on the subjects' personal lives and eccentricities rather than chronologies of their masterpieces. A few notes on major artworks follow each biography. Among the 19 artists discussed are Leonardo, Bruegel, Cassatt, Van Gogh, Picasso, O'Keefe, Dali, Noguchi, Rivera, Kahlo, and Warhol. Each chapter begins with one of [Kathryn] Hewitt's distinctive portrait paintings, handsome caricatures of the artists and a few significant or distinctive objects indicating their interests and individual traits. A lively, entertaining presentation.

Lauren Adams

SOURCE: A review of *Lives of the Artist: Masterpieces, Messes (and What the Neighbors Thought)*, in *The Horn Book Magazine*, Vol. LXXII, No. 3, May-June, 1996, pp. 349-50.

The author and illustrator of *Lives of the Musicians* and *Lives of the Writers* team up a third time to present twenty of the world's greatest artists. Once again, Krull's brief biographies provide basic facts as well as intriguing details of unusual circumstances or personality traits. The selection of subjects ranges from the famous (Michelangelo Buonarroti) to the infamous (Andy Warhol) to the less well known, including Sofonisba Anguissola, an Italian Renaissance painter who achieved great success in her time in spite of the generally accepted belief that women were "inferior versions of men." [Kathryn] Hewitt's cariacature-like illustrations reflect and extend the lively text, which focuses on the subjects' lives. As in previous volumes, only brief notes about the creators' works appear at the end of each chapter, and reproductions are conspicuously lacking in this full-color illustrated volume. Still, the accessible introduction to these fascinating individuals should spur readers' interest in the even more fascinating world of their art.

📖 *WILMA UNLIMITED: HOW WILMA RUDOLPH BECAME THE WORLD'S FASTEST WOMAN* (1996)

Kirkus Reviews

SOURCE: A review of *Wilma Unlimited: How Wilma Rudolph Became the World's Fastest Woman*, in *Kirkus Reviews*, Vol. LXIV, No. 6, March 5, 1996, p. 450.

Only after reading this book does the subtitle—"How Wilma Rudolph Became the World's Fastest Woman"—

appear rife with understatement. In spite of a low birth weight and childhood bouts with scarlet fever and polio (the doctor said Wilma would never walk again) and after years of painful, relentless exercise, she not only walked, she ran: to college on scholarship, and to the Olympics, where she became the first American woman to win three gold medals in the same games. Krull tells the inspiring tale in rolling, oratorical prose; [David] Diaz, coming off his Caldecott-winning work for Eve Bunting's *Smoky Night* (1994) again lays stylized painted scenes over textured background photos—here, sepia-toned close-ups of fences, ivy, and bare footprints in loose dirt. Though a mannered, blotchy typeface (also Diaz's creation) gives the pages an overly designed look, the book as a whole is a dramatic commemoration of quite a heroic life. Rudolph died in 1994; her post-Olympic accomplishments are described in an afterword.

Betsy Hearne

SOURCE: A review of *Wilma Unlimited: How Wilma Rudolph Became the World's Fastest Woman,* in *Bulletin of the Center for Children's Books,* Vol. 49, No. 8, April, 1996, p. 269.

Picture-book biography has entered an innovative stage with the likes of Jonah Winter's *Diego,* Diane Stanley's *Peter the Great,* and Allen Say's *El Chino.* Now Krull and [David] Diaz join the ranks with an inspiring success story about a baby born with the odds against her: she weighed only four pounds at birth, she was black and poor in a racist southern town during the 1940s, and she was crippled with polio as a child. But she had four points in her favor: a devoted mother, supportive brothers and sisters (twenty-one of them, in fact), a deep religious faith, and an inner strength that pushed her to work through her paralysis, onto the basketball court, and all the way to three Olympic gold medals as a sprinter. If there's any stinting in this simply phrased, sensitively selective account, it's in the stage of her training on the track. In a single sentence Rudolph leaps from discovery by an athletic coach to triumph in Rome, but perhaps it's valid to emphasize the childhood struggles in which her achievements were rooted. Diaz' artwork reinforces the mythic-hero aspects of the narrative with deeply framed compositions featuring stylized, statuesque figures of robotic power. In fact, the one quibble with his depictions might be the Herculean stoutness of Wilma jumping over a wagon, an illustration that faces a sentence stating "she was always so small and sickly." As he did in the Caldecott Medal book *Smoky Night* by Eve Bunting, Diaz has textured the background paper here according to story motifs—straw packing material for the picture in which Wilma and her mother send the hated leg-brace back to the hospital, netting for a basketball game, dirt for a race, the stars and stripes for an award ceremony, footprints on the endpapers. Because these backgrounds are all brown-hued, and brown skin tones dominate the illustrations, there's no distraction of focus despite the ambitious layout and complex typeface. With the kind of concentration that Rudolph mustered to win her way, Diaz rivets our

attention with thick outlines and organic shapes that carry us from enforced stillness to driving motion in the sweep of one brief book.

Publishers Weekly

SOURCE: A review of *Wilma Unlimited: How Wilma Rudolph Became the World's Fastest Woman,* in *Publishers Weekly,* Vol. 243, No. 18, April 29, 1996, p. 73.

"No one expected such a tiny girl to have a first birthday," begins this inspiring biographical sketch of a legendary track star. Born in 1940 in Tennessee, the chronically sickly though "lively" Rudolph contracted polio just before her fifth birthday. Though not expected to walk again, the fiercely determined girl persevered with her leg exercises; by the time she was 12, she no longer needed her steel brace. Eight years later, Rudolph represented the U.S. in the 1960 Olympics in Rome, where, despite a twisted ankle, she became the first American woman to win three gold medals during a single Olympic competition. Krull's (*Lives of the Musicians*) characteristic, conversational style serves her especially well here. Through her words the nearly superhuman Rudolph seems both personable and recognizable. Rendered in acrylic, watercolor and gouache, Caldecott Medalist [David] Diaz's (*Smoky Night*) imposing, richly hued illustrations have a distinctive, cubist feel. The artist's bold design superimposes this art against sepia-toned photographs of relevant background images: playground sand, wooden fence slats, the gravel of a running track. This juxtaposition yields busy, effectively textured pages, flawed only by the text's curiously embellished font—the letters look as though they have been speckled with either ink blots or dust. A triumphant story, triumphantly relayed.

Michael Cart

SOURCE: A review of *Wilma Unlimited: How Wilma Rudolph Became the World's Fastest Woman,* in *Booklist,* Vol. 92, No. 17, May 1, 1996, p. 1503.

Wilma Rudolph was a wonder. Though partially paralyzed by polio as a child, she managed—through indomitable spirit and unlimited determination—to transform herself from a disabled 5-year-old to a world-class runner at age 20, the first woman ever to win three gold medals in a single Olympics. In this biography for younger readers, Krull skillfully demonstrates that in achieving her historic triple victory, Rudolph also claimed victory over three obstacles: a normally crippling illness, growing up African American in the segregated South of the 1940s, and competing in what was then regarded as a men's sport. The never didactic text includes a suspenseful and dramatic retelling of Rudolph's triumphant participation in the 1960 Summer Games in Rome. Enhancing the text are Caldecott medalist [David] Diaz's richly colored, stylized illustrations that—though painted—have the look and permanence of wood carvings. These single-and double-page pictures are set on sepia-tone backgrounds that, like his Caldecott Medal-winning art for *Smoky Night* (1994), Diaz assembled and photographed. He has also created a striking new font called Ariel for the display and text type. Both Krull's words and Diaz's illustrations are celebrations of an inspiring life that deserves to be remembered. An appended author's note offers additional historical context.

Ellen Fader

SOURCE: A review of *Wilma Unlimited: How Wilma Rudolph Became the World's Fastest Woman,* in *The Horn Book Magazine,* Vol. LXXII, No. 5, September-October, 1996, p. 617.

An inspiring picture book tells the story of the indomitable Wilma Rudolph, who, although she weighed only a little more than four pounds when she was born and contracted polio when she was five, went on to become the first American woman to win three gold medals at a single Olympics. The book's design is similar to that of the Caldecott medalist's *Smoky Night,* in that brightly colored acrylic, watercolor, and gouache paintings are placed against equally dynamic sepia-toned photographic backgrounds, creating juxtapositions that thoughtfully extend both the text (which is in an unfortunately distracting typeface) and the pictures in the foreground. [David] Diaz creates illustrations of Rudolph that artfully capture her physical and emotional determination as well as the beauty of her body in motion. Krull's understated, well-paced conversational style is perfectly suited to tell Rudolph's remarkable life story. (An author's note provides information on the athlete's later life.) A winning biography that highlights perseverance and true heroic courage.

Additional coverage of Krull's life and career is contained in the following sources published by Gale Research: *Contemporary Authors,* Vol. 106 and *Something about the Author,* Vols. 39, 52, 80.

Sam McBratney

1943-

Northern Irish editor and author of picture books, fiction, nonfiction, and plays.

Major works include *Jimmy Zest* (1982), *Colvin and the Snake Basket* (1985), *The Ghosts of Hungryhouse Lane* (1988), *Put a Saddle on the Pig* (1992; published as *You Just Don't Listen!*, 1994), *Guess How Much I Love You* (1994).

INTRODUCTION

The popular and prolific author of over fifty books for children and young adults, a selection of which have been published in the United States, McBratney is praised for his insightful characterizations, refreshing literary style, skill with narrative and dialogue, and offbeat humor. Although he has written in a variety of genres—picture books, mysteries, informational books, fantasy, science fiction, humorous and realistic tales and short stories for primary and middle graders, and realistic novels for teenagers—McBratney is best known as the author of *Guess How Much I Love You*, a tender picture book featuring a bedtime game between Little Nutbrown Hare and Big Nutbrown Hare that has become an international best-seller and is often viewed as the successor to Margaret Wise Brown's *Goodnight Moon*. McBratney, who includes both human and anthropomorphic animals as protagonists in his works, is often lauded for accurately representing the perspectives of all of his characters, both young and old. Several of his books feature young siblings who are initially naughty or self-absorbed but who learn lessons about such subjects as giving and friendship. McBratney is also the author of several stories for beginning readers that are considered both excellent introductions to good literature and accessible, entertaining romps for their intended audience; in addition, many of McBratney's works lend themselves for reading aloud.

Biographical Information

Born in Belfast, Northern Ireland, McBratney grew up in Lisburn, a town ten miles away, because his family was forced to relocate after air raids on the Belfast shipyards near their home. After attending a Quaker grammar school, McBratney went to Trinity College in Dublin, graduating with an honors degree in modern history and political science. He then became a teacher, working at the primary, secondary, and university levels while writing books for children and young people and raising a family of three children; in 1990, he became a full-time writer.

Of his work, McBratney has noted, "I write everything for all ages: historical fiction, science fiction, light-heart-

ed ghost stories, real-life angst, short stories, zany things, serious pieces, BBC radio plays, and television educational programmes. . . . My problem was that I never became known for a style or a genre—I write because the act of imagining makes me feel good, and I never got much of a buzz out of writing the same sort of thing twice." Regarding his success with *Guess How Much I Love You*, McBratney said, "My career with its ups and mostly downs, reached its apotheosis recently with [this] picture book, . . . a four hundred word story about two hares in a field. It describes the attempts of Little Nutbrown Hare and Big Nutbrown Hare to put into words the love and the need that a wee one feels for a big one, and vice versa."

Major Works

McBratney began his career with two realistic stories, one for middle graders and the other for teenagers: in *Mark Time* (1976), he addressed the situation in Northern Ireland by describing the battle between two rival gangs of preteen boys, one Catholic and one Protestant, while *A Dip of the Antlers* (1977) depicts how the tensions between two secondary school students of opposite temperaments leads to a bloody fight. Reviewers acknowledged both books for their authenticity in setting and feeling as well as for their excitement. McBratney published another realistic young adult novel, *Boy Blue* (1979), and two science fiction stories for young people, *The Final Correction* (1978) and its sequel *From the Thorensen Dykes* (1980), before introducing one of his best-known characters, Jimmy Zest, who appears in four short story collections for primary graders. McBratney portrayed the comic adventures of the ingenious Jimmy and his classmates at a multiracial Irish school in works characterized by both warmth and hilarity. In his review of the first book in the series, *Jimmy Zest*, Steve Bowles said, "There are very few stories of junior school life as good as this on the market." Another popular creation is Colvin, the mischievous small boy whose favorite sanctuary is a laundry basket and who is the title character of *Colvin and the Snake Basket.* Liz Waterland praised the uniqueness of *Colvin,* saying it was due to "the insight we as readers are given into Colvin's view of the world."

The Ghosts of Hungryhouse Lane, a humorous story for middle graders, marked the first appearance of McBratney's books in the United States. In this work, three "ex-human beings" find their "Unwakeful Serenity" disturbed by the Sweets, three unruly children whose family has rented the haunted residence. The children, who are initially disrespectful of the ghosts, become their unexpected allies when they discover a missing will. In *The Ghastly Gerty Swindle: With the Ghosts of Hungryhouse Lane* (1994), the Sweets help their ghostly friends recover antiques stolen by the nasty housekeeper Gerty and her son Alexander. In 1993, McBratney received a Bisto Award from the Irish Children's Book Trust for *Put a Saddle on the Pig,* a young adult novel that was published in the United States as *You Just Don't Listen!* The book outlines how sixteen-year-old Laura comes to terms with her mother, a widow who wants to marry a man who owns a farm fifty miles away. Praised as a direct and well-written delineation of teenage emotions, *Put a Saddle on the Pig* is also acknowledged for accurately representing the viewpoints of both mother and daughter. With *Guess How Much I Love You,* McBratney continued his fascination with parent/child relationships in what is considered an especially affecting—and successful—manner. Told in simple yet poetic language, the story describes a gentle contest held by Big Nutbrown Hare and Little Nutbrown Hare to see who loves the other the most. Most critics were charmed by the story: for example, a reviewer in *Publishers Weekly* described the story as "[fresh] as a fiddlehead fern in spring." McBratney is also the author of nonfiction, short stories for children and adults, and radio plays and educational programs for the BBC; he has also provided the text for a graphic novel for teenagers and has edited two collections of stories from BBC Northern Ireland Schools Radio.

Awards

Besides his Bisto Award for *Put a Saddle on the Pig,* a

prize he also won in 1994, McBratney received the Bass Ireland Literary Prize in 1980 and the Silvern Griffel Award from the Children's Book Association of Holland in 1995. *Guess How Much I Love You* was named an ALA Notable Children's Book in 1996.

TITLE COMMENTARY

MARK TIME (1976)

David Rees

SOURCE: "Ulster Unrealities," in *The Times Literary Supplement,* No. 3879, July 16, 1976, p. 878.

We like to think of ourselves in matters of history or contemporary events, whether in the class-room or in the pages of a children's novel, as a nation who may have made mistakes but whose mistakes are of a less grave nature than those of other countries. So Ireland is usually ignored. Cromwell, the penal days, 1798 (the "year of liberty"), the Famine, the Easter Rising, all provide material for the historical novelist as rich as that of any nation, but it is rarely used. We are too ashamed of it. It is, therefore, heartening to see that the current situation in Northern Ireland has not been totally ignored in recent children's fiction, but **Mark Time** by Sam McBratney raises a number of misgivings. The main event of the story is a battle between two rival gangs of teenagers, one Protestant and one Catholic, but no attempt is made at any point to relate this to the larger issues that bedevil life in Ulster, and the result is that Mark's problems and concerns could be those of any urban child anywhere. The dust-jacket mentions "the harsh realities of Northern Ireland", but they simply do not exist in this book.

There are no bombs, no IRA, no religious hatreds, and as the writer conveys other aspects of modern city life, the reader is left with some feeling of incredulity. One can understand the caution of both writer and publisher; no one wishes to fan the flames of sectarian violence, but to ignore what is going on so totally as this book does is not helpful: once again one feels that Ireland is being swept under the carpet, ignored because it is too painful to contemplate.

Having said that, there is little else to find fault with. Sam McBratney writes with a refreshingly individual style, witty and assured; his characters, both children and adults, are clear and convincing; the relationship between Mark and his father is particularly good. Also well handled is Mark's interest in Emily, a girl in his class at school. Mark is only ten, and the adults find his feelings a source of much amusement; their insensitivity on this score and his own sensitivity to her and annoyance with them come over very truthfully. This sort of puppy love is common enough in real life, but hardly ever finds its way into children's books.

Margery Fisher

SOURCE: A review of *Mark Time,* in *Growing Point,* Vol. 15, No. 3, September, 1976, pp. 2940-1.

Violence breeds friendships of a fragile, dangerous kind. In **Mark Time** a boy of nearly eleven who has blithely accepted that he owes loyalty to the Shampoo Kid's gang against the "Fenians" from "across the line" finds himself wondering how he can stand up for himself without telling tales and why the Shampoo Kid's campaigns have ceased to be fun and become missions of hate. Belfast is the setting and a quasi-military operation on waste ground (with Mark as runner and stone-collector) the central scene in a book which offers, without comment, an example of the effect of violence on the young as searching in its way as Joan Lingard's *Twelfth of July* was. The strength of this story, exciting as it is in action and vigorous in description, lies most of all in the development of character, particularly of Mark with his uncertainties and worries and of his jocular, tolerant father; this is not a "working-class" stereotype of a family but a group of individuals in a run-down urban setting. . . .

The book is enlivened by an offhand humour and it has all through it a spontaneity in dialogue and narrative which gives it an authentic air.

G. Bott

SOURCE: A review of *Mark Time,* in *Junior Bookshelf,* Vol. 41, No. 1, February, 1977, pp. 40-1.

Although this story is set in Northern Ireland, the violence of the political and religious conflict is not allowed to intrude into what is basically a study of an eleven-year-old boy. Gang warfare is part of Mark's life and much of the book is a build-up to the battle between the Shampoo Kid's lot and the Fenians, though fortunately the account of the actual fight is not prolonged.

Mark is about to start at the local grammar school, an academic achievement that tends to make him something of an outsider. We share his first stirrings of affection for Emily, his fears and hopes, his mother's ambitions for her son, his dislike of being called nicknames, his relationships with other members of the gang—convincingly explored and recorded by Sam McBratney with an authenticity that captures not only the bewilderment of early adolescence but also the atmosphere of the Belfast wastelands.

A DIP OF THE ANTLERS (1977)

Peter Fanning

SOURCE: "Ganging Up," in *The Times Educational Supplement,* No. 3251, September 30, 1977, p. 24.

A Dip of the Antlers brings social realism to a simple story about a fight beside a canal. Sam McBratney traces the thought and lives of four people involved up to the crisis and terrible denoument: two boys, one teacher and one policeman. The antlers are those of the warring factions.

It's a gruesome short story, tough and credible, in a world which has no room for winners. There are only losers and beautiful losers. The theme is more direct and treated with more assurance than in Mr. McBratney's first book, **Mark Time,** and there's a wealth of realistic detail (like the ghastly horrors of first time dating) which leaves the characters sharply defined and our sympathies evenly divided.

Margery Fisher

SOURCE: A review of *A Dip of the Antlers,* in *Growing Point,* Vol. 16, No. 6, December, 1977, p. 3221.

[*A Dip of the Antlers* takes place in] an urban setting where the secondary buildings and the Grove estate are described in a general rather than a localised way. A sardonic teacher stops a fight between John Turkington, son of an accountant, and the studious Barry Freeman. From this point the incident is seen and discussed from various points of view and the subsequent troubles of Turk, led into pointless acts of destruction by his cowardly side-kick Monkey Reynolds, are seen as the possible results of an adolescent testing of power. The book is open-ended, so that this particular theory, put forward by a reporter talking to the police, at the climax of the action, is by no means a dogmatic one. The atmosphere of tension and rivalry at school is strongly felt through the book but the author is happier describing action than he is with his long, sententious discussions of the state of mind of one character after another. This would have been a better book if he had allowed the reader more freedom to make his own assessments.

A. R. Williams

SOURCE: A review of *A Dip of the Antlers,* in *Junior Bookshelf,* Vol. 41, No. 6, December, 1977, pp. 359-60.

[The] title is simply a journalist's expression to describe the contest between two boys of diametrically opposed temperaments and abilities within the setting of a secondary school realistically yet sympathetically appraised. The disciplinary dilemma of a humane young teacher in a modern context is convincingly analysed. *A Dip of the Antlers* belongs to an enlarging genre in which "skool" is neither guyed nor sentimentalised . . . and a balance of sympathy is achieved. Perhaps the main theme of antagonism between the boy from an unsettled home and another whose academic potential is bolstered by domestic toleration may not be novel, but John Turkington and Barry Freeman emerge as individuals as well as representative characters, the current climate of mindless vandalism and comparatively precocious behaviour among teenagers are sensibly integrated with the main conflict and social comment on the insolubility of certain aspects of delinquency are not too artificially incorporated through the reactions of a young policeman engaged in investigating the destruction of a graveyard by the moronic "Monkey" Reynolds and the truanting "Turk". Dialogue, though a trifle "strong" in places, is more than adequately handled, too. In so short a book one cannot expect real depth but it is peopled with more than merely lay figures.

Stuart Hannabuss

SOURCE: "Beyond the Formula: Part II," in *Junior Bookshelf,* Vol. 46, No. 5, October, 1982, p. 174.

The theme of confrontation has been handled with great insight by some of [the writers reviewed in this essay]. Sam McBratney's impressive *A Dip of the Antlers,* for instance, takes up the familiar matter of suspicion and hatred between two boys at school, and builds up the external and internal tensions until the only outcome is a bloody fight between them. There is no superfluous word in this story: its bare bones tell all the tale, the events, the feelings, the different viewpoints, the revealed prejudices. Even the conflict implied by the very title is a matter of brief and ironic self-awareness by the central characters. They are aware of how rituals, social forms, pressures of family and school, expectations and roles, manoeuvre people into certain actions, and McBratney is realistic enough to force his characters, like his readers, to work out things for themselves. There is no compromise with language either: 'Turkington and Freeman eyed one another in a silence that affected not only those who had come to fight but also those who had come to watch. Nothing moved in those early seconds; nothing of any substance. Wild grasses twitched; hairs on foreheads sprang in and out of place on the breeze; and scum drifted on the stagnant waters of the canal at a pace determined by nature: but the central characters saw none of these things and the total impression was one of absolute stillness. They had confronted one another at last, the pair of them, and for a brief time the capacity to act had deserted both'. Taut, gripping, realistic: none of these qualities is lost in a book aiming higher than the obvious and making more demands than usual on the reader.

📖 THE FINAL CORRECTION (1978)

Alan Ryan

SOURCE: "Spook Plugs," in *New Statesman,* Vol. 96, No. 2485, November 3, 1978, p. 594.

Tanith Lee's *The Castle of Dark* is well up to her usual standard. . . .

The Final Correction by Sam McBratney is equally good value; what it forgoes in the way of atmosphere it picks up with its curious echoes of 18th-century anthropological speculation. The descendants of juvenile delinquents

shipped out from Earth 2,000 years before live in a child's world, cared for by a machine which manifests itself as 'Mother-person' to her/its charges. To keep the human race going, the machine has chosen to keep them in a state of mindless innocence; but over the millennia, external dangers have multiplied. Mother-person's final correction to the programme in order to defeat these is to take the risk of allowing one human being to grow up with a memory, a sense of identity and all those dangerous traits which Rousseau long ago picked out as the source of humanity's greatness and misery alike. It's a good adventure story, too, which is more than can be said for Rousseau's *Nouvelle Héloïse.*

Peter Fanning

SOURCE: "Out of This World," in *The Times Educational Supplement,* No. 3308, November 24, 1978, p. 50.

Sam McBrantney's *Final Correction* is an adventure story fraught with heavy symbolism. Set on a distant planet whither earth's delinquents have all been shipped, this confused, fantastic and violent allegory feeds its hero on the Tree of Life; while elsewhere on the planet, innocent children live blissfully in Fool's Paradise. They are supervised by the "Mother Person" and live a blinkered prey to the menace of the "Clickers".

As usual Sam McBrantney looks to violence for his theme. What motivates aggression? Several old friends crop up along the wayside: the ageing Fairy Godmother, a pack of talking dogs and of course the clicking Big Bad Wolf. He vindicates aggression as the one survival instinct in a world grown woolly and supersoft. "Rollerball" violence—where camera pans smartly away at the moment of contact—and grim epigrams underline every moment and make this a readable and gripping book in spite of the spoonfuls of fashionable clichés.

David Burns

SOURCE: "Space-Trail," in *The Times Literary Supplement,* No. 4000, December 1, 1978, p. 1396.

The Final Correction is traditional "sci-fi" with alien planets and gadgetry. It is also complex and thought-provoking, releasing seemingly random pieces of a jigsaw which spans two thousand years. The novel traces the efforts of Alkin to discover his origins after he frees himself from the stifling control of the machine Motherperson. The entire future of the family of Man on planet Alanto depends on Alkin's success in rediscovering his natural human instincts.

📖 BOY BLUE (1979)

Robin Barlow

SOURCE: A review of *Boy Blue,* in *School Librarian,* Vol. 27, No. 4, December, 1979, pp. 382-3.

Like many of his age, John Tavener has had enough of school by the time he is sixteen. Like few of his age, he runs away from home, school and friends to take stock of his life and declare his independence. Tavener makes his new home in a scruffy bedsitter and becomes involved with the other people in the house. He has fantasies about the attractive middle-aged divorcee upstairs, but his dreams of an affair come to nothing. A petty criminal who tries to involve Tavener in a 'job' is refused, out of fear rather than through any concern with morality. Eventually Tavener returns home.

Presumably this story is intended to give some insight into how a teenager copes with the problems of maturity; but Tavener's experiences are so untypical and the plot so thin that this never quite comes off.

J. Russell

SOURCE: A review of *Boy Blue,* in *Junior Bookshelf,* Vol. 44, No. 3, June, 1980, p. 145.

This short tough novel is for older children faced, like its hero Tavener, with leaving school and home and leading an independent life. John is 16, he runs away and finds himself in a scruffy bed-sittingroom in a house full of characters like Myles Naylor—the petty thief, and Mrs. Redmond—the divorcee with whom Tavener imagines he is in love.

It will be much enjoyed by readers who may glamorise the idea of living alone when reality is loneliness and one more tin of baked beans.

📖 *FROM THE THORENSON DYKES* (1980)

R. Baines

SOURCE: A review of *From the Thorenson Dykes,* in *Junior Bookshelf,* Vol. 44, No. 4, August, 1980, p. 194.

The community shielded by Dyke One has brought a sandman creature from the shore, protected it by building a house around it and fed it abundantly. Now it is enormous. They worship it and demand tribute from the residents on other Dykes. Capoquin, on Dyke Three, opposes payment. His problems are increased when his son Laar determines that An-Thanya, who lives behind Dyke One and is promised to his friend, shall be his wife.

The family solves its immediate difficulties by leaving the Dykes. The first half of the book has been devoted to a leisurely account of parochial difficulties, the second is crammed with a pell-mell record of their discoveries about the planet they inhabit and earlier colonists. Perhaps readers of Sam McBratney's earlier book will find interest in this headlong progress through many years. Considering the book in isolation, it gives an unbalanced and confusing effect.

Norman Culpan

SOURCE: A review of *From the Thorenson Dykes,* in *School Librarian,* Vol. 28, No. 3, September, 1980, p. 290.

From the Thorenson Dykes is also science fantasy, but offers more, and makes more demands [than Douglas Hill's *Deathwing over Veynaa.*] Before the story begins, a spaceship from Earth has landed on the far planet Alanto. Three members of the group leave in shuttle ships to escape tyranny, and land at various parts of the planet, where one, at least, Thorenson, founds a community. For some 2,000 years at Thorenson's Dykes they live without much technology at, say, a Saxon level of civilisation, until tyranny is threatened here, too. One family, a father and his wife, his son and his son's wife and baby, take to the sea to search for their fabled ancestors. These, in fact, have retained their advanced technology, are aware of the voyaging group, but refrain from giving aid until the small family overcome many dangers and themselves make the reunion. The narrative is interesting and full of action. Human relationships are important throughout, both in their own right and as action motivators. The nature of democracy, the impact of advanced technology on primitives, the intrepidity of the human spirit at its best are not preached about, but are an integral part of the story. Though younger readers and those who are less sophisticated will find much of this out of their range, and may also be thrown by the time scale and the alternating point of view of narration, this novel offers a great deal to brighter fourteen- and fifteen-year-olds. It is not a superb book, but it is a good one.

📖 *JIMMY ZEST* (1982)

D. A. Young

SOURCE: A review of *Jimmy Zest,* in *Junior Bookshelf,* Vol. 46, No. 6, December, 1982, p. 225.

Jimmy Zest is one of those folk heroes in the *Just William* style created by Richmal Crompton. Jimmy always has the best, the most zany and the most outrageous ideas amongst his small circle of friends. He makes a corner in egg-boxes to produce the largest ever model of a dinosaur. He discovers an alien being in a Mrs Cricklewood-Holmsy's garden which turns out to be the lady herself geared up for bee-keeping. He has an aunt in the country who could be a witch.

There are six stories in the present volume which will be enjoyed by eight-year olds—both boys and girls. The sentences are short and the vocabulary well within the grasp of early readers but in no way stilted.

Steve Bowles

SOURCE: A review of *Jimmy Zest,* in *School Librarian,* Vol. 31, No. 2, June, 1983, p. 146.

Ghastly jacket and illustrations [by Thelma Lambert] do

nothing to draw an audience for what is an interesting sequence of stories about a group of junior school children. Unusually, the longest story—the first in the book—is the best. Jimmy's obsession with collecting egg boxes and secretiveness about his purposes provide an excellent link for a series of comic escapades. Sam McBratney's refusal to parade his characters, allowing action and dialogue to speak for themselves directly, makes a refreshing change and maintains the pace of the narrative. None of the remainder quite lives up to this opener, although they are all lively and swift moving. Regrettably, Jimmy becomes a little too like a Bill Naughton figure at times, but the characters around him prevent this from becoming too obtrusive. Overall, a collection that's well worth knowing about. There are very few stories of junior school life as good as this on the market, though it might need some promotion to bring it the readership it deserves.

ZESTY (1984)

E. Colwell

SOURCE: A review of *Zesty,* in *Junior Bookshelf,* Vol. 48, No. 5, October, 1984, p. 209.

The story is made up of a series of episodes involving a class of junior school boys and girls. They are entertaining reading for the children are wholeheartedly, and sometimes fiercely, concerned with the happenings of their daily life. Zesty, about whom the author has already written several stories, is a central figure. An enterprising lad, he conceives a scheme for insuring his school mates' belongings for ten pence a week. His efforts to reimburse himself for his losses involve the whole class. Then there are the girls, by no means the weaker sex. Their reaction to such graffiti as 'Mandy Taylor loves . . .' is forceful.

One feels that the author is poking fun affectionately at children he knows well. This is not a sentimental book but it has a warmth which is refreshing. Perhaps the most amusing, yet moving, event in the book is the class's gift to a loved teacher when she leaves. They give her a secondhand mahogany hatstand, chosen by Zesty. 'I like it. It's unusual', says Zesty and the teacher replies sincerely, 'I'm going to miss you people very much'. So will the young readers as they reach the end of this enjoyable book.

Bill Boyle

SOURCE: A review of *Zesty,* in *Books for Keeps,* No. 36, January, 1986, p. 15.

Five more school stories in this second collection about the life, times and schooldays of Jimmy Zest and gang. Lots of kiddiespeak here, with Gowso Knuckles, Legweak and Shorty illustrating the author's observation of children's obsession with nicknames for their mates. The stories are undemanding and not tremendously original, but they are quite fun to read aloud, and will be enjoyed

in class sessions I'm sure. The best one is the first in the book, with a novel insurance scheme worked out by Jimmy to cover loss or theft of rulers, pens and sweets.

COLVIN AND THE SNAKE BASKET (1985)

Naseem Khan

SOURCE: "Yukky Dip," in *New Statesman,* Vol. 110, No. 2850, November 8, 1985, p. 26.

The blurb for David Henry Wilson's *Do Goldfish Play the Violin?* tells us that Jeremy James has been bringing laughter to children and parents ever since an elephant sat on Daddy's car. Well, there's no accounting for taste, but as far as I and my children (Amelia Tasneem, ten; George Haroun, eight) are concerned, we would have been rather happier if the elephant had sat on Jeremy James.

Colvin, of Sam McBratney's *Colvin and the Snake Basket,* is another candidate for the elephant. Colvin is also a cutie. Of indeterminate age (but the big print suggests six or seven), his favourite reading is a mail-order catalogue and his favourite haunt an Ali Baba laundry basket. Like Jeremy James, he is for ever getting into scrapes: his big sister's doll gets vandalised, the class gerbil comes to a sad end (and is swiftly replaced by an identical gerbil), his pet monkey gets chomped by a dog. At least there are hints of real life in Colvin's relationship with his big bossy sister and a suggestion of a multiracial school.

Chris Brown

SOURCE: A review of *Colvin and the Snake Basket,* in *School Librarian,* Vol. 33, No. 4, December, 1985, p. 334.

The snake basket is a type of Ali Baba laundry basket that serves as Colvin's refuge at times of being out of sorts with the world. Colvin gets into the sort of difficulties that make him feel the need for a refuge quite frequently, especially as he is a middle child, coming between big sister, Beccy, and the useless and messy baby, Lamb Chop. The seven linked stories read aloud well and they also have some unusually less than happy, so all the more real, endings. It is certainly true to life to have an escaped gerbil 'zapped' by Queenie the dog and, while I would be inclined to be cautious over reading that particular passage with some young children, on the whole the realistic detail creates involvement and interest.

Liz Waterland

SOURCE: A review of *Colvin and the Snake Basket,* in *Books for Keeps,* No. 47, November, 1987, p. 18.

Colvin is a thoroughly realistic little boy in a very recognisable home and school setting. The snake basket of the title is the washing basket that Colvin hides in whenever life becomes too much for him . . . such as when he cuts his sister's doll's hair off to enter her in a competition or after the awful affair of the school gerbil. The difference between this and many other tales of naughty children is the insight we as readers are given into Colvin's view of the world and the reasons for his actions. Like the adults in his world, we know that his thinking will lead to disaster but like Colvin we feel it is unfair that it should!

It is a very funny book. To an adult reader the dialogue, especially of the school scenes, is just right; to children Colvin is just *them* in all their hopefulness and good intentions. My school loved it.

It is a longish book, split into chapters; one for fluent readers (right up to adulthood) or for having read to you if you are, at a guess, six or older.

Stephanie Nettell

SOURCE: A review of *Colvin and the Snake Basket,* in *The Times Literary Supplement,* No. 4416, November 20-26, 1987, p. 1286.

Colvin Matthews is as rare and wonderful a creation as Little Pete, and deserves to live as long. McBratney is without parallel in his insight into life as seen from the middle of the family sandwich, by an engaging small boy who is in love with his infant teacher and at war with Rosy Tea Cosy, who retires to the laundry basket and hides under the dirty socks when he's miserable, and gives world-beating Ribsquashers and Neckbreakers when he's happy. The spirited humour and affection appeal as much to adult readers as young listeners.

📖 THE JIMMY ZEST ALL-STARS (1985)

Margery Fisher

SOURCE: A review of *The Jimmy Zest All-Stars,* in *Growing Point,* Vol. 24, No. 6, March, 1986, p. 4594.

Jimmy Zest, exuberant and overflowing with ideas, decides to approve of the new class-teacher after all when he strongly supports Zesty's decidedly unorthodox football team in appealing against what seems to them an entirely unjust disqualification. A lost pet rat, a birthday party from which boys are excluded, the theft of a goldfish, all give the author opportunities for racy dialogue and boisterous humour, supported by illustrations in cartoon-style [by Thelma Lambert]. The third instalment of the exploits of a group of primary school pupils in an Irish town.

Julia Marriage

SOURCE: A review of *The Jimmy Zest All-Stars,* in *School Librarian,* Vol. 34, No. 2, June, 1986, p. 154.

The antics of Jimmy Zest and his friends remind me of

the best of television situation comedy. The situations portrayed in these stories are slightly beyond belief but never preposterous. Among them are the possibilities of a rat breaking loose in the borough Public Health Department, and a flask passed hand to hand, rugger-ball style, round the class and smashing at the last moment. Both are convincingly described. Sam McBratney has a sharp eye for incident and a well-tuned ear for dialogue which is fast, witty and born of the perception of how children interact. This book will read aloud well and would be good for those occasions when one is looking for sheer enjoyment. Give it to good middle and top junior readers, and to reluctant ones as well. It says a great deal beneath the comedy about humanity and tolerance and the way we judge ourselves and others.

Pat Thomson

SOURCE: A review of *The Jimmy Zest All-Stars,* in *Books for Your Children,* Vol. 21, No. 2, Summer, 1986, p. 10.

Jimmy has gathered around him a very lively little junior school gang. They start by having difficulties with a new teacher and pass, via the rat in the Town Hall fiasco and the untimely demise of the carp in the ornamental pond, to a final triumphant football match. Clearly, a life pocked with incident, and a life which includes the girls on equal terms. The book is easily read and very well written with a vivacity which cheers the reader like sunshine.

📖 THE MISSING LOLLIPOP (1986)

Elizabeth J. King

SOURCE: A review of *The Missing Lollipop,* in *British Book News Children's Books,* September, 1986, p. 33.

The Missing Lollipop tells of old Mr Harris, the crossing-man, who has lost his precious 'lollipop', which Peter suspects is stolen. Peter's attempts to track this down with his chief suspect being one Carolyn Hinds, whom he cannot stand, seem to end up with him in front of the headmaster with increasing frequency. The daily life of a primary school is very well portrayed and the story also shows how easy it is to suspect someone just because you do not like him or her.

📖 UNCLE CHARLIE WEASEL AND THE CUCKOO BIRD (1986)

Maisie Roberts

SOURCE: A review of *Uncle Charlie Weasel and the Cuckoo Bird,* in *British Book News Children's Books,* September, 1986, p. 35.

Uncle Charlie Weasel and the Cuckoo Bird is not for reading to the faint-hearted or lily-livered. The animals here are certainly not sentimentalized. When Mr Stoat brings back stolen birds' eggs for breakfast, Uncle Charlie has his eye on the largest, but, before he can devour it, it hatches. The rest of the story is concerned with the Cuckoo Bird and how it outstays its welcome. While some children will undoubtedly enjoy the exploits of disgusting Uncle Charlie and his rat friends, I found the descriptions too vividly vile for reading to the very young.

Colin Mills

SOURCE: A review of *Uncle Charlie Weasel and the Cuckoo Bird,* in *Books for Keeps,* No. 50, May, 1988, p. 12.

Endearing tale about a family of stoats who adopt a chick as a pet. Story is enlivened by the dourest of characters, Uncle Charlie, who pours scorn on sentimentality, and saves the family (and the tale) from tweeness. This writer has a lively, immediate voice. There's a good sense of action, too. Catch the same writer's *Jimmy Zest* and *Zesty,* if you don't know them.

📖 *CLAUDIUS BALD EAGLE* (1987)

Pat Thomson

SOURCE: A review of *Claudius Bald Eagle,* in *Books for Your Children,* Vol. 22, No. 3, Autumn-Winter, 1987, p. 17.

Claudius has a pretty good opinion of himself and the other forest animals are indignant at the way he uses his gentle friend, Edward Moose. Edward is melancholy about his antlers and begs the Repulsively Ugly Troll to change them for a nice, red chicken's comb. And that happens on the day when millionaire Harry is planning to shoot Edward for his magnificent set of antlers. This wonderfully bizarre plot bounces along, fired by retro-jets of sharp dialogue and good jokes. Edward's problems can only be solved by an act of true friendship which adds warmth to the story and a further satisfaction is produced when Harry, stunned by his experiences, exchanges his guns for gold-plated golf clubs and leaves the forest in peace.

📖 *UNCLE CHARLIE WEASEL'S WINTER* (1988)

Fiona Maceachin

SOURCE: A review of *Uncle Charlie Weasel's Winter,* in *British Book News Children's Books,* June, 1988, p. 27.

Uncle Charlie Weasel's Winter charts the welcome return of Sam McBratney's delightfully horrid Uncle Charlie. The thoroughly nasty weasel in this tale finds himself terribly unprepared for the coming winter, so can hardly believe his good fortune on finding the perfect Winter Palace. There is only one problem however—Henry Streetmouse and his friends already live there. Uncle Charlie evicts them, but they retaliate with remarkable ingenuity.

Action packed and fast moving, with continuous excitement, adventure, great dialogue, a whole host of interesting characters and vivid descriptive language, this tale exemplifies that good will triumph. It should provoke much discussion, and comes again highly recommended.

George Hunt

SOURCE: A review of *Uncle Charlie Weasel's Winter,* in *Books for Keeps,* No. 56, May, 1989, p. 11.

The villainous Charlie Weasel, thief, liar and wino, evicts a band of courageous mice from a mysterious item of discarded furniture, before using it as a base from which to conduct a campaign of plunder against the winter foodstocks of the other forest animals. A simply told, knock-about tale, spiced up with a couple of touches of Dahlian muckiness, that would probably appeal to lower juniors seeking a slightly gutsier perspective on woodland life than that provided by [Beatrix] Potter and [Kenneth] Grahame.

📖 *THE GHOSTS OF HUNGRYHOUSE LANE* (1988)

Kirkus Reviews

SOURCE: A review of *The Ghosts of Hungryhouse Lane,* in *Kirkus Reviews,* Vol. LVII, No. 5, March 1, 1989, p. 380.

Three "ex-human beings"—Lady Cordelia, Sir James, and Bobbie (a chimney-sweep girl)—find their "Unwakeful Serenity" shattered by the three young Sweets ("interesting children but not particularly nice"), whose newly rich parents have rented the house where the ghosts had quietly resided with old Mercia Porterhouse. After the kids inadvertently dump frog spawn on James (in the bottle where he lives), Cordelia attempts a diplomatic meeting. Her pleas for understanding are met with curiosity but disrespect; the ghosts are forced to call in a *really* frightening reinforcement in the form of a Stone Age Scottish ghost before the children become their unexpected allies.

Besides the refreshingly ornery kids and their oblivious, backgammon-hooked parents, there's a lot of humor in the new "facts" introduced about ghosts: they inhabit things rather than places, float upside-down when perturbed, and must concentrate to pass through walls. This one would be fun to share aloud. Frequent full-page black-and-white illustrations add to the humor.

Publishers Weekly

SOURCE: A review of *The Ghosts of Hungryhouse Lane,* in *Publishers Weekly,* Vol. 239, No. 9, March 10, 1989, p. 89.

Three ghosts reside contentedly in Mercia Porterhouse's

home on Hungryhouse Lane, in a tranquil state called "Unwakeful Serenity." When Mercia dies, the house is rented out to the Sweet family and their three naughty, bickering children, and all signs of tranquility vanish. Zoe, Bonnie and Charlie create havoc around the house, discovering and destroying each ghost's special habitat. And they decide to charge other children fees for glimpses of the spooks. The ghosts only want to resume their peaceful existence; they get their wish when the children have a change of heart. But that's not all—a will is unearthed that names Mercia's friend Amy as the new, quieter owner of the house, and the beleaguered ghosts are once more left in peace. The Sweet family may strike readers as a little too shrill; their exploits are unappealing to the end. And the line drawings, [by Lisa Thiesing] while conveying some of the story's humor, seem an inappropriate match for the formal tone of the prose. Despite this, the book has amusing moments, and whether or not those will be enough to satisfy readers depends on how diehard they are about ghost stories.

Denise Wilms

SOURCE: A review of *The Ghosts of Hungryhouse Lane,* in *Booklist,* Vol. 85, No. 15, April 1, 1989, pp. 1387-8.

The ghosts of Hungryhouse Lane are quite upset: the Unwakeful Serenity that they have enjoyed while Mercia Porterhouse was alive is gone, gone, gone and replacing it is the severely disruptive chaos of the three Sweet children, who have boldly destroyed the reclusivity of the ghosts. Their friend, Amy Steadings, who was to inherit Mercia Porterhouse's abode, would love to help them but can't, for the will Mercia left is missing; without it, Amy has no control over the house. Even her suggestion to invite a scary ghost to do some heavy-duty haunting fails, for the incorrigible Sweet children prove more than a match for the imported specter. The victimized spirits are about to give up when the children, finding Mercia's will, realize that the ghosts are vulnerable and need protection. McBratney's story is told with considerable wit. His sly narrative pokes fun at both the preoccupied parents and the rambunctious children, all of whom are too self-absorbed to sense the crisis they present to the ghosts. Intelligent comedy that's illustrated with occasional, pen-and-wash drawings.

Bruce Ann Shook

SOURCE: A review of *The Ghosts of Hungryhouse Lane,* in *School Library Journal,* Vol. 35, No. 9, May, 1989, p. 110.

The wealthy Sweet family moves into their new rental home. The three unruly children quickly discover that they are sharing their quarters with three eccentric ghosts. By rights the house should belong to Miss Amy Steadings, best friend of the recently deceased owner, Mercia Porterhouse; however, no one can find Mercia's will. The ghosts are subjected to all sorts of indignities by the noisy,

precocious children, who are not the least bit frightened by the resident spooks. In fact, the ghosts are more than a little intimidated by the antics of the children. The Sweet children find the will and move out so that Amy can assume her role as caretaker of the ghosts. This is a lightweight, cleverly told tale with a distinct British style, enhanced by a number of amusing drawings [by Lisa Thiesing] that enable readers to see what the ghosts actually look like. The Sweet family is mildly reminiscent of Helen Cresswell's "Bagthorpes." The dotty parents play endless games of backgammon and remain oblivious to the uproar going on around them. Thoughtful readers may wonder why the dear departed Mercia did not become a ghost herself, or why some dead souls must linger on while others do not. Most young people, however, will enjoy the story for what it is: a humorous romp with some non-threatening spirits. This is one ghost story that will evoke chuckles, not shivers.

FUNNY, HOW THE MAGIC STARTS (1989)

Sheila Allen

SOURCE: A review of *Funny How the Magic Starts,* in *School Librarian,* Vol. 37, No. 3, August, 1989, p. 114.

A delightfully innocent story for teenagers. A tale of the blossoming of young love between the new boy, with the improbable name of Seymour Brolly, and Monica, the 'author' of the book, whose mother asks her to befriend her new neighbour. There are the usual characters to be found in any fifth form and in any staffroom but each one is almost a caricature. Seymour's attachment to his binoculars, his passion for all forms of wild life, and his campaigns to save animals border on the ridiculous. He works hard to establish his rights and his beliefs but all his endeavours bring him into conflict with authority. Yet somehow his integrity ensures his superiority. In addition there is the relationship between Monica and her best friend, Debbie, that of Monica and her parents, and those between teachers and pupils, all just a little larger than life but so recognisable! The book is totally inconsequential; a lighthearted, enjoyable read.

THE SECRET OF BONE ISLAND (1989)

George Hunt

SOURCE: A review of *The Secret of Bone Island* and *When I Lived Down Cuckoo Lane,* in *Books for Keeps,* No. 60, January, 1990, p. 8.

The Secret of Bone Island treads ominously familiar ground: three siblings unearth a treasure map and set off to explore a reputedly haunted island. The book conveys an atmosphere of Blyton with extra adjectives, but a couple of clever twists in the plot rescue the story from blandness. . . . [*The Secret of Bone Island* provides] nonstrenuous literary entertainment, and therefore [earns its] place on the Junior bookshelf.

Joan Nellist

SOURCE: A review of *The Secret of Bone Island,* in *School Librarian,* Vol. 38, No. 1, February, 1990, p. 19.

Four books [*Squonk* by Julia Jarman, *The Trouble with Herbert* by Heather Eyles, *The Party in the Lift* by Jacqueline Wilson and *The Secret of Bone Island*] for that difficult gap which comes between newly fluent readers and voracious (we hope) older bookworms. They are all attractively presented and keep well within a limited storyline. They are not too long, have clear print and relevant illustrations [by Hernesh Alles in *The Secret of Bone Island*], extend vocabulary as well as giving plenty of reinforcement, and are very much geared to children's interests.

The Secret of Bone Island, the meatiest of the four, is a typical island adventure with a good twist in the tail. It is quite challenging in its structure and plot and could be a class story as well as an individual reader.

PUT A SADDLE ON THE PIG (1992; U.S. edition as *You Just Don't Listen!*, 1994)

R. Baines

SOURCE: A review of *Put a Saddle on the Pig,* in *Junior Bookshelf,* Vol. 56, No. 4, August, 1992, p. 165.

Jim Mulholland has emerged from the past of Laura Clement's widowed mother, and Victoria Clement is of a mind to marry again. The changes that this would mean for her sixteen year old daughter are encapsulated in the fact that the marriage would necessitate moving fifty miles away to another house, and consequently involve changing schools, losing friends, and possibly ending a burgeoning romance. Laura becomes immensely territorial, opposing the move with all her might and main.

The relationship between mother and daughter, rich in love and caring but short on intimacy and understanding, is well drawn, and Sam McBratney is generous in his perception of the differing viewpoints of each generation of the Clement family. However, a very high proportion of this story is told through conversation, usually between females and frequently between young people. Perhaps because the author is a mature male this dialogue is not always entirely convincing.

Joanna Porter

SOURCE: A review of *Put a Saddle on the Pig,* in *The Times Educational Supplement,* No. 3979, October 2, 1992, p. 9.

Victoria Clement in *Put a Saddle on the Pig* is a talented, capable and attractive widow who likes parallel lines and right angles, cups on hooks and washing hung properly on lines. Yet when she meets childhood friend turned pig-farmer Jim Mulholland, she rediscovers her adolescent penchant for Wordsworth, blushes at bouquets and astounds her teenage daughter Laura with plans to move to the country.

Laura cannot credit that her mother might be drawn to one whom she herself recalls "waddling through the muck like a duck in wellies". Mum can ponder over the still, sad music of humanity and her "good, quiet man" all she likes: daughter is busy finding a man of her own, thanks, and is set on staying put.

In this elegantly written novel, Sam McBratney is as likely to appeal to an adult as to a teenage audience. The case for both older and younger female is relentlessly argued, but McBratney still manages to promise something beyond dogged stalemate without resorting to a facile solution. Despite this, I'm not sure that we ever quite lose sight of Laura's duck in wellies and when Vicky's heart quickens to Jim's flat-vowelled insistence that a spade is a spade is a spade, it's rather hard to know what all the fuss is about.

Val Biernan

SOURCE: A review of *You Just Don't Listen!,* in *Books for Keeps,* No. 91, March, 1995, p. 16.

This was first published in hardback under the title *Put a Saddle on the Pig*—a more attention-grabbing one than the paperback! Conflict and emotions run high when 16-year-old Laura finds out that her widowed mother is not only seeing another man but plans to move to the country. Faced with the prospect of leaving her friends and the city life she enjoys, she rebels and feels betrayed at her mother's lack of consultation. Eventually, acknowledging that her mother too has the right to make her own life, Laura makes a fragile truce. The author describes teenage feelings with accuracy and style in a book which was chosen by young people in Ireland as the Bisto Book of the Year.

J. Jarman

SOURCE: A review of *You Just Don't Listen!,* in *Books for Your Children,* Vol. 30, No. 2, Spring, 1995, p. 30.

When 16 year old Laura discovers that her widowed mother is planning to move fifty miles away—to live in the country—she is appalled. When she learns that her mother is thinking of marrying again she is devastated. How dare she? The author tells the story showing all points of view—mother's, daughter's, and the might-be step father's and by the end mother and daughter come to see each other's point of view. It's a rather chastening experience for Laura, but young people in Ireland voted this story Bisto Book of the Year—proving, I think, that lots of teenagers like their literature to be unsentimental and unpatronising—in a word—REAL!

📖 *THE GREEN KIDS* (1992)

Margery Fisher

SOURCE: A review of *The Green Kids,* in *Books for Keeps,* No. 77, November, 1992, p. 40.

[*The Green Kids*] is not an addition to the lengthening list of conservation stories but a neat conjunction of two popular subjects—children sampling country ways and the discovery of a friend in an unexpected place. The squabbling trio upsetting the journey (by white Rolls, no less) to a remote Irish mountainside in the Easter holidays are sharply outlined—Charlie currently obsessed by collecting bones, Shelley daintily affronted by a lack of bathroom facilities and TV, and spoilt little Lottie whose rag doll Lubylou includes in her many roles the dangerous one of scapegoat (a role sometimes shared by Neptune, the much put-upon family dog). Driven out to perform the unwonted exercise of walking, the Greens find their first surprise—a supermarket trolley standing idly beside a gorse bush, one feather caught in its meshes. Only mildly interested at first, the Greens are gradually drawn into stranger affairs. Their theory of secret cock-fighting in the district is exploded when the uncouth figure in tattered coat and black wellies proves to be harmless, except for the determination to fly, with home-made wings, from the considerable height of the Black Cliff.

Thatcher Collins is eccentric; he is also nature-wise; before this compact layered tale comes to an end, lessons—like moderation, bread making and good manners—have been well learned. There is skill in the way the behaviour of the children is poised just on the edge of improbability, as the unpromising new environment has its slow effect on them. The prose is simple enough for a newly-fledged reader around 8 or 9 but a nice turn of phrase refreshes the ordinary. The Green children 'squabbled and fought rather like starlings round a single crust of toast on a frosty morning'; Shelley, watching a fanatic trying to fly like the birds, feels the wind is playing with him 'before blasting him away like the seed-head of a dandelion or some other inconsequential thing'; the breakfast porridge which is part of Mr Green's disciplinary scheme seems to Charlie like 'microwaved frogspawn'.

Scrawly drawings [by Virginia Chalcraft] punctuate the pages but are hardly needed in such a vigorous, craftsmanlike mixture of pathos, sparkling humour, such an expert moulding of insistent personality and calmly enduring landscape.

A. R. Williams

SOURCE: A review of *The Green Kids,* in *Junior Bookshelf,* Vol. 56, No. 6, December, 1992, pp. 243-4.

'Remote from public road or dwelling' as the poet described it sums up the situation of the Green family on their arrival at their holiday cottage in their white Rolls Royce which there represents the height of incongruity. Included are Mum and Dad, easy-tempered and delighted with the solitude; twelve-year-old Shelley, bossy but bold; Charles, whose main occupation apart from his collection of bones seems to be the taunting and teasing of his more babyish sister, Lottie, and abusing her treasured doll, Loubyloo; and the snob dog, Neptune, stubbornly disdainful of even the priciest dog-food. Not much of a welcome in the hillsides, either, since conditions in this back of the beyond are what are popularly referred to as primitive by seasoned town-dwellers. Three (no, four) to a bed, too. As for having to go for a walk! Intrigued by the discovery of a still serviceable shopping trolley among the heather the children explore beyond the crest and find the dilapidated residence of the ageing 'Thatcher' Collins who aims to *fly* with his home-made wings (transported to take-off in the trolley). Mr. Collins turns out to be an interesting source of information on a number of country matters so that the holiday looks like being not such a dead loss after all. Mr. Green voices his misgivings over Mr. Collins and his obsession, fears justified by the bird-man's plan to descend from the top of a neighbouring eminence named Black Cliff. His inevitable dead fall leads to an action-packed rescue operation of which the family are part. The style of the tale is racy at least if not pleasurably slangy and there are no dull moments, what with the suspense over Thatcher's daring and the children's bickering, so the tale moves at a good pace.

Ann Jenkin

SOURCE: A review of *The Green Kids,* in *The School Librarian,* Vol. 41, No. 1, February, 1993, p. 22.

The Green kids, selfish, argumentative and noisy, but quite intelligent, are dragged off by their parents for a quiet country holiday in a mountain cottage which has few modern amenities and no TV. Their father has nostalgic dreams of returning to his childhood haunts. The children have other ideas. They find the whole prospect boring and alarming and they quarrel more than ever. However, when they discover a supermarket trolley on an old mountain track and then a tumbledown cottage with a dead thing on the wall, their adventures begin. They meet the cottage's strange inhabitant and discover a different way of life from their own pampered existence. They also begin to care for someone other than themselves, and are concerned for his safety as he embarks on his own great and dangerous adventure on the Black Cliff.

The story is lively and fast-moving. It will be a good read for young fluent readers, though some of the long difficult words seem out of keeping with the large print, uncomplicated style, and simple line illustrations. Phrases like 'horrendous proportions' and 'excellent qualities' will be heavy-going for eight- to ten-year-olds. However, naughty children, a dog, and adventures are always popular, and the jokey style and the humour will appeal to most readers of that age.

Pam Harwood

SOURCE: A review of *The Green Kids,* in *Books for Keeps,* No. 85, March, 1994, p. 11.

The Greens take a holiday in a mountain cottage. Mr and Mrs relish the simple, wholesome quality of life but Sally, Lottie and Charlie, the little Greens, are frankly horrified at their loss of the 20th century. It proves not to be an idyllic break as the children fight and squabble between themselves and it's only the appearance of Thatcher Collins that stops them in their tracks. He wants to be a birdman and has spent ages collecting feathers to this effect—never mind aerodynamics or hollow bones, one of our last glimpses is the flap of huge, sinister wings as they launch off Black Cliff into swirling, empty air.

A witty tale with a depth and sensitivity of feeling that's rare in books for the newly competent reader.

📖 *ART, YOU'RE MAGIC!* (1992)

Marion McLaughlin

SOURCE: A review of *Art, You're Magic,* in *School Librarian,* Vol. 40, No. 4, November, 1992, p. 146.

Young Arthur Smith never intends to be naughty. He only wants to be as popular as Mervyn Magee and to keep out of the hated Henrietta Turtle's way, but trouble seems to seek him out. In the end, Art saves the day—and the class play, *Daniel in the Lions' Den*—when he steps into the role of Daniel at the last minute. These gentle, undemanding stories of Art's misadventures at home and in school are ideally suited to beginning readers. The book has been carefully designed to appeal to young children, with colourful dust jacket and large, well-spaced print, perfectly complemented by amusing black and white illustrations [by Tony Blundell].

📖 *A CASE OF BLUE MURDER* (1993)

Tom Deveson

SOURCE: "To Be Continued," in *The Times Educational Supplement,* No. 4016, June 18, 1993, p. 16.

[*A Case of Blue Murder* is] part detective story, part adventure tale, with a murdered racing pigeon and an Iron Age camp. Why were Jenny's slippers with the pink tufts ruined? Why did two policemen collapse with laughter? What was the secret of the football stickers? The answers are found in this cheerful colloquial first-person narrative.

D. A. Young

SOURCE: A review of *A Case of Blue Murder,* in *Junior Bookshelf,* Vol. 57, No. 4, August, 1993, pp. 138-9.

The gang from *The Thursday Creature* is back! It was Ernie Kilbride's idea to build an underground hut in the field at the back of the street so that they could be primitive people for a while. Somewhat reluctantly Jenny, Melanie and Craig agreed. Ernie gave the instructions and the other three did the work. Joker and his lot must come along to find out what this hole in the ground covered with planks and sheets of tin was all about. Then the dead pigeon is found. Ernie conducts a post-mortem only to discover the pigeon was shot. Now they have a murder investigation on their hands. How it happened and who did it are the questions which keep Ernie and his friends busy during the tailend of the boring summer holidays.

Jenny tells the story which brings out the characters of the other children. Grown-ups are relegated to a shadowy background on the periphery of events out of touch with the children's activities. Who needs parents when the omniscient Ernie is at hand? The conversation is amusing and the story moves convincingly to the discovery of the culprit, a bout of fisticuffs and a broken leg for Joker.

This addition to the Superchamp series for established readers has colourful cartoon style illustrations [by Terry McKenna] which match the liveliness of the text. It is a great argument for the notion that reading books can be fun.

📖 *GUESS HOW MUCH I LOVE YOU* (1994)

Prue Goodwin

SOURCE: A review of *Guess How Much I Love You,* in *School Librarian,* Vol. 43, No. 1, February, 1995, pp. 17-8.

Every so often you come across a book that you know, now you have it, you will not be able to live without. For me, *Guess How Much I Love You* is such a book. From the moment I met Big and Little Nutbrown Hare on the front cover, followed them into the book and found them looking out from the title page to check that I was there, I was hooked. This book doesn't really tell a story. It is a description of that time each evening when children realise that bed is imminent unless they can distract the adults' attention. Little Nutbrown Hare embarks on a contest to see who loves the other the most. Big Nutbrown Hare always manages to 'win' the competition but Little Nutbrown Hare keeps trying until, at last, tiredness gets the better of him. That is what happens—but what is it about? The words 'I love you' can become meaningless if repeated too often but in this case, when Big Nutbrown Hare says them on the final page, any parent will know what they mean.

I believe this to be an exceptional book. For me it encapsulates the warmth and security we wish for every child. The profundity of its theme is made more powerful by the apparent simplicity of the pictures. It is a book to share with the very young but it is also a book for any adult who wants a reminder of those magic moments spent with a child before the world intrudes on their relationship and changes it forever.

Publishers Weekly

SOURCE: A review of *Guess How Much I Love You,* in *Publishers Weekly,* Vol. 242, No. 11, March 13, 1995, p. 68.

Fresh as a fiddlehead fern in spring, this beguiling bedtime tale features a pip of a young rabbit and his indulgent parent. Searching for words to tell his dad how much he loves him (and to put off bedtime just an eentsy bit longer), Little Nutbrown Hare comes up with one example after another ("I love you as high as I can hop!"), only to have Big Nutbrown Hare continually up the ante. Finally, on the edge of sleep, he comes up with a show-stopper: "I love you right up to the moon." (Dad does top this declaration too, but only after his little bunny falls asleep.) Effused with tenderness, McBratney's wise, endearing and droll story is enriched by the near-monochromatic backdrop of Jeram's pen-and-wash artwork, rendered earthy tones of moss, soft brown and gray for a visually quieting effect just right for that last soothing tale before sleep.

Stephanie Zvirin

SOURCE: A review of *Guess How Much I Love You,* in *Booklist,* Vol. 91, No. 14, March 15, 1995, p. 1328.

An endearing nursery game is beautifully revitalized in this comforting, sleepy-time picture book. A little hare tests his father's love by declaring his own: "Guess how much I love you . . . This much." [Anita] Jeram's double-page-spread watercolors are just right for the gentle competition that ensues as parent and child each avow affection in ever more expansive terms. Neither sugary nor too cartoonlike, the watercolors, in soft shades of brown and greens with delicate ink-line details, warmly capture the loving relationship between parent and child as well as the comedy that stems from little hare's awe of his wonderful dad. The story ends with a declaration of love so great it reaches "right up to the moon," and little hare finally falls fast asleep. There's not a wrong note in this tender tale, which should become an enduring bedtime favorite—right up there with *Goodnight Moon.*

Susan Patron

SOURCE: A review of *Guess How Much I Love You,* in *The Five Owls,* Vol. IX, No. 4, March-April, 1995, p. 82

Like that of Margaret Wise Brown's bunny and his mother in *Runaway Bunny,* Little Nutbrown Hare's dialogue with Big Nutbrown Hare suggests an attentive and loving parent-child relationship. "I love you as high as I can

reach," says Little Nutbrown Hare, and raises his forearms straight up, as his much larger father watches. Then, on the next page, the father replies, "I love you as high as *I* can reach," which is, of course, much higher.

On one level, McBratney's story stays close to truths of childhood, realistically capturing the preschooler's efforts to describe a feeling so big, so all-important, as love. But each heartfelt effort is topped by dad, whose love always comes out to be higher, farther, wider, bigger. After several playful but serious verbal rounds with his father, Little Nutbrown Hare's final, poetic choice of metaphor, "I love you right up to the moon," is once again bested by dad.

Margaret Wise Brown's 1944 story, a still-popular bedtime book, offers reassurances about parental love to a small child testing boundaries and ends on a light note, as the mother says, "Have a carrot." But where the dialogue and resolution in *Runaway Bunny* satisfy, *Guess How Much I Love You* leaves this reader wishing that the child could have the last word—or at least be able to show his own love to be just as huge as dad's.

Still, their gamelike dialogue is fueled by love, and listeners should be of a mind, at the end, to nod off cozily.

Diane Roback with Bella Stander

SOURCE: "U.K. Sleeper a Hopaway Success," in *Publishers Weekly,* Vol. 242, No. 37, September 11, 1995, p. 33.

It's not a new phenomenon—*Stellaluna, Time for Bed* and *Mama, Do You Love Me?* come to mind—the sweet, unassuming picture book that is a natural handsell to any parent looking for the perfect bedtime story. A book for which a publisher has modest hopes but one that proceeds to sell and sell and sell.

During the last several months the picture book with legs has been *Guess How Much I Love You* by Sam McBratney, illustrated by Anita Jeram, which was released in March by Candlewick Press. Originally published by Walker Books in the U.K., the book has been (or will be) published in 15 countries so far, and boasts worldwide sales of one million copies. Its initial 30,000-copy printing in the U.S. sold out long before pub date, it has appeared on *PW*'s children's bestseller list since April (it debuted at #2), and it's been flying off bookstore shelves in record numbers.

How does one explain such an extraordinary success? First off, most agree, it's a very soothing, affectionate story. According to Judy Bulow, children's backlist buyer at the Tattered Cover in Denver, "It's a reassuring book for both the parent and the child, because it reinforces the idea that parent-child love is always there no matter what happens. It transcends time or place or ethnicity, and it has a universal appeal because of the animals [Big Nutbrown Hare and Little Nutbrown Hare] in the illustrations."

Janis Fields, co-owner of B. Dolphin Books for Kids in Greensboro, N.C., adds another reason—because it's about a father, for a change, rather than a mother, and also because "the pictures are cute but aren't overly gorgeous. Kids can't relate to some overly gorgeous pictures that adults can."

When parents read the book in her store, Fields comments, "they say it's such a sweet story, and it's exactly what they're looking for. It's something they can read to the children to calm them down right before bed, but it's not just a bedtime story."

At the Tattered Cover, where the children's department is located on the lower level, the book achieved instant success when it was put on the first floor's "Staff Recommends" shelf. "I noticed that within an afternoon, I had to replace it three times," Bulow reports.

"We were handselling it for a while, but now it's word of mouth," she continues. "People hear about it from their friends." And those friends are obviously telling *their* friends, to the point where Candlewick couldn't ship the book fast enough to fill orders.

"I liked it from the moment the rep handed it to me," Bulow says. "I showed it to everyone in my store and anxiously awaited for it to come in. Then we sold out and couldn't get any more."

"We knew it had the potential to be big, but nothing like this," says Joanne MacKenzie, publicity manager for Candlewick Press. "In England it has sold about 30,000 copies, which is a lot there; the equivalent here would be about 90,000. Instead we've sold 580,000. It's been a challenge for us to keep up with the demand."

The company has changed its production methods to stay on top of that demand: the books, which were originally printed in Italy, are also being printed in several locations throughout the U.S. "We worked it so that a new printing would arrive every month throughout the summer," MacKenzie explains. "With larger accounts and some independents, we have offered layaway buying, where they don't have to commit to books from a certain print run. So they've been able to get them as they've needed them and it's helped us plan our print runs."

She says that the book is selling in a "pretty balanced" way to chains and independents. It's on Barnes & Noble's and Media Play's bestseller list, has appeared on Baker & Taylor's bestseller list for libraries every month since publication, and "there are literally dozens of independents that have sold over 100 copies of this book," MacKenzie says.

In celebration of the millionth copy sold, Candlewick is bringing Sam McBratney over from Ireland for an author tour this month; he'll be appearing at three of the regional bookseller trade shows, as well as many of the stores that have sold large quantities (including the Tattered Cover, which has sold around 1000 copies), and even a regional

managers meeting at Barnes & Noble (where 20,000 copies have been sold chain-wide).

According to MacKenzie, McBratney is "stunned" by **Guess How Much I Love You**'s success. "I asked him how he felt that a million copies of his book were out in the world," she says. "He said what was unimaginable to him was that a million parents were out there sharing this book with a million children. I don't think he ever conceived that he would have that kind of impact on people."

HURRAY FOR MONTY RAY! (1994)

Gill Roberts

SOURCE: A review of *Hurray for Monty Ray!*, in *Books for Keeps*, No. 89, November, 1994, p. 11.

It's a real problem for Monty Ray that baby brother 'Lamb Chop' is still without a name, especially when Myrtle Stackpole, the class creep and clever-clogs, finds out and won't stop making fun. However, the fifth boy of the family is eventually named and taking 'rotten old burned toast' to school isn't as strange as Myrtle presumes. After a worrying time, Monty can relax. The bold print is interspersed with clear and often coloured illustrations [by Robert Bartelt] on every page. 7-year-olds enjoyed this and established readers will read it for themselves.

THE GHASTLY GERTY SWINDLE: WITH THE GHOSTS OF HUNGRYHOUSE LANE (1994)

Mary Harns Veeder

SOURCE: A review of *The Ghastly Gerty Swindle with the Ghosts of Hungryhouse Lane*, in *Booklist*, Vol. 91, No. 5, November 1, 1994, p. 500.

In this sequel to **Ghosts of Hungryhouse Lane,** the Sweet children (who aren't particularly sweet) visit their elderly friend Amy Steadings and the ghosts in her attic. The English village backdrop and the great house filled with antiques may seem remote to some kids, but the Sweets will win readers. The feisty brood, whose sibling rivalries are brilliantly evoked in a few choice phrases, are actually more interesting than the ghosts, with their eighteenth-century manners and their whining about the hardships of ghosting. The housekeeper, Ghastly Gerty, who helps her larcenous son steal antiques from the house, is also memorable—because she's so sour. Young readers will enjoy the Sweets' squabbles and their lively, nondemanding adventures.

Cheryl Cufari

SOURCE: A review of *The Ghastly Gerty Swindle: With

the Ghosts of Hungryhouse Lane, in *School Library Journal,* Vol. 40, No. 12, December, 1994, pp. 110-11.

In this sequel to **The Ghosts of Hungryhouse Lane** obnoxious, brazen Gerty Swindle and her son, Alexander the Grate, form a plan to relieve kind, elderly Amy Steadings of her many antiques. They carry it out when Amy goes off on a picnic with the three Sweet children, who have come back to Hungryhouse Lane to visit. Alexander empties the furniture into his van, but in so doing also removes the ghosts that dwell in Amy's attic. After the deed is done, the children gather clues and the spirits use their powers to draw police attention to the thieves. Thanks to this combination of efforts, the criminals are found out and the mystery of the missing antiques is solved. Although this brief novel contains numerous characters, McBratney works them into the plot smoothly, endowing each with unique qualities. His writing exhibits energy and humor and sustains suspense. Occasional full-page, black-and-white illustrations [by Lisa Thiesing] extend the action. An enjoyable addition where mysteries are needed.

📖 THE STRANGER FROM SOMEWHERE IN TIME (1994)

S. M. Ashburner

SOURCE: A review of *The Stranger from Somewhere in Time,* in *Junior Bookshelf,* Vol. 59, No. 1, February, 1995, pp. 22-3.

This is one of the 'Banana Book' series, described as for 'newly fluent readers'.

It is an amusing story of how a group of children decide to make and bury a time capsule, filled with items typical of today. Some of them are tricked by a 'stranger from somewhere in time'.

The format of the book—it is small and easy to handle—and its overall appearance make it initially appealing. However, despite this, and its colourful, lively illustrations [by S. Anderson] and fairly good characterisation, the book is generally mediocre. The story lacks sparkle and has a rather too predictable ending. It might be reasonably popular with the lower junior school age-range.

📖 FLASH EDDIE AND THE BIG BAD WOLF (1994)

B. Clark

SOURCE: A review of *Flash Eddie and the Big Bad Wolf,* in *Junior Bookshelf,* Vol. 59, No. 2, April, 1995, pp. 71-2.

Flash Eddie organises a T.V. Chat Show for Fizz T.V. and is worried. Every month the number of viewers falls sharply, so he is desperately looking for a really interesting person to be interviewed. Then someone calls at Fizz

T.V. saying he is the Big Bad Wolf. Eddie's assistant says "He gives me the creeps" and seems reluctant to shake hands. When questioned about his friends "Wolfy" says that the few friends he had never seemed to last. "Why was that, Wolfy," asks Eddie. "I ate them," says Wolfy. Eddie goes to see Wolfy in his own home, and Wolfy says "Let's think about lunch". "Lunch" croaks Eddie. "You know, I have never tasted a T.V. personality before," the Big Bad Wolf smiles with teeth as sharp as icicles, "and certainly not a chat show host."

So at Fizz T.V. Eddie's assistant has been promoted. To read this story is hilariously amusing—not perhaps for the very timid child, but even for such readers the "fun" level seeps through, and most children will revel in the sheer impossibility of it.

Cherie Gladstone

SOURCE: A review of *Flash Eddie and the Big Bad Wolf,* in *The School Librarian,* Vol. 43, No. 2, May, 1995, p. 64.

This modern cautionary tale has sophisticated but credulous chat-show host, Flash Eddie, believing his own media hype and forgetting self-preservation. With his ratings going down dramatically, he seizes the chance to interview the villain of many a tale—the Big Bad Wolf—who seems elderly and toothless but turns out to be just as sly and cunning as ever.

The story is episodic which makes it ideal to read aloud over a period of time. The child's interest is maintained as the suspense builds up—will the wolf really eat Eddie? The ending is very satisfying (not a cop-out) and the reader has clues as to what is going to happen. Women are shown as powerful, sensible and independent in contrast to Eddie, the embodiment of an egoistic, exploitative media personality, who gets his come-uppance. I can imagine this being noisily popular with children of 8 upwards. There is a lot of potential for audience participation.

📖 FRANCIS FRY PRIVATE EYE (1995)

Steve Rosson

SOURCE: A review of *Francis Fry Private Eye,* in *Books for Keeps,* No. 94, September, 1995, p. 7.

My own favourite [of the books reviewed] is **Francis Fry Private Eye.** Sam McBratney and Kim Blundell's detective has got the lot—trench-coat, fedora, overflowing waste-paper basket and revolving office chair—but boy is he dim? On the trail of a stolen parrot, he discovers that more and more tropical animals are disappearing but the reader will twig the 'baddie' long before he does. As usual from 'Jets' there are speech bubbles, press-cuttings and other printed stuff to hurry the story on and the big, bold, colour illustrations are a treat. When Fry does finally stumble over the 'villain', there's a nice green twist at the end.

📖 *SUZUKI GOODBYE* (1995)

Dennis Hamley

SOURCE: "Revving Up for Reluctant Readers," in *The Times Educational Supplement,* No. 4134, September 22, 1995, p. R11.

[*The following excerpt is from a review of several volumes from the Collins Comets series, a set of graphic novels that are designed for teenagers who require special encouragement in reading. In addition to* Sukuzi Goodbye, *the novels considered are* Ricky and the Ram-Raiders *and* Hell-Ride Tonight *by David Clayton,* The Exterminators *by Ian Gregory, and* The Soldier Who Never Was *and* Sir Gawain and the Rugby Sevens *by Mick Gowar.*]

At its best, the graphic novel is a hybrid art form with its own rules, purposes and integrity. But in adapting this deceptively straightforward genre for reluctant readers, is there not a grave risk of its becoming a half-hearted comic, no more than an attempt to dilute text by slipping it in between a lot of pictures? . . .

I soon found that at the very least I was reading fast, compulsive narratives which were all well served by their illustrators, with a good balance of picture to text, using the genre's conventions well. . . .

Suzuki Goodbye tells of Caroline, John and Bill and the comeuppance of a crooked motorcycle dealer. As one would expect from Sam McBratney, a tragic element is beautifully handled. . . .

In interest levels and reading difficulty, these carefully edited books hit, I think, their intended readership, and I rate the pack as one of the best things to appear for special needs English for years.

📖 *THE FIRETAIL CAT* (1995)

Liz Baynton-Clarke

SOURCE: A review of *The Firetail Cat,* in *School Librarian,* Vol. 43, No. 4, November, 1995, p. 153.

Sharkbait! Such is the likely fate of anyone unfortunate enough to find themselves aboard the good ship *Belinda,* under the direction of the evil Captain Pegg. Until the day when Pegg, searching for a creature to rid the ship of rats, happens to acquire a 'firetail cat' in error. Ignoring warnings that 'cats like 'em is never lucky on board ship', Pegg and his crew soon find themselves helplessly beset by the catalogue of troubles which will ultimately be their downfall. Not everyone suffers, however, and for cabin-boy William Trevithick, press-ganged aboard in the same sack as the unfortunate cat, the magic of the firetail proves far from harmful.

Recommended by the publishers as 'suitable for readers who are confidently reading by themselves', this book will provide encouraging and enjoyable reading for many 6 to 8-year-olds. All in all, this is another good yarn from Sam McBratney. Coupled with Scoular Anderson's sparky illustrations, the story has every chance of becoming 'childbait'. We'll forget the sharks for now!

📖 *THE DARK AT THE TOP OF THE STAIRS* (1995)

Kirkus Reviews

SOURCE: A review of *The Dark at the Top of the Stairs,* in *Kirkus Reviews,* Vol. LXIV, No. 1, January 1, 1996, p. 70.

In this book, McBratney has crystallized every single detail into part of a winning formula. There is little story: Three mice—Cob, Hazel, and Berry-Berry—tell an older, wiser mouse that they would like to go see the monster at the top of the cellar stair. He is understanding and allows them to recover from their journey, during which they were terrified by the sight of the cat's shadow, without comment. The narrative is comic and catchy, with all the dialogue arranged with flawless symmetry. It is set against dramatic crayon pencil illustrations [by Ivan Bates], in which everything is depicted from the perspective of the mice (a door looms like a skyscraper). In his first book, Bates chooses a palette of dark purples, browns, and ambers; the mice seem sculpted from the gloom of the cellar.

Publishers Weekly

SOURCE: A review of *The Dark at the Top of the Stairs,* in *Publishers Weekly,* Vol. 243, No. 3, January 15, 1996, p. 461.

As in his *Guess How Much I Love You,* McBratney spins an ample, emotionally ripe tale out of a familiar, even slight premise. A wise old mouse lives with his three young mice in the corner of a cellar, and at bedtime he asks them what they'd like to do the next day. One night, all three clamor to see "the dark at the top of the stairs" where the "monster" lives, and the old mouse, who knows that "sooner or later all young mice will try to see the dark at the top of the stairs," agrees to take them. Perfectly capturing the edgy glee and derring-do of a trip to dangerous territory, McBratney builds the suspense with each well-chosen word. When the four finally reach the door at the top of the stairs, a glimpse of the shadow of a seemingly gigantic cat sends them scurrying ("bumpety-bump and slippity-slide and tumble-thump") back down the staircase, "where they landed in a wriggle and a heap before making a dash for warm, safe, wonderful home." In his picture book debut, [Ivan] Bates provides endearing depictions of these (at least temporarily) bold mice; his compositions and mouse's-eye perspectives create enticingly eerie shadows and angles. Rendered on textured surfaces, his crayon-pencil art at times has the feel of needlepoint, sweetly balancing the shivers in this tale.

John Peters

SOURCE: A review of *The Dark at the Top of the Stairs,* in *School Library Journal,* Vol. 42, No. 3, March, 1996, p. 178.

McBratney follows up his cozy, warm *Guess How Much I Love You* with a real change of mood. Though their wise old mentor tries to entice them outdoors to play, three young mice insist on seeing what lives behind the dark at the top of the stairs. Its single word—"MEOW"—sends them "bumpety-bump and slippity-slide and tumble-thump" all the way back down. Bates gives readers a mouse's-eye view of the adventure: topped by a towering door, the huge stairs loom above a shadowed, cobwebby, cluttered cellar lit in dim, ominous blues and grays. Like Michael Rosen and Helen Oxenbury's *We're Going on a Bear Hunt,* this book invites youngsters to venture out into the unknown, offering the reassurance of a haven at the end, and the exhilaration of a mad scramble to get there.

IN CRACK WILLOW WOOD (1995)

Angela Redfern

SOURCE: A review of *In Crack Willow Wood,* in *The School Librarian,* Vol. 44, No. 1, February, 1996, p. 21.

This book of five short stories is intended for reading aloud to children at KS1 and is centred on the antics of a group of woodland friends, namely Stoat, Vole, Rabbit, Badger, Hog and Weasel. Each story takes place in the familiar setting of the classroom or the home. Billy Weasel is a pivotal figure, a mischievous class prankster rather than an out and out bully, whose humour errs towards the mean and is not appreciated by the rest of the group nor by his teachers. With a quiet, gently humorous tone that contrasts nicely with Billy Weasel's boisterousness, the book manages to resolve the situation and Billy is eventually integrated into the group. The stories provide opportunities for discussing the complexities of friendship, unacceptable, hurtful behaviour, and revenge. It is also a useful book for introducing the short story genre to a class of young children.

F. Ball

SOURCE: A review of *In Crack Willow Wood,* in *Junior Bookshelf,* Vol. 60, No. 3, June, 1996, p. 111.

Crack Willow Wood is the setting for a series of adventures featuring a homely group of anthropomorphic animals. The five friends are Harvey Stoat, Billy Weasel, Charity Rabbit, Olivia Vole and Badger. They attend the local school where they are taught by Miss Findley, an erudite duck. Their adventures—described in five stories

which could be read independently but are linked by the characters and setting—include incidents likely to appeal to older infants and younger juniors. Billy Weasel is the naughtiest creature in the group, easily getting all the others into trouble. In the first story, Harvey Stoat becomes fed up with school after some of Billy Weasel's pranks. His solution is to tie up the hands of the village clock so that it will never again be time to go to school. Next, Harvey Stoat tries to exclude Billy Weasel from his party but he still turns up. The other children manage to trick him into running off by starting a game which ends with the refrain ' . . . the last one home's a Custard Bun!' In the third story, Billy Weasel gets Charity Rabbit into trouble. The next story shows Harvey Stoat discovering how disappointing it can be if you believe totally in stories like the tooth fairy. And the final story shows how they all cheer up badger when he is feeling low.

The five stories are full of the kind of detail and dialogue that will sound familiar to young schoolchildren. Although the incidents are often amusing, the concerns of the friends are treated seriously. The black and white illustrations [by Ivan Bates] create traditional images, and although the school has modern details such as a lollipop lady, and the party includes food such as pizzas, the whole book has a timeless quality.

Maurice Saxby

SOURCE: A review of *In Crack Willow Wood,* in *Reading Time,* Vol. XL, No. III, August, 1996, p. 27.

Labelled 'A Walker Read Aloud', that is just what it is—a simple text about frisky little animals for unsophisticated children making their own way into reading. Charity Rabbit, Billy Weasel and Olivia Mole won't mean much to Australian kids, although the tooth fairy is common currency (no pun intended!). School pranksters are universal as are birthday parties that include pizza pieces and sausages on sticks, I suppose. This is a nice little book to handle: clear print set in well leaded lines. The black and white line illustrations have a slight touch of Ernest Shepard, about them, and I also found myself thinking of Alison Uttley (the Little Grey Rabbit books) and the safe conservation of forty years ago. I would like to think that such texts still have a place in our schools, but I doubt it.

OLIVER SUNDEW, TOOTH FAIRY (1996)

Gill Roberts

SOURCE: A review of *Oliver Sundew, Tooth Fairy,* in *Books for Keeps,* No. 98, May, 1996, p. 13.

It's said that Oliver Sundew isn't an obvious choice for the special team of tooth fairies set to bring back a particularly special tooth. But, though disappointment is great, he's good-naturedly pleased at his friends' selection, and then, dramatically, his swimming talents make his help crucial to the final success of the expedition.

Full of urgency and fun, this well-illustrated tale [with pictures by Dom Mansell] also suggests that tooth fairies consider a tooth's condition when assessing which coins to leave! Subject interest from 6+ but the humour was more fully appreciated by slightly older children.

📖 *THE CATERPILLOW FIGHT* (1996)

Stephanie Zvirin

SOURCE: A review of *The Caterpillow Fight,* in *Booklist,* Vol. 92, No. 18, May 15, 1996, p. 1593.

Professional comedians tell us that some things are inherently humorous—pigs, for example. McBratney adds caterpillars to the "funny" list with this playful picture book: "One naughty caterpillar,/in the middle of the night,/Woke the other caterpillars/for a caterpillow fight." The simple setup, the catchy rhyme, the wordplay, and the ultimate resolution will be greatly appealing to little ones, and [Jill] Barton's sweetly comical illustrations, crowded with colorful caterpillars, are a perfect match. A bedtime backdrop but an anytime read.

Additional coverage of McBratney's life and career is contained in the following source published by Gale Research: *Something about the Author,* Vol. 89.

Jenny Nimmo

1942-

English reteller and author of fiction and picture books.

Major works include *The Snow Spider* (1986), *The Chestnut Soldier* (1989), *Ultramarine* (1990), *Rainbow and Mr. Zed* (1992), *Griffin's Castle* (1994).

INTRODUCTION

Considered an accomplished writer whose works are often lauded for their distinctiveness and outstanding literary quality, Nimmo is the creator of complex fantasies as well as picture books, retellings, and stories for beginning readers and primary graders. Her books, which are often set in the author's adopted homeland of Wales, reflect Nimmo's appreciation for the Welsh countryside and its people as well as a strong environmental consciousness. She is perhaps best known as the author of the "Snow Spider" trilogy of fantasies for middle graders and young adults—*The Snow Spider, Emlyn's Moon* (1987; U.S. edition as *Orchard of the Crescent Moon*), and *The Chestnut Soldier.* These works, which are influenced by and include characters from *The Mabinogion,* a collection of medieval Welsh legends and hero tales, are noted for being demanding but rewarding. Nimmo is often praised for successfully interweaving magic and other supernatural elements with realistic social and personal issues in her books. Acknowledged for the rounded characterizations of her young male and female protagonists, she is well regarded for her understanding of children as well as for her accurate portrayals of family life. As a writer, Nimmo is celebrated for her lyrical prose style and storytelling ability; she is also credited with investing her short books for beginning readers with the depth of her books for older children and young people. Critics are nearly unanimous in their praise of Nimmo's talents: for example, Marcus Crouch calls her "an important writer" who is the "master of a formidable technique and a deep understanding of people and their environment," while Gillian Clarke names Nimmo a writer of "outstanding quality."

Biographical Information

Born in Windsor, Berkshire, England, Nimmo was educated in private boarding schools before becoming an actress and assistant stage manager for Theatre Southeast in Sussex and Kent. She also worked as a governess in Amalfi, Italy, before becoming a photographic researcher, assistant floor manager, writer, and director for "Jackanory," a popular children's television program produced by the BBC in London. While with "Jackanory," Nimmo produced a children's version of "Cuhweh and Olwen," a story from *The Mabinogion;* this experience led to her fascination with the Welsh tales. In 1974, Nimmo married artist David Wynn Millward, with whom she had three children, and settled in Wales. In 1975, she became a full-time writer. Nimmo once wrote, "I live and work in a rural community in Wales where my three bilingual children are growing into an old but vigorous culture. Here . . . it seems to me that the past is still part of the rhythm of everyday life. My books are concerned with the very real problem of growing children, and most of them are set in a landscape which is undeniably magical; they are described as fantasies."

Major Works

Nimmo began her writing career with *The Bronze Trumpeter* (1975), a story set in Italy during World War I. The book describes how Harlequin and his troupe of comedians, a group of villagers, and a garden statue foil a plot devised by the boy's evil governess to kidnap the young son of a count. In her review of the title, Ann Thwaite commented that "Jenny Nimmo is a new writer of considerable imagination and skill." Nimmo's next book, *Tatty Apple* (1984), is the first of her works to be set in Wales as well as her first contribution to the beginning reader genre; the story outlines how a small boy, Owen-Owen, learns to cope with the death of his father through the aid of a magical green rabbit, Tatty Apple. Bob Jay noted that *Tatty Apple* "makes demands of its readers which are fully repaid."

In *The Snow Spider,* the first book of her trilogy, Nimmo introduces young readers to ten-year-old Gwyn, a Welsh boy who is having a difficult time adjusting to the death of his sister and to his father's accusations that he is to blame. When he is given five birthday gifts by his grandmother, Gwyn must look within himself to find the magical powers that are his by birthright. The title of the book comes from one of the gifts, a brooch that turns into a silver spider. As the snow spider spins webs, Gwyn sees the reincarnation of his sister, a vision that helps to reconcile father and son; at the end of the novel, Gwyn is able to accept himself as a magician. In her next novel, *Emlyn's Moon,* Nimmo focuses on Gwyn's neighbor, seven-year-old Nia, who has been labeled "Nia-can't-do-nothing" by her family. With help from Gwyn and his grandmother, Nia becomes more self-assured and begins to discover her talents as an artist; the combination of Nia's gifts and Gwyn's power help to save Gwyn's cousin Emlyn when he is threatened by supernatural forces. In her review of the U.S. edition, *Orchard of the Crescent Moon,* Beth E. Andersen called the book a "little gem," and Matthew Sweeney noted that the book's blend of magic and realism "is so distinctive as to make this a special performance." The last book in the trilogy, *The Chestnut Soldier,* is usually considered the most ambitious of the series. Gwyn, who is now nearly fourteen, allows the angry spirit of a dark prince from *The Mabinogion* to escape from the tiny wooden horse that he received from his grandmother on his tenth birthday. When Evan Llyr, a wounded Northern Irish major who is the cousin of Nia from *Emlyn's Moon*, becomes possessed by the spirit, Gwyn must use his grandmother's magic wand and the assistance of his uncle Gwydion to exorcise the demon. Virginia Golodetz praised Nimmo's work in *The Chestnut Soldier*, saying that she "has skillfully woven the ancient story into the modern one, making it accessible to those who do not know the legend."

With *Ultramarine*, Nimmo created her first major fantasy that does not refer back to *The Mabinogion*. The story concerns ten-year-old Ned and his younger sister Nell, who have lost their father in a drowning accident. The children, who themselves have an affinity for the sea, are befriended by a strange man whose name, Arion, is that of the son of Poseidon. Ned and Nell, who help Arion rescue drowning sea birds covered in oil, learn that Arion, a kelpie, is their real father and that their mother, Ultramarine, drowned several years before while rescuing the birds. Marcus Crouch stated that *Ultramarine* "is the work [Nimmo's] admirers have been looking for, and she fulfils their expectations in generous measure." Its sequel, *Rainbow and Mr. Zed,* centers on shy Nell, who is lured to an island by her mysterious uncle. Nell discovers that Mr. Zed plans to take over the world by exploiting the sea crystals that hold the key to the origins of life; Zed wants to use Nell's unique power to hear the voices of the crystals to aid him in his evil plan. In thwarting her uncle, Nell grows more self-confident and learns her true name, Rainbow. Regarding the novel, Marcus Crouch advises readers to "be prepared for the imagination to be stretched, the emotions assaulted, as never before." With *Griffin's Castle,* Nimmo uses an urban setting for the first time in one of her longer works. Eleven-year-old Dinah and her mother move into a handsome but dilapidated old house in Cardiff that Dinah dubs Griffin's Castle. When Dinah's security is threatened by her mother's boyfriend Gomer, who sees the house as a moneymaking scheme for himself, she finds allies in three of the carved animals that line the walls of Cardiff Castle, as well as two school friends who share her secret that the beasts have come to life; at the end of the novel, when Gomer is defeated and Donna finds a home outside of Griffin's Castle, she learns that the animals have gone. Marcus Crouch calls *Griffin's Castle* Nimmo's "most substantial offering since the 'Ultramarine' sequence" and notes that all readers "will surely have lost their hearts" to Dinah. In addition to her stories for older children, Nimmo has written a number of books for primary graders, several of which showcase the author's humor. Among her most popular works for this audience are two tales about a magical cat that casts spells on dogs, *Delilah and the Dogspell* (1991) and *Delilah and the Dishwater Dogs* (1993). Nimmo is also the author of two picture books illustrated by her husband, David Wynn Millward, and the reteller of the Cinderella story, which she set in Ireland, as well as a Celtic tale about how two brave tomcats rescue some children enchanted by witches.

Awards

Nimmo received the Smarties Prize in 1986 and the Tir na n-Og Award—both the grand prix and the prize for books for children ages seven to eleven—from the Welsh Arts Council in 1987 for *The Snow Spider.*

GENERAL COMMENTARY

David Bennett

SOURCE: A review of *The Snow Spider* and *Emlyn's Moon,* in *Books for Keeps,* No. 55, March, 1989, p. 19.

[*The following excerpt presents criticism of* The Snow Spider *and* Emlyn's Moon.]

Seen separately or as a pair, award-winning Jenny Nimmo's contribution to the fantasy library is considerable. **The Snow Spider** has recently had a TV screening which will ensure its popularity.

The 'realness' of the child characters, despite their close access to ancient magical powers, is no mean feat, especially Gwyn in the first book, who so unwillingly accepts his birthright of Welsh magicianship and then uses the odd gifts from his eccentric, gaudy grandma to solve the unnatural disappearance of his sister, lured, as he discovered, to a world of ice and silver, where evil is latent.

That same world threatens to snatch his cousin Emlyn in the second book, where family enmity and moon-struck magic conspire to create a devastating conclusion that Gwyn must again avert and for which he needs the powers of Nia Lloyd, Nia-in-the-middle, Nia-can't-do-nothing, who has yet to discover her own unique gift.

Jenny Nimmo gradually piles layer upon fine layer in both stories, weaving gentle, intriguing spells, which should captivate most imaginative youngsters and which I suspect will read aloud well.

Donna White

SOURCE: "Welsh Legends through English Eyes: An American Viewpoint," in *The School Librarian,* Vol. 39, No. 4, November, 1991, pp. 130-1.

Jenny Nimmo is a relative newcomer to children's fantasy. Although her first book, **The Bronze Trumpeter,** came out in 1975, she did not become a full-time writer until the 1980s, when her children were of school age. The English-born Nimmo married a Welshman in 1974 and settled in mid-Wales. Her three children are fluent Welsh speakers, whereas she is only a learner, but Wales has a powerful hold on her imagination.

Early in her career as an adaptor/director for BBC Television's *Jackanory* programme, Nimmo produced a children's version of 'Culhwch and Olwen', and she has been fascinated with the Mabinogion ever since. The two legendary characters who most stimulate her imagination are Gwydion the magician and Efnisien, the ambiguous figure in 'Branwen Daughter of Llyr' who mutilates the Irish horses, murders his own nephew, then sacrifices himself to destroy the Cauldron of Rebirth. Gwydion and Efnisien are central figures in Nimmo's **'Snow Spider'** trilogy.

The Snow Spider, the first book in the series, is for children aged seven to eleven. The protagonist, nine-year-old Gwyn, discovers that he has inherited magical abilities from his ancestors, the ancient magicians of Welsh legend, and he uses his new-found powers to discover the fate of his older sister Bethan, who disappeared four years earlier.

In the second book, *Emlyn's Moon,* young Nia helps Gwyn save his cousin from a fate similar to Bethan's. Along the way Nia discovers a few talents of her own. Of the three books, this one is least dependent on the Mabinogion as a source.

The third volume is *The Chestnut Soldier.* Intended for a slightly older audience, this longer and more complex novel traces Gwyn and Nia's efforts to free a Welsh soldier from demonic possession by the spirit of Efnisien. The figure of Efnisien and the image of a mutilated horse play important roles in the book-symbols of the tragically flawed hero and his deep psychic wounds.

Her English upbringing coupled with her new life in Wales makes Jenny Nimmo an excellent cultural interpreter. When she published *The Snow Spider,* Nimmo was extremely careful in her presentation of Gwyn's Welsh family, friends and culture. Both dialogue and description are simple and straightforward; only the setting and character names establish the sense of Welshness in the book. After the success of the first book of the trilogy, however, Nimmo became more daring in her use of Welsh words and Anglo-Welsh dialect. The Welsh language and culture are much more evident in *Emlyn's Moon* and *The Chestnut Soldier.* By the time she wrote the third book in the series, Nimmo had read *The owl service;* Garner's influence is apparent in both structure and style. Nimmo's characters are caught up in a re-enactment of 'Branwen' just as Garner's are entangled in the legend of Blodeuwedd. However, Nimmo's own creative talents overcome the possibly crippling effect of Garner's influence; she is instead stirred to new depths. She draws a brilliant analogy between the modern 'Troubles' in Northern Ireland and the legendary war with Ireland in 'Branwen'. By capitalising on the Irish connection and making her Welsh soldier a veteran of the Troubles, Nimmo succeeds in extending her cultural bridge to a third culture.

The Chestnut Soldier is Jenny Nimmo's best book to date. It deserved the Tir na n-Og Award even more than *The Snow Spider,* which won the award in 1987, but the

award committee chose not to present an English-language prize in 1990. . . .

In recent years, . . . the award committee has been unhappy about the quality of the English-language nominees and for several consecutive years has decided to withhold the award. Under more favourable circumstances *The Chestnut Soldier* would surely have been recognised. Both *The Snow Spider* and *Emlyn's Moon* have been filmed for children's television, and plans are afoot to adapt *The Chestnut Soldier* as well. . . . Meanwhile, Nimmo has gone on to other writing projects for the moment, but she thinks she may someday continue the adventures of her **'Snow Spider'** characters.

Marcus Crouch

SOURCE: A review of *The Starlight Cloak* and *The Witches and the Singing Mice,* in *Junior Bookshelf,* Vol. 58, No. 1, February, 1994, pp. 25-6.

[*The following excerpt presents criticism of* The Starlight Cloak *and* The Witches and the Singing Mice.]

Here are two folk-tales retold with the help of illustrations from two distinguished artists [Justin Todd and Angela Barrett], making attractive and desirable books with pictures (rather than picture-books). *The Starlight Cloak* is an Irish 'Cinderella' with some neat individual twists. The finding of the slipper and the marriage of Oona and her prince, far from being the climax of the story, comes half-way through, and Oona's anguish is prolonged through a war and a last attempt on her life by one of the stepsisters. (She finds refuge, Jonah-like, in the belly of a whale.) Justin Todd has made full use of the period setting with special attention to architecture and costume.

I prefer *The Witches and the Singing Mice* which is a folkish, perhaps not an authentic folk-tale, from Scotland. Jenny Nimmo releases the scary details of her macabre story with full regard to their effect. It deserves to be read aloud just-so, for every syllable counts. This time Ms Nimmo has support from Angela Barrett at her best. Splendid contrasts here between the safety of home and the terrors of the mountain where the witches set up their instant depot. Here is a valuable addition to the storyteller's repertoire and most effective beside the fire on a winter's evening.

Caroline Axon

SOURCE: A review of *The Witches and the Singing Mice* and *The Starlight Cloak,* in *The School Librarian,* Vol. 42, No. 2, May, 1994, p. 56.

[*The following excerpt presents criticism of* The Witches and the Singing Mice *and* The Starlight Cloak.]

In the first book, something strange happens one night in

Glenmagraw: the blacksmith's cat and the carpenter's cat sense it. Mystery, intrigue and witchcraft come to cause havoc among the children of the village. The witches have the legendary singing mice in their power and they send them to put the children of Glenmagraw to sleep if the villagers do not obey their every demand. Everyone is afraid except for the two brave cats, who are determined to save the children and rid the village of evil. This excellent and courageous story is almost overshadowed by the bewitching illustrations [by Angela Barrett]. The sleeping children are as pale as ice while the witches are as black as night, especially when they transform themselves into witch-cats with glowing coal-red eyes.

The Starlight Cloak is a Celtic version of the well-loved Cinderella story with Oona as the youngest princess in Ireland. She is treated like a slave by her two cruel sisters who disobey the king's instructions to treat her with love and care. Life at the castle is miserable and Oona wishes for her foster mother to be there. Her wish comes true and Mother Brigid comes to her rescue. She is unlike any other mother as she can weave magic with the help of her starlight cloak. The princess faces some difficult times but the magic and the care of her friends make for a fairytale ending. The beautiful illustrations [by Justin Todd] are rich and colourful, especially when they depict the gleaming starlight cloak.

Both books would be perfect for reading aloud as the language used is very evocative and gives the feeling of magic in the air. The words are enhanced by the superb illustrations which capture the imagination.

Marcus Crouch

SOURCE: "Green Rabbit to Griffin: Jenny Nimmo," in *Junior Bookshelf,* Vol. 59, No. 6, December, 1995, pp. 195-200.

It all began, for me, with *Tatty Apple* in 1984. Not that the first impression offered anything more than gentle pleasure. A slim book of less than a hundred pages, generously illustrated [by Priscilla Lamont], it seemed just a good example of the early reader, one of Methuen's 'Read Aloud' books. Realisation came in the first page. There are writers whom one grows to respect. There are others one learns to love. A few rare spirits establish from the beginning a very personal rapport with their readers. In this precious category I put Jenny Nimmo, and that first linking of writer and reader has been repeated time and again over ten years.

Owen-Owen, who is very much the hero of *Tatty Apple,* is Welsh. Of that there is no question. A few hints dropped in the early chapters led me to his home in the village of 'Llanibont'. It took longer to discover that his creator too lived in this delectable country beside the 'green river' and within earshot of the little red engine which runs down to Llyndu (which we know less evocatively as Welshpool). It is still a green land, 'trees, meadows, hedges, the winding river and the mossy stones beside it'.

Tatty Apple is green too. Owen-Owen finds the green rabbit when, seeking a bribe to coax his sister to take him on the railway, he dares to confront Mr. Evans of Ty Uchaf, a notoriously taciturn farmer, and gets as a gift a red hen for Elin and, looking down, there is his own gift, a green rabbit. Any green rabbit is magic, and Tatty Apple has more than most and uses it to some purpose, mischief as well as magic. Through several chapters fun predominates, but when Owen-Owen and his sister take the promised train ride the mood darkens. Local bullies threaten and there are less identifiable terrors. A happy ending is deeply satisfying; it grows naturally from a conjunction of magical countryside and the characters of Owen-Owen and his family.

In its freshness, its humour and its joyous reaction to landscape and people the brief story seemed an ideal first step in a writing career. It was not until 1989, when I was writing Jenny Nimmo's entry in *Twentieth-Century Children's Writers,* that I discovered that there had been an earlier book, and later still, through the kindness of the author, I acquired a copy of *The Bronze Trumpeter*, a book by then long out-of-print but still with something important to say to today's children. It was a book of Jenny's pre-Welsh days. In the year of its publication she married David Wynn Millward, an artist with a rare gift for recording the Welsh scene, and the years of her involvement in BBC television came to an end. The inspiration for *The Bronze Trumpeter* came perhaps from an earlier experience when as a young woman she worked for a time as a governess in Italy.

On the surface the theme of *The Bronze Trumpeter* may seem conventional. A small boy, with no parents to support him and suffering hostile adult domination, wins through by his own persistence and the support of friends. How these bare bones are clothed in living flesh is by no means conventional. The boy is the son of an Italian count during and just after the First World War. His father is missing, believed killed, his mother has become a recluse, and he is at the mercy of an unloving and unlovable German governess. Fraulein Helga is a horror. She recalls for me, but perhaps for no one else including Jenny Nimmo, another evil fictional governess, Mme de la Rougierre in Le Fanu's *Uncle Silas*. There is a difference. Helga is apparently not acting on behalf of a superior villain; her malice is purely her own. She emerges perhaps not from a literary parallel but from a folktale tradition, and certainly there are folk elements in much of this novel although no direct magic. The many folk stereotypes to be found in the story have been subtly transformed in the author's hands. A most memorable part of the story comes with the arrival of the Comedians, a mysterious and largely unexplained company of travelling players who revive the count's disused garden theatre. They come straight out of the *commedia del' arte* with their conventional characters, their improvisation and their ability to slot appropriate modern and local commentaries into the old plays. The Comedians help Paulo to face his problems and to confound the governess and her allies. This is a fine book, as relevant today as when it was published. A new edition is long overdue.

Like others coming to live in Wales Jenny Nimmo came under the spell of the *Mabinogion,* that haunting collection of medieval legends, romances and histories. For her, fascination turned into inspiration, and her **Snow Spider** trilogy tested her resources to the limit and led to a spectacular success, awards (the Smarties Grand Prix and, less lucratively but I suspect more rewarding, for it demonstrated her adoption by the country she had adopted, the Tir na'n Og Award), and three television serials adapted with due respect for the originals and brilliantly presented and acted. The three novels are too familiar for detailed description here, but it may be appropriate to mention some of the elements that distinguish this trilogy from others. The first is consistency. There are no contradictions, in action, characters and setting. The children and their parents and other adults change under the weight of events, but this is growth, not denial of basic characteristics. Next is the reconciliation of the supernatural and the normal. In spite of all the terrors that assail them, Griffiths, Lloyds and Llewelyns remain ordinary people, the grown-ups preoccupied with the economics of farming and shopkeeping, the children involved in the normal problems and pleasures of school and play and (as they grow) sex. Lastly magic. A common ingredient of many stories, here we accept it without question because it comes naturally out of the land and its history and, frightening as it often is, it has the right scale. Gwyn, descendant of Gwydion, master magician in the far-distant past, is a small boy called upon to meet imminent threats to family and friends. Not for him the great war of good and evil in which many of his fictional counterparts are engaged in the imaginings of other writers.

Above all these three stories deal with people. Gwyn, nine as **The Snow Spider** begins, is hovering delicately on the brink of adolescence when **The Chestnut Soldier** ends. He meets the demands of his magical powers reluctantly but with increasing responsibility. He grumbles about his 'batty' Nain who has awakened understanding of his ancient inheritance, but he does his job when he must. I am more fond of his friend Nia Lloyd, a girl overshadowed by brothers and sisters, who grows slowly and sometimes painfully through three books, and who comes of age after the stresses of three testing adventures. The adults are equally interesting and convincing, not just Evan Llyr the 'Chestnut Soldier', most enigmatic of all and, when taken over by the spirit of Efnisien, most evil and puzzling of all the *Mabinogion* characters, the most dangerous, but Gwyn's angry father, Nia's dad Iestyn, cheerful and feckless whether dealing with his big family or playing the butcher in Pendewi, or Llewelyn, the sad, wise, compassionate artist who dominates *Emlyn's Moon*.

The **Snow Spider** trilogy was a difficult act to follow. Jenny Nimmo no longer had the *Mabinogion* to draw upon directly, although she was still aware of the special nature of Welsh magic. There were other pressing concerns, including the protection of a threatened environment and the dilemma of children who do not fit into a society or a school where the norm is exclusively favoured. Somewhere along the line of creativity the sea came in too, a sea by no means governed by normality and peculiarly prone to damage in a conflict between nature and commerce. The result was a pair of novels (a third is still to come) displaying great depths of understanding and stylistic subtlety. **Ultramarine** and **Rainbow and Mr. Zed** are not easy books. The reader has to make a positive commitment to them. They represent however the writer's richest and most rewarding work to date.

The setting has changed. These are stories of sea and coast, and the precise models are not easy to identify. Ned and Nell live within reach of the sea, Ned's dreams filled with 'a sensation of being carried by infinitely loving waves', Nell hearing 'the ocean's footsteps'. Is Jenny thinking of the Lleyn, farthest western peninsula in the North of Wales, or the equally dramatic, if more crowded, coast of Pembrokeshire in the South? Perhaps some features of both are blended with the author's own imagined landscape. Certainly her powerful prose is filled with images of the sea. Ned and Nell are brother and sister, Ned strong and clear-headed, Nell confused and often troubled. School is 'a terrible intrusion on her thoughts'. She is, to use a jargon word which remains unspoken here, dyslectic. Her finely tuned intelligence is at odds with her inability to join letters and words together. There are problems of identity too. Father is dead, or is he? Mother (Leah) is loving but caught up in her own work. The children seem to have inherited nothing from her. Their names too seem homely for such an individual pair. Then everything changes. A man enters their lives from the sea, setting them inexplicable puzzles to solve. Leah remarries, leaving them for her honeymoon in the care of an unknown grandmother. There could be no greater contrast with Gwyn's Nain (in the **Snow Spider** trilogy). Grandmother makes it clear that she hates them, and everything she does (which is little enough, for she stays mostly in her room) offends their deepest instincts.

The story ends satisfactorily (grandmother is dead!), but questions remain unanswered. **Rainbow and Mr. Zed** presents further problems, and these are for Nell alone. Ned is away on holiday without her, and Nell has sunk into despair. Out of kindness neighbours take her with them for a few weeks in their beach-house along the coast. Lively confident Menna will keep her company. Menna's father works for the mysterious Mr. Zed, a millionaire who owns an offshore island, and very soon Mr. Zed invites them to stay, an invitation which is a command. Nell, shy and unhappy, goes with great reluctance, although she finds herself thoroughly spoilt, given the best of rooms and a chest of clothes specially chosen for her. At this point Nell is about to be called on to meet the most serious challenge of her life. She must change if she is to survive, and change she does in a characteristically Nimmo way. After an angry rejection of her new dresses she decides that she had better wear just one. She surrenders to temptation and unexpected vanity, and chooses a sundress of all the colours of the rainbow. 'The dress was a perfect fit and Nell danced downstairs in bare feet to match her new tropical image.' She is heading for danger and temptation, but her character has toughened to cope with both.

(I am reminded of two earlier occasions when a similar image is evoked. In **Emlyn's Moon** Nia, angry with herself and the world, changes into some of her mother's outdated clothes and goes for a walk in the busy shopping town. She is jostled and knocked down in the crowd and her mother's fine high heels go missing. It is a situation for broad comedy and so most of the witnesses treat it. But the artist Llewelyn, in whose forbidden home she takes refuge, offers her nothing but understanding, and he sketches her for a portrait, bare feet and all. Nia is never quite the same after this experience. And as the trilogy approaches its crisis in **The Chestnut Soldier,** Catrin, most beautiful of the Lloyd girls, leaves her sunbathing to answer the phone. The caller is her cousin Evan Llyr, and the brief conversation is to have a profound effect on her. She runs upstairs. 'Her feet were bare and her swirling skirt made mysterious shadows on her long golden legs.')

Jenny Nimmo is masterly in her handling of many contrasting characters, but here there are few and only two (three if one includes the enigmatic grandfather, who is dead) are explored in depth. It is a battle, not only of words, between Nell, who is Rainbow, and Mr. Zed, who is her evil uncle Zebedee. There are terrifying as well as exhilarating moments before the story moves to a close which is satisfying but still inconclusive.

Jenny Nimmo's most recent long novel, **Griffin's Castle,** has some familiar ingredients, but the treatment is so individual that its ability to surprise, shock and delight the reader is unimpaired. Unlike all the earlier work this is a story with a city setting. A preliminary note asserts that the setting is fictitious. The city however has something of Cardiff in it, including the castle. The principal character, a remarkable girl named Dinah, accepts city life with some reluctance, not surprisingly because, as is revealed as the action progresses, she has country blood in her. Her great-grandmother, who lies buried in a city churchyard, had been married to a hill-farmer in North Wales with 'only sheep for company'. Dinah is one of this author's finest creations. Living with her mother, beautiful and improvident Rosalie, she has grown a tough skin in order to face a restless life wandering 'between rented and borrowed rooms' and at one low point taken into care. Her classmates discover that Dinah 'gets everything right all the time', partly through natural intelligence, partly as a cover for her uncertainty about her future. Barry, from her school, observes shrewdly that 'something horrible' has happened to her and she has 'just put it by so that she can keep an eye on it'. At last, thanks to her mother's latest man, the worldly ruthless Gomer, she has a real home of her own, even if the house is falling down graciously. Griffin's Castle (a broken carving of the mythological beast lies in the garden to welcome the newcomer) needs her love; it needs too, it seems, the protection of the fierce animals which have jumped down from their home on the castle walls to impose their will upon her. Even arrogant Gomer is no match for a stone lioness and bear. As her castle crumbles around her Dinah's future becomes ever more uncertain, but salvation arrives, heralded by an old and battered cat,

in the shape of an old man come to take her home. It is a wonderful story (with far more in it than can be contained in a brief summary) rich in atmosphere, in observation of adult and child characters, in social awareness, in invention.

Alongside these full-length novels have appeared a succession of shorter—I would not say minor—works. They include **The Red Secret** (1989), her only story with no hint of magic in it. It is unusual too for its setting, across Offa's Dyke in England (Shropshire) and its presentation of a community involved in the activities of ordinary country folk. Several stories allow expression to the humour latent in all her writing. Two of these feature Delilah, a forceful cat with a talent for magic. Another which I enjoyed greatly, **Wilfred's Wolf** (1994), is her only collaboration so far with her husband, David Wynn Milward, whose line drawings show a real talent for gentle caricature. One book stands out, and its rare quality gained it a 'Highly Commended' from the Carnegie Medal jury. This is **The Stone Mouse** (1993) which has a setting straight out of **Ultramarine** but a theme all its own. The stone (Stone Mouse only to those with a special quality of vision and understanding like Aunt Maria and Elly) can move no more than any other small mineral but he can observe and think. He can talk too, but only to those of the right mind, like Elly who comes to the seaside for a holiday with her family. Her brother Ted comes too, reluctantly. He is consumed with anger, and he shuts himself off from healing influences, even that of a stone mouse, and many hazards must be overcome before the boy can face the origin of his anger. What part the Stone Mouse plays in his cure is the subject of a small book (62 pages shared with plentiful illustrations by Helen Craig) exquisitely written and capturing the serious comedy of the story to perfection. One can find parallels here with other writers, Andersen, de la Mare, Farjeon, and yet this is Jenny Nimmo's book, uniquely imprinted with her personality. If, Desert-Island fashion, I had to choose just one of her books, I could not split up either of the trilogies and I suspect that my final choice would fall on **The Stone Mouse.** Happily I am not prone to desert islands, and am free to delight in everything that this remarkable writer, as gifted in storytelling as she is original in her creation of landscape and character, has made for the enrichment of her readers. It has been a privilege, as well as a joy, to witness her development.

TITLE COMMENTARY

THE BRONZE TRUMPETER (1975)

Ann Thwaite

SOURCE: "Time and Again," in *The Times Literary Supplement,* No. 3813, April 4, 1975, p. 362.

[As does *The Stone Angel* by Pamela Rogers,] **The Bronze**

Trumpeter also centres around a statue: this time in a garden in Sicily belonging to the Count of Montorella. The Count has gone off to the Great War, leaving his wife moping in her room, and his son Paolo in the control of a mysterious and frightening governess. After a poor opening section, the story is complex and highly romantic. Jenny Nimmo is a new writer of considerable imagination and skill. Her cast of characters includes Harlequin and his friends who form the troupe of Comedians (ageless and yet vulnerable), the fisherman, the bandits known as the Vitelli brothers, and the household servants. In the battle between the governess and the bandits on the one hand and Paolo's friends on the other, a blast on the statue's trumpet causes Etna to erupt in the nick of time. Miss Nimmo cannot resist describing the Comedians' play in some detail—which slows up the action at a crucial point—but on the whole she copes admirably with her extraordinary story. The only trouble is that Paolo is not quite solid enough for us to care what happens to him.

Pamela T. Cleaver

SOURCE: A review of *The Bronze Trumpeter,* in *Children's Book Review,* Vol. V, No. 2, Summer, 1975, pp. 63-4.

This is an immensely complicated story which seems at times to have run away with its author: Paolo is the son of the Count of Montorella who has gone away to the First World War. His mother droops in seclusion leaving Paolo with a sinister German governess. Paolo's only comfort is a wild part of the garden where he finds a hidden fountain in the shape of a bronze trumpeter. Then the Comedians (Harlequin and his company) arrive in the village and strange things begin to happen. It is never clear how real they are nor why the governess takes one of the comedians as her servant when she knows that it was he who stole away her mother when she was young. As if these complications were not enough, there are strange bandits in the hills to whom the governess applies to have Paolo kidnapped. However Harlequin, Paolo and the bronze trumpeter, aided by the villagers, foil the bandits with the help of a well-timed eruption of Mount Etna. The comedians give their performance in the hidden theatre in the wild garden, restoring happiness to the villagers and, as they leave, Count Montorella arrives explaining to Paolo that he has had amnesia.

There is much that is good in this book, especially the descriptions and the feeling of authentic magic, but it is a pity that the plot was not simpler and less melodramatic and that Paolo's character was not more strongly drawn. The dust jacket is attractive but the black and white illustrations [by Caroline Scrace] are ugly and the reader would have been better off without them, supplying the pictures in his own mind. However, I am sure the book will be enjoyed by top juniors and, because Jenny Nimmo writes with feeling, that the author will produce better books.

TATTY APPLE (1984)

Marcus Crouch

SOURCE: A review of *Tatty Apple,* in *Junior Bookshelf,* Vol. 49, No. 1, February, 1985, pp. 28-9.

By now Jenny Nimmo and her talented illustrator Priscilla Lamont may be regretting that they squandered so many good ideas and characters on a 'Read Aloud' book. The series has its limitations, especially of scale, and *Tatty Apple* is potentially a very big book. It is a long time since I last saw such rich promise.

The scene is Wales, the central character a small boy called Owen-Owen. Owen-Owen wants a ride on the Engine that, in typical Welsh fashion, takes visitors and locals alike on a trip through the hills and valleys. The widowed mother will not let him go alone, and his sister Elin, remembering the effect of the bench seats on her bottom, is unwilling to take him unless he gets her a red hen. So Owen-Owen goes into the hills (a more perilous enterprise, one would have thought, than a ride on the little train) to interview Mr. Evans who has hens and a bad temper. Surprisingly Mr. Evans gives him a hen, named Poppy by Elin, and while he is at the farm Owen-Owen also finds a green rabbit called Tatty Apple (because he looks like an apple that has waited too long to be picked).

With this information we are ready for a splendid story of magical adventure in the homeliest of settings. Apart from Tatty Apple's skill in teleportation, which is very great, everything that happens springs from the situation and the people. There is no contrivance. Quietly, and with a fine sense of timing and an unfailing supply of humour, Jenny Nimmo tells her tale and holds the reader in her hand. The book is full of characters clearly evoked and full of interest. If only she had room to realise them to the full. Next time—for she has surely got other good stories in her head—she must be allowed the space in which her invention can expand.

I must save a little of my enthusiasm for Priscilla Lamont whose admirable line drawings complement the text perfectly. She never imposes her view on the reader, but her (apparently) swift impressions give a useful hint at the characters and the country in which they operate.

Bob Jay

SOURCE: A review of *Tatty Apple,* in *Books for Keeps,* No. 40, September, 1986, p. 25.

Owen Owen and his three siblings are being reared by their widowed mother in the Welsh hills. It is spring and Owen remembers his father's last visit home from the oil rig when he promised a ride along the valley on the steam train—just the two of them.

Tatty Apple is a magical rabbit who pops into Owen's

life and becomes his 'pet'. Through the mischievous and delightful rabbit Owen is helped to do a lot of growing up; coming to terms with his grief at his father's death and learning to experience and cope with conflicting emotions.

The mix of reality and fantasy succeeds in many ways. It does not patronise its young readers either in language or content, presenting a convincing and sympathetic picture of hectic family life. (The one dud patch is Mrs Drain, a stereotyped 'wicked old woman'.)

The story is tightly knit and fast-moving, the characters are three-dimensional, a strong sense of place is evoked. The book makes demands of its readers which are fully repaid.

THE SNOW SPIDER (first novel in the "Snow Spider" trilogy, 1986)

Marcus Crouch

SOURCE: A review of *The Snow Spider,* in *Junior Bookshelf,* Vol. 51, No. 1, February, 1987, pp. 46-7.

As has happened before the ideas contained in these 'Pied Piper' books are rather too big to submit to the constraints of the series. Moira Miller, for example, who takes her overlong title [*Did You Think I Would Leave You Crying?*] from a somewhat maudlin poem which provides the prelude and postlude to her book, gives us six short stories dealing, sensitively and imaginatively, with what Wilfred Owen called 'War and the pity of War'. . . . I felt all the time that she needed more space in which to realise her full potential. Hers is an admirable book; I hope that next time the publisher will allow her a larger canvas.

In welcoming Jenny Nimmo's first book *Tatty Apple* a year ago I expressed a similar hope. In *The Snow Spider* she is able to do more justice to her unusual talents, but the 'Pied Piper' formula is stretched to the limits and beyond to contain what she has to say about tradition and the imagination. This is the story of Gwyn who is nine and a magician, not by choice but by inheritance, for he is in the direct line from Math, Lord of Gwynedd. We are in the realm of Celtic mysticism, a place made acceptable and indeed accessible because it is also the modern world of Welsh country folk with their ordinary as well as extraordinary problems. Four years before, Gwyn's sister Bethan went up the mountain and never came down. Now Gwyn has the birthday presents given him by his strange grandmother to help him solve the mystery of her disappearance. The gifts take him into some wonderful and frightening adventures and eventually, and most convincingly, to the solution of the riddle. The story, like *The Owl Service,* is full of echoes of *The Mabinogion;* as in [Alan] Garner's book too, the fantasy is made acceptable because of the accuracy with which the modern actors are presented, especially the neighbour Lloyds squeezed into their farmhouse. Jenny Nimmo writes beautifully, but even

her most eloquent evocations of the countryside are never just for effect but spring from the occasion and the people caught up in it. Excellent stuff this—and admirably supported by Joanna Carey's fine illustrations—leaving me more than ever convinced that this is a writer to be reckoned with. Next time perhaps she will have another hundred pages or so in which to expand her lively and original ideas.

Colin Mills

SOURCE: A review of *The Snow Spider,* in *British Book News Children's Books,* March, 1987, p. 31.

In *The Snow Spider* the Welsh legends that nine-year-old Gwyn is told mesh with reality when he is given five gifts for his birthday. He has magical powers, and in a carefully structured, but undeveloped, quest he uses them to unlock the unhappiness that surrounds his parents and his home. The writer controls her plot, but I think the book falls short of its ambitious aim. To give its implied readership (nine to twelves?) a sense of the numinous, there needs to be more lightness and poetry in the surface text. The adults are not well enough drawn for the young to feel sympathy for them.

Margery Fisher

SOURCE: A review of *The Snow Spider,* in *Growing Point,* Vol. 25, No. 6, March, 1987, p. 4773.

The five gifts which Gwyn's grandmother gave him on his ninth birthday were far from ordinary and so were the events and visions they inspired—mysterious but beneficent when tin whistle and metal brooch were exchanged for a magical pipe and a strangely prescient spider, visionary when the yellow scarf vanished on the wind, dangerous when the broken model horse conjured up a storm. The boy's short, practical name is used by his father in preference to his true name of Gwydion but his grandmother puts him in touch with the strange powers of his legendary Welsh ancestors, bringing other-world help to the perplexities of Gwyn's family, saddened by the disappearance of his sister Bethan for which his father has always blamed him. Celtic beings of legend are invoked against a background of mountain and farmland which helps to hold the supernatural in contact with the reality of a bitterly reserved father and a sensitive son, in a story simple to read but rich in implied feelings and strange appearances.

Zena Sutherland

SOURCE: A review of *The Snow Spider,* in *Bulletin of the Center for Children's Books,* Vol. 40, No. 11, July-August, 1987, p. 216.

Nimmo's fantasy—smoothly meshed with its realistic matrix—is set in Wales. Gwyn, on his tenth birthday, received odd gifts from his eccentric grandmother, who said it was time to find out if he were a magician. One of the magic elements is a silvery spider whose web holds images, and out of this conjuring appears a pale, silvery girl who seems to be a reincarnation of a sister who died years before. Through Eirlys, the girl in the web, Gwyn's parents are finally able to accept his sister's death, and his father is able to forgive Gwyn's role in that tragedy. Cohesive and compelling, this tautly-structured story has depth and nuance that never interfere with its clarity.

Lucy Hawley

SOURCE: A review of *The Snow Spider,* in *School Library Journal,* Vol. 33, No. 11, August, 1987, p. 87.

Gwyn's birthday is the anniversary of his sister's unexplained disappearance. Nain, Gwyn's grandmother, presents him with a collection of strange items including a brooch which eventually turns into a silver spider. Nain, either mad or a witch, looks for special powers of the ancestral magicians to be found again in Gwyn and tries to convince him that the magicians of the old Welsh legends are reborn in him. As the snow spider spins webs that reveal another world, Gwyn comes to understand that he is a magician, and he yearns for his heart's desire, the return of his sister. A new classmate enters his life and is befriended by his family. She is surely Bethan, the sister who had been taken to the other world seen in the web. The occurances of arcane and bizarre wonders increase extravagantly, almost out of control. But the reality of Gwyn, his parents, and the Welsh setting give this fantasy equilibrium and an appealing warmth. The pace is brisk and captivating. A good choice to lead into "The Dark Is Rising" series by Susan Cooper.

Mary M. Burns

SOURCE: A review of *The Snow Spider,* in *The Horn Book Magazine,* Vol. LXIII, No. 5, September-October, 1987, pp. 613-4.

"Gwyn's grandmother gave him five gifts for his tenth birthday. They were very unusual gifts, and if Gwyn had not been the sort of boy he was, he might have been disappointed." These two simple sentences could be the opening of an everyday family story, but they are the author's method of enticing the reader into suspending disbelief before introducing elements of fantasy. Until that tenth birthday Gwyn Griffiths thought of himself as an ordinary boy with problems stemming from the strange disappearance of his older sister, Bethany, four years earlier: his mother's constant fretting; his father's heartless accusations that he was to blame for the tragedy. But now his eccentric, colorful grandmother has made him extraordinary by announcing that the time has come to determine if he has inherited the magic powers of his Welsh ancestors. The birthday gifts—a piece of seaweed, a yellow scarf, a tin whistle, a twisted metal brooch, and a small broken horse—are the means by which he would

attain his heart's desire. Unfortunately, Gwyn demonstrates his lack of maturity—first, by disobeying the interdiction to keep his powers secret and, second, by unleashing forces beyond his control. But he receives unexpected help from a mysterious girl, a pale reincarnation of the missing Bethany, who tells him of the other world that is now her home. At story's end he must choose between journeying with her to that world or remaining in his own. Gwyn's visions of the other world in the translucent web of an elfin spider, the eerie ship conjured into existence through casting the fragment of seaweed to the wind, and his obsession with following his destiny recall segments from *Close Encounters of the Third Kind.* Yet the story is not derivative but rather a fascinating reflection of contemporary idioms. Gwyn is a very real ten-year-old, bewildered by the sorrows that have divided his family, conscious that he is different from his classmates, touchingly anxious to belong and to be loved. The combination of his personality and the author's power of description makes the story believable.

EMLYN'S MOON (second novel in the "Snow Spider" trilogy, 1987; U.S. edition as *Orchard of the Crescent Moon,* 1989)

Marcus Crouch

SOURCE: A review of *Emlyn's Moon,* in *Junior Bookshelf,* Vol. 52, No. 1, February, 1988, p. 51.

When Jenny Nimmo's **The Snow Spider** appeared I made a plea to her publisher to allow her greater scope for her unusual talents. I can't claim any credit for this larger book. The fact that the earlier book collected awards including the Smarties Prize (in money terms, I believe, the most rewarding of all) must have given Methuen the broadest hint that they had a treasure on their list.

Emlyn's Moon confirms all our hopes. This is a rich, moving and amusing story, one which demands and receives the reader's total capitulation. It is described as a sequel to **The Snow Spider,** which it is, but it can be read with enjoyment and full comprehension by those unfortunates who missed the earlier story. The setting is the same—mid Wales—and so are some of the characters, although the spotlight has moved from Gwyn, hereditary magician, to his neighbour Nia, one of the numerous Lloyds. The Lloyds have abandoned their unprofitable farm and moved into town, where Mr. Lloyd has become the butcher. Nia, a girl in the middle and lacking the beauty and cleverness of her sisters, has been labelled 'Nia-can't-do-nothing'. It is mainly Emlyn Llewelyn and his artist-father, themselves cold-shouldered by the community, who break down the wall of failure that has been built around the troubled girl. Magician Gwyn and his uncanny Nain help too. The story is worked out with great skill. The writing is as evocative as ever, and Jenny Nimmo benefits from the opportunity to explore her creations at greater length and in more depth. She handles the supernatural elements with Welsh confidence. I hope that now she will make a book out of the everyday life of the country folk she knows so well. Meanwhile, very grateful thanks for this rewarding excursion into the wonderland of Welsh mythology.

Matthew Sweeney

SOURCE: A review of *Emlyn's Moon,* in *British Book News Children's Books,* March, 1988, p. 28.

[Thea Bennett's] *The Gemini Factor* is based on a TV series by another writer, and it shows . . . *Emlyn's Moon,* for slightly younger readers, is much subtler and better written. Set vividly in Wales, it is a story of magic that's been passed through generations to a boy, Gwyn, and how he uses this power constructively. It is also a natural story, well-paced, about a young girl moving from a farm to a town, and the mysteries she encounters. And how she discovers she is not useless after all. If, inevitably, the magic gets fuzzily mystical at times, the realism regains control and the overall blend is so distinctive as to make this a special performance.

Denise Wilms

SOURCE: A review of *Orchard of the Cresent Moon,* in *Booklist,* Vol. 85, No. 22, August, 1989, p. 1980.

In this sequel to **The Snow Spider** the focus has shifted from Gwyn Griffiths, who learned he was a magician, to seven-year-old Nia Lloyd, middle child in a family of seven, who has begun to believe her family's refrain "Nia-can't-do-nothing." When Nia's family moves into town, she meets Gwyn's cousin Emlyn, who lives with his artist father in a converted chapel. Although Nia has been warned away from Emlyn because of ill will between Gwyn's and Emlyn's families, she warms to his friendship. Gradually she learns what happened to Emlyn's mother and how Gwyn's father was involved. Gwyn's wisdom allows him to rise above some of the strife, and his power, coupled with Nia's intuitive sense of people and of magic, is what saves a forlorn Emlyn when he is about to be stolen away by the same evil creatures that took Gwyn's sister years before. Nimmo's sequel has a more pronounced structure than her previous story, making its magical elements easier to believe. The fantasy aspect combines nicely with the development of Nia into a more self-assured child who is beginning to know her considerable strengths. It's not only fantasy fans who will enjoy the transformation.

Elaine Fort Weischedel

SOURCE: A review of *Orchard of the Crescent Moon,* in *School Library Journal,* Vol. 35, No. 12, August, 1989, p. 142.

The characters that first appeared in Nimmo's **The Snow Spider** return in this sequel. This time the central character is Nia Lloyd, the middle child of a large Welsh family. Upset by the family's move from their farm to the nearby town where her father is to be a butcher, Nia is equally unhappy with her reputation as "Nia-can't-do-nothing." Once settled in the town, Nia rapidly becomes involved in the feud between the Llewelyn and Griffiths families. Along the way she discovers her own special artistic talent and finds that she can do something after all. While the narrative alludes to events in the first book, the sequel can be read independently. Nia is a believable protagonist, and readers will empathize with her problems. If the Llewelyn family troubles seem a bit melodramatic, fantasy lovers will nonetheless be caught up in Nia's desperate attempt to save her friend Emlyn from the spirit world that threatens to claim him. A cut below the fantasies of Susan Cooper or Patricia Wrightson, this should still find a ready audience where fantasy is popular.

Beth E. Andersen

SOURCE: A review of *Orchard of the Crescent Moon,* in *Voice of Youth Advocate,* Vol. 12, No. 4, October, 1989, p. 215.

In this sequel to Nimmo's well-received **The Snow Spider,** young Nia Lloyd is the overlooked middle of seven children, and another sibling is on the way. Despondent over the move from her beloved Welsh mountain farm (her father buys a butcher shop in town), Nia flounders in her new life until she befriends schoolmate Emlyn Llewelyn and his artist father who has transformed their dwelling, a converted chapel, with his brilliantly colored, floor-to-ceiling murals of rainbow-draped fields and floating butterflies. Nia is troubled by the dark secrets hovering over the Llewelyns, but continues to disobey her parents who have forbidden her to spend time at the chapel.

Nia is soon caught in the middle of the feud between the families of Emlyn and his cousin Gwyn Griffiths. Gwyn's sister disappeared into the mountain about the time his father was accused of luring Mrs. Llewelyn and her infant son away from her husband and Emlyn.

Nimmo's tale is steeped in magical powers and sinister ethereal events. There is not much logic to the spells cast and broken but *Orchard of the Crescent Moon* reads beautifully as Nia learns to recognize her own special gifts to make a difference in the lives of those she loves.

This is a lovely story, a perfect read-aloud book. Unfortunately, the youth of the main characters will turn away many YA readers, unless they are shown the way to this little gem.

📖 *THE RED SECRET* (1989)

Marcus Crouch

SOURCE: A review of *The Red Secret,* in *Junior Bookshelf,* Vol. 53, No. 2, April, 1989, pp. 65-6.

Limited physical scale is not new to Jenny Nimmo. She

made her debut with a book of about this length, and she seems to thrive on the discipline that such writing demands. For the first time she sets a story outside Wales (but not far away) and puts no supernatural element in it. The magic in *The Red Secret* is that of nature. Tom does not enjoy his new school. It is in the country (a new experience for a city boy) and being the headmaster's son is a poor recommendation to his peers. One of these, Glyn, gives Tom a 'puppy' which is in fact a fox cub, a half-malicious joke which misfires, because the challenge of looking after a helpless wild thing is just what Tom needs. There are some exciting moments before Tom's secret comes out into the open, and he takes a first step towards entry into the rural community. The simple story is told with professional ease and with a warm appreciation of the countryside and its people.

Margery Fisher

SOURCE: A review of *The Red Secret,* in *Growing Point,* Vol. 28, No. 1, May, 1989, p. 5172.

When his father becomes head of a primary school near the Welsh border, Tom and his sister Daisy have to get used to country ways, especially to the teasing of their schoolfellows, who resent their different accents and scorn Daisy's frilly skirts and hair-bows. For both, the way to friendship is by way of a fox with a wounded leg which local children offer to the townies as a puppy. Recognising the animal, Tom hides it in a shed in the woods and manages to steal food for it. When he discovers that Gwyn Bowen, one of his persecutors, had hoped to save the cub after its mother was killed, their alliance begins and is cemented when the young animal is safely released in the wild. Roughly outlined figures of children and landscape in the drawings [by Maureen Bradley] may be less useful to the young reader tackling this 'Antelope' than the concise, pictorial and energetic prose in which an encounter important to an animal as well as to a human is recorded.

THE CHESTNUT SOLDIER (third novel in the "Snow Spider" trilogy, 1989)

Susan Cooper

SOURCE: "Caught in the Web," in *The Times Educational Supplement,* No. 3828, November 10, 1989, p. 60

Writing the last in a linked series of books is a horrendous task, especially if the earlier books have had some success. The author wants the final volume to be a triumphant climax, better than its predecessors; to be the glittering spire on the cathedral. As a result, he or she is perilously vulnerable to an ailment known as trying too hard.

Having once suffered from it myself, I think I see the symptoms of this condition in Jenny Nimmo's new book *The Chestnut Soldier*. This is the third fantasy novel of

a trilogy set in Wales; the earlier volumes were *The Snow Spider* and *Emlyn's Moon*. The new book is the most ambitious of the three, and while its treatment of human relationships is very accomplished, its use of fantasy is less so.

The Snow Spider was a novel about Gwyn (short for Gwydion) Griffiths, a nine-year-old boy named for, and perhaps descended from, the mythic magician of the Mabinogion. In the book, Gwyn discovers that he too has magical powers, after acquiring five gifts from his witchlike grandmother. He discovers too that his elder sister Bethan, who vanished two years earlier when looking for Gwyn's favourite sheep on the mountain, did not die, but was carried off by a magical ship to "another planet" which is a chilly cousin of Tir na n-Og, the land of the ever-young. Bethan comes back briefly in the form of another girl, and helps reconcile Gwyn and his bitter father Idris, who has always blamed the boy for her loss. Of Gwyn's five gifts, all used in the story, the most haunting is a broken model horse in which is trapped the dreadful ferocity of Efnisien, arch-villain of the Mabinogion story of the Children of Llyr.

In *Emlyn's Moon,* Gwyn is joined by his cousin Emlyn Llewellyn, and by Nia Lloyd, sister of his best friend. This second book focuses on Nia and her search for identity. She feels deeply ordinary: "a moth in the middle, with two butterfly sisters and an older brother who could mend anything; with two younger brothers who could stand on their heads, and an even younger one who got by just because he was the youngest, and had curls." In the course of a story which interweaves Gwyn's magic and Emlyn's haunted family, Nia finds out that after all she is not "Nia-can't-do-nothing", but a very particular person.

Nia's quest is not over; it runs on through *The Chestnut Soldier*. And although this book is designed as a reflection of the story of Efnisien, the dark prince caught in Gwyn's model horse who tries to funnel his power into a modern soldier called Evan, it is at its best when dealing with the relationships between Nia and her sisters. The dreams and jealousies of adolescent girls all captivated by the same adult male are conjured up much more vividly than the modern echoes of ferocious myth. After reading these three books in succession, I found myself hoping that Jenny Nimmo's considerable talent for writing about real young people would in her next books escape from the framework of fantasy; it's like Efnisien, trying to get out of that horse.

Fantasy—"high fantasy", as opposed to amusing whimsy, is an odd business. You can't write it on purpose; it requires the indefinable, effortless quality of imagination which infuses that best of all retellings of a Mabinogion element, Alan Garner's *The Owl Service*. The power of the myth throbs out of that book, overwhelming the characters; set against it, *The Chestnut Soldier* is an elaborate contrivance in which strong characters glow out, but the author's deliberate patternings of myth remain dim. Jenny Nimmo is a good novelist; we have some fascinating books ahead if she breaks out of the snow-spider's web and strikes out on her own.

Margery Fisher

SOURCE: A review of *The Chestnut Soldier,* in *Growing Point,* Vol. 28, No. 5, January, 1990, pp. 5263-4.

Jenny Nimmo brings Celtic legend into the everyday lives of Welsh hill farmers with confidence, casting mist over very simple building blocks of everyday—mealtimes, shops, bus journeys—by virtue of strange happenings and by the emotional intensity which these happenings visit on the characters. *The Chestnut Soldier* follows *Snow Spider* and *Emlyn's Moon,* linked to them by the people concerned and by the small mutilated model of a horse which once again revives its sinister power against Gwyn Griffiths, farmer's son, and his friend Nia, whose father has left their farm to run a butcher's shop in the town. As in the earlier stories the routine of two respectable households is upset, this time when a soldier cousin of Gwyn's, Evan Llyr, comes to visit his relations and is caught up in ancient wrongs, his mind taken over by the spirit of a former antagonist in the legendary contest against Gwyn's impressive ancestor, the hero Gwydion. In spite of this revival of tradition the book in fact is more about people than about magic. Evan, who has performed heroic feats in Northern Ireland, is a flawed person: to Nia he is a prince, to Gwyn a possible arsonist and certainly an adversary. Water and fire play their part in a duel which ends when Gwyn uses his grandmothers's powerful wand to exorcise the demon which has driven Evan to outrageous behaviour, but many readers will find the interaction of children and their elders the most powerful and interesting part of the book.

Marcus Crouch

SOURCE: A review of *The Chestnut Soldier,* in *Junior Bookshelf,* Vol. 54, No. 1, February, 1990, p. 49.

Jenny Nimmo brings to a dramatic close her trilogy of 'Mabinogion' novels which began with *The Snow Spider* in 1986. The focus is again on Gwydion Gwyn (as his fey grandmother calls him) whose wish to enjoy the ordinary life of a Welsh country schoolboy is in conflict with his destiny as the descendant of a great magician from the Celtic dawn. Much of this story—much the longest that Miss Nimmo has so far written and one in which she clearly enjoys the greater scope for her rare talents—is concerned with Gwyn at home and school and in the company of his friends. We are allowed to see more of the Lloyds, the large and lively family of the butcher of Pendewi, especially the sensitive Nia and her gorgeous elder sister Catrin whom Gwyn sees as 'probably the most beautiful girl in Wales'. The reader, as much almost as Gwyn and some of the Lloyds, regards as an unwelcome intrusion the arrival of Evan Llyr, a Lloyd cousin who is convalescing after suffering severe injuries (whose scars are not visible) in a terrorist attack in Northern Ireland.

Major Llyr is big and handsome and strangely sinister. Gwyn is reminded of a snake 'with enough venom in its tongue to kill an army'. Evan makes divisions in the happy family. Catrin is captivated and love makes her seem even more like a princess. Powerful forces have been let loose in the Welsh countryside, and Gwyn, reluctantly calling upon his magic resources, does not help when he loses the most dangerous of his birthday gifts, the mutilated horse which is a direct link with that most enigmatic and tormented of all *Mabinogion* characters, Efnisien. The very elements are harnessed against the once-happy community. The resolution is not achieved without suffering and sacrifice.

Masterly as are the supernatural episodes in this novel Miss Nimmo shows her true mettle in her domestic scenes. Her sympathetic and affectionate portraits, not only of the principal characters, bring warmth and colour to them. Hers is a real community, interdependent and tightly united yet subject to disturbance and conflict. The writer is outstanding too in her feeling for the countryside and in her use of natural description as an agent in her narrative. Now that she has got this story out of her system—and it clearly had to be done—may we hope for the novel of Welsh countryfolk in an entirely naturalistic context which the author is outstandingly qualified to write? Meanwhile, let us give thanks for a rich and rewarding experience in this powerful and moving story.

Virginia Golodetz

SOURCE: A review of *The Chestnut Soldier,* in *School Library Journal,* Vol. 37, No. 7, July, 1991, p. 74.

This suspenseful fantasy concludes the trilogy begun in *Snow Spider* and continued in *Orchard of the Crescent Moon.* Like the others, it is set in a village in the hills of Wales, with their aura of mystery and danger. Much the strongest of the three books, *Soldier* draws heavily on the second part of the Mabinogion tales. In the first book, young Gwyn Griffiths was given responsibility for guarding a tiny chestnut-wood horse that contained the restless, angry spirit of Efnisien, the mad dark prince of the old tale. Gwyn is careless with the horse, and the prince's negative energy is inadvertently released. Immediately, it finds its way into the soul of a troubled Welsh soldier visiting in the village. Disturbing events ensue, and Gwyn knows who is responsible. He also knows that he must use his inherited magic powers to recapture it before greater harm is done. He tries several spells but the maleficence proves too strong for him. He calls on his grandmother, and on his friend Nia, the heroine of the second book, and on his ancient uncle Gwydion, the magician of Mabinogion fame. With their help, the spirit is recaptured and peace is restored. Nimmo has skillfully woven the ancient story into the modern one, making it accessible to those who do not know the legend. This satisfying fantasy introduces young readers to the genre, and to other works that draw on the ancient Welsh legends, such as those by Lloyd Alexander, Susan Cooper, and Alan Garner.

Beth E. Andersen

SOURCE: A review of *The Chestnut Soldier,* in *Voice of Youth Advocate,* Vol. 14, No. 4, October, 1991, p. 248.

In *The Chestnut Soldier* the final story in Nimmo's *The Snow Spider* trilogy, 30 year old cousin Evan Llyr comes to Wales to the Lloyd residence to recuperate from a terrible accident he survived as a soldier in Belfast. Evan, who as a child witnessed his older brother's fatal fall from a tree, now seems possessed by his dead brother's wicked spirit. Or is it more sinister than that? As Evan's presence in the Lloyd household becomes more disruptive to the family of eight children, 11 year old Nia Lloyd's friend Gwyn Griffiths, fast approaching his 14th birthday, reluctantly feels ever more compelled to use his magical gifts to exorcise the evil in Evan's soul, a dark force which is not his dead brother but rather a 2000 year old mythical demon prince named Efnisien.

Bad storms, broken bones, and wild rides on horses by caped madmen clash with the details of modern life (Land Rovers and flying jets). Everyone in this story is a tortured soul. The relentlessly oppressive moodiness of the Lloyd siblings, Gwyn's grandmother, and the ever-wild Evan drag on to a disappointingly anti-climactic finish. Whereas an earlier entry (*Orchard of the Crescent Moon*) in the *The Snow Spider* trilogy soared with lyrical magic, *The Chestnut Soldier* clunks along, more a story of a lot of people in a bad mood than a tale of fantasy.

JUPITER BOOTS (1990)

Marcus Crouch

SOURCE: A review of *Jupiter Boots,* in *Junior Bookshelf,* Vol. 55, No. 1, February, 1991, p. 26.

Like the best of these 'Banana Books' *Jupiter Boots* is a novel in miniature; that is, it has a plot, defined characters, a setting and a philosophy. All this in 42 pages of large and generously leaded print and with many illustrations [by Paul Warren]. Divided into chapters, it gives the struggling reader the challenge as well as the delight of a real book. Timothy, who tells his own story, is at odds with the world. As he writes in his essay 'about yourselves', 'My name is Timothy and my feet hurt.' Mum has lost her feckless husband and is having a tempestuous relationship with an Italian waiter. She struggles with the problem of three very young children. No wonder there is no money for shoes for Timothy, and he is growing. No wonder too that he yields to impulse and 'borrows' a pair of Jupiter boots from Heale & Hyde's sale. Maybe these are magic boots, maybe the relief of comfortable footwear uplifts Timothy's spirits; anyway he undergoes an experience which changes him permanently. Even the heavy hand of the Law can be endured. Whether magical or psychological, Timothy's tale is told with all Jenny Nimmo's quiet assurance and her instinct for the right turn of phrase and word-pictures.

Carol Fox

SOURCE: "Independent Points of View," in *The Times Educational Supplement,* No. 3894, February 2, 1991, p. 29.

It is still rare to read about children in this society who have very little, but in *Jupiter Boots* by Jenny Nimmo Timothy Starr is a child from a large family with a low income. But this is no weepy, self-pitying story. Tim's feet may be almost deformed from shoes which pinch, but he possesses imagination and love. A lot is packed into this little tale—some excellent school scenes, a magical episode, and some strong domestic detail.

Linda Saunders

SOURCE: A review of *Jupiter Boots,* in *The School Librarian,* Vol. 39, No. 2, May, 1991, pp. 61-2.

'Banana Books' have hit on a winning formula—good writers, short and interesting stories, colour illustrations, attractive layout and a bright cover. This has made them justifiably popular with many children and I am sure this book will also be popular.

Tim's shoes are too small and worn out but his mother doesn't have the money to buy him a new pair. Then one day, on his way home from school, he sees the jupiter boots in a shoe shop window. They draw him into the shop and he has to 'borrow' them. When he tries them on they take him on an amazing journey through space and away from all his troubles. However, he has stolen them and justice must be done—though everything does end happily. While this is not the most exciting 'Banana Book,' it is a warm-hearted story about hope and care triumphing over misfortunes.

ULTRAMARINE (1990)

Marcus Crouch

SOURCE: A review of *Ultramarine,* in *Junior Bookshelf,* Vol. 55, No. 1, February, 1991, pp. 37-8.

Ultramarine represents a long stride forward for Jenny Nimmo. Having got the *Mabinogion* out of her system (at least temporarily), this most talented writer is exploring fresh ground, topographically and imaginatively. In this new book too she shows greater maturity in the handling of words and ideas. This is the work her admirers have been looking for, and she fulfils their expectations in generous measure.

This time the story is not of mountain and river but of the sea. Instead of the complex society of village and small town, attention is focussed on barely more than half a dozen characters whose interactions are explored in depth. Important as these people are, the real hero, whose presence is sensed on every page, is the sea.

Ned and Nell live happily with their loving and scatterbrained mother Leah. Work—she is a makeup artist for television—limits what she can do for the children, but Ned has developed his own resources for dealing with domestic crises. He has become expert in forging letters of excuse to explain absences and late arrivals at school. Ned has learnt to live with the tragedy in which his father died and he and Nell narrowly escaped drowning, although he still has recurrent nightmares. For Nell, too young to remember the accident, the sea has no menace. Nell is not retarded, or (as Leah is almost tempted to hope as a softer option) deaf, just absorbed in her inner life to which school is a distraction. Both children are so closely identified with the sea that it comes as no great surprise when a strange man comes into their lives seemingly on the crest of a wave. He calls himself Arion, and seems to be inexplicably well informed about them. Arion (a book tells them that he is the son of Poseidon, and this confirms their impressions) is dedicated to the sea and its creatures and he is engaged in a ceaseless war with those who pollute it. He still makes time to help Ned and Nell in their dealing with the half-mad grandmother who, in the temporary absence of Leah, is nominally in charge of them. During the conflict many ghosts from the past are stirred up. The complex story works its way to a satisfactory conclusion in which no one's status remains unchallenged.

Although this is the closest knit and most absorbing of all Jenny Nimmo's plots, it is not the story that stays longest in the reader's mind. Nor is it the characters, beautifully and consistently presented as these are. This is a novel of atmosphere, of the moods of nature dictating the reactions of the players in the strange drama. Miss Nimmo uses prose like a poet, matching every action and idea with words and images chosen with great precision yet giving always the impression of spontaneity. Most of them are drawn from the sea. Ned, his fears eased by Arion, 'was all at once supremely happy, as though all the aching corners of his life had been soothed by invisible waves'. Rhoda, the sensitive and sympathetic aunt who acts in some sort as a catalyst in the action, says 'water soothes us when we watch it . . . like a visible lullaby rocking us back to babyhood . . .'. The constant presence of the sea, and the exquisite language in which it is invoked, help Ned and Nell to follow their difficult path, so unlike 'the path that carried other people securely through everyday events'. The children's quest for identity is full of hazards but by no means devoid of happy moments, when warmth and love and triumph over obstacles put the confused malice of Grandmother McQueen into perspective. *Ultramarine* can be read with immediate delight in its mysteries, its sea-pictures and its vivid characters. Each re-reading will reveal fresh felicities of phrase, unsuspected layers of meaning. For the first time in a major book Jenny Nimmo eschews magic and has no need of it. The wonder in her story comes out of the realities of nature and the human mind.

Margery Fisher

SOURCE: A review of *Ultramarine,* in *Growing Point,* Vol. 29, No. 6, March, 1991, pp. 5482-3.

The voice of the sea, its colour and movement, strike a receptive reader at the very start of *Ultramarine,* introducing quietly the extra-ordinary element of a tale of two children dealing with an important change in their lives. Ten-year-old Ned and his younger sister Nell have grown up happily with their widowed mother since the accident which robbed them of their father and left both of them (infants then) with a strange affinity with ocean worlds. Then a stepfather comes into their home. Accepting balding, friendly Mark is not hard but the unknown grandmother, almost blind and shocked by the loss of her island home in a landslide, is another matter, and even with the help of sturdily supportive Aunt Rhoda, the witchlike old woman seems to the children like an enemy. In their bewildered alarm they readily accept the help of Arion, who seems to have come out of the sea with a mysterious knowledge of their problems and their past. The accretion of magical interventions is gradual, growing in tension and meaning as the story proceeds, the extra-natural being proposed very simply:

> "Before he went downstairs he picked up Arion's mirror again. Now things seemed to move beneath the glimmer; there was a strange green light behind his mirrored face, as though he was not sitting in his room but squinting up through water. He quickly shut the mirror in a cupboard, not ready to recognise the Ned who seemed to belong to a region of fishes."

Two elements of reality (the rescuing of oiled birds and endangered sea-mammals and the ancient wrongs from the past which involve the identity of the two children and the reasons for their grandmother's hostility towards them) are irradiated by the mysterious influences and enlightenment which come from the sea and from the significantly named Arion who comes and goes like the tides. The psychology of a tormented family and children caught in emotional tangles from the past is subtly developed in this notable book as the almost poetic backing of an oceanic direction of human sensibilities.

Kevin Crossley-Holland

SOURCE: A review of *Ultramarine,* in *The Times Educational Supplement,* No. 3897, March 8, 1991, p. 31.

Two horrible old women, spewing poison and uniting beleaguered children; broken marriages, second marriages, stepchildren, foster-children; two ghastly threats to the environment; seabirds as victims, seabirds as saviours; and the always-ocean, moody and mysterious, dividing and linking us: these two dramatic novels [*Ultramarine* and *Crow's Head* by Anna Lewins] share an uncommon number of themes and preoccupations and, indeed, show most interestingly where the fantasy writer *moyen sensuel* is likely to come down.

Jenny Nimmo's Ned and Nell are brother and sister, and they are both much involved with the sea. Nell says she can hear "the ocean's footsteps", while Ned longs to find out about the car crash in which his father was drowned.

When their mother, Leah, remarries and goes off to the Algarve for a honeymoon, Ned and Nell are looked after by Scottish relatives unknown to them—friendly and capable aunt Rhoda, and their threatening and angry grandmother.

Down on the beach, Ned and Nell meet Arion. But is he flesh and blood, or is he a sea-spirit, with salt water coursing through his veins? Ned confides in Arion, telling him about his lost father, absent mother, destructive grandmother, and step by step, Arion is able to lead the children on a quest to recover the lost first chapter of their lives.

It's a gruelling journey, punctuated by violent events (the grandmother's self-destructive fury when confronted with past events with which she has never come to terms, her sudden death, and a serious oil spillage) and culminating in stunning discoveries.

Bristling with ideas, and by turns tender, humorous and harrowing, *Ultramarine* is a fine and courageous book. One would expect of Jenny Nimmo that the narrative momentum should be well-sustained and the characterisation subtle and convincing, and so they are; but what impresses me above all is the penetrating understanding of the inner world of children—the charting of their hopes and sorrows, the recognition of their powers of assimilation and endurance. It is a book about beginning to know oneself—beginning to grow up—and when I finished it, I felt as if I had been led through a frightening thicket by a confident and knowing guide.

Joan Zahnleiter

SOURCE: A review of *Ultramarine*, in *Magpies*, Vol. 6, No. 2, May, 1991, p. 33.

Jenny Nimmo creates such compelling fantasy that she has the reader securely emmeshed in it right to the end of the book. Despite the fact that it is difficult to determine the audience for this one, her fans will not be disappointed.

Ned and Nell both feel an overpowering affinity for the sea which, they are sure, has its origins deep in their past—a past which their mother, Leah, avoids discussing. In time they are brutally confronted with the truth by their malevolent grandmother, but not before they meet Arion, the mysterious man from the sea. Who is he? Is he a kelpie? If so, he is a benevolent one, intent upon saving sea creatures from the depredations of man. There is even a suspicion that he may be the children's father.

This gripping mystery story, full of symbolism, is a very complex book in which the sensitive issues involved warrant discussion if it is to be used with a group. It is also a book worth introducing to secondary readers who may be put off initially by the younger protagonists. Ned is 11 and Nell is 8, but this is definitely not a book for that age group.

The dramatic cover shows Arion, an attractive well-muscled young man, clad only in wet jeans, rising out of the sea. Above him float the brooding faces of the two children. It promises what the book is likely to deliver. Not to be missed.

Publishers Weekly

SOURCE: A review of *Ultramarine*, in *Publishers Weekly*, Vol. 239, No. 13, March 9, 1992, p. 58.

With their mother away on her honeymoon, Ned and Nell face a week alone with their Aunt Rhoda and their frightening Grandmother McQueen, neither of whom they have met before. Haunted by memories of the ocean, the two children discover the truth about their past: Their real mother drowned when they were babies, and their father may be a seal-man, or kelpie. Surrounded by a cornucopia of seashore images, Nell and Ned start to understand both their family's tragedy and the mysterious nature of their father, who spends his life sailing the globe and rescuing marine life from ecological disasters. As in *The Tempest*, the water-images add resonance to the plot, giving it a sea-change into something rich and strange. Nimmo (*The Snow Spider*) again combines fantasy elements with the psychological growth of her protagonists to weave solid entertainment. Seamless writing and a deft touch of family humor round out Nimmo's gifts in this engrossing novel.

Virginia Golodetz

SOURCE: A review of *Ultramarine*, in *School Library Journal*, Vol. 38, No. 5, May, 1992, p. 116.

This story interestingly interweaves fantasy with realistic fiction, but is somewhat burdened by an excessively complex and mysterious set of family relationships. Ned, 11, and Nell, 8, are forced to face their true origins when their half-crazed grandmother reveals that the woman who has lovingly cared for them all their lives is not their birth mother. Rather, it was Grandmother's daughter, Ultramarine, who drowned several years before while rescuing sea birds. They also learn that the shipwrecked sailor whom they meet on the beach, and whom they help to care for oil-covered birds, is their real father. He had deserted his young family years ago to travel wherever sea birds were endangered and needed rescue. Is this man really half kelpie, as the story hints? And how did the ocean rescue the children from the accident that years ago killed the man they had believed to be their father? Neither of these questions is satisfactorily resolved. Sometimes the thread of fantasy strains credulity and disrupts the story, as when the sea apparently enters the house to soothe the children. On the realistic side, the plight of oil-injured creatures is vivid, but there is no hint of any solution to this distressing situation. Because these ambiguities are not satisfactorily developed, the book is not completely successful. Readers who enjoyed the author's *Snow Spider* trilogy may be disappointed.

THE BEARS WILL GET YOU! (1990)

Nick Tucker

SOURCE: A review of *The Bears Will Get You!*, in *Books for Your Children*, Vol. 26, No. 2, Summer, 1991, p. 11.

Never deny the existence of bears underneath when stepping on a crack in the pavement. If you do, you are sure to fall straight into the otherwise settled homestead of Mr and Mrs Bear. This is exactly what happens to the boy, girl, window-cleaner, cat and furniture-remover featured in this amiable picture-book. But fortunately, their reception is quite friendly, and return to the normal world is no problem. Wendy Smith's fuzzy, relaxed drawings are perfectly in tune with this affectionate, charming story.

DELILAH AND THE DOGSPELL (1991)

Margery Fisher

SOURCE: A review of *Delilah and the Dogspell*, in *Growing Point*, Vol. 30, No. 4, November, 1991, p. 5602.

Delilah and the Dogspell uses the natural antagonism between cats and dogs in a nonsense tale which supposes that a finely bred feline has the power to turn dogs to miniature size, a power which she exercises with increasing success till she goes too far in casting a spell on the Prime Minister's beloved pet Hodgson. Delilah's activities are being observed by tiny Prince, adopted as a stray by Annie Watkin, whose longing for an animal of her own is gratified by parents who could hardly object to such a small and amenable animal. Summoning a number of Delilah's victims, Prince organises her capture and threatens her with a bath unless she promises not to minify any more dogs or turn them invisible; the contract works two ways, for the dogs have to agree in their turn to stop chasing cats. The possibilities for comedy reach a climax when Prince is restored to his proper size as a Saint Bernard while he is perched in a tree. Alert drawings [by Emma Chichester Clark] fill out this event and many others in a racy bit of nonsense based on a sturdy recognition of the relationship of dogs and cats which adds noise and confusion to the lives of most pet-owners.

David Churchill

SOURCE: A review of *Delilah and the Dogspell*, in *The School Librarian*, Vol. 40, No. 1, February, 1992, p. 21.

An exotic cat that can cast spells on dogs which annoy her, a boy and a girl who each need a friend, two pairs of slightly odd parents, all blended in a crackling style of storytelling, make this a most attractive read. The fantasy moves at a very fast pace and increases in entertainment right up to the moment when the writer shocks a laugh out of us by springing the surprise effect of a huge St Bernard stranded at the top of a very spindly tree. The book is a romp, splendidly done, and must be a delightful

choice either for reading aloud to any primary class or for displaying on the bookshelves.

R. Baines

SOURCE: A review of *Delilah and the Dogspell*, in *Junior Bookshelf*, Vol. 56, No. 4, August, 1992, pp. 147-8.

The cat Delilah has been given magical powers and begins this book by shrinking an enormous, menacing dog until he is "tiny as a kitten, miserable as a half-eaten mouse". This thin and bedraggled creature, mysteriously endowed with the gift of speech, is befriended by Annie; Delilah arrives next door when an apparently unhappy and unfriendly family moves in.

Jenny Nimmo's fantastic plot includes a legion of tiny dogs, all shrunk by Delilah, and who are sometimes invisible: an idea which reaches its climax when all the dogs materialise, at their full size, in the bathroom of Annie's house. The complexity of the story is increased by telling it sometimes as an account of Annie's experiences and sometimes from Delilah's viewpoint.

RAINBOW AND MR. ZED (1992)

Marcus Crouch

SOURCE: A review of *Rainbow and Mr. Zed*, in *Junior Bookshelf*, Vol. 56, No. 4, August, 1992, pp. 158-9.

This is described as a sequel to the author's ***Ultramarine***. As we know from Jenny Nimmo's earlier sequence, her sequels are not like other people's. For one thing she herself develops as well as her characters. Although the magic is fundamentally much the same this author is now master of a formidable technique and a deep understanding of people and their environment. So, in enjoying ***Rainbow and Mr. Zed***—and it is an immensely enjoyable book—be prepared for the imagination to be stretched, the emotions assaulted, as never before.

The new story drove me back to reread ***Ultramarine***, and the exercise was a reminder of how carefully, and with what control, Jenny Nimmo releases information. At the end of the earlier book we did not know many vital facts about Nell and Ned and their curious domestic and family set-up. I am not sure if we are fully in the picture when ***Rainbow and Mr. Zed*** reaches its devastating climax, which makes it seem likely that there is one more book in the sequence still to come. This is all to the good. Characters as complex as this are not to be comprehended easily. The author needs space and time in which to explore them for our understanding and delight.

This is Nell's book (Rainbow is her real name, as only her father and her sinister uncle know). She has previously been sustained by her brother Ned, in whose company she can hear the ocean's footsteps. Without him she has 'a tendency to sink'. Now Ned is far away, and Nell is at the mercy of the extrovert Menna and her parents whose life-style and interests are remote from hers. Worse still, Menna's father is summoned to his employer, the mysterious Mr. Zed, on his Atlantic island, and to her horror Nell is included in the invitation. Zed's wishes are commands, and Nell has to go. In physical terms it might be worse. Zed lives in great luxury and Nell has everything she could want. Zed's son Dylan proves friendly. Even the family ghost, although smelling strongly of fish, is amiable. But Zed? I was suspicious about Zed's limp. Would he turn out to be the Devil? No, Zed's powers, although extraterrestrial, are not diabolic. Zed is in fact long-lost Uncle Zebedee whose lust for power is compromised a little by his hatred of his brother, Nell's environmentally-friendly father.

No more of the plot which can only be diminished in summary. It is exciting, moving, and deeply committed to the preservation of the world. These big and important themes are interpreted in terms of people, and especially of Nell who grows before our eyes, her personality developing as the cocky Menna, a delightful creation, shrinks. As always Ms Nimmo underpins her plot with a sound philosophy and with an exquisitely lucid style, rich in relevant imagery. No space for quotation here, but in a long and complicated story every image, beautiful in itself, fits securely into the overall structure. Great stuff this, with much fun to match the terrors, an exciting adventure worked out in terms of vividly realised characters, all confirmation—if such were needed—that here is an important writer at the height of her powers.

Ingrid Broomfield

SOURCE: A review of *Rainbow and Mr. Zed,* in *The School Librarian,* Vol. 40, No. 4, November, 1992, p. 159.

Jenny Nimmo has the ability to anchor fantasy so firmly in the details of everyday reality that her magic becomes totally believable, and this novel is no exception. It features shy Nell, who is separated from her family for the first time when she holidays with some distant relatives. Summoned by the mysterious Mr Zed to a remote island in the Atlantic, Nell becomes aware of strange voices whispering to her from the crystal tower that Mr Zed has built. She also finds a ghost, a boy who can swim like a fish, and finds that Mr Zed knows her true name—Rainbow. The plot escalates as Mr Zed tells Nell what he wants from her and she learns that he and her father are old enemies. By the end of the book Nell has grown as a person, she has made a new friend, found an uncle and a cousin, and achieved her dream of sailing to the furthest ocean with her father. Throughout the descriptions are vivid and exact. Mr Zed's island is bright with sunshine and colour, his house and garden are precisely detailed, and the ghost has a smell and a substance that are wholly convincing. Characters and the relationships between them are also fully realised, the author is skilled at conveying feelings, and she has a fine ear for dialogue. The book reads very easily but there are deeper layers of meaning linked to underlying themes of good and evil, friends and

family, the environment, and responsibility. It is a sequel to *Ultramarine,* but stands on its own as an excellent read to be recommended to fluent readers of ten and upwards.

Neil Philip

SOURCE: A review of *Rainbow and Mr. Zed,* in *The Times Educational Supplement,* No. 4003, March 19, 1993, p. 11.

Rainbow and Mr Zed is a sequel to Jenny Nimmo's *Ultramarine* a powerfully-conceived fantasy with an ecological theme. In the first book, a brother and sister, Ned and Nell, discover the truth about their heritage: their real names are Albatross and Rainbow, and they have kelpie blood. Their innate affinity with the sea comes from their magical father Arion, whose life is devoted to environmental rescue. In *Ultramarine* those haunting television images of seabirds drowning in spilled oil formed a potent focus both for a traditional fantasy of good and evil and a modern treatment of green issues.

Rainbow and Mr Zed revisits some of the same territory and, like *Ultramarine,* is a beguiling read, with moments of real tension and poetry. It lacks, however, some of the emotional punch. Largely this is because the children's terrifying witchlike Granny is dead, and the vortex of twisted emotions and guilty secrets which stormed about her has been quieted. In the new story, her place is taken by an evil uncle, Zebedee, who as Mr Zed, plots to take over the world by exploiting the secrets of the sea: "He has this ambition to be the most powerful man in the world does Zed, not just the richest. And his future is in the crystals. He's going to blast the ocean apart to find more. . . ."

There are echoes in Mr Zed of a long line of power-hungry scientists, notably T. H. White's *The Master.* Like the Master, Zed lives on an island, to which he lures Rainbow, in order to make use of her unique ability to hear the voices of the sea crystals. But Zed has "eyes so black they showed Nell only herself," while the Master has eyes with "lids . . . drawn down at the outer corners, hooding them in the calm, yellowish, distant, cellular, reserved antiquity of the vellum death mask—a mask which lived its life inside." Zed's is too blank a character to carry the authentic charge of fear and mystery which his role requires.

Nevertheless the character of shy, nervous Rainbow is convincingly developed over the course of the story, and while her brother never appears, his place is satisfactorily filled by Zed's merboy son, Dylan.

Ultramarine's strikingly original concept has been put at the service in *Rainbow and Mr Zed* of a rather old-fashioned tale, but now Dylan has been added to the cast, the children's adventures may take a more thought-provoking turn.

Jenny Nimmo's special qualities as a writer—her quietly

rhythmic prose, her gift for the telling phrase, her sensitivity to childhood worries—certainly stand out in comparison to the formulaic competence of Frank Rodgers's *The Drowning Boy* and Robert Swindells's *Inside the Worm*. These are two well-constructed and utterly forgettable books on too-tired themes: the haunting of a young girl by an old tragedy; the possession of a group of schoolchildren by an ancient evil. Nimmo's alertness to environmental issues has at least opened up a new area for children's fantasy novels to explore: Rodgers and Swindells are both living in the past as the well-observed Fifties setting of *The Drowning Boy* confirms. Mentions of McDonald's are about all that prevent the reader from assuming that *Inside the Worm* is set in the same era.

J. Jarman

SOURCE: A review of *Rainbow & Mr. Zed*, in *Books for Your Children*, Vol. 29, No. 1, Spring, 1994, p. 24.

Nell, the Rainbow of the title, describes herself as 'a bit different from other people'. Well, yes! Her mother came from the sea. Her father is an albatross—sometimes. One grandfather is a ghost, the other a kelpie, a mysterious sea creature. Mr. Zed, her Prospero-like uncle, is an enchanter with a pillar of crystals stolen from the secret depths of the sea. These crystals call to Nell in sad whispers, telling how the world began, but only Nell can understand them. It's a secret Mr. Zed yearns to know, but she won't tell him—so he takes her prisoner.

It sounds weird and unbelievable, but fantasy and reality are melded in language so precise, that it's utterly believable and deeply moving. The happenings are strange and exciting. The characters are convincing both as modern and mythical beings and it's a powerful story about the quest for knowledge, its attractions and dangers.

Elizabeth Bush

SOURCE: A review of *Rainbow and Mr. Zed*, in *Bulletin of the Center for Children's Books*, Vol. 48, No. 6, February, 1995, pp. 210-11.

The continuation of *Ultramarine* finds Nell (Rainbow) in early adolescence, painfully aware of her own social backwardness and envious of older brother Ned's chance to sail off on an animal rescue mission with their mysterious, adored father. Nell stoically accepts an invitation to visit with distant relatives in hope that "the timorous bits of her would be snipped away," but she is lured to an island by the reclusive Mr. Zed—Nell's Uncle Zebedee, an evil enchanter who, in his lust for power, has plundered from the Furthest Ocean crystals which hold the secret to life's origins. Zebedee is certain that Nell's kelpie heritage will enable her to interpret the tiny voices of the crystals, and he holds his niece virtually hostage while awaiting both her acquiescence and a final confrontation with his childhood enemy—Nell's father. If the delicately ambiguous relationship between fantasy and reality that

graces *Ultramarine* is missing from the sequel, Nimmo more than compensates with a coming-of-age tale of equal delicacy. Nell's self-doubt and self-discoveries are subtle, complex, and thoroughly believable as she tests the strength of her absent father's love, even while tearfully admitting her bond to Zebedee, who "saw me as someone special, someone he wanted with him—always."

THE WITCHES AND THE SINGING MICE: A CELTIC TALE (retold by Jenny Nimmo, 1993)

Hazel Rochman

SOURCE: A review of *The Witches and the Singing Mice*, in *Booklist*, Vol. 89, No. 22, August, 1993, p. 2067.

"On a stormy night, when wolves still roamed the Highlands, three witches came to Glenmagraw." From the first line, Nimmo's lyrical version of a Celtic tale draws you close against the fearful outside. Three wicked strangers come to town; they demand that impossible tasks be done; and suddenly children are held fast in a terrible enchantment. The strangers are witches who turn themselves into cats with razor-sharp claws and teeth that sink into the very bone. But two brave domestic tomcats go out into the dark forest and defeat the monsters in a fight to the death. [Angela] Barrett's light-filled paintings of family and pets in the orderly village are set against the dark swirling monster world of storm and wolves, black and fiery red. Great storytelling for a dark and stormy night.

Joy Fleishhacker

SOURCE: A review of *The Witches and the Singing Mice*, in *School Library Journal*, Vol. 39, No. 8, August, 1993, p. 166.

In this dark retelling of a Celtic tale, two tomcats battle a trio of witches. After arriving in Glenmagraw on a stormy eve, three evil sisters take over an abandoned house. One by one they visit the village and make impossible demands on the local craftsmen. As each one is denied, she snarls, "Then it will be the worse for you." The blacksmith's daughter and the carpenter's son fall into a deathly sleep, victims of magical rodents who hadn't bothered the townspeople in years. Tam and Rory spy on the witches, see them transform into horrible black cats, and learn that they had been forcing the fairy mice to bite the children. Following the villains into the forest, the brave felines combine courage with quick claws to defeat them and bring back the remedy for the sleeping spell. Nimmo's tale is filled with wonderfully gruesome details and images. Unexpected plot twists heighten the suspense, as the clever cats solve the mystery of the singing mice. Although she provides no source, Nimmo successfully mixes folkloric elements with lots of action. [Angela] Barrett's shadowy, full-color paintings create a misty, mysterious setting. The witch-cats, with their red-flecked eyes, razor-edged claws, and unnaturally stiff postures, are powerful and frightening. The lengthy text and complicated story line might limit this book's appeal to more tenacious folklore fans.

Publishers Weekly

SOURCE: A review of *The Witches and the Singing Mice: A Celtic Tale,* in *Publishers Weekly,* Vol. 240, No. 31, August 2, 1993, p. 81.

In this energetic retelling of an old Celtic tale, three witches spread magic and terror in Glenmagraw village. The ghoulish night visitors make impossible demands of local craftsmen and, their requests refused, send two children into a deep sleep. Local cats Tam and Rory must hunt down singing mice to rouse the sleepers and prevent the witches from striking again. Clear, evocative prose ("ancient trees grinned and threatened, tangled roots caught and tripped the nimble paws"), imbued with a musical lilt, races the text to an uplifting conclusion. Nimmo skillfully combines the legend's romanticism with a pleasingly down-to-earth briskness. Scenes of magic are portrayed with wispily textured artwork while village scenes have a naïve freshness. Especially well drawn are the witches transformed into black cats with wild eyes and "knife-edged" claws. Their fight with Tam and Rory is all movement, hiss and flying fur. This fine picture book's frisson of fright has the reassuring fillip of a happy ending.

 **THE BREADWITCH** (1993)

Chris Stephenson

SOURCE: A review of *The Breadwitch,* in *The School Librarian,* Vol. 39, No. 11, November, 1993, p. 153.

The Breadwitch . . . deals in the fantastic. Toddler Belinda spoils family mealtimes in the Eatwell household by being faddy with her food. In desperation her brother Peter seeks the help of the Breadwitch, whose magic bread has the power of increasing the eater's appetite. Belinda is cured, but not before morsels of the bread have been fed to the dog, the cats and the birds—with hilarious consequences.

THE STONE MOUSE (1993)

Sue Smedley

SOURCE: A review of *The Stone Mouse,* in *The School Librarian,* Vol. 41, No. 4, November, 1993, p. 157.

This story of a stone mouse, who can speak, is a strangely engaging read. Elly has conversations with the mouse, much to her brother Ted's annoyance. Ted tries to get rid of the mouse by throwing it in the sea and then by burying it. The mouse survives both ordeals and eventually helps Ted by befriending him. . . .

The reader is invited to consider many themes, such as

the relationships between brothers and sisters, between children and parents, and the importance and significance of friends. This is a good book to read aloud, chapter by chapter, to younger children and also a good read for older, more experienced readers.

Marcus Crouch

SOURCE: A review of *The Stone Mouse,* in *Junior Bookshelf,* Vol. 57, No. 6, December, 1993, p. 235.

Jenny Nimmo has always shown a special kind of mastery in the little book, of which this, although divided into eight chapters, is an example. With a good type, generous leading and plenty of pictures, **The Stone Mouse** is a short story presented to young readers as a challenge to master a whole book. The gentle, humorous, intensely human story should encourage even the reluctant reader to overcome a few difficulties. Miss Nimmo, like Beatrix Potter, loves the resonant phrase, the colourful word. I like the moment when the stone mouse, through the malice of Ted, finds himself in the sea, where he spends a restless night that nevertheless feeds 'his mousy curiosity'. 'Only the pebbles worried him with their smooth, eyeless surfaces and lack of conversation.' What seems at first to be a conventional story about gentle young sister and rough unsympathetic brother turns out to be far subtler. There is reason behind Ted's anger, and the stone mouse helps to defuse it. A highly satisfactory little book, written with charm and wisdom, and finished with a set of illustrations by Helen Craig which never usurp the reader's right to form his own images.

Carol Fox

SOURCE: A review of *The Stone Mouse,* in *The Times Educational Supplement,* No. 4044, December 31, 1993, p. 17.

In complete contrast [to *48 Hours with Franklin* by Mij Kelly and *The Ghost That Lived on the Hill* by Jean Ure] is Jenny Nimmo's **The Stone Mouse,** though there is still a fantasy character, a pebble mouse that talks. The mouse is used to show up and explore the anger of Ted, Elly's brother. I enjoyed the scene where the two cats, Moss and Minnie, sit silently by Ted's bed, staring him out in a quiet but menacing way, finally forcing him to go and dig up the stone mouse from the rose bed where he has spitefully buried him. The book is written in a direct and unsentimental style that is a pleasure to read. Helen Craig's drawings are finely tuned to the story and beautifully executed.

DELILAH AND THE DISHWATER DOGS (1993)

Janet Sims

SOURCE: A review of *Delilah and the Dishwasher Dogs,*

in *The School Librarian,* Vol. 42, No. 2, May, 1994, p. 62.

This book, a sequel to **Delilah and the Dogspell,** is exciting, funny and extremely readable. Delilah, a magical cat, described as 'queen of the night garden' is kidnapped by the wicked fortune teller, Bianca Bono. The rest of the cats in the neighbourhood, each with a clearly drawn character, description and name, come to her rescue and the day is finally saved by Tudor, the timid kitten.

The story is well delivered, with increasing and stretching vocabulary. Tension mounts towards the climax and the loose ends are all neatly tied up at the end with, of course, a most satisfactory ending. Awareness of the natural world, as well as humans with personalities, all adds to the roundedness of this story. The book is nicely presented, with clear line illustrations throughout and chapters with titles. Headings like 'Into the Mountains' and 'Tudor's Finest Hour' will you to read on. A highly recommended book, with a stylish cover, for 7 to 10s.

A. R. Williams

SOURCE: A review of *Delilah and the Dishwasher Dogs,* in *Junior Bookshelf,* Vol. 60, No. 4, August, 1996, pp. 150-1.

The flamboyant Bianca Bono, failed witch and discarded conjuror is the villainess of Jenny Nimmo's two-layered tale of trouble among cats and dogs. Delilah, the cat *supreme* is abducted by Diana in a dishwasher into which Delilah has inserted herself to investigate the kitten, Bugo's claim that Bianca has magicked the new machine with miniature dogs. Tudor enlists the neighbouring cats, family pets or not, in the search for Bianca's van into which, by representing herself as an electrical engineer, she has managed to load the dishwasher and make off. The reader follows the endeavours of the cat posse in alternating suspense and chagrin as they roam the village and the woods, having to contend with Bianca's over-sized dog as well as darkness and growing despair. Hugo plays a valiant part and at the end feels himself accepted as a full member of the cat community. There are many disappointments following the initial Catastrophe (sorry!) but what sounds like a complicated plot is firmly controlled. La Bono's nostalgic recollections of her earlier life are a story in themselves and one can even begin to feel a sneaking sympathy for this misguided lady as she reveals a colourful past. Humans, children and adults, provide necessary background to the goings-on. Ben Cort's illustrations are well-suited to the 6+ age group for which the book is intended; he is at his best with Annie's fall from her bicycle.

THE STARLIGHT CLOAK (retold by Jenny Nimmo, 1993)

Beth Tegart

SOURCE: A review of *The Starlight Cloak,* in *School Library Journal,* Vol. 39, No. 9, September, 1993, p. 216.

A Celtic variant of the Cinderella story that combines traditional folk figures with new adventures and characters. Oona, the youngest daughter of a widowed Irish king, is treated cruelly by her two elder sisters. It is only with the magical assistance of her foster mother's cloak that she is able to dress in fine clothing and meet the handsome prince, who was once engaged to one of her sisters. The couple marry, but three years later the jilted sister pushes Oona off a cliff into the sea, where she is swallowed by a whale. Once again the cloak comes in handy, and Oona is saved, assuring a happily-ever-after ending. The story is intriguing at times, but grows tedious as readers follow the poor young woman through all of her trials. The writing is hindered by too many extraneous details. The pleasant, full-page illustrations [by Justin Todd] are done in soft watercolors in the classic fairy-tale mode, with lots of blues, greens, and purples, but the characters appear flat and washed out. This is an interesting version of the tale, but not a first purchase.

Kristina Lindsay

SOURCE: A review of *The Starlight Cloak,* in *Magpies,* Vol. 9, No. 23, July, 1994, p. 29.

This is a delightful retelling of the Cinderella story drawn from traditional Celtic roots. The story is set in Ireland where a widowed king had three daughters. The two oldest were mean and cruel; Oona, the youngest, was fair and beautiful. Made to work day and night in the big, cold castle Oona was visited by her foster mother who was able to give her a magic dress, cloak and shoes and a snow white mare to take her to church. There the prince of Ermania awaited the three princesses as he was betrothed to the eldest daughter. However, when he spied Oona his heart was captured. The story does not finish when they marry but adds an extra dimension to this well loved fairy tale.

The illustrations by Justin Todd are of high quality and truly add to this magical story.

Gill Roberts

SOURCE: A review of *The Starlight Cloak,* in *Books for Keeps,* No. 91, March, 1995, p. 11.

A beautifully written and illustrated fairytale. It has parallels with the traditional Cinderella, but is further extended so that once Oona and the prince have married, one of the ugly stepsisters seeks revenge.

Cormac (who is Oona's foster-mother's grandchild) witnesses the crime and it's due to his faithfulness and his grandmother's magic powers that there's a happy ending. A truly magical tale—a Jenny Nimmo classic which will encapture readers of all ages.

GRIFFIN'S CASTLE (1994)

Jenny Nimmo

SOURCE: "Building a Castle," in *Books for Keeps,* No. 89, November, 1994, p. 29.

When I was very small I had great need of a ghost; I don't mean an imaginary friend whom I could call up or banish at will, but rather someone who lived in my house, someone I could hear and often glimpse going about their business: a comforting presence. And, perhaps because I believed in him utterly, he was there. We moved house when I was seven and the ghost was left behind.

In *Griffin's Castle,* Dinah Jones has need of the supernatural. The real World has been found wanting. Although her mother has never abandoned her, she has been continually uprooted; she has lived in squats, in damp bedsits, in hostels and in care. Dinah is exceptionally gifted, a condition that isolates her as much as a learning difficulty can isolate the children who are struggling to keep up with their peers—not because they are rejected by other children, but rather because there is no shared experience, no level at which they can easily communicate.

In Dinah's case her early maturity is beginning to distance her from her mother. They have reached a stage where they are both aware that their relationship is about to change irrevocably; henceforth they are inevitably bound upon separate courses. The realisation is painful for both of them. To make matters worse they are living in a house that is due for demolition; the floorboards are rotten, the walls crumbling, the electricity supply erratic and dangerous. But Dinah sees the house as it once was, a fine building furnished, curtained and carpeted in gleaming antique colours, a castle to be defended at all costs. At 11 years old she has decided she cannot exist without a place to call her own, a place of safety.

The animals on the wall outside Cardiff Castle are startling to anyone who comes across them for the first time. To someone like me, in search of a story, they were a gift; a perfect link between Dinah and the supernatural. When the stone lioness leaps over the traffic to Dinah, it is a repetition of the flight the animal took in my imagination, in the dusk of a winter's afternoon.

Children often turn to animals for comfort when they feel betrayed and insecure. The presence of a being that accepts them, listens and never censures, is infinitely reassuring. Dinah wants a real animal but as this is impossible she chooses the stone creatures. There they sit, regarding her from the wall, waiting for life. It seems inevitable that she should give it to them.

Three of the fifteen creatures answer Dinah's call: the lioness, a bear and a wolf. The animals, luminous replicas of the stone images, come to inhabit Dinah's garden at night. They are the barrier between her and a World she has ceased to trust. But like many metaphorical walls that desperate people build around themselves, Dinah's animal wall becomes too strong, too real, and she finds she cannot escape from it.

Lonely children are often more sensitive to things running just below the surface of normality. And this is the case with Barry Hughes and Jacob Rose, both of them loners in need of a friend. It's their craving to understand Dinah that plunges them into her mysterious Other-world, the world that her extraordinary energy has conjured up.

It has been said that the supernatural is a ruse, a device to make a story out of a routine event; but I see it as the very fabric of a story. The oldest tales in the World deal with the supernatural. They would not exist without it. The precise meaning of each tale has probably been lost, but we do know that they represent the everlasting human struggle to bring about a better World, the battle between good and evil. They are tales of wonder and imagination and they liberate us from our often troubled existence, and allow us to hope.

Children often receive a bad press these days, but there are thousands who should be applauded for their courage, energy and determination. Dinah is such a child. She became very real for me. Through her I was able to acclaim all those small brave fighters, who deserve better than they get and, if they read *Griffin's Castle,* allow them to hope.

A deep and often neglected human instinct is the wish to belong, to be part of a tribe that we can recognise, to know where we came from. In Dinah, because she's never had a home or been welcomed by her family, the wish to belong becomes overwhelming. Having nothing, she is too proud to accept the hospitality Jacob and Barry offer her, she is searching for something older and deeper, a link with the past, and a place that she can claim as her own.

The greatest bonus for an author, it seems to me, is freedom to choose our protagonists' fate; we can reward, elevate, punish, humiliate and even kill off, should the story require it. I relished the rewarding of Dinah Jones. Perhaps I only built the wall that threatened to extinguish her, in order that I could rescue her. Although she was in thrall of the supernatural, she is saved by a real and predictable event, and it is a real, albeit damaged and forsaken, animal that leads her to the person who we know will keep her safe. So the reader cannot say, 'This happy ending couldn't happen. It's fantasy.' It could. Dinah is rewarded because she is brave, thoughtful and determined—human characteristics that we all possess.

Marcus Crouch

SOURCE: A review of *Griffin's Castle,* in *Junior Bookshelf,* Vol. 58, No. 6, December, 1994, pp. 229-30.

Jenny Nimmo's new novel, her most substantial offering since the **'Ultramarine'** sequence was temporarily put on hold, marks another change of direction and a step forward for this remarkable writer. For the first time in an important work she has an urban scene. She combines timeless magic with a contemporary social problem, laughter with tears, all in a story which is unrelentingly readable.

Dinah's beautiful and feckless mother Rosalie is a drifter, living always in a vain expectation that things will get better. Perhaps this time her hope will be proved true, for they are moving into a house, a house of character which to Dinah seems, in the dark, as big and strong as a castle. Even in the moment of their arrival she picks up carved broken stones and christens her new home Griffin's Castle. The 'castle' comes with the blessing of Rosalie's new boyfriend Gomer, who is no Father Christmas but a ruthless go-getter who looks for pay in some form or other. Dinah sees Griffin's Castle as the final answer to her need for a home. To Gomer it is a potential building site. Dinah fights him with the aid of the carved animals who line the castle walls (the city has something of Cardiff in its topography) and who, it seems, roam the streets at night. Lioness, wolf and bear should be a match for a smooth operator like Gomer. Dinah finds allies too at school in the shape of Jacob and Barry who sink their own differences in their devotion to the strange, wayward, imaginative girl.

No more of the plot, except that it maintains its pressure to the last page. Some readers may feel that the happy ending, however well earned by Dinah, has a touch of contrivance about it. All will surely have lost their hearts to her and will be glad that she, through the good offices of a scruffy stray cat, finds a family and a home far from the decaying walls of Griffin's Castle. As ever Jenny Nimmo uses her setting as a key character in her story. More than ever she is in control of a flexible style which meets the demands of ever changing crises and moods. Beautifully written, finely imagined to the last detail, this is a fantasy the more powerful because it obeys strict rules and reconciles the differences of magic and reality.

Gillian Clarke

SOURCE: "Mythical Beasts," in *The Times Educational Supplement*, No. 4106, March 10, 1995, p. III.

Here are two novels [*Griffin's Castle* and *Flex* by Philip Gross] set geographically worlds apart, that share the common ground of the imagination. They show the significance of fantasy in modern life, and exemplify the psychological importance of myth. The works of two writers of outstanding quality who understand the young, these books deal with magical transformations, adventure based on fantasy and the search for love. . . .

In *Griffin's Castle* the "real" life of Dinah Jones is a harder one [than in *Flex*] and one memory out of which her mythical beasts arise is the tragic death of a baby in her arms. The baby died in circumstances of poverty into which many single mothers fall. Dinah cannot forget it. Her mother, 17 when Dinah was born, has a rich suitor

who owns the beautiful, disintegrating old house where mother and daughter make yet another temporary home. Their long lost roots lie far away in Snowdonia with great grandfather Tomos Gwalchmai. Dinah and the lover are enemies at first sight. Her mother is torn between her lover and her brilliant, wayward daughter.

The story, set in Cardiff, is Dinah's search for roots, a family and a home. The mythical beasts are sculpted in stone on the city's famous animal wall where generations of children and imaginative grown-ups must have walked, certain they heard a lioness, a lynx, a bear or a wolf slip like a shadow from the wall to follow them.

Dinah is clever, admired at school, but remote from the two boys who share the secret of the beasts that come, one by one, at night to prowl before her on the lawn. "She did not need to see the creature. It was there, very close, dangerous and savage." Her jealousy and frustration summon them out of the trees, and they fulfil Dinah's need for an embodied rage. When her enemy collapses, it is not she but her beasts that harm him. Only in ultimate fulfilment does she find they have gone away.

📖 ***WILFRED'S WOLF* (illustrated by husband, David Wynn Millward, 1994)**

Marcus Crouch

SOURCE: A review of *Wilfred's Wolf*, in *Junior Bookshelf*, Vol. 58, No. 6, December, 1994, p. 218.

After the turmoil and the mystery of *Griffin's Castle* Jenny Nimmo relaxes with an agreeable frolic. For the first time, I think, she collaborates with her husband, the distinguished artist David Wynn Millward, and a very successful partnership it proves. Mr. Millward adds his own dimension to the story, finding some excellent jokes which are barely hinted at in the text. Don't look for subtleties. The maitre d'hotel of The Plush, best in London, is Mr. Spite, and when justice catches up with him he is replaced by Ms Elda Berry who adores wolves. Wilfred, head chef and the wolf's protector, loves Eclair, the baker's daughter. These and other innocent inventions are welded together in a narrative which, for all its brevity, is full of neat phrases and sound observation. A great book for bedtime (or any other time).

📖 ***RONNIE AND THE GIANT MILLIPEDE* (1995)**

Marcus Crouch

SOURCE: A review of *Ronnie and the Giant Millipede*, in *Junior Bookshelf*, Vol. 59, No. 6, December, 1995, pp. 214-5.

This is Jenny Nimmo in relaxed mood. Ronnie is a descendant of Rumpel Stiltskin and has inherited his ancestor's predilection for stamping. In his birthday boots he wreaks havoc with furniture and floors and then turns his attention to insect life, notably millipedes. In the end a giant millipede turns the tables on him, and he is lucky to survive with no more than six hundred and fifty bruises. A genial moral tale is told briskly with easy-to-read typography and many illustrations by David Parkins which, to my mind, go just a little over the top. Young readers would not agree.

THE WITCH'S TEARS (1996)

Judithe Hall

SOURCE: A review of *The Witch's Tears,* in *Reading Time,* Vol. XL, No. 3, August, 1996, p. 28.

When a series of strange things happen at Theo's house he starts to wonder. Is Mrs Scarum, a total stranger who has taken shelter at his house from the freezing hail and howling wind, a witch? The signs are all there: the story-telling, the black cats . . . even tears which turn to crystal. He wishes his father would return home from his travels, and the clocks which he fixes would stop behaving strangely. This award-winning author has created a gently, but wonderfully atmospheric story which will be sure to enthral many young readers. It is at once moving, exciting and gripping, with characters both believable, and yet a little mystical as well. The softness of the illustrations [by Paul Howard] supports the story's mood beautifully, and the simple but powerful language keeps the reader on the edge of their seat.

F. Ball

SOURCE: A review of *The Witch's Tears,* in *Junior Bookshelf,* Vol. 60, No. 5, October, 1996, p. 194.

As Theo runs home from school one stormy night, his neighbour is looking for his cat. Theo stops briefly and Mr. Oak says it will be a good night for witches. Theo asks how you can tell if someone is a witch, and Mr. Oak says that witches' tears turn to crystal as they fall—but witches rarely cry.

Later that night Mrs. Scarum arrives, complaining that she has lost her cat Harum, and needs shelter. Theo is convinced she is a witch. His mother tells him that is nonsense and says the old woman must stay. Mrs. Scarum wants Theo's cat to keep her feet warm but he refuses. Surprised at his behaviour, his mother still makes Mrs. Scarum welcome. As night comes, Theo, his sister Dodie, his mother and Mrs. Scarum prepare for the cold. Mr. Blossom is away working and they are rather worried about him. He is due to take Theo's mother to a dance the next day. They had been looking for her crystal necklace

before Mrs. Scarum arrived but Mrs. Blossom has now explained that she had to sell it when they ran short of money. Next morning, as she prepares to move on, Mrs. Scarum briefly cries, and her tears turn to crystal. They are swept up with the hailstones and thrown into the snow. Later, a sudden squall sends a crystal necklace to earth—then Mr. Blossom returns.

As the story unfolds, Mrs. Scarum's deeds gradually become more witch-like. Events build towards a climax which reveals her as a witch, resolves the problem of the missing necklace, and sees the safe return of Mr. Blossom. The storm, snow, and tear crystals combine to create a magical winter night. Children of junior age who would enjoy a story of benevolent witchcraft will discover various witchy deeds in the Blossoms old cottage at the edge of the wood. Paul Howard's pencil illustrations capture the essential details of Mrs. Scarum's eccentricity, and Theo's wonder and worry, against the background of the storm.

John Sheppard

SOURCE: A review of *The Witch's Tears,* in *Carousel,* No. 4, Winter, 1996, p. 19.

This is a delightfully told short story, gentle as well as scary, very descriptive but moving with pace. There is mystery too, with the reader having to decide whether the strange visitor is a witch or not. With Theo and Dodie's father missing in a blizzard and their next door neighbour having lost his cat, the odds seem to be that she must be. However, as Dorothy was relieved to discover in 'The Wizard of Oz' there are good witches as well as bad . . .

ALIEN ON THE 99TH FLOOR (1996)

A. R. Williams

SOURCE: A review of *Alien on the 99th Floor,* in *Junior Bookshelf,* Vol. 60, No. 4, August, 1996, p. 150.

Fred reluctantly accompanies his mother on a shopping expedition and, in the store, escapes into the lift from which he is 'beamed up' to a rooftop where he finds a stranded, disabled space 'Bubble' and a desolate Alien. Having restored the craft's functions Fred is invited to share the Alien's cloak of invisibility and together they create a mild mayhem in the departments below especially among the toys. Fred is eventually 'found' by distracted mother and staff and receives an unexpected reward. All rapid-fire high jinks with splendidly funny illustrations [by M. Chatterton], Floor 99 turns out a right whizz and Jenny Nimmo's plot a real hoot.

Additional coverage of Nimmo's life and career is contained in the following sources published by Gale Research: *Contemporary Authors,* Vol. 108; *Contemporary Authors New Revision Series,* Vol. 52; and *Something about the Author,* Vol. 87.

Paul Yee

1956-

Chinese-Canadian children's and young adult author.

Major works include *Teach Me to Fly, Skyfighter!* (1983), *The Curses of Third Uncle* (1986), *Tales from Gold Mountain: Stories of the Chinese in the New World* (1989), *Roses Sing on New Snow: A Delicious Tale* (1992), *Breakaway* (1994).

INTRODUCTION

A writer of nonfiction and fictional stories for children and young adults, Paul Yee is best known for his fictional works which effectively relate the Chinese-Canadian experience of a world filled with cultural traditions and new influences. He is often credited for addressing complex themes such as racism, social and sexual discrimination, alienation, and New World versus Old World, which not only reflect the Chinese-Canadian experience but other multicultural groups as well. Yee is also noted for his historical fiction which contains Chinese immigrants arriving or living in the New World, some whose hopes and dreams were quickly dashed due to discrimination. Drawing upon his experiences of growing up in Vancouver's Chinatown, Yee sets most of his stories in Vancouver. "When I write for children, I have a fairly good idea of where I want to take the novel . . . ," Yee explained in an *Emergency Librarian* interview. "Usually my themes are about history, identity and the acceptance of who one is. Those are the basic ideas that I seem to go back to over and over."

Biographical Information

Yee was born in Spalding, Saskatchewan, Canada, but moved as a young child to Vancouver's Chinatown after his parents died. He and his older brother were raised by a strict elderly aunt and uncle who didn't allow them to watch television or to speak any English at home lest they forget how to speak Chinese. After graduating from high school Yee attended the University of British Columbia as a language major. He quickly discovered, however, that a career as a translator or interpreter was not for him. He also realized that he missed Chinatown and its community, so he started doing volunteer work there. Not only was Yee helping the community, but he was also rediscovering his own Chinese roots. By his third year of college, Yee decided to major in history and graduated the following year. While working at the City Archives in Vancouver, Yee was contacted by a publishing company to write stories about children from various Canadian neighborhoods, especially Chinese, for juveniles. Yee accepted the invitation and created *Teach Me to Fly, Skyfighter!,* drawing upon his own experiences as a Chi-

nese Canadian. He has since written other books for a variety of audiences, including preschoolers and adults.

Major Works

Yee's first work, *Teach Me to Fly, Skyfighter!,* contains four separate stories, each featuring a fifth grade student who must address situations that conflict with his or her own cultural or social background. Several critics appreciated the way Yee approached the topics of racism and multiculturalism. A reviewer in *Children's Book News* felt that "children of all backgrounds will identify with these stories." *The Curses of Third Uncle,* a historical novel set in Vancouver in 1909, involves Lillian, a fourteen-year-old Chinese-Canadian girl searching for her missing father. While her father is gone, his younger brother (Lillian's third uncle) tries to take over the family but is squelched by Lillian. Much of this story is based on the experiences of Yee's aunt as a young girl growing up in Vancouver's Chinatown in the early 1900s. Raymond E. Jones described *Curses* as combining "romantic suspense and gritty historical realism." Containing eight original short stories, *Tales from Gold Mountain: Stories of the*

Chinese in the New World focuses on the dreams of Chinese immigrants and their experiences in and contributions to North America. Gernot and Alexandra Wieland stated that "there is not much description, but when there is, it is accomplished in a few short and powerful sentences." *Roses Sing on New Snow: A Delicious Tale,* a picture book for young children, is a feminist story set within the patriarchal society of late nineteenth-century Chinese immigrants. While Maylin cooks delicious meals each day in her father's Chinatown restaurant, her lazy brothers receive all the credit. When the family is asked by an important official to prepare in his presence Roses Sing on New Snow—one of Maylin's special New World dishes—the truth becomes known to all. Karen Hutt wrote that "Yee tells his 'delicious tale' with grace and economy." Yee again focuses on racism and cultural clashes in *Breakaway,* another historical novel for young adults, set in 1932. Kwok-ken Wong has trouble understanding his father and his traditional ways and is often ignored or mistreated by his white schoolmates and others. After playing in a championship soccer game for his Chinese community, the eighteen-year-old boy comes to terms with his heritage and his father. Margaret Mackey felt that *Breakaway* "contributes a valuable picture of a fascinating and complex time and world."

Awards

In 1990 *Tales from Gold Mountain: Stories of the Chinese in the New World* won the National I.O.D.E. Book Award, the British Columbia Book Prize for Children's Literature, and the Egoff Award. It was also a Parents' Choice Honor book.

AUTHOR'S COMMENTARY

Dave Jenkinson

SOURCE: "Portraits: Paul Yee," in *Emergency Librarian,* Vol. 22, No. 5, May-June, 1995, pp. 61-4.

"Totally a fluke!" is how Paul Yee describes his getting into writing for juveniles. In the early 80s, James Lorimer Publishers was working on a series of stories set in different Canadian neighborhoods. "They'd done Toronto and Edmonton, and came to Vancouver and said, 'We want to do Vancouver's Chinatown and need a writer who knows the community.' They found somebody else, but it didn't work out. My name came up because I was known as a community volunteer, and I'd published one or two adult short stories I had written about my own parents and Saskatchewan. They approached me, and I said, 'Sure, I'll give it a try.'"

Born October 1, 1956, in Spalding, Saskatchewan, Paul grew up in Vancouver's Chinatown. His parents passed away when he was just a young child. "I have an older brother, and we were split up for a short while after my parents' death. He went first to live with my Aunt Lillian and Uncle Foon in Vancouver, and I went off to foster parents in Saskatchewan. These white folks wanted to adopt me, but my aunt said, 'No, I think the brothers should be together.' My aunt and uncle were not wealthy. They were in their sixties and retired when they decided to raise us." Their decision to take in these two young children, Paul explains, was only partly cultural. "I think there was a sense of a family responsibility as well as a personal need on my aunt's part. She was a very strong personality. None of her own children that she gave birth to survived. She had adopted an earlier child, and, when we came along, I think she had another opportunity to become a mother. She said, 'It's like raising chickens. You raise one; you raise two; it's all the same thing.'

"As a child, I certainly didn't have aspirations of being a writer. In fact, I really had no kind of career aspirations. When asked, 'What do you want to be when you grow up?', I would say, 'Teacher,' because that was really all the exposure I'd had to an adult world. I had a fairly 'confined' childhood. My aunt was very strict. Despite the fact that she spoke fluent English, my aunt didn't want a TV in the house. Another of her rules was that we were not allowed to speak English at home. She said, 'I don't have any fears that you're going to learn English because you speak it at school. I do fear that you're not going to speak Chinese.' And so we went to Chinese school. That rule lasted probably until we started high school.

"From an early age, I understood from my aunt that she wanted both my brother and I to go to university. She didn't really care what we studied. Going to university was a ticket out of Chinatown and out of poverty. It was the classic way of escaping one's economic background. I started off at the University of British Columbia in the Faculty of Arts thinking I was going to study languages—Japanese, Mandarin Chinese and French—and become a translator or interpreter. By the end of the first semester, I'd dropped Japanese and knew I wasn't going to go through with the language program.

"By the time I started university, I was becoming involved in the Chinese community in Chinatown. In an ironic way, the very time that we moved away from Chinatown was the point that I decided to go back there to do volunteer work. I'd lived in Chinatown during the '60s, a decline period for the area. Businesses were closing, and people were moving away from Chinatown and Strathcona, the residential neighborhood around it. By the time I was in high school, very few of my classmates were still living in Chinatown-Strathcona. The area was very much a 'halfway house.' Immigrants landed there and then moved away. Nobody wanted to stay in Chinatown-Strathcona. It just wasn't considered a desirable area to live in.

"My going back to do volunteer work was part of the third generation of English-speaking Chinese-Canadians rediscovering their roots. We were a group of young

Chinese-Canadians who wanted to get back into China-town. There was a lot of analysis of why we had been dispossessed of our own heritage and of our own connections to the community. One of those reasons was that we didn't know a lot about our history. Our own families had decided not to tell us a great deal about the past because it had been so dark and gloomy, and they didn't want to scar us. They just wanted us to get out of Chinatown and get good jobs. The flip side to not knowing our history was that, if you knew your history, you controlled the destiny of your community, of how it would move ahead. Those concepts were very exciting to me, and so finally in the third year of my BA, I figured out my major, which was history.

"During my fourth and final year, I was really perturbed about what I was going to do with this degree. I'd applied for library school and got accepted, but, when it came down to it, I thought, 'This really isn't quite it.' I took a year off and worked part-time in Chinatown and part-time at the City Archives in Vancouver. By the end of that year, I realized I was more intrigued with working with an archives because it was closer to history. I eventually found a full-time position at the archives and started on an MA program in history part-time, finishing in 1983."

It was while Paul was employed full-time at the archives that Lorimer approached him. "They had a very firm idea of what they wanted: working-class stories, plus a mix of characters and ages. Nothing was to be either totally good or totally bad, and I had to provide social explanations for problems. I gave them about nine story outlines, and they chose four which became the stories in *Teach Me to Fly, Skyfighter!*"

Each of *Skyfighter*'s stories can stand alone as a separate read, but they are linked via a group of grade 5 schoolmates. Though the children engage in typical kid activities, they all feel some form of insecurity because of their backgrounds. For example, in the title story, Canadian-born Sharon Fong dislikes living in Chinatown because it is so "Chinese," and the unilingual Sharon also feels awkward around immigrant Samson Wong, who, she believes, is talking about her in Chinese to his immigrant friends. Two of the other stories use immigrant children as their central characters: Samson from Hong Kong and John Chin from China. The final story features a white girl, Christine Thomas, who lives in the local housing project.

"Part of my living in Chinatown went straight into *Skyfighter* because it was very much about the neighborhood and kids growing up there. I was in about grade 4 when the first wave of kids coming over from Hong Kong began. As children, we saw them as different. They dressed differently, they couldn't speak English and they clung together. There were derogatory terms for them—CBs, meaning China-born. Certainly there was a sense of looking down at the newcomers, and we didn't see ourselves as one community. But, by high school, the barriers were down, and the groups were quite integrated. As long as

the immigrant kids spoke English, they were accepted, and there were a lot of friendships.

"The physical school in *Skyfighter* is my school, but Strathcona School had changed by the time I was writing about it. During the '60s, the classes were almost 100 percent Chinese, but these stories are set in the early '80s, and Chinatown had changed. There was an adventurous middle class moving back, and it was more racially mixed. And it was also culturally mixed, in the sense that there were also the Chinese from Vietnam. I went back to my elementary school and sat in to see what the kids were like. The majority were still Chinese, probably 70 percent, but there was a much stronger non-Chinese base.

"After *Skyfighter* came out, I was relieved to know that I could, in fact, write for children. Lorimer had said, 'If you want to do more stories, we'd be interested.' *The Curses of Third Uncle* was not actually the novel I wanted to do next. I did an outline for a soccer story, and, at the same time, I also did a story outline for *Third Uncle*. For whatever reason, Lorimer thought *Third Uncle* was more appealing. I believe they were trying to launch a series, 'Adventures in Canadian history,' and so they were looking for historical material.

"*Third Uncle* was essentially my aunt's stories about her childhood in Vancouver. I took one or two pivotal events from her history which I then expanded and took liberties with and made into this story. She was born in Vancouver's Chinatown in 1895 and had enormous links and memories of that place. By being raised by her, I got a sense of the immense vibrancy of an earlier community that wasn't around when I was there. Her memories and descriptions of people and my interactions with the friends of my aunt and uncle gave me indications of the past glories of Chinatown.

"My aunt's father came from China to San Francisco for the gold rush in the 1860s and then trekked up to B.C. where he ultimately became a merchant tailor in Vancouver. He brought a wife over from China, and they had about six or eight children. On a business trip to China at the turn of the century, he passed away, leaving his wife and children in Vancouver. My aunt's stories were always about how the family struggled to survive with her widowed mother leading and trying to provide for the family, and having an uncle who was very disdainful of women and thought that all girl children were not useful. The story was built up around that and what Lillian would do to try and help. My aunt was, herself, taken out of school in grade 3 and sent to work in a white household as a servant."

The Curses of Third Uncle, though set in Canada, uses the revolution in Imperial China as its backdrop. In 1909, Vancouver's Lillian Ho, 14, and the eldest of four daughters, goes searching for her father, who, after five months, has not yet returned from a mysterious trip. Traveling to Revelstoke, she learns that her father had been collecting funds for Dr. Sun Yat-sen's fight against the empire. In Lillian's father's absence, his younger brother, the title's

Third Uncle, tries to claim headship of the family, and threatens to send these "totally useless" women back to China. As the plot unfolds, Lillian discovers that her wastrel uncle has betrayed his own brother to the Empire's agents.

Paul's next book, *Saltwater City: The Chinese in Vancouver,* was for adults, and developed out of his volunteer work. "The year 1986 was Vancouver's centennial, and we in Chinatown decided to do a museum exhibit on 100 years of the Chinese. We went on a major artifact hunt looking for stuff, and then we mounted everything professionally. Having come up with a descriptive catalog of the pieces, we thought we should try and publish it. We took it to an editor who said, 'This is not a catalog. It's a book.' Because we were all volunteers, we needed somebody to write the history portion, and that 'somebody' turned out to be me. I took a leave of absence from work for about five months to do all the research, to do the interviews and to pull the book together."

Profusely illustrated with photographs, "*Saltwater City*'s main text is essentially a narrative, an educational text. The sidebars and the personal stories are to let people speak for themselves. I very much believe that oral history provides a sense of power that comes from the first-person voice. In a way, it's for people to put at peace what they have to say about certain issues and memories. There's a range of voices, regret, bitterness, anger. I wanted to convey that mix because ultimately that was the humanity of that community. I think it's very hard in this day and age to imagine a society that was so openly racist that it was alright to write violently racist things or for young children to throw stones and rocks at Chinese. The narrative text of *Saltwater City* sets out the skeleton of the system. It doesn't give any emotional sense of how these people lived with it, coped with it, survived. That part comes from oral history."

The concept for *Tales from Gold Mountain,* Paul's next children's book, he attributes to two sources. "I was reading an Edgar Allen Poe short story which started off, 'In the little town of . . . ,' and then Poe goes on to tell the story. And I thought, 'This is quite amazing. This man is writing a story that is so known that he has to conceal the identity of the place. This was the exact opposite of what I was working with, because here we have a people and a history that are absolutely not recognized.' I thought of 'ghost stories,' because, while my aunt was not a great teller of stories, she did have great fears of ghosts. When we were children, she would tell us about these fears of hers, and they used to terrify me because they were essentially about Chinese people, people I could understand.

"What I was trying to do with *Tales* was to pull together history and mythology and elevate history into another realm. It's fine for me to write narrative chronologies of what happened, but I was trying to hit another nerve in people, the nerve of their imagination, the point where we get surprised or slightly scared, and I think that happens best through fiction. With history, because it's 'this is

how it happened,' there is some sort of distance. No matter how well you write history, people don't value it. It's the past, and it's not relevant, but fiction has a broader appeal. It works on the mind in a different way, and so I was trying to write historical fiction through folktales.

"I wrote about 13 original stories, and Douglas & McIntyre selected eight for *Tales from Gold Mountain: Stories of the Chinese in the New World*. In the 19th century, 'Gold Mountain' was the term used in China for North America which was seen to be a land of riches by the poor peasant farmers." Winner of the 1990 National IODE Book Award, the tales vary greatly in their content and mood, but all expose aspects of the immigrants' experience in this new country. For instance, "The Revenge of the Iron Chink" is a powerful and clever story which reveals how some Chinese salmon factory workers "repaid" their greedy employer, who had callously replaced them with automated canning equipment.

One of the 13 original *Tales* stories also became a separate picturebook, *Roses Sing on New Snow*. The story, Paul says, "deals with one of the contradictions in Chinese-Canadian history, in that it's a predominantly male history, and that's because the first people who came over were predominantly male. The sex-ratio figures were horrifyingly high. However, there were small pockets of women, and I felt the need to write about them. As well, in this day and age, one cannot simply write about the stories and experiences of men, certainly not in an educational context.

"Additionally, I react against how girls are often raised in traditional Chinese families. I've been in classrooms where I see Chinese girls who are very quiet, timid and well behaved, while the boys are raucous, noisy and lively. In my mind, I know these are children being raised by immigrant parents. I want to give girls images of stronger, interesting women, and I think certainly *Curses of Third Uncle* was another attempt.

"I also attribute my inclusion of strong women to my aunt, simply because, being the kind of woman she was, she was a major influence on my life. My uncle was more of a distant person and not around. He certainly didn't tell me stories, and so my aunt was always more accessible. I certainly draw from her life more than I do my uncle's. I was just closer to her."

Subtitled *A Delicious Tale, Roses Sing on New Snow* is the story of Maylin, who toils thanklessly seven days a week cooking in her father's New World restaurant. Whenever anyone compliments the chef, Maylin's father says that his two sons are responsible for the food. On the occasion of the governor of South China's visit to Chinatown, each restaurant is invited to create a special dish for a banquet, and Maylin concocts something she calls "Roses sing on new snow." The governor is so impressed by Maylin's dish that he requests its creator show his own cook how to make it, so that he can present it to the emperor. Naturally, Maylin's father gives the credit to his two fat, lazy sons, but they cannot replicate the dish's taste. Finally, Maylin's father must reveal her role, and she finally gets the respect and honor due her.

Paul's most recent book is a novel, *Breakaway*. "Very early in my research into Vancouver's Chinese community, I came across the Chinese Students Soccer Club, a trophy-winning team with tremendous community support. They'd always been heroes to me, and I wanted to do something with them. The idea of writing a story around the soccer team was a very strong motivation, but the story has changed incredibly from the time I originally wrote the outline, somewhere about 1983–84. It shifted away from the soccer team itself, as this sort of heroic role model that I had in my mind, to focus more on an individual 'teacher,' Kwok, who has his own struggles. In a way, the soccer team becomes a backdrop, an option to him. The new focus surprised me, because it switched from the team to a character who is more central and sympathetic for the readers."

Set in Depression-ridden Vancouver of 1932, *Breakaway* effectively utilizes the enduring adolescent theme of identity while exposing historical, yet contemporary, social issues. Though the title could refer to a scoring opportunity in soccer, a sport in which 18-year-old Kwok-Ken Wong, a second-generation Chinese-Canadian, excels, it more aptly indicates Kwok's desire to escape both his Chinese heritage and his immigrant father's expectation that he will eventually take over the family's debt-ridden farm. Kwok and older sister Ying are the only Chinese students in their all-white, friendless high school. In one pivotal day, a helpless Kwok twice feels racism's harshest stings. Not only is the academically well-qualified Kwok denied the scholarship he requires for university tuition, but he is dropped from the city's all-star soccer team because he is a "Chinaman." Kwok's mother, determined that her son will secure a better life via a university education, is prepared to marry Ying to a Chinese businessman in order to secure the "bride money." When another financial opportunity—in the form of a wealthy white land developer—presents itself, Kwok unsuccessfully tries to persuade his father to sell the farm. Ultimately, by playing on Vancouver's Chinese Soccer Team against Caucasian teams, Kwok discovers who he really is, and learns that his identity can include his cultural roots and his father's values.

Paul characterizes *Breakaway* as "a major undertaking to write. One of the advantages of my Vancouver job was that we were on a four-day work-week. We worked long days from 8:30 to 5:30 with short lunches. Because we had a three-day weekend, I was able to use that time to write *Curses*. We got down to the serious writing of *Breakaway* after I moved to Toronto in 1988, to become first the multicultural coordinator for the Archives of Ontario, and then a policy analyst in Ontario's Ministry of Citizenship. Here I was, in what were rather stressful jobs, struggling to write a long novel. Getting into the writing of a novel is very hard if you don't have large chunks of time set aside for it. It was very easy for me to write *Tales* while I was working because they were shorter pieces and easier to think through. But doing a novel while I was working was very difficult and took a long time. By the time I came to Toronto, *Saltwater City* and *Tales* were essentially done. We spent about five years to-and-froing over the soccer story, recasting the outline, writing the complete manuscript and then rewriting the manuscript over and over. It was very trying to find time to focus and pull things together, but I have a really fine editor, Shelley Tanaka. It's been a good experience. I'm one writer who works *with* editors. All of my writing gets a fair amount of editorial critique. It usually gets chopped down in length. I lose about 50 to 100 pages by the time we settle on the final draft."

Young readers can anticipate two more Yee titles. "Groundwood has said they'd like to do another of the folktales as a picturebook, and they already have the story. Since *Tales* has come out, I've probably written another dozen or so. I'm also finishing a nonfiction historical piece. Basically, it's a fairly straightforward history of the Chinese in Canada from 1858 up to the present, looking at recent immigrations and the more recent issues, but couched in very broad terms to make it accessible to school users in grades 6 up."

Speculating on the future, Paul says, "My own personal interest right now is to work on something at a more adult level, to address different issues and to look at the creative process differently. When I write for children, I have a fairly good idea of where I want to take the novel in terms of what the novel is saying to children. Usually my themes are about history, identity and the acceptance of who one is. Those are the basic ideas that I seem to go back to over and over. For adults, you look at different issues, and you write more broadly for them. There's more leeway given to you about what you can create and entertain adults with. So, I'm thinking of writing a novel, again in the historical context, about the Chinese in Vancouver, but it would be different from all of these things which have been mainly aimed at children."

This is not to say that Paul has abandoned his juvenile audience forever. "I have other outlines, and, if somebody were to approach me to say, 'We would really like you to do a historical novel,' I might do it."

TITLE COMMENTARY

TEACH ME TO FLY, SKYFIGHTER! (1983)

Children's Book News

SOURCE: A review of *Teach Me to Fly, Skyfighter!*, in *Children's Book News*, Toronto, Vol. 6, No. 2, September, 1983.

Vancouver author Paul Yee has written four short stories dealing with the Chinese community in Vancouver. They centre on a group of grade 5 students who have become friends. Despite their friendship, however, there are trying times for all of them which sometimes lead to arguments.

Some of the children are second-generation Canadians, others are recent immigrants from Hong Kong and at least one is from a rural community in China. The differences in their attitudes towards social customs and their approach to life in Canada are focal points in the book.

The stories point out the effect on children of racism, of being a Chinese-Canadian who can't understand or speak the language of parents or grandparents, and of being unable to understand a new language or culture.

Children of all backgrounds will identify with these stories, but they will be particularly appreciated by children who have recently arrived in Canada or who are members of a visible minority born in Canada.

Frieda Wishinsky

SOURCE: A review of *Teach Me to Fly, Skyfighter!: And Other Stories,* in *Quill and Quire,* Vol. 49, No. 10, October, 1983, p. 16.

Teach Me to Fly, Skyfighter! is a series of four related stories about four children—three of them are Chinese and one Caucasian—living in the Strathcona area of Vancouver, a predominantly Chinese and immigrant neighbourhood. Author Paul Yee has succeeded in portraying the personalities, interests, and dreams of four 11-year-old friends whose voices ring true throughout.

The title story, about our need for links to the past, is perhaps the most powerful. Sharon, a second generation Chinese girl, feels distant from her rich Chinese heritage until she meets Skyfighter, an old friend of her grandfather and a talented kite-flyer. Skyfighter tells her how kite-flying helped him escape from the hardship and loneliness of an immigrant's life. "You can't work and sleep your whole life away without finding something to make you smile," he tells her.

The other three stories are about a first generation Chinese boy who wants to become "Canadian" as quickly as possible, a new immigrant from Hong Kong who learns kung-fu to gain confidence, and a Caucasian girl who wants to prove herself as more than just a girl from a housing project.

The book ends with a short history of Strathcona and the Chinese community in British Columbia, which ties in well with the stories. *Teach Me to Fly, Skyfighter!* is not only a useful addition to the study of multiculturalism but also a moving collection of stories about young Canadians.

Mary Ainslie Smith

SOURCE: "Great Escapes," in *Books in Canada,* Vol. 12, No. 10, December, 1983, p. 17.

Teach Me to Fly, Skyfighter! is the title of a book of four stories by Paul Yee, illustrated by Sky Lee. Each story features one of four young friends who live in the Strathcona neighbourhood of Vancouver. Three are Chinese Canadians, two recent immigrants, one Canadian-born. Their stories tell of their responses to the conflict between their heritage and their own personal aims and ambitions. For instance, Sharon, the Canadian-born one, rebels at the way Chinese things are forced on her. She is resentful that she looks Chinese, because she feels Canadian. A kite given to her by an old friend of her grandfather's in Chinatown flies beautifully, and at last something Chinese makes sense to her and she can feel happy and proud of what she is.

The last story is about Christine Thomas, the non-Asian member of the group. She lives alone with her mother in a housing project and is considered a problem at school. Her decision to try out for an all-girls soccer camp at last gives her a sense of direction, while the support she receives from her friend Sharon increases her sense of self-worth. These stories are sensitively written and nicely capture the home, school, and leisure life of the four friends.

THE CURSES OF THIRD UNCLE (1986)

Mary Ainslie Smith

SOURCE: A review of *The Curses of Third Uncle,* in *Books in Canada,* Vol. 15, No. 9, December, 1986, p. 18.

Paul Yee's *The Curses of Third Uncle* is set in the Chinese community of Vancouver in 1909. The main character, 14-year-old Lillian, is frustrated in many ways by her Chinese heritage. She is painfully aware of the way most whites treat the Chinese, but she is impatient that some Chinese living in Canada are not as anxious to assimilate as she is. She is also frustrated by the curtailed roles assigned to mere daughters, and wants to live her own life in spite of these restrictions.

Lillian's life is disrupted by the distant revolution in China. Her father—who, as she finds out, has been secretly collecting money in support of the revolution—disappears, and the family, having no livelihood, might be sent back to China. Lillian sets out to discover what happened to her father, and in spite of herself comes to understand more about what special gifts her heritage can give her.

Annette Goldsmith

SOURCE: "Illuminating Adventures with Young People from Long Ago," in *Quill and Quire,* Vol. 52, No. 12, December, 1986, p. 14.

Paul Yee's *The Curses of Third Uncle* focuses on a second-generation Canadian's ambiguous feelings towards her double heritage—a theme first explored in his previous book, *Teach Me To Fly, Skyfighter.* Lillian Ho is a 14-

year-old Chinese, Canadian-born, who lives in Vancouver's Chinatown in 1909. Her family is poor, with another baby on the way. Suddenly Lillian's father, the principal bread-winner, disappears. Gradually, Lillian discovers that her father raises money from local supporters for Dr Sun Yat-Sen's revolution in China. The more she pieces together, the greater her fear and determination to find her father—especially when she learns that the unscrupulous Third Uncle, her father's brother, is plotting against him.

The Curses of Third Uncle is an exciting, fast-paced, well-written tale of intrigue in a society where Chinatown is home and a wealthy white neighbourhood strange and exotic. The dialogue, however, sounds somewhat too contemporary for the period. The pencil illustrations also have too modern a feel.

The strong female characters are made all the more prominent by references to women warriors of Chinese legend. The book teeters dangerously on the brink of despair when Lillian learns of her father's death, but she and her mother rally at the end.

The reader might balk at some unlikely circumstances in the plot. Would Third Uncle really hide an important letter where Lillian could so easily find it? And would two young women be allowed to embark on a train journey to an isolated town on their own?

Raymond E. Jones

SOURCE: "Different Dragons," in *Canadian Literature,* No. 116, Spring, 1988, p. 168.

Paul Yee's *The Curses of Third Uncle* . . . combines romantic suspense and gritty historical realism. Set in British Columbia in 1909, the tale traces the efforts of a young Chinese girl, Lillian (Ah-Lai) Ho, to find her father, who has been trying to gather funds for the revolutionaries in China. Lillian's circular journey takes her to the wilderness outside Revelstoke, where she discovers her inner strengths. Returning to Vancouver, she is able to stop a counter-revolutionary plot and to accept that her father has been murdered. She displays such courage in overcoming her fear of being sent to China that her mother overcomes her own fear of Canada and decides that the family can stay in their new land.

Although part of a publisher's series designed to make Canadian history interesting for children, Yee's novel avoids the cloying didacticism and boring pedagogy of a series book. Yee's glimpses into Chinese-Canadian life are as relevant as they are fascinating. They create an exciting, exotic atmosphere, and they intensify respect for Lillian's courage when she proves that Chinese girls are not, as her "third uncle" declares, "garbage." Like the female warriors in the traditional tales, Lillian proves they can be heroes. Yee falters when he tries to connect the girl's personal struggle with her people's similar struggle with fear of the Chinese emperor. The connection is nei-

ther as smooth nor as coherent as it should be, but it does suggest that a people's courage begins with courageous individuals like Lillian and her father.

SALTWATER CITY: AN ILLUSTRATED HISTORY OF THE CHINESE IN VANCOUVER (1988)

Bruce Serafin

SOURCE: A review of *Saltwater City,* in *Books in Canada,* Vol. 18, No. 4, May, 1989, p. 5.

Excellent layout, superb photographs, and an artful combination of photography and the printed word make *Saltwater City,* by Paul Yee, resemble a good modern textbook. There are photographic captions in bold face, sidebars printed on grey-tinted paper that generally run along the bottom of the page and tell a story separate from the main narrative, photographic reproductions of documents and newspaper stories, italicized columns that give the transcribed voices of various members of Vancouver's Chinese-Canadian community, and a master text in wider columns that pins the whole thing together. The disadvantage of this textbook format is that it gives *Saltwater City* a somewhat impersonal tone; rhetoric and prose style have been subordinated to allow the quick comprehension of a huge mass of information. The photographs themselves, however, encourage reflectiveness: seen in sequence like this, they tell a story that is both wretched and triumphant. To compare the Wongs and Lees of contemporary Vancouver to the skinny young labourers dressed in nothing but loincloths that you see in one stunning picture is to experience the shocking force of historical change over a century.

TALES FROM GOLD MOUNTAIN: STORIES OF THE CHINESE IN THE NEW WORLD (1989)

Peter Carver

SOURCE: A review of *Tales from Gold Mountain,* in *Quill and Quire,* Vol. 55, No. 12, December, 1989, p. 23.

The jacket copy for this handsome collection of stories about the Chinese in the New World describes Paul Yee as "a typical Chinese-Canadian . . . caught between two worlds and yearning to move away from the neighbourhood."

It is fortunate for young readers that Yee resisted the temptation to turn away from his heritage. Already he has two children's books about the Chinese-Canadian community to his credit, and this book is a powerful distillation of his people's experiences as they came to seek a new life across the Pacific.

Coming to North America more than 150 years ago, the first Chinese immigrants did not have an easy time of it.

They were visibly different from the host populace, and their capacity for hard work was exploited in the building of railroads and other great 19th-century industrial projects.

But Yee's stories are anything but gloomy. He tells us about the beautiful Yenna, who puts a light in her window for the young man she loves when he leaves for the northern gold-fields. He has taken with him her gift of ginger root to remember her by—and the ginger finally brings him back to her. In another tale, young Chu comes to North America to find his father among the thousands of Chinese working on the railway. When the son joins the work gangs, he discovers his father's fate and is able to appease his tortured spirit. In another, a greedy boss literally explodes when he is tricked into eating too much bread.

The stunning illustrations of Simon Ng add great resonance to the book. The end result is a collection of absorbing yarns that will be enjoyed by young readers from a variety of backgrounds.

In addition, *Tales of Gold Mountain* is important for its assertion of the Chinese tradition in a North American context, evidence of the richness that this most ancient of cultures has brought to the New World.

Betsy Hearne

SOURCE: A review of *Tales from the Gold Mountain: Stories of the Chinese in the New World,* in *Bulletin of the Center for Children's Books,* Vol. 43, No. 7, March, 1990, p. 178.

Eight original stories—brilliantly illustrated [by Simon Ng] with eerily textured, mask-like portraits—make a haunting companion to use with the tales in Laurence Yep's *The Rainbow People,* which were drawn from a WPA oral narrative project. Yee never indulges in stylistic pretensions as he releases these dramatic blends of realism and legend from what seems long silence. The manager of a fish cannery turns trickster to foil a greedy boss, a young man arranges burial for a group of Chinese railroad workers after meeting his father's ghost in a deserted tunnel ("Take chopsticks; they shall be our bones"), a young woman's gift of ginger root saves her betrothed's life and, eventually, their love. A few of the tales focus on the personal price of clashes between old traditions and new influences. From romance to sly humor to conflicts of the living and dead, these carry mythical overtones that lend the characters unforgettable dimension—humans achieving supernatural power in defying their fate of physical and cultural oppression. The combination of Yee's piercing portrayals and Ng's monumental images against background effects of cracked canvas must—as the author hopes in his afterword—"carve a place in the North American imagination for the many generations of Chinese who have settled here as Canadians and Americans, and help them stake their claim to be known as pioneers, too."

Hanna B. Zeiger

SOURCE: A review of *Tales from Gold Mountain: Stories of the Chinese in the New World,* in *The Horn Book Magazine,* Vol. LXVI, No. 4, July-August, 1990, pp. 459-60.

The eight stories in this collection are original; however, they are firmly rooted in the real experiences of the Chinese who came to North America seeking the prosperity of Gold Mountain. Though Mr. Yee has drawn on tales he heard growing up in Vancouver's Chinatown and on research into the lives of the Chinese who settled in Canada, the stories contain many parallels with the experiences of the Chinese in the United States. Told in richly evocative language, the stories skillfully blend the hardships and dangers of frontier life in a new country with the ancient attitudes and traditions brought over from China. In **"Spirits of the Railway,"** young Chu crosses the ocean to try to find news of his father. Having gotten a job on the railway tunneling through "towering ranges of dark raw rock," he is confronted one night by the ghost of his father, whose body, along with other Chinese workers, was dumped into the river after a premature dynamite blast. Performing a ritual burial, the son is able to bring peace to his father's spirit. Discrimination and racial hostility are the basis for two of the stories. In **"Forbidden Fruit,"** Farmer Fong watches his only daughter pine away because his prejudice has separated her from Farmer Johnson, the man she loves. **"Gambler's Eyes"** is a haunting tale of a young man mocked for his mixed blood who goes through life with his eyes sealed shut until, one day, his eyes flash open. "They glinted blue-green, sharp as mountain ice, hard as emeralds." The monumental figures in Simon Ng's illustrations seem chiseled in stone, as if they were statues paying belated homage to the dignity, courage, and perseverance of these pioneers. The images in this book will stay with the reader for a long time.

Gernot Wieland with Alexandra Wieland

SOURCE: "Familiarity and Alienation," in *Canadian Literature,* No. 130, Autumn, 1991, pp. 142-3.

The Chinese immigrant experience is explored in eight stories in this handsomely produced book: **"Spirits of the Railway," "Sons and Daughters," "The Friends of Kwan Ming," "Ginger for the Heart," "Gambler's Eyes," "Forbidden Fruit," "Rider Chan and the Night River,"** and **"The Revenge of the Iron Chink."** The stories can be classified as "folk tales," sometimes with fairy tale motifs, sometimes without. Obviously the book is not meant to be a chronicle of the Chinese coming to Canada, but the reader is presented with the floods and famines which drove many Chinese from their homeland; he is likewise presented with the harsh realities facing the newcomers in the New World where they yet had to establish themselves. Though racism is not an overt topic, several scenes in which the white man exploits the Chinese gently hint that the newcomers had to suffer that indignity, too.

Several of the stories can be grouped together thematically. **"Spirits of the Railway"** and **"Rider Chan and the Night River"** are ghost stories in which a fearless hero comes to face the world of the dead and by righting a wrong that had been done to them overcomes the obstacles they place in the path of the living. **"Ginger for the Heart"** and **"Forbidden Fruit"** are love stories, the first ending happily with the couple getting married, the second unhappily with the woman wasting away and dying. **"Forbidden Fruit"** also touches on the tensions arising from an interracial relationship, especially when the partner of the other race also happens to be poor. Interracial problems are also explored in **"Gambler's Eyes,"** the story of a man who pretends to be blind because his white mother had given him blue-green eyes, and whites and Chinese alike had mocked his mixed blood. **"The Friends of Kwan Ming"** and **"The Revenge of the Iron Chink"** deal with exploitation of the Chinese at the hands of white men, and the solidarity of the Chinese that makes them triumph over their tormentors in the end. **"Sons and Daughters"** stands alone; it deals with a rich Chinese merchant who is disappointed at having only daughters since that means to him that the family name will not survive into the next generation. Merchant Moy tries to trick fate, but is tricked in turn.

These brief plot summaries suggest the range of the stories. The stories themselves are told in a simple, straightforward style. There is not much description, but when there is, it is accomplished in a few short and powerful sentences, as in this passage from **"Spirits of the Railway"**:

> When the morning mist lifted, Chu's mouth fell open. On both sides of the rushing river, gray mountains rose like walls to block the sky. The rock face dropped into ragged cliffs that only eagles could ascend and jutted out from cracks where scrawny trees clung. Never before had he seen such towering ranges of dark raw rock.

The style obviously suits the simplicity of the folk tale; it evokes rather than exhausts.

The stories entertain children and adults alike; I read the book to my seven-year old daughter and she was delighted. The sparsity of illustrations [by Simon Ng] (only one per tale) did not bother her; she was willing to let her imagination roam in the landscapes presented to her. She "liked" each one of the stories, but to my surprise she showed a marked preference for the two ghost stories; I had kept these last because I did not know how she would react to the more scary scenes, but she put my parental caution to shame by wishing to have these stories read repeatedly. She enjoyed the thrill of danger and was relieved by the positive outcome.

Some of the distinctly Chinese flavour of the book may be beyond the grasp of a seven-year old, but it adds a special dimension for the adult reader who, whether he is Chinese or not, will find himself both within and without

the story; the universality of the folk motifs pulls him into it, the foreignness of the characters leaves him without. In so doing, Paul Yee creates for the reader the same sense of familiarity and alienation which the Chinese immigrants must have felt when they first set foot in a Canadian Chinatown.

ROSES SING ON NEW SNOW: A DELICIOUS TALE (1992)

Karen Hutt

SOURCE: A review of *Roses Sing on New Snow: A Delicious Tale,* in *Booklist,* Vol. 88, No. 13, March 1, 1992, p. 1288.

Seven days a week, Maylin cooks in her father's restaurant in Chinatown, but her culinary successes are attributed to her fat, lazy brothers. When the governor of South China comes to town, Maylin creates a delectable dish called "roses sing on new snow" for a banquet in his honor. The governor is so impressed with the dish that he wants to present it to his emperor. He orders that it be prepared in front of his cook, but the brothers' culinary efforts are unsatisfactory. Even cooking side-by-side with Maylin, the governor is unable to re-create the dish. As Maylin explains to him, "This is a dish of the New World. . . . You cannot re-create it in the Old." Yee tells his "delicious tale" with grace and economy, and [Harvey] Chan's memorable watercolors portray scenes of Chinatown in the early 1900s, depicting characters full of emotion and expression. With both substance and visual appeal, this is a book to savor.

Elizabeth S. Watson

SOURCE: A review of *Roses Sing on New Snow: A Delicious Tale,* in *The Horn Book Magazine,* Vol. LXVIII, No. 2, March-April, 1992, p. 196.

Delectable from beginning to end, this feminist story, set in the late nineteenth century in a generic, nonspecific New World Chinatown, is delicately told and illustrated. Maylin is the primary cook in her father's restaurant but receives no recognition; indeed, her slothful brothers are reputed to be the geniuses behind the restaurant's best dishes. When a government official asks for a particular dish—called Roses Sing on New Snow—to be prepared in his presence, the truth begins to emerge. Moving swiftly to a satisfactory conclusion, the tale offers a slice of life from immigrant Chinese history that could have played out in either the United States or Canada. The pictures [by Harvey Chan], full of drama and movement, are equally strong in establishing a setting and depicting the characters in the story.

Betsy Hearne

SOURCE: A review of *Roses Sing on New Snow: A De-*

licious Tale, in *Bulletin of the Center for Children's Books,* Vol. 45, No. 11, July-August, 1992, p. 307.

Like the stories about Chinese immigrants in Yee's *Tales from Gold Mountain* this crosses realism with tradition for a folkloric effect. Young Maylin is a heroine whose victimization by her father and two brothers backfires when an Imperial governor from the old country discovers she's the superlative cook who has created a dish called "Roses Sing on New Snow." No longer can the men in her family take credit for the restaurant's superior food; nor, as it turns out, will the Emperor of China ever taste it, for Maylin's talent is uniquely her own and uniquely of the New World. Chan's watercolors cast the Canadian frontier setting in ruddy tones. Most telling is his varied use of perspective, including a closeup of the furious governor's eyes and nose and later a picture of the diminutive Maylin flanked by towering guards. Vivid art and clean writing are graced by a neatly feminist ending: "From that day on Maylin was renowned in Chinatown as a great cook and a wise person."

Marnie Parsons

SOURCE: "Changing Tunes," in *Canadian Children's Literature,* No. 70, Summer, 1993, pp. 93-4.

Maylin, the heroine of Paul Yee and Harvey Chan's *Roses Sing on New Snow,* has a voice of her own and uses it to advantage in what has been subtitled "a delicious tale." Another "tale from gold mountain," this story continues Yee's project of giving voice to the Chinese experience in North America through the forms of traditional folktales. The occasional awkward phrase aside, Yee's text is interesting and nicely paced. The story of how Maylin gets the kudos she deserves for her delicious new dish, "Roses sing on new snow," despite her father's and two brothers' attempts to take the credit, and of how she stands up to the governor of South China to teach him and her family a necessary lesson about the importance of culinary individuality, is clearly in sympathy with feminism, even if the heroine does spend most of her time in the kitchen. Maylin is a bold, creative and hard-working woman who defines the patriarchal structures of the story's historical period to make a statement about her own identity and abilities. Her defiance effectively changes the tune of the men in the story, liberating herself in the process.

A marvellous complement to Yee's story are the illustrations by Harvey Chan.

BREAKAWAY (1994)

Patty Lawlor

SOURCE: A review of *Breakaway,* in *Quill and Quire,* Vol. 60, No. 4, April, 1994, p. 39.

Fiction, non-fiction, picture book, short story. You name

it, and Paul Yee has written it to let readers, young and older, know about the Chinese experience in Canada.

Breakaway, Yee's latest offering, is young-adult fiction. In its setting, this book is a companion piece to Yee's 1986 *The Curses of Third Uncle.* Although *Breakaway* takes place twentysomething years after *Curses,* British Columbia is, again, the story's backdrop. A struggle between generations and cultures is, again, at the heart of the story. Old-World politics are still a major concern for the Chinese community in Canada. The Chinese in B.C. are still very much a people apart.

Breakaway's Kwok-ken Wong is 18 years old. He is Canadian-born and wishes his name were Clark. It is 1932, and his parents, pig farmers and market gardeners, are struggling to break even. To Kwok, his father is obsessively thrifty, traditional to the extreme, and far too attached to his land. Kwok believes his mother deserves a much better life. He can't understand why his sister might agree to an arranged marriage to help bolster the family finances. He is appalled that his parents would expect or ask it of her when, in his eyes, a recent offer of $1,200 for their land represents a fortune. Kwok's outrage at his parents' treatment of his sister would ring truer if he didn't discredit her himself by claiming to be "the only Chinese" in the school they both attend.

At school, Kwok is a good student. Encouraged by his school principal, he has applied for a university scholarship. His soccer skills have earned him a place on the Selects, an all-star team with corporate sponsorship. But when his scholarship application is rejected without explanation and he's cut from the Selects for being "a Chinaman," Kwok sees the world closing in on him. He desperately wants to fight back. By agreeing, at last, to play for the Chinese community's own soccer team in a championship game, he discovers a sense of community and pride. At the same time, circumstances cause him to rally to his father's cause in a bittersweet conclusion to the story.

Breakaway is a well-written novel with staying power. Because it presents examples of the stupidity, violence, and ugliness associated with culture clash, the book will be useful in senior-elementary and high-school programs about other cultures and racism. But the story that Yee has so deftly created will also appeal to readers for its sports and family aspects.

Margaret Mackey

SOURCE: A review of *Breakaway,* in *CM: A Reviewing Journal of Canadian Materials for Young People,* Vol. 22, No. 4, September, 1994, p. 139.

Paul Yee has written a rich and detailed account of one boy's life in the Chinese community around Vancouver during the Great Depression. Kwok-ken Wong works hard on his father's farm, studies intensively to meet his mother's ambition for him to attend university, and plays soccer with the school team. Poverty plagues the farm, and racism in the white community undermines his other activities.

Kwok does not seem to belong anywhere. His white schoolmates ignore him and he is banned from the local all-star team and rejected for a scholarship because he is Chinese. On the other hand, he does not want to associate with the Chinese community in Vancouver; he scorns their drinking and gambling ways.

Yee does a good job of conveying the complexity and ambivalence of Kwok-ken's life. He does not gloss over the drawbacks of life on a poor farm, and he makes no attempt to disguise the crippling sexism in Chinese customs which deny all opportunities to Kwok's sister Ying. Kwok's increasing bitterness over his inability to fit in anywhere is well handled.

The ending is rather abrupt and somewhat sentimental. The white characters are, without exception, weak and prejudiced. Nevertheless, this book contributes a valuable picture of a fascinating and complex time and world.

Ronald Jobe

SOURCE: A review of *Breakaway,* in *Journal of Adolescent & Adult Literacy,* Vol. 39, No. 5, February, 1996, pp. 431-2.

What was it like to be the only Chinese high school student in Vancouver during the depression of the 1930s?

Although he is a good student and an exceptional soccer player, Kwok-ken Wong has to face reality. He and his sister live with their parents in a small house on the river flats. His father raises pigs for sale, and Kwok must go with him to Chinatown to collect the slops for pigfood. It is a dirty, smelly task done amidst racist taunts from bystanders.

Kwok wants to go on to University and to continue to play soccer, but he has to help his father with the farm. Land is everything to Kwok's father, and despite the hard times he is the last of the Chinese immigrants to still have any. When Kwok does not get a soccer scholarship because of his Chinese name, and when White business interests apply pressure to buy his father's land, Kwok realizes he must give up his dreams to help his family. Even his sister agrees to marry a man she does not particularly like because he is successful in business and will be able to help the family.

Yee gives a sensitive yet hard-edged portrait of the life facing a talented young Chinese man in the 1930s. Readers glimpse the stern reality of the depression—lack of jobs, shortage of money, and constant worry about food. The physical requirements of daily life make it seem almost overwhelming. The novel contains a marvelous image of a determined mother, one who insists her son stay in school and do well, ignoring the objections of her husband.

Yee's novel gives great insight into the feelings and actions of a teenager. Through the lively and at times intense dialogue and personal introspections readers are able to sense Kwok's frustration, hopes, dreams, and defeating reality. I have found that encouraging students to write a journal or diary, as if they were Kwok, during the reading of the novel, gives them an opportunity to internalize Kwok's feelings and may indeed give them a brief opportunity to walk in his shoes.

Additional coverage of Yee's life and career is contained in the following sources published by Gale Research: *Contemporary Authors,* Vol. 135; *Junior DISCovering Authors (CD-ROM);* and *Something about the Author,* Vol. 67.

Jane Yolen

1939-

American author of fiction, nonfiction, poetry, literary folktales, and plays.

Major works include *Dragon's Blood: A Fantasy* (1982), *Children of the Wolf* (1984), *Owl Moon* (1987), *Piggins* (1987), *The Devil's Arithmetic* (1988).

INTRODUCTION

A prolific versatile creator of both fiction and nonfiction for children and young adults, Yolen is best known for her inventive use of folk themes, her storytelling skill, and her musical use of language. Ranging from picture books to poetry, Mother Goose to musical plays, a time fantasy about the Holocaust to humorous science fiction for beginning readers, nonfiction about kite-flying to the life of George Fox, Yolen's more than one hundred twenty-five books reflect her literary heritage, the influence of religion and song, and her deep and absorbing love of folk culture. The settings of her stories reveal her wide travels, from Greek olive groves to Welsh seasides, while her three growing children expanded her repertoire from juvenile to young adult fiction. Whether writing for children or teenagers, however, Yolen's fascination with traditional literature, including the Arthurian legends and ethnic folktales, and her commitment to pass on the stories she discovers led her renowned editor Ann K. Beneduce to dub her the "American Hans Christian Andersen."

Biographical Information

Born in New York City to a family of storytellers and writers, Yolen learned to read at an early age and was writing plays, songs, and stories from first grade on. After sixth grade, she attended Hunter, a school for the gifted, and continued to write stories and songs, and to perform as a ballet dancer, alto soloist, and pianist. Yolen, born a Jew, attended a Quaker camp for two summers as a youngster, where she learned about pacifism and storytelling, and later worked at an American Friends Service Committee work camp in Ohio. Her best friend in high school introduced her to the rituals of Catholicism. All three religions influence her writings. After majoring in literature and minoring in religion at Smith College, where she wrote poetry and sang folk songs to earn pocket money, Yolen moved to Greenwich Village and began to work for various New York publishing houses. In 1962, she married David Stemple, a computer programmer and photographer, and began work as an assistant editor at Alfred A. Knopf. Three years later, Yolen and her husband both quit their jobs, bought a Volkswagen camper, and made a nine-month tour of Europe. Once back in the United

States, they settled in Massachusetts where they began to raise their family—Heidi, Adam, and Jason. Yolen also acquired an agent and began to see her books emerge in print. Today she and her husband live on Phoenix Farm in western Massachusetts where she writes her music and books. Yolen also writes fiction and nonfiction for adults. Her daughter Heidi, a probation officer, coauthored *Meet the Monsters* (1996), son Adam wrote the musical arrangements for two of her books, and son Jason took the photographs for two others, including the autobiographical *Letter from Phoenix Farm* (1992).

Major Works

Dragon's Blood: A Fantasy, the first book in Yolen's "Pit Dragon" trilogy, features fifteen-year-old Jakkin, who steals and trains a hatchling dragon with whom he discovers an extraordinary mental bond. The suspenseful tale, involving secretly training the dragon to be a champion fighter, a touch of romance, and the plausible details of a society based on bond servant and master on the planet Austar IV has been favorably likened to Anne McCaffrey's popular Pern books. In *Children of the Wolf,* Yolen began with the true story of a 1920s case in India where two little girls who were raised by a wolf were found and brought to an orphanage. Taking the point of view of fourteen-year-old Mohandas, a resident orphan, the author describes his frustrations as he tries to teach the sisters human speech and behavior. At the same time, Yolen raises the larger question of the validity of the effort to forcibly humanize feral children. A delightful spoof on British mysteries for the younger crowd, *Piggins* is the pig-butler who serves dinner to the starchy guests of the foxy Reynards. When the lights go out and a diamond necklace disappears, Inspector Bayswater, a hound dog, is nonplussed, but Piggins picks up the clues and pinpoints the culprits. The picture book *Owl Moon* is a memorable account of Yolen's husband taking their daughter out on a New England winter night to look for an owl. Matching the spare, telling text, fellow owler John Schoenherr's Caldecott-winning watercolors dramatically evoke the night life, the cold, and the quiet. Although a Jew and a writer, Yolen had never been looked upon as a Jewish writer until *The Devil's Arithmetic*. Thirteen-year-old Hannah is bored by the annual Seder where her grandfather always recounts memories of how he and his sister survived death camp. Suddenly Hannah is transported back to 1942 where she is the Polish girl Chaya, caught among the villagers who are taken to a death camp, there to volunteer to die in the place of another girl Rivka. Instead of dying, she finds herself back in the present with a new appreciation of her heritage and the significance of memory.

Awards

Dragon's Blood was selected as a Children's Choice book from the International Reading Association and the Children's Book Council in 1983 and won the Parents' Choice Award in 1982 and the CRABbery Award in 1983. *The Stone Silenus* received the Parents' Choice Award in 1984, while *Piggins* and *The Three Bears Rhyme Book* won it in 1989. *Heart's Blood* was selected one of American Library Association's Best Books for Young Adults, 1984, and then Yolen received the 1986 Daedelus Award for "a body of work—fantasy and short fiction." *The Lullaby Songbook* and *The Sleeping Beauty* were each selected as a Child Study Association of America's Children's Book of the Year in 1987, and *Owl Moon* won the Caldecott Medal in 1988. In 1988 Yolen received the World Fantasy Award for *Favorite Folktales from around the World;* the Parents' Choice Silver Seal Award, the Jewish Book Council Award, and the Association of Jewish Libraries Award for *The Devil's Arithmetic;* and the Kerlan Award for "singular achievements in the creation of children's literature." In 1989 *The Devil's Arithmetic* was declared a Judy Lopez Honor Book and Nebula Award finalist, and *Piggins* won the Golden Sower Award from the Nebraska Library Association and the Charlotte Award from the New York State Reading Association. In 1990 Yolen received the Skylark Award and the Smith College Medal for her body of work; she received the Regina Medal in 1992. Many of her books have been selected by the Junior Literary Guild, and some of her manuscripts are held in the Kerlan Collection.

AUTHOR'S COMMENTARY

Jane Yolen

SOURCE: "Magic Mirrors: Society Reflected in the Glass of Fantasy," in *Children's Literature Association Quarterly,* Vol. 11, No. 2, Summer, 1986, pp. 88-90.

It surprises no one that authors are mired in society and that their work reflects current thinking. Though one must always take into account that books will be a year or more in production, such titles as Norma Klein's *Mom, the Wolfman, and Me* and Judy Blume's *Are You There God, It's Me, Margaret?* followed closely on the heels of the sexual revolution; Virginia Hamilton's *Zeely* and *The Planet of Junior Brown* appeared after the onset of President Johnson's "Great Society," and fictional accounts of child abuse, Indian rights, women's issues, and nuclear concerns all have been published in the decade of public awareness and social legislation on such issues.

It is a bit more difficult to track such authorial politics in fantasy books; but the issues and prejudices are still there if one digs deeply enough. Fantasy authors reflect the society they live in just as authors of realistic fiction do, though their work is like the wicked queen's magic mirror that did not always give her the answer she expected.

In Charles Kingsley's *Water Babies,* the picture of society's underbelly and the plight of the poor chimney sweeps is only the outward reflection, the first casting of the mirror. Kingsley's anti-black, anti-Jewish, and anti-Catholic attitudes, quite typical of a Victorian gentleman, are easy to excise in bowlderized editions of the book. But he also disguises his good fairy in the one impenetrable mask he can devise, that of an Irish washerwoman, and thus shows his anti-Irish and anti-female sentiments in the magic mirror.

Rudyard Kipling's otherwise brilliantly conceived fantasy *The Jungle Books* is marred for the in-depth reader by its jingoism and wog-hating attitudes. The feral child Mowgli is a "Godling" but he is also *only* an Indian, and Kipling's white English sentiments can be seen in the portraits of the other Indians in the book who are without exception venal, stupid, cruel, or helpless.

Hugh Lofting's *Dr. Dolittle* and Mary Travers' *Mary Poppins* share a cultural bias against peoples of color, though it was years before those beloved books were taken to task for their prejudices. The original Oompaloompas in Roald Dahl's *Charlie and the Chocolate Factory* have skin that is "almost black" and are "Pygmies . . . [i]mported direct from Africa." Imported as if they were no more than yardgoods. In later printings of the book, their skin color and place of origin are changed, but not the fact of their importation.

That is the bad news. The good news is that fantasy books deal with issues as thoroughly as realistic fiction—but one step removed. Randall Jarrell's *The Bat Poet* is about the artist in society. Robin McKinley's Demar books (*The Blue Sword, The Hero and the Crown*) are about active women in restrictive societies. Patricia Wrightson's *A Little Fear* is as effective and affecting a piece about old age as one might find.

It is the phrase "one-step removed" that we must consider. Fantasy fiction, by its very nature, takes us out of the real world. Sometimes it places us in another world altogether: Demar, Middle Earth, Earthsea, Prydain. Sometimes it changes the world we know in subtle ways, such as telling us about the tiny people who live behind the walls of our houses and "borrow" things. Or that in a very real barn, but out of our hearing and sight, a pig and a spider hold long, special conversations. Sometimes what makes a book a fantasy is the traveling between planets (Madeleine L'Engle's *A Wrinkle in Time*), between worlds (the Narnia and Oz books), between times (Pearce's *Tom's Midnight Garden* or Twain's *A Connecticut Yankee in King Arthur's Court*); or the traveler him/her/itself is from somewhere else, such as Nesbit's psammead.

By taking that one step away from the real or actual world, the author allows us to pretend that we are not talking about the everyday and the society in which we live. It is simply a convention we all agree to. A mask. In eighteenth century Venice, when masked balls were common, it became a convention that a person who wished to go about the street and be treated as if he were disguised needed only to wear a pin in the shape of a mask on his lapel. Thus accoutred, he was considered suitably masked and could act any part he wished without fear of shame or recognition. So fantasy novels go capped and belled into literate society, and we acknowledge that convention, saying in effect: this is not the real world we are talking of, this is a faerie land, a make-believe, where bunnies wear britches, bi-colored rock pythons speak, and little girls converse with packs of cards.

However the adults who write the books understand that beneath the pin there is a very real lapel. It is the children who do not always understand the convention. They mistake the pin for the lapel. They write to Maurice Sendak and ask for directions to the place where the wild things are. To them Narnia, Middle Earth and the Land Beneath the Waves are as real—indeed often more real—than the every day. And that is because the world of fantasy has three very persuasive parts to it. First, it has identifiable laws that always work. Second, it has a hero or heroine who is often lost, unlikely, powerless at first glance, or unrecognized, which makes him or her easy for the child reader (who feels lost, unlikely, unrecognized or powerless) to identify with. And third, in a fantasy world things end justly though not always happily. (G. K. Chesterton once wrote something to the effect that children desire justice in their stories because they know themselves innocent, while we fear ourselves guilty and so naturally prefer mercy.)

Therefore, it is important that writers of fantasy be doubly aware of the moral underpinnings of their work. As Lloyd Alexander wrote, "Fantasy, by its power to move

us so deeply, to dramatize, even melodramatize, morality, can be one of the most effective means of establishing a capacity for adult values."

Recently, I have been involved in the third book of a trilogy that has taken me over five years to write. The world of Austar IV, like its actual counterpart Australia in the 18th century, is a penal colony, a dumping ground for earth's jails. It is an arid, metal-poor planet, with great warm-blooded dragons its most outstanding animal-life. As I got deeper and deeper into the first novel, I realized that I did not like the social structure but, given the parameters I had carefully set up, it was a proper extrapolation of two centuries of settlement by a criminal fringe on a marginal world. It is a sexist, brutal, nasty world lit by a stark but beautiful landscape and a wonderful animal population, of which I was becoming more and more fond.

Now there is this to be understood about writing novels: novelists know very little about what they are doing when they start, and learn more and more as events, characters, and landscape take form. Every plunge into a new novel is a parallel adventure—for hero or heroine and novelist. Like our fictional counterparts, we are taking a journey into the unknown. Joseph Campbell's definition of the hero is a definition of an author as well: "A hero ventures forth from the world of common day into a region of supernatural wonder: fabulous forces are there encountered and a decisive victory is won: the hero comes back with the power to bestow boons on his fellow man." The author is *the hero venturing forth from the world of common every day* (my writing room is typical of its kind, the floor littered with research books, the pile of unanswered mail in the in-box, etc.). *Into the region of supernatural wonder,* which is what the fantasy world of the novel is because it only exists in the author's mind until it takes form on the page. And what of the *fabulous forces encountered?* Any writer who has ever struggled with slippery words, monstrous unwieldy plot elements, or a wildeyed character who will not be tamed, understands that phrase. *The decisive victory won* is not the Newbery Medal, or the ALA Notable List, or the Golden Kite Award; is simply getting the story down on paper recognizable as a novel. This is a victory indeed. (No mythic hero knows a thing about revisions. Once a battle is won, a grail discovered, a dragon slain—it does not have to be done again.) And what the novelist as hero *comes back with* is the power to enchant others with the story and inculcate his or her own particular moral vision. Only one letter needs to be changed to turn *boon* into book.

When I had gotten into the middle of **Dragon's Blood** and discovered I did not like the society in which women were considered second-class citizens, in which the best of the young people were ground into the dust, in which the supercilious Darwinism of the masters and the passive acceptance of the bonders made slavery a given, I had three choices. I could give up on the book, I could change the parameters of the society, or I could foment a revolution.

That, of course, is how book number two was conceived,

as the beginnings of a revolution. *Heart's Blood* took me into the bowels of a rebellion at a time when the real world was in turmoil with mini-rebellions in every continent. I penetrated into the cell-structure of an ugly movement, where terrorism is a commonplace, and discovered with my hero and heroine that the kind of "freedom" offered was not what any of us had in mind.

And so I came to the third book in the Pit Dragon trilogy, the way my young hero did, by living through the first two books. When I was thinking about the three books, from the vantage point of a small mountain in the middle of book one, I believed that my hero and his friend could save the world all on their own. But by the time I reached the middle of the third book, my own children were teenagers. They had little power, a lot of heart, and a capacity for suffering that I had forgotten from my own adolescence. And I know now that my hero Jakkin and his friend Akki will come back from their adventure to the place where all life begins—the nursery. To the home they left, the home they *had* to leave because of forces they set in motion by living. They will return with the power to bestow knowledge—which is humankind's greatest power—on those who love them the most. So the trilogy I am writing is formed and shaped by the world in which I am living, a very twentieth century kind of novel, a quest in the modern sense because Jakkin leaves as hero and returns as servant. You see, I grew up believing Kennedy's "Ask not what your country can do for you, but what you can do for your country." As Lloyd Alexander said when he accepted the Newbery Award for his very wise Prydain books, "At heart, the issues raised in a work of fantasy are those we face in real life."

Jane Yolen

SOURCE: "The Eagle and the Hummingbird," in *The Writer,* Vol. 98, No. 3, March, 1988, pp. 5-6.

It is late afternoon. Outside my workroom window, shadows lengthen by the trees. My golden tomcat is prowling across the field. In my typewriter are the last lines of a story, and I have just typed the period that ends the work that I have held in my heart, in my head, and in my fingertips for the past few months. I should feel elated. Instead, I am struck by the growing dark shadows, the cat's fruitless search, and the day punctuated by a story's end.

All my stories end that way, with a small keening note. Oh, I am glad enough to have done the work, and finished within my self-imposed deadline. The images seem good enough. The sentences flow. There is a beginning, a middle, and a satisfying conclusion. Why then this letdown, this incomplete feeling, this sense of mourning?

Something Edith Wharton once wrote always strikes me at this time: "I dream of an eagle, I give birth to a hummingbird."

When I begin a story, it is a great eagle of a tale. The strong pinions, the mighty wingbeat, the slashing beak and talons of my story will strike at my gut—I am sure of it—like Prometheus' implacable fate. It is, in my first imaginings, a story that will be the greatest ever written, will move the reader to laughter or tears, will bring about world understanding, universal brotherhood, and peace. *That* kind of writing.

And then I start to transplant the images in head and heart into black dots on a page. Perhaps I am just a poor translator. Words are never sharp enough to get at what it is I am dreaming. "Human language," wrote Flaubert, "is a cracked kettle on which we beat our tunes for bears to dance to when all the while we wish to move the stars to pity."

I try. Oh, I certainly try. I read my story aloud, trying to suck out the marrow from the dry bones of sentences. I polish, I rewrite, I close my eyes and snatch, like an incompetent fisherman, for that bright silver flash of word.

Sometimes I get very close to my eagle. Catch a few feathers of his tail. I suppose I can count on the fingers of two hands stories I have clothed in eagle feathers: "The Girl Who Cried Flowers," "The Lady and the Merman," "The White Seal Maid," "Brother Hart," "Greyling," "The Hundredth Dove." As it happens, they are not necessarily the ones critics have liked best or the ones that have been reprinted the most. One man's eagle is another's dove.

It is late afternoon. Outside my workroom, the lengthening shadows, like dark fingers, point away from me. The cat lies in wait by the door. A new story is teasing its way into my head, like a dark shadow, like a prowling cat. I again recall Edith Wharton's sentence—"I dream of an eagle. I give birth to a hummingbird"—but this time something different strikes me: It is not the dream that is important, but the birth. Where one ends, the other begins. The hummingbird is a bright little thing; it cannot be captured, and with almost defiant energy, it flies. How it flies!

Jane Yolen

SOURCE: "An Empress of Thieves," in *The Horn Book Magazine,* Vol. LXX, No. 6, November-December, 1994, pp. 702-5.

My winter house is in New England, in a small Polish farming community along the Connecticut River. Summers I spend in Scotland, where the *haar* blows across the garden, the mist from the North Sea.

But I was born and brought up in New York City, reading endlessly while curled up on a windowseat overlooking Central Park West. For two years of my childhood, we lived with my maternal grandparents in Virginia while my father was off in Europe during World War II. Often my cousin Michael and I walked along the oil-fouled waters of Hampton Roads, watching the big ships sail off, packed with American troops.

My father's family came from Ukraine, near Kiev, in an area known as the "Fields of Rest." He came over as a four-year-old and swore he had no memory from his time there. It was only after he died that his younger brother told me all about the family homestead in the now-lost town of Ykaterinislav. I thought my father had been born in Connecticut.

So what is my tradition? What box do I check on the census reports? I was a New York City child who knew every change on the subway systems and regularly stole empty bottles from drunks in the park to play with. I was a Hampton Roads girl who went fishing with the boys in the local streams. I was a Connecticut teenager who was both the shortest member and captain of the girls' basketball team. Part of me, too, are the stories of the family compound in Ykaterinislav, where my father's eldest siblings died in a smallpox epidemic.

My own three children will have all this plus their father's West Virginian heritage, a liberal mixing of Scots-Irish and German. I expect that any grandchildren will be even more ethnically mixed. In America we are all great thieves. That is what multiculturalism is about: our children and our children's children.

As a writer I am the empress of thieves, taking characters like gargoyles off Parisian churches, the *ki-lin* (or unicorn) from China, swords in stones from the Celts, landscapes from the Taino people. I have pulled threads from magic tapestries to weave up my own new cloth.

If I borrow a Scottish Border ballad like "Tam Lin" (having not a bit of Scottish blood in my veins), I will—without willing it—re-invent it from a modern feminist perspective. If I borrow Taino and Spanish materials to create *Encounter*, the book is nevertheless infused with my 1990s take on the Columbus story. If I borrow from the Shakers, I will of necessity tell the story from a twentieth-century mother's perspective. Like all writers, I am what I write.

Borrowing is a hazardous occupation, as Mary Norton told us. When I speak of borrowing, I am always aware of the absolute necessity for research—cultural, physical, historical. All translations are off-center somewhere. The Italians say, "Translations, traitors," meaning that to some extent any translation misrepresents. And anytime one borrows from another culture, another time, another gender, it is translation. But our very lives are borrowed—from our own pasts, from the pasts of others. It cannot be otherwise. As Hazel Rochman has written, a good story "makes immigrants of us all."

We all view the world through individual lenses. Even those things which actually happened can be reported upon in a number of ways. When I wrote *All Those Secrets of the World*, a story based upon a childhood memory of walking with my cousin Michael along the shore and longing for my father, who was in Europe making the world safe for democracy, I wrote it from my exclusive memories. A few weeks ago I saw my cousin Michael

again, for the first time in thirty years. He told me: "It didn't happen that way. We used to wade in Robinson Creek, not Hampton Roads, not the Chesapeake Bay. We would never have been allowed alone in the big water." I have to add that Robinson Creek is narrow enough to walk across in a few seconds. No big boats go along there. Michael's memories and mine do not match at all. Is it the fault of our synapses? Or a gift of the storyteller?

It is both. Michael remained in Virginia while I went back to New York City when my father returned—wounded but alive—from the war. Michael's memories of time and place are chock-a-block with many childhood memories of the creek and the bay. Mine are much simpler. But also, once the storyteller got hold of the memory, much was added. I *remembered* the wading, but the conversations in the book are all made up. The family story says that my baby brother would not let his returning father—a virtual stranger—kiss my mother until he was given a box of chocolates. But the storybook makes no mention of sweets. The story in the book is Janie's story, not the brother's. So we remake our memories to serve a higher function—that of literature.

I have in the past few years worked on four Jewish books—*The Devil's Arithmetic, Briar Rose*, and the forthcoming *And Twelve Chinese Acrobats* and *Milk and Honey: A Year of Jewish Holidays*. I had to do as much research for those books as any non-Jew would. Perhaps more—because my memories were not particularly consistent with common Jewish practice and ritual. In fact, I feel more cultural compatibility with my beloved Arthurian stories than I do with the rabbinical tales that I read for several of those books. I resonate more clearly with the Scots among whom I live in the summer than the Polish-American farmers I live among in the winter. The Highlands speak to me more forcibly than the concrete canyons of New York City, though I have only visited the former and spent most of my childhood among the latter.

What we are seeing now in children's books is an increasing push toward what I can only call the "Balkanization" of literature. We are drawing rigid borders across the world of story, demanding that people tell only their own stories. Not only does this deny the ability of gifted storytellers to re-invigorate the literature with cross-cultural fertilization, but it would mean that no stories at all could be told about some peoples or cultures until such time as a powerful voice from within that culture emerges. Thus we may be excluding the Gypsy, the Inuit, the Amazonian forest people, for example. And what if the culture is for all intents and purposes dead? These people would, in very real terms, become invisible. Surely that is not the goal of multicultural education.

We humans are made up of stories. Almost all those stories have already been cross-fertilized by other cultures, other tongues. A gifted storyteller can plumb a culture not her own. To arbitrarily set borders for our writers, boxing them in with rules, is to do literature the gravest disservice. And in the end it does a worse disservice to the children.

Children's literature is about growth. Just as we do not put heavy weights on our children's heads to stunt their growth, we should not put weights on our writers' heads. To do so is to stunt story forever. Stories go beyond race, beyond religion—even when they are about race and religion. The book speaks to individuals in an individual voice. But then it is taken into the reader's life and re-created, re-invigorated, re-visioned.

That is what literature is about.

GENERAL COMMENTARY

Cheryl Abdullah

SOURCE: "Story for Story's Sake: The Gift of Jane Yolen," in *The Book Report,* Vol. 7, No. 2, September-October, 1988, pp. 26-8.

Once upon a time in Bar Harbor, Maine, a fire blazed in the hearth behind a storyteller as she spun the story of Perseus killing Medusa. The children who were gathered around hung on to every word, but one small child in particular was mesmerized, and her brown eyes glazed as she saw snakes curl around the storyteller's wrist. . . .

Today Jane Yolen is not sure why she thought she saw snakes that night at camp 43 years ago ("Because I ate hot dogs for dinner?"), but she is sure that story affects the teller and listener. "Storytelling is having a renaissance . . . we now tell stories adult to child. It used to be adult to adult, with children listening in." She notes that a warmth occurs between people in storytelling, "something missing in popular entertainment today."

This is the decade in which Jane Yolen's gift of story has been recognized. In 1989, she is taking a sabbatical from her busy routine of lecturing and teaching, a routine that requires one and one-half weeks out of each month on the road. "We are human because we recount and project," she preaches, "and that's what makes us different from animals. We're always telling stories . . . we're people of stories." *Touch Magic,* her book of ten essays for adults, discusses the importance of story.

Yolen's great-grandfather, an innkeeper, told *bubba meises* (Yiddish "grandma tales") in the Finno-Russian village from which her father's family eventually emigrated to America. Her father, a public relations executive, wrote, compiled, and edited several books. Her mother's family had an academic bent, so, when Jane was born on February 11, 1939, odds for a healthy respect of literature were in her favor.

An avid reader and writer by second grade, Jane excelled in schoolwork and pursued music, sports, dance, and horseback riding. She survived the high school popularity gauntlet by telling funny stories, thereby getting "in" with various crowds. (Puns are a Yolen forte; the Commander Toad and Piggins series abound with groaners.) Her first job was as a library page in Westwood, Connecticut. She has always been a library "regular." "I can remember the physical feel of the door handle of the Newport News library. We used to take long bus rides there twice a week—by the time we got home, I would have finished one of the books I checked out."

During her years at Smith College, Yolen generated lots of poetry. She also performed folk songs, some of which inspired later stories. Majoring in English and Russian literature, Yolen minored in religious studies. Her interest in not only her Jewish and Quaker backgrounds but other beliefs and rituals would influence *The Magic Three of Solatia*.

Though her main love has always been writing, Yolen worked at various jobs in the publishing industry, including editing. A college professor who thought well of her writing abilities gave her a good recommendation when she was ready to publish books, and *Pirates in Petticoats* came out in 1963. Averaging several books a year since then, Yolen will have published over 90 titles by 1989 (not to mention her short stories, poetry, articles, book reviews, and essays). Her ideas come from newspapers, magazines, music, paintings, dreams, children, her family—"The more I write, the more ideas I get," she says.

Prolific at writing stories, Yolen also tells stories, and with superb style. "I used to read my stories to audiences at libraries. One day a little boy shouted out, 'Hey, she's not looking at the book!'" Through practice, she developed an oral style that captivates. She'll sway ever so slightly with the rhythm of what she speaks, and her listeners barely breathe. A Yolen lecture flows in and out of story mode, and, for every point she wants to make about fantasy in our lives, there is a story in the wings of her memory available for the telling.

Story has been therapeutic in her own life. When her father died, a Bedouin tale about every home containing some degree of grief consoled her feeling of loss. "What I got from that story was that we cannot outrun our fate—no one has been able to avoid pain," shares Yolen. "'Bibliotherapy' is simply what librarians have been doing all along: choosing the right book for the right person at a moment of crisis." . . .

To Yolen, the bottom line of fiction is story. "A good story is a good story is a good story." In her popular fantasy, the Pit Dragon series, three books (and there will probably be a fourth) are set on the planet of Austar, a former penal colony whose inhabitants must cope with a harsh environment. The characters who discover Austar's potential are two youths in love, Jakkin and Akki, whose unique connection to their world is truly romantic—and replete with stimuli for young intellects. Yolen's dragons are endearing, too. "They're a combination of dragons from Western mythology and my husband's research on early birds—their bone structure, flight muscles, and the fact that they were warm-blooded." Ssargon, whom she fondly calls "the Howard Cosell of dragons," is a good example of her ability to bring character to life. Yolen gets many long letters from readers who were touched by this series. "One teen told me he has read all three books 13 times!"

Those who want to develop storytelling skills should consider Yolen as a resource say Augusta Baker and Ellin Greene in *Storytelling: Art & Technique.* Her shorter books and story collections such as ***Sleeping Ugly, The Transfigured Hart,*** and ***The Girl Who Cried Flowers*** would provide excellent practice for students wanting to recite for drama, English, and child care classes, or, best of all, fun. Yolen herself suggests that hopefuls "search for storytelling groups, conventions, and conferences. NAPPS, the National Association for the Preservation and Perpetuation of Storytelling, is an excellent resource to write to. If there are no active groups or events nearby, there are always video and cassette tapes available."

Writing Books for Children, champions quality story and contains a wealth of ideas, quotes, and insights. In it, Yolen cites the need for dedicated authorship: "Books . . . change lives. When you think of it that way, asking a little bit of homework from the author is not asking too much." . . .

Yolen writes in the third-floor attic of her home, a huge, old, New England farmhouse. Full of bookcases, the attic consists of two rooms. One room is for editing and the other, for writing, has three wings: a writing area, a copier/filing cabinet area, and a reading area (where a sofa currently serves as an "in" basket). From her typewriter she often looks out over her family's 15 acres of farmland (12 of which are rented out to truck farmers). "There is nothing modern," she notes about the view, complete with occasional foxes and a small forest. For a practical realist creating timeless fairytales, that comes in handy. Her library consists of one wall of folklore and mythology books, one of poetry, two walls of science fiction and fantasy, and a vast (as in "I can't count them all") collection of children's literature. (This does not include what her husband and three children own!) She also keeps many of her out-of-print books on hand in case people write to her about acquiring them.

In her local area, she participates in a weekly writer's group whose members critique one another's manuscripts. A close friend, fellow member of that group, and former student of Yolen's is Patricia MacLachlan, *Sarah, Plain and Tall* author. "Jane calls out the best in people," says MacLachlan. "She demands high quality, but she is generous with beginning authors. Many writers and illustrators owe their first contact with children's literature to Jane . . . she's provided the world with better reading."

Yolen distinguishes literature from what she terms "litterature," the publication of books that are no more than "product." Harcourt Brace Jovanovich has recently announced the addition of Yolen as an out-of-house editor, and Jane Yolen Books, the resulting imprint, will generate four to six books per year beginning in fall of 1990.

Bonnie Ingber, Jane's editor at HBJ, is excited about the development: "People here at HBJ respect Jane, her work, her values, her talent. . . . She has a limitless imagination."

Yolen will not accept unsolicited manuscripts but will instead work with writing acquaintances and students. "I want to publish what I would have loved to read when I was a child: picture, science fiction, and fantasy books." . . .

[***The Devil's Arithmetic***] is one of Yolen's best. When recently describing research efforts for this Holocaust story to a class of 8th-graders, one boy asked her if "the stuff about the concentration camps" was true. "This," adds Yolen, "was in a school where two teachers who are concentration camp survivors work." Hannah, the 13-year-old protagonist of this time-travel novel, understands by book's end what is difficult for today's youth to comprehend. And, when the fate of two girls is imminent, Hannah lovingly puts her arms around them and says, "Let me tell you a story." It was, in Yolen's way, the human thing to do.

Lee Bennett Hopkins

SOURCE: "O Yolen: A Look at the Poetry of Jane Yolen," in *Teaching and Learning Literature,* Vol. 6, No. 2, November-December, 1996, pp. 66-8.

[Yolen's] love of poetry began as a young child and never ceased. She was born on February 11, 1939, in New York City, and grew up in a literary environment. Her father, Will Hyatt Yolen, was an author of books and radio scripts; her mother, Isabelle Berlin Yolen, was also a writer and composer of crossword puzzles, many of which appeared in children's magazines.

While in college Jane wrote poetry and sang folk songs professionally to earn money for living expenses. Upon receiving a B.A. degree in 1960, from Smith College, she was a production assistant for *Saturday Review* magazine for six months, followed by a long career in publishing that continues today. Currently, she is the editorial director of her own imprint, Jane Yolen Books, for Harcourt Brace.

In 1963, her first book in rhyme, ***See This Little Line?*** appeared. Yolen was off and rhythmically running!

I asked her, "As a multi-faceted writer, how do you decide when you are going to do a book in poetic form?"

Her reply came quick, terse: "I don't decide," she said. "I *never* decided. The book decides. I follow!"

Her first two books of poems both appeared in 1980: ***Dragon Nights and Other Lullabies,*** and ***How Beastly! A Menagerie of Nonsense Poems***.

Although ***Dragon Nights . . . ,*** a collection of sixteen lullabies a variety of animals might sing to their young, is out of print, several of the songs such as "Grandpa Bear's Lullaby" and "Caterpillar's Lullaby," have been reprinted in numerous anthologies.

How Beastly! began her foray into nonsense verse. The book features twenty-two selections of "never were" creatures including "The Bluffalo," "The Centerpede," and "The Dinosore" who is so heavy that "The poundage gets him down. / He gasps and gasps some more. His aching feet, they have him beat, / That's why he's Dinosore."

Since the publication of the two volumes, Jane has created over twenty books of original poetry and anthologies for readers of all ages from the playful, *The Three Bears Rhyme Book,* and *The Three Bears Holiday Rhyme Book,* with illustrations by Jane Dyer, to the elegantly produced young adult collection, *Among Angels,* which she co-authored with Newbery Medalist, Nancy Willard.

"What is poetry?" I posed. "What is poetry to you?"

She replied: "I think of poetry as the soul of literature. It is what we see and hear the moment before sleep takes us. It is the space between wingbeats. The pause between heartbeats. The first touch of the drumstick on the tight stretch of drum hide and the slight burring after."

"Do you know what else it is, Lee? It is:

> Hard work.
> A single great line.
> A word discovered after an afternoon of trying.
> An emotion caught in the hand, in the mouth.
> Two words that bump up against one another
> and create something new.
> A song between friends.
> Hard work.
> *Hard* work.

"And the problem is that, as John Ciardi once wrote, 'A poem is never finished, it is abandoned.' And, as Robert Graves reputedly said, 'A perfect poem is impossible. Once it is written, the world would end.' In other words, I am never satisfied. I can approximate. And sometimes, if I am lucky, I come pretty close to what I am trying to do.

"Since I write both humorous / light verse and serious poems I find it difficult to speak about poetry without hedging. I enjoy writing funny poems and I think children and teachers find those the most accessible. My more serious poetry, and to my mind, better poems, are not as easy to discover. What the serious poems tend to have in common is a singability, driven by a line that often ends with a single strong stress syllable. I am, and have always been, quite musical which informs a great deal of my poetry. I am also an admirer of the bardic and psalmic traditions and often consciously, and unconsciously, use those rhythms in my work."

I asked if she had a favorite among her books of poetry. "Every author has trouble singling out a favorite book or favorite poem," she stated, "but *Ring of Earth* holds a special place in my heart."

Ring of Earth: A Child's Book of Seasons, handsomely illustrated by John Wallner, views the four seasons from the perspective of a weasel, spring peeper, dragonfly, and a goose, who, in part, admonishes: "We fly but wingtips apart, / No compass, no compass but the heart. / *Kerhonk. Kerhonk. Kerhonk.*"

"Three of my poetic influences are John Donne, William Butler Yeats, and Dylan Thomas. My favorite poets for children are David McCord (*the* master), Mary Ann Hoberman (brilliant rhymes), Lilian Moore (who creates little masterpieces and who is a Grand Lady), and Edward Lear." . . .

May the pen of Yolen never run dry. The world of children's literature has been, and will continue to be, richer for her vast talents.

TITLE COMMENTARY

COMMANDER TOAD IN SPACE (1980)

Kirkus Reviews

SOURCE: A review of *Commander Toad in Space,* in *Kirkus Reviews,* Vol. XLVIII, No. 18, September 15, 1980, p. 1232.

A feeble whimsy presented as a ha-ha space adventure. Commander Toad ("brave and bright, bright and brave") and his froggy crew discover a watery planet, effect a landing on a rubber lily pad, and attract the attention of a Loch-Ness-y monster—whose waves sink their "sky skimmer," cutting off their exit. To distract the monster, brainy Mr. Hop asks him riddles ("What is a monster's favorite ballet?" *"SWAMP LAKE!"*) and ex-warbler Lieutenant Lily (late of *"Warts and Peace"*) inveigles him into singing-along . . . while commander Toad inflates the lily pad—via "special candles"—until it's a hot-air balloon capable of carrying the trio back to their spaceship. Unbelievable and unfunny.

Judith Goldberger

SOURCE: A review of *Commander Toad in Space,* in *Booklist,* Vol. 77, No. 6, November 15, 1980, p. 464.

Any beginning-to-read book with brave space explorers, a ship named the *Star Warts,* and a monster who calls himself Deep Wader would be popular almost by definition. The bonus here is that the adventure of Commander Toad and his colleagues is a clever spoof and really funny reading. Yolen pokes fun at two beloved space-age cult-sagas, but not too much: there is good drama in the dilemma faced by the *Star Warts* crew. [Bruce] Degen picks up on it by drawing mock-serious amphibious characters and a horrible, yet somehow foolish, Wader. This hits the nail on the countdown button for primary as well as some older problem readers.

School Library Journal

SOURCE: A review of *Commander Toad in Space*, in *School Library Journal*, Vol. 27, No. 4, December, 1980, p. 66.

Commander Toad in Space goes where no frog has gone before, with his trusty spaceship the *Star Warts* and his able amphibian crew: Lt. Lily, Jake Skyjumper and Mr. Hop. Exploring a watery planet in their inflatable rubber lily pad, they are nearly done in by the evil Deep Wader but Commander Toad saves the day. A hoppy combination of good story and clever media exploitation, Jane Yolen's frogs-in-space spoof meets the need for good easy-reading science fiction. The illustrations by Bruce Degen are toadally appropriate, adding funny froggy touches as well as action and personality. This one holds water.

DRAGON'S BLOOD: A FANTASY (first novel in the "Pit Dragon" trilogy, 1982)

Sally Estes

SOURCE: A review of *Dragon's Blood*, in *Booklist*, Vol. 78, No. 18, May 15, 1982, p. 1236.

Fifteen-year-old Jakkin, whose master is the best dragon breeder on Austar IV, follows the established but risky tradition of stealing a hatchling to raise and train in secret for the gaming pits so that he can win his freedom from bondage. To Jakkin's amazement, he and his "snatchling" soon forge a mental link uncommon among men and dragons—one that enables the pair to work as one mind. The plot moves right along and suspense is well maintained, but the story's highlight is definitely the imaginatively defined dragon lore, particularly as it is reflected in the relationship between Jakkin and his dragon. What's more, Yolen has created a world that is convincing both in physical and societal aspects, though occasionally expository passages intrude, and her characterizations have vitality and charm. Open to a sequel, this engaging story will attract the audience that already savors Anne McCaffrey's adult and juvenile dragon series. . . .

Zena Sutherland

SOURCE: A review of *Dragon's Blood*, in *Bulletin of the Center for Children's Books*, Vol. 35, No. 11, July-August, 1982, p. 220.

On the planet of Ausdar there is only one way to become free if you are a bond servant, and that is to buy freedom. Jakkin decides that he will earn money by training a fight-

ing dragon, since the planet's gaming pits are a large part of the economy. He steals a hatchling, takes it to a hidden oasis, and there trains the rapidly growing dragon to be a superb fighter, in part by having him respond to telepathic commands. The story ends with a dramatic flourish, when Jakkin's dragon wins his first fight, and Jakkin learns that his master had known all along about the theft and the training but had felt the boy's prowess should be encouraged. He also learns that Akki, the girl he loves, is his master's illegitimate daughter. Akki leaves, telling Jakkin he is too young, an ending that seems to indicate the probability of a sequel. The genre and the subject indicate a strong potential for the popularity of this story and any that may follow; in some ways reminiscent of the series *(Dragonsong, Dragonsinger)* by Anne McCaffrey, this is not derivative; it is written with good structure and pace, has a wholly conceived fantasy world, and is much better in writing style than Yolen's earlier books for younger readers.

Ann A. Flowers

SOURCE: A review of *Dragon's Blood*, in *The Horn Book Magazine*, Vol. LVIII, No. 4, August, 1982, pp. 418-9.

The story about the boy Jakkin and how he raised his stolen dragon to be a great fighter is set on the planet Austar IV. Once a penal colony, Austar IV was a dry desert planet, whose one resource was great dragons—unpredictable and dangerous—selectively bred and raised for their fighting abilities. The societal structure was composed of bond servants and masters; one could buy one's way out of bondage, but money to do so was hard to come by. Jakkin, a bond boy who worked in Master Sarkkhan's "dragonry," was determined to buy his freedom, so he stole a hatchling and raised it in his carefully prepared secret oasis. Not only did his dragon, Heart's Blood, prove to be a fine, bold fighter, but Jakkin was able to achieve the mental link with her that was possible only to the best trainers. When Heart's Blood won her first fight, Jakkin's freedom was ensured. The planet is completely realized—the flora and fauna, the care and feeding of dragons, the planet's economic and societal structure. Although there are some similarities to the mental telepathy between beast and master in Anne McCaffrey's books about the dragons of Pern, the relationship on Austar IV is predicated upon quite different principles. An original and engrossing fantasy.

Patricia Manning

SOURCE: A review of *Dragon's Blood*, in *School Library*, Vol. 29, No. 1, September, 1982, p. 146.

As on McCaffrey's Pern, we have specially bred dragons on Austar IV, but the telepathic gentle giants of Pern might meet their match in Yolen's fierce fighters. Raised and trained to compete in the pits, a brave canny fighter may parlay a simple bet into freedom for a bondservant—or an empty bag. Yolen has created a new world, complete with traditions, legends, ecology, social strata; where bond-servants can earn their freedom by careful saving, wise betting or—as Jakkin does—by stealing a hatchling from an owner's brood barn and raising it to be a fighting champion. Aided by Akki, a bond girl training for medicine, Jakkin rears his hatchling into a prime pit beast, maintaining a telepathic mind-touch to help control the dragon. A fascinating glimpse of a brand new world.

Mary M. Hamilton

SOURCE: A review of *Dragon's Blood,* in *Voice of Youth Advocates,* Vol. 5, No. 4, October, 1982, p. 51.

Dragon's Blood is a thoroughly delightful fantasy which takes place on the planet of Austar IV in the Erato Galaxy. Austar IV is well-known for its dragon breeding and fighting. The central character in *Dragon's Blood* is Jakkin, a bond slave, who dreams of stealing a baby dragon to raise and train for fighting in order to buy his bond and become his own master. The book describes the carrying out of his plans with the help of the girl, Akki, and Jakkin's own perseverance.

I was impressed with the author's imagination, conciseness, ability to describe surroundings, and nice style of writing. The pace of the story never slowed, as I found myself "caught up" in the imaginary world of Austar IV. It seemed like such a place was within the realm of possibility. Traits of friendship, love, truth and hard work are often lacking in so many of the "real world" books written today. I shall look forward to more books written by Jane Yolen. The ending in *Dragon's Blood* left me hoping to soon pick up a second tale from Austar IV. . . .

Neil Philip

SOURCE: "Out of this World," in *The Times Educational Supplement,* No. 3507, September 16, 1983, p. 24.

Jane Yolen has envisaged an entire world dependent on cock-fighting: Austar IV, "one of the better-known R & R planets in the explored universe". An economy based on gaming removes the need for political complexity; a barren, desert landscape avoids the need for geography, botany, zoology, ethnology; recent settlement sidesteps history; a society derived from a convict/guard hierarchy, consisting of masters and bond slaves, reduces social issues to a similar manageable simplicity. The stage is set, then, for a straightforward science fiction story about a boy proving his worth in a competitive male atmosphere and establishing his deepest bond not with another human but with an animal: in this case the fighting cock which will allow him to "fill his bag" and buy his freedom. The bag, which all bond slaves wear around their neck, contains a "grave coin" and whatever money the slave can earn or steal; it is a useful image both of servitude and possible liberation, with undertones of meaning which allow some clever coinages; the brothels to which most female slaves are consigned are known as "the Bagger-

ies". The boy is Jakkin (that tiresome double k recurs in all proper names—another labour saving device). He steals a hatchling from his master Sarkkhan, raises it and trains it in secret, and, with the help of a girl, Akki, and Sarkkhan's acquiescence, enters it for the fight which will make or break him. He achieves a great success, but, in a touch which promises a sequel, refuses to "fill his bag" till he can mortgage his freedom to Akki.

All this is competently done. The disappointing thing is that in providing an appealing daydream for readers contemplating, like Jakkin, the transition to manhood, Jane Yolen makes no attempt to step outside the strict limitations of her one-dimensional world, despite having demonstrated in her *Touch Magic: Fantasy, Faerie and Folk-lore in the Literature of Childhood* a real understanding of the ways in which story can enlarge our capacities. Her one imaginative act—and that necessary to mask the cruelty of her central idea—is to replace spurred poultry with fire-breathing dragons; her insistence on referring to these creatures as cocks and hens mars the intended effect of majesty.

Pauline Thomas

SOURCE: A review of *Dragon's Blood,* in *The School Librarian,* Vol. 31, No. 4, December, 1983, p. 384.

On harsh, arid Austar IV, dragon fighting is the only entertainment, except for visits to the brothels or 'Baggeries'. Most bond boys spend their money there, and will never have enough to buy their freedom. Jakkin decides that his only hope of escape is to steal a hatchling from the dragon nursery where he is in bond, and bring it up in the desert as a fighting dragon. He must evade the fatal chill of desert night, the attacks of pterodactyl-like drakks and the enmity of Likkarn, the old weed-crazed dragon trainer. The life of the nursery is brilliantly described. The author explains little, letting the reader work out the details of geography, natural history, social structure and sexual mores. The result is remarkably convincing. Austar IV is a world as real as Earthsea; but Jane Yolen must yield to Ursula Le Guin over characterisation. Jakkin's personality is not very interesting, and he finally achieves his ambition with disappointing ease once the early adventures are over. The marvellous dragon is a more complex character than his trainer, with whom it communicates telepathically in rainbow colours. Splendid entertainment, and, like many American books, a much quicker read than its 243 pages suggest.

CHILDREN OF THE WOLF (1984)

Jean Hammond Zimmerman

SOURCE: A review of *Children of the Wolf,* in *School Library Journal,* Vol. 30, No. 7, March, 1984, p. 177.

Since the time of Romulus and Remus, men have been fascinated by the idea that abandoned children might be cared for by wolves. Yolen offers a realistic look at life for these feral children when they are returned to the human world. Based on a controversial case reported in India in the 1920s, the tightly-knit novel relates how Amala and Kamala are taken from the large empty termite mound they share with a wolf family to an orphanage run by a British missionary. Mohandas, the teenage narrator who is sympathetically drawn to the girls, is asked by Mr. Welles, the missionary, to teach them language and human ways. After the younger girl dies, Kamala becomes more dependent on Mohandas and learns rudimentary language and how to stand upright. Despite her limited capabilities and animal-like innocence, the girl inspires hatred and jealousy in one of the other orphans, who torments her. The frightened Kamala retreats to the jungle where, after a dangerous search, Mohandas finally finds her hiding in another mound. The experience causes Kamala to lose the little language she has learned and to live the rest of her short life as an animal. The intelligent and sensitive Mohandas develops compassion and courage while caring for the two girls. Yolen shows not only the plausible alienation of Kamala but also the contradictions and dilemmas confronting Mohandas as an Indian orphan attempting to become a British Christian. The language is clear and so well used that it performs well without drawing attention to itself. *Children of the Wolf* engages readers in a real world and creates an admirable hero who humanizes and strengthens himself by his failure to humanize Kamala.

Publishers Weekly

SOURCE: A review of *Children of the Wolf,* in *Publishers Weekly,* Vol. 225, No. 13, March 30, 1984, p. 57.

It seems inevitable that the sensitive author of over 70 acclaimed books should write this story, based on children taken from the wolf that had fostered them in India during the 1920s. The orphan Mohandas narrates Yolen's version of events at the orphanage where the boy lives under the guardianship of a minister and his wife. Sacrificing the companionship of his friend Rama—who despises the dirty, ugly, feral wolf girls brought to the home—Mohandas helps care for the disoriented pair. He feels an affinity with the foundlings, dispossessed like him and forced to adapt to alien ways. Naming them Amala and Kamala, Mohandas tries to gain their trust, a mission he almost despairs of when Amala dies. Kamala retreats further from him in her terror and grief. Gradually, though, she responds to the boy's kindness and begins to learn words. Kamala's progress ignites the minister's hopes of converting her to Christianity but after a sneak attack by the asylum's bully, she runs away. The denouement makes an indelible impression on the reader. Perceptive Mohandas asks the question implicit in the novel: has society the right, for humanitarian or any purpose, to "rescue" living beings from their environments and compel them to conform?

Ethel R. Twichell

SOURCE: A review of *Children of the Wolf,* in *The Horn Book Magazine,* Vol. LX, No. 2, April, 1984, pp. 205-6.

In 1920 two small feral girls were discovered in a remote village in India. Rescued and brought by the Reverend J. A. L. Singh to his orphanage in Midnapore, the children continued to move about on calloused hands and knees, to eat raw meat, and to refuse to wear clothing. Despite his efforts, the younger one died after a year, and the other lived only eight more years, having learned to walk upright and to speak with a vocabulary of thirty words. She was, however, never able to describe her earlier life. Out of these facts taken from Dr. Singh's diary published in *Wolf-Children and Feral Man* the author has developed a fictionalized account. She tells the story through the narrative of an intelligent young orphan, Mohandas, who is asked by the head of the orphanage to care for the two girls and to teach them the essentials of speech and behavior. At first repulsed by their animallike ways and taunted by the other orphans, the gentle Mohandas gradually gains the girls' trust and achieves an odd friendship before their early deaths. The author has credibly fleshed out the story and has just as convincingly described the three children and the Indian setting of the book.

Zena Sutherland

SOURCE: A review of *Heart's Blood,* in *Bulletin of the Center for Children's Books,* Vol. 37, No. 10, June, 1984, p. 197.

Mohandas, fourteen, tells the story, based on fact, of Amala and Kamala, two feral girls reared by wolves in 1920s India. Villagers believe the two are *manush-baghas,* ghosts, but Mr. Welles (who runs the orphanage where Mohandas lives) is determined to civilize the girls and bring them to Christianity. While the girls are feared and taunted by the other orphans, Mohandas feels a kinship with their alienation, and so they become his responsibility. "Tame them," says Mr. Welles. The story of these "wild children" has inherent interest, and Yolen brings a strong pathos and drama to the story. Kamala and Amala never adjust to human society, and Kamala, particularly, in her torn up dress, clutching her rag doll, mumbling her few words, is affecting.

Ilene Cooper

SOURCE: A review of *Children of the Wolf,* in *Booklist,* Vol. 80, No. 22, August, 1984, p. 1631.

Based on a true incident that occurred in India in the 1920s, this novel recounts the discovery of two feral children by a Christian missionary, Mr. Welles, who has been asked by local peasants to rid their village of ghosts. The story's narrator is Mohandas, a 14-year-old Indian boy who lives at Mr. Welles' orphanage. Present when the two wolf girls are routed from their lair, Mohandas feels both revulsion and a responsibility toward them.

When Mr. Welles puts their care and education into his hands, Mohandas dedicates himself to civilizing the girls. He soon learns society can be as dangerous and cruel as anything that they have had to face in the jungle. Children, naturally curious about the feral phenomenon, will find this story engrossing. The characters are varied and true, their individual dramas played out against the backdrop of the feral children's lives. Yolen adeptly weaves mundane details together with sweeping sociological and psychological implications into a full-bodied work. A vivid piece that has the capacity to stir readers and to make them think. An afterword details Yolen's sources.

HEART'S BLOOD (second novel in the "Pit Dragon" trilogy, 1984)

Sally Estes

SOURCE: A review of *Heart's Blood,* in *Booklist,* Vol. 80, No. 14, March 15, 1984, p. 1040.

The sequel to *Dragon's Blood* continues the story of Jakkin, now a free dragon trainer, and his beloved dragon, Heart's Blood, with whom Jakkin enjoys a closer mental and emotional link than is usual between human and dragon. The pressure on Jakkin mounts as the hatching of Heart's Blood's first clutch looms and he is asked to infiltrate rebel forces and rescue Akki, his former master's daughter, whom he has been trying (unsuccessfully) to forget. The narrative is full of action as Jakkin bonds his dragon's five hatchlings, works dragons in the gaming pits, and is drawn into a rebel cell—becoming caught up in intrigue, as pawn and scapegoat in a deadly act of terrorism. He and Akki are forced to flee into the desolate wilderness, where their final metamorphosis is both convincing and right. Once again, dragon lore carries the story, backing up Yolen's fine world building and vital characterizations. Readers of the first episode will welcome this one with delight.

Charlotte W. Draper

SOURCE: A review of *Heart's Blood,* in *The Horn Book Magazine,* Vol. LX, No. 2, April, 1984, p. 206.

In a sequel to *Dragon's Blood* Jakkin, who has already purchased his freedom from bondage and has become Dragon Master, learns that his new status does not automatically make him a man. The new book details Jakkin's growth as his attention shifts from the narrow world of the dragon nursery and the fighting pit to the arena of Austar politics. After his girl friend Akki is abducted by rebels, he is drawn to confront issues of freedom and responsibility he previously ignored. Founded as a penal colony generations ago, Austar has evolved a complex caste system of masters and bond slaves economically grounded in the raising, training, and fighting of the great pit dragons domesticated by

early colonists. Jakkin's tie with the dragon Heart's Blood deepens into an almost mystical communion. Heart's Blood has fought for Jakkin in life; she continues to insure his survival in death. During the rebels' pursuit of Jakkin and Akki, Heart's Blood is killed; in order to survive the murderous cold of night, called After Dark, the fugitives take shelter inside her carcass. Emerging the next morning, Jakkin and Akki recognize that they are changed by this rebirth; they will henceforth bring the "gift of dragon's sight out to the others." Rich in symbolism, eloquent in the evocation of a culture which carries within it the seeds of its own destruction, the book stretches the reader's conception of human capability.

Dorcas Hand

SOURCE: A review of *Heart's Blood,* in *School Library Journal,* Vol. 30, No. 8, April, 1984, p. 129.

This sequel to *Dragon's Blood* can hardly be said to stand independently, but the saga is exciting and leaves readers waiting for the third volume of the "Pit Dragon" trilogy. In the first book, Jakkin paid off his bond and took his fighting dragon Heart's Blood to the pits where she was a constant winner. As the second book opens, Heart's Blood is just laying her first clutch of eggs; two days later, five tiny dragons hatch and Jakkin can prepare her to fight again. In the midst of all this, Jakkin is contacted by an offworlder who wants him to infiltrate a rebel group in search of his girlfriend, Akki. The story proceeds at a rapid pace; Akki is found and the two are assigned a rebel delivery. They discover that the package is a powerful bomb which destroys The Rokk, a major city, and they flee. The authorities follow and eventually corner them. Heart's Blood does her best to protect them, but dies trying. Jakkin and Akki survive, with new powers which will undoubtedly serve them well when the story continues. Despite a certain similarity to Anne McCaffrey's "Pern" series, these books are enjoyable light fantasy. Character development is minimal, but the quick pace overcomes the other weaknesses. Readers of *Dragon's Blood* will certainly want to keep up with the story.

Zena Sutherland

SOURCE: A review of *Children of the Wolf,* in *Bulletin of the Center for Children's Books,* Vol. 37, No. 10, June, 1984, p. 197.

In a sequel to *Dragon's Blood* this second volume in a planned trilogy describes the efforts of the former bondsman Jakkin to rescue the woman he loves from the toils of a dangerous group of rebels. This science fantasy is set on a distant world where much of the economy is based on the rearing of fighting dragons; Jakkin's dragon, Heart's Blood, with whom he has telepathic communication, is killed in defending him. A soundly-structured story has good pace, color, and suspense.

📖 *THE STONE SILENUS* (1984)

Zena Sutherland

SOURCE: A review of *The Stone Silenus,* in *Bulletin of the Center for Children's Books,* Vol. 38, No. 2, October, 1984, pp. 37-8.

A year after the death of her father, a poet she idolized, Melissa meets a boy who looks so much like her father and so much like a faun that she almost believes that the "faun-boy," Gabriel, is a reincarnation of her father. Melissa finds it as hard to accept some of the truths about her father (conveyed by her mother) as to accept his death, or to accept her mother's announcement that she is marrying again. It all comes to an unconvincing climax when Melissa finds Gabriel in her bedroom at night and is frightened; he proves to be a look-alike student with a history of mental illness and—somehow—this helps Melissa to accept reality, including the upcoming marriage. A diffuse story in which the only firmly established character is the dead poet, an aging Pan whose rejection by a college girl had led to what his wife is firmly convinced was not accident but suicide.

David Gale

SOURCE: A review of *The Stone Silenus,* in *School Library Journal,* Vol. 31, No. 2, October, 1984, p. 172.

While unusual elements are incorporated into Yolen's story of a 16-year-old girl coming to terms with her father's death—and his life—they don't help to make this novel anything more than standard fare. Melissa Stanhold believes that the strange boy she meets on the beach is a faun, the reincarnation of her poet father. The boy/faun quotes Stanhold's poetry, knows details of his family's life and, to Melissa, looks like Stanhold. Her meetings with the boy first reinforce her denial of her father's death and further alienate her from her mother, who is continuing with her life; when she realizes he is a fraud, she gains the strength to see her father as the man he was rather than as the idealized image she had of him, to accept his death and to stop resenting her mother. The puzzle of the boy/faun lacks credibility and is not well integrated into the story; and the climax, which might have been terrifying, is played out too quickly to engender any strong feelings from readers. Yolen's use of language and her style are impressive, and she does a remarkable job of defining a multi-dimensional character (Stanhold) strictly through the eyes of those who loved him. Nevertheless, this book does not have the strength of some other novels about accepting the death of a parent. . . . Whether or not readers consider Yolen's frequent references to mythic creatures pretentious, it is unlikely that they will be led to further study or appreciation of mythology. The most thought-provoking question that comes of reading Yolen's novel is how Stanhold could have built such a major reputation on the basis of the mundane poetry quoted here.

Alethea K. Helbig

SOURCE: A review of *The Stone Silenus,* in *Children's Book Review Service,* Vol. 13, No. 3, November, 1984, p. 33.

Obsessed with the memory of her dead father, poet Joshua Stanhold, Melissa believes that a handsome young faun-like stranger is her father reincarnated. Electra complex, grief, and rebellion against mother shatter when the youth attempts to rape her, and Melissa must come to terms with her fixation, her mother's impending marriage, and the reality of her father's less-than-godlike personality and death. Although mythological allusions occur so frequently that they become monotonous, the gradually revealed character of Joshua sets Melissa's infatuation in bold relief. Yolen skillfully controls the tension, making Melissa's obsession and terror so palpable that the revelation at the end, about the youth's identity, is something of a letdown.

Anne Frost

SOURCE: A review of *The Stone Silenus,* in *Voice of Youth Advocates,* Vol. 7, No. 6, February, 1985, p. 334.

Melissa's father, the prize winning poet, had been dead for a year, but she continues to walk on the beach in the fog, trying to feel his presence. One afternoon she encounters a stranger—he is about her age and looks like a faun boy from a Greek vase. He reaches for her, and she runs, hearing his call of "Wait, Issa. Wait, Issa." "Issa" was her father's pet name for her. How does this boy know it? And who or what is he? She encounters him on other occasions—always on the beach—and grows more alarmed by his presence. He knows a lot about her and her father—things only the family should know. Is he real? Is he a reincarnation of her father? Melissa must find the answers to these questions and resolve the adversary relationship with her mother before she can accept her father's death and begin to live her own life.

Yolen has written another excellent book, with just the right amount of intrigue to appeal to YA readers. Melissa is a well-developed character, and Melanie, her younger sister who quotes lines from movies, adds just the right "family" touch.

📖 *PIGGINS* (1987)

Kirkus Reviews

SOURCE: A review of *Piggins,* in *Kirkus Reviews,* Vol. LV, No. 4, February 15, 1987, pp. 304-5.

In a picture-book mystery for young readers, Yolen pays homage to the world of *Upstairs, Downstairs,* to Beatrix Potter's animal/human characters, and to not only Agatha Christie but Conan Doyle.

The servants' preparations are complete; the Reynards are ready to receive. Piggins the butler announces Inspector Bayswater (a hound), his friend Professor T. Ortoise, Lord and Lady Ratsby, and elderly explorer Pierre Lapin with his three unmarried sisters. In the midst of dinner, the lights go off; in the confusion, Mrs. Reynard's diamond necklace disappears. Bayswater is stumped, but the alert Piggins assembles several clues and pinpoints the Ratsbys as culprits; the Misses Lapin foil a getaway attempt; then Piggins oversees the washing up and concludes the evening with a pot of tea.

Yolen's staccato style gives this the air of a satirical synopsis; the events are barely mysterious, but they're humorous and fun. [Jane] Dyer's carefully detailed interiors have the charm of a period dollhouse; her animal characters have a comic individuality. There aren't many mysteries available on this level; this one should serve nicely.

Ilene Cooper

SOURCE: A review of *Piggins*, in *Booklist*, Vol. 83, No. 14, March 15, 1987, p. 1132.

Readers will know they are in for some fun the moment they see the supercilious pig dressed as a butler who adorns the dust jacket. Set in the Edwardian household of Mr. and Mrs. Reynard, two foxes, this mysterious romp takes place on the night of an elegant dinner party. Among the guests are Professor T. Ortoise, explorer Pierre Lapin, and Lord and Lady Ratsby. The Reynards are thinking of selling a diamond lavalier that they believe is cursed, but when the lights go off during dinner, it is stolen. It's up to butler Piggins to figure out who is the thief. [Jane] Dyer has captured the upstairs-downstairs atmosphere of Edwardian life in her highly detailed pictures. Some of her colors (the greens, for example) are a bit harsh, but other aspects of the artwork—showing the whole house in dollhouse style—capture attention in full-page pictures that are as amusing as they are individual. Yolen and Dyer make a good team. Here's to more Piggins mysteries.

Betsy Hearne

SOURCE: A review of *Piggins*, in *Bulletin of the Center for Children's Books*, Vol. 40, No. 8, April, 1987, p. 160.

A witty, sophisticated collaboration between author and artist results in a mystery-spoof of Sherlock Holmes vintage. Piggins, the portly butler at Mr. and Mrs. Reynard's wealthy home, welcomes the guests one night at a dinner party arranged to show off—and sell—Mrs. Reynard's diamond lavaliere, reputed to have a curse that brings bad luck. In the midst of the soup course, the lights go out and the necklace disappears. Even Inspector Bayswater finds only a few disparate clues. Piggins however, is not stumped. He collars the thieves, Lord and Lady Ratsby, plucks the lavaliere from the chandelier, and finishes the evening as he had begun it, trit-trotting up and down stairs

to finish his chores. Both the narrative and art contain nuances that lend depth to rereadings. In addition to consistently elegant drafting and watercolor detail, the pictures characterize each of the guests in perfect coordination with the verbal descriptions. Professor T. Ortoise, who "is famous for his conversation," introduces the evening with a comment on the weather. The "world-famous explorer Pierre Lapin" has three unmarried sisters and mutters, after the dining room commotion, "In my youth, I stole into a farmer's garden and made much too much noise." The rats, particularly, are expressive in showing their greed as they pocket the cheese hors d'oeuvres and scamper toward the table before the rest of the company. Yolen's pacing and use of the present tense add an immediacy that counteracts any off-putting effects of the elitist tone, which listeners will actually enjoy once they catch on to the setting. [Jane] Dyer, too, has taken special care to reflect the upper-crust atmosphere in costumes, furnishings, and design touches such as the shadow profiles facing several full-page illustrations. This has all the appeal *Upstairs Downstairs* had for adults, plus notes of humor and suspense that flavor it for a child's palate.

Karen K. Radtke

SOURCE: A review of *Piggins*, in *School Library Journal*, Vol. 33, No. 7, April, 1987, p. 91.

A sophisticated English mystery parody for the primary set. The Reynards throw a dinner party to show off Mrs. Reynard's new diamond lavaliere and to explain why they must sell it. As Mr. Reynard is relating the story of the necklace's curse, the lights go off; when they are restored, the necklace is gone. All the dinner guests are stumped, but Piggins, the very proper butler, explains to all how it was done and who did the evil deed. Yolen utilizes word play in the names—Professor T. Ortoise is an elderly turtle. Her plot is clever, but with enough obvious clues for first or second graders to solve the mystery on their own. Some of Yolen's understated humor may not be appreciated by children, but an adult reader will enjoy sharing this book with children. The color pencil and watercolor illustrations complement the text in every way. Each textual detail is meticulously expressed in the pictures. The animal characters have human expression while still remaining true to their animal natures—the rats, of course, are the thieves. The Edwardian details in decor and costuming are fun to examine and yet do not interfere with the action or visual flow of the illustrations. One of a kind—and sure to provide a great deal of fun for many readers and listeners.

Ann A. Flowers

SOURCE: A review of *Piggins*, in *The Horn Book Magazine*, Vol. LXIII, No. 4, July-August, 1987, p. 459.

The influence and popularity of the British television series "Upstairs, Downstairs" has penetrated all aspects of American life, even picture books. A mystery episode is set in a ménage closely resembling that of the Bellamys but with a cast composed of animals. The master and mistress of 47 The Meadows are Mr. and Mrs. Reynard, and the servants are Cook (a hedgehog), Sara and Jane (crocodiles), and the butler Piggins (perfectly obvious). A grand dinner party is underway—among the guests are Lord and Lady Ratsby, Pierre Lapin and his three well-known sisters, Professor T. Ortoise, and Inspector Bays-water, a Sherlock Holmes-like hound dog. When the lights suddenly go out during dinner, Mrs. Reynard's valuable but hexed diamond lavaliere disappears. Piggins, of course, supplies the solution. The illustrations perfectly depict the pomp and circumstance of the era—the ladies at dinner in their feathered and bejeweled hats, the fluted caps of the maidservants, the gleaming silver, the portly and reassuring Piggins, the personification of all a good butler should be. The book is clearly not for the preschool crowd, who are presumably ignorant of lavalieres, much less of Edwardian dinner parties. But it's lots of fun for middle and older readers, who will enjoy solving the mystery, spying out the villains and the hiding place of the jewelry, and who just might make the connection with "Upstairs, Downstairs."

THE THREE BEARS RHYME BOOK (1987)

Publishers Weekly

SOURCE: A review of *The Three Bears Rhyme Book,* in *Publishers Weekly,* Vol. 232, No. 11, September 11, 1987, p. 92.

The wonderfully paired team of Yolen and [Jane] Dyer has created another winner with this collection of 15 rhymed poems narrated by the smallest bear of the familiar three bears story. This insouciant, bright-eyed cub tells about the things that interest him—birthdays, flowers, rain or what happens "When a Bear Gets Mad." The designs of Dyer's vivid pages are exceptionally clever, and the illustrations are a snug match for Yolen's lilting text. Dressed in red pajamas, the irresistible cub settles on his mother's lap while outside his window a winged dragon, a castle and pirate ship move dreamily across a starry sky. "Read to me riddles / and read to me rhymes, / read to me stories / of magical times," he says, and "when you are finished—please read them again!" Children will say the same.

Ilene Cooper

SOURCE: A review of *The Three Bears Rhyme Book,* in *Booklist,* Vol. 84, No. 5, November 1, 1987, p. 486.

Using the story of "The Three Bears" as a jumping-off point, Yolen and [Jane] Dyer combine their talents to bring little ones into the world of whimsy and rhyme. In these 16 poems, readers see the bears walking, thinking about porridge, and sitting in chairs ("But of all bears' chairs, / the very best / is to lie against / your poppa's chest / and cuddle up / to take a nap / upon the chair /

that's Poppa's lap"). But these offerings travel far beyond the events in the tale; they find the little bear complaining he's too old for naps, Goldilocks appreciating the beautiful blossoms in her garden, and Mama and Baby Bear discovering the joys of reading aloud. The universality of the events will certainly appeal to young listeners who'll find the words mirroring their own everyday activities. . . . It's clear that this book was carefully crafted by everyone involved, and children, who'll enjoy looking at it over and over, will reap the benefits of that eye for detail and concern.

Ellen Fader

SOURCE: A review of *The Three Bears Rhyme Book,* in *School Library Journal,* Vol. 34, No. 6, February, 1988, p. 71.

The 16 poems offered here assume that Goldilocks and the three bears maintain a close friendship in spite of their initial encounter, which is not mentioned. The verses describe familiar activities such as taking a walk, eating porridge, having a birthday party, and going out in the rain. Some of the poems explore, in a reassuring way, common feelings: getting mad, being afraid of nighttime monsters, feeling too old to take a nap. The narrator's voice varies from poem to poem, with the little bear's point of view most often represented. Although these changes are jarring, the majority of the verses will appeal to children. . . .

A SENDING OF DRAGONS (third novel in the "Pit Dragon" trilogy, 1987)

Publishers Weekly

SOURCE: A review of *A Sending of Dragons,* in *Publishers Weekly,* Vol. 232, No. 16, October 9, 1987, p. 90.

The final volume in the Pit Dragon trilogy—which began with **Dragon's Blood**—concludes a riveting saga that intertwines elements of fantasy and science fiction. The planet of Austar, whose climate and history have much in common with Australia's, serves as backdrop to the social hierarchy of the descendents of the original criminal/warden settlers. This book forces Jakkin and his friend Akki—who became part dragon in the last book, **Heart's Blood**—underground, where they encounter a horrifying race of not-men, whose society is also based on the breeding and destruction of dragons. Yolen's tightly plotted, adventurous trilogy constitutes superb storytelling. She incorporates elements of freedom and rebellion, power and control, love and friendship in a masterfully crafted context of a society sick with perversion. All phenomena relating to dragons—birth, mating, physiology, telepathy, their training, breeding and care—are meticulously evoked. The world of the dragons, which are complex creatures, provides a unique foundation for this compelling finale.

Sally Estes

SOURCE: A review of *A Sending of Dragons,* in *Booklist,* Vol. 84, No. 5, November 1, 1987, pp. 467-8.

On a par in quality and probable popularity with **Dragon's Blood** and **Heart's Blood,** the conclusion to Yolen's trilogy continues the adventures of Jakkin and Akki, who—with the deceased Heart's Blood's five fledgling dragons—have escaped capture to make a home in the wilderness. However, a searching helicopter forces them to flee farther into the mountains, and after an arduous trek they enter a hidden tunnel where they are captured by an underground tribe of primitive people who are also bonded to dragons through a terrifying and bloody rite. When Jakkin discovers a river that flows out of the mountain, he and Akki determine to escape, taking with them a gravid dragon they have befriended and a fledgling they helped birth. Once outside, they are confronted by their searchers and make a choice to return to the city. As in the preceding stories, the author combines well-wrought dragon lore with exciting adventure and good characterization, and her scenes of human-dragon interaction are captivating and convincing. Not so tightly wrapped up that she could not continue it, the trilogy deserves a place on the shelf with McCaffrey's Pern series and Shirley Rousseau Murphy's *Night Pool* and *Ivory Lyre.* All are of special appeal to dragon lovers.

Kirkus Reviews

SOURCE: A review of *A Sending of Dragons,* in *Kirkus Reviews,* Vol. LV, No. 21, November 1, 1987, p. 1582.

The concluding volume in the Pit Dragon trilogy: Akki, Master's daughter, and Jakkin, former slave and dragon trainer, achieve full rapport with the dragons—and discover both the promise of their planet and the obstacles to its fulfillment.

At the end of **Heart's Blood,** Akki and Jakkin were fleeing from both government and rebel factions on Austar IV. They survived the harsh night only by burrowing in the body of Heart's Blood, the dragon that Jakkin had raised and who had died in their defense. The experience, heartbreaking for Jakkin, brings telepathic rapport between the two, and opens full communication with the children of Heart's Blood. In exploring the mountain fastness, they find a hidden race of men who have discovered not only the telepathy induced by dragon's blood but the way to extract metals on resource-poor Austar IV. Realizing that neither the hidden race nor the government recognizes the full potential of the dragons and of Austar IV, Akki and Jakkin escape—with a resolve to use their new knowledge to bring an end to the feudalism and dragon enslavement on their planet.

Yolen has created a full, passionate world to engage our concern; we care about Akki and Jakkin, about the dragons, and about the resolution of Austar IV's conflicts. If the concluding volume seems to end too abruptly, and

with questions unanswered, mark it to the gathering storm on Austar IV and not to its historian. Engrossing and engaging.

Michael Cart

SOURCE: A review of *A Sending of Dragons,* in *School Library Journal,* Vol. 34, No. 5, January, 1988, pp. 87-8.

Here is the third and concluding volume in the indefatigably creative Jane Yolen's "Pit Dragon" trilogy. Jakkin and Akki, whom readers met in the two preceeding volumes, have survived in the Austarian wilds through bonding with the dragon Heart's Blood, and in this volume continue their harrowing journey to freedom and spiritual enlightenment. Like the two volumes preceeding it, *A Sending of Dragons'* particular strengths are in the almost encyclopedic detail which Yolen has lavished upon her fully realized alternative world of Austar IV, in her sympathetic portrayal of the dragons as both victims and telepathic partners, and in the symbolic sub-text which enriches her narrative and reinforces her universal theme of the inter-dependency and unique value of all life forms. Similarly the shortcomings reflect those of the two companion volumes: these include certain stylistic shortcomings and a tendency toward one-dimensional characterization. Nevertheless the trilogy remains an ambitious and rewarding work of speculative fiction. The two previous volumes should be read for a more complete understanding and appreciation of this concluding volume.

Carole A. Barham

SOURCE: A review of *A Sending of Dragons,* in *Voice of Youth Advocates,* Vol. 10, No. 6, February, 1988, p. 293.

Like the other titles in Yolen's *Pit Dragon Trilogy,* *A Sending of Dragons* is absorbing and powerful, rich in the fantastic and yet with the essential realism necessary to draw the reader into a world of rainbow-colored telepathic communication and dragons. After the revolt on Austar IV, Jakkin and Akki are forced to hide with five young dragons, Heart's Blood's hatchlings, their only companions. The hatchlings are bonded to the young couple in a special way: before Heart's Blood's tragic death she had sheltered Jakkin and Akki in her body in the very chamber which had recently carried the five eggs. Jakkin and Akki emerged able not only to withstand the cold of "Dark After," but to communicate telepathically with dragons. When search parties force them to leave their hiding place, Jakkin and Akki discover an underground world of primitive people who are also bonded to dragons and their terrifying ritual of bloody sacrifice. Watching the horrifying spectacle, Jakkin realizes that he and Akki must go home and set things right.

Reminiscent of McCaffrey's Pern dragons, Yolen's tale is original and engrossing. Although it can stand on its own, YA fantasy fans will want them all.

Ann A. Flowers

SOURCE: A review of *A Sending of Dragons,* in *The Horn Book Magazine,* Vol. LXIV, No. 2, March-April, 1988, p. 216.

In the concluding volume of the Pit Dragon trilogy the story is resumed after Jakkin and Akki are saved by sheltering themselves from the fatal cold of the night under the body of Heart's Blood, Jakkin's beloved dragon. The dragons on the planet Austar IV can form telepathic and emotional bonds with their masters, and Jakkin is heartbroken at the loss of Heart's Blood, who has died defending them. But the experience has also changed them: they are now able to survive Dark After; they see colors more clearly; and Jakkin and Akki have learned to communicate with each other telepathically. They have made a new life in the wilds with Heart's Blood's hatchlings Sssasha, Sssargon, Tri-sss, Tri-ssskkette, and Tri-sssha. The two run away still further to evade the searchers, who suspect them of participation in a revolt and find themselves in a dark, dismal, and dangerous cave. They are captured by members of a primitive civilization, which resembles that of prehistoric man, and are horrified to discover these people practicing ritual sacrifice of dragons. Anguished over the fate of the dragons, Jakkin and Akki manage a desperate escape through an underground stream, taking with them the dragon Auricle and a hatchling. Finally discovered by friends, the two can return to their old lives prepared to introduce their unique skills to the inhabitants of Austar IV. The amusing antics of the hatchlings, particularly the egocentric Sssargon, bring humor and lightness to a basically serious book. With the final volume the author has concluded the construction of an alternate world, complete with a believable social system, an evolving history, and an especially interesting and ecologically sound flora and fauna—notably the magnificent pit dragons.

OWL MOON (1987)

Kirkus Reviews

SOURCE: A review of *Owl Moon,* in *Kirkus Reviews,* Vol. LV, No. 20, October 15, 1987, p. 1524.

A rare reappearance of a fine illustrator, whose watercolors here follow a father and small child as they seek an owl beneath a winter moon.

In Yolen's spare, graceful text, the child recounts their trudge through snow, long past bedtime, with Pa repeating an owl call until he is rewarded with a reply plus the sighting of the owl, for a minute or "maybe even a hundred minutes." [John] Schoenherr catches the deep, misty blues and soft browns of night—contrasting them to the snow's stark white so sharply that the bite of the cold is palpable—and hides a wild creature in tree or wall in almost every vista of the farmland landscape. Yolen hints at a philosophical overtone ("When you go owling you don't need words or warm or anything but hope . . . the

kind of hope that flies on silent wings . . ."), but the shared experience of the mysterious, natural night-world seems the more important message of this lovely, quiet book.

Publishers Weekly

SOURCE: A review of *Owl Moon,* in *Publishers Weekly,* Vol. 232, No. 26, November 13, 1987, p. 68.

A girl and her father go owling on a moonlit-winter night near the farm where they live. Bundled tight in wool clothes, they trudge through snow "whiter than the milk in a cereal bowl"; here and there, hidden in ink-blue shadows, a fox, raccoon, fieldmouse and deer watch them pass. An air of expectancy builds as Pa imitates the Great Horned Owl's call once without answer, then again. From out of the darkness "an echo / came threading its way / through the trees." [John] Schoenherr's watercolor washes depict a New England few readers see: the bold stare of a nocturnal owl, a bird's-eye view of a farmhouse. In harmony with the art, the melodious text brings to life an unusual countryside adventure.

Kay E. Vandergrift

SOURCE: A review of *Owl Moon,* in *School Library Journal,* Vol. 34, No. 4, December, 1987, p. 78.

Owl Moon is as expansive as the broad sweep of the great owl's wings and as close and comforting as a small hand held on a wintry night. The poetic narrative is told from the point of view of a child who "had been waiting to go owling with Pa for a long, long time." The father and child venture forth on a cold winter night not to capture, but to commune with, the great horned owl. The illustrations perfectly match the mood and sensitivity of the verbal imagery. The human characters are most often pictured small against sweeping lines which convey distance and the vastness of the natural world that they share with other creatures. The visual images have a sense of depth and seem to invite readers into this special nighttime world. Although the words are the child's, the view is that of the owl looking down on the human scene or of some omnipresent being looking down on both. The play of shadows, the contrast between light and dark, and the way in which the woods make an irregular frame around the words all contribute to the total unity of the book. This is a loving book that readers, male or female, young or old, will want to make a part of their lives.

Phillis Wilson

SOURCE: A review of *Owl Moon,* in *Booklist,* Vol. 84, No. 8, December 15, 1987, p. 714.

An exquisite mood piece, *Owl Moon* is a poetic story of

a winter-wrapped little girl and her father's owling adventure. The elusive magic and gentle shivery excitement that accompany the twosome are felt by the reader. The late-night walks are steeped in family tradition, no words are exchanged, but the companionship of the elusive quest speaks volumes. "When you go owling / you don't need words / or warm / or anything but hope. That's what Pa says." The integrity of Yolen's pleasure in writing about her subject is evident, and [John] Schoenherr, also an owling enthusiast, captures the stark blue-black majesty of the nighttime forest in his powerful and evocative watercolor illustrations. Excellent for one-on-one or read-aloud groups.

Zena Sutherland

SOURCE: A review of *Owl Moon,* in *Bulletin of the Center for Children's Books,* Vol. 41, No. 5, January, 1988, p. 107.

Oversize pages are used in a remarkably effective way by [John] Schoenherr, whose watercolor paintings, in double-page spreads, are economically composed scenes of a winter night that are strikingly dramatic and truly evocative of the cold and silence described in the text. The latter is also spare and poetic, a child's account of going, silently, with her father in hopes that an owl will answer Pa's imitation of an owl's cry. This is a fragment, but a memorable one, in which story and pictures are nicely matched, each reinforcing the other.

Ethel R. Twichell

SOURCE: A review of *Owl Moon,* in *The Horn Book Magazine,* Vol. LXIV, No. 2, March-April, 1988, p. 198.

The story of a child's nighttime walk with her father in search of a great horned owl unfolds against a backdrop of extraordinarily handsome illustrations. Well-wrapped against the cold, the two leave their farm, stepping high over the drifted snow, and wait, listening breathlessly in the shadowy woods for an answer to Pa's call, "'Whoo-whoo-who-who-who-whoooooooo.'" The moon-washed, double-page-spread snowscapes capture the brooding silence of the night and the chill expectancy of father and child. Rough barked and gnarled trees lean under their burden of snow and are a striking setting for the hushed moment when the great owl lifts itself from a nearby tree and is caught, yellow-eyed, in the glare of Pa's flashlight. The delineation of the owl's barred feathers, white bib, and curved talons will satisfy the sharp-eyed birder, but, more than that, the huge bird is imbued with a looming presence and mystery which transcends the description of his appearance in the text. It is splendid to find [John] Schoenherr, known for his pictures in *Rascal, Gentle Ben,* and *Julie of the Wolves,* turning his hand to illustrations in a book which blends a quiet and reflective text with powerful and boldly conceived watercolor paintings.

THE DEVIL'S ARITHMETIC (1988)

Jane Yolen

SOURCE: In a speech delivered in 1990 at the Sydney Taylor Book Awards, in *Judaica Librarianship,* Vol. 5, No. 1, Spring, 1989-Winter, 1990, pp. 52-3.

[The following excerpt is Jane Yolen's acceptance speech for the Children's Book Award.]

I am a Jew. And I am a writer. But I have never been considered a Jewish writer, that is, one who invariably uses Jewish themes or characters in a book. In fact, except for a couple of poems in the *Chicago Jewish Forum* back in the '60s, and three short stories published between 1982 and 1985, I never touched on the matter of Jewishness until I wrote *The Devil's Arithmetic,* the children's novel about the Holocaust that you are honoring tonight. So, in one sense, I feel a fraud in speaking to you. In another, I am extremely grateful for the welcome home.

For that homecoming, it is important that I first thank the people who helped me find the way: my editor, Deborah Brodie, for nagging me to write this particular book after I told her the idea over lunch a number of years ago; my husband, David Stemple, who was furious with me for walking in on him as he was finishing his critical reading of the manuscript, because I caught him crying and he had to flee to the bathroom to scrub away the tears; my agent, Marilyn Marlow, who has supported me unfailingly through 24 years and over 100 books. And, of course, I have to thank my writing group of five women who listened carefully—sometimes in tears—to the chapters as they developed: Patricia MacLachlan, Ann Turner, Shulamith Oppenheim, Judy Karasik, and Zane Kotker. Finally, a special thank you to Barbara Diamond Goldin, who helped me ask some of those unbearable questions of survivors to make my story real.

I am a Jew, but I am a child of American assimilation. I was raised on stories in the Andrew Lang color fairy books, on tales of King Arthur and Robin Hood. I was a fanatical reader of fantasy and magic, history and adventure. I was interested in Camelot, not Haifa, and in laws of chivalry, not the laws of *kashrut.* What I knew of my Jewish heritage came from family weddings, bar mitzvahs, and seders, like the one with my Uncle Louis that was reproduced in my book. But the Yolen versions of Judaica have always been somewhat antic. I had a great-grandfather, a storyteller, who told Yiddish versions of Shakespearean plays and passed them off as his own.

There are books one writes because they are a delight. There are books one writes because one is asked to. There are books one writes because . . . they are there. And there are books one writes simply because *the book has to be written. The Devil's Arithmetic* is this last kind of book. I did not just write it. The book itself was a mitzvah.

Researching it was a trip through an appalling landscape.

Yet reading the dry role of history has its comforts: statistics, maps, diagrams can all help distance the researcher from the drama. And anyone working exclusively on Holocaust material must construct a careful wall between himself or herself and the reality, or be destroyed by it. Oh, I knew the names, dates and the bitter roll call of the camps that read like a dark, malevolent poem. But my goal was—at first—to learn, not to weep. Facts . . . FACTS . . . were the wall behind which I prepared for the story. But, of course, the cracks in the wall appeared.

My cracks began with the movie "Shoah" and with Victor Frankel's book *Man's Search for Meaning*. I remembered, with sudden clarity, a friend telling us about his childhood in a camp where the children had to dive into the midden pile whenever the commandant visited. That image—of children saving their lives by becoming garbage—struck me as central to the story I had to tell.

My book begins in the 1980s, with an almost thirteen-year-old girl, Hannah Stern, who is tired of being forced to learn the history of her people. She refuses to listen to the stories of her grandparents' past. But she is whirled into that very past, drawn through the door opened at the seder for Elijah, that consummate traveler in time. So Hannah—and through her, all the young readers of the book—rides the whinwind of years back. I am hoping that once the door is opened and the child reader steps back willingly with Hannah, then history itself will not let him (or her) go.

While I was in the middle of writing *The Devil's Arithmetic*, I was invited to Indianapolis to spend a week in a private school where the boys and girls had studied my books. I spent an hour in each classroom, K-8th grade, and spoke with the teachers as well. How I remember the discussion in one of the eighth grade classes; I had just told a story called "Mr. Fox," and we got into a discussion of the story, a very scary Bluebeard variant, in which the emphasis is on the dreaded stranger who comes to town. It led into a debate about who are the strangers we fear, and from there, into talking about black/white, Arab/Jew, American/Russian—even to rivalries in team sports. And somehow, we segued into concentration camps. So I began to tell them about *The Devil's Arithmetic* and, finally, one boy raised his hand, asking tentatively, "You're making all this stuff up, right?"

Making this stuff up. He meant about the ovens and the starvation and the *Sonderkommandos* and the rest. About the numbers tattooed on the arms, and the shaven heads, and the death showers. About the cattle cars and the lime pits and the babies torn from their mothers' breasts.

Making this stuff up. I said that they had two teachers in the school who were Holocaust survivors, one who had been in the camps. And when they asked me how I—who had been there only a single day so far—knew this, and asked who the teachers were, I replied: "This is your assignment: to find them and to learn that I was not making this up."

This year, I was at another school, in Colorado, where again the students had spent weeks studying my books. The two fifth grades had heard *The Devil's Arithmetic* read aloud.

"How did you do it?" I asked the teachers.

They replied: "At the end, we all put our heads down on the desk, and we all wept. And then we discussed the book."

But one fifth grader from that school slipped a note into my hand. It said: "I am a lot like Hannah. I didn't want to have to hear any more history. But after reading your book, I understand why I must remember. Now can I talk to you about Hebrew School?"

There is a wonderful story about the Baal Shem Tov that is, to me, a core story about being Jewish. It goes like this:

> Whenever misfortune threatened the Jews, the great rabbi, the Baal Shem Tov, would go to a special place in the forest. There he would light a ritual fire and say a special prayer. And misfortune would be averted.
>
> In the passing of time, the Baal Shem Tov died, and the task of leading the people fell to another rabbi. And whenever misfortune threatened the Jews, he, too, would go to that special part of the forest and light the ritual fire. But he had never been taught the prayer. Still, it was enough—and misfortune was averted.
>
> He, too, at last came to the end of his days, and another rabbi led the people. Whenever misfortune threatened, he would go at once to the special part of the forest. But he had never been taught how to light the ritual fire and, of course, he had never been told the special prayer. Still—it was enough, and misfortune was averted.
>
> At last he, too, died, and the task of leading the people fell to Rabbi Israel of Rizhin. Whenever misfortune threatened the Jews . . . well, of course, he did not know the prayer, or how to light the ritual fire. He did not even know the special place in the forest. All he knew was how to tell this story.
>
> And it was enough.
>
> (From: *Favorite Folk Tales from Around the World,* ed. by Jane Yolen. New York: Pantheon, 1987)

I was not there in the special part of the forest, where all the Jews were taken from their homes. My family was among the lucky ones. We came over at the turn of the century. The family joke among Yolens is now: If we had *only* escaped the Cossacks, we would have been wiped out by Hitler. If we had *only* escaped Hitler, we would have been done in by Chernobyl. Very lucky indeed.

I did not light any ritual fires, nor did I have relatives burned alive in the Holocaust. My immediate family was not among those counted by the hideous Nazi mathematics, where humans were numbers tattooed on the inside of the wrist or scrawled in smoke against the sky.

I did not even know the ritual words, having been little educated in Jewish tradition or Jewish law.

Still, I could tell the story—the story that whispered in my ear for a number of years, and whose voice could not be denied. A story for young readers, about a Jewish girl from today who opens the door at the family seder and is whisked back to a small shtetl on the Polish-German border in 1942, where she is taken—along with the other villagers—to a death camp. All the stories of the Holocaust—fact and fiction—must be told over and over and over again, whether we remember the place in the forest, or the way to light the fire, or how to say the special prayers. The stories must be told because it is my story, your story, our story, *history.*

And perhaps it will be enough. Thank you.

Kirkus Reviews

SOURCE: A review of *The Devil's Arithmetic,* in *Kirkus Reviews,* Vol. LVI, No. 16, August 15, 1988, p. 1248.

Yolen is the author of a hundred books, many of which have been praised for their originality, humor, or poetic vision, but this thoughtful, compelling novel is unique among them.

Hannah, 13, finds the annual Seder—which calls up her grandfather's memories of the death camp he and his sister Eva survived—tedious, the facts distant and unreal. Chosen to perform the ritual of opening the door to Elijah, she finds herself in rural Poland in 1942, as Chaya (life), the heroic girl whose Hebrew name she bears. There, she shares the experiences of villagers who are interrupted during a wedding, transported in a grueling four-day train journey, and delivered to a camp where the commandant routinely chooses victims for the gas chambers. At the camp another girl, the indomitable Rivka, teaches her how to survive, and she learns an unforgettable lesson: some must live, at whatever cost, to bear witness. When Rivka is "chosen," Hannah goes to her death in her place—and awakes to find herself returned to the family Seder, recognizing Aunt Eva as the beloved friend she saved.

In less skillful hands, such a story would risk being either didactic or irreverent, but Yolen has so completely integrated her deep concern with the structure and movingly poetic language of her story that the meaning shines clear. Symbolic details—such as the role memory plays in Hannah's response to her experiences—are meticulously worked out. A triumphantly moving book.

Roger Sutton

SOURCE: A review of *The Devil's Arithmetic,* in *Bulletin*

of the Center for Children's Books, Vol. 42, No. 2, October, 1988, pp. 23-4.

Time-travel fantasy can be an honorable form of historical fiction, but how effective is it as an introduction to the Holocaust? In Jane Yolen's engrossing new fantasy, *The Devil's Arithmetic,* the thirteen-year-old heroine, Hannah, slips back in time when, as part of the Passover feast, she opens the door to welcome Elijah. The prophet isn't there; instead, Hannah finds herself looking out from a door into a pastoral landscape. The people in the unfamiliar house call her Chaya ("Life," and also the Hebrew for Hannah) and excuse her confusion with the explanation that her parents died of sickness, as Chaya nearly did herself, and so she has been sent to them—from *Lublin*—to recover. The date is revealed when Hannah and her new-found family, on their way to a wedding, encounter soldiers. Implausibly, no one else seems even aware that there is a war going on, but Hannah, after ascertaining the year (1942), understands. "The men down there, they're not wedding guests. They're Nazis. Nazis! Do you understand? They kill people. They killed—kill—will kill Jews. Hundreds of them. Thousands of them. Six million of them. I know." Along with other villagers, the wedding party is packed into a freight car and taken to a concentration camp. Hannah's warnings seem crude. The victims certainly think so (and refuse to listen), and the reader feels bludgeoned as well. But captivated, too: Yolen has shaped the traditional suspense of the time fantasy—how will she get back?—with a sensational twist: will Hannah be murdered in the gas chambers?

Yes, and no. Hannah survives in the camp (a fictionalized Auschwitz) for months, and the depiction of the horrors she sees is more graphic than any we've seen in holocaust fiction for children before. She is forced into the showers and is relieved to find only water coming from the spouts. When her head is shaved, Hannah loses her memories of the future. Her arm is tattooed. She sees friends murdered, survives several "choosings," and watches helplessly as a little boy is taken "to be with his mother" by the Mengele figure, Dr. Brauer. She endures the slaps and barked commands (*"Schnell!"*) of the three-fingered guard, the *blokova.* The sweet-faced *sonderkommando* who carries to the crematorium the bullet-ridden body of Chaya's friend Fayge "as one might carry a loved one, with conscious tenderness and pride" will survive, unbelievably, to become Hannah's grandfather, the one who raves at family gatherings about the number on his arm.

Jane Yolen has written a powerful, not easily forgotten, story, but is it a story about the Holocaust? The horror—and the history—are betrayed by the essentially comforting vision of the story and its time-travel form. There is a future, and those who are brave, and good, can live to see it. Near the end of *The Devil's Arithmetic,* three of Chaya's friends are chosen for extermination, to enter the place called "Lilith's Cave" by the prisoners. Tearing Rivka's kerchief from her head, Chaya places it on her own. Her memory has returned. Arm in arm with the other two (and how that choosing must have felt!) she walks into the gas chamber saying "Ready or not, here we come," a flip Americanism that serves as epitaph for Shifre and Esther, but as Dorothy's slippers for Hannah herself, who suddenly finds herself once again at the door of her grandparents' apartment. With her grandfather, the *son-derkommando,* and with beloved Aunt Eva, who, it turns out, was Rifka.

The lesson of Yolen's book is that we have survived the Holocaust, we have lived the future. We have learned, as Yolen says in her afterword, that "swallows still sing around the smokestacks." This optimistic, neatly rounded lesson fits comfortably into children's literature, a genre that, despite well-known exceptions, demands a hopeful conclusion. How much hope can be extracted from the Holocaust? The stories of survivors can be inspiring, but, as survivor Primo Levi writes in *The Drowned and the Saved,* those of the dead are the truer stories. And which is Hannah's? She is neither victim nor survivor, nor, despite Eva/Rifka's claims, is she a heroine; she was never really there.

Publishers Weekly

SOURCE: A review of *The Devil's Arithmetic,* in *Publishers Weekly,* Vol. 234, No. 16, October 14, 1988, p. 78.

The Holocaust was so monstrous a crime that the mind resists belief and the story must be made new for each individual. Yolen's book is about remembering. During a Passover Seder, 12-year-old Hannah finds herself transported from America in 1988 to Poland in 1942, where she assumes the life of young Chaya. Within days the Nazis take Chaya and her neighbors off to a concentration camp, mere components in the death factory. As days pass, Hannah's own memory of her past, and the prisoners' future, fades until she is Chaya completely. Chaya/Hannah's final sacrifice, and the return of memory, is her victory over the horror. The book's simplicity is its strength; no comment is needed because the facts speak for themselves. This brave and powerful book has much it can teach a young audience.

Susan M. Harding

SOURCE: A review of *The Devil's Arithmetic,* in *School Library Journal,* Vol. 35, No. 3, November, 1988, p. 114.

In this novel, Yolen attempts to answer those who question why the Holocaust should be remembered. Hannah, 12, is tired of remembering, and is embarrassed by her grandfather, who rants and raves at the mention of the Nazis. Her mother's explanations of how her grandparents and great-aunt lost all family and friends during that time have little effect. Then, during a Passover Seder, Hannah is chosen to open the door to welcome the prophet Elijah. As she does so, she is transported to a village in Poland in the 1940s, where everyone thinks that she is Chaya, who has just recovered from a serious illness. She is captured by the Nazis and taken to a death camp, where

she is befriended by a young girl named Rivka, who teaches her how to fight the dehumanizing processes of the camp and hold onto her identity. When at last their luck runs out and Rivka is chosen, Hannah/Chaya, in an almost impulsive act of self-sacrifice, goes in her stead. As the door to the gas chamber closes behind her, she is returned to the door of her grandparents' apartment, waiting for Elijah. Through Hannah, with her memories of the present and the past, Yolen does a fine job of illustrating the importance of remembering. She adds much to children's understanding of the effects of the Holocaust, which will reverberate throughout history, today and tomorrow.

Cynthia Samuels

SOURCE: "Hannah Learns to Remember," in *The New York Times Book Review,* November 13, 1988, p. 62.

In recent years the device of time travel has become steadily more popular with young readers. But in her brave and moving novel *The Devil's Arithmetic,* Jane Yolen has brought the time travel convention to a new and ambitious level. Instead of fantasy she offers a sober and enriching dose of history.

Ms. Yolen has chosen to take her young heroine, Hannah, not to a make-believe land but to a grim past—pushing her back in time to become a Jewish teen-ager in the midst of the Holocaust. And though heroism is very much a part of the story, it is not the swaggering heroism of rescue and escape but the stoic courage of the condemned as they help one another to end their days with as much dignity as they can muster.

Hannah is a modern, assimilated Jewish teen-ager (she is "nearly" 13) in New Rochelle, N.Y., who complains to her mother, "*All* Jewish holidays are about remembering, Mama. I'm tired of remembering." Comfortable in the suburban ordinariness that probably mirrors that of many adolescent readers, Hannah resents going to the Bronx for the annual family seder with her elderly relatives who survived the concentration camps. For her the rituals of Passover evoke references to "Darth Vader, or Robin Hood, or . . . or the Easter Bunny. . . . No one believed those superstitions anymore." What happens to Hannah, then, is a reply to her all too typical scorn for her heritage: an attempt to demonstrate the values of both a religion and culture that were nearly destroyed, and to depict the evil of the regime whose purpose was their extermination.

An adult's first instinct may be to recoil from the idea of fictionalizing the Holocaust for young adults. We don't want our children to know too much too soon; we'd like to give them as much as we can of what is good about the world before we must tell them about the unspeakable; we hesitate to cross the bridge from one to the other. And we're right.

But so is Ms. Yolen. As she sets Hannah on an irrevocable course made all the more horrible by her understanding of what is to come, she provides companions whose decency steadfastly affirm basic human values. At the seder, the girl opens the door for the spirit of the prophet Elijah and finds herself, with her modern memory, in a Jewish village in Poland in 1942.

She is in a farmhouse, just at dusk. She is Chaya now, a niece of the family, recently come from the city where her parents have died. Her uncle is to be married in the morning. Everyone is excited. But the next day Nazi troops load the villagers into trucks and take them to the railroad station.

Though the reader is not shielded from the details, their intensity is muted. Ms. Yolen has wisely chosen to omit the sort of graphic descriptions that might overwhelm youngsters and has balanced Hannah's story with moments of heroism and generosity.

Of course Hannah tries to warn her new family and friends, to urge them to flee. But just as many of the Jews of Europe refused to listen then, so they refuse to heed this child for whom their future is the past. And because their refusal is accurately and compassionately portrayed, it seems inevitable—evoking sorrow in the reader rather than alienation or anger.

But Ms. Yolen resists making the reader feel utterly powerless against evil: she allows Hannah a critical choice. The decision Hannah makes, and the life she saves, return her to the present and offer her the opportunity to give the gift of life to someone she cherishes.

"I remember. Oh, I remember," Hannah tells her assembled family as she returns to the present and the seder table. And indeed she does. Her decision, unlike that of William Styron's Sophie, offers affirmation and identity.

Ms. Yolen, a prolific writer for children and adults who has worked in the genres of folklore and science fiction, says on the dust jacket that she wrote *The Devil's Arithmetic* for her children, who need "to learn, and to remember." This is a book parents should want to read first. And while many young people who read it may turn to their parents for interpretations and comfort, the story's impact seems vastly different from that of, say, Elie Wiesel's *Night,* another book about the Holocaust they might encounter. His was a testament—an offering of evidence to a world that could not fathom such evil. Ms. Yolen's novel is more of a bridge to the receding past, and it concludes on a note of redemption and love. Sooner or later all our children must know what happened in the days of the Holocaust. *The Devil's Arithmetic* offers an affecting way to begin.

BEST WITCHES: POEMS FOR HALLOWEEN (1989)

Kirkus Reviews

SOURCE: A review of *Best Witches: Poems for Hallow-een,* in *Kirkus Reviews,* Vol. LVII, No. 15, August 15, 1989, p. 1253.

Twenty-four mostly new poems to celebrate the many-faced holiday—ranging from the sprightly and easily accessible ("The Magic House": "We should have known when we tasted the eaves, / Breaking them off like toffee . . . But it was only when we saw the witch / That we knew we were in deep, deep trouble") to the comically gruesome ("The Fossilot," about a fossil that consumes the scientists who have reassembled it) to the thought-provoking ("The wand's a symbol / of a treasure. / It's heart—not hand— / one has to train") to a touch of real evil ("The Witch's Cauldron": "Strong as a wish, / Hard as hate, / Full as a moon, / Brutal as fate"). With full-color illustrations on every double spread, [Elise] Primavera ably reflects the poems' many moods, making the popular images funny and idiosyncratic enough to be interesting—and tempering the frightful so that it's scary but not too frightening. Good quality, lively entertainment.

Susan Scheps

SOURCE: A review of *Best Witches: Poems for Hallow-een,* in *School Library Journal,* Vol. 35, No. 13, September, 1989, p. 270.

Yolen has concocted a delightful volume of 21 poems that introduce witches and spectres of all types: feisty modern singles and tombmates with marital problems; witch druggists, pizza bakers, and school witches; old fashioned broom riders and spell makers; and one who rides a flying carpet. Many of her poems are the humorous, upbeat sort that attract young readers like magic. She has also included some silly poems, jump-rope rhymes, and several of a more sophisticated nature. [Elise] Primavera has painted a panorama of witch personalities ranging from orange-haired vamps to knobby-chinned broomstick riders with frizzled hair—from ugly old hags to young wide-eyed children. A sense of humor pervades. Most of the two-page watercolor illustrations are painted on color-washed backgrounds. Special effects—misty, ghost-like apparitions, shadowy monsters, sparkling stardust, and creeping fog—highlight many pages. Only three poems mention Halloween; children will enjoy this collection all year long.

Zena Sutherland

SOURCE: A review of *Best Witches: Poems for Hallow-een,* in *Bulletin of the Center for Children's Books,* Vol. 43, No. 2, October, 1989, p. 48.

There's nice control of form, meter, rhyme, and scansion in this collection; there are moments of spine-chill that middle-grades readers will enjoy; there is, as prime appeal, a humor that has verve and sophistication but is never inaccessible. The ebullience of Yolen's poetry is matched by that of [Elise] Primavera's paintings, which are colorful but pleasantly gruesome, with a great deal of vitality and antic humor.

Margaret A. Bush

SOURCE: A review of *Best Witches: Poems for Halloween,* in *The Horn Book Magazine,* Vol. LXV, No. 6, November-December, 1989, p. 786.

Colorful comic scenes aptly convey the lighthearted tone of these often humorous verses. Takeoffs on current culture mark the lives of many of the witches. "Oh, I'm the model of a major modern witch," sings a redhead in a satin jump suit, ankle socks, and spike heels as she dances around her condominium. Pizza parlors, department stores, television game shows, and a "used-carpet" salesman are all features of this world of witches. To be sure, the traditional elements of witchcraft are not forgotten: spells and symbols, cats and caldrons appear in the twenty-one poems, which vary widely in shape, meter, and tone. Not all of the poems feature witches, nor are they all humorous. Clever parodies contrast with occasional somber pieces that are sometimes beyond the ken of the intended audience. The lovely reverie "Magic Wands," the philosophical "Old Man of the Wood," and the surrealistic "Ivy" are thought-provoking contrasts to poems modeled on jump rope rhymes or those playing on children's interests in corny riddles, extinct animals, and Halloween night. Most of the poems have not been previously published, but it seems likely that many will reappear over time in diverse collections.

📖 THINGS THAT GO BUMP IN THE NIGHT: A COLLECTION OF ORIGINAL STORIES (edited by Jane Yolen and Martin H. Greenberg, 1989)

Roger Sutton

SOURCE: A review of *Things That Go Bump in the Night: A Collection of Original Stories,* in *Bulletin of the Center for Children's Books,* Vol. 43, No. 1, September, 1989, pp. 23-4.

Yolen's own contribution to this anthology has a can't-miss title—"The Baby-sitter"—and is the most effectively frightening tale in the book: Hilary learns a ghost-warding trick from the twins that comes in real handy when a Halloween-masked intruder comes to call. "All she could see was a crumpled gorilla mask, a piece out of a green shirt, and a dark stain on the floor that was rapidly disappearing, as if someone—or something—were licking it up." William Sleator's story about a claustrophobia-causing elevator is creepy, and Diana Wynne Jones spins a crankily humorous story about a chair that comes to obnoxious life. Most of the other fifteen writers will be unknown to YA readers; some are practiced, others promising. Midori Snyder's "Jack Straw" is a quiet, moody standout about a girl's two encounters with Death, once deferred and once accepted. As in the best ghost stories, this

one leaves the reader with both exhilaration and horror. Like many written-to-order collections, this one has some stories that suffer a lack of imaginative spark or are over-ambitious, but most demonstrate verbal nerve and a fair degree of ghostly chill.

Barbara Hutcheson

SOURCE: A review of *Things That Go Bump in the Night: A Collection of Original Stories,* in *School Library Journal,* Vol. 35, No. 14, October, 1989, p. 139.

A collection of original chillers. Several of the contributors are well known in the genre (Yolen, William Sleator, Bruce Coville, Diana Wynne Jones, and Anne E. Crompton), and others less so. The settings are mostly contemporary, urban America, but China, Canada, Britain, and the Philippines are also represented. Most represent a fairly straightforward prose narrative style, but there are two with a folklorish tone, and even a movie script. All are suitably creepy, although not lacking in humor. The gender balance of protagonists is a little better than usual, with nine stories featuring a male main character, five female, and four shared or not indicated (and irrelevant). Inanimate objects, some of them disturbingly active, feature prominently, as the title suggests. The pieces vary in length from a three-page quickie to a novella. There is a short introduction that may or may not be read, as it's a somewhat self-conscious apologia for this type of fantasy. There are some welcome notes on the contributors. The only real fault is the predictable one for this type of anthology: the quality of the selections is uneven, with some stories first-rate and others only so-so. Yolen's *The Babysitter* and Sleator's *The Elevator* are real heart-pounders, but Jones' *Chair Person* is a one-joke piece that goes on far too long. *The Scarlet Batling* rates top marks for authenticity, but only a passing grade for child appeal. On the other hand *Duffy's Jacket* would be a perfect Friday afternoon classroom read-aloud or book-talk centerpiece. Overall, worth recommending for selective reading and as a good alternative to less-suitable horror titles demanded by this age group.

📖 DINOSAUR DANCES (1990)

Kirkus Reviews

SOURCE: A review of *Dinosaur Dances,* in *Kirkus Reviews,* Vol. LVIII, No. 17, September 1, 1990, p. 1255.

Suppose dinosaurs dressed like people and cavorted in dances like the waltz or the hula, to the sound of disco or hard rock. Wordsmith Yolen turns out 17 witty poems on this theme, playing expertly with both sound ("When the allosaurus / Does a rumba / Does she lumber? / Is she limber?") and sense ("Dress Code: A Sedimental Journey": " . . . A fad is a fad . . . And that's why no clothes are imprinted on stones: / Only the remnants of dinosaur bones"). Dinosaurs are sure-fire popular; the fun of [Bruce] Degen's lively rendition of them frolicking in fancy dress outshines Yolen's rather quietly satirical comparison with their human cousins. It's too bad that editors still don't excise casual mention of the never-existent brontosaurus; still, sprightly, clever good fun.

Ilene Cooper

SOURCE: A review of *Dinosaur Dances,* in *Booklist,* Vol. 87, No. 5, November 1, 1990, p. 52.

You can't miss with dinosaurs, and this group is particularly appealing, dressed to the teeth for a dance. Yolen offers 17 amusing poems detailing what the high life was like at the remains of a "prehistoric party." Perhaps the most amusing pairing of art and rhyme is in "Tyrannosaurus," where the prehistoric beast assumes a John Travolta-like disco dancer persona. "He strides onto the dance floor / Each and every weekend night / With his head slicked down with hair oil / and his suit a brilliant white." In most cases, children will probably like [Bruce] Degen's entertaining two-page spreads more than the poetry, which sometimes seems rather adult in tone. The book's cover, with two dinos tripping the light fantastic, and looking very Fred and Ginger-ish, is pure fun.

Publishers Weekly

SOURCE: A review of *Dinosaur Dances,* in *Publishers Weekly,* Vol. 237, No. 44, November 2, 1990, p. 74.

The terpsichorean dinosaurs in this collection of whimsical poems allemande left and pirouette in high style. Although Yolen's verses often scan raggedly and require no small knowledge of fossils in order to comprehend the humor and puns, [Bruce] Degen's witty dinosaurs never miss a beat. A brontosaurus Fred Astaire sports a monocle and lace cravat while waltzing to "a rhythm that pounds / All the way down the street." A Carmen-like ankylosaurus dances with a rose in her teeth, and hard rock dinosaurs blare bedrock music. Degen's detailed drawings brim with fun, as in the picture of two dinosaurs preparing for the dance at a beauty parlor littered with magazines—on the cover of *Reptilian Quarterly,* a dandified tyrannosaurus is "Puttin' on the Rex."

Cathryn A. Camper

SOURCE: A review of *Dinosaur Dances,* in *School Library Journal,* Vol. 36, No. 12, December, 1990, p. 97.

Dinosaur Dances sound like fun, but it's [Bruce] Degen's illustrations that shake a tail feather here, not the rhymes. Yolen's idea of connecting poems and prehistoric prancing is a good one, but the contents of these verses seem more directed toward adults than children. Kids will appreciate some of the sillier sounding rhymes—"When the allosaurus / Does a rumba / Does she lumber? / Is she limber?"—and they'll recognize some of the dances and

music Yolen describes. But the poems about dress codes, love, and choosing dance partners would be of little interest to young readers, were it not for Degen's boisterous illustrations. His bright colors and energetic style will hold even nonreaders' attention. Often, the humor of the drawings surpasses that of the text; for example, a T. Rex drawn as John Travolta. A smaller complaint is that these dinos reenact some rather tired stereotypes, such as the ugly female wallflower—albeit humorous, it lacks originality. . . .

SKY DOGS (1990)

Publishers Weekly

SOURCE: A review of *Sky Dogs,* in *Publishers Weekly,* Vol. 237, No. 39, September 28, 1990, p. 101.

In this lyrical tale drawn from Blackfoot legend, an old man recounts the origin of his name, He-who-loves-horses. He describes the coming of horses. "Sky Dogs," from across the plains, and the wonder and awe he and his people felt when they first saw these "big . . . elk, with tails of straw." He-who-loves-horses, then a lonely boy, learns to care for and ride the beautiful animals, and his knowledge and abilities help him earn a place on the council of warriors—and a sense of self-worth. His story is made all the more poignant by the elderly narrator's revelation that "now I sit in the tipi, and food is brought to me, and I do not ride the wind." [Barry] Moser's sun-and-earth-toned watercolors, of the plains and of the main character as both boy and man, are lovely and haunting.

Kirkus Reviews

SOURCE: A review of *Sky Dogs,* in *Kirkus Reviews,* Vol. LVIII, No. 19, October 1, 1990, p. 1399.

Drawing on Native American tales, Yolen creates her own story (as she meticulously explains in a note) about how horses might first have come to the Blackfeet: An old man tells why he is called "He-who-loves-horses." When he was a boy, three large beasts (so awe-inspiring that people called them "Sky Dogs") arrived bearing dying members of a hostile tribe, and stayed to become an important part of his tribe's life and lore. Yolen's dignified, lyrical style turns the episode into an event that resonates with significance; [Barry] Moser's stunning watercolor illustrations—in sunset gold and the rich hues of shadowed sandstone—shine with the glory of remembered youth. . . .

Leone McDermott

SOURCE: A review of *Sky Dogs,* in *Booklist,* Vol. 87, No. 6, October 15, 1990, p. 453.

Drawing on a number of Blackfoot Indian stories, Yolen

Jane Yolen talks with students, Texas, 1983.

has fashioned a spare, realistic tale of how the Blackfeet first acquired horses. A young boy of the Piegan band relates the time when three Kutani Indians arrived on doglike animals as big as elk. Many Piegan feared the strange creatures, but Long Arrow pronounced them "sky dogs," a gift sent from heaven by Old Man the creator. This simple, undramatic account, which focuses largely on people's immediate reactions, has a feel of authenticity. Young readers, however, might have benefited from more details on how the horses changed the Indians' way of life. [Barry] Moser's sweeping watercolors drawn on handmade paper glow in sunset tones and range from detailed portraits to silhouettelike panoramas.

Patricia Dooley

SOURCE: A review of *Sky Dogs,* in *School Library Journal,* Vol. 36, No. 11, November, 1990, pp. 100-1.

Many legends reflect the radical difference the advent of the horse made in the life of the Plains Indians. In fluid storytelling style, Yolen melds the mythic and the realistic modes in the emotions and reactions of her narrator, a

motherless Piegan boy, on the day the first "sky dogs" come to his band. Fear and disbelief are tempered by wonder and gratitude. The horse brings the hero a substitute mother and status in the tribe, as it would bring success to all the Plains people. Goble's retelling in *The Gift of the Sacred Dog* emphasizes the legendary over the realistic, and his slick, flat, brightly colored illustrations are the antithesis of [Barry] Moser's. Moser's palette is all ochre, yellow, and umber, red earth and golden sky. Against the low horizon and dry prairie, humans and horses loom, at once significant and insignificant. Two portrait roundels are as revealing and moving as Catlin's or Bodmer's 19th-century "noble savages." Writer and artist together have produced a fine evocation of a place and a people.

Hanna B. Zeiger

SOURCE: A review of *Sky Dogs,* in *The Horn Book Magazine,* Vol. LXVII, No. 1, January-February, 1991, p. 62.

This story of a band of Blackfoot Indians' first encounter with horses is told as a first-person account. The narrator, now an elder of the tribe, recalls his childhood and the day the Sky Dogs first came over the horizon from the west. Some members of his tribe are uneasy and frightened and run away, but, since the boy's mother is dead, he has no one to run to, so he stays and watches "with big eyes." Of the three sick Indians who ride into the village with these strange creatures, only one survives. She becomes his father's new wife and teaches the boy how to feed, care for, and ride the Sky Dogs. Because he is the first one brave enough to approach the animals, his courage earns him the name of He-who-loves-horses. The author has drawn from parts of different stories and legends about the coming of horses to the Plains Indians to create the story of a little boy and the Sky Dogs. Barry Moser's illustrations are full of dignity and drenched with the bright sunlight of the plains.

Zena Sutherland

SOURCE: A review of *Sky Dogs,* in *Bulletin of the Center for Children's Books,* Vol. 44, No. 6, February, 1991, p. 156.

Yolen's postscript explains that she has drawn from history and from Blackfeet legends to tell the story of how the first horses (Sky Dogs) came to the Piegan Indians (a Blackfeet band). The narrator is an elderly man who was a boy when this occurred, and he describes the apprehension and awe that gave way to pride and affection, as he and others learned to care for and ride the Sky Dogs that so greatly changed their lives. The text is smooth, poetic, and nicely suited to reading aloud or telling. [Barry] Moser's paintings—all red, gold, and brown—are starkly effective: spacious in the outdoor scenes, beautifully detailed in the portraits of the narrator, He-who-loves-horses, and of his chief, Long Arrow.

📖 *BIRD WATCH: A BOOK OF POETRY* (1990)

Kirkus Reviews

SOURCE: A review of *Bird Watch: A Book of Poetry,* in *Kirkus Reviews,* Vol. LVIII, No. 20, October 15, 1990, p. 1461.

Celebrating an activity that is companionable as well as scientific ("I will miss these conversations . . . where I listen carefully / then answer / only with my eyes") and that fosters a special bond with the natural world, Yolen presents 17 melodious evocations of particular species and the ruminations they've prompted. Her images are in tune with her subjects, and her language is concrete, its simplicity often merely the surface of a more profound thought, as in "Time Piece": "Which is more fleeting: / the flicker / of swallow wings / in a field of insects, / the hover / of a hummingbird / over a flower's invitation, / or the footprints / of sandpipers / before an incoming tide?" [Ted] Lewin's lovely watercolors, precise enough to serve for identification, provide a perfect backdrop—or, for those unfamiliar with the birds, a vivid sense of their character. A last page offers notes on most of the birds. A book to bring nature- and poetry-lovers together.

Publishers Weekly

SOURCE: A review of *Bird Watch,* in *Publishers Weekly,* Vol. 237, No. 43, October 26, 1990, p. 71.

From its arresting cover of a vee of geese stretching across the "earless / face of the moon" to the songbirds that sit "along the wires / like scattered notes / on lines of music" on the last page, this soaring collection of poems about birds will delight young ornithologists. Though some of the poems deal with subjects beyond the experience of most children, all are carefully wrought and thoughtful. [Ted] Lewin's breathtaking watercolors marvelously complement Yolen's graceful language and gentle humor, and a glossary at the end supplies interesting facts about each species of bird included in the volume. Like Yolen's winter finches at their feeder, these elegant poems and unforgettable pictures will last "long, long / past the turning of the year."

Hazel Rochman

SOURCE: A review of *Bird Watch,* in *Booklist,* Vol. 87, No. 5, November 1, 1990, pp. 520-1.

Bird watchers are silent, says Yolen in the first poem in this collection, "I listen carefully / then answer / only with my eyes." She and artist [Ted] Lewin do observe birds with quiet attention, and they neither intrude nor prettify. Yolen's witty metaphors swoop from the wild to human activities: the woodpecker's *ratatatat* is like a casual jackhammer on a city street, like an oil drill, a record needle, a dentist's probe. In dramatic double-page spreads Lewin paints single birds, like swan, robin, swell-

ing turkey, and scarlet cardinal, or a flight of geese against the sky or finches on a branch. A few poems are flat, but in some of the best pages, image, movement, sound, and ideas seem to blend in words and pictures—as in "Calligraphy," about the dark ducks on a pond, the tracings of their backwash, and their muted reflections in the gray water. With brief notes about each bird at the back of the book, this is a treat for nature and poetry lovers.

Betsy Hearne

SOURCE: A review of *Bird Watch: A Book of Poetry,* in *Bulletin of the Center for Children's Books,* Vol. 44, No. 4, December, 1990, p. 106.

Like Marilyn Singer's fine *Turtle in July,* this nature poetry is paired with evocative watercolor art that gives young readers plenty of space to consider the graphic verbal images. Some of the lines are solemn: "From the lake / laughs the last joke / of a solitary loon. / Winter silences us all." Others are satirical, as in the poem about choosing a supermarket tom over a wild turkey ("In matters of eating, / our minds do what they can"). "Swan" offers rhymed humor with a contrast of the bird's stately appearance above the water, versus its functional feet underneath. [Ted] Lewin's pictures strike just the right tonal balance, neither glamorizing the birds nor distracting from the poetry. The swan picture, for example, is a deep blue wash with the white bird framing the poem in white print. A last page gives the names and a bit of information about each bird.

Kay E. Vandergrift

SOURCE: A review of *Bird Watch,* in *School Library Journal,* Vol. 36, No. 12, December, 1990, p. 97.

Yolen and [Ted] Lewin have combined verbal and visual images in an expression of reverence for and joy in our feathered friends. But this is not, in any way, a preachy book. Yolen's startling descriptions almost jump off the page, reminding readers of what they may have watched but never truly saw. Sometimes the images will cause readers to stop and then break into laughter, as when a woodpecker's ratatat is described as "as cleansing as a dentist's probe / in a mouthful of cavities." There is a poignancy in "Nestlings," which states that, "All babies / are born / ugly / and unfinished. / But today / I found a nest with / three / baby / robins / and they were / beautiful / because they were mine." Each double-page spread contains a single poem and corresponding picture. The birds are beautifully, vibrantly, and realistically portrayed in Lewin's watercolor paintings that perfectly match the words of the poems. The cardinal, "a brilliant blot / on winter's page," is indeed a bold red on the upper left of two stark, snowy pages. The Great Blue Heron is smaller against the dark autumn colors, revealing the complete mirrored reflection of this bird "Motionless, a painted hunter / upon a painted pond." Scientific descriptions of the birds at the end of the book help to assure readers of the accuracy of their portrayal. This is a book that naturalists, artists, and poets, young and old, will enjoy.

Elizabeth S. Watson

SOURCE: A review of *Bird Watch,* in *The Horn Book Magazine,* Vol. LXVII, No. 1, January-February, 1991, p. 80.

Set against an interesting variety of paintings depicting different species of North American birds, these seventeen poems range from short but elegant comments to longer descriptive works. Using a variety of forms, meters, and rhyme schemes, the author fits her poems to the bird in question, catching the personality and characteristics of the particular species. Her language is rich in imagery and metaphor. Although most of the poems are serious, often reflective, humor is found in several. Ted Lewin's paintings are in turn lush and spare, showing the birds against very detailed backgrounds or isolated in white space. Featuring a beautiful blend of text and illustration, the collection is a lovely accompaniment to Peterson or Audubon for the young birder. A section of brief scientific information about each bird is appended.

WIZARD'S HALL (1991)

Sally Estes

SOURCE: A review of *Wizard's Hall,* in *Booklist,* Vol. 87, No. 18, March 15, 1991, p. 1494.

"Talent don't matter . . . It only matters that you try," states 11-year-old Henry's mother as she packs him off to Wizard's Hall, where he's admitted and renamed Thornmallow ("prickly on the outside, squishy within"). Thornmallow is the last student admitted, number 113, the exact number the wizards need to stand up to The Quilted Beast and its evil master. Unfortunately, the novice wizard can't seem to get any spells right, not to mention Changes and Transformations, but he means well and he tries. As it turns out, that is exactly what is needed when the 113 students and 13 wizards confront their nemesis in the Great Hall. A simply told story filled more with whimsical humor than a true sense of dread, though the fast-paced action surges to a satisfying climax. A tale that may well introduce readers to the fantasy genre as well as appeal to established fans.

Publishers Weekly

SOURCE: A review of *Wizard's Hall,* in *Publishers Weekly,* Vol. 238, No. 18, April 19, 1991, p. 66.

The instant Henry casually "mention[s] wizardry to his dear ma," she packs him off to Wizard's Hall, with little more than a change of clothes and the advice that, whatever he might encounter, "it only matters that you try." Once at Wizard's Hall, Henry discovers that his magical talents are at best limited, but that even so, he must fulfill an ancient prophecy and help overthrow a powerful, evil wizard. Although he wants to give up, Henry—now dubbed Thornmallow—perseveres and tries his hardest. *Wizard's Hall* has it all: fairy tale wonder, baffling mystery, captivating magic, edge-of-the-seat suspense, wry humor and a well-taught moral. This captivating package is neatly tied up by the marvelous bow of Yolen's masterful prose, with a few lilting verses thrown in.

Kirkus Reviews

SOURCE: A review of *Wizard's Hall,* in *Kirkus Reviews,* Vol. LIX, No. 9, May 1, 1991, p. 611.

Latest and 113th recruit at a school for wizards, Henry is given a new name (Thornmallow: prickly outside but "squishy within") and is soon making friends and discovering that—despite a becoming humility and lamentable tone-deafness—he has an unusual, as yet uncharted, power to make magical things occur. This is fortunate, because the school is under threat from a disaffected wizard who used to be the 14th "magister" (teacher) and his monster, a patchwork dragon constructed from negative traits and entire personalities. Piecing together information from the library with his other scant knowledge, Thornmallow manages to stop the beast just before it adds him to its grisly bulk, then rescue the rest of the already-devoured school.

Yolen skillfully blends the traditions of fantasy and school story, giving her theme a special twist: Thornmallow is not the expected powerful enchanter but an "enhancer" who makes his contribution as a catalyst for others' magic and whose heroism consists of trying hard and not giving up. Briskly told, with plenty of engaging humor and wordplay—plus the unique, truly gruesome beast (splendidly colorful on Trina Schart Hyman's jacket, but not nearly so scary as in the text). Good, imaginative fun.

Margaret A. Chang

SOURCE: A review of *Wizard's Hall,* in *School Library Journal,* Vol. 37, No. 7, July, 1991, pp. 75-6.

An experienced storyteller blends wizardry and enchantment in fluid, graceful prose. Young Thornmallow, "prickly on the outside and squishy within," leaves his "dear Ma" and follows his smudgy nose to Wizard's Hall, where walls move, portraits talk, and clothes clean themselves. Disconcerted by the atmosphere of enchantment, Thornmallow nevertheless makes friends with his fellow apprentices; struggles with such classes as Cursing, Spelling, and Names; and ponders his destiny as the 113th student at Wizard's Hall. It is evident that he is inept and without talent, although he means well and he tries. Yet the Magisters welcome Thornmallow as their last hope to defeat the evil Master Nettle, who threatens Wizard's Hall with his terrifying Quilted Beast. While the happy ending is never in doubt, readers will share Thornmallow's surprise at the discovery of his own unique strengths. This school of wizardry is a jollier, warmer place than Le-Guin's Roke Island in *A Wizard of Earthsea* and less competitive than McCaffrey's Harper's Hall in *Dragonsinger.* Drawing familiar ingredients from the cauldron of story, Yolen serves up a light, palatable brew that will satisfy younger readers with a taste for entertaining fantasy.

Roger Sutton

SOURCE: A review of *Wizard's Hall,* in *Bulletin of the Center for Children's Books,* Vol. 44, No. 11, July-August, 1991, p. 280.

Henry "never wanted to be a wizard," but that seems to be his destiny, so off he goes to Wizard's Hall to receive instruction and a new name: Thornmallow, "prickly on the outside, squishy within." As student number one-hundred-and-thirteen, Thornmallow discovers that something special is going to be demanded of him; and, sure enough, it is he—"small and thin and often smudgy of nose"—who defeats the Beast and its Master. Although Yolen is a good storyteller and any tale of a child-hero conquering monsters has appeal, the writing here is often Disney-cute and the theme ("Try") didactically overpointed. The exact nature of the Beast is obscure and underdeveloped, but the story is suspensefully spun out to a satisfying, if predictable, ending.

Tony Manna

SOURCE: A review of *Wizard's Hall,* in *Voice of Youth Advocates,* Vol. 14, No. 3, August, 1991, pp. 184-5.

If there ever was an unlikely candidate for mastering the art of wizardry it is young Henry, the sheltered farmboy who, in the course of Yolen's enticing tale of initiation, proves just how deceiving first impressions can be. Scrawny, smudge-nosed, uncertain, and socially inept, Henry, a thoroughly likable kid, is suddenly thrust out of the familiar and into the unknown when his practical-minded mother decides, on a whim, that he might just make a good wizard. And so, buoyed by one of his mother's copious adages ("It only matters that you try," in this case), and filled with consternation, Henry at age 11, makes his way to Wizard's Hall, the legendary training school for the magical arts to which, he soon learns, no one, especially himself, is called without design. At once Henry is dubbed "Thornmallow" (prickly on the outside, squishy within) by one of the Hall's altogether mysterious mentors ("magister" is their title of choice), each of them a seasoned practitioner of a particular brand of magic. Determined and well-meaning, Thornmallow muddles along from lesson to lesson with the help of other novices, and though he lacks a natural talent for metaphysical pursuits, he possesses by the spadeful a host of respected attributes, not the least of which are selflessness; honesty; healthy motivation; and, yes, a desire to try. In fact, as it turns out in the tale's most compelling

scenes, it is Henry who saves the day. Gradually and suspensefully he and his cohorts discover that their community is about to come under the spell of a former magister turned sorcerer who, to avenge himself for having been expelled from Wizard's Hall for misusing his knowledge, is bent on turning both students and teachers into the pieces of a terrifying living quilt, otherwise known as Beast. Not to worry! By hook, crook, and a good deal of ingenuity, Henry, keeping his wits and determination about him, comes to the fore in the nick of time to subdue Nettle's acrimonious plan in a harrowing episode that overflows with edge-of-your-seat, *Star Wars*-like suspense. It is indeed a genuine celebration of the power of human virtue when, in the end, Thornmallow is heralded by all, not for his potential as a wizard, but rather as an agent of goodness whose belief and obstinancy and altruism save and sustain others in the worst of times. As a fantasist Yolen's gift is her power to engender belief in an uncommon world and from this stance to remind us of what matters in our own.

ALL THOSE SECRETS OF THE WORLD (1991)

Publishers Weekly

SOURCE: A review of *All Those Secrets of the World,* in *Publishers Weekly,* Vol. 238, No. 14, March 22, 1991, p. 80.

The highly prolific Yolen here relates a bittersweet memory from an important period in her childhood: the two years during which her father was away at war. She recalls the fun she and her cousin Michael had when the family piled into the car to go see Daddy's ship off at the docks—the children ate ice cream cones, but Mama "cried all the way home." At the beach the next day Janie and Michael see some tiny spots on the horizon. Michael tells her that they are ships, but Janie doesn't believe him. (The specks are so small, she says, and her daddy's ship was so big. . . .) Five-year-old Michael teaches her a "secret of the world"—as he moves further away from her, he gets smaller. When father returns and tells his daughter that she is "lots bigger than I remembered," Janie explains, "Now you are here, so I am big." This timely, nostalgic story is told with simple grace, and Janie's thoughts and experiences are believably childlike.

Roger Sutton

SOURCE: A review of *All Those Secrets of the World,* in *Bulletin of the Center for Children's Books,* Vol. 44, No. 8, April, 1991, p. 208.

Gentle yet direct, this small story of a girl's experience of a father gone to war has the sense of children's reality. . . . Four-year-old Janie (the dedication seems to indicate an autobiographical source for the story) is excited when her father ships out: he gives her a hundred kisses, she gets to wave a flag, she and her cousin are treated by Grandma to ice cream. But the next day, when Janie and Michael are playing at the beach, she becomes frightened when he runs off into the distance to show her how things look smaller when they're far away. "'Come back, come back,' I cried, suddenly afraid he'd disappear forever like the ships gone from the horizon, dropped over the edge of the world where no policeman could ever find him." The metaphor is unforced and apt, especially so when a two-years-older Janie recalls it upon her father's return: "When you are far away, everything is smaller. But now you are here, so I am big." Yolen's text is comfortably poetic, if occasionally self-conscious, and finds a quiet match in [Leslie] Baker's watercolors, which capture the World War Two setting in cool blue-green tones. While both words and pictures have the perspective of memory, they are not nostalgic, and may well evoke an empathic response from children scanning an uncertain horizon today.

Kirkus Reviews

SOURCE: A review of *All Those Secrets of the World,* in *Kirkus Reviews,* Vol. LIX, No. 7, April 1, 1991, p. 477.

In a gracefully cadenced text with telling echoes of ideas and images, an apparently autobiographical story: when Jane is four, she and her family see Daddy off on a crowded troopship to WWII; only Mama cries. Soon after, on a forbidden trip to wade in the nearby Chesapeake, Jane's five-year-old cousin Michael demonstrates that the small-looking ships they see are actually big, like Daddy's—Michael moves away while Jane compares his size to her own hand. Two years later, Daddy comes home. "Everyone cried, except Mama," and Janie tells him why she seems bigger: "... you were so far away, Daddy. When you are far away, everything is smaller. But now you are here, so I am big." ... A poignant, beautifully wrought book.

Hazel Rochman

SOURCE: A review of *All Those Secrets of the World,* in *Booklist,* Vol. 87, No. 17, May 1, 1991, p. 1723.

[This] is a quietly emotional picture book about a child who watches her father go off to war and longs for his return. Yolen's plain, poetic text is autobiographical: Janie is four years old and the time is World War II. The book begins with good-byes, kisses, and flag-waving as the troopship leaves. The next day, in a game at the beach, Janie's older cousin Michael explains to her why the distant ships on the horizon look so small—it's because they're so far away. And two years later, when her father returns and tells her she's much bigger than he remembered, she whispers Michael's secret in his ear: "That's because you were / so far away, Daddy. / When you are far away, / everything is smaller. / But now you are here, / so I am big." [Leslie] Baker's exquisite watercolors express what the words mean but leave largely unspoken: the sadness beneath the determined gaiety, the memory of

separation within the circle of the family embrace. Some pictures stretch out with a wide view connecting sea and sky and countryside; some focus close up on family members holding each other tight. Adults who remember the time will feel the truth of the experience; so will today's kids who have come to know about parting and reunion in wartime.

Phyllis G. Sidorsky

SOURCE: A review of *All Those Secrets of the World,* in *School Library Journal,* Vol. 37, No. 7, July, 1991, p. 66.

Yolen once again demonstrates her unique ability to use a small incident to reveal a profound idea. When her father leaves port on a ship departing for the war, four-year-old Janie relates the experience from a child's point of view. A few days later while wading along the shore, her older cousin Michael points to ships in the distance also bound for the fighting. Janie is sure her father left on a big boat, not a speck on the horizon. Michael demonstrates the concept of linear perspective by running off down the beach. Several years later her father comes home and tells her how big she has grown, and it is at this poignant moment that Janie comes to understand the world's secrets. . . . An affecting piece without an extraneous word and one that is particularly timely today.

ENCOUNTER (1992)

Carolyn Phelan

SOURCE: A review of *Encounter,* in *Booklist,* Vol. 88, No. 13, March 1, 1992, p. 1281.

Written from the point of view of a Taino Indian boy, this unusual picture book presents the first encounter of native Americans with Columbus. One night, the boy awakens from a terrifying dream about three predatory birds riding the waves, only to see three strange ships anchored in the bay the next day. Alternately frightened, amused, and fascinated by the strangers who come ashore, he warns his chief not to welcome them; but he is brushed aside, his alarm seen as the result of a child's nightmare. Besides, the Indians covet the weapons and trinkets the white men possess. The boy's fears come true, both for himself and his tribe. He and several other Indians are taken as slaves, and though he jumps overboard and escapes to warn other tribes of the danger, it is to no avail. At the end of the narrative, the Taino wiped out, the boy, now a ghostly old man, sits alone, saying, "So it was we lost our lands to the strangers from the sky. . . . May it be a warning to all the children and all the people in every land." [David] Shannon's striking acrylic paintings illustrate the story with imagination and power. Yolen weaves historical data into a narrative that holds together well, yet readers may feel her presence and point of view more strongly than the narrator's. Notes on the historical basis for the text and artwork are appended. While the portrayal of Columbus as evil may strike traditionalists as heresy, he did hunger for gold, abduct native people, and, ultimately (though unintentionally), destroy the Taino. This book effectively presents their point of view. . . .

Kirkus Reviews

SOURCE: A review of *Encounter,* in *Kirkus Reviews,* Vol. LX, No. 6, March 15, 1992, p. 402.

A poignant account of Columbus's landfall in the Americas, from a Taino boy's point of view. After a terrible prophetic dream, the lad begs his elders not to welcome the strangers, but they disregard him. He sees how they look at his people's gold; he temporarily becomes their captive; and at the end, as an old man, he sadly notes: "We lost our lands . . . we gave our souls to their gods . . . our sons and daughters became their sons and daughters, no longer true humans. . . . " [David] Shannon's dark, richly colored paintings brilliantly capture the story's emotion and the sense of worlds colliding; Europeans are rendered with a rugged realism that strongly recalls the work of N.C. Wyeth, and the Native Americans look like polished wooden figurines—with the border between these two realities shifting and changing. The author closes with a historical note, while the illustrator ends with an apology for adding loincloths to his figures. *O tempora! O mores!*

James C. Juhnke and Jane Yolen

SOURCE: "An Exchange on Encounter," in *The New Advocate,* Vol. 6, No. 2, Spring, 1993, pp. 94-6.

[The following excerpt is from a letter by James Juhnke, a professor of history at Bethel College in North Newton, Kansas, and a reply from Jane Yolen.]

James C. Juhnke's Second Thoughts about *Encounter*

Jane Yolen's children's story of the coming of Europeans to the new world, told through the eyes of a Taino boy, is among the most powerful and disturbing publications of the Columbian Quincentennial. It is a dark story, both in text and illustration. The Taino lad has an ominous warning vision of approaching disaster, warns the chief not to welcome the strangers from the three ships, and is rebuffed. The white strangers take him captive, but he jumps overboard and escapes back, continuing to warn the people. On the last page he is an old man who no longer can dream. But he has a message: "May it be a warning to all the children and all the people in every land."

Encounter is effectively written with concrete imagery and is supported by illustrations that convey an almost overpowering sense of foreboding. But the greatest achievement is the reversal of perspective. This book forces us to confront what a disaster it was for the Taino people to be discovered and destroyed by Europeans.

Readers young and old will fervently wish never to be encountered by such "strangers from the sky."

For all its pioneering brilliance, however, this book falls short of an ideal standard for children's literature of the encounter between Europeans and Native Americans. Although Jane Yolen succeeded in reversing the traditional perspective, she has not solved the need for a narrative structure authentic to Native American culture. Yolen's story is about a child who has a personal vision which is set over against the ignorance, compromises, and anti-youth biases of the elders. The story celebrates—if such a dark tale can be called celebrative in any sense—the insight of a lonely individual. In this sense, Yolen's story remains trapped within a European mindset and mythology. Indeed, in its structure this is a transposed version of the traditional western image of Christopher Columbus as a lonely struggler against stupid kings and bishops who resisted his insights.

The Taino culture was destroyed and is not available for research. But all anthropology speaks of the communal nature of traditional cultures. A story of the "Encounter" which wants to be both authentic and positive would need to build upon the affirmative values of the native communal culture. Rather than setting a lone ranger child in opposition to the community, the story could show how a child cooperates heroically with others. There could be small triumphs in the context of a larger, tragic defeat. It takes a modern author of unusual imagination to make a convincing portrayal of positive communal values as they existed in pre-modern culture.

Our literature of the early encounter between Europeans and Native Americans should tell the truth about the cause of tragic depopulation of native peoples. We know in fact that the overwhelming majority of deaths were due to epidemic diseases to which the natives had no natural immunities—smallpox, measles, typhoid, cholera, and others. The European invaders did not intend these epidemics, nor did they have the capacity to control them. The author's note at the end of *Encounter* speaks of this awful depopulation, but neglects to mention the disease factor. To omit such vital information comes short of truthfulness as surely as to tell of a heroic Columbus and leave out his cruelty and his enslavement of Indians.

Finally, we must give attention to the moral of this historic encounter. Yolen's story, despite its reversal of perspective, does not derive its moral from the culture of the assaulted people. If hospitality was one of the prime virtues of Taino culture, the message of this story is to abandon that virtue. The old man has learned a powerful lesson: It is dangerous to be hospitable to strangers. But is this lesson, which seems to fit quite well on the streets of modern American cities, any credit to the Tainos? Would their fate have been better, would they have survived any longer, if they had behaved like modern Americans and met the invaders with suspicion and hostility? If they lived by an ethic of hospitality, should we impose our ethic of hostility? How can we tell this story in a way that respects the integrity of cherished native values?

Yolen's *Encounter* has broken new ground. Perhaps the popular success of her book will empower other writers and illustrators to work for the same reversal of perspective and to move even more creatively and sympathetically into the hearts and minds of the people who welcomed Columbus in 1492.

Jane Yolen Replies:

All first steps are just that—first steps. When I wrote *Encounter* I assumed it would be one of a number of books from the Taino perspective of that first meeting between Columbus and the people he called "Indians." Imagine my surprise when the only other children's books out during the Quincentennial year were a nonfiction book, *The Tainos* by Francine Jacobs and a novel, *Morning Girl* by Michael Dorris—both excellent, but far fewer than I expected.

However, Dr. Juhnke's thoughtful letter, while correct in wanting authentic voices (and acknowledging how little we know about the Taino and their destroyed culture) makes an anthropologically incorrect assumption about story. He writes that "all anthropology speaks for the communal nature of traditional cultures. A story of the 'Encounter' . . . would need to build upon the affirmative values of the native communal culture." His assumption is that all stories out of such communities would have the child attended to, listened to. He forgets the many Native American stories of isolated, lonely, exiled child heroes ("Arrow Boy" of the Cheyenne and "Orphan Boy" of the Blackfeet are but two examples). My pattern was theirs.

I am pleased that Dr. Juhnke and other readers have given *Encounter* much thought; even more pleased by the response I have gotten from teachers, librarians, and children across the country. If my book becomes a first step towards the exploration of the meeting between Columbus and the indigenous peoples—and its tragic aftermath—then it has done its work, whatever its flaws, perceived or real. In fact, the moral dilemma of the *Encounter* story is that the only way the Taino might have salvaged their lives and their culture was to have abandoned some of their most cherished tenets—such as hospitality. We cannot change history. But we—and most especially our children—can learn from it so that the next encounters, be they at home, abroad, or in space, may be gentler and mutually respectful. It is a large hope but it is, perhaps, all that we have.

📖 *JANE YOLEN'S MOTHER GOOSE SONG-BOOK* (with arrangements by son Adam Stemple, 1992)

Publishers Weekly

SOURCE: A review of *Jane Yolen's Mother Goose Songbook,* in *Publishers Weekly,* Vol. 239, No. 44, October 5, 1992, p. 72.

Yolen, [Adam] Stemple and [Rosekrans] Hoffman make

beautiful music together. Forty-nine nursery songs and rhymes reclaim their sociopolitical roots in Yolen's pithy introductions ("Sing a Song of Sixpence," notes Yolen, may allude to Henry VIII, Catherine of Aragon and Anne Boleyn; "Goosey, Goosey, Gander" commemorates the murder of an English cardinal). Hoffman's colored-ink illustrations wholeheartedly embrace the songs' fantastical elements without shying from their darker undercurrents: she builds an idiosyncratic style with slightly skewed perspectives, vivid and playful borders, fanciful details (a child crouches before the Muffin man, his mouth wide open as if to receive a communion wafer, while a cat and a frog line up behind him) and characters whose eyes fairly sparkle with caprice. Arrangements for piano and guitar, by Yolen's son Stemple, are simple and clear. Bringing out the special pleasures of each entry, this trio's fine work explains anew the timelessness of Mother Goose.

Hazel Rochman

SOURCE: A review of *Jane Yolen's Mother Goose Songbook,* in *Booklist,* Vol. 89, No. 8, December 15, 1992, p. 740.

The brief folklore and history notes with each nursery rhyme will make this Mother Goose collection attractive to older kids and adults who share the traditional verses with very young children. Yolen's son has provided simple piano arrangements with guitar chords as well. Surrounding the musical notation, the illustrations in bright colored inks are also adult in appeal, full of verve and character. The pictures, within shifting, patterned borders, are sometimes complex and surreal, picking up the violence and wild fantasy of the rhymes, though, as Yolen points out in her introduction, the rhymes have long outlived their political and ritual meanings. For "Oranges and Lemons" there's a droll play with fruits, bells, and people. "Mary Had a Little Lamb" shows a prim, bespectacled sheep at a desk. The old street rhyme "Goosey, Goosey, Gander" celebrated a terrible murder, and the illustrations are appropriately bright and ominous. For most of us, whether child or adult, the pleasure in these rhymes is in the sounds and nonsense, and being made to think about the meanings at all is a bit unnerving. Blackbirds in a pie? Three blind mice?

Jane Marino

SOURCE: A review of *Jane Yolen's Mother Goose Songbook,* in *School Library Journal,* Vol. 39, No. 1, January, 1993, p. 95.

A visually pleasing collection of 49 rhymes set to music. Selections range from classics, such as "Mary Had a Little Lamb" and "Old King Cole," to lesser-known ones such as "Michael Finnigin" and "My Dame Hath a Lame, Tame Crane." Through a brief, informative forward and short notes, Yolen places the rhymes within a historical context that will add to the understanding as well as the enjoyment of each. The two-handed piano arrangements are accessible and fun to play with music that varies from high drama in "Who Killed Cock Robin" to soothing familiarity in "Twinkle Twinkle Little Star." [Rosekrans] Hoffman's wonderful watercolor illustrations combine vibrantly colored accents and borders, which give the whole a rich look, and small, delicately featured figures that fairly dance across the pages. This collection celebrates the heritage and musical tradition of Mother Goose in the same way that *Songs from Mother Goose,* compiled by Larrick, and Glazer's *The Mother Goose Songbook* do. But the high quality and distinctive personality of Yolen's book merit its consideration even if these titles are part of the collection.

📖 *LETTING SWIFT RIVER GO* (1992)

Heather Vogel Frederick

SOURCE: "Tales Kids Can Curl Up With," in *The Christian Science Monitor,* November 6, 1992, p. 10.

A river is the central character in [this] picture book . . . for a slightly older audience. Jane Yolen's *Letting Swift River Go* takes a nostalgic look at the "drowning" of the Swift River towns in western Massachusetts to form the Quabbin Reservoir. Told through the eyes of young Sally Jane, the tale traces the bittersweet chain of events that follow the vote—houses moved or bulldozed, trees cut down, families relocated. Yolen's fluid, poetical style is superbly matched by two-time Caldecott winner Barbara Cooney's luminous landscapes.

Noel Perrin

SOURCE: "Bulldozer Blues," in *The New York Times Book Review,* November 8, 1992, p. 54.

If there were a modern equivalent of Aesop, it would probably be Jane Yolen. Aesop told stories in order to teach lessons. The story of the mouse and the lion teaches that small creatures can sometimes save the lives of big ones—a thrilling lesson for a young child to learn. The story of the tortoise and the hare teaches two lessons at once. From the tortoise you learn that less talented people can surpass more talented ones, if they persist. From the hare you learn that overconfidence can get you in big trouble.

Ms. Yolen also tells stories in order to teach lessons. Sometimes it's a lesson that Aesop also taught. (This is no criticism. The great lessons number only a hundred or so.)

For example, *The Emperor and the Kite* tells the story of a Chinese ruler long ago who had eight children. Four are tall sons, and three are strapping big daughters. The eighth child is a tiny little daughter named Djeow Seow. It is she who rescues her father from the evil plotters.

Sleeping Ugly shows that you must not judge people by their looks. *The Girl Who Loved the Wind* demonstrates that a true life must include sorrow as well as joy.

These are all storybooks for younger children. I don't mean to say that every illustrated book for which Ms. Yolen writes the text is Aesopian. Some, like *Piggins,* are content to be playful variations on a genre—in this case the stock English detective story.

But it is books with morals that one thinks of as most characteristic of the prolific Ms. Yolen, and it is the absence of a clear moral that makes her new book so puzzling. *Letting Swift River Go* is an environmental picture book, or at least it seems to be.

The central character is a little girl named Sally Jane who lives in a beautiful valley in western Massachusetts. The time is about 60 years ago. Sally Jane tells about the idyllic life she has: sleeping out under the backyard maples, fishing in the river, helping with maple sugaring in the spring.

But then some men come from Boston, 60 miles away, and explain that the city needs a new reservoir. The people in Sally Jane's town and three other towns all have to move. Where the idylls have taken place, bulldozers will be pushing down the beautiful old houses. Every maple will be cut.

In a preface written for adults, Ms. Yolen makes clear she understands that there's a trade-off here. Yes, much beauty was destroyed to build the Quabbin Reservoir. But new beauty was created. The Quabbin is now, she says, "a lovely wilderness," complete with eagles and deer.

In the story, however, the child gets no glimpse of the lovely new wilderness. It is all loss. And how should Sally Jane deal with that loss? Her father takes her every Friday to watch the bulldozers, and to fix the scene in her mind. "You've got to remember, Sally Jane," he says. "Remember our town."

But her mother tells her all things pass and change. Back when she and her friends caught fireflies in jars, her mother would say, "You have to let them go." And at the end of the book, grown-up Sally Jane is out in a boat on the reservoir with her father. And she hears her mother's voice, speaking "over the drowned years."

"You have to let them go, Sally Jane." Clearly "them" is no longer fireflies but memories of rural America. So what's the lesson? Fight development or accept it? Who knows?

But if the text is ambiguous, the pictures are not. Barbara Cooney's illustrations (and they are glorious ones) say plainly that it was wicked to flood the valley and to cut down all those trees. In fact, despite their beauty, some of her illustrations might scare a small child, because they say that America eats its past. This is probably not a bedtime book.

Cathryn M. Mercier

SOURCE: A review of *Letting Swift River Go,* in *The Five Owls,* Vol. VII, No. 2, November-December, 1992, p. 36.

From its glossy-wet cover, this book tackles the challenges when "powerful thirsts" of economic, industrial, and urban growth imbibe the resources of traditional, peaceful, rural communities. The story is based on true events that occurred between 1927 and 1946 in western Massachusetts, when villages in the Swift River valley were moved and the valley flooded to create the Quabbin Reservoir and thereby meet Boston's need for water.

The author effectively adopts the voice of a child. However, Sally Jane tells her story in retrospect, a technique that irreversibly sets the events in the past and lends a distinctive note of nostalgia. Yolen's exquisite control as a storyteller enables this to be truly Sally Jane's story, not just a performance of authorial ventriloquism aimed at memorializing an historical past.

In serene language laced with metaphor, Sally Jane recalls her early childhood. She remembers tender family moments and the adventures of good friends. Most of all, she places her growth within the physical and human communities of Swift River, a place providing freedom and obligation for all.

As everything begins to change from Sally Jane's perspective, Barbara Cooney shifts the tone of her luminescent, porous watercolors. Their drama increases as Cooney populates scenes with more bodies, larger and disproportionate. The illustrations echo Sally Jane's worries as they make vivid the voraciousness, the unquenchability of the outsiders. Similarly, the text names directly the willingness of the adults in town to "trade water for money."

Sadness tinged with consent pervades the dismantling of the town as it yields its history and identity. Yolen's selected details of "buttons, teeth, and a few thin bones" magnify the loss by casting it in individual terms. Families relocate, friends disperse. Sally Jane's deceptively straightforward voice describes the demolition of cemeteries, houses, and buildings. The singularity of the community drowns with its monuments and landscape in the new reservoir.

The book moves between pictorial vignettes amidst text, single-page illustrations, and double page spreads. Cooney floods one double-page spread in the variegated blues of water, the midnight blues of hills after nightfall, the sky blues of calm weather. Only the words of a displaced Sally Jane, now grown, disturb this tranquility.

M. Jean Greenlaw

SOURCE: A review of *Letting Swift River Go,* in *The New Advocate,* Vol. 6, No. 3, Spring, 1993, p. 146.

The city of Boston was in need of water so it was decided to build the Quabbin Reservoir in a valley called Swift River. To create the reservoir, people had to be displaced and towns disassembled and covered with water. Yolen highlights the poignancy of this upheaval by using one child to detail the joys of living in her community and the subsequent disquiet as she sees graves and houses being moved, trees cut down, and friends moving, never to be seen again. The final acceptance is a satisfying conclusion to a thoughtful book. [Barbara] Cooney's palette is perfect for rendering the New England countryside. Though a picture book, this could be used through high school for discussion of the consequences of change and its effect on people.

WELCOME TO THE GREEN HOUSE (1993)

Joanne Schott

SOURCE: "The Stuff of Legends," in *Quill and Quire,* Vol. 59, No. 2, February, 1993, p. 37.

The sights and sounds of the rainforest are celebrated in Yolen's brief, poetic, simple text. It is descriptive and full of movement, changing pace and rhythm as she focuses on new images. The pictures, in [Laura] Regan's début as a children's illustrator, earn more than equal billing. Her accurately-detailed, softly-outlined paintings present a panorama of the jungle's life, from flowers and ferns to ocelot, sloth, orange frogs, and striped lizards. Dappled light and shadow and the green of leaves and moss, layered on layer in a seemingly infinite jungle, create the image of a place with a special reality.

The beauty and wonderful variety of the rainforest is the book's only message, being reasons in themselves to know that this space must be preserved. A brief note on the fragility of this beauty and the threats to its existence is confined to an afterword.

Ellen Fader

SOURCE: A review of *Welcome to the Green House,* in *School Library Journal,* Vol. 39, No. 4, April, 1993, p. 116.

Yolen explores a tropical rain forest in an entrancing poem full of internal rhyme, alliteration, and evocative images. "But it is not all green / in the hot green house: / a flash of blue hummingbird, / a splash of golden toad, / a lunge of waking lizards, / a plunge of silver fish. . . ." These are only a few of the many creatures that the author catalogs and [Laura] Regan depicts in her lush gouache paintings. The illustrations include all of the animals mentioned in the brief text, but readers are left to their own devices to identify the extra treats the artist includes. Ideal for introducing rain forest ecology in the primary grades, this book may be also be used by preschool teachers. Its many animal sounds and closeup views of snakes, sloths, and primates will perfectly suit their inquisitive students. A page of remarks about the continuing destruction of tropical rain forests and an address where youngsters may write to obtain information about preserving them is appended. The next best thing to a guided tour.

Stephanie Zvirin

SOURCE: A review of *Welcome to the Green House,* in *Booklist,* Vol. 89, No. 15, April 1, 1993, p. 1435.

Dramatic paintings of tropical rain forest flora and fauna will entice children into this quiet plea to protect the environment. Capturing the scenery from a variety of perspectives—ground level, aerial, etc.—the resplendent double-page spreads, dappled with shadows, surround the reader with forest activity. Brilliant blue butterflies flit around bright orange blossoms, an ocelot prowls the forest floor, golden frogs slide into crystalline pools. The steady rhythm of Yolen's brief, evocative text gives voice to the noises of the "hot green house"—"the *kre-ek, kre-ek, kre-ek* of the keel-billed toucans" and "the *pick-buzz-hum-buzz* of a thousand thousand bees"—while a follow-up note reminds us how quickly the forest paradise will disappear if nothing is done to preserve it. A beautiful book, with pages large enough and artwork distinctive enough to make it valuable for group sharing.

Publishers Weekly

SOURCE: A review of *Welcome to the Green House,* in *Publishers Weekly,* Vol. 240, No. 16, April 19, 1993, p. 60.

In the current freshet of rainforest books, Yolen's rises to the surface not as a mere tour guide, but a gracious host to earth's "dark green, / light green, / emerald green / bright green / copper green, / blue green, / ever-new green house." The author's atmosphere-laden free verse, which falls into unexpected, pleasing rhyme and repetition, correlates with [Laura] Regan's sumptuous gouache artwork. While the text focuses on the relentless noise of forest inhabitants, borderless, painterly illustrations seem to spill off the pages in their intricate depictions of animals cavorting amidst tropical flora. The illustrations are just literal enough—allowing youngsters to match familiar and unknown species with names in the text. Yolen's language begs for reading aloud but for a common problem: her generous use of onomatopoetic translation of animal calls and other sounds may be difficult for readers to imitate without jarring the beauty and rhythm of the language. A stimulating challenge, however, in a strikingly vibrant package.

Kirkus Reviews

SOURCE: A review of *Welcome to the Green House,* in *Kirkus Reviews,* Vol. LXI, No. 9, May 1, 1993, p. 606.

Taking as her text a sentence from Darwin's *Voyage of the Beagle*—"The land is one great wild, untidy luxuriant hothouse, made by nature for herself"—Yolen lyrically compares a house to the rain forest (" . . . no roof in the green house, / only the canopy of leaves") and notes its animals ("the quick-fingered capuchin/make their slow-quick ways / from room to room . . . a splash of golden toad, / a lunge of waking lizards, / a plunge of silver fish") and their sounds. [Laura] Regan makes an outstanding picture-book debut with lush full-bleed spreads rendered in gouache, with luminously diffuse light, exquisitely detailed wildlife, and decorative forms—close to the picture plane—that recall Leonard Weisgard's art. Unlike the plethora of contrived or sentimental books on the subject, this one is simplicity itself—eloquent and effective.

📖 *RAINING CATS AND DOGS* (1993)

Kirkus Reviews

SOURCE: A review of *Raining Cats and Dogs,* in *Kirkus Reviews,* Vol. LXI, No. 20, October 15, 1993, p. 1340.

It's hard to know which end's up when it's "raining cats and dogs." This engaging collection of poems, nine about each of the classic antagonists, does a flip-flop to read from both ends to the middle, with an additional symmetry in its subject sequence ("I Am Cat" / "I Am Dog"; "Alley Cat Speaks" / "House Dog Speaks," etc.). Yolen brings insight and affection for both species, plus her usual wry wit and deft versifying, to the poems (all but three new), tying the book together in the middle with a topsy-turvy spread accommodating the punning nonsense of "Raining Dogs" ("Dogmatically, / They're splashing down, / And currents cover / Half the town") and "Raining Cats" ("A cataract, / A waterfall . . . Catastrophe, / They're purring down / On top of me"). Meanwhile, [Janet] Street captures the lighthearted spirit of the verse and the movement of the creatures in exuberant stylized illustrations in rainbow bright colors. A pleasure.

Nancy Palmer

SOURCE: A review of *Raining Cats and Dogs,* in *School Library Journal,* Vol. 39, No. 12, December, 1993, p. 110.

The first nine poems in this collection feature dogs. Turn the book upside down and start from the other end to find cat poems. The half-and-half format is a good foil for the mostly clever canine/feline lines here. From "I Am Cat" ("I am silk and velvet, / I am spit and squall . . . I am creep of claw clicks. / I am corduroy tongue . . .") to "My Hound's Nose" ("What a wonderful thing / Is the nose of my hound . . ."), the character and behavior of these creatures are plumbed in verses ranging from bouncy rhyme to haikulike spareness. The print is large, but the language runs from simple to sophisticated, the voices from first-dog or cat to bemused owner's to detached observer's. The watercolor illustrations use basic shapes and the occasional squiggly detail to form their large-eyed flattish creatures—these are smooth beasts from a vaguely postmodern brush. The full-color compositions fill each double-page spread, providing a background for the one or two accompanying poems. Aileen Fisher's *My Cat Has Eyes of Sapphire Blue*, Nancy Larrick's *Cats Are Cats*, Lee Bennett Hopkins's *I Am the Cat* and *A Dog's Life*, and William Cole's *Good Dog Poems* all have more selections, but Yolen's book has a unique combination and format. It's not a must, but it's fun.

Carolyn Phelan

SOURCE: A review of *Raining Cats and Dogs*, in *Booklist*, Vol. 90, No. 7, December 1, 1993, p. 696.

This upside-down volume can be read from either direction: one half is a collection of nine short poems about dogs, but flip the book over to find a second title page and nine cat poems. The feline and canine meet midway through the book in a double-page spread with merging, dreamlike illustrations of the two poems "Raining Cats" and "Raining Dogs," featuring dozens of dogs and cats held aloft by parachutes as they gently fall toward streets below. Kids will enjoy the creative format and the bright, naive watercolor artwork as much as the poems themselves, which are generally pleasing and often clever, though seldom memorable. An attractive picture book of poetry on a popular subject, or rather two popular subjects.

HONKERS (1993)

Kay Weisman

SOURCE: A review of *Honkers*, in *Booklist*, Vol. 90, No. 5, November 1, 1993, p. 533.

When her mother is sent to bed for the duration of a difficult pregnancy, five-year-old Betsy travels alone by train to stay with her grandparents, Nana and Grandy. She is very homesick until Grandy shows her an abandoned nest containing three goose eggs. Together they tend the nest, and later, Betsy mothers the new goslings through the summer months. As the "honkers" mature and gain independence, so does Betsy, and, shortly after the birds migrate south in the fall, she returns home to her parents and new baby sister. [Leslie] Baker's soft watercolor paintings, rendered in earth tones highlighted in blue, suggest a turn-of-the-century setting that complements Yolen's lyrical text. A great choice for spring or fall story hours, this will also make a useful addition to primary units on birds or the farm.

Susan Scheps

SOURCE: A review of *Honkers*, in *School Library Journal*, Vol. 40, No. 1, January, 1994, p. 102.

A heartwarming tale of birth and growth, of loving and

belonging. It is the story of a little girl who is sent to spend the summer with her grandparents while her bed-ridden mother awaits the birth of a new baby. Clinging to her silky blanket, Betsy arrives at the farm to find three Canada goose eggs that Grandy discovered abandoned by the river. The child watches the goslings hatch, then grow quickly into lovely young geese that fly off in the early fall, just as it's time to head home to her parents and new sibling. [Leslie] Baker's realistic watercolors have a haziness that surrounds the sunbathed fields and barn, their ocher and gray-green tones perfectly capturing a turn-of-the-century family and farm as in a series of enlarged snapshots. The flow of Yolen's writing and Grandy's terse conversational style, the warm loveliness of the illustrations, and the subtleness of the story itself combine to form a poignant book with a quiet but powerful message that is sure to be enjoyed by young and old alike.

Miriam Martinez and Marcia F. Nash

SOURCE: A review of *Honkers*, in *Language Arts*, Vol. 71, No. 4, April, 1994, p. 298.

Betsy isn't sure she wants to spend the summer on Nana and Grandy's farm, but Mama must stay in bed awaiting the birth of the new baby. So Betsy journeys to the farm all alone on the train. Once there she discovers the special surprise her grandparents have for her—three abandoned goose eggs which Betsy is to care for. Betsy begins by turning the eggs twice a day. Then, when the goslings make their way out of the eggs, she is the first one they see, and so she becomes their mother. With growing geese to care for, the summer passes more quickly; fall arrives, and suddenly it is time for both Betsy and the geese to leave the farm. For Betsy this means a train trip home to her parents and the new baby sister; for the geese it means their first trip south. Yolen tells a warm story about a little girl who makes important discoveries about mothering and independence. . . .

HERE THERE BE DRAGONS (1993)

Publishers Weekly

SOURCE: A review of *Here There Be Dragons*, in *Publishers Weekly*, Vol. 240, No. 44, November 1, 1993, p. 81.

Dragon-lovers and maybe even dinophiles will unite to celebrate Yolen's virtuosic poems and stories about dragons. Some new, others previously published, the entries cover a spectrum of genres: tales of heroic battles, romance, fantasy, science fiction (one story is set on another planet), occasional blood and guts, a story of Chinese origin, an ancient story retold (Merlin is a dragon) and even borscht-belt humor ("'Is that all you can say?' asked the dragon. 'I tell you I am The Dragon and all you can answer is *oh?*'"). Yolen introduces each selection, supplying its genesis and adding invitingly personal anecdotes (e.g., her son had a tattoo made from an illustration for the poem "The Making of Dragons").

Susan L. Rogers

SOURCE: A review of *Here There Be Dragons,* in *School Library Journal,* Vol. 39, No. 12, December, 1993, p. 118.

Here there be dragons, indeed—in original poetry and prose, fiction, and original folklore—a total of five poems and eight stories from the prolific Yolen. Each selection is preceded by a chatty introduction explaining some aspect of where, when, how, or why she wrote it. She has clearly given much thought to dragons, and presents them convincingly from many points of view. "Great-grandfather Dragon's Tale" is a plausible, if revisionist, retelling of the legend of St. George. "The Dragon's Boy" is an episode in the early life of Artos and Merlin in the spirit of T. H. White's *The Sword in the Stone.* "Cockfight" is a story about Jakkin of Austar IV and his red dragon, which led to Yolen's well known trilogy of dragon novels. "The King's Dragon" and "One Ox, Two Ox, Three Ox, and the Dragon King" are pieces that have the familiar motifs and rhythmic cadences of authentic folktales, making them good read-aloud choices. There are evil dragons as well as good ones in this collection, and after experiencing their variety and might, readers won't be able to help echoing the author's hope that they will return some day.

Kirkus Reviews

SOURCE: A review of *Here There Be Dragons,* in *Kirkus Reviews,* Vol. LXI, No. 23, December 1, 1993, p. 1532.

New, reworked, or reprinted—13 stories and poems. Here, St. George is not a dragonslayer but a friend; the dragon pits of Austar IV test trainers as well as dragons; the healer Tansy is no healer to dragons, while dragonslayer Lancot is no hero at all, except to Tansy; and, in "The Dragon's Boy"—a short story that was a predecessor of the novel of the same name—old "Linn" (a.k.a. Merlin) makes a bad dragon but a good teacher for Artos. These stories and poems are a little uneven, with language and ideas extending over a considerable span of difficulty and sophistication. Still, most have at least a glimmer of an idea, and there continues to be a ready market for dragons. And [David] Wilgus's full-page illustrations, in soft pencil emulating the effect of lithographs rendered on stone, are especially appealing—beautifully modulated forms, subtle characterizations, classic images of dragons, handsome, formally structured compositions. Inviting.

M. Jean Greenlaw

SOURCE: A review of *Here There Be Dragons,* in *The New Advocate,* Vol. 7, No. 3, Summer, 1994, p. 219.

Dragon lovers of all ages will resonate to this creative melange. The striking cover shows a dragon embedded within an almost freefloating eye, and if the eye is the window to the soul, there are surely dragons embedded deep within each of us. Yolen prefaces each of her pieces with a musing on its origin, revealing parts of herself as well. There are poems and short stories, some of which led to full novels, and emotions run from humor to poignancy. The storyteller's craft is evident and this is a wonderful collection for reading aloud.

📖 THE GIRL IN THE GOLDEN BOWER (1994)

Susan Dove Lempke

SOURCE: A review of *The Girl in the Golden Bower,* in *Bulletin of the Center for Children's Books,* Vol. 48, No. 2, October, 1994, p. 71.

A magic comb, a mysterious beast, an innocent maiden and a wicked sorceress are some of the traditional fairy tale elements Yolen weaves together in this original tale. A child is born to a woodsman and his wife, whom he had found wandering lost in the woods. They name their daughter Aurea, but, after their death, the sorceress renames her Curry, because of Aurea's habit of grooming the woodland animals with a comb she has inherited from her mother. The sorceress eventually realizes that the comb is the charm she has been searching for, but when she attempts to starve Curry to death so she can "cut the comb from the dead child's hair," the animals build the sleeping girl a nest and use the comb to create a golden bower. Yolen's phrases are lyrical, with some powerful passages and a particularly poignant ending, but many parts of the story are summarized so quickly, particularly in the opening, that the story is confusing and less than satisfying. [Jane] Dyer's watercolors saturate each page in glowing golds with touches of green; romantic curves, curls, and tendrils are everywhere. The pictures are lovely, but one's eyes may yearn for more variety by the end. One double-page spread has only a border accompanying the text, but the story is sufficiently involving at this point that groups may be willing to listen without pictures.

April Judge

SOURCE: A review of *The Girl in the Golden Bower,* in *Booklist,* Vol. 91, No. 4, October 15, 1994, p. 440.

Searching for a great treasure, a sorceress disguised as a cook gains a position in the home of a woodsman, his wife, and young daughter, Aurea. Near death from a poisoned stew prepared by the cook, the wife gives her daughter a prized possession—a russet-colored comb—and says that the comb will always watch over her. Realizing that Aurea has the magic piece, the sorceress tries to outwit the girl, but Aurea's animal friends alter the wicked spell and keep her alive. The text and illustrations are printed on paper that has been painted to resemble parchment. The double-page watercolor spreads, featuring portraits of the characters and detailed, swirling garlands of flowers and plants that spill over the borders, are executed in a palette of yellows, golds, light browns, and greens that beautifully complement the story's setting and tone. The lyrical language Yolen employs makes this an excellent choice for reading aloud.

📖 *GOOD GRISELLE* (1994)

Hazel Rochman

SOURCE: A review of *Good Griselle*, in *Booklist,* Vol. 91, No. 3, October 1, 1994, p. 335.

The angels and gargoyles carved on an old cathedral are the characters in an original fairy tale about an ugly changeling. Set at Christmas, this is also a kind of Nativity story. Griselle is so beautiful and good that she gives away half her food to the cats and birds. The grumbling gargoyles can't stand her, and they have a wager with the angels to test Griselle's goodness by sending her an ugly and unlovable child. He arrives at her door on Christmas. She takes him in and loves him. Nothing will make her abandon him, not even the man she loves, not even her own safety. She is the child's savior, and her love transforms him. The book design is handsome, with some hand lettering and with watercolor paintings of depth and mystery that evoke the sculptured figures in stone shades of gray and brown. Some pictures are like panels; some show the gargoyles bursting out like evil happenings and ugly feelings. One realistic view of the child clutching the battered mother is a heartbreaking madonna image. Like Winter's illustrated version of Lagerlof's *The Changeling,* this may appeal more to adults than young children, but it will touch anyone who imagines a story about those strange figures carved in stone.

Kirkus Reviews

SOURCE: A review of *Good Griselle*, in *Kirkus Reviews,* Vol. LXII, No. 20, October 15, 1994, p. 1419.

In old Paris, a wager is placed between stone angels standing tall on a cathedral wall and stone gargoyles squatting precariously on cathedral ledges. The gargoyles, speaking in voices "passersby mistake for the rumbling of carts," bet that the good, kind lacemaker Griselle cannot love an ugly little boy; the angels, cooing like pigeons, smugly bet that she can. The angels win. Griselle welcomes the ugly boy, who smells as ripe as "a dish of milk left out too long" and is as heavy "as a sin," and she dresses him in clothes fashioned from her own, including her pearl-studded wedding dress. Although she is cruelly tested, she proves her worth and loves the child—she even scolds the angels for calling him ugly. When Griselle dies, her boy disappears. But one can still see him at the cathedral, writes Yolen: He is the ugly little stone angel with the "absolutely angelic smile."

Told with language as precise—and illustrated with watercolors as delicate—as the "miracles of lace" the heroine creates.

Publishers Weekly

SOURCE: A review of *Good Griselle*, in *Publishers Weekly,* Vol. 241, No. 42, October 17, 1994, p. 81.

Yolen reaches new heights in this flawless tale. Patterned after the story of Job, it concerns one Griselle, a lace maker in Paris of long ago. Reports of her goodness so enrage the gargoyles on a nearby cathedral that they place a wager one Christmas Eve with their holy counterparts, the stone angels. Their bet? To test Griselle's goodness by thrusting upon her "an ugly and unlovable child." The angels consent, and the gargoyles send a hideous, squalling imp to the woman's doorstep. Though the foundling tests her sorely indeed, Griselle proves faithful, and in a particularly poignant ending, her place in heaven and that of her homely but much loved son are assured. The prose is lush but exquisitely restrained, and moves to the measured cadences of another, more gracious era. The story creates new opportunities for [David] Christiana's brooding, mysterious watercolor art. Part impressionist, part Arthur Rackham, wholly original, rendered largely in shades of gray but with an occasional touch of color, the illustrations reveal a world where crouching gargoyles hint of dark purposes and the shadowed and oblique are infinitely more intriguing than the overt. In a word, heavenly.

Karen Williams

SOURCE: "Readable Gifts for Under the Tree," in *The Christian Science Monitor,* December 13, 1994, p. 10.

Award-winning author Jane Yolen has written an original tale with Gothic overtones in ***Good Griselle***. Stone gargoyles and angels on a cathedral in Paris argue about lacemaker Griselle's unflagging goodness. In a Christmas Eve pact, they send an ugly child to test her. Griselle proves her goodness but not without heartbreaking trials. The watercolors by David Christiana are exquisite, depicting Europe of centuries past. The book embraces many different religious themes, some of which may warrant explanation by parents.

📖 *HERE THERE BE UNICORNS* (1994)

Chris Sherman

SOURCE: A review of *Here There Be Unicorns, Booklist,* Vol. 91, No. 5, November 1, 1994, pp. 492-3.

Yolen's latest collection of stories and poetry on a single theme will appeal to unicorn lovers, to readers who enjoy tales based on old lore, and to teachers who want fine examples of fantasy to read aloud to their classes. All the selections are intriguing, but "Unicorn Tapestry," the 50-word poem "The Promise," and "De Natura Unicorni," which contains the traditional themes associated with unicorn lore (healing, true goodness, and unqualified love), are particularly good. The poems, which are written in a variety of styles, including some that are quite challenging, are sure to generate interesting discussions about creative expression. In brief notes preceding each selection, Yolen lends insight into the background of the myths and into her own creative process. These notes are as thoughtful and entertaining as the selections and add much to the enjoyment of the stories.

Kirkus Reviews

SOURCE: A review of *Here There Be Unicorns,* in *Kirkus Reviews,* Vol. LXII, No. 22, November 15, 1994, p. 1546.

The prolific Yolen follows her collection of stories and poems about dragons, **Here There Be Dragons**, with this similar collection about unicorns. In these 18 original pieces with accompanying autobiographical introductions, Yolen attempts to convey the majesty of this beloved mythical creature. Unfortunately, most of her stories are merely workmanlike, and the poems, with the exception of "The Hunting of the Narwhale" ballad, are unspectacular. Two stories that stand out, however, are "An Infestation of Unicorns" and "The Boy Who Drew Unicorns." While the surprise ending of the former will only be a surprise to the most unsophisticated of readers, the story is still witty and fun to read. The latter is about a damaged little boy who is healed by a unicorn, and Yolen expresses both the boy's heartache and his recovery with painful clarity. The accompanying pieces, in contrast, while intending to teach the reader about the writing process, are boring and provide little enlightenment. If anything, they prove Yolen to be a great recycler of old material— not all of it her own. She would do better to let the works speak for themselves, as they occasionally say something worth hearing. [David] Wilgus's illustrations, on the other hand, are magnificent.

The unicorn deserves better.

Cheri Estes

SOURCE: A review of *Here There Be Unicorns,* in *School Library Journal,* Vol. 41, No. 1, January, 1995, p. 110.

The majesty and mystery of these mythical beasts are explored in original stories and poems that draw on both Western and Eastern traditions and have strong heroines and heroes. Yolen prefaces each selection with a note that includes facts and folklore. Masterfully woven together are tales both romantic ("Unicorn Tapestry") and humorous ("An Infestation of Unicorns"). "The Unicorn and the Pool" incorporates the legend of the creature's horn as protection against poison and is a profoundly affecting allegory. The touch of the horn heals a traumatized child who has lost the desire to speak in "The Boy Who Drew Unicorns," a story that previously appeared in Bruce Coville's *Unicorn Treasury.* Most of the tales are set in "fairy-tale times," but a few are contemporary. Mature readers will appreciate the poetry, which is more abstract than, but reinforces, the stories. Yolen is adept at setting

a scene and evoking emotions without being effusive, and readers will delight in her use of irony. . . .

AND TWELVE CHINESE ACROBATS (1995)

Hazel Rochman

SOURCE: A review of *And Twelve Chinese Acrobats,* in *Booklist,* Vol. 91, No. 14, March 15, 1995, p. 1331.

Set in a village in old Russia, Yolen's warm chapter-book comedy is based on her own family stories about her father's beloved older brother. Lou is in so much trouble in the village that he gets sent away to military school, but he runs away from there and is never heard from again, until one day he returns home to the village with a troop of Chinese tumbling acrobats. In the tradition of Singer and Sendak's *shtetl* stories in *Zlateh the Goat,* both words and pictures have a dancing energy and absurdity, with wonderful confrontations between the shocked village elders and Lou's somersaulting troop. The mind has to "bend and stretch like an acrobat" to hear what the visitors tell about a world so different from the cozy little village. In the end, Lou is the one chosen to immigrate to America to find a home for the family. He's a character many children hear about: the beloved, outrageous relative, always in trouble, never able to fit in, who causes uproar in the old country and leads the way to a new life.

Kirkus Reviews

SOURCE: A review of *And Twelve Chinese Acrobats,* in *Kirkus Reviews,* Vol. LXIII, No. 8, April 15, 1995, p. 564.

A colorful episode from the history of Yolen's family— her grandparents and their eight children—marinaded in Old World nostalgia.

The oldest son, Lou, is a charming no-goodnik who keeps getting in trouble and finally is sent away to school. Everybody becomes sad—especially Wolf, Lou's younger brother (and Yolen's father), who idolizes him. When they learn that Lou has been dismissed for gambling, everybody seems even sadder. The next time Lou shows up, he is the manager of a troupe of 12 Chinese acrobats whom he met while working in a Moscow circus. When the acrobats leave the *shtetl* in the spring, Lou's father sends him to America to find a place for the family. Yolen's animated narrative, liberally sprinkled with Yiddish, sticks to Wolf's point of view, and accordingly alternates between acute happiness and sorrow. [Jean] Gralley's antic b&w pictures are mildly Sendakian; her characters, with pointy ears and round foreheads, are simultaneously good-looking and peculiar in appearance. A book radiating family warmth, in words, art, and remembrance.

Emily Holchin Ferren

SOURCE: A review of *And Twelve Chinese Acrobats,* in

Children's Book Review Service, Vol. 23, No. 10, May, 1995, p. 116.

Jane Yolen reaches into her rich family history and weaves "a true story, as true as I can make it." It is the story of her father's oldest brother who was always a rascal and a trouble maker. He runs away from military school and brings 12 Chinese acrobats to his small Ukrainian village. [Jean Gralley's] illustrations perfectly complement the frolicking adventures of the acrobats in the town. The black-and-white pictures have an old-fashioned mood that joyfully carries along the story.

Betsy Hearne

SOURCE: A review of *And Twelve Chinese Acrobats,* in *Bulletin of the Center for Children's Books,* Vol. 48, No. 10, June, 1995, p. 365.

A family story about Yolen's mischievous Uncle Lou coming of age in a Ukrainian village, this centers on the pranks that lead to his leaving (in disgrace) for military school in Moscow. Everyone misses his wild sense of humor, especially his younger brother Wolf—the author's father—and when Lou returns (again in disgrace), the troop of Chinese acrobats he brings with him attests to his new career in a Russian circus. The relationship between the two brothers, Lou and Wolf, lends an immediate dynamic to the historical setting; while simply told, the story is nevertheless detailed and individualized enough that it does not become oversimplified. The compressed narrative, brief chapters, spacious format, large print, and vivaciously drafted pen-and-ink illustrations dancing across almost every page all make this a prime choice for young readers venturing into historical fiction for the first time, or, for that matter, considering a probe into their own family stories.

Carolyn Noah

SOURCE: A review of *And Twelve Chinese Acrobats,* in *School Library Journal,* Vol. 41, No. 6, June, 1995, pp. 115-6.

Lou the Rascal crosses the line of acceptable humor when he "borrows" lambs from all the farmers in his village for a prank. His father sends him to a military school in Kiev, where "He will learn to march in an orderly fashion . . . and to go in a straight line." Not surprisingly, he is expelled; when he returns home months later leading a team of Chinese acrobats, his father recognizes his managerial ability and sends him to America to find a place for a "troop of Yolens" to stay. Told from the perspective of Lou's younger brother, who later became Jane Yolen's father, this nostalgic story sits comfortably in the niche where family folklore and historical fact grow together. Mood and setting are especially well conveyed. Readers get a sense of a 1910 Ukranian village through the actions of its residents, and especially of Lou's boisterous and loving family. Though the author explains that "Jew-

ish boys simply did not go to army schools . . ." because they could not maintain religious observances there, she never alludes to the political reasons they avoided the Russian military. [Jean] Gralley's pencil illustrations are robust and animated, and evoke Maurice Sendak's early work in their high-density characterizations. All told, this tale has the tone of a personal tribute. Though it's well written and illustrated, its appeal for the intended audience is limited—it's long on description and short on dialogue and plot.

THE BALLAD OF THE PIRATE QUEENS (1995)

Susan Dove Lempke

SOURCE: A review of *The Ballad of the Pirate Queens,* in *Bulletin of the Center for Children's Books,* Vol. 48, No. 8, April, 1995, p. 290.

Long after hearing this story-poem, listeners will find themselves chanting the chorus: "And silver the coins and silver the moon, / Silver the waves on the top of the sea, / When the pirate ship comes sailing in, / That gallant *Vanity.*" Yolen never forces a rhyme or makes a misstep in this true adventure about the female pirates Mary Reade and Anne Bonney. The story is a thrilling one, as Captain Calico Jack Rackham and his men stay below decks playing cards and drinking while Anne and Mary attempt to fight off the "bristling man-o'-war" the *Albion:* "So shoulder to shoulder and back to back, / Stood Mary and stood Anne; / Never was it said that they / Were feared of any man." Of course all are taken, and when Anne passes by Calico Jack's prison cell, she tells him, "If you'd fought like a man, / My Jack, you'd need not die." The men are hanged, but Anne and Mary are both pregnant and therefore escape the gallows; according to Yolen's note at the end, Mary may have died in prison, but the story chooses the happiest of the possible scenarios, as "Anne and Mary's children's children / Round their households play," while Jack and his men rise from their graves to sail a ghostly *Vanity.* [David] Shannon's acrylic paintings are magnificently dark and spooky. Rich and full of accurately portrayed historical detail, these are illustrations that children will want to pore over, especially those of the two ships. The faces of the pirates are particularly vivid and intense, and each painting has a hand-lettered caption, which sometimes includes the words supposedly used in real life, as when Anne tells Rackham, "Hang like a dog!" The closing note gives just enough factual background to send readers back to the beginning to read it through again: "Silver the coins and silver the moon. . . ."

Leone McDermott

SOURCE: A review of *The Ballad of the Pirate Queens,* in *Booklist,* Vol. 91, No. 18, April 15, 1995, p. 1501.

Finally, equal time for female ruffians. In this picture book for older readers, Yolen's ballad recounts the last stand of Anne Bonney and Mary Reade, real-life women pirates of the early 1700s. When a government vessel attacked their ship, Anne and Mary fought back fiercely. Although they called to their fellow pirates for help, their male comrades (including the women's "husbands") lolled below deck, drinking rum and playing cards. The men were hanged, but the women "pled their bellies," and the judge freed the pregnant pirates. Yolen's jingly rhymes are a little forced in places but lend themselves well to theatrical reading aloud. [David] Shannon's very handsome acrylic paintings convey the tale's excitement with dramatic compositions in bold reds against smoky backgrounds. The eighteenth-century feeling is enhanced by pen-and-ink borders and the use of a parchment-colored background for the text. Pirate fans will enjoy Yolen's informative author's note—and the alluring skull and crossed swords on the back cover.

Publishers Weekly

SOURCE: A review of *The Ballad of the Pirate Queens,* in *Publishers Weekly,* Vol. 242, No. 16, April 17, 1995, p. 59.

This rollicking ballad springs from an actual incident: captured in 1720 aboard the sloop *Vanity* when their dilatory mates "below, did drink and sport," the "pirate queens" Anne Bonney and Mary Reade escaped hanging because they were pregnant. Author and artist imagine them later, roughhousing with their grandchildren, while their fellow pirates are fated to sail a ghost ship ("And silver the coins and silver the moon, / Silver the waves on the top of the sea, / When the ghostly ship comes sailing in, / That gallant *Vanity*"). Yolen and [David] Shannon sail a different course than the one they plotted for the darker and more tragic *Encounter.* Yolen approaches this almost farcical incident in simple, occasionally rough verse. Ironic in their stateliness, Shannon's paintings—framed, captioned in a scrawled script and otherwise composed to evoke the 18th century—display a sly humor; Mary and Anne in profile "pleading their bellies" before a judge will elicit chuckles. Not for everyone, but offbeat and grimly amusing.

Helen Gregory

SOURCE: A review of *The Ballad of the Pirate Queens,* in *School Library Journal,* Vol. 41, No. 6, June, 1995, p. 126.

"And silver the coins and silver the moon, / Silver the waves on the top of the sea . . ." Yolen writes a most unusual ballad of pirate adventure that sings the history of Anne Bonney and Mary Reade, the only 2 women of the 12 pirates aboard the *Vanity.* They defend the ship from the men of the governor's man-o'-war, *Albion,* while their captain and the rest of the crew are below drinking rum and playing cards. The females are absolutely the best and bravest of this bad lot. The *Vanity* is taken; all are brought to trial, but Anne and Mary escape hang-

ing by "pleading their bellies" (claiming they are pregnant), a page taken from history for which Yolen provides notes. . . . This is not for the faint of heart—no good pirate story is—as pirates are not a God-fearing lot. But it is for those who crave high adventure, death-defying acts, and an unflinching glimpse into history. A rousing read-aloud.

THE WILD HUNT (1995)

Kirkus Reviews

SOURCE: A review of *The Wild Hunt,* in *Kirkus Reviews,* Vol. LXIII, No. 10, May 15, 1995, p. 718.

A gruesome fantasy, as cold and disturbing as a blood-stained suit of armor in a field of wildflowers.

The story concerns two boys, Jerold and Gerund, who exist in parallel realities and become pawns in an evil knight's quest. Yolen strips the genre down to the bare bones. All the elements of epic fantasy are present: good and evil, darkness and light, a black knight, young hero, castle, creatures. There are no real relationships presented; each character seems to wander alone through the mists, trying to figure out what is happening in this sad and lonely work. Readers drift through an evocative netherworld, as if the traditions and symbols of this literature are in themselves, enough. That may be true, in another book. Yolen *could* have been writing a meditation on the genre by trying to evoke the actual experience of reading a fantastic mystical work; and the work *could* have been a presentation of classic symbols in a sort of visionary hieroglyph that would speak to readers directly, unburdened by a conventional narrative. But the elements just never come together; readers may not understand the deeper meanings, because—perhaps—there aren't any. The language can't sustain the book's dreamlike qualities, and its few bright flourishes get buried.

Roger Sutton

SOURCE: A review of *The Wild Hunt,* in *Bulletin of the Center for Children's Books,* Vol. 49, No. 1, September, 1995, p. 35.

With each chapter divided into three layers (Chapter One, Chapter One—Sort Of, Chapter One—Almost, et seq.) that measure the spaces between reader and story, Yolen's latest novel is too artful for its own good. We see a boy named Jerold and another named Gerund who live in the same house sort of/almost; there's a mysterious cat who roams as she pleases, and the Wild Hunt that Jerold reads about and Gerund seeks rides through all. The book is not easy to get into; readers will need to be patient in settling into the contrapuntal narratives that, after a while, create a structural tension that matches the suspense of the story itself. The cat is actually the White Goddess; the leader of the Hunt, the Horned King, is her husband, and the two are enacting a cyclical ritual in which she chooses a hero

(Jerold) whom her husband must name and capture. There is much power in Yolen's writing ("the dog's howl filled the house, pushing every bit of silence into the corners like dirt"), and there's enough pathos and humor to balance the essential solemnity of the tale. Still, you can't help thinking that the author would have done better to tell her story straight out; the narrative play is interesting in a somewhat recursive way but gives the proceedings an abstract quality that keeps the reader at a distance.

Joan Zahnleiter

SOURCE: A review of *The Wild Hunt,* in *Magpies,* Vol. 10, No. 4, September, 1995, p. 30.

Yolen's superb skills in writing fantasy are well in evidence in this complex version of the ancient Scandinavian tale of the Wild Hunt. Penelope Lively's *The Wild Hunt of Hagworthy* incorporated the tale of the menacing dark rider in the antlered helm in a story grounded in reality. Yolen plucks two very different boys from the real world and places them separately in a fantasy world based on a mysterious Gothic mansion. Ringed about with rowan trees the house stands in a bitterly snowy landscape. It is presided over by an enigmatic white she-cat. Neither boy can recollect where he came from.

Jerold, quiet and reflective reads the strange books in the library. He becomes the hero of the story. Gerund, running, falling, leaping, flopping, slipping, sliding, scrambling, tumbling, from the other side of the house, has a large noisy hound dog, Mully, as his companion. It is through Mully that the boys eventually meet and join cause against the forces of darkness as personified in the Horned King, with his troop of invisible horsemen riding 'mine-black horses', the pack of 'sod-coloured dogs with fluorescent muzzles' and the hairy, tree-like Moss-man. The boys are also in thrall to the cat/woman who is quite ruthless in her role as Queen of Light, the Now and Future Queen. The fortunes of all three turn on the naming of names for naming gives power in the battle for supremacy fought at the year's turning between the Lord of Dark and Queen of Light. The manner of telling the story is tantalising. The reader is kept guessing even as the boys are. The pace is leisurely but nevertheless suspense is maintained. There is a curious arrangement of the chapters, each is in three parts, e.g. Chapter Nine; Chapter Nine-Sort of; Chapter Nine-Almost—Some are only one or two paragraphs long. These short passages usually consist of vivid description setting the scene for what is to follow. [Francisco Mora's] illustrations in charcoal acrylic reflect the black atmosphere. They maintain the mystery of the story but do not surpass the powerful imagery of Yolen's text. The whole book is aesthetically very pleasing.

However it does seem more 'a rare book for a rare child' rather than one with instant popular appeal. It would lend itself very well to story reading, (especially round the fireside on winter nights).

HERE THERE BE WITCHES (1995)

Kirkus Reviews

SOURCE: A review of *Here There Be Witches,* in *Kirkus Reviews,* Vol. LXIII, No. 18, September 15, 1995, p. 1360.

The third entry in the series that spawned *Here There Be Unicorns* and *Here There Be Dragons* has 17 stories, clever poems, rousing parodies, and short pieces in diverse genres about different varieties of witches and wizards, including the hags from Macbeth, Baba Yaga, Pythagoras, an Arapaho Indian shaman, Merlin, and an assortment of others. The pieces are prefaced with chatty introductions in which Yolen tells readers her inspiration for the stories, sources of various lines or ideas, what she did in elementary school, for whom she was waiting when she started writing a particular tale, her daughter's problems, etc. With works ranging in length from brief poems to a 30-page story about King Arthur, the book's strengths are its variety and sense of humor; the latter informs all aspects of the volume in which Yolen gracefully combines things magical with things psychological. Following series format, [David] Wilgus's detailed and extremely polished pencil drawings are included, but this time appear somewhat staid in the midst of Yolen's happy-go-lucky structure.

Karen Hutt

SOURCE: A review of *Here There Be Witches,* in *Booklist,* Vol. 92, No. 4, October 15, 1995, p. 39.

Similar in format to *Here There Be Unicorns,* Yolen's latest collection of short stories and poetry on a single theme provides a wide variety of selections about witches in all shapes and forms. From a tale about a young girl unjustly hung as a witch in seventeenth-century England to a twist on the sword-in-the-stone legend, these stories vary in length as well as tone. Yolen shares the inspiration for each work in chatty introductory notes, and compelling black-and-white pencil drawings by David Wilgus provide an added dimension to the collection. An intriguing and entertaining compilation that will appeal to young adolescent readers with an interest in the scary and supernatural.

Donna L. Scanlon

SOURCE: A review of *Here There Be Witches,* in *School Library Journal,* Vol. 41, No. 12, December, 1995, p. 110.

Seven poems and ten short stories present views of witches that range from humorous to poignant. A boy from a long line of sorcerers completes a routine homework assignment in "When I Grow Up, by Michael Dee." Yolen takes a sly poke at political correctness in "The Passing of the Eye," and brings Baba Yaga into the 20th century in "Boris Chernevsky's Hands." Gleanings from historical accounts serve as the seeds for "The Witch's Ride," which is about a lovely young woman beyond suspicion of witchcraft, and "Witchfinder," which takes a look at different sides of the same story. Some of the pieces have a darker note, such as "Circles," in which a young woman learns the true shape of her power, and "Weird Sisters," a poem about how some evil spells are cast by ordinary human beings. A strong, imaginative sense of story and clear, crisp language are trademarks of Yolen's work, and this collection is no exception. . . .

WATER MUSIC: POEMS FOR CHILDREN (with photographs by son Jason Stemple, 1995)

Susan Dove Lempke

SOURCE: A review of *Water Music,* in *Booklist,* Vol. 92, No. 4, November 15, 1995, p. 558.

A mother and son combine their talents in a book that builds on the theme of water in its various forms. [Jason] Stemple's photographs, which Yolen notes preceded the poetry, are imaginatively composed and crisply focused. Never merely attractive landscapes, they actively draw the reader's attention to the special qualities of water wherever it is found. Yolen's 17 poems (including haiku and concrete poetry) invite us to consider water's mysterious sounds, paths, and powers. Many are easy to understand, though a few require reflection, and one. "The Rock Cries Out," may puzzle younger children. Useful in a primary science unit and for inspiring children to attempt poetry of their own.

Reading Teacher

SOURCE: A review of *Water Music: Poems for Children,* in *Reading Teacher,* Vol. XLIX, No. VIII, May, 1996, p. 649.

Another book with wet images is Jane Yolen's *Water Music: Poems for Children.* Color photographs from the mountains of Colorado, the California Big Sur shore, and Yolen's Massachusetts home are provided by Yolen's son, photographer Jason Stemple. After seeing her son's slides, Yolen wrote the reflective poems. Some poems directly respond to the pictures, but the photographs serve as starting points for other rhymed and free verse poems.

MERLIN AND THE DRAGONS (1995)

Leigh Dean

SOURCE: A review of *Merlin and the Dragons,* in *Children's Book Review Service,* Vol. 24, No. 4, December, 1995, p. 45.

In a drafty tower of a medieval castle, a compassionate magician named Merlin spins a story from his own boyhood to comfort and instruct a young King Arthur of Pendragon. It is a magnificent tale about a boy who had visions. There is the mystery of a stone tower that keeps collapsing. There is the hatching of two fierce dragons and their battle to the death. The secret of Arthur's true and rightful parentage is revealed. Here are words that enchant and paintings that bedazzle and hold readers spellbound.

Susan Powers

SOURCE: A review of *Merlin and the Dragons,* in *School Library Journal,* Vol. 42, No. 3, March, 1996, p. 198.

Drawing once again upon Arthurian legend, Yolen has created a stirring tale within a tale. Young Arthur wakes one stormy night from uneasy dreams and seeks out the company of Merlin. Sensing the boy's readiness to learn of his legacy in claiming the crown he wears without conviction, Merlin tells him of another fatherless boy, Emrys, who dreamed baffling dreams of dragons and crumbling stone towers. When the cruel Vortigern attempted to take over all of Britain, Emrys's dreams became prophetic and catalytic. Merlin ends his tale cryptically, as a certain knight advances toward Vortigern's tower. When Arthur cries out for a proper ending, Merlin draws him into the story and it becomes revelatory—at last he is able to call the crown his own. Yolen goes beyond her sources—folklore and history—and moves expertly into the realm of invention. Matched with [Li Ming's] arresting oil paintings, the legend comes alive on a grand scale, the dramatic narrative and well-wrought dialogue heightening the theatrical effect and inviting a fast-paced read-aloud. . . .

Howard George

SOURCE: A review of *Merlin and the Dragons,* in *Reading Time,* Vol. XL, No. III, August, 1996, p. 23.

Merlin tells the boy, Arthur, how he came to tell the fate of the cruel king Vortigern when Merlin, himself, was a boy. In the hearing of the tale young Arthur begins to understand something of what is needed in a truly great king. Yolen weaves her magical skill as a storyteller in this fabulous tale and draws in the actual reader as she does Arthur. [Li Ming's] illustrations are broad and sweeping although they depict the romance of medieval times rather than the earlier era when Arthur was thought to have existed. It is, however, these paintings with their show of raw energy joined with the sense of the mystical which initially captures the reader. Yolen has written a boy's tale for boys who will be set to dreaming of created lands and dragons.

O JERUSALEM (1996)

Kirkus Reviews

SOURCE: A review of *O Jerusalem,* in *Kirkus Reviews,* Vol. LXIV, No. 1, January 1, 1996, p. 76.

In honor of Jerusalem's upcoming 3000th anniversary, Yolen offers a series of poetic meditations on its history, people, and symbolic meaning. In a tone that is reverent throughout, she gives Muslim, Christian, and Jewish traditions equal time, visiting landmarks, describing customs, and explaining in prose notes the references in each preceding poem. [John] Thompson, using warm golds and browns applied in complex textures, creates spread-filling acrylics that range from impressionistic views of towering clouds to a larger-than-life, carefully detailed pilgrim's hand gathering a few pinches of earth from the Mount of Olives. Two potentially confusing notes: In a poem about the nine "measures of beauty" God gave the city, readers may count more than nine; in the poem titled "Jerusalem 3000," the number refers not to the city's anniversary but to the (Christian) year 3000, when the city and the world might, finally, be at peace. That's a fairly gloomy forecast if readers accept the number literally and not as a typographical error. Otherwise, this is an uplifting companion to Karla Kuskin's *Jerusalem, Shining Still.*

Ilene Cooper

SOURCE: A review of *O Jerusalem,* in *Booklist,* Vol. 92, No. 4, February 1, 1996, p. 93.

Jerusalem is a holy place for Judaism, Christianity, and Islam. In her poetry, Yolen captures the feelings all three of these religions have toward the city, and [John] Thompson brings them to life in his exquisite paintings. The poems thoughtfully explore moments of history and myth: the life of young David and his effect on the Jewish people, the meditations of the angels as they watch pilgrims make their way to Jerusalem to honor Allah, and the hope and horror that are sealed in the city's stones. Each double-page spread has a poem and a bit of narrative that tells about the history from which the poem springs. But it is Thompson's pictures that really call to you. He manages a sensitivity and beauty that is equally strong in each picture, whether he is drawing a panoramic view of the city at dawn or a single one of its stones. A book that will linger in your memory.

Renee Queen

SOURCE: A review of *O Jerusalem,* in *Children's Book Review Service,* Vol. 24, No. 8, March, 1996, p. 93.

This book defies categorization for it is poetry, history, geography and religion accompanied by art gallery quality illustrations. Ms. Yolen has written an explication of the background for each poem. While the poetry is engaging and lyrical, the religious significance extends the meaning. The text and poetry help to clarify the importance of Christianity, Judaism and Islam in this one small nation. Adults and children will share many thoughts through this lovely book.

SACRED PLACES (1996)

Patricia (Dooley) Lothrop Green

SOURCE: A review of *Sacred Places,* in *School Library Journal,* Vol. 42, No. 3, March, 1996, p. 217.

Holy in the distant past (Delphi), or still sacred today (Mecca), the sites of Yolen's poetic tributes include some of the world's most celebrated spiritual and cultural power centers. The poems evoke, rather than describe, their subjects, with brief additional information on each provided in an appendix. Nevertheless, many of the references to places, gods, and concepts require further research for comprehension. Of the 12 sites chosen, one is in the U.S., one in Honduras, two each in the Middle East and the Pacific, and three each in Asia and Europe. Since one of the "places" in Europe is the vast category "cathedrals," Europeans appear disproportionately blessed with sacred sites. An otherwise helpful map unavoidably highlights the utter absence of sacred places in Africa and South America. The familiar "Ayers Rock" is rightly called Uluru, but Jerusalem's Western Wall is still tagged "Wailing Wall" here. [David] Shannon's paintings are compelling. Recognizably realistic, they are nevertheless given expressionistic emphasis, from point-of-view, composition, coloring, or simplification of form, to suggest their spiritual dimension. Browsers may be attracted by the pictures, and if the text is too allusive for some readers, others may accept the mysteries as part of the allure of the sacred.

Leigh Dean

SOURCE: A review of *Sacred Places,* in *Children's Book Review Service,* Vol. 25, No. 1, September, 1996, pp. 9-10.

I would like to believe that a majority of adults knows what the words "sacred place" mean, but I suspect that here, in the U.S., only a small minority of spiritual and New-Age seekers know or care. This insures that the powerful beauty of the artwork and the condensed, jewel-like poems filled with the images and symbolic words of each sacred place will leave more adults and most children disoriented. At the back of the book, there is a brief historical paragraph about each site, but this additional information does not solve the problem.

PASSAGER (first novel in the "Young Merlin" trilogy, 1996)

Miriam B. Holm

SOURCE: A review of *Passager: The Young Merlin Trilogy,* in *Children's Book Review Service,* Vol. 24, No. 9, April, 1996, pp. 104-5.

An excellent book that recreates the story of Merlin the wizard who was abandoned in the woods at age eight. He forgets what it is like to be civilized and becomes wild learning survival techniques. A falconer finds him and tries to teach him much the same as he teaches his birds. This is the first of the trilogy. I'd love to read the others!

Susan L. Rogers

SOURCE: A review of *Passager,* in *School Library Journal,* Vol. 42, No. 5, May, 1996, pp. 118-9.

Eight-year-old Merlin lives alone in a medieval forest. Surviving on plants and fish and sleeping in trees to avoid wild dogs, he gradually forgets the habits and language of those who abandoned him. One day a man comes to the forest with a hunting hawk, and the fascinated boy follows him out of the woods to the first bed, bath, and bread he has seen in a year. Struggling against captivity at first, he is gradually won over by kindness. In a final electric moment, the man introduces him to his falcons, and readers share the youngster's shock of recognition when he is " . . . given back his own true name." There is no magic or fantasy in Yolen's stark, poignant, and absorbing tale. Readers feel the sun, rain, hunger, and fear as the child does, along with the intense curiosity and longing that lead him back to civilization. This "skinny" book will entice reluctant readers, but its rich language and poetic phrasing make it compelling and challenging. Some readers may not catch the similarities between the boy and the passager, but all will anxiously await the next volume in what promises to be an outstanding trilogy.

Ann A. Flowers

SOURCE: A review of *Passager,* in *The Horn Book Magazine,* Vol. LXXII, No. 4, July-August, 1996, p. 466.

This slight book, almost an episode, is nonetheless a worthy introduction to Arthurian legend for the younger reader. A feral child wanders the woods, sleeping in trees, fending for himself against cold, hunger, and wild animals. He has forgotten where he came from and lost his ability to speak. After some time, a kindly falconer comes across the wild boy; he captures and tames him. As the boy slowly recovers his ability to speak, he learns to be friends with the falconer's dogs and birds and, in a moving conclusion, remembers that his name is Merlin. This first book of the Young Merlin Trilogy will have readers awaiting the sequels.

📖 *MILK AND HONEY: A YEAR OF JEWISH HOLIDAYS* (1996)

Janice M. Del Negro

SOURCE: A review of *Milk and Honey: A Year of Jewish*

Holidays, in *Bulletin of the Center for Children's Books,* Vol. 50, No. 3, November, 1996, p. 119.

This is a thoughtfully written, attractively designed overview of a year of major Jewish holidays, beginning with Rosh Hashanah and concluding with Shavuot, with a closing section on the importance of the Sabbath. Each chapter opens with a brief history of each holiday, followed by an explanation of various celebratory customs. Short original poems, stories based on traditional sources, and lyrics and music for holiday songs are included. [Louise] August's oil-painted, linoleum-block prints add a lovely luminosity to the text; her full and half-page paintings and thematically appropriate vignettes help to make this combination of history, religion, and story (it even includes a Purim play) rich and rewarding. Similar in concept to Drucker's extensive compendium *The Family Treasury of Jewish Holidays,* this has a warmer, more intimate, and more cohesive execution. The index is divided into non-fiction, poems, plays, songs, and stories. The notes are very general, and no sources are indicated.

📖 *MEET THE MONSTERS* (with daughter, Heidi E. Y. Stemple, 1996)

Maxine Kumin

SOURCE: A review of *Meet the Monsters,* in *Children's Book Review Service,* Vol. 25, No. 3, November, 1996, p. 33.

An attractive collection of monster poems which will alternately make you chuckle and cringe. Each double-page spread is complemented by colorful, exciting illustrations [by Patricia Ludlow Walker]. Facts about the monsters are so cleverly hidden within the verse that readers will not realize they are learning. Most important is the information telling how to get rid of the monster! "Gargoyle" is my favorite. This first joint effort between mother and daughter was created over the Internet!

📖 *HOBBY* (second novel in the "Young Merlin" trilogy, 1996)

Ann A. Flowers

SOURCE: A review of *Hobby,* in *The Horn Book Magazine,* Vol. LXXII, No. 6, November-December, 1996, p. 741.

This second book of the Young Merlin trilogy continues the adventures of Merlin as a boy. When his adopted family dies in a tragic fire, the boy sets out to find a new life. On his journey, he is taken up by a sinister and cruel thief, but escapes to become the apprentice to an apparently kindly traveling magician, Ambrosius, who names him Hobby. He finds Ambrosius's magic deceptions distasteful, however, and realizes that only truth will serve him and his dreams in the future. We find him at the end of the book escaping once more into an unknown future. Slight but winning, this is an enjoyable introduction to Arthurian fantasy.

Additional coverage of Yolen's life and career is contained in the following sources published by Gale Research: *Authors and Artists for Young Adults,* Vol. 4; *Children's Literature Review,* Vol. 4; *Contemporary Authors New Revision Series,* Vols. 11, 29; *Dictionary of Literary Biography,* Vol. 52; *Junior DISCovering Authors (CD-ROM); Major Authors and Illustrators for Children and Young Adults; Something about the Author,* Vols. 50, 81; and *Something about the Author Autobiography Series,* Vol. 1.

CUMULATIVE INDEXES

How to Use This Index

The main reference

lists all author entries in this and previous volumes of *Children's Literature Review.*

The cross-references

See also CA 103; 108; DLB 22; JRDA;
MAICYA; MTCW; SATA 18; TCLC 7

list all author entries in the following Gale biographical and literary sources:

AAYA = Authors & Artists for Young Adults
AITN = Authors in the News
BLC = Black Literature Criticism
BW = Black Writers
CA = Contemporary Authors
CAAS = Contemporary Authors Autobiography Series
CABS = Contemporary Authors Bibliographical Series
CANR = Contemporary Authors New Revision Series
CAP = Contemporary Authors Permanent Series
CDALB = Concise Dictionary of American Literary Biography
CLC = Contemporary Literary Criticism
CLR = Children's Literature Review
CMLC = Classical and Medieval Literature Criticism
DAB = DISCovering Authors: British
DAC = DISCovering Authors: Canadian
DAM = DISCovering Authors Modules
    DRAM: dramatists module
    MST: most-studied authors module
    MULT: multicultural authors module
    NOV: novelists module
    POET: poets module
    POP: popular/genre writers module

DC = Drama Criticism
DLB = Dictionary of Literary Biography
DLBD = Dictionary of Literary Biography Documentary Series
DLBY = Dictionary of Literary Biography Yearbook
HW = Hispanic Writers
JRDA = Junior DISCovering Authors
LC = Literature Criticism from 1400 to 1800
MAICYA = Major Authors and Illustrators for Children and Young Adults
MTCW = Major 20th-Century Writers
NCLC = Nineteenth-Century Literature Criticism
PC = Poetry Criticism
SAAS = Something about the Author Autobiography Series
SATA = Something about the Author
SSC = Short Story Criticism
TCLC = Twentieth-Century Literary Criticism
WLC = World Literature Criticism, 1500 to the Present
YABC = Yesterday's Authors of Books for Children

CUMULATIVE INDEX TO AUTHORS

Bashevis, Isaac
  See Singer, Isaac Bashevis

Baum, L(yman) Frank 1856-1919 . . . . **15**
  See also CA 108; 133; DLB 22; JRDA;
  MAICYA; MTCW; SATA 18; TCLC 7

Baum, Louis F.
  See Baum, L(yman) Frank

Baumann, Hans 1914- **35**
  See also CA 5-8R; CANR 3; SATA 2

Bawden, Nina (Mary Mabey) 1925- **2**
  See also Kark, Nina Mary (Mabey)
  See also CA 17-20R; CANR 8, 29, 54;
  DAB; DLB 14, 161; JRDA; MAICYA;
  SAAS 16; SATA 72

Baylor, Byrd 1924- **3**
  See also CA 81-84; MAICYA; SATA 16, 69

Beckman, Gunnel 1910- **25**
  See also CA 33-36R; CANR 15; CLC 26;
  MAICYA; SAAS 9; SATA 6

Bedard, Michael 1949- **35**

Belaney, Archibald Stansfeld 1888-1938
  See Grey Owl
  See also CA 114; SATA 24

Bellairs, John (A.) 1938-1991 . . . . **37**
  See also CA 21-24R; 133; CANR 8, 24;
  JRDA; MAICYA; SATA 2, 68;
  SATA-Obit 66

Bemelmans, Ludwig 1898-1962 . . . . **6**
  See also CA 73-76; DLB 22; MAICYA;
  SATA 15

Benary, Margot
  See Benary-Isbert, Margot

Benary-Isbert, Margot 1889-1979 . . . . **12**
  See also CA 5-8R; 89-92; CANR 4;
  CLC 12; MAICYA; SATA 2;
  SATA-Obit 21

Bendick, Jeanne 1919- **5**
  See also CA 5-8R; CANR 2, 48; MAICYA;
  SAAS 4; SATA 2, 68

Berenstain, Jan(ice) 1923- **19**
  See also CA 25-28R; CANR 14, 36;
  MAICYA; SAAS 20; SATA 12, 64

Berenstain, Stan(ley) 1923- **19**
  See also CA 25-28R; CANR 14, 36;
  MAICYA; SAAS 20; SATA 12, 64

Berger, Melvin H. 1927- **32**
  See also CA 5-8R; CANR 4; CLC 12;
  SAAS 2; SATA 5, 88

Berna, Paul 1910-1994 . . . . **19**
  See also CA 73-76; 143; SATA 15;
  SATA-Obit 78

Berry, James 1925- **22**
  See also CA 135; JRDA; SATA 67

Beskow, Elsa (Maartman) 1874-1953 . . . . . **17**
  See also CA 135; MAICYA; SATA 20

Bess, Clayton 1944- **39**
  See also Locke, Robert

Bethancourt, T. Ernesto **3**
  See also Paisley, Tom
  See also AAYA 20; SATA 11

Bianco, Margery (Williams) 1881-1944 . . . **19**
  See also CA 109; 155; DLB 160; MAICYA;
  SATA 15

Biegel, Paul 1925- **27**
  See also CA 77-80; CANR 14, 32;
  SAAS 18; SATA 16, 79

Billout, Guy (Rene) 1941- **33**
  See also CA 85-88; CANR 26; SATA 10

Biro, B(alint) S(tephen) 1921-
  See Biro, Val
  See also CA 25-28R; CANR 11, 39;
  MAICYA; SATA 67

Biro, Val **28**
  See also Biro, B(alint) S(tephen)
  See also SAAS 13; SATA 1

Bjoerk, Christina 1938- **22**
  See also CA 135; SATA 67

Bjork, Christina
  See Bjoerk, Christina

Blades, Ann (Sager) 1947- **15**
  See also CA 77-80; CANR 13, 48; JRDA;
  MAICYA; SATA 16, 69

Blake, Quentin (Saxby) 1932- **31**
  See also CA 25-28R; CANR 11, 37;
  MAICYA; SATA 9, 52

Bland, E.
  See Nesbit, E(dith)

Bland, Edith Nesbit
  See Nesbit, E(dith)

Bland, Fabian
  See Nesbit, E(dith)

Block, Francesca (Lia) 1962- **33**
  See also AAYA 13; CA 131; CANR 56;
  SAAS 21; SATA 80

Blos, Joan W(insor) 1928- **18**
  See also CA 101; CANR 21; JRDA;
  MAICYA; SAAS 11; SATA 33, 69;
  SATA-Brief 27

Blue, Zachary
  See Stine, R(obert) L(awrence)

Blumberg, Rhoda 1917- **21**
  See also CA 65-68; CANR 9, 26; MAICYA;
  SATA 35, 70

Blume, Judy (Sussman) 1938- **2, 15**
  See also AAYA 3; CA 29-32R; CANR 13,
  37; CLC 12, 30; DAM NOV, POP;
  DLB 52; JRDA; MAICYA; MTCW;
  SATA 2, 31, 79

Blutig, Eduard
  See Gorey, Edward (St. John)

Blyton, Enid (Mary) 1897-1968 . . . . **31**
  See also CA 77-80; 25-28R; CANR 33;
  DLB 160; MAICYA; SATA 25

Bodker, Cecil 1927- **23**
  See also CA 73-76; CANR 13, 44; CLC 21;
  MAICYA; SATA 14

Bond, (Thomas) Michael 1926- **1**
  See also CA 5-8R; CANR 4, 24, 49;
  MAICYA; SAAS 3; SATA 6, 58

Bond, Nancy (Barbara) 1945- **11**
  See also CA 65-68; CANR 9, 36; JRDA;
  MAICYA; SAAS 13; SATA 22, 82

Bontemps, Arna(ud Wendell) 1902-1973 . . . . **6**
  See also BLC; BW 1; CA 1-4R; 41-44R;
  CANR 4, 35; CLC 1, 18; DAM MULT,
  NOV, POET; DLB 48, 51; JRDA;
  MAICYA; MTCW; SATA 2, 44;
  SATA-Obit 24

Bookman, Charlotte
  See Zolotow, Charlotte S(hapiro)

Boston, Lucy Maria (Wood) 1892-1990 . . . . **3**
  See also CA 73-76; 131; DLB 161; JRDA;
  MAICYA; SATA 19; SATA-Obit 64

Boutet de Monvel, (Louis) M(aurice)
  1850(?)-1913 . . . . **32**
  See also SATA 30

Bova, Ben(jamin William) 1932- **3**
  See also AAYA 16; CA 5-8R; CAAS 18;
  CANR 11, 56; CLC 45; DLBY 81;
  INT CANR-11; MAICYA; MTCW;
  SATA 6, 68

Bowler, Jan Brett
  See Brett, Jan (Churchill)

Brancato, Robin F(idler) 1936- **32**
  See also AAYA 9; CA 69-72; CANR 11,
  45; CLC 35; JRDA; SAAS 9; SATA 23

Brandenberg, Aliki Liacouras 1929-
  See Aliki
  See also CA 1-4R; CANR 4, 12, 30;
  MAICYA; SATA 2, 35, 75

Branley, Franklyn M(ansfield) 1915- **13**
  See also CA 33-36R; CANR 14, 39;
  CLC 21; MAICYA; SAAS 16; SATA 4,
  68

Breinburg, Petronella 1927- **31**
  See also CA 53-56; CANR 4; SATA 11

Brett, Jan (Churchill) 1949- **27**
  See also CA 116; CANR 41; MAICYA;
  SATA 42, 71

Bridgers, Sue Ellen 1942- **18**
  See also AAYA 8; CA 65-68; CANR 11,
  36; CLC 26; DLB 52; JRDA; MAICYA;
  SAAS 1; SATA 22, 90

Briggs, Raymond Redvers 1934- **10**
  See also CA 73-76; MAICYA; SATA 23, 66

Brink, Carol Ryrie 1895-1981 . . . . **30**
  See also CA 1-4R; 104; CANR 3; JRDA;
  MAICYA; SATA 1, 31; SATA-Obit 27

Brooke, L(eonard) Leslie 1862-1940 . . . . . . **20**
  See also DLB 141; MAICYA; SATA 17

Brooks, Bruce 1950- **25**
  See also AAYA 8; CA 137; JRDA;
  MAICYA; SATA 72; SATA-Brief 53

Brooks, George
  See Baum, L(yman) Frank

Brooks, Gwendolyn 1917- **27**
  See also AAYA 20; AITN 1; BLC; BW 2;
  CA 1-4R; CANR 1, 27, 52;
  CDALB 1941-1968; CLC 1, 2, 4, 5, 15,
  49; DA; DAC; DAM MST, MULT,
  POET; DLB 5, 76, 165; MTCW; PC 7;
  SATA 6; WLC

Brown, Marc (Tolon) 1946- **29**
  See also CA 69-72; CANR 36; MAICYA;
  SATA 10, 53, 80

Brown, Marcia 1918- **12**
  See also CA 41-44R; CANR 46; DLB 61;
  MAICYA; SATA 7, 47

Brown, Margaret Wise 1910-1952 . . . . **10**
  See also CA 108; 136; DLB 22; MAICYA;
  YABC 2

Brown, Roderick (Langmere) Haig-
  See Haig-Brown, Roderick (Langmere)

Author Index

CUMULATIVE INDEX TO NATIONALITIES

CUMULATIVE INDEX TO TITLES

Title Index

Title Index

Title Index

Title Index

Title Index

ISBN 0-7876-1138-7

90000

9 780787 611385